Presidential Temperament

*The Unfolding of Character in
the Forty Presidents
of the United States*

Ray Choiniere
David Keirsey

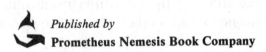
Published by
Prometheus Nemesis Book Company

©1992 David Keirsey and Ray Choiniere

First Edition
Printed in the United States of America

10 9 8 7 6 5 4 3 2 1

ISBN 0-9606-954-6X

PREFACE

This book is about persons and character. Specifically, it is a look at the Presidents of the United States, as seen through the special lens of temperament and character study.

Our experience is in psychology, particularly its applications to psychotherapy, psychopathology, and the theory of temperament and character. We are not biographers or historians, and our excursion into biography is just that: an excursion. Accordingly we wish to express our appreciation for the extraordinary devotion many biographers have brought to their work, and we acknowledge our great debt to them.

We have made use of the biographical and historical works readily available to the interested reader, just as we have avoided the more controversial interpretations of presidential history. There are many authors quite prepared to turn history into controversy, and we gladly leave that pursuit to them. Also, some biographers engage in lavish praise of those Presidents they favor, and in excessive censure of those whom they hold in disfavor. We have tried as best we can to distance ourselves from both kinds of bias.

We anticipate that applying the powerful perspective of temperament and character theory to the lives of the Presidents will have at least four useful effects. First, it may bring the Presidents to life as far more memorable characters than they usually are. Second, it may offer an engaging introduction to the study of character and temperament. Third, it may provide a structure for examining the most basic similarities and differences between all human beings. And fourth, it may help voters make more informed choices about political candidates, better able to see behind the façades of political campaigns.

Dedication

With appreciation to three wonderful Idealists:

Diane Crosby, who first proposed this book, and who in its early stages provided a wealth of encouragement and of presidential research;

Sharon Summer, who has filled these four years of writing with her infectious enthusiasm, her unstinting appreciation, and her constant and gracious support;

Alice Keirsey, whose boundless energy and delightful enthusiasm have been (as always) invaluable, and whose compassion has tempered our sometimes harsh judgments about our subjects.

CONTENTS

PRESIDENTIAL SKETCHES

Franklin D. Roosevelt	1933-1945	72
Harry Truman	1945-1953	267
Dwight D. Eisenhower	1953-1961	436
John F. Kennedy	1961-1963	83
Lyndon Johnson	1963-1969	96
Richard M. Nixon	1969-1974	283
Gerald Ford	1974-1977	344
Jimmy Carter	1977-1981	296
Ronald Reagan	1981-1989	139
George Bush	1989-	354

ABOUT THE QUESTIONNAIRE

We have found that many of those who encounter temperament theory are soon interested in determining their own temperament. To accommodate interested readers we have included in the Appendix a brief questionnaire and instructions on how to score it. If you would like to use the questionnaire we strongly recommend you do so before you begin Chapter Two. In this way you are less likely to accidentally bias your answers because of what you have already read.

A better course might be to put off scoring the questionnaire until you have read the book. In that way you will be able to keep a fresh, unbiased view of the material, and you may enjoy figuring out your temperament as you read. It is likely that you will discover that you don't need the inventory to feel sure of your own type.

Please understand that *all* such questionnaires at best offer only rough indicators of how people actually behave. They are only starting points in the process of self-description and self-definition. The best way to determine character type is always to watch behavior itself, in different places and at different times, quite independent of *any* written device.

Chapter One

PATTERNS

The year 1912 was a presidential election year, and former President Theodore Roosevelt was again campaigning for the nation's highest office. By the evening of October 14 his campaign had carried him to Milwaukee, Wisconsin, where he was to deliver a speech in the city's public auditorium. The time was nearing for him to speak, so he strode from his hotel onto the sidewalk outside, where a car was waiting to take him to the auditorium.

As Roosevelt walked toward the car a man suddenly stepped up to him and pointed a pistol at his heart. The gunman pulled the trigger and a bullet burst from the pistol and smashed its way into Roosevelt's chest. His shirt was suddenly spattered with red, and more blood immediately began seeping from the ugly hole. The bullet had come to rest against his rib cage, a mere half inch from his lungs.

"He pinked me!" shouted Roosevelt, as bystanders rushed to subdue the gunman, John Shrank. They wrestled Shrank to the ground and then, seeing Roosevelt's bloody clothing, prepared to rush him to the hospital. But they found Teddy Roosevelt a more difficult man to deal with than the would-be assassin. "TR" adamantly refused to go for help. "You just stay where you are!" he thundered. "I am going to make this speech and you might as well compose yourself."[1]

Teddy Roosevelt was as good as his word that October evening. Still wearing his torn and red-stained shirt, he had himself driven to the auditorium and there, Shrank's bullet lodged in his chest, he pulled out

---

1 *Presidential Campaigns,* 195.
  (Abbreviated citations are given in the footnotes. Complete listings will be found at the end of the book under "Bibliography of Works Cited.")

his blood-spattered notes and gave his speech. "I have a message to deliver," he declared to the stunned audience, "and I will deliver it as long as there is life in my body."[2]

It was a rousing performance. Roosevelt was a wonderful, charismatic orator under any circumstance, and the sight of his spattered shirt and notes added a spectacular portion of drama to his speech. Only after he had completely finished his performance did he take time to go to a hospital and have the wound tended.[3]

Perhaps Americans were more shocked than surprised by the shooting. After all, only eleven years earlier, in September of 1901, President William McKinley had also been the victim of a gunman. The details of McKinley's shooting were almost identical to Roosevelt's: a famous political figure is walking in public; a lone madman steps up and fires a pistol point blank into his chest; the gunman is immediately wrestled to the ground while the bloodied victim, still conscious, sees his assailant subdued.

In President McKinley's case, however, the rest of the story is quite different. As the mortally wounded McKinley watched the madman Leon Czolgosz being subdued, he cried out, "Don't let them hurt him!" Then, to his secretary George Cortelyou he gasped, "My wife—be careful, Cortelyou, how you tell her—oh, be careful!" Then as his supporters rushed him to the hospital he sighed, "It must have been some poor misguided fellow."[4]

Two shootings, two very different responses from the victims. Though we can never be entirely certain how anyone will respond to critical events, no one knowledgeable about temperament theory would have been surprised by either man's reaction to these extraordinary circumstances. Roosevelt responded to the shooting like the vigorous and sometimes fierce bulldog he had been all his life. McKinley, though he too was a persistent and determined man, was naturally more gentle and considerate. His immediate display of worry and compassion for his

---

2 *Presidential Campaigns,* 195.

3 *Presidential Anecdotes,* 200. Roosevelt was fortunate to be alive. The bullet had been slowed when it struck the case for his glasses and, directly behind it, the thick wad of paper on which he had scribbled the notes for his speech. Otherwise his wound would probably have been mortal.

4 *Presidential Anecdotes,* 192.

assassin and his wife was typical of him, just as a fiery, impetuous response was typical of Roosevelt. Roosevelt and McKinley both reacted to the shooting in ways quite consistent with their life-long, unchanging *temperaments:* Roosevelt as a spontaneous, ebullient adventurer, and McKinley as a serious and kindly caretaker.

The forty men who have been President of the United States have behaved in a remarkable variety of ways. Some have been commanding figures, others have been timid; some have been remarkably vigorous, others have been almost inert; some have been recognized by history as heroic, others have been brushed aside as pedestrian. Certain American Presidents might remind us of foxes, wily, solitary creatures on the lookout for their advantage, or like playful dogs, looking for an exciting romp or a good chase. Other Presidents have been more reminiscent of beavers, busy, socially cooperative creatures, carefully building and guarding their communities. Still others are like the silent owl, sitting high in his tree, moving only when there is a target worthy of his concentration.

The premise we will be exploring in the pages that follow is that the widely different actions of our Presidents arise from the temperament each was born with. To understand a person's behavior requires us to recognize what is unique in an individual, and what social forces are at work on the individual. But that will never be enough. To try to understand a person without recognizing that person's *character,* his or her gradually emerging, lifelong pattern of behavior, is always to miss the mark, for our character arises from the interplay of our environment and our temperament.

There are four basic temperaments out of which our character can be fashioned, and each temperament is quite different from the other three. Teddy Roosevelt, for example, with his remarkable bravado, is an engaging example of the venturesome *Artisan* temperament. And as an Artisan he resembles some of our most colorful Presidents, daring and charming men like Andy Jackson, John F. Kennedy, Lyndon Johnson, and Ronald Reagan.

William McKinley, in contrast, is a fine example of the steadfast *Guardian* temperament, and joins the distinguished company of American Presidents like George Washington, Grover Cleveland, and Harry Truman, all sober and serious men.

There are two other temperaments. One, the analytic *Rational*, has given us some of our most far-sighted and controversial Presidents, men of theory and strategy such as Thomas Jefferson, James Madison, and Abraham Lincoln.

The other temperament, the *Idealist*, has provided one of the great surprises in this study of character: we find that there has never been an Idealist President in all the two hundred year history of The United States of America. We will comment later on this curious void in American politics, and we will look extensively at one Idealist, Eleanor Roosevelt, who came close to wielding presidential power, and another, Mahatma Gandhi, who was more powerful than some United States Presidents ever hoped to be.

Presidents, like all of us, are complex creatures. To understand them, biographers must study the effects upon their lives of family background, education, economic conditions, and social status, as well as the particular events and the general circumstances of their times. But we believe the *temperament* a President is born with is a more fundamental determinant of his behavior than the complex of extrinsic influences usually studied by biographers. Many of these biographical studies are excellent, and demonstrate scholarship and creativity of the highest order. Nonetheless, something is missed when the qualities of the seed and the tree, of temperament and character, are overlooked.

For example, three very different Presidents, Lyndon Johnson, Harry Truman, and Dwight Eisenhower (an Artisan, Guardian, and Rational respectively), were from rural backgrounds. Their families frequently had to struggle to stay solvent, and each young man had to find jobs to help pay the family's bills. Eisenhower attended West Point because it was a tuition-free college; Johnson worked as a manual laborer and then had to struggle to make ends meet in college, even leaving school for a year to work; Truman never attended college at all. On the other hand, three other very different Presidents, John Kennedy, Jimmy Carter, and Thomas Jefferson (another Artisan, Guardian, and Rational), were never confronted with these struggles. Each, at least in terms of his own community, was from birth a part of the aristocracy; each was free from financial worry; and each attended college as a matter of routine.

In spite of the parallels in their social or family histories, however, the cunning Johnson's character could never be confused with the self-controlled Eisenhower's, nor the stylish Kennedy's with the moralistic Carter's. Essential similarities in character cut across enormous differences in social background and historical context, just as essential differences in character clearly separate people of the most similar backgrounds. The Rational farm boy Eisenhower would have no difficulty making sense of the Rational aristocrat Jefferson's absorption in designing both the buildings and the curriculum of the University of Virginia. Nor would the Guardian aristocrat Carter have trouble comprehending how the Guardian farm boy Truman arrived at his decision to drop the atomic bomb on Hiroshima. And the charismatic Artisan aristocrat Kennedy may have disliked—and been disliked by— the hard-living rural Artisan Johnson, but each could readily take the other's measure, and knew what to expect from the other in the political arena.

We are not suggesting here that social background and personal history are unimportant. Far from it; our social context stamps us inevitably and indelibly. But we feel quite safe in proposing that our life-long patterns of action, our character, will always arise from and be consistent with our temperament. Thus William McKinley and Teddy Roosevelt, each of a different temperament, could never have developed similar characters, similar ways of looking at and responding to the world. They saw differently and they responded differently, quite consistently with their differing temperaments, even to the almost identical traumas of their shootings.

Temperament, then, is a lifelong predisposition toward certain identifiable patterns of behavior. Dogs are predisposed to chase cats, beavers to dam up streams to create quiet ponds, and owls to hunt in the dark. Each, unless impaired by its environment, subsequently develops the habit of (respectively) chasing cats, damming up streams, and hunting at night. So with the Presidents, we can say that Andy Jackson and Teddy Roosevelt, predisposed by their Artisan temperament to act spontaneously and with impact, inevitably made a habit of doing so. These actions became part of their character. Thus the innately vigorous Artisan Teddy Roosevelt could rejoice, "A President has a great chance; his position is that of a king and a prime minister rolled into one,"[5] and

---

5 *From George ... To George*, 5.

his habitual behavior would consistently reflect this dynamic Artisan perspective.

Similarly, Calvin Coolidge, with his Guardian's propensity for taking the cautious and pessimistic perspective, for anxiously building and guarding his territory, made his worried pessimism part of his character. Thus in 1928, while the country seemed to be riding comfortably and cheerfully on an ocean swell of great prosperity and hugely profitable speculation, Coolidge could warn that the country was prospering, but "having reached this position, we should not fail to comprehend that it can easily be lost."[6]

In the same way, the Rational Thomas Jefferson, with his penetrating vision, was naturally given to long-range, strategic planning and to architectural design, whether of buildings, curricula, or nations; such behavior was a life-long habit, part of his character. So Jefferson could declare that the United States was not merely another nation, but an "experiment to show whether man can be trusted with self-government."[7]

In short, each man's temperament, in interaction with his circumstances, gave rise to his character. And so it has always been. Twenty-five hundred years ago Hippocrates took note of four fundamental and distinct patterns of human behavior, and he observed that each of us consistently displays only one of these patterns. Thus we could be either Sanguines, or Melancholics, or Phlegmatics, or Cholerics. From Hippocrates' time on the same four patterns have been described with such consistency that we may assume that they are rooted in our biological heritage, and that temperament is oblivious to gender, age, nationality, religion, race, and geography. Humanity seems designed on the same four fundamental patterns of speech and action that we have introduced in these pages as the Artisan, Guardian, Rational, and Idealist temperaments.[8]

---

6 *From George ... To George*, 49.

7 *From George ... To George*, 107.

8 So true is this that we can parallel contemporary observations about temperament and character with the observations made by Hippocrates. Teddy Roosevelt, for example, would be a Sanguine, Thomas Jefferson a Phlegmatic, Harry Truman a Melancholic, and our look at the Idealist Eleanor Roosevelt will allow us to match her nicely with Hippocrates' Cholerics.

The following list mentions some important contributors to the study of temperament, the times in which they wrote, and the names of the four classes they noted. A quick scan of the list will demonstrate the remarkable diversity of interest and observation brought to the study of the four character types. If you will scan the labels they used for the types, you may see in them parallels with the distinctions presented here.

The Observer, his time, and the four classifications of character

Hippocrates	550 BC	Choleric	Phlegmatic	Melancholic	Sanguine
Paracelsus	1540	Nymphs	Sylphs	Gnomes	Salamanders
Adickes	1907	Dogmatic	Agnostic	Traditional	Innovative
Spränger	1914	Religious	Theoretic	Economic	Aesthetic
Kretschmer	1920	Hyperesthetic	Anesthetic	Melancholic	Hypomanic
Fromm	1947	Receptive	Marketing	Hoarding	Exploiting
Myers	1956	Feeling	Thinking	Judging	Perceiving
Keirsey	1958	Schizoid	Obsessive	Depressive	Manic
Keirsey	1978	Apollonian	Promethean	Epimethean	Dionysian
Keirsey	1987	Idealist	Rational	Guardian	Artisan

Hippocrates' descriptions of character concerned themselves with what we might loosely call a person's prevailing mood. In fact his terms (or their linguistic descendants) are still used to describe certain moods or emotional states. We may still hear a typically calm and detached person called "phlegmatic," an often downcast person labelled "melancholic," a frequently cheerful person described as "sanguine," and a person typically given to quick anger called "choleric." Other observers have focused on other facets of character, as the table indicates, but what is important is that each of the ten observers has uncovered four fundamental styles of behaving, or what we call the four temperaments, and the ten classifications of temperament are consistent with one another.

Temperament

We have said that temperament is a lifelong predisposition toward certain identifiable patterns of behavior, and that what we call character is simply a person's habitual way of acting out his temperament.

Character is a pattern of behavior, and therefore observable, while temperament is the biological substrate out of which character emerges. The four temperaments might be more clearly represented in a four cell matrix:

Idealists	Rationals
Guardians	Artisans

The position of each temperament in the matrix is quite important, for it points up certain relationships among the temperaments. Thus, there is a characteristic that the Idealist shares with the Guardian, which sets both off from the Rationals and Artisans, and vice versa. Similarly, there is a characteristic the Rationals and Idealists share which differentiates them from the Artisans and Guardians, and vice versa. The vertical and horizontal orientations of the matrix suggest these parallels between the four temperaments. In fact the temperaments are very intimately related, and though we will not discuss their relationships extensively in this book, it is important to point them out before going on.

Moral Sanction And Pragmatic Utility

The first of these constants in human action is a very fundamental difference between persons. It is the difference between *sanctioning* and *utilizing*. The sanctioning kind of people, the Idealists and Guardians, do things and want others to do things that are legitimate, in full accord with the rules (though Idealists and Guardians have rather different rule books). The utilizing kind of people, the Rationals and Artisans, do things and would like others to do things that work, that get people where they want to go (though the Rationals and Artisans, as we shall see, have different criteria for what works).

The point is not that the sanctioning types, the Idealists and Guardians, don't care about getting results; certainly they do care. It is just that they are naturally drawn to, and value highly, cooperative, sanctioned interaction with those they are close to, with their families, and with the groups with which they identify themselves. Because of this they naturally think about the issue of results in this context. Sanctioners are not averse to making headway, but they consider the utility of an action as *secondary* to whether it is ethically or morally sanctioned.

In opposite fashion, the utilitarians are strongly and naturally oriented to producing results, and the matter of sanctioning is secondary to the matter of results; they will inevitably consider the matter of cooperation in the light of its effect on producing results. They don't refuse to observe the rules, but their observance of the rules is *secondary* in selecting their behaviors, coming only after the matter of how well the behavior works in achieving their aims.

Concrete and Abstract Speech

While difference between the sanctioners and utilitarians is very great, there is a second constant in human action we must consider: all of us are either primarily *concrete* or primarily *abstract* in what we think about and talk about. For example, we may think and talk about food, clothing, cars, grades, or other particulars, or we may think and talk about epistemology, electronics, causality, consciousness, or other generalities. But we cannot choose both at once, and we will usually show a strong preponderance of one over the other. At times, of course, we all have rather concrete things to talk about, while at other times we may need to speak in abstract terms. But all of us make a habit of speaking mostly one way or the other, and may even seem to have a "deaf ear" for the other sort of conversation.

Not that concrete characters are oblivious to hypotheses, analogies, or symbolic expressions (abstract considerations) any more than abstract characters are oblivious to the concrete world of colors, textures, or harmonies. It's just that for each the liveliness, the immediacy, and the significance of life is found in one world, while what is most central to the others' world seems relatively unimportant. When we read about Abraham Lincoln, for example, we will find this abstract Rational a remarkable contrast with the Guardian George Washington, a man whose world was unalterably concrete. Both were patriots, both were Presidents, both are revered. Yet they might have had a rather troublesome time trying to understand each other.

Most of us are habitually concrete in our thought and speech, while only a few of us, perhaps only 15%, are abstract. Most of us live in a very concrete world which concerns itself primarily with food, clothing, shelter, transportation, and recreation. Very few of us really have time for and interest in esoteric matters like science, technology, engineering, and philosophy. Those who do have the time and interest find little opportunity to talk about these matters with others unless their work involves such concerns. Further, since there are so few of the abstract types around, the difference between the abstracts and concretes is rarely noticed.

We can now classify the four temperaments according to whether they are sanctioning or utilitarian in choice of method, and whether they are concrete or abstract in thought and speech. As the matrix now shows, the Idealists are Abstract Sanctioners, while the Guardians are Concrete Sanctioners, and the Rationals are Abstract Utilitarians while the Artisans are Concrete Utilitarians.

	Sanctioners	Utilitarians
Abstract	Idealists	Rationals
Concrete	Guardians	Artisans

Variants

What is more, careful observation will show that we can divide each temperament into two variants. A President may be an Artisan, for instance, but he may be either the *Operator* variant of the Artisan personality or the *Player* variant. If a President is a Guardian, we will see that he is either a *Monitor* Guardian or a *Conservator* Guardian. In the same way, Rationals are either *Organizer* or *Engineer* Rationals, and Idealists are either *Mentor* or *Advocate* Idealists. In matrix form:

The *Idealists* may be either *Mentors* or *Advocates*	The *Rationals* may be either *Organizers* or *Engineers*
The *Guardians* may be either *Monitors* or *Conservators*	The *Artisans* may be either *Operators* or *Players*

The differences between the two variants of each temperament are not as fundamental as the differences between the personalities themselves. Nonetheless they help us refine our ability to understand character, and they add some intriguing variations to our study.

Directing and Reporting

These eight modifications are not mere random variations. All four pairs arise through a difference in one single factor. Quite simply, some people in their relationships naturally give commands or directives, while others just as naturally give reports. The pair of variants found in each temperament distinguishes the Directors of that temperament from the Reporters of the same temperament.

The fun-loving Artisan Warren Harding, for example, was a *Reporting* Artisan, never a commanding presence (literally or figuratively), while Andrew Jackson was an extreme example of the *Directive* Artisan, whose communications were invariably commanding. Of course each could, and at times did, communicate in the other's style; even Reporters must sometimes command, and Directors must sometimes explain or describe. But both kinds were usually rather uncomfortable doing so, for they were acting against their own inherent leaning.

Similarly, the Guardian Washington was a Directive communicator: he naturally gave orders, and naturally expected that others would obey. The Guardian William McKinley naturally reported in his communications; he naturally sought to lead by providing information.

And Thomas Jefferson was an Reporter Rational. He preferred to explain, to define, to describe; to lead with information. In contrast John Adams was a Director Rational, a man who naturally gave directives and rarely tried to lead by report.

It is not, by the way, that the Director characters want to dominate while the Reporters don't, or that one deliberately seeks to withhold information while the other does not. There is nothing suspect or culpable in either style of communication. There is merely a natural preference for one style rather than the other. Whether one uses that preference for ill or for good depends on the person, not the temperament.

This is of course only a brief exposition of this matter of the four temperaments and their Directive and Reporting variants. As we examine each of the Presidents, the difference between temperament types, and between the Reporters and Directors of each type will become increasingly clear. For the moment we can simply add the distinctions to our matrix of the types.

	Sanctioners	Utilitarians
Abstract	**Idealists** Mentors: Directive Advocates: Reporting	**Rationals** Organizers: Directive Engineers: Reporting
Concrete	**Guardians** Mentors: Directive Conservators: Reporting	**Artisans** Organizers: Directive Players: Reporting

Now that we have completed our overview of the matrix of temperament and character, we can enrich our understanding of its implications. In the chapters that follow we will look at the Artisan temperament in particular, along with its two variants, and then the Artisan Presidents. Then we will move on to the Guardian and Rational temperaments, their variants, and their presidential representatives. Then, since there have been no Idealist Presidents, we will complete our survey with a look at two outstanding Idealists who, though they never ran for high political office, became world-renowned and greatly loved.

A final chapter will offer some conclusions about temperament, character, and the presidency, and the reader will find a short appendix which comments briefly on some of the theoretical underpinnings of personality type studies. Some readers will be familiar with the letter designations used by the Myers-Briggs Type Indicator. A brief appendix has been included for those readers, which correlates the "MBTI" letter codes with the names used in this book.

For those interested in perusing the background of this study of temperament and character, we have appended a brief listing of books on that topic.

A Brief Bibliography of Characterology

Allport, G.	*Personality*
Angyal, A.	*Neurosis and Treatment*
Adickes	*Charakter und Weltanschauung*
Cleckley, H.	*The Mask of Sanity*
Goldstein, K.	*Abstract and Concrete Behavior*
Fromm, E.	*Man For Himself*
Hippocrates	*Human Nature*
Jung, C.	*Psychological Types*
Keirsey, D.	*Please Understand Me*
Keirsey, D.	*Portraits of Temperament*
Keirsey, D.	*Temperament: the Graces and Foibles of Human Conduct*
Keirsey, D.	*The Gentle Art of Taking Over Character Games*
Kretschmer, E.	*Physique and Temperament*
Kretschmer, E.	*The Psychology of Men of Genius*

Laing, R.	*The Divided Self*
Maslow, A.	*Motivation and Personality*
Montgomery, S.	*The Pygmalion Project: I The Guardian*
Montgomery, S.	*The Pygmalion Project: II The Artisan*
Montgomery, S.	*The Pygmalion Project: III The Idealist*
Myers, I.	*The Myers-Briggs Type Indicator*
Paracelsus	*Nymphs, Gnomes, Sylphs, and Salamanders*
Roback, A.	*The Psychology of Character*
Shapiro, S.	*Neurotic Styles*
Sheldon, W.	*Varieties of Temperament*
Spränger, E.	*Types of Men*

Chapter Two

THE ARTISANS

"I say we must act now!"

Artisans who have been American Presidents

Andrew Jackson	1829-1837
Martin Van Buren	1837-1841
Zachary Taylor	1849-1850
Franklin Pierce	1853-1857
James Garfield	1881
Chester Arthur	1881-1885
Theodore Roosevelt	1901-1909
Warren Harding	1921-1923
Franklin Roosevelt	1933-1945
John Kennedy	1961-1963
Lyndon Johnson	1963-1969
Ronald Reagan	1981-1989

Even before the United States became embroiled in World War II, President Franklin Roosevelt was eager for the country to take aggressive action to prepare itself for the conflict. Over the last few years there have been more, and more public, suggestions that Roosevelt was cooperating secretly with the British war effort. He had learned from the British Prime Minister, Winston Churchill, that British Intelligence had infiltrated German Intelligence with counterspies. Thanks to a very effective espionage agent known as "Intrepid,"[1] the British had also cracked the most secret German code and could

---

1 William Stevenson's *A Man Called Intrepid* offers an account of that remarkable agent.

anticipate well in advance many of the maneuvers of German armed forces. Though the United States was far from entering the war officially, the adept Artisan Roosevelt, and the equally clever Artisan Churchill, agreed to protect the British intelligence effort by housing Intrepid and his staff in America.

In hindsight, aiding the British war effort this way was a wise action. But at the time anti-war sentiment in the U.S. was loud and growing louder, and the President's conspiring with one foreign government against another, no matter how noxious the other might be, would not have been approved by a cautious Congress. So Roosevelt took action on his own. But he didn't stop at the espionage game; he also contrived by all sorts of ploys to equip Britain with munitions and other military resources, including no fewer than fifty World War One destroyers, which the British desperately needed to combat the dangerously effective German submarines.

Some have argued in the last decade that Roosevelt knew the Japanese were planning an attack against Pearl Harbor, but that he chose to keep the information secret.[2] In this view he feared that if he announced the information the Japanese would drop their plan for the attack and wait for a more favorable opportunity. FDR, it is argued, did not want to delay the showdown so he did not speak out. There is little support for this thesis, but it is interesting that an Artisan would be suspected of such maneuvering. Roosevelt's maneuvering of the Navy's role in the North Atlantic is a far better example, as we shall see.

Whatever his moves, the Artisan FDR was successful not only in creating an "arsenal of democracy," as he called it, but in converting that arsenal into the primary defender of democracy. He did it almost single-handedly, secretly, and with astonishing virtuosity. Some might argue that his deeds were wrong, but no one can argue that they were not effective.

The observer of presidential character finds plenty of evidence that Artisan Presidents in general are prone to such extra-legal—and sometimes frankly illegal—activities when they have decided to pursue a particular course of action. The Artisan President Teddy Roosevelt's

---

2 *Sacrifice at Pearl Harbor*, a videotape broadcast on public television in December of 1990, presented this argument.

high-handed actions in Panama at the turn of the century, the Artisan Andy Jackson's military forays into Spanish Florida, the Artisan Ronald Reagan's pursuits in Nicaragua, and Artisan Franklin Pierce's intrigues in the Caribbean are noteworthy examples of this sort of activity. Men such as FDR and TR, Jackson and Pierce, are naturally drawn to taking effective actions, whether or not those actions are unauthorized. They also tend to be exceptionally talented at such behavior. Guardian and Rational Presidents have been much less likely to engage in such machinations, and far less adept at them than the clever Artisans.

The Artisans can be characterized by their remarkable attentiveness to immediately practicable changes in the physical world. They have what we may call a *variational mentality*.

Artisans are drawn to change, but this doesn't mean that just any kind of change will do. Mere disruption or distortion may be considered change, but they will not suffice, for they are only the forerunners to anarchy. The Artisan's change will be a fitting or an artful change, which is to say a thematic change. It is, for example, the sort of change that in music is called "variation on a theme," in which a simple theme is varied by turning it upside down or playing backwards or overlapping itself, as in a fugue or canon, for instance, "Three Blind Mice" or "Frère Jacques," or Pachelbel's well-known D-major *Canon*. Thematic variation can also be found in the meshing gears of a bicycle, where the power from the pedals is varied when it reaches the sprockets on the rear wheel; or even in the 90 degree change of direction that comes with dovetailing two pieces of wood in making the corner of a drawer. Art, like mechanics, is constancy under variation. If we can understand this, then we can understand those who become artists and mechanics—the Artisans.

An Artisan is a person skilled in *any* of the arts.[3] The domain in which the Artisan is most at home is an earthy, Dionysian world: the domain of the visible, audible, and palpable, the world of objects and events which can be made and manipulated. This means that whatever is abstract and whatever is not practical is of little interest to the Artisan. If

---

3 These include at least the athletic, culinary, graphic, linguistic, martial, musical, and plastic arts. We must not confine our conception of the arts to the so-called "fine" arts.

it cannot be seen, heard, or touched, who needs it? If it can't be used, why pick it up?

But if it can be used, then *use* it! In fact Artisans cannot, and would not want to, resist "picking it up." They *must* pull the trigger, climb the mountain, fly the plane. What has been called their "function lust" shows up very early in life in Artisans, amounting to a compulsion in the more reckless and energetic Operator Artisans like Teddy Roosevelt and John Kennedy.[4]

Artisans see themselves, and wish to be seen by others, as bold, impressive, competitive, and sophisticated. Their self-confidence, self-respect, self-esteem, and self-presentation depend upon their ability to act daringly, impressively, competitively, and with suave and urbane sophistication. They will not be cowardly, they will not be unimpressive, they will not be outdone or overtaken, they will not be naive; for to be any of these would diminish their self-regard. Moreover these innovative characters are the most hedonic of all the types. In their view doing things that aren't fun is a waste of time. And along with this love of pleasure is an abiding optimism: the next gamble, the next move, shot, ploy, or gambit, will be a lucky one. Nothing is as enjoyable to the Artisan as a run of luck, and along with their love of pleasure they have an incorrigible belief that they live charmed lives.

As already suggested, Artisans show little interest in or patience with mere abstractions. To bother with symbols, theories, or generalities is to waste one's time, unless they immediately abet an action which is already of interest to the Artisan. (The abstraction will still be uninteresting, mind you; it merely becomes useful.) No high-flown speculation for the Artisan, no deep meaning or introspection. Leave to others the philosophical inquiry, the inward search. Goals and reflection are, after all, the enemies of impulse and action. Consider the distinction between technique and technology, a distinction which helps separate the Artisans from their utilitarian cousins, the Rationals. The Artisan strives for technique, but is bored by technology. Technology, after all, is the *study* of how things are made or done while technique *is* the making or doing. Technology is abstract, technique concrete.

---

4 *Child Development*, the English translation of Karl Bühler's *Entwicklung des Kindes*, offers an important discussion of the concept of function lust.

The Artisans, with their concrete utilitarian outlook, think and speak descriptively. Their language is usually colorful and cast in the vernacular, which is usually quite concrete, for they tend to pick up the regional jargon, slang, shoptalk, and street talk wherever they go. Even their analogies are concrete. The splendid and eloquent language of the famous Artisan, Winston Churchill, certainly shows us this. And the Artisans' high-minded language quickly leads to concrete action, as did, for instance, Churchill's breathtaking speech during the darkest moment of World War II:

> We shall defend our island, whatever the cost may be, we shall fight on the beaches, we shall fight on the landing grounds, we shall fight in the fields and in the streets, we shall fight in the hills; we shall never surrender!

Finally, all the splendid talk about lofty principles and long-term goals leads the Artisan to action, whole-hearted action—or it is abandoned. So, said Teddy Roosevelt, "It isn't how long you are President that counts, but what you accomplish as President."[5] Again, don't philosophize, don't just maintain the status quo, but *make something happen.*

Impulse and action are very important to the Artisan, whose motto might be "Go for broke when you're on a roll." It doesn't take much, by the way, to convince them that they're on a roll. They are usually excited about something, after all, and if they are not excited then they are looking for the chance to become excited. The Artisans are easily excited, and they wish to be excited easily. They are in love with their impulses, they detest routine, which suppresses their impulsive behavior and quickly bores them. Andy Jackson, as an especially noteworthy example, would fly instantly into a rage if anyone spoke badly of his wife, Rachel, and for thirty-seven years he kept a pair of duelling pistols loaded and ready for action in defense of her (and of his own) honor.

Of course impulse takes many forms. Since their deaths, anecdotes about John Kennedy's and Lyndon Johnson's private lives have steadily surfaced, offering us pictures of both men that contrast sharply with their carefully cultivated public images. We see the Artisan's love of impulse and excitement showing up in their behavior toward women. Both men,

---

5 *From George ... To George,* 5.

according to these tales, indulged themselves in unsanctioned relationships with women frequently and boldly. The story is told of an attractive young woman, for instance, an aide to Lyndon Johnson, who woke in the middle of the night to see the shadow of a man standing by her bed. It was Johnson, who playfully commanded her, "Move over; this is your President."[6] Stories in a similar vein have been told about John Kennedy. One writer captured the issue most succinctly when he predicted after Kennedy's election that the Kennedy administration would do for sex what the Eisenhower administration had done for golf.

The Artisans love activity, they seek out adventure, they display a constant hunger for pleasure and stimulation. Their great fear is boredom, and since they become bored very easily, they will try desperately to relieve boredom when it occurs, even at times engaging in illegal or immoral activities to do so. Legal or otherwise, they must *do* something. Franklin Roosevelt understood himself well in this regard. He once commented that

> I sometimes wish I could find some spot on the globe where it was not essential for me to start something new—a sand bar in the ocean might answer, but I would probably start building a sea wall around it and digging for pirate treasure in the middle.[7]

During most of his adult life FDR had a severe disability: he suffered from the crippling effects of polio, with severe restrictions on his mobility. Yet in 1928, at age forty-six, he undertook a rigorous political travel campaign that lasted for several long and exhausting weeks. While those around him were ready to collapse from the stresses and fatigue generated by this arduous trek across the entire United States, Roosevelt cheerfully proclaimed that "if I could keep on campaigning twelve months longer, I'd throw my crutches away."[8]

Because of their penchant for unfettered action, Artisans are sometimes thought to be uncooperative, even willfully oppositional, but this is quite unintentional (unless someone is trying to fetter them). What the Artisans are usually trying to do is get something done, to produce some result. If their actions displease someone, then that's too bad. They

---

6 *Fall From Grace*, 209.

7 *Franklin D. Roosevelt's Own Story*, 91.

8 *Presidential Style*, 290.

may not wish anyone harm, but Artisans balk at doing useless things just to avoid offending someone's rules of seemly or decorous conduct.

Artisans live with great immediacy, intensely absorbed in the present moment and in whatever they are doing (if it engages their interest at all) to the exclusion of everything else. Consider the following description of John F. Kennedy. It is an extremely accurate description of the Artisan in general:

> Kennedy is a man completely and vigorously engaged in events of the moment. Thus he regards his past acts as more or less irrelevant prologue; his future acts as something to be determined under future circumstances. One could talk to him all day and be unable to say what his attitude toward business will be, because what he says or thinks on that day has a bearing only on the effect his is trying to achieve that day.[9]

In the same way, when Artisans practice something their practice is neither onerous nor even "practice" in the usual sense of mere drill and repetition, a "getting ready to." It is rather *doing itself,* usually perfecting some absorbing variation on a theme. It is a matter of pushing the activity to its limits, of skating near the edge, and of crashing or missing or falling many times until the furthest limits of the activity have been explored, that is, until mastery of the activity is reached. Testing limits is absorbing, entrancing, mesmerizing to them; no other character can match the Artisans in their capacity for being caught up totally in some action. This may be one reason that the Artisans are so well represented among performing artists such as actors, dancers, skaters, musicians (whether classical or popular), and professional athletes. It is also one reason that Artisans such as John Kennedy, Franklin Roosevelt, and Ronald Reagan are so often great political campaigners: they readily become absorbed in the action, the intense schedule, the chance to make an impact. They find themselves living for it, feeling enlivened by its demands when most of us would be exhausted by the same demands.

Virtuosity in performance, then, is the domain of the Artisans, which follows rather naturally from their love of action and impact. Virtuosity after all is the result of endless activity, endless absorption, endless perfecting. If Artisans are not caught up in the activity, if it does not happen to appeal to them, it will be very difficult to hold them to it

---

9 Louis Banks, later managing editor of *Fortune*, quoted in *Roosevelt to Reagan,* 75.

(as so many parents, teachers, and employers have discovered). But if Artisans become fascinated by the activity, endless absorption and repetition are to be expected of them.

Such absorbed rehearsal may look like drudgery to people of other character and because of this the Artisans are sometimes considered "compulsive." They will themselves sometimes claim that they can't help themselves; they have to behave in a particular way. Thus they may admit to being "compulsive gamblers," or "compulsive drinkers" for instance, and are likely to be diagnosed as such by therapists who encounter them. But while compulsions are experienced as burdensome and even tortuous (and in their obsessional form are also the province of the Rational), the impulsive "compulsions" of the Artisan are almost irresistibly exhilarating and absorbing.[10]

The same absorption with theme and variation is found in the way the Artisans' work on people. Artisan salesmen or politicians will test out their tactics, expand their repertoire, and refine their methods over and over again. James Garfield and Ronald Reagan, for example, became flawless orators in this manner. It is not merely because it is useful to do so, but rather because such "practice" is an engaging activity in itself. As a great pianist plays the keyboard with breath-taking virtuosity, so the great con-artist plays his victims with a virtuosity that may be less admirable but no less breath-taking. Lyndon Johnson, for example, loved to maneuver people. It was rather like a hobby with him. He was a virtuoso who knew how much wheedling to do, how much bullying, how much flattering—and when to do each. Like most Artisans, he also knew how to speak about his own behavior in a way that dressed it up nicely. In a speech in 1963 he promised that the first duty of a professional politician is to "appeal to the forces that unite us, and to channel the forces that divide us into paths where a democratic solution is possible."[11] Franklin Roosevelt, another Artisan, commented in 1936 that "The science of politics...may properly be said to be...the adjustment of conflicting group interest."[12] Dispassionate words,

---

10 Some courts of law recognize the "irresistible impulse" as an excuse for otherwise illegal action.

11 *From George ... To George*, 37.

12 *From George ... To George*, 37.

obscuring nicely Roosevelt's lust for challenge, for action, and for impact.

Impact, and especially social impact, is profoundly important to the Artisans. To be without influence is to be without oxygen. The Artisans love to "make it happen," whether the "it" is an outrageous party, a stunning performance on a stage or in a competitive game, a spectacular maneuver in the world of stocks or corporate business, or on a battlefield or, of course, in the political arena. This intense absorption in having impact may be part of what has made them, in the twentieth century United States at least, some of the most likely candidates for public office. It also helps to explain why so many professional politicians are Artisans: the political arena allows for maneuvering, for excitement, for risk—and for impact, even on a world-wide scale.

The Artisans are remarkably acute observers of the present. They will notice the smallest details, the most subtle shifts in nuance, the slightest changes in both foreground and background. This, combined with their constant activity and their venturesomeness, is why the Artisans are the most charismatic of all temperaments. They "practice" their presentation, they observe sharply the effect their efforts are producing, they vary the theme and try again and again and again until even their most off-the-cuff speeches can seem to be masterful. John Kennedy could address a crowd in beleaguered West Berlin and declare, "Ich bin ein Berliner" ("I am a Berliner") and the roar of crowd was so great that it seemed it would be heard around the planet. It didn't matter that Kennedy's accent was bad; his boldness and vigor were apparent, his intensity infused his voice, his words had already set the stage for a dramatic moment. Kennedy was there, his practised charisma was irresistible, and his impact was enormous.

Boldness and daring are virtues in the eyes of the Artisans, while timidity is a vice. Their self-respect lies in behaving with boldness, and they will feel guilty if they turn down a challenge or a dare, or otherwise fail to act with boldness. Andrew Jackson, for example, was a veteran of scores of lethal duels as an adult, and dozens of brutal fights as a youth.

As their self-respect is found in bold action of every kind, their self-esteem is rooted in their competitiveness. Teddy Roosevelt's insistence on assaulting the Spanish entrenched on Kettle Hill in 1898, and his desire to serve in France during World War I, even though he was already forty years old, are obvious examples of the Artisan's attraction to competition and contest, the source of their pride.

In turn, Artisan self-esteem emerges from their ability to take on the competition and defeat it under almost any circumstances. John F. Kennedy was a very proud man, usually with good reason. He was a man who had cheated death when his PT boat was blown out from under him during World War II, who had defeated the political odds against a young, rich Roman Catholic reaching the presidency, and who had even taken tactical command—by telephone—of the United States Naval forces blockading Cuba against Russian shipping.

Their self-respect, their pride, and their confidence all stem from their willingness and ability to take on challenge boldly, and to win. They are therefore understandably the world's greatest risk-takers. They delight to put themselves at risk, to take a chance, to adventure, whether the adventure be physical or political or financial. They may find risk so irresistible that they court it again and again, even while knowing that to do so will be terrifying.[13] It is likely that most skydivers, motorcycle racers, and mercenary soldiers, for instance, are Artisans who have become absorbed in the thrills of risk-taking.

Of course not all risks are physical. The most devoted Wall Street wheeler-dealers and high-rollers are probably Artisans while, closer to home, we can watch young Artisans playing arcade games where they will be found intently absorbed in destroying the next enemy tank, starfighter, wizard, or monster. It is not difficult to imagine them as young Wyatt Earps, the Artisan hired gun moving in to clean up Tombstone in a deadly showdown. In more "civilized" times, the arcade game takes the place of the shoot-out at high noon.[14]

Excitement need not always be tumultuous, challenges need not always be dramatic. The Artisans working at their potter's wheel or developing their computer programs, working on their paintings or

---

13 Actually, such adventures are terrifying, only before, not during, their execution. The risk-taker is much too busy concentrating on what is being done to be frightened by any possible mishaps.

14 The arcade game may be challenging, the "high score" listing may call forth their competitiveness, but the non-lethal character of the arcade game, though it may reduce the Artisan's satisfaction in the activity, may be a disguised blessing. More than a few Artisans have gone impulsively for the showdown in life without sufficient practice, and as a result have been eliminated from life entirely.

musical compositions or developing a new sales pitch or a new political maneuver will not seem dramatic to the casual observer. But the careful observer will see the same absorption, the same intensity, the same aliveness to the activity so apparent in the more outgoing Artisan.

It has already been said that Artisans are impulsive, impetuous, given to whim. Let us add that when they cannot feel the impulse to act rising up in them, or when they cannot move freely to accommodate that impulse, they quickly become bored. Boredom is one of the most painful conditions an Artisan can experience and if it continues for long Artisans are likely to do almost anything to relieve the condition. Thus a Franklin Pierce may gallop down a Washington street, putting at risk anyone in his path, or an Andrew Jackson may engage in scores of duels which led to the death of other men (and could have led to his own death), or a John Kennedy may pull strings to get himself assigned to the very exciting but very dangerous "PT boats" during World War II. Often what they will do to relieve their ennui will be disturbing to most of those around them, as countless teachers have found out. Most public schools, with their regulation and regimentation, have been among the worst possible environments for young Artisans, which may be one reason that there are relatively few Artisan teachers.[15]

There is an intriguing converse to this pattern which deserves mention. When Artisans finally lose interest in exploring the limits of a particular behavior, they will either abandon it or reduce it to mindless routine so they can get on with more exciting things. Routine is ordinarily abhorrent to the Artisans, but one still finds them eventually reducing many of their frequently-occurring activities to automatic, hard-and-fast routines. These behaviors become their "modus operandi," that is, their standard mode of operating in a particular situation. Observers of the early political involvements of Ronald Reagan, for example, wrote often of the presentation that he gave, time and again, always the same, with only minor variations on the theme. So unchanging was it that some finally dubbed it "The Speech." The same kind of "M. O." can be found among Artisans in the criminal world, where the M. O. of a professional criminal can become as distinctive as

---

15 See *Please Understand Me* for more about the traditional school's neglect and occasional persecution of the Artisan student.

his fingerprints. Determining the criminal's modus operandi can become quite valuable to the police since it helps them predict where and how the criminal will commit his next crime.

As long as an action can still command their attention the Artisans will continue with their themes and variations. But when the excitement and challenge have disappeared even a politician's presentations or a criminal's risky behavior may be reduced to nothing but doing a job.

The most important thing to understand about the Artisans in considering their performance as Chief Executives is the kind of competency they bring with them upon entering office. Their talents are the practical, here-and-now talents, the *tactical* talents, and their tactical leadership is what distinguishes them from Presidents of other temperaments. Tactics are always relevant to a specific moment, a particular time-place-personnel-materiel situation; the tactical leader is one who looks for the best angle of approach, for that particular angle that *at the moment* gives one the greatest advantage, who is able to devise effective maneuvers on the field of combat and in the heat of battle. The Artisan, more capably than all others, sees such second-by-second opportunities, and takes advantage of them with quick, fluid, and effortless gracefulness. In the inevitable confusion of combat, whether on the battlefield or in the political arena, the Artisan is by nature extremely adept at surviving and flourishing—and producing the results he goes after.

As we noted in the first chapter, there are two variants of the Artisan: the Operators, who naturally give directives; and Players, who naturally give reports. The United States has elected six Operator Artisans and six Player Artisans to the presidency, so both variants have been well-represented in the White House.

The Operator Artisans

Andrew Jackson	1829-1837
Martin Van Buren	1837-1841
Theodore Roosevelt	1901-1909
Franklin Roosevelt	1933-1945
John Kennedy	1961-1963
Lyndon Johnson	1963-1969

The Operator Artisan has a special fondness and talent for manipulation. Whether dealing with people or with tools, the Operator inevitably operates on them, or operates with them, on anything and on anybody. Sometimes he will operate with an agenda in mind; both Teddy and Franklin Roosevelt operated beautifully on the reporters who surrounded them, and both used the press as if it were their own publicity machine. They are the experts in expedience, seeing instantly the quickest route to whatever payoff they are interested in. Literally, they can expedite almost any activity more quickly and decisively than anyone else. In prison populations they will be the masterminds, the maneuverers, the scroungers par excellence. But even if there is no particular purpose being served the Operators are still likely to maneuver and manipulate, simply because of their love of operating. Lyndon Johnson couldn't resist cajoling, arguing with, and smooth-talking even unimportant visitors to the White House or to his Texas ranch.

The Operators, even more than the Players, cannot resist besting others, whether in combat, in wheeling and dealing, or in clever maneuvering. A weak, ineffective performance embarrasses them and, like an impulse denied, can leave them feeling quite badly about themselves. But an Operator who has been able to pull off a clever maneuver, or create a dramatic impact, especially where the risk is high, is a person who will hold himself in high regard indeed, at least for the moment.

If they feel insecure the Operators are more prone to bragging than any other character type. They can become insufferable braggarts, seemingly oblivious to how their self-aggrandizement is being received by others. While all Operators are prone to some bragging, the more upper-class Operators are usually trained to control this tendency, so their natural glibness and brashness remain hidden under a veneer of social decorum. This training was especially obvious in, for example, John Kennedy, while unfettered bragging was equally obvious in his successor, Lyndon Johnson.

Operators may be drawn to carpentry, auto mechanics, sales, or computer programming because these are wonderful arenas for manipulating objects and events. Similarly many and perhaps most great battlefield generals are Operator Artisans, including Alexander the Great, the Union commander Phil Sheridan and the Confederate commander J. E. B. Stuart during the Civil War, and Generals Patton and Rommel of World War II fame. And of course one may add to the list of successful Artisan field generals the names of Andy Jackson and Zachary Taylor, both of whom became American Presidents. (The directive habit patterns of the Operators typically serve them very well in the domain of on-the-field generalship, though there are exceptions, as the history of the impetuous general George Armstrong Custer shows.)

The field general poised at or near the front lines (in contrast to the staff general who must sit behind a desk far from the battlefield) has a marvelous opportunity for maneuvering people and machines. In their position the action is here and now, the need is here and now, the opportunities are here and now—and, in combat, the heat of battle is intense and immediate.

Operators typically demand of themselves that they be tough. There is no room for "chickening out" in the Operator's world, and to be bold, to rise to a challenge, to conquer: these require toughness of body and mind. Furthermore, toughness has its own virtue for the Operators, and they look upon those who do not show it with contempt. The meek, the weak, and the powerless are somehow tainted. If a person is weak and timid and if things do not go well for him, then he probably deserves what he gets. Andrew Jackson was physically frail, both as a youth and as an adult. Yet he was frequently in fights that he deliberately brought upon himself. If he lost he would get up off the ground, challenge his opponent again, and keep going until he won. In one duel, fought with a famous duelist named Dickinson, Jackson was shot in the chest by Dickinson, who had fired first. Jackson stood his ground, carefully aimed and fired his own weapon, and killed Dickinson. "I intended to kill him," said Jackson later. "I would have stood up long enough to kill him if he had put a bullet in my brain."[16]

The powerful competitive streak of the Operators sometimes leads them into a remarkable intensity of performance. Virtuosity and a willingness to dare are still the name of the game. The Operator Artisans are therefore the people most likely to become "top gun," whether they are flying a warplane in combat, ramrodding a battlefield command, or

16 *Presidential Anecdotes,* 68.

performing as Wall Street wheeler-dealers, or corporate raiders—just as they are the people most likely to push events too far and to crash and burn.

The Player Artisans

Zachary Taylor	1849-1850
Franklin Pierce	1853-1857
James Garfield	1881
Chester Arthur	1881-1885
Warren Harding	1921-1923
Ronald Reagan	1981-1989

The Player Artisans are drawn even more strongly than the Operators to excitement, to intense sensation and to playing games, whether they be games of poker, tennis, basketball, seduction, or politics. Players can handle being excited for periods of time that would leave most other people utterly exhausted, and the more outgoing Players are the ultimate "party animals." Their problem is never how to sustain themselves through prolonged excitement, but rather how to manage themselves after the excitement subsides. When the excitement disappears they may become painfully bored, and boredom is the worst possible condition for the Player.

As the name "Player" suggests, they are more playful in attitude and behavior than the Operators. In fact the Players are more interested in pleasure than any other type. Their interest in pleasure is quite natural to them and it seems immoral to them to pass up the opportunity for pleasure, for fun, for enjoyment. Many Players have a great fondness for recreational sex, and it may be that Players are those most likely to become persistently involved in destructive drug usage. This may be especially likely if such indulgence will help them avoid ennui. But in spite of the extremes to which they may sometimes go to avoid tedium, playing is still their choice of recreation.

Player Artisans don't maneuver and manipulate the way the Operators do. That sort of cleverness is not their style. Instead the more gregarious of the Players will impress the observer with their flair and their energy. They are often wonderful performers who seem to have a special ability to "read" their audiences and their audiences' moods as they perform. But that very ability to read and manage their audiences seems to engender in them a certain cynicism, similar to the harder-edged cynicism of the Operators, and just as deep-seated. People allow themselves to be maneuvered, say the Players, as the Operators also say, but the Players don't share the contemptuous perspective of the Operators, who will hold the malleable "sheep" in contempt for their malleability.

The more outgoing of the Players are natural-born performers and showmen, and blossom when given a chance to show off. The less outgoing of them may put together a musical composition, a choreographic design, or an outstanding exhibition of some special skill. As the Operators are expediters, the Players are synchronizers, bringing together disparate elements into one coherent party, construction, or performance. They are the reporting Artisans, and it is a part of their talent that they are able to bring together and synchronize all these elements using their own informative language patterns, without special reliance on the directing patterns of the Operators.

As in the case of the Operators, the Players' self-confidence comes from besting others, whether in creating things or in performing. As with all Artisans, competitiveness is important to them, and there is little they will undertake which does not have some element of competition and risk to it. A Player out for a friendly game of golf is unlikely to get through a single hole without placing a bet of some kind on the outcome. As with the Operators, clumsy performance or poor workmanship can embarrass them and, like an impulse denied, can leave them feeling very uncomfortable indeed.

We now offer a visual summary of the facets of the Artisan character. The "wheel" is divided into four quadrants, indicating the Artisan character's natural leadership patterns, most central values, facets of the Artisan's most satisfying self-image, and the work (vocation, avocation) which the Artisan most naturally and most ably performs. The four centered labels identify the central characteristic of each of these, and the "spokes" specify their most salient aspects.

The Artisans

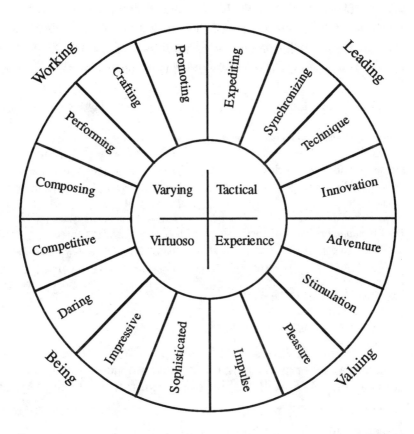

For those who would like to read further about Artisans, Kretschmer's "hypomanic" type, Adickes's "Innovative" type, Spränger's "aesthetic" type, and Keirsey's "Dionysian" and "Artisan" types present the full range of Artisan traits of character. Biographies are an excellent source of Artisan portraits, since there are so many famous Artisan warriors, athletes, and artists who have become the subjects of biographical study. Famous painters such as Rembrandt and Gauguin, flamboyant musicians like Mozart and Wagner, and noted writers like Hemingway and Fitzgerald, all make for fascinating biographical subjects. There are also many famous female Artisans—actresses, athletes, even pilots—who have been described very well by biographers. Novelists, playwrights, and screen writers certainly seem to understand the Artisan character, perhaps more than do biographers and psychologists, so there are countless fictional studies of the amusing and sometimes outrageous escapades of Artisan characters. Montgomery's account of the Artisans' manner of interacting with their mates is especially rewarding reading for those who have such a mate.

Non-fiction	Fiction
Character Structure and Impulsiveness (Kipnis)	*Wuthering Heights* (Brontë)
Please Understand Me (Keirsey)	*The Great Gatsby* (Fitzgerald)
Portraits of Temperament (Keirsey)	*The Sun Also Rises* (Hemingway)
Physique and Character (Kretschmer)	*Lady Chatterley's Lover* (Lawrence)
Hemingway (Meyers)	*The Natural* (Malamud)
The Pygmalion Project: Artisans (Montgomery)	*Gone with the Wind* (Mitchell)
Autobiography of B. F. Skinner (Skinner)	*The Entertainer* (Osborne)
Types of Men (Spränger)	*The Taming of the Shrew* (Shakespeare)
Impulsive Personality (Wistonce)	*Huckleberry Finn* (Twain)
Yeager (Yeager)	*A Streetcar Named Desire* (Williams)

The United States's first Artisan President was **Andrew Jackson**, a clever and daring man whose impact on the nation was remarkable. We will begin our exploration of the Artisan Presidents with him.

The Artisan Presidents

.The Directive Artisans: The Operators		The Reporting Artisans: The Players	
7 Andrew Jackson	1829-1837	12 Zachary Taylor	1841-1845
8 Martin Van Buren	1837-1841	14 Franklin Pierce	1853-1857
26 Theodore Roosevelt	1901-1909	20 James A. Garfield	1881
32 Franklin D. Roosevelt	1933-1945	21 Chester Arthur	1881-1885
35 John F. Kennedy	1961-1963	29 Warren G. Harding	1921-1923
36 Lyndon B. Johnson	1963-1969	40 Ronald Reagan	1981-1989

Directive Artisan Presidents: The Operators

Andrew Jackson

"Let the people rule!"

Operator
Born: March 15, 1767
Died: June 8, 1845
Presidency: 1829-1837

From Washington's first term of office in 1789 until the election of 1828 almost fifty years later, four Rationals and two Guardians had served as President. Each of these men had been born in either Massachusetts or Virginia, each was an aristocrat, and each (except Washington of course) served as Vice-President or Secretary of State before becoming President. But by 1828 there had been an important change in the way many voters saw their relationship with their national leaders. Instead of exalting aristocrats and Revolutionary War heroes by electing them to the presidency one after another, the voters gave thought to electing "a man of the people," someone more like themselves.

Perhaps, without knowing it, the voters felt a need for a change in the function of their government. George Washington had done well his Guardian's job of conservation and monitoring, and Americans held title to their land thanks to him. The three Rationals that followed him, Adams, Jefferson, and Madison, had applied their architectural skills to make more complete the design of an elegant edifice of government. The Guardian Monroe had presided over a stable and peaceful time and the recent Rational John Quincy Adams had tangled with the unsettled times beginning to emerge. Now the nation's circumstances and temper called for something else than construction and consolidation and maintenance of the status quo. What exactly that something might be could be perceived only vaguely; perhaps it was known more by what it was not than by what it was. Perhaps for a while there had been enough careful self-discipline and high-flown thinking.

The year was 1828. One could feel a sea change in national sentiment—and there stood Andy Jackson. He was a genuine hero, strikingly colorful and outrageously different from all his presidential predecessors. He was a man of action, constrained by neither conservatism nor abstraction. The voters knew the rough-hewn frontiersman was a military hero and an exciting presence, but they could also see in Andy Jackson, the son of poor Irish immigrants, a slightly larger-than-life version of themselves. They had not the foggiest notion of what he was otherwise, but they voted for him anyway, and in 1829 the Operator Artisan General Andrew Jackson, "Old Hickory," Indian fighter extraordinaire and victor over the British in the battle of New Orleans, assumed the mantle of the President of the United States.

Jackson was a remarkable choice. President Andy Jackson was the same man who had received an unexpected inheritance at age sixteen and promptly and enthusiastically spent it on the quick pleasures of alcohol, horse races, cards, dice, fancy clothes, and the raucous camaraderie of the local taverns. The new American President was the same Andy Jackson who was later described by an old acquaintance as "...the most roaring, rollicking, game-cocking, horse-racing, card-playing, mischievous fellow, that ever lived in Salisbury."[17]

---

17 An old Salisbury resident quoted in *Presidential Anecdotes,* 73.

Jackson certainly knew how to have fun; Artisans (especially the Players) usually do. But he also knew how to be angry and to desire revenge, and he was far more likely than most to act on his desire. Even when he was a child his aggressive style was obvious, and his pugnacious determination remarkable. Though was a slender, rather fragile youngster, he was nonetheless:

> always itching for a fight with anyone he felt was slighting or maligning him. Though he seldom won these adolescent battles, he constantly came back for more, taking on any boy, regardless of size or ability, with the kind of temper typically ascribed to a red-headed Irishman.[18]

None of his aggressiveness was lost when he became an adult. Then, as in his childhood, he was restless and combative and would not back away from a fight regardless of his still-frail constitution.[19] Compared especially to his presidential predecessors, the hell-raising Jackson was incredibly pugnacious, raw, narrow-minded, ill-spoken, and poorly educated. But of course these characteristics, other than his remarkable aggressiveness, did not make him so very unusual. The same things might have been said about almost any man raised in a frontier society. It was a time when all of the frontier, including its people, was rough-hewn; the dictates of survival did not allow for a great deal of personal polish.

Jackson had been born on the impoverished frontier of South Carolina where he and his family lived in deep poverty. In his teen years, after the death of his mother, he lived as a poor relation subsisting largely on the generosity (or the sense of obligation) of others. He felt his inferior position very strongly and responded to it by developing a very strong code of "honor," the basic tenet of which was quite straightforward: to attack anyone who suggested that he was not honorable. Not unexpectedly his code, along with his hasty Irish temper, led him into innumerable confrontations and, later in life, duels.

Jackson of course shared the prejudices and beliefs of his frontier culture. He took great pride in comparing himself and his rugged frontier fellows with what they all saw as the dishonest, greedy, soft and less

---

18 *Presidential Courage*, 37.
19 As an adult he stood more than six feet tall but weighed only 140 pounds.

vital Easterners. As he grew he also observed the powerful impact of the
Eastern establishment on the lives of people on the Western frontiers.
The unofficial but powerful Eastern government-by-economics could
and often did make or break the fortunes of small, hard-working
Westerners. Andy Jackson saw the often damaging effects of that
establishment and despised it and the people who made it up. Jackson
hated energetically, as he did everything, and in later years the Eastern
establishment would have cause to regret his hatred.

Jackson's feelings are not hard to understand. Artisans in general,
and perhaps especially very energetic Artisans, regard social
establishments of any kind as useless. Even worse, they may regard
them as confining, and it is not surprising that the powerful and
dominating eastern establishment caught Jackson's attention and
fostered in him a powerful fury. The establishment, he believed, was
smothering the freedom of action of the young Jackson, of his friends, of
his neighbors, and of what little family he had. It was depriving them all
of the opportunity to win, he felt, and he never forgot these early years
of poverty or the struggles through which he saw those plain and honest
folks suffer. Nor did he ever surrender his view that it was the monied
East that caused so much of their suffering. No Artisan is likely to be
able to resist, or even want to resist, the temptation to strike back at such
an oppressive enemy.

Perhaps this is part of what led Jackson eventually to take up the
practice of law, though it is hard to imagine that he would have been so
far-sighted. Young Andy had learned to read by the time he was of
school age and, as one of the very few literate people in his community,
served as a public reader of newspapers there. All the same, he claimed
later to have read only one book in his life (*Blackstone's Commentaries,*
a book on law), and, since he did not often find time for study among his
other pursuits, his progress in reading law was slow.

But Jackson could not be stopped once something captured his
attention, and in fact many Artisans develop a taste for the practice of
law. The courtroom or boardroom contest, so often fought for high
stakes and using any kind of tactics both fair or foul, can be an
Operator's dream. Apparently it caught Jackson's fancy, and even
though he continued raising hell with his friends he did manage to
become a practicing lawyer, though a poorly-prepared one in the formal

sense. He also developed a taste for land speculation as well. This also fit well with his character, for neither the practice of frontier law nor speculating in land requires that one severely restrict one's other activities, such as persistent carousing.

Along the way Jackson also acquired a taste for the military life, was appointed to the Tennessee militia, showed tactical talent and aggressiveness in the field, and eventually became a militia general.

He was a brilliant military leader and a tough disciplinarian who was willing to suffer in the field the same privations as did his troops. (It is said that in one campaign through wilderness country he walked several hundred miles so that a wounded soldier could ride his horse.) His fearless obstinacy and raw-boned resourcefulness won from his men the admiring nickname "Old Hickory," just as his on-the-field generalship won their admiring loyalty. As a fighting general Jackson was a prodigal; he was disciplined, cool, and showed that tactical brilliance which often characterizes the Artisan, and especially the Operator, field commander. He proved his ability in a number of campaigns between 1814 and 1815, conducted primarily against restive Indian tribes.

Of course his most famous battle was his splendid victory near New Orleans during the War of 1812. The war had dragged on for almost three years and the British had landed a force near New Orleans at the mouth of the Mississippi River. Jackson prepared to repel the British advance on the city with the only troops available: a rather motley, ill-trained and ill-disciplined force of Americans half as numerous as the British. In spite of this handicap he successfully turned back the attacking force of well-trained British regulars and in the process inflicted approximately 2,000 casualties on the attackers. The losses to the American force were astonishingly light: eight men killed and thirteen wounded![20]

The outcome of the battle was a delight to the people of the embattled United States, and their satisfaction was increased when it was realized that the badly mauled British force was the same one that had burned Washington earlier in the conflict. We might as well add here that it was in this military action that Jackson made use of the men

---

20 *The American Presidents,* 72.

of the colorful French pirate, Jean Lafitte, who appears to have been another venturesome Artisan.[21] Lafitte may have been unsavory, but the pragmatic Jackson would take any step he could to win. Allying himself with a bold pirate was, if nothing else, a *useful* thing to do.

Accompanying the color and the glory of this battle there is an inescapable tragedy. The war had been concluded at the peace table in Belgium several weeks earlier, but it took considerable time for the news to travel across the Atlantic, and the British and Americans fought the Battle of New Orleans ignorant that the war was already over. The slaughter need never have happened. Nevertheless, Jackson's dramatic success as a military leader, his popularity with his troops, and his charismatic manner earned him a reputation which made him a very attractive presidential candidate. The party politicians knew that the vigor of populism, especially in the West, made a successful, pugnacious, hell-for-leather character like Jackson very promising. In contrast Jackson's political opponent, the aristocratic, austere, and graceless Rational John Quincy Adams, made a perfect foil for him.

Jackson was unquestionably a fascinating hero. An early biographer wrote of him that

> He was the most candid of men, and was capable of the most profound dissimulation. A most law-defying, law-abiding citizen. A stickler for discipline, he never hesitated to disobey his superior. A democratic autocrat. An urbane savage. An atrocious saint."[22]

The extravagance of this description is not mere hyperbole, for Jackson was himself capable of great extremes. The writer's immediate juxtaposition of extremes is also warranted; so violently could Jackson leap from one extreme to the other that he was sometimes called "the Tennessee Firecracker."

Note the emphasis on issues of authority and obedience in the above description. Authority is a source of conflict for most Artisans, and for larger-than-life Operator Artisans such as Jackson it is likely to have larger-than-life proportions. In a sense, all directive types (including our

---

21 It is difficult to imagine a privateer or pirate or corsair commander not cut from the same cloth as Jackson. Both jobs require absolute fearlessness, tactical virtuosity, and high intelligence in executing variations on a theme—in the case of Jackson, the theme of military maneuver, in the case of pirates, the theme of plunder.

22 *Presidential Courage*, 46.

Operator, Organizer, and Monitor Presidents) naturally prefer issuing directives to obeying them; it is natural and inevitable. But Jackson in particular could no more contain his own impulse to give direction than he could contain his impulse to disobey those in authority. And Jackson was a man of powerful and urgent impulses that demanded immediate discharge.

If Jackson's skirmishes with those who tried to dominate him were the hub of his impetuous life, his spotless honor was its rim. Artisans usually covet "honor" far more than most other character types and for Andy Jackson honor was a matter of life and death; quite literally he would kill for it. He was willing, even eager, to jeopardize his own life in defense of his honor and did so many times. He could be frighteningly impetuous in defense of his honor, as well as being a man who took his revenge seriously. Those who knew him knew he was absolutely ruthless and totally fearless where either was concerned. Important as these matters may be, Artisans are loath to appeal to the law to set things right for them. In the Artisan view the task of exacting revenge cannot be honorably transferred to others, hence the Artisan's sometimes relentless pursuit of the skills and employment of the means of vengeance. (The old Code Duello was undoubtedly their invention, bent as they are on honor at any price.)

Jackson is said to have fought more than one hundred duels. Whatever the count might have been, he carried with him many of their scars, including a bullet which had penetrated his chest and come to rest next to his heart. He had acquired this painful souvenir during a duel with a Charles Dickinson. Dickinson was an exceptional marksman and generally considered to be best shot in Tennessee. His shot lodged in Jackson's chest, but Dickinson paid the full price for his success: Jackson's own shot killed him outright.

Jackson's idea of honor was not entirely self-directed. He had a markedly chivalrous bent, as if he were a knight of old, and some of his duels were with those he thought had defamed women or any other persons he had decided to defend. Because of this his marriage to Rachel Robards in August of 1791 became the occasion for considerable mayhem.

The marriage was apparently a happy one. Rachel and Andy seemed to understand each other well and to love each other greatly. She, like

Andrew, grew up in the rough and vigorous atmosphere of the American frontier, though (unlike Andrew's) her family did have some wealth. She was vigorous, sturdy and tanned, largely uneducated and able to read and write only slightly. Because of this she was never at ease with the more "feminine," pale-complexioned, salon-worshipping society of Washington. She had spent time in the city with her military hero husband, and though he was lionized she was never accepted by Washington's upper crust who in fact treated her cruelly. Washington society and the Washington press mocked and disparaged her for her rough appearance and manners. She was accused of what would have been a very demeaning act for a woman in those times: smoking a large corncob pipe. Though the accusation seems to have had no foundation in fact it was still widely circulated and still finds its way into print occasionally.[23]

Even so, when Jackson won the presidency the tough, high-spirited and courageous Rachel determined to go to Washington again, this time as First Lady. If nothing else, she was intent upon showing her enemies that they couldn't cow her. Sadly, she did not have the opportunity. Three months before her husband's inauguration, at the age of sixty-one, Rachel Jackson died of a heart attack. Her death may have been hastened by her terrible upset when she discovered her unwitting role in the presidential campaign of 1828. It was a remarkably vicious campaign, and Rachel Jackson's character and behavior were favorite topics for some of the most vicious slanderers. She was accused of wantonly betraying her first husband, Lewis Robards, in order to run off with Jackson. Stories were circulated that she had deserted Robards and been caught in bed with Jackson while still married to Robards, and other similar tales were presented which portrayed both her and Jackson as evil, cruel, flagrantly and wantonly adulterous.

The facts of the matter did not help the Jacksons greatly. Granted, Robards was by other accounts a mean-spirited, high-handed, jealous and unfaithful husband. Rachel Robards tried in spite of this to live with him, but eventually found the marriage intolerable. She finally ran off to

---

23 The film version of Jackson's life, for instance, with Charlton Heston cast as Andy Jackson, showed Rachel Jackson puffing on a pipe of sorts. (Heston, by the way, is probably not an Artisan, and so his Andy Jackson did not come off as an Artisan character.)

Natchez to avoid Robards, and Jackson accompanied her on the trip, presumably as friend and protector. Upon hearing that Robards had divorced her Jackson returned to Rachel in Natchez and married her himself.

However there are some problems with this version of events. Lewis Robards did not in fact divorce Rachel at that time; there is evidence to suggest he was trying to find her rather than to leave her. Nor is there a record of Andrew and Rachel's marriage to be found in Natchez where the marriage is supposed to have occurred. And the young lawyer Jackson seems to have been rather careless about whether the divorce from Robards was in fact ever granted. It was an unlikely oversight for a lawyer, though not an impossible one for a wily and impulsive Artisan like Andy Jackson. Artisans as a rule are keenly aware of custom, protocol, and tradition. They can sniff out the regional patterns wherever they go and whatever they do. They surpass even Guardians in ascertaining these patterns, and of course are masterful in making use of the information. Under the circumstances it may have appeared to Jackson that he and Rachel Robards could marry and live as husband and wife without difficulty. Then, when it became known that Robards had not divorced Rachel until after 1791, Andy and Rachel simply had another wedding ceremony (in 1794) to settle any doubts about the legality of their union.

In spite of painful rumors, vicious accusations and possible improprieties, the Jacksons' marriage was overall a very good one. He was tender with her and considerate of her and he usually tried to subdue his impetuosity (with mixed results) for her sake. She was similarly considerate of him, and though she missed him when he was gone she never tried to discourage his enormous political ambition. When she died in 1828 he was heartbroken.

But as one might expect of this action-loving Artisan, Jackson carried out his presidency powerfully, and even outrageously. As President he was still the charismatic general and still the wily Artisan, and he conducted his presidency like a military leader conducting a military campaign. In Jackson as in his fellow Artisans, excitement was the prevailing mood, adventure the prevailing search, stimulation the prevailing hunger, victory the prevailing source of pride. To win, to defeat his foes decisively, that's living! The issues were black and white, the ends justified the means, loyalty and courage were rewarded. Charisma was necessary to such a campaign; the passionate loyalty of the troops was more important than matters of rightness of cause or justification of tactics. And subordinates were to be rewarded or rebuked as if they were his subordinate field officers. Thus "let the people rule!" was a Jacksonian campaign slogan, but the equally famous sentiment "to the victors belong the spoils" spoke more clearly of the style of his administration.[24]

Jackson had little political experience at the national level. Between 1796 and 1825 he had spent four years in the United States Congress, to be sure, but he had held office primarily at a state or county level in North Carolina and Tennessee. However, this flamboyant, clever, and energetic man was an Operator, and he brought a wealth of the Operator's tactical agility and love of excitement to his administration.

Jackson conducted a very personal administration. Just as he was inconsistent in his opinions, his administration was inconsistent in its policies (when it had any). Just as he was changeable in his actions his administration was erratic in its procedures. Where consistency was found in his presidency it was found in what was consistent in Jackson's views and style. It was, first above all, Andy Jackson's presidency.

It was the period of spacious opportunity following a successful military campaign. It was a time when Jackson's own views, friends, and agendas could be given priority and those of his vanquished opponents merely tolerated when necessary, destroyed when possible. But Jackson was sixty-one years old when he took office. He was irascible, weary, and sick, and his administration was in the hands of those who had managed his election campaign, including the clever Martin Van Buren. Tired and aging poorly, paying the price for living his life so wildly, Jackson could no longer concentrate well and left much of the everyday conduct of government in the hands of his managers who were, by and large, an unscrupulous collection of self-serving and vicious opportunists. It was as if the general were being kept isolated in his tent while the spoils of victory were distributed among his subordinates and their cronies.

---

24 Eric Fromm in his splendid treatise on human nature, *Man For Himself*, referred to the kind of personality as possessed by the likes of Jackson as "exploitative."

But Jackson was still a spoilsman and he saw in his behavior no violation of the letter or spirit of the Constitution. In his own words, "It was settled by the Constitution, the laws, and the whole practice of the government that the entire executive power is vested in the President of the United States."[25] Thus he was free to do what he wanted with the executive branch, including what was called "rotation of office": the practice of firing supporters of one's political enemies and replacing them with one's own followers.

Jackson's assertion about the powers of the presidency is quite remarkable since it was written at a time when the Congress was considered by most to be the most powerful branch of government. By contending that all necessary and sufficient legislation for the conduct of national affairs was already in the constitution, Jackson could portray the Congress as a rather useless appendage of government. As far as he was concerned all legislative policies were fixed and pre-set; it was his job to get on with the business of executing them without interference from mere Senators and Congressmen. Similarly he held the Supreme Court in complete contempt. Their rulings could not influence the presidency, he contended, and in fact they did not influence his presidency. Rule as they might wish, he need only ignore them.

Jackson's stance about the powers of the presidency relative to those of the Congress and the Supreme Court created an issue that would not disappear even after Jackson was gone. As one writer notes,

> It would be a source of irritation, sometimes becoming a critical issue, for a long time to come. It would torment Lincoln in his day and almost lead to his successor's impeachment. It would result in substantial failure for Wilson's peace plans, and it would force the liquidation of much of F. D. Roosevelt's New Deal. It was a quarrel inherent in the constitution so soon as a strong President should assert the powers derived from his independent position.[26]

All that would be in the distant future, of course, a time with which Artisans rarely concern themselves. There was opportunity for immediate action. As we have already noted, opponents were to be treated as enemies, and for the Westerner Andy Jackson, an important enemy of the frontiersman was still the hated Eastern money

---

25 *The American Presidents*, 72.
26 Rexford Tugwell, *How they Became President*, 95.

establishment. There were no shades of gray in Jackson's world, no nuances; things were good or bad, issues were black or white, one was for him or against him. And the Eastern establishment was bad, it was the enemy, and nothing further need be said. Artisans, as noted earlier, have a knack for blaming others for their own shortcomings and misfortunes, and Jackson appears to be no exception to this rule. Throughout his life Jackson considered himself one of those "plain and honest folks" so oppressed by the Eastern money and power center, and they wildly reciprocated his simple, unquestioning identification with them. On the day of his inauguration there were people who had trekked five hundred miles to attend the event; at least some of them could be found standing with their muddy boots planted firmly on the White House furniture in order to get a better look at their hero.27

So when the inaugural dust settled Jackson could go about his vendetta. When it was time for the routine rechartering of the Second Bank of the United States, a very large and powerful Eastern bank, he refused, loudly, to renew the charter. "This monster must perish!" he declaimed. "Until I can strangle this Hydra of corruption, the Bank, I will not shrink from my duty or my part."28 It was an interesting contrast in styles. Bank president Nicholas Biddle retaliated for Jackson's veto by refusing to make any further loans available. As he expected, his action precipitated a financial panic; money was desperately needed, but money was not to be found. Biddle hoped that the people and the Congress would turn on Jackson and force his compliance. Instead Biddle himself was eventually censured by the Congress, but still he would not back down. Money was power and he intended to use that power to defeat Jackson. But the savvy Jackson was able to gather and maintain the political support he needed, and the banker's power tactics eventually collapsed. A worthwhile lesson: head-on tactics against a talented and reckless Operator are usually ill-advised.

The same lesson might be learned from watching Jackson respond to rumblings of certain southern states. "States' rights" as opposed to

---

27 Jackson, 61 years old and in poor health, eventually became weary of the whole affair. He finally escaped his wildly enthusiastic supporters, it is said, by slipping out of the White House through a side window and settling down for the night at a local tavern.

28 *Presidential Courage*, 55.

Federal rights was an increasingly heated issue, and secession from the United States was already being spoken of by some influential Southerners. It was moot whether individual states had any "right" to secede or even to decide when Federal rulings must be obeyed. Jackson, whatever else he may have been, was an unflinching and unquestioning patriot. He ignored any congressional or judicial dictates that he take any action which would impair the soundness of the Federal position, and he would clearly have marched into the South with Federal troops had any southern state attempted to secede. He may have been unruly and impulsive, he may have been a spoilsman, and he may even have held the Supreme Court and the Congress of the United States in contempt, but Andy Jackson was a patriot and a military virtuoso who would probably have made mush out of any headlong attempt to split the Union.

Jackson served two very active terms as President of the United States even though he may have been one of the most physically impaired of all our Presidents. He was aging rapidly and he not only suffered painfully from the bullet in his lung (the legacy of his duel with Charles Dickinson), but also from recurring fevers, problems with breathing, infections and hemorrhaging, colitis and dysentery, smallpox, very severe tooth decay, and almost constant insomnia associated with his illness and pain. Yet he did not seek out for his cabinet men who could stand in his place if he became too ill. This is not what one would expect of an Artisan who relished the opportunity to create his own impacts. Instead he selected cabinet members who were faithful followers, good aides-de-camp, men who would do his bidding in the manner of good and faithful junior officers. Partly because he surrounded himself with weaker men he was able to insist on the smooth but suspect Martin Van Buren as the man who would succeed him as President.

Andrew Jackson died in June of 1845, eight years after leaving office. His frail body was finally overborne by the effects of a life energy spent profligately and the severe damage acquired in the course of his intemperate battles with his many enemies.

In Jackson's life we can find much of the best and much of the worst of the Operator Artisan character, unfettered and undisguised by the niceties of "gentlemanly" social breeding. Rash impulsiveness which in some Artisans is burning enough to die for; instant vengefulness even at the price of challenging death; a simplistic but tightly held "code of honor," never examined and never surrendered. Reckless and relentless pursuit of advantage and of the spoils of conquest; total focus on whatever he happened to be doing; complete lack of fear; and a prodigal tactical sense. All this along side an easy generosity, frankness and forthrightness in manner, and great decisiveness. One commentator expressed beautifully the essence of Andrew Jackson (and of the Operator Artisan character itself) when he wrote in 1855 that

> Swords, not words, were his arguments....Action followed speech, as thunder the lightning....With him, to think and to do were not so much two things as one.[29]

Bibliography

Bassett, J 1967	*The Life of Andrew Jackson*
Belohlavek, J 1985	*Let the Eagly Soar: The Foreign Policy of Andrew Jackson*
Buel, A 1904	*History of Andrew Jackson, Pioneer, Patriot, Soldier, Politician, President*
Curtis, J 1976	*Andrew Jackson and the Search for vindication*
Davis, B 1977	*Old Hickory: A Life of Andrew Jackson*
Eaton, J 1971	*The Life of Andrew Jackson*
Hoffman, W 1958	*Andrew Jackson and North Carolina Politics*
James, M 1933	*The Life of Andrew Jackson*
Johnson, G 1927	*Andrew Jackson, an Epic in Homespun*
Latner, R 1979	*The Presidency of Andrew Jackson: White House Politics*
Ogg, F 1919	*The Reign of Andrew Jackson: A Chronicle of the Frontier of Politics*
Remini, R 1967	*Andrew Jackson and the Bank War; a Study in the Growth of Presidential Power*
Remini, R 1977	*Andrew Jackson and the Course of American Empire*
Remini, R 1984	*Andrew Jackson and the Course of American Democracy*
Remini, R 1988	*The Legacy of Andrew Jackson: Essays on Democracy, Indian Removal, and Slavery*

---

29 J. G. Baldwin, Quoted in *The Presidency*, 73.

Rogin, M 1975 *Fathers and Children: Andrew Jackson and the Subjugation of the American Indian*

Stone, I 1951 *The President's Lady; a Novel about Rachel and Andrew Jackson*

Sumner, W 1899 *Andrew Jackson*

Syrett, H 1953 *Andrew Jackson: His Contribution to the American Tradition*

Wellman, P 1962 *Magnificent Destiny: A Novel about the Great Secret Adventure of Andrew Jackson and Sam Houston*

Martin Van Buren

"The Sly Fox"

Operator
Born: December 5, 1782
Died: July 24, 1862
Presidency: 1837-1841

Most of the men who were United States Presidents during the country's first century have been the objects of lengthy and intense scrutiny. George Washington, Thomas Jefferson, Andy Jackson, and Abraham Lincoln, for instance, have repeatedly captured the interest of biographers. In comparison with these men, relatively little has been written about Martin Van Buren. He was neither a popular presidential figure nor a charismatic one, nor a man whose personal life has been especially accessible to the biographical researcher. Even his autobiography is more a simple narrative of his political activities than a portrait of his personal life. The autobiography doesn't even mention his wife, Hannah Hoes Van Buren, who died when Van Buren was still a young man.

The sketchy record should probably not surprise us; Martin Van Buren was instinctively a quiet man. He rarely let himself be pinned down on an issue, especially if it promised to be controversial. Even when he spoke he often managed to be as elusive as a ghost. He might speak at length, but when he had finished one still could not be quite sure whether he had committed himself to a definite point of view. Extracting a definite opinion on anything from Van Buren was hard work, and the attempt to do so became something of a pastime among his colleagues.

Van Buren offered his political commitments, like his opinions, only after searching out every possible source of opportunity. Even with issues that seemed trivial he was likely to go through a carefully calculated inquiry: asking for information, seeking others' opinions, considering, shrewdly reconsidering, checking for problems, traps, pitfalls. He absorbed information and sought commitment, giving in return as little as he could. He was so adroit, commented one of his enemies, that "Van Buren glides along as smoothly as oil and as silently as a cat."[30] His enemy had right lubricant in mind, but the wrong animal; Van Buren was no cat, but a most stealthy fox, perhaps the stealthiest of all the fox-like Artisan Presidents.

Martin Van Buren married Hannah Hoes in 1807. She bore four children but died of tuberculosis in 1819 when she was only thirty-five. Van Buren himself was only thirty-six when she died, and it would be almost twenty years before he became President. Even though he was therefore still a relatively young man he never remarried and never showed any inclination to do so. Little is known of Hannah Van Buren, and Martin Van Buren's failure to mention her in his autobiography is another sign of his intensely private and impersonal approach to life and his typically Artisan here-and-now frame of reference. Personal history was for him another of those books best kept closed, to be opened to public view only for specific purposes, just as the veteran gambler plays

---

30 James Hamilton, quoted in *The Presidency of Martin Van Buren,* 30.

his card close to his chest, and lays them down to public view only when he must.[31]

Of course, "the Red Fox of Kinderhook," as some called him (he was born in Kinderhook, New York), did on occasion take a definite and public position about matters. But when he did it was usually with some personal advantage in mind. Van Buren once committed what appeared to be an uncharacteristic slip while talking to a gossipy woman who happened to have then-President Andrew Jackson's ear. Van Buren praised Jackson openly but then begged the woman, "Don't tell Jackson I said he was a great man." Of course he knew full well that his apparently careless and confiding comment would reach the President. And of course he also understood that he would gather political advantage thereby, though that advantage might not show itself for quite some time. The Operator Van Buren was a master of maneuver, for he had developed to a very high degree his ability to find and use whatever tactics were necessary to get him where he wanted to go. He was naturally very clever in this regard, and he coupled cleverness with slow, calculated movement, a wary fox approaching a watchful farmer's hen house. And his maneuvering usually paid off. In fact Andy Jackson, himself a fox, though a less stealthy one, became so fond of Van Buren that in 1836, when he himself decided not to run again for office, he forced Van Buren's candidacy on the Democratic party.

It seemed an unlikely choice in some respects. Andy Jackson was a tall, lean, whip of a man, more than six feet tall and constantly in restless motion. Though by 1836 he was a gaunt and sick old man, Jackson was still the imperious general. Van Buren, on the other hand, was only five and a half feet tall, and though handsome enough as a younger man, he had become comfortably obese. Along side the severe and rather rude-mannered General Jackson, Van Buren gave the appearance of a plump dandy. He had developed a taste for good wines and for the social life of the political and monied elite, and he had readily adopted the signs and styles of the upper classes. "Ease and grace of movement, meticulous

---

31 When he later took office as President, the work of the First Lady was taken over by Angelica Van Buren, Van Buren's daughter-in-law. Angelica also happened to be one of Andrew Jackson's nieces, and was apparently a kind and charming woman, but she has garnered little recognition, and has gone largely unremarked by historians.

dress and grooming, the glow of health and good cheer—all suggested the drawing room or a caucus more than the battlefield."[32] And his Artisan's suaveness and sense of humor and his conversational gifts made him a popular figure in the "best" circles, whether in Washington or London.

Of course his Artisan character also meant that he was not inclined to abstract thought or speech. He had, by his own admission, a "disinclination to mental efforts,"[33] and he claimed to read only for amusement—when he read at all. Though he showed little ability or interest in shaping his own ideas, he was expert at adopting and making practical use of the ideas of those around him. In the typical tactical style of the Artisan, "as a lawyer he responded to the case at hand, as a governmental official he reacted to events more than he tried to shape them,"[34] and in this he was extraordinarily clever.

His cleverness was respected by both friends and enemies, but while his allies might admire him as an able politician, his enemies (including the outspoken Davy Crockett) portrayed him as nothing more than a small-minded, unprincipled opportunist. He was interested only in personal power and prestige, they declared, and they awarded him a number of unflattering nicknames, including "the Little Magician" and "Weasel." Whether they admired or detested him, called him "fox," "weasel," or "wizard," none who knew him doubted Van Buren's capacity to manage political events expeditiously, and few could fail to recognize his instinctive ability (found often among the Artisans) to anticipate the winning side in a dispute and to ally himself with it.

His history up to the time he entered the White House showed this ability nicely. He had studied law as a young man and was admitted to the bar in 1803 when he was only twenty-one, but he quickly became active in politics, which was always his first love. Then, in 1808, he was awarded his first political prize: appointment as a county judge. His political star was rising, and only a few years later he was elected to the New York State Senate, and then served as Attorney General of New York. He gradually took control of "the Albany Regency," a political

32 *The Presidency of Martin Van Buren,* 22.
33 *The Presidency of Martin Van Buren,* 23.
34 *The Presidency of Martin Van Buren,* 24.

machine that became the powerhouse of New York state politics, and therefore an important part of national politics. In 1821 he was elected to the U. S. Senate, but while in the Senate he still managed to maintain his grip on the New York political machine, which operated much as if he were still there.

During John Quincy Adams's administration (1825-1829), Senator Van Buren was the leader of congressional opposition to the President, and he played a major role in negotiating the political coalition that defeated Adams and elected Andrew Jackson in 1828. (Artisans, especially the Operators, can become master negotiators because of their view that everything anyone values is negotiable. This view gives them a flexibility that their opponents are unlikely to be able to match.) Van Buren himself was elected Governor of New York in 1828, though he resigned the governorship after a few months to become newly-elected President Andrew Jackson's Secretary of State. His progress had been carefully crafted, smoothly executed, and largely without hindrance, and now he would demonstrate his abilities as a king-maker.

Until the campaign of 1828, presidential candidates had been selected from among the country's aristocrats: the landed, the educated, and the privileged. It was Martin Van Buren as much as anyone who recognized the political power in the unspoken, even unrecognized wish of the common people of the country to see "one of their own" capture the highest office in the land. It was also Van Buren who saw Andrew Jackson's candidacy as a way of harnessing this unrecognized political sentiment.

Jackson was a comparatively uneducated backwoods hell-raising lawyer, and a populist who could be portrayed easily as a "man of the people." He also had the political virtue that he was a military hero who was somehow a bit larger than life. Jackson's enormously effective presidential campaign with its late-night torchlight parades and his campaign slogan, "Let the people rule," a nation-wide, rip-snorting, carefully choreographed populist donnybrook, was largely composed, promoted, and steered by Martin Van Buren. Van Buren was the man who most deliberately introduced into political campaigns the evasive speeches by candidates, and the friendly but meaningless handshaking, back-slapping, and baby-kissing. Such was the Little Magician's impact on the campaign that Daniel Webster, hardly a political amateur himself, said later that no ten men had done as much to elect Jackson as had Van Buren. In fact it was Van Buren's remarkable skill in shaping and managing the machinery of the American political system that earned him the sobriquet "the Little Magician." The organization and functioning of our modern political parties is in important part the direct result of Van Buren's work.

His fascination with the nature of party politics puts Van Buren in sharp contrast with the Guardians and Rationals who had preceded him in American politics. With the single exception of the Artisan Andrew Jackson, Van Buren's predecessors (and many of his contemporaries) worked to create and stabilize a thoughtfully organized, durable, and effective structure for governing. His predecessors drew their inspiration largely from the Constitution which, for the Rationals, was both the product of and the continuing inspiration for their preoccupation with government as a structure built consistent with the canons of science and logic. These men envisioned government as something to be designed, as an elegant building is designed, and most of them found abhorrent and even menacing the emergence of political parties with their divisive, self-interested agendas.

Martin Van Buren did not wish to be alienated from the political support Thomas Jefferson could still offer, and he was careful to assume the position espoused by the former President. Van Buren did seem to admire Jefferson, and sometimes visited him at Monticello. Jefferson believed that party distinctions were inevitable in a free republic. Certain groups, said Jefferson, would inevitably mistrust others. There would always be those who trusted the people but not a centralized government, as the Jeffersonians did, and there would always be those who trusted to centralized power and strong connections between political and economic leadership, as the more aristocratic Hamiltonians (whom Jefferson detested) did. Party coalitions would inevitably arise to express this fundamental division, and a democracy must be prepared for them. Van Buren greatly respected Jefferson and his own political philosophy, insofar as he could be said to have one, was rooted in Jefferson's.[35]

---

35 Van Buren had to hide his opinion to some degree from Jackson, though in most regards the two could talk with one another very openly. Though Jackson was rather

The ambitious craftsman also saw in the principles of state rights and limited government, both consistent with Jefferson's outlook, practical ways of defusing the nation's political problems, and especially those associated with the slavery issue. That issue was already leading to sectional sentiments so strong that some feared—and others hoped—that they would result in the secession of the Southern, slave-holding states from the United States (as would happen less than twenty-five years later). Van Buren knew better than anyone how to resolve differences and establish consensus, and his greatest successes had come through his use of the power of party organization. As one of the foremost inventors of the party, he not only knew the importance of party discipline and party loyalty, but he thought the party system might be enough to break the grip of sectional factions and increase the likelihood of disciplined cooperation across sectional boundaries. He hoped that organized political parties could foster (and manage) local initiative, the rights of the individual states could be protected, and any measures that invited more sectionalism could be avoided.

Indeed Van Buren thought that effective government required such interplay of organized political forces, and he therefore applauded and encouraged party politics. Not only did party politics seem to him the best way to keep the government stable and attuned to Jeffersonian principles, but it was also the game he most enjoyed and the one he was best at. Because of belief as well as inclination, then, Van Buren devoted himself to the art of political maneuver, the use of governmental structure and process to achieve specific political ends. He focused on the election of his own party's candidates, and he became a master of behind-the-scenes maneuvering to assure passage of desired legislation, exhibiting a tactical virtuosity perhaps not equalled until the coming, a century later, of another astute "fox," Lyndon Johnson.

Van Buren recognized quite early in his career that unnecessary trouble could arise from letting a political struggle become too personal, and he made it a life-long habit to keep his political animosities to himself. He was not unique in this habit of course; it is characteristic of

---

republican, or Jeffersonian, he saw no conflict in his effort to maintain a strong central position for himself. But then Artisans do not worry about philosophical consistency in any event.

most experienced politicians. When they see that nothing is gained and much may be lost by expressing their ire publicly they will curb their impulse to do so. Van Buren expertly managed his own anger, and even in the midst of heated political campaigns he showed a facility for avoiding most of other people's anger or disfavor. Thus, though he might never become a figure popular with the public at large, he could still talk and work with opposing political factions with equanimity and without alienating any faction. He might be a political opponent; he could usually avoid becoming a political enemy. He was in this regard one of the first truly professional American politicians, a careful practitioner of the political art, the essential Operator Artisan.

Van Buren consistently downplayed the importance of his own position, though insiders recognized clearly the power he wielded. He preferred, to use a European image, to be the power behind the throne, the shadowy figure who quietly and often secretly advises and even dominates the person sitting on the throne. There is a certain shrewdness in this: Van Buren was undoubtedly aware that kings are sometimes beheaded; only rarely do their advisors share their fate.

Not that Van Buren was timid; timidity is not a characteristic found in the Artisans. During his time as a U. S. Senator, in fact, matters became so heated at one point that certain of his political opponents threatened his life. Van Buren, a quiet man but no coward, went about his business in the Senate in his usual fashion—while carrying with him, where all could see them, a pair of loaded pistols. We can hardly help being reminded of the inimitable Operator general, George Patton of World War II fame, and the pair of ivory handled pistols he wore so ostentatiously.[36] (The Operators, with their penchant for taking all dares and assaulting all challenges to their bold and hard image, are the people most likely to exhibit this sort of behavior.)

In spite of his political skills, his polish, and even the occasional brace of pistols, Martin Van Buren was not a charismatic person, and his soft-spoken calculating style did nothing to fire the public's imagination. Though he was a powerful party politician, he became President only

---

36 Contrary to the usual story, they were not pearl handled pistols. Patton, in his typical, rather Jacksonian Operator style, claimed that only someone who worked in a whorehouse would own a weapon with pearl handles.

because Andy Jackson, retiring after his second term, hand-picked him over the protests of the party bosses and forced his candidacy on the party in 1836. Van Buren knew that he was seen as an indecisive, slippery intriguer, and he worked hard to show himself an absolutely reliable supporter of the party's programs and ideology. Neither charismatic like Jackson, nor an intellect like Jefferson, Van Buren became a doctrinal purist. In this he presented himself—successfully enough to become President—as the absolute opposite of the Artisan opportunist he really was.

Van Buren was elected easily but, hand-picked favorite or not, espouser of Jeffersonian principles or not, skillful mediator or not, he did not establish a popular or a potent presidency. A different set of skills were required of the occupant of that highly visible office, and Van Buren did not have them sufficiently. The Wizard Van Buren, like the fictional Wizard of Oz, seemed to lose much of his power when he was exposed to public view. Nonetheless, in easier times Van Buren might have become a more popular leader. But times were not easy, and Van Buren inherited a number of difficult problems from his Artisan predecessor. For instance, international relations were troublesome, and some people were eager to declare war against England. There were skirmishes going on in Maine between Canadians and Americans, each marauding across the international border, and many angry and ambitious Americans wanted to invade Canada and annex it, just as had been attempted during the War of 1812. Van Buren struggled to avoid this hotheaded and dangerous course of action.

Furthermore, the economy was in terrible shape. The economy seemed to be booming and speculation had become quite fevered during Jackson's terms of office. The boom was cheered by many, especially those with access to credit, and the speculative rashness which often accompanies optimism was abundant. But Jackson's war with the banks had unsettled the credit markets badly, and the economy still had not settled down when Van Buren took office. Two months after Van Buren's inauguration, many banks stopped making "payments in specie": they wouldn't honor their own banknotes. In effect, no money and no credit were available; the economy was frozen. The great Panic of 1837 ensued, more than 600 banks failed over the course of the next year, and a depression followed which lasted until after Van Buren had left office. In fact the financial storm was severe and lasting enough that when he ran for re-election in 1840 his opponents could call him "Martin Van Ruin," though the depression was not of his making.

Even more menacing, the question of slavery had become dangerously troublesome, and the national temper became increasingly feverish as abolitionist outrage and secessionist anger inflamed one another. As was noted earlier, Van Buren tried to work his magic and create a political compromise about the slavery issue. He sought to satisfy southern interests by adhering to a strict state's rights policy on slavery, by appointing a largely Southern cabinet, and by promising to veto any legislation about the matter which did not meet with Southern approval. He also tried to placate the Northern abolitionists by opposing the expansion of slavery into new territories. In fact he went out of his way, like Jackson before him, to oppose expansionist policies, which would add new states to the Union. Thus when Texas declared its independence from Mexico in 1836 Jackson, and then Van Buren, refused to support the popular move for its annexation.

Ultimately Van Buren's efforts failed to satisfy many, for the South resented (among other things) his refusal to admit Texas as a slave state, while the North was unhappy with his pro-state (which to them meant pro-slavery) stand. The struggle over slavery was a vicious one, and even Van Buren's tactical gifts could not subdue the gigantic forces angrily arrayed against each other.

Given how difficult he was bound to find his presidential term of office, it might be that Van Buren's decision to run for the presidency when he did was one of the few significant political errors the Fox of Kinderhook ever made.

It is ironic that when Van Buren ran for re-election in 1840 he found himself the victim of more than the economic difficulties plaguing the nation and the poisonous slavery issue: he was also a victim of the populist style of his opponent's campaign. For entertainment in the White House under Van Buren had become far more leisurely and the atmosphere more formal than it had been under Jackson. There were guards now to prevent citizens from walking in unannounced, noisy receptions were replaced with quiet, polite dinners, with meals prepared by Van Buren's imported chef. In contrast, the opposition candidate, William Henry Harrison was presented to the public as another Andrew

Jackson, another man of the people, another military genius. Van Buren, "The American Talleyrand" (implying that he was a devious and royalist aristocrat) could not counter the presidential campaign strategy that he himself had helped formulate for Andrew Jackson twelve years earlier. And though Van Buren was in fact no aristocrat, and though Harrison was far from being another Jackson, their public images were enough to sway the election in favor of "the man of the people." Van Buren was defeated.

Van Buren's defeat showed once again that he was right: except in the best of times the reign of aristocracy (real or perceived) could no longer survive the populist challenge. However, given the problems his administration faced, it can be said that Van Buren had done a creditable job in running the country. His last address to Congress, a few months before the election of 1840, pointed to the relative quiet along the nation's frontiers, which was an indication of his effectiveness in foreign affairs. He also pointed out that he had not increased taxes, had not created any new government indebtedness, and had not turned to a new national bank system which would have replaced the imperious bank killed off by Andrew Jackson. Van Buren didn't even mention abolition because he had been able to keep things reasonably quiet on that front and saw no need to stir them up again. Thus, in spite of the difficulties involved, he had been able to manage a reasonable, even though temporary and very delicate consensus about the most urgent matters facing the nation.

It wasn't a bad performance for a President in those troubled times, and though he has not been widely credited for his performance, Van Buren used his tactical leadership in a way which served not just his own interests, but those of his country as well. Perhaps he was not so far from the truth seeing himself as "a man of national principles who was seeking to preserve the Union as he thought the fathers had made it."[37]

Politics was deep in Van Buren's blood and after his defeat he tried for the presidency again in 1844 (though his nomination was blocked by southern Democrats) and once again in 1848. He was defeated both times, and though he was disappointed, perhaps in the final analysis his failures were less than heartbreaking. He was after all at his best as a

---

37 *The Presidency of Martin Van Buren*, 209.

party politician rather than as a chief executive, and he wryly commented toward the end of his life that the two happiest days of his life were the day he entered the presidency and the day he surrendered it.

Van Buren died in 1862, a comfortable gentleman farmer living on his estate in New York, but witness to the opening stages of a calamity not even a politician as clever as he could avert: that terrible blood-letting known as the Civil War.

Bibliography

Alexander, H 1935	*The American Talleyrand*
Bancroft, G 1889	*Martin Van Buren to the End of His Public Career*
Bowers, C 1923	*The Party Battles of the Jackson Period*
Bradford, G 1932	*The Prince of Darkness—Talleyrand*
Butler, W 1862	*Martin Van Buren: Lawyer, Statesman and Man*
Crocket, D 1835	*The Life of Martin Van Buren*
Curtis, J 1970	*The Fox at Bay: Martin Van Buren and the Presidency*
Dawson, M 1840	*Sketches in the Life of Martin Van Buren*
Hoyt, E 1964	*Martin Van Buren*
Fitzpatrick, J 1920	*The Autobiography of Martin Van Buren*
McBain, H 1907	*De Witt Clinton & the Origin of the Spoils System in New York*
Meyers, G	*A History of Tammany Hall*
Parton, J 1860	*The Life and Times of Aaron Burr*
Werner, M 1928	*Tammany Hall*
Wilson, M 1984	*The Presidency of Martin Van Buren*

Theodore Roosevelt

"Wherever you are; get action!"

Operator
Born: October 27, 1858
Died: January 6, 1919
Presidency: 1901-1909

Theodore Roosevelt, the quintessential Operator Artisan, was among many other things a cowboy, a mountain climber (he had climbed the famous Matterhorn in the Alps), a big game hunter in Africa, the pre-eminent figure among the famous Rough Riders in the Spanish American War, Governor of the State of New York, Vice-President, and finally the youngest President of the United States.

Roosevelt had been born to money. He grew up in the atmosphere of Eastern wealth and sophistication and almost as a matter of course received his education at Harvard University. Though his family was not extremely wealthy it was still a patrician family, and the Roosevelts' aristocratic background lent itself to a rather elitist view of people and politics. But Teddy Roosevelt was quite unimpressed by wealth and social station. Throughout his life he was passionately committed to a democracy that functioned in the interests of all the people rather than of only a limited aristocratic or power elite. He was a powerful advocate of honesty and fairness, and had a passionate interest in improving the position of the underdog, the ordinary citizen.

During his long political career he was actively and enthusiastically engaged in political reform of various kinds, but he is especially well-known as the supreme "trust buster." There were a number of giant monopolies whose power dominated American commerce in the early days of the twentieth century. Roosevelt used anti-trust legislation to break these monopolies' stranglehold and showed that he was not afraid to go after the "big boys" in his efforts. On one occasion Roosevelt brought suit against one of the giant organizations of J. P. Morgan, the financial prince, thereby tackling one of the most powerful men in the country. But that should surprise no one; the Artisan Teddy Roosevelt had a strong competitive streak, he was completely fearless, and he probably enjoyed the challenge thoroughly.

His interest in honesty and fairness and his activity in support of "the little guy" were very appealing to most Americans. But there have been others with these characteristics whose popularity did not begin to approach Roosevelt's. Teddy Roosevelt, known affectionately as "TR" by millions of people, had a flair, a magnificent charisma that was irresistible to most people. His overwhelming zest for life and his remarkable ebullience were legendary and captivating, as were his self-confidence and fearlessness and his enormous capacity for simply enjoying himself. Energetic and athletic, Teddy Roosevelt was action personified and action glorified. He lived fully the advice he gave so enthusiastically to others: "Get action; do things...create, act, take a place wherever you are; get action."[38]

The opportunity for action can be found anywhere, and TR knew it. The story is told that when Roosevelt in his early career found himself

---

[38] Quoted in *The American Political Tradition*, 210-211.

the new commissioner of a corrupt police force he decided instantly to put an end to the corruption. Unwilling to confine himself to taking only administrative action (such as forcing the chief of the city's uniformed police to resign), he adopted the habit of donning a black cape and prowling the city's streets nightly in search of policemen who were not doing their duty properly. Though his nightly forays made good newspaper copy and also made him very popular, his popularity was dimmed considerably—at least in New York—when he also acted to enforce the law requiring that all taverns be closed on Sundays. Roosevelt's family background was rather Victorian, and there is no one more assiduous in demanding adherence to the rules than an Artisan who has taken them on as his own.

Like his Operator Artisan precursor Andrew Jackson, Teddy Roosevelt was prodigious in his ability to capture the confidence of ordinary men and women. He brought to all his projects a flair which made them seem somehow like heroic battles. Consider his announcement that he intended to run for the presidency again in 1912: "My hat is in the ring! The fight is on and I am stripped to the buff!"[39] Roosevelt, to hear him report it, was not initiating a political campaign; he was participating in a heroic bare-knuckled prize fight.

Probably the appeal that Artisan politicians in general and TR in particular have for ordinary people is their versatile use of what might be called "contest" metaphors and similes. Artisans are usually avid fans, if not participants, of all sorts of fights, games, and debates; they are first to volunteer when war breaks out, and they quickly pick up the argot or slang that emerges in such contests of daring and prowess. Wherever they adventure they become proficient extremely quickly in their comrades' lingo, and they are masterful at finding and making use of its impact. TR, master Artisan, was a master of lingo.

TR had become a member of the New York State Assembly in 1882. Next he was on the U. S. Civil Service Commission, was appointed the New York Police Commissioner, and then during 1897-98 served as Assistant Secretary of the Navy. He had been highly active in each of these offices, as his nightly prowls while Police Commissioner suggest, and he always found a way to have fun even as his positions of

---

39 Quoted in *Presidential Campaigns*, 192.

authority and responsibility became more noteworthy. During an absence of Navy Secretary John Long, it was the job of the Assistant Secretary, Teddy Roosevelt, to manage the American Navy. TR was able to hold the reins of command in his own hands for a brief time and held them, one suspects, a bit more tightly than was necessary. He loved the power and freedom of command. As he wrote to a friend, while Secretary Long was absent, "I'm having immense fun running the navy." Secretary Long was not as pleased; he nicknamed his Assistant Secretary "The Bull in the China Shop," reminding one of the not altogether successful adventures of another American naval Artisan, Admiral "Bull" Halsey in WW II.[40]

Similarly, when TR eventually became President he felt rather constricted by the counterbalancing structure of the executive, legislative, and judicial branches of national government. He had his objectives to pursue and his enthusiasms to indulge, and the checks and balances of government were quite annoying to him. He was eager for more freedom of action, so he wanted much more authority to reside in the executive branch. This would mean added authority for the office of the presidency, but would also make available more power and freedom of action for the current CEO, Theodore Roosevelt.

Not that the dynamic TR always waited for explicit legislative sanction for his exercises of power. For example, at one point he decided it would be desirable to sail the United States Fleet around the world to demonstrate the country's power, an exercise in jingoism called "showing the flag." An irate congressman, upset by Roosevelt's expensive plan in a time of tight budgets, told TR that Congress might well refuse to provide funds for the venture. Roosevelt replied that he already had enough funds to sail the Fleet half way around the planet. He would leave it up to Congress to decide whether to provide the money necessary to bring the Fleet home from there.

A reasonable degree of involvement in exciting events was rarely enough for Roosevelt. There just was not enough action, not enough

---

40 See *The History of Naval Warfare in the Pacific* by Sam Morrison, official naval historian for WW II. Morrison's analysis of the battle of Leyte Gulf shows Halsey impetuously leaving his post to chase after a decoy dangled deliberately in front of him. The Artisan Halsey had missed most of the immediate action so far and couldn't resist the temptation, even though he almost caused a disaster for the American forces.

impact, not enough risk entailed in reasonable involvement.[41] When the Spanish-American War broke out in 1898 Teddy Roosevelt resigned his position as Assistant Navy Secretary and volunteered to lead a combat unit against the Spanish. He provided financial backing for, and was appointed a Lieutenant Colonel of the now famous 1st U. S. Volunteer Cavalry regiment, the "Rough Riders."[42] Those who knew the unit considered it a rag-tag collection of adventurers, cowboys, and "odd characters." But when the regiment, with TR second in command, advanced in a well-publicized assault against the Spanish on Kettle Hill (now known as San Juan Hill) both the regiment and Teddy Roosevelt quickly became legends.

The whole affair was typically TR. It was exciting, it was challenging, it made him look good, and it was well-covered by the press. It did not seem to matter to him (or to the press) that the assault was poorly conceived and sloppily executed, that the rather ill-conceived "charge" was a dismounted uphill trudge against an entrenched enemy, or that American casualties were painfully and unnecessarily high. Always excited by both the prospect and the memory of adventure, Roosevelt later commented about the San Juan Hill action, "Oh, but we had a bully fight!" He was intoxicated by the event, and while Artisans of any stamp are typically hungry for stimulation (especially during periods of quiet), TR seems to have had a ravenous appetite for it.

The "charge" took place in 1898, and it helped make him as a politician. The Spanish-American War had been popular and most people were delighted two years later when Roosevelt was acclaimed as his party's vice-presidential choice for the campaign of 1900. But Mark Hanna, the party's national chairman, protested. He saw the impulsive and even rash side of Roosevelt's character much more clearly than most, and he was worried. "Don't any of you realize," he protested, "that there's only one life between this madman and the White House?"[43] By

---

41 Artisans of all types are usually hungry for stimulation. This characteristic was studied and those who shared it were called "the sensation seeking personality." (See M. Zuckerman's papers in the *Journal of Consulting Psychology:* "The Sensation Seeking Scale," 1964, 477-482, "The Validity of the Sensation Seeking Scale," 1968, 420-426, and "What is the sensation seeker?" 1972, 308-321.)

42 This sort of appointment was not unusual in the United States at that time. Many military formations were backed by men who were then, almost automaticaly given high command within them.

43 *The American Presidents,* 221.

and large Hanna need not have worried so much. TR was impulsive but not mindlessly so. Usually the moment consumed him only after he had made certain that he could afford to have it do so.

Roosevelt had an instinctive sense of the power of the press and was extremely careful about his relationships with its members. A master promoter and negotiator, he was always adept at arranging to become its darling and its hero. Even though he was only second in command of the 1st Volunteer Cavalry, for instance, the regiment, by virtue of TR's careful management of the gentlemen of the press, became known by everyone as "Teddy Roosevelt's Rough Riders." His careful management of reporters' locations, of their comfort, of what they could access, and of his relationships with them bore this kind of fruit time after time.

TR understood the value of managed news and enjoyed the activity. He was, after all, an Operator. But even more he openly and enthusiastically glorified physical adventure and contest, and he found great joy in the sense of triumph that could come only from the clash of arms. Expressing his dissatisfaction at one point with what he considered a certain flabbiness of the American population, he commented to Henry Cabot Lodge that "This country needs a war!" Direct action, physical action, elemental risk-taking: here was the tonic the nation needed, he believed. Here would be found the inspiration for the country's greatness, that greatness that the passionate nationalist Teddy Roosevelt valued so highly.

Roosevelt had no love for pointless brutality or for destruction or for any of the other horrors and tragedies of war. He was drawn rather to the glory and the adventure that he associated with battle. For example, in 1905 Russia and Japan had become involved in a fruitless and highly destructive war which had become hopelessly stalemated. It was TR's own idea to take upon himself the difficult task of mediating peace talks between the two combatant nations. So successful was he in this difficult endeavor that he was later awarded the Nobel Peace Prize, making him one of only two American Presidents to be so honored. (Woodrow Wilson was the other.)

Roosevelt the mediator displayed a consistent interest in maintaining good relations between the United States and the other nations of the world. Even so Roosevelt the enthusiastic patriot was eager to assert what he saw as the rights and powers of the United States. His decision to send the American fleet around the world was not mere whimsy; he wanted to remind the world of American might and power. "Speak softly, and carry a big stick" he said. Don't go looking for trouble, but if you find it, be prepared to give better than you get.

His eagerness to assert the preeminent position of the United States is obvious in his treatment of the Monroe Doctrine. This Doctrine, the result of the collaboration of President James Monroe and John Quincy Adams, declared that the countries of North and South America were to be free of domination and colonization by the European powers. The United States would stand as the protector of these small nations against any European encroachment. The bold and energetic TR took the Monroe Doctrine a very considerable step further in what has been called "the Roosevelt Corollary." He declared that these protected little countries could not always be counted upon to conduct themselves properly if they were free of any accountability for their actions. Therefore the United States had the responsibility for seeing to it that the countries of the American continents behaved themselves as responsible members of the world community. Default of debts, mistreatment of alien citizens, or other actions by the nations of the Americas which showed insufficient regard for the rights and interests of foreign countries or their citizens would be dealt with by these nations' protector, the United States.

Thus the adventurous Roosevelt provided a rationale for paternalistic interventions by the United States throughout the Western Hemisphere. These interventions were frequent during the early years of this century and are still resented in many places south of the United States' border. In some areas the recent invasion of Panama and deposition of the dictator Manuel Noriega is seen as merely another example of the "imperialism" promulgated by Teddy Roosevelt. And it must be acknowledged that his paternal interest was far from altruistic. He took great pride, for instance, in having brought about the creation of the Panama Canal, a resource which has been vital to the interests of the United States.

The Canal almost wasn't built, for there had been a hitch in negotiations with Colombia. (Panama was a province of Colombia at that time.) Rather than allow the hitch to scuttle the deal Roosevelt encouraged a Panamanian revolt. (He even had United States warships standing by to make sure nothing went wrong.) The revolt was successful and enabled Panama to throw off Colombian rule. Roosevelt immediately recognized the new country of Panama and found no further difficulty in his negotiations for the Canal. Word of his action got out and he tried to defend it, but for a change he had little success. His Secretary of War, Elihu Root, commented to him that "You have shown that you were accused of seduction and you have conclusively proved that you were guilty of rape."[44] This is the sort of outrageously high-handed but often remarkably effective maneuvering that one comes to expect of the Artisan, particularly the Operator Artisan.

If Roosevelt was an aggressive, adventurous, spirited Artisan who was in love with action and who from time to time acted rashly and with questionable intentions, he was also finally a man of overall good intentions. As President he sponsored a great deal of pivotal legislation, including anti-trust laws, the Pure Food and Drug Act, and various conservation measures. He also invited Booker T. Washington to dine with him during his presidency, and Washington thereby became the first Black in American history to be an invited guest to the White House.

Of course the event was not well-received in all quarters. But Roosevelt was a man quite willing to invite impassioned controversy. In fact he usually relished the opportunity to do so. He could not have been terribly upset, and was probably exhilarated when one southern newspaper called the dinner "the most damnable outrage ever."

Roosevelt's high level of physical and political activity were accompanied by considerable academic ability, and his display of virtuosity could be considerable even in intellectual pursuits. For instance he was a good scholar when he chose to be and a prolific writer. He authored several dozen books, most of which are still quite readable and interesting today. He was fond of American history. Perhaps his best respected work is his three-volume history with the lovely Artisan title, *The Winning of the West*. Verbal fluency and cheerful enthusiasm, love of action and a sense of impact, hard work and boundless energy: each

---

44 *One Night Stands with American History*, p. 190, drawn from *The Panama Canal*, Walter Lafeber, Oxford University Press, New York, 1978.

of these contributed its share to his charisma, his ability to capture the enthusiasm and loyalty of his followers.

TR's love of activity and his inveterate good cheer were also reflected in his family life. His first wife, Alice Lee Roosevelt, died of Bright's disease when she was only twenty-three, four years after their marriage. His mother died of typhoid on the same day, February 14, 1889, and the double tragedy struck Roosevelt very hard. About his wife he wrote "When my heart's dearest died the light went from my life forever."[45] Well, perhaps not that long. TR was rigidly Victorian in his outlook on sex, so much so that the question of the appropriateness of his own second marriage was a major issue. But Artisan impulsiveness soon triumphed over Victorian upbringing. Fidelity, seemliness, conventionality in sexual mores were important to him, but still, when a healthy and vigorous and passionate man is a widower...

Teddy Roosevelt, no matter how powerful his sense of loss, could not settle for a tragic life. He quickly plunged back into action, for action was the Great Healer to a man like Roosevelt, and then, less than three years later, he remarried. His second wife, Edith Carow Roosevelt, was probably an Organizer Rational. She was a rather regal and commanding presence who appeared "supremely confident, in command of herself and often, it seemed, of those around her."[46] So well organized and certain of herself did she seem that some wags claimed she had never made a mistake. Perhaps those around her couldn't help comparing her behavior with that of the many nearby Artisans. Rationals, though quite capable of error, try very hard never to repeat an error. Artisans, on the other hand, can rather cheerfully make the same error over and over again. They sometimes seem to learn nothing from experience, perhaps because they so often blame others (or "the breaks") for their setbacks and losses and thereby fail to recognize their own mistakes.

Edith Roosevelt bore five children and took care of the one child from TR's first marriage. She was a rather aloof person and though she

---

45 *The American Presidents,* 218.
46 *A Ford, Not a Lincoln,* 118.

apparently did not disapprove of TR's irrepressible frolicking with their children, she did comment that having her ebullient husband around seemed to her rather akin to having a seventh child to manage. He was apparently a rather difficult "child," rough-housing, sliding down banisters, roaring through the house, and generally encouraging their children in all sorts of mischief. It was a blessing that Edith Roosevelt was such a fine manager and administrator; not only did she manage to keep the White House organized, but she also managed to subdue some of the most potentially embarrassing of her husband's impulses (for instance his propensity for wearing gaudy military uniforms when given half a chance). Even so it wasn't easy to manage the crowd, as may be noted by the fact that the Roosevelt children became known as "The White House Gang."

Edith Roosevelt also showed herself to be unflappable about life in the public eye. During Teddy's governorship of New York, for instance, she discovered that she would not be required to shake hands while standing in a reception line if she were holding a bouquet of flowers. So she immediately adopted the practice and continued it when she reached Washington. She also showed her Organizer's proclivities when she calmly and systematically assigned to subordinates many of the minor details and routine tasks formerly carried on the sometimes frail shoulders of the First Ladies.

Though she was capable of almost complete detachment from whatever was going on around her, apparently impervious to the stresses and strains that afflict most White House wives, beneath her cool exterior she was still capable of considerable graciousness. The story is told that at a White House entertainment she noted a woman being snubbed by the other guests. The woman had fallen into financial difficulty and become a sales clerk, and Edith Roosevelt knew her because she patronized the store where the woman now worked. The terribly embarrassed guest was preparing to leave to avoid the painful snubbing when Mrs. Roosevelt noted what was happening. The President's wife immediately went up to her, held out her hand, and said, "I think we need hardly be introduced, since we are old

friends. I am so glad to see you here." Then she put her arm
around the woman's waist, led her to a sofa, and sat and chatted
with her for fifteen or twenty minutes.[47]

Teddy Roosevelt ran for office a second time and was easily
elected. Four years later, however, he decided to step aside though he
was still a young man. No one had ever been elected to three terms as
President, and he apparently wasn't interested in breaking the two-term
precedent established by George Washington. Besides, there were new
adventures calling to him. He chose William Howard Taft to be his
successor, the man who would carry out Roosevelt's programs while TR
himself was off on other adventures. Roosevelt was later to regret his
decision about Taft, who turned out to have a mind of his own.

TR, indignant about Taft's course of action, and eager to take up the
political life again, four years later ran against Taft for the presidency.
He formed a new party, the Progressive Party, known popularly as the
"Bull Moose" party. The party was composed mostly of disaffected
Republicans and Roosevelt's candidacy split in the Republican vote so
badly that neither he nor Taft could win. Instead the Democrat Woodrow
Wilson won and the Progressive Party, which existed chiefly as a result
of Roosevelt's charismatic popularity, dissolved soon after. This was a
painful outcome for TR, who hated Wilson. Soon after Wilson took
office, in Auguast of 1914, war broke out in Europe. Roosevelt, still the
adventurous Artisan, again sought command of a military unit, which he
would then lead in the fighting in France. Wilson prevented him from
doing so, and TR never forgave him.[48]

When Roosevelt died in 1919, ten years after leaving the
presidency, his son sent a cable to friends in Europe with the simple
announcement: "The lion is dead." TR's own comment about his
presidency could equally well have been about his own life. It seems a
fitting epitaph for this ebullient Operator: "No President has ever
enjoyed himself as much as I have enjoyed myself, and for the matter of
that I do not know any man of my age who has had as good a time."[49]

---

47 *Presidential Wives,* 199.
48 Professor Richard Burns, who reviewed this manuscript, commented "I've heard that
   TR's personal letters contain so many 'four letter' words that trying to edit [them] for
   publication was almost impossible."
49 *The American Presidents,* 217.

Bibliography

Beale, H 1956	*Theodore Roosevelt and his Time*
Burton, D 1968	*Theodore Roosevelt, Confident Imperialist*
Chessman, G 1965	*Governor Theodore Roosevelt*
Cutright, P 1956	*Theodore Roosevelt the Naturalist*
Davis, O 1925	*Released for Publication: Some Inside Political History of T. Roosevelt*
Dunn, A 1922	*From Harrison to Harding*
Hagedorn, H 1921	*Roosevelt in the Badlands*
Hagedorn, H 1954	*The Roosevelt Family of Sagamore Hill*
Harbough, W 1961	*Power and Responsibility; the Life and Times of Theodore Roosevelt*
Inglehart, F 1919	*Theodore Roosevelt, the Man as I Knew Him*
Leupp, F 1904	*The Man Roosevelt: a Portrait Sketch*
Lorant, S 1959	*The Life and Times of Theodore Roosevelt*
May, E 1961	*Imperial Democracy: The Emergence of America as a Great Power*
Putnam, C 1958	*Theodore Roosevelt. Vol I. The Formative Years 1858-1886*
Robinson, C 1921	*My Brother Theodore Roosevelt*
Roosevelt, T 1913	*An Autobiography*
Roosevelt, T 1924	*Diaries of Boyhood and Youth*
Viereck, G 1919	*Roosevelt; a Study in Ambivalence*
Wagenknecht, E 1958	*The Seven Worlds of Theodore Roosevelt*
Wister, O 1930	*Roosevelt—The Story of a Friendship*
Wood, F (ed) 1930	*Roosevelt as We Knew Him: Personal Reflections of 150 Friends*

Franklin Delano Roosevelt

The long, difficult Happy Days

Operator
Born: January 30, 1882
Died: April 12, 1945
Presidency: 1933-1945

The somber shadow of the Great Depression lay over the nation when Franklin Delano Roosevelt came to the White House in 1933. Unemployment was at an all-time high (and even after six years under Roosevelt it would be at an astonishing 25% of the work force), people were selling apples on street corners and living in cardboard "Hoovervilles." Some men left their families behind to wander, in some cases all the way across country, in search of work. In 1933 life was grim for many people and it looked as if conditions would never improve. The persistent grimness of the times left many people desperate, and of course helped Roosevelt and the Democratic Party defeat the incumbent Republican, Herbert Hoover.

The contrast of those harsh times with the new President's lively character and stirring promises could hardly have been more striking. Even the song that marked his successful 1932 election campaign, "Happy Days are Here Again," proclaimed the difference between the smiling and optimistic Franklin Roosevelt and the frowning and skeptical Hoover.

Franklin Roosevelt's presidency did not come about as the final achievement of a man struggling to earn his living as a professional politician; Roosevelt was not a man who needed to earn a living. He was born to wealth and privilege, leisure and amusement, and the arduous struggles most people face in life seemed over for him before they could properly begin. He had grown up in the protected environment of his family's Hyde Park estate and the family compound on Campobello. His early education came from tutors and governesses and he went through school in the classrooms of the privileged at Groton School and Harvard University, where he enjoyed an ample allowance and had as his associates other young men equally privileged. Upon graduation Roosevelt studied law but found it boring and was at best a dilettante lawyer. He could have settled for a very easy, comfortable and idle life had he wished to, but an easy and comfortable life, and especially an idle life, was not enough for him. There was no risk, no excitement, no adventure, no challenge in such a way of living.

The energetic and gregarious Operator Franklin Roosevelt loved freedom, activity, excitement, and impact. He was exhilarated by them, almost transported. To be able to take action, preferably dramatic action, to rise to a difficult challenge, to impose his prowess on events: these were what made life worth living. There was no room in such a life for either scientific or ethical inquiry into the realm of the mind. Concrete utility was his talent, and concrete utility the key to living happily; abstract reflection was the enemy, for abstract reflection kills the opportunity for expedient action.

Consider FDR as a political campaigner. He had entered politics almost as a dare. He was already moving in political circles because of his family and school connections, and some Democrat friends proposed to him that he run for the New York state senate in an area always controlled by Republicans. There was little chance that he could win, but it would be a useful and interesting experience. Roosevelt agreed that it was a sporting proposition and undertook the campaign, and to everyone's surprise he won.

Most people who understand the rigors of an intense election campaign quail at the thought of its demanding, even exhausting schedule. But Roosevelt loved campaigning from the very first. As time went by he became more and more versatile at electioneering and consumed energy at a rate and with a cheerfulness that astonished those who were with him. He was a fine, charismatic speech maker who could excite his audiences in the same way as did his fifth cousin, the ebullient Artisan and spellbinding orator, Teddy Roosevelt.

FDR enjoyed spur-of-the-moment activities as well as political campaigning, and his later press secretary, Steve Early, recalled that in those early years the candidate was "just a playboy" who spent a great deal of time playing cards, feeling quite free to put off the preparation of his speeches until he was almost ready to deliver them. Still FDR's speeches could be splendid. Roosevelt could persuade himself as well as the public with ingenious and stirring oversimplifications. "Let it be from now on the task of our Party to break foolish traditions....This is more than a political campaign; it is a call to arms. Give me your help, not to win votes alone, but to win in this crusade to restore America to its own people" he declaimed in his acceptance speech for his party's presidential nomination; and when he later uttered his famous "we have nothing to fear but fear itself," he seemed uplifted by the assertion as much as were so many of his listeners.[50]

Such inspiring pronouncements, even if they are not especially realistic, often swing affairs in favor of the person uttering them. FDR certainly understood this, as have generations of successful politicians. Artisans, especially the Operators, recognize this especially well and habitually say whatever they have to get what they want. FDR was a master at doing just that, just as he was a master at putting together ambitious reforms and agencies, as the people of New York saw during his governorship, and as the nation was to see when he became

---

50 *Presidential Campaigns*, 233.

President. It was his vigorous governorship that helped make him a contender for the presidency in 1932.

On his way to the White House, by the way, he had the fun of being an undersecretary of the Navy as had his predecessor Teddy Roosevelt. Naval matters were a hobby of his and during his time as undersecretary Franklin Roosevelt became an enthusiastic advocate of a large navy. When the First World War broke out he tried to get himself assigned to duty at sea with the Navy, and was discouraged when he was refused on the grounds that his skills were needed where he was.

When he became President in 1933 Roosevelt put together a group of professors, analysts and other thinkers of various disciplines. He called the group, somewhat mockingly, "the brain trust." Roosevelt's "brain trust" were his advisors; they could take care of thoughtful analysis and present him their findings when he wanted that sort of thing. But they did not have the status for FDR that they might have had for a President of another character type. Roosevelt would listen to their conclusions and if he agreed with them (which did not always happen), he might act on them, for they could serve to rationalize his actions. If he didn't agree then he could quite comfortably ignore "the brain trust" and take the action he had intended all along.

He enjoyed watching advisors of different opinions vie against one another for his favor, and was not above deliberately setting them at each others' throats. Artisans often find enjoyment in conflict, unlike the Guardians and Idealists, who prize cooperation. And FDR could get away with his maneuvers. As his wife Eleanor later wrote, "Franklin had the gift of being able to draw out the people whom he wished to draw out and to silence those with whom he was bored, and in both cases the people were greatly charmed."[51]

Even when relaxed Roosevelt was not interested in waiting for an extended analysis. He wanted to do something, and he wanted to do it now. This was true whether the issue was recreation or a problem that needed handling. The first three months he was in office demonstrates nicely his approach to problem solving: he quickly established and set in motion a diversity of largely uncoordinated federal programs to deal with the nation's severe economic difficulties. It was as though he

---

51 *The Autobiography of Eleanor Roosevelt*, 132.

wanted to get everything happening all at once. So striking was the flurry of activity he began during this brief time, and so intense his absorption in making things happen after the cautious actions of the Hoover administration, that those three months are still remembered as "The 100 Days." And cheering as the idea of action might be, there was often little to recommend the actions he took other than the fact that they were action. He generated agency after agency, project after project, piled one on top of the other, appointed roving troubleshooters, and generally created very confused lines of authority.

> Examine closely the product of the 100 days and you will find no coordinated plan of action, no master program. He was really playing it by ear; he later likened himself to a quarterback who waits to see what one play accomplishes before deciding on another.[52]

Roosevelt was not a long-term strategist in the fashion of the Rationals. But he was a prodigal tactician, a very clever maneuverer of people and immediate events with the extraordinary sense of timing so often seen in the Artisan. Behind the wide and winning smile, the playful sense of humor, the friendly wave of his arm, the enormous charisma, there was a cunning mind at work and a love of making an impact. FDR understood clearly the power of his smile, the confident warmth suggested by the casual wave of his arm. He knew well the intense impact that his words and phrases could have on his listeners.

His confidence seemed unshakeable, and in FDR's case it was quite understandable. Whereas the self-confidence of Rationals rests on their strength of will, that of Guardians on their acceptability as members in good standing, and that of the Idealists on their empathic bonds with others, self-confidence in Artisans rests on their ability to impress their audience. Should this recede, so too does their self-confidence. But FDR seemed able to impress everybody all the time, so that his self-confidence never had occasion to flag.

Like his Operator predecessor Theodore Roosevelt, FDR had a powerful grasp of the uses of the press. But Franklin Roosevelt also had available a new medium: the radio. He knew the persuasiveness of his words and the stirring resonance of his voice. He recognized that the radio was a means by which he could address the entire nation directly

---

52 *Presidential Style*, 327.

without being edited by the newspapers. That marvelous, magical charisma of his could be sent electronically all over the nation, all of it at once, and his "fireside chats" became as popular as Jack Benny and Fibber Magee and Molly.

Eleanor Roosevelt once commented that "The President used those who suited his purposes. He made up his own mind and discarded people when they no longer fulfilled a purpose of his."[53] Though his spontaneous enjoyment of others and his sense of fun were surely natural to him, the appearance of great warmth that he exuded, the friendly teasing and the cheerful informality, were also purposeful. His easy-going interactions in fact incorporated quite calculated action designed to produce a particular impact. For FDR, as for so many assertive and directive Artisans, the spontaneous and the calculated were intertwined so naturally and inevitably that it could be extraordinarily difficult to tell where one ended and the other began. "Everyone is useful; everything is used": this was inherent in Roosevelt's style from beginning to end.[54] Even when he had nothing at stake Roosevelt would often be devious simply for the pleasure it afforded him, and he was clearly a virtuoso in this realm, the ultimate concrete utilitarian:

> Evasiveness, duplicity, underhandedness are generally taken as imperfections of character...in the case of FDR [they can be seen as] skills of a high order in the fine art of ambiguity...it is the art of keeping one's own counsel while giving others the exhilarating impression they are on the inside. In this art FDR was peerless.[55]

But Roosevelt did not always search for the most cunning or devious stratagem. The occasional power play would do nicely at times. At the beginning of the Second World War, for instance, he had great difficulty trying to persuade steel manufacturers to expand their production. They were concerned that if they did so they would spend the last of their capital and find that they had an insufficient market for their goods. Roosevelt, tiring of gentle persuasion, made the straightforward and enormously high-handed threat that the government would open its own steel mills and leave the private sector high and dry. If they would not cooperate, then they would have to shift for

---

53 *Eleanor and Franklin,* 510.
54 *The FDR Memoirs,* 258.
55 *The FDR Memoirs,* 205-206.

themselves and the devil take the hindmost. Business rapidly capitulated and the American war effort did not falter for lack of steel.

Charismatic and powerful he might have been, but Franklin was not the only famous Roosevelt in town. His wife Eleanor Roosevelt became so well-known in her own right that at times she would almost overshadow him. Eleanor Roosevelt is discussed at length later, as an example of an Idealist with very nearly presidential power, so little will be said about her here. For the moment let it be noted that from the shy and naive wife of an aspiring politician she became one of the world's best-known and best-loved women, an energetic and highly public figure with a deep dedication to a wide variety of humanitarian causes. As we will note later, it was as if the most unpleasant of Franklin Roosevelt's cunning manipulativeness and lust for the exercise of power were being turned upside down, transformed by Eleanor Roosevelt into generosity, devotion to others' well-being, and constant concern for the disadvantaged.

FDR's own vision for the country and for humanity was not especially lofty, nor did it have the depth of compassion of his wife's. He was not a deep or far-sighted thinker nor did he ever wish to be; he was instead a practical man in every sense of the word. His vision was not exalted or profound but was instead broad and spacious. He seemed to assume that humanity would naturally take advantage of opportunities to improve its own condition if it were truly given the freedom to do so—and if it didn't first sink itself entirely in the mire—just as an Artisan might be expected to do.

Perhaps his own unflinching resilience helped shape his attitudes about helping others. Nothing, not even cunning, wealth, and status can protect one from all the tragedies life may visit upon us; at 39 years of age, and already a very successful politician, Franklin Roosevelt was stricken with severely crippling infantile paralysis in August of 1921. FDR was still the adventurous and optimistic Artisan, however, and would not accept the profound restrictions this disease would normally mean. Instead he fought back vigorously against the effects of the illness. In less than six months he had been fitted with steel leg braces and was already making agonizing attempts to stand. The braces were terribly heavy, weighing thirty pounds, but they could be locked at the knees so Roosevelt could keep his legs stiff and swing his body from side to side. In this fashion he could throw his stiffened legs forward, one after the other and thus "walk." He kept working at it until he eventually mastered the ability to get about rather well on his crutches.

After his paralysis his family encouraged him to abandon politics, but before long they recognized that FDR's real mortal enemies were leisure and boredom. Of the four temperaments, Artisans are most subject to and offended by boredom. When ennui overtakes them they will do almost anything to dispel it, and so it was with Roosevelt. Thus, six years later, in 1928, Roosevelt ran successfully for Governor of New York State. (It was on this campaign that he became so exhilarated that he made the previously noted comment that if he could keep on campaigning twelve months longer he would be able to throw away his crutches.[56])

Roosevelt was a man who was always on stage, always in role, and always posing. Even the effects of his illness could either be put to his advantage or at least mitigated. Confined to his wheelchair, Roosevelt knew full well that he was in the disadvantageous position of having to look up at others. So he put what was left of his body to work for him.

> With his inborn sense of staging, he used his prominent chin to execute an upthrusting impression that in effect carried him to a higher level. It was positive, optimistic, a gesture of great confidence and so much a symbol that caricatures of the man could capture his whole being and outlook with a few clever lines.[57]

Nor would he ever allow his disability to appear to be a sign of weakness. Artisans usually try to hide their disability or wounds; note for instance that when a baseball player is hit by a pitched ball he does not rub the sore spot. He acts as if he feels nothing, when in point of fact the pain is sometimes almost unbearable. In the same spirit FDR seemed determined to show that he could triumph over his enormous handicap. Even at home he would refuse assistance. When he tried to ascend the staircase he would use his upper body to drag himself from one step to the next. "The sweat would pour off his face, and he would tremble with exhaustion," wrote John Gunther.

> Moreover he insisted on doing this with members of the family or friends watching him, and he would talk all the time as he inched

---

56 *Presidential Style*, 290.

himself up little by little, talk, talk, and make people talk back. It was a kind of enormous spiritual catharsis—as if he had to do it to prove his independence, and had to have the feat witnessed, to prove that it was nothing.[58]

All this energy, all this resolution, all this effort should be enough to accomplish almost anything. Yet though Roosevelt had come into the presidency partly because of the effects of the Great Depression, all his vigorous and dramatic efforts to return the country to economic well-being seemed largely ineffectual. Though he became recognized as a great war leader during World War II, some have judged that FDR's ability to direct the long-range consequences of the war (especially the behavior of Stalin and the USSR) was defective. Given his special talents in maneuvering difficult people, including gifted but difficult strategists such as General MacArthur, Roosevelt has been criticized for letting himself be outmaneuvered by Joseph Stalin at the Yalta Conference in February of 1945, in which important agreements were made about how the post-war world would be (in effect) divided up. Others, however, have noted that FDR recognized that the Soviet Union would not disappear after the war concluded, and that the political reality was that the Soviets and the United States would have to accommodate to each other. The best course, he probably felt, was to establish ties as friendly as possible now, and manage the post-war realities later on the basis of those ties.

Even if FDR's critics are correct, his lack of foresight and his strategic failure should not be a great surprise. The Operator has the ability to work with the concrete and immediate, but shows neither an enduring interest nor any special talents in the arena of broad, long-term, complex issues. He has the ability to pinpoint advantageous immediate gains, but little interest or flair for long-range goals. Roosevelt was an Artisan and therefore an optimist. He had a war to fight, and Stalin and the Russians were important allies. Winning the war was what he wanted now; the final fate of Europe could wait and one way or another he would handle it.

Furthermore, Roosevelt's physical health was already very poor and the Yalta environment was terrible for even a healthy man. Winston

---

57 *Presidential Courage*, 107-108.
58 *Presidential Courage*, 194.

Churchill, who also attended the Yalta Conference, later wrote that "If we had spent ten years on research we could not have found a worse place in the world than Yalta....It is good for typhus and deadly lice, which thrive in those parts."[59] It is unlikely that Roosevelt, now only two months from death, was able to muster his usual observational and tactical skills at this absurdly inhospitable site.

In spite of his increasing infirmity and painful physical disabilities, in spite of his failing intellectual powers, and in spite of the obvious signs of deteriorating health, Roosevelt seemed to be in remarkably good spirits even at Yalta. Perhaps Robert E. Sherwood described the Roosevelt of that time best in his *Roosevelt and Hopkins:*

> Although crippled physically and prey to various infections, he was ... gloriously and happily free of the various forms of psychic maladjustment which are called by such names as inhibition, complex, phobia. His mind, if not always orderly, bore no trace of paralysis and neither did his emotional constitution, and his heart was certainly in the right place.[60]

In any event, it seemed that nothing, including his own gradually worsening health, could impair Franklin Roosevelt's cheerfulness, his political power, or his personal popularity. His impact on the country during the Depression and the war years from 1941 to 1945 was often more dramatic than effective, but it was still well-received by the majority of the voters. Hopeful activity has its own potent impact and FDR became the only person ever elected to four terms as President of the United States.

His presidency, which had begun in the early days of the Great Depression, did not end until he died in office in April of 1945. World War II had been consuming the people and the resources of the planet since 1939 and when Roosevelt died the United States and its allies were only four short months from victory over the Axis. It is sad that he did not live those few additional months so he could witness the conclusion of his most important campaign.

---

59 *Presidential Courage,* 187.
60 *Presidential Courage,* 201.

Bibliography

Asbell, B 1973	*The FDR Memoirs*
Beard, C 1948	*President Roosevelt and the Coming of the War, 1941*
Burns, J 1956	*Roosevelt, the Lion and the Fox*
Day, D 1951	*Franklin D. Roosevelt's Own Story*
Einaudi, M 1959	*The Roosevelt Revolution*
Flynn, J 1948	*The Roosevelt Myth*
Freidel, F 1952	*Franklin D. Roosevelt*
Gosnell, H 1952	*Champion Campaigner: Franklin D. Roosevelt*
Greer, T 1958	*What Roosevelt Thought*
Gunther, J 1950	*Roosevelt in Retrospect, a Profile in History*
Halasz, N 1961	*Roosevelt through Foreign Eyes*
Hatch, A 1947	*Franklin D. Roosevelt, an Informal Biography*
Hill, C 1966	*Franklin Roosevelt*
Jackson, R 1941	*The Struggle for Judicial Supremacy*
Kingdon, F 1947	*Architects of the Republic: Washington, Jefferson, Lincoln, Roosevelt*
Ludwig, E 1938	*Roosevelt, a Study in Fortune and Power*
Marloff, M 1964	*Mr. Roosevelt's Three Wars: FDR as War Leader*
McKenzie, C 1944	*Mr Roosevelt*
Reed, L 1934	*Frankie in Wonderland: With Apologies to Lewis Carroll*
Rollins, A 1960	*Franklin D. Roosevelt and the Age of Action*
Roosevelt, E 1946	*As he Saw it*
Roosevelt, J 1959	*Affectionately, FDR; a Son's Story of a Lonely Man*
Roz, F 1948	*Roosevelt*
Stetinius, E 1950	*Roosevelt and the Russians; the Yalta Conference*
Tugwell, R 1958	*The Art of Politics, as Practiced by Three Great Americans*
Tugwell, R 1957	*The Democratic Roosevelt; a Biography of Franklin D. Roosevelt*
Wann, A 1968	*The President as Chief Administrator; a Study of Franklin D. Roosevelt*
White, W 1961	*Majesty and Mischief: A Mixed Tribute to FDR*

John Fitzgerald Kennedy

Camelot lost

Operator
Born: May 29, 1917
Died: November 22, 1963
Presidency: 1961-1963

Only forty-three years old when he became President, John Fitzgerald Kennedy was the youngest man ever to be elected to that office. He brought to the White House not only his youthful vigor but an almost irresistible charisma. Kennedy also brought an engaging "style," as it was often called, which fascinated and beguiled multitudes of Americans and Europeans alike. As a Congressman he sometimes appeared on the floor of the House in chino pants and tennis shoes, and though he didn't work very hard he did have that special insouciance, that special flair. So great was his flair, in fact, that it eventually became fashionable to compare the Kennedy White House with King Arthur's Camelot, that marvelous kingdom of the hero king, valiant knights, and noble ladies.

In that comparison there is even today a certain sadness, a wistful remembrance of what once was—or what appeared to be—before it was stolen from us by an assassin.[61] Never mind that there was the Bay of Pigs fiasco. Never mind that the Cuban missile confrontation could have set off World War III. John F. Kennedy's charm and grace, his boldness and energy, his obvious brilliance and his lighthearted wit are what most people best remember of him. His vitality and his exuberance and his celebration of the best and the most accomplished come to mind far more readily than the misjudgments he made or the dangerous risks he took.

History might finally have appraised him less graciously if the bullets aimed at him in Dallas had missed their mark, for JFK was a man who courted challenge and adventure, who loved risk and excitement, and who expended energy liberally but not thoughtfully. He fought for the sake of winning, rather than for the sake of a principle or an agenda; he loved the competition and the victory. As one observer noted of Kennedy's ambition, it "was an ambition almost totally empty of any purpose for the country. The object of winning was to win."[62] Where these characteristics, so typical of the Artisan, might eventually have taken the nation we can of course never know.

Much of John Kennedy's style is reminiscent of Franklin Roosevelt's. Both men were born to wealth and privilege. Both were men of superior ability and energy who were educated in prestigious institutions in the East but who failed in spite of their endowments to achieve significant academic distinction. At Harvard Kennedy was usually a "C" student but he did manage to graduate with honors largely on the strength of a thesis he wrote which concerned the Munich agreement between Hitler, France, and Great Britain. The subject matter, concerned largely with duplicitous political tactics and the cost of wishful thinking, was a splendid study for an Artisan postmortem.

---

61 Kennedy's biographer William Manchester characterized the Kennedy era with the poignant book title, *One Shining Moment*.

62 *Roosevelt to Reagan*, 70.

Roosevelt and Kennedy shared an attraction to the Navy and to excitement and action and challenge. And in spite of their privileged backgrounds both men knew how to appeal to all elements of American society, from the intellectual elite to the uneducated laborer. If FDR could be described as an urbane patrician, JFK manifested that same urbane quality and added to it a flair that was youthful and unpretentious. In doing so he brought back to the presidential scene a personal charisma not seen since the early years of the Roosevelt administration.

Kennedy managed to see active duty and combat, by the way, becoming a hero in the process, something that Franklin Roosevelt failed to manage. But then Kennedy wasn't Undersecretary of the Navy when he made his attempt to join the Navy, and so was less constrained. Another notable difference between the two men (though perhaps reminding us of the earlier Teddy Roosevelt) is found in Kennedy's ferocious enthusiasm for sports. A friend of his commented that Kennedy was always far more excited about sports than by academics.

> During his freshman year he tried out for football swimming and golf and crowded in some softball too. As he had at Choate, he played furiously, but his drive was greater than his athletic skill. He was fearless and willing to fight until the game was over.[63]

Like most Artisans, Kennedy was excitable and venturesome. He hated routine, he hated rules, he hated boredom.

> To Jack the cardinal sin was boredom; it was his biggest enemy, and he didn't know how to handle it. When he was bored, a hood would come down over his eyes and his nervous system would start churning. You could do anything to him—steal his wallet, insult him, argue with him—but to bore was unpardonable.[64]

A writer intimately acquainted with the Kennedy reign, recalled that the White House constantly "crackled with excitement" under JFK. Kennedy's speeches reflected this quick, electrifying Operator's style.

> No speech was more than twenty to thirty minutes in duration. They were all too short and too crowded with facts to permit any excess of generalities and sentimentalities. His text wasted no words and his delivery wasted no time. Frequently he moved from one solid fact to

---

63 Quoting James MacGregor Burns in *John Fitzgerald Kennedy*, 22.
64 *Among Those Present*, 71.

another, without the usual repetition and elaboration, far too quickly for his audiences to digest or even applaud his conclusions.[65]

Kennedy was enormously energetic, but energy seeks excitement, and excitement usually involves risk-taking. Thus during the Second World War John Kennedy, son of Joseph Kennedy, the powerful and wealthy United States Ambassador to Great Britain, found himself ensconced in a comfortable and safe desk job—and hating it. He pleaded with his father to get him transferred to more exciting duty and soon found himself commanding a "PT boat," a small patrol-torpedo boat. The "PT" was a boat designed originally for reconnaissance and for launching torpedoes at enemy ships. It had large and powerful engines but its hull was chiefly reinforced plywood, making it very fast, highly maneuverable, exciting, but also a very dangerous command. (Kennedy found out soon enough about the danger; his boat was sunk in combat and two crewmen were lost.)

Kennedy, like Roosevelt before him, struggled with physical problems. He had a back injury which could cause him pain great enough almost to immobilize him. But just as FDR's disability could not stop him, Kennedy's back pain could not suppress his activity, nor could physical pain or the trials of office suppress his sense of humor. Like the Roosevelt humor, Kennedy's was clever, witty, and usually friendly. "It flowed naturally, good-naturedly, casually. It was dry, wry, ironic, and irreverent."[66] And like so much of the Operator Artisan's natural charm, it was also a powerful political asset which he was able to use to good advantage.

The White House was a place of action and intensity and wit and irreverence. But it did not become a place of profound inspiration or of great ideas under Jack Kennedy, however much it might have been compared to Camelot. Kennedy was completely absorbed in the immediate, practical, concrete change. He had little or no interest in science, technology, philosophy, ethics, or even aesthetics. He was concrete and literal in his thinking, with a superb memory for details. He was curious and penetrating and incisive when immediate problems and immediate opportunities were at issue. Looking for action, he would

---

65 *Kennedy,* 1965, 61.
66 *Kennedy,* 1965, 369.

present many different reasons for an operation rather than producing one single, overarching reason. He used his mind, filled with its myriad of discrete facts, to overwhelm his listeners rather than to win them over with abstract and figurative finesse.

Like some of the other Artisan Presidents, Kennedy had scholarly talents which showed up well when he chose to make use of them. His Artisan preferences did not prevent him from majoring in government and international relations at Harvard and graduated cum laude, a testament to what a bright Artisan, interested in a topic, can accomplish even in academia. Moreover he was a fine writer. His senior thesis on England's failures in the face of Nazi territorial adventures was later published under the title, "Why England Slept." And of course there was finally his prize-winning *Profiles in Courage*.

But he preferred action, and however he might go about it he was always exhilarated by the game of persuasion and maneuver and the search for advantageous compromise. Kennedy's approach is a definitive display of the approach of the Artisan, particularly the Operator. The Operator is not harnessed to rules, regulations, policies, or traditions. He is riding whatever crest of opportunity may present itself, ready to exploit whatever advantageous compromise may be available. Everything is negotiable and nothing is sacred. Kennedy himself captured much of the Operator pattern when he wrote that

> Some of my colleagues who are criticized today for lack of forthright principles—or who are looked upon with scornful eyes as compromising 'politicians'—are simply engaged in the fine art of conciliating, balancing, and interpreting the forces and factions of public opinion, an art essential to keeping our nation united and enabling our government to function. Their consciences may direct them from time to time to take a more rigid stand for principle—but their intellects tell them that a fair bill or a poor bill is better than no bill at all, and that only through the give-and-take of compromise will any bill receive the successive approval of the Senate, the House, the President, and the nation.[67]

This is an eloquent statement of the sophisticated Concrete Utilitarian's approach to living, and as such it warrants careful reading by anyone interested in understanding the world of Operator Artisan. Especially important is Kennedy's recognition that negotiation is an art,

---

67 *Profiles in Courage*, 1955, 26.

not a science. This of course places negotiation squarely in the Artisan's domain, along with the other performing arts.

Kennedy once commented that "happiness is the fullest use of one's powers along the lines of excellence,"[68] and he was drawn to operations that were excellent in the sense of being better than others. Kennedy wanted to be the best and be with the best. He wanted to be in the company of those who stood out, those who, like himself, were the most daring and successful competitors. These were the sorts of politician about whom he wrote in his book *Profiles in Courage,* which won him a Pulitzer Prize in biography.[69] He brought to his search the same thing he brought to everything: his irrepressible energy and his love of challenge and excitement.

Thus in JFK's administration "the zest for life was everywhere and competition was king."[70] Kennedy's love of competition was also found among what he sometimes called his "band of brothers," his group of top advisors. Kennedy's description, "band of brothers" is an expression of his fierce fraternalism, something often found among the Artisans. And, comments one Kennedy observer, the White House atmosphere did remind one of a fraternity house. "The tensions were there as they had to be in such a collection of ambitions and energies....What held them together was Kennedy."[71] But whether with or away from his "band of brothers," Kennedy was obviously a very successful competitor. He worked long, long hours, moved at an incredibly rapid pace, rarely slowed down, and demanded from his "band of brothers" the same high-pitched, high-energy behavior.

He didn't save his energy for the execution of his official duties. Such prudence would have been unlike him. When he managed to be with his family on weekends, whatever the difficulties he faced, he would "devote every inch of mind and body to leisure as intensively as

---

68 *Among Those Present,* 80.
69 Even here some of the less savory aspects of Kennedy's behavior show up. According to Hedley Donovan, *Profiles in Courage* was largely ghostwritten by Ted Sorenson (See Donovan's *Roosevelt to Reagan*).
70 *Among Those Present,* 77.
71 *Presidential Character* 1977, 316.

he had to work, completely shaking off and shutting out the worries of the world beyond."[72] No matter what,

> the dynamo would not—or could not—slow down. He was always in the process of going or coming. Friends noted with a smile that of the first six words Caroline had learned at a year and a half—daddy, airplane, car, shoe, hat, and thank you—at least three had something to do with motion.[73]

During the 1960 presidential campaign a reporter asked him why he wanted to become President. He responded with the previously mentioned comment that "happiness is the fullest use of one's powers along the lines of excellence." But among his intimates the response was a bit different and considerably more clear: he wanted the presidency because "that's where the power is."[74] Kennedy wanted power, but as a Concrete Utilitarian, an Artisan, he sought something different than the power sought by the Rational, the Abstract Utilitarian. Being the extremely versatile Operator that he was, he was after the power to move men and machines, while the Rational seeks the power to explain, predict, and control the forces of nature.

Of course, the White House is also where the action is. Kennedy wanted action, and in his lust for action he was quite willing to throw away routines and the carefully engineered procedures which had been thoughtfully constructed over the years. His immediate predecessor Dwight Eisenhower had gathered an undeserved reputation as a passive President, in part because he had so carefully organized the White House operations that he did not usually need to look active. The operations he designed took care of most matters very nicely without presidential flailing and floundering. But when Kennedy came into office he disposed of most of the established procedures, including Eisenhower's. He preferred to get his finger directly into any pie that interested him and he didn't want to wait for committees or to have to pay attention to lines of authority. He would quite readily ignore organizational boundaries and speak with White House subordinates rather than taking the more indirect (and slower) route of channelling his communications through lines of authority.

---

72 *Kennedy*, 1965, 377.
73 *John Kennedy: A Political Profile*, 217.
74 *Among Those Present*, 75.

A telling example of this is found in his handling of the Cuban missile crisis. In its most critical stage it involved a United States naval blockade around Cuba; Cuban ports were off-limits to certain Russian vessels. As Russian ships approached the island Kennedy himself was on the phone in direct tactical command of the blockading forces. At the beginning of the blockade at least, it was Kennedy himself who gave moment-by-moment operational instructions for confronting the Russian cargo ships. Kennedy did not want to lose control of the situation for even a moment and could not bear to leave operations in the hands of the naval officers on the scene. As it happened, of course, matters turned out to the United States' distinct advantage. The Russian ships changed course away from Cuba rather than risk being sunk—and the beginning of a third world war. In this brief but dangerous skirmish Kennedy used disinformation in combination with confrontation. The tactics are very much like those of a poker player, and involve both calculation of the odds, and use of available chips, and the "disinformation" we know as bluffing.[75] In this game Khrushchev was no match for Kennedy.

Kennedy managed the White House in a way that gave him the opportunity for as much direct action with as little restraint as possible. He thereby lost access to some of the thoughtful deliberation which intact executive structures could have provided. It may be that loss of this thoughtful but constraining deliberation was part of the reason that Kennedy mishandled the Bay of Pigs adventure. An invasion had been designed to unseat Cuba's Fidel Castro, the plans for which had been begun during Eisenhower's administration. Kennedy was fascinated with the scheme. He followed it through with relatively little counsel from his subordinates, and when it failed miserably he publicly shouldered the blame. (Many of those who had initial responsibility for formulating the plan nevertheless disappeared quietly from their jobs over the next few months.)

Jack Kennedy's zest for action and challenge was not confined to politics or family football. Though it was rarely spoken of while he was alive, for instance, Kennedy engaged in a great deal of sexual adventuring. Apparently his marriage to Jacqueline Bouvier and his stay

---

75 *How Real is Real?* by Paul Watzlawick offers an illuminating analysis of the nature and importance of disinformation in conflict situations.

in the White House did not bring an end to these adventures, and though he did relatively little to keep his promiscuous behavior secret the press tended to be careful that his activities did not become public knowledge. But Kennedy was no fool, and we might speculate that in the 1980s he would have been considerably more careful. Otherwise, given the new interest of the media in exploring publicly every aspect of a candidate's life there is a question about whether he could be elected at all. The media's treatment of Gary Hart (also likely and Artisan) in 1987-88 was a notable demonstration of the shift.

Kennedy was not merely given to illicit liaisons. He was also fascinated by the sex lives of others, enjoyed talking about them, and was not above the occasional vulgarity. "When one bachelor ambassador went through a White House receiving line, he told me later that he was astonished when the President asked him, 'Are you getting any lately?'"[76]

Jacqueline Kennedy was not oblivious to the whispers about her husband's promiscuity. But she seemed to deal with them with remarkable equanimity, at least outwardly. Once when showing a visitor the White House she opened the door to an office in which a secretary was busily at work. "And this," she commented dryly, "is a young lady who is supposed to be sleeping with my husband," closed the door and continued the tour.[77]

Whatever quiet difficulties their marriage might have had, Jacqueline Kennedy was a remarkable public complement to Jack Kennedy. Like her husband she was born to wealth and privilege and educated at the "best" schools. When she finally left school she was given a job at a Washington newspaper and soon had her own column, "Inquiring Reporter," whose quality was sufficient to guarantee its continuation regardless of her family connections.

She was too fiercely independent and enterprising, too talented and hard-working to ignore. For a while after her marriage to Jack her independent behavior sometimes threatened to become a significant liability. But in spite of her strong-minded and sometimes willfully flip manner she managed, apparently with very little effort, to become a

---

76 *Among Those Present*, 75.
77 *Presidential Wives*, 376.

powerful asset to Jack Kennedy's political aspirations. Though she was bored with politics and had little patience with its demands, Jackie Kennedy was an Artisan, probably a Player, and, as Players often do, she had an understanding of and love for the arts. She consistently projected an aura of elegance and good taste which, along with her beauty and personal charm captivated many Americans and made her a fashion trend-setter. In fact it was Jackie Kennedy's sense of taste, for which Kennedy wisely made room, which helped make the vision of Camelot compelling.

Jacqueline Kennedy was only thirty-one when her husband assumed the presidency but with her natural confidence and independence she soon felt quite comfortable being First Lady. She was in fact extraordinarily quick to begin asserting the powers of the position. Even before JFK was inaugurated she announced her intention to make the White House a showcase of American history and American art, and once installed in the White House she refused to attend most of the routine events (formal luncheons and teas, etc.) which typically fill the First Lady's social calendar. She was usually quite diligent with respect to events which affected her plans for the White House or other projects in which she had taken an interest, but she was determinedly absent from most of Washington's usual social functions. Typically, the only excuse she would give for her absences was the rather transparent claim that her duties with her children were too demanding.

Jacqueline Kennedy was clearly her own person, and her position as the President's wife equally clearly did little or nothing to change that. She could still take luxurious vacations abroad, riding elephants in India (on what was touted as a good-will journey) and sojourning with the charming Aristotle Onassis and friends on his yacht in the Mediterranean. She could still take daughter Caroline on sight-seeing trips to Italy and in general carry on with all the style of the rich and privileged. She could even find herself subject to rumors of infidelity, though these rumors were largely suppressed, just as rumors of her husband's infidelity were largely suppressed. What is most remarkable about Jacqueline Kennedy is that she could do all this without alienating the admiration and the affection which so many felt for her.

Jackie Kennedy, though she was herself a very active and energetic Artisan, remarked of her life with John Kennedy that "it was like being married to a whirlwind,"[78] and there is no question that Kennedy's administration was a busy one. But it was far from the most productive of the nation's presidential administrations. There was the aberration of the Bay of Pigs, and Kennedy did send more U. S. troops into the growing quagmire of Viet Nam. (Their numbers during his administration were gradually increased from Eisenhower's 600 or so "advisors" to more than 16,000 combat troops.) Kennedy spoke eloquently about civil rights, but did relatively little to press for passage of civil rights legislation. He did initiate the Peace Corps, though that was originally an idea of Hubert Humphrey's. And, when the Soviets put up the Berlin Wall, with its implied threat to East-West stability, he did go to Berlin and give his enormously well-received "Ich bin ein Berliner" speech to signal that the West would not accept further Soviet encroachments. But the consequences of most of these actions were either negative or insignificant.

Perhaps most important and valuable of all his actions was the negotiation of a nuclear test treaty with the Soviets. The treaty came after some Cold War saber-rattling at the Communist world, including the frightening Cuban missile crisis, and perhaps this helped point up the urgent importance of East-West cooperation. Nonetheless the pattern of negotiation which emerged in his work for the treaty has been characteristic of all successful U. S.-Soviet negotiations since that time. It seems quite fitting that an important part of Kennedy's legacy would be related to (in his words) "the fine art of conciliating, balancing, and interpreting the forces and factions" of which the Operator is the natural master.

Kennedy was assassinated on November 22, 1963 in Dallas. His death was mourned deeply by people of almost every nation of the world. The shock of the assassination and the angry suspicions which continue to enshroud it are still very vivid for many people. The Report of the Warren Commission, intended to provide the definitive answers to the questions about Kennedy's death, is considered by many to be either a masterpiece of incompetence or a cover-up for some dark secret associated with his death. For many the terrible crime against John Kennedy and against the United States is still unexplained and unavenged.

---

78 *Kennedy*, 1965, 37.

In spite of his charisma, in spite of his contributions, and in spite of the trauma surrounding his death, Kennedy is not generally considered a great President, and though he was enormously charismatic, history will probably not consider him a President of any special nobility. Kennedy was too much the Artisan opportunist and, however beguilingly, the Operator playboy for that assessment to stand.

Indeed, a respected British scholar of the American presidency has recently written, "It's taken quite a while for me to demystify and demythologize Kennedy. The general feeling now is that he was all front, isn't it?....Kennedy's womanizing didn't seem to matter, but he didn't seem to have much taste."[79]

All the same, in death and in memory perhaps even more than in life, the charismatic Operator John Fitzgerald Kennedy reminds us of Camelot, the mythical realm of great knights and great deeds. As one historian has concluded, "For millions, not just in America, John Kennedy is the romantic hero, martyred and forever young. More than any concrete deed or policy, his greatest achievement is precisely his legend."[80]

Bibliography

Bernstein, I 1991   *Promises Kept: John F. Kennedy's New Frontier*
Berry, J 1987   *John F. Kennedy and the Media: the First Television President*
Brauer, C 1977   *John F. Kennedy and the Second Reconstruction*
Brown, T 1988   *JFK, History of an Image*
Burner, D 1988   *John F. Kennedy and a New Generation*
Donald, A 1966   *John F. Kennedy and the New Frontier*
Donovan, R 1961   *PT 109, John F. Kennedy in World War II*
Firestone, B 1982   *The Quest for Nuclear Stability: John F. Kennedy and the Soviet Union*
Heath, J 1969   *John F. Kennedy and the Business Community*
Thompson, K (ed.)   *The Kennedy Presidency: 17 Intimate Perspectives of John F. Kennedy*

---

79 Marcus Cunliffe, quoted in the *Los Angeles Times*, 11/21/88.
80 *Roosevelt to Reagan*, 5.

Levine, I 1970   *Young Man in the White House: John Fitzgerald Kennedy*

Lieberson, G 1965   *John Fitzgerald Kennedy. As We Remember Him*

Lincoln, E 1965   *My Twelve Years with John F. Kennedy*

Lowe, J 1961   *Portrait: The Emergence of John F. Kennedy*

Manchester, W 1967   *Portrait of a President: John F. Kennedy in Profile*

Menendez, A 1978   *John F. Kennedy, Catholic and Humanist*

Miroff, B 1976   *Pragmatic Illusions: The Presidential Politics of John F. Kennedy*

Paper, L 1975   *The Promise and the Performance: The Leadership of John F. Kennedy*

Parmet, H 1980   *Jack: The Struggles of John F. Kennedy*

Strousse, F 1965   *John F. Kennedy, Man of Courage*

Lyndon B. Johnson

A fox on a leash

Operator
Born: April 27, 1908
Died: January 22, 1973
Presidency: 1963-1969

November 22, 1963: John F. Kennedy was dead in Dallas, killed by
an assassin. Jacqueline Kennedy, her clothes still spattered with her
husband's blood, stood beside Vice-President Lyndon Baines Johnson as
Johnson took the presidential oath of office. Camelot was suddenly and
shockingly gone. In the passage of a few jolting hours King Arthur had
been replaced by the crude, graceless, but no less energetic Lyndon
Johnson, the professional politician from Texas.

The contrasts between the lives and manners of Lyndon Johnson
and the charming, charismatic, socially and economically privileged

Kennedy were obvious. Johnson was born to a Texas family that had fallen on hard times. He worked his way through high school and then left for California to find a decent job. Finding only poorly-paid laborer's work he soon returned to Texas where he ended up doing heavy manual labor for a while on a Texas road gang. Eventually he decided to begin college, beginning with $75 he had available and working again to pay the rest of his tuition. His was not the prestigious education of the Eastern elite; he graduated from Southwest Texas State Teachers College. Nor was his education paid for by his family; Johnson had to leave college for a year in order to earn enough money to complete his education.

During that year he was a teacher for the Hispanic children of the small town of Cotulla, Texas. His experience there taught him much about the plight of minority groups and seemed to touch him in some special way. Perhaps it helps account for the vigor with which he pursued the civil rights legislation about which Jack Kennedy had done little more than speak eloquently.

Of course Lyndon Johnson's expenses were not confined only to the purchase of books and typing paper. As an Operator, Lyndon loved a good time and he loved to show others a good time. He was a natural swaggerer who enjoyed bragging about himself and his accomplishments, and boasting about the influential connections he claimed to have. Living the life he preferred was rather expensive for a college student, and he was constantly in debt. He often had to borrow money from one source to pay off loans overdue to another source. Much of the money he earned during his year in Cotulla was apparently devoted to repaying the various debts he had contracted while attending school in his preferred style.

It is worth noting that living by one's wits this way is not in the least worrisome to Artisans such as Johnson, though it might be very hard on the other temperaments. On the contrary it is highly stimulating and enhances the Artisan's self-respect and self-confidence. After all, the ability to get friends and acquaintances to keep on lending him money must have revealed to him that he was good at encouraging people to have confidence in him. The development of his budding talent in gaining others' confidence would pay off handsomely in the Congress he was later to dominate.

Still it is perhaps fortunate that there was really nothing in the tired little town of Cotulla for Lyndon to spend his small salary on. Saving was not the problem it would have been in a place where he had more opportunity for strutting and impressing. He was therefore able to return to college with most of his debts retired. This left him more freedom which he used to become quickly an energetic and important part of the campus's political scene. He eventually earned his bachelor's degree, and soon after leaving school he became a campaign worker and an office assistant for a local politician. The politician was impressed by Johnson's work and gave the young man a job in Washington.

When Lyndon Johnson reached the nation's capital he had found his true home.

Johnson lacked Kennedy's social breeding, Kennedy's wealthy background, Kennedy's Eastern connections and style, Kennedy's urbane wit and grace. Where Kennedy was polished, Johnson was bluff; while the Kennedy wit could be like a rapier, Johnson's was more like an axe; while Kennedy tended to be subtle and artful in his political combats, Johnson preferred, when he could, to be brazen and pugnacious. He was, in comparison to Kennedy rude, unpolished, a country bumpkin with none of the appreciation of "the finer things" and the social graces that were associated with the Kennedys. But underneath these striking differences were equally striking similarities. Both men were enormously energetic; both loved the process of politics; and both were gregarious Operators. And both had a fondness for women.

Not that Johnson was interested merely in bedding women.

> Often what he really wanted was nothing more than a playmate. His ego needed such nurturing and his energies were so inexhaustible that it was beyond the ability of any one person to handle. Ladybird tolerated—in fact, welcomed—such companions, who were usually nothing more than an adoring audience.[81]

All his life Johnson reached for adulation, admiration, the rapt audience for his narratives about his own accomplishments. Still, his interests were far from merely conversational, and he could relish the chase as much as the capture. When President Johnson met with Nehru,

---

81 *Among Those Present*, 158.

the head of state of India, Johnson described their meeting as being like seducing a woman: "with great relish he talked about winning one point in the conversation; according to him, it was 'just like putting your hand up her leg.'"[82]

From the time he reached Washington Johnson knew the world he wanted to be part of. He knew where the power was, he knew the people to cultivate, and if he was not rich in dollars still he was rich in cunning, ambition and energy. When John F. Kennedy eventually ran for the presidency in 1960 he was not sure how much support he would have in the South. To strengthen his position in that area and to keep harmony within the Democratic party he selected the Southerner Lyndon B. Johnson, by then a powerful Texas Senator, as his vice-presidential campaign partner.

The two Operators had no special fondness for each other but, Operators that they were, they found their association useful. Johnson had hoped to become the Democrat's presidential nominee, and when Kennedy was selected instead Johnson was in agony. Nonetheless when Kennedy proposed the partnership Johnson decided to agree to it. The Kennedy-Johnson ticket squeaked by the election in 1960, Kennedy was assassinated in 1963, and the rough but cunning Lyndon B. Johnson was President of the United States.

Johnson loved politics. It was for him the greatest, most exhilarating and fascinating game to be found anywhere. He loved to persuade, to blandish, to maneuver. He had an insatiable appetite for using the machinery of government, employing the rules and regulations as his own personal tools. His natural style was to attack, overpower, and bury his opposition, whether it be a person or an idea. It didn't matter whether it was a major matter or a trivial one. He loved contest and he had to win. In spite of his fondness for steam roller power plays, however, he recognized with the Artisan's special tactical prowess the importance of subtlety and dexterity, of deceit and seduction. And recognizing them, he used them. "I'm just like a fox" he once said. "I can see the jugular in any man and go for it, but I always keep myself in reign. I keep myself on a leash, just like you would an animal."[83]

---

82 *Among Those Present*, 87.
83 *Among Those Present*, 177.

Lyndon Johnson was disinterested in ideas that didn't have direct application to his immediate interests. His relationship with the press reflected his Operator's tactical viewpoint. He didn't like the press and he didn't trust journalists, and he had no patience with the notion of the importance of a free press.

> You were either for him or against him, and he gave only lip service to the right of the press to find fault...when he believed that he was doing his best for his country, he thought that any rejection of him or his politics was unpatriotic, if not treasonous.[84]

Nor was he interested in books. His preferred reading material was newspapers and magazines and government reports and documents related to pending legislation. These were the materials that demanded his attention; they were the materials that could make the difference between winning and losing. During his presidency Johnson also had a prodigious three-screen television console in his bedroom, complete with a playback device, so he could watch three network news programs simultaneously and replay anything of interest (anything, that is, that he could use). It was immediate action, not philosophical rumination, that fascinated Johnson; it was the contest that fascinated, not the cause.

In spite of his surface roughness Johnson was a highly gifted negotiator. His belief was that the government of any country was in the hands of a small group of powerful men; therefore he was interested in working with these small power elites, in negotiating and persuading and maneuvering them. As Johnson saw it, the entity which needed to be maneuvered or conciliated was not so much "the people," but rather that special club for which eligibility was rooted in power and maintained through quid pro quo. Perhaps this helps to account for the fact that Johnson was never a charismatic public figure in the fashion of Kennedy or the Roosevelts, and never seemed interested in trying to become one. He preferred the bluff, down-home, one-on-one approach where his own personal forcefulness could accomplish in a few minutes or a few hours what might require months to accomplish if the issue were taken to "the people." This preference also helps to explain Johnson's love for the telephone. His favorite desk phone came complete with forty-two

---

84 *Among Those Present*, 135.

buttons, and it seemed to his brother that the "mere act of calling was often more important than anything he had to say."[85]

It's intriguing that this clever, cunning, and dynamic Operator might manage to look dignified when delivering a presidential address, but only at the price of appearing dull and even stodgy. As President he never seemed able to evoke the warm and enthusiastic response in his mass audience that so many of his Operator predecessors were so good at eliciting. Yet when he was on the campaign trail and face to face with the public he became animated, and responded in typical outgoing Operator fashion. As with the Roosevelts and Kennedy, when he was about to address an audience his eyes would glint, his fatigue would disappear, and he would suddenly come to life as if he had just received a dose of fresh blood or an infusion of some other wondrous, life-giving elixir. Endlessly sociable, Johnson seemed happiest when he was surrounded by a group of admirers or a group of people he wanted to win over. At such times he could be absolutely tireless in his efforts to charm, to cajole, to argue the other to his own point of view.

His effort to persuade Claudia Alta Taylor ("Bird" to her friends, "Lady Bird" to most others) to marry him was typical of his persuasive style. He had known her less than two months but had already decided to marry her. One day he roared into town from Washington and took her for an automobile ride during which he proposed marriage. When Lady Bird appeared uncertain about this remarkable turn of events Lyndon flattered, pleaded, threatened, and cajoled. Finally, flustered and dazed, she agreed to marriage. Within two months of their first meeting Lyndon and Lady Bird were married.

Bird Taylor's early life had not been especially happy. Her mother died when she was six and her father, not sure what to do with her, left her largely in the hands of a well-intentioned but rather frail and sickly aunt who could teach her little about getting along with her peers. Bird was a very bright student and graduated high school at age fifteen. But her lack of social skills, her youth, and her natural shyness had made her time in school very painful and left her feeling like (and largely being seen as) a maladroit and isolated wall flower. Though her father was rather wealthy she spent very little on her own appearance and comfort.

---

85 *My Brother Lyndon*, 171.

Her choices in clothing were often considered to be rather tasteless, almost designed to show her at her worst. All the same she attended the University of Texas, adjusted to the new environment, and did very well there. She earned a B.A. in the liberal arts, attended school for another year and earned a degree in journalism, pursued a teaching certificate, and developed skills in typing and stenography. She was quite sure she wanted this variety of skills. Uncertain about her own future, Bird did not intend to be caught unready for whatever might come.

Of course, she could not know that one of the things that might come would be Lyndon Baines Johnson. She met LBJ, was swept off her feet by his ardent proposal, was married, had a quick honeymoon, and was launched into a career as a politician's wife all within the course of a few months. Over the next several years she gradually learned the ropes of political life, taught by the wildly energetic and enormously demanding Lyndon.

She became proficient enough that she garnered considerable respect for her abilities. Lady Bird, a Guardian, eventually came to demonstrate both a personal warmth and graciousness and a remarkably practical business sense that served her well when she eventually became First Lady. (These skills were also useful to her in the monitoring of the business interests she had inherited from her father and that she had ferreted out and purchased on her own.) She pursued her project for the "beautification" of America and her interest in Head Start programs with considerable energy and skill and she also demonstrated an ability to organize her own staff at least as well as Lyndon organized his. Like Eleanor Roosevelt before her, Lady Bird Johnson found the challenge of her husband's life the springboard for an assertion of her own interests and individuality.

Unlike Eleanor Roosevelt, however, Lady Bird Johnson did not become a world traveller or an entity existing independently of her husband. There was always a sense of the connectedness of Lyndon and Lady Bird, and though Lyndon was clearly and adamantly the dominant force in the relationship and though he might insist on a dominant role in their marriage, Lyndon did take great pride in her abilities. At one time, after she had completed a difficult, multiple city speaking tour which was compressed into only a few long and busy days, he commented on the skill and energy with which she had performed and exclaimed, "I'm proud to be her husband."

Lyndon Johnson was a powerful politician; he understood the game well and played it energetically, shrewdly, and unflinchingly. He was a crafty, hard-working opportunist, able to use any event to accomplish a goal. He could be underhanded, unprincipled, devious, brazen, menacing, and downright dirty in the way he played the game of politics. Like all Operators, he played hard and he played to win. Yet it must be acknowledged that his administration and policies were shaped by something within the man that stood beyond mere political expedience. Though a great deal of the legislation he sponsored during his presidency originated with someone else, his pursuit of its passage was earnest and energetic. He brought his own powers to bear on much of that legislation with such implacable resolve that, regardless of where it originated, it can truly be called Lyndon Johnson's.

While he was still a Congressman he was influential in bringing into being the Civil Rights Act of 1957. While in the White House he pressed for (and got) more civil rights legislation through the Congress. Bills were sponsored for voting rights, mass transit, medicare, support for low-income families and the aged, federal aid to education. All these were a part of Johnson's "Great Society," part of his own personal "war on poverty." His early days of financial hardship and his experience working with the Hispanic children in Cotulla, Texas apparently had not been forgotten.

And though he was a masterful wheeler-dealer, capable of great cynicism and sometimes shamefully underhanded dealings, still he did seem to want to be respected, to be admired, to be loved. He was enormously self-confident but he still wanted to be looked up to, to be "somebody." He was the underdog, determined to win and bone-deep eager to be admired for his victories. On the domestic scene he accomplished a great deal.

Perhaps without the Viet Nam conflict his presidency would have been regarded by some as nearing greatness. He had inherited the Asian conflict from Eisenhower and Kennedy and, hating to lose, he tried to bull his way through to a successful outcome. But his efforts to deal with the Viet Nam conflict have the Artisan's stamp of improvisation. There were continually larger numbers of men being sent in response to new incursions and pressures, the debatable Gulf of Tonkin Resolution, and his decisions about bombing North Viet Nam. All seemed designed moment by moment to try to force something to happen militarily; few seemed to be based on any sort of thoughtful strategy for dealing with the Viet Nam war as the manifestation of a complex political situation. And all were destined finally to fail, for he was not confronting a simple military matter.

Perhaps in his dealings with foreign policy Johnson was brought low by his own weaknesses: ignorance about the political and ideological history of southeast Asia; ignorance about what the people of the United States were willing to pay for a war that had little importance for them; ignorance about people with whom he could not sit face-to-face and who were not part of the political machinery so familiar to him. With a distressingly simplistic view of the world, a world of "us" and "them," he tried to improvise complex negotiations with strangers who were moved by fundamentally unfamiliar beliefs and motives. His downfall was the result of his failure to comprehend sufficiently the power of their ideology.

It was foreign policy and especially the Viet Nam conflict that broke Johnson's presidency. As the time for the presidential primaries approached in early 1968, it appeared that he might have to struggle against anti-war candidates in his own Democratic party—and that he might lose to these upstarts. Perhaps this prospect helped him decide not to run for re-election.

For that was his decision: on March 31, 1968, near the end of his second term of office, he announced his decision not to run again. The game of politics was over for Lyndon Johnson. He and Lady Bird retired to their ranch in Stonewall Texas where they lived until his death less than four years later, in January of 1973. They were not good years for him.

> He was not cut out to be Cincinnatus. After the White House, he lived just four restless years, prowling the ranch and Austin, not greatly esteemed or consulted as any sort of elder statesman, never settling into a reflective, semischolarly mode.[86]

Lady Bird was stricken deeply by his death, but gradually her own vitality reasserted itself. She eventually took on a schedule almost as busy as she had maintained during her White House days, working with

---

86 *Roosevelt to Reagan*, 105.

various projects and charities in which she had a special interest. But she has never stopped remembering and loving her dynamic husband Lyndon, the man about whom a friend once commented:

> He hates more, he loves more, he eats more, he sleeps more, he drinks more, he has more kindness, he has more contempt, he saves more, he spends more, he does everything more. He's just more.[87]

Bibliography

Amrine, M 1954	*The Awesome Challenge: The Hundred Days of Lyndon Johnson*
Berman, L 1989	*Lyndon Johnson's War: The Road to Stalemate in Vietnam*
Bornet, V 1983	*The Presidency of Lyndon B. Johnson*
Caro, R 1982	*The Years of Lyndon Johnson*
Conkin, P 1986	*Big Daddy from the Pedernales: Lyndon Baines Johnson*
Deakin, J 1968	*Lyndon Johnson's Credibility Gap*
Dugger, R 1982	*The Politician: The Life and Times of Lyndon Johnson*
Evans R, 1966	*Lyndon B. Johnson: The Exercise of Power, a Political Biography*
Geyelin, P 1966	*Lyndon Johnson and the World*
Goldman, E 1969	*The Tragedy of Lyndon Johnson*
Goodwin, D 1976	*Lyndon Johnson and the American Dream*
Johnson, S 1969	*My Brother Lyndon*
Pool, W 1965	*Lyndon Baines Johnson: The Formative Years*
Reedy, G 1982	*Lyndon B. Johnson, a Memoir*
Rulon, P 1981	*The Compassionate Samaritan: The Life of Lyndon Baines Johnson*
Shandler, H 1977	*The Unmasking of a President: Lyndon Johnson and Vietnam*
Sidney, H 1968	*A Very Personal Presidency: Lyndon Johnson in the White House*
Thompson, K (ed.)	*The Johnson Presidency: 20 Intimate Perspectives of Lyndon B. Johnson*
Turner, K 1985	*Lyndon Johnson's Dual War: Vietnam and the Press*
White, W 1964	*The Professional: Lyndon B. Johnson*

---

87 *Roosevelt to Reagan*, 106.

Reporter Artisan Presidents: The Players

Zachary Taylor

Old Rough and Ready

Player
Born: November 24, 1784
Died: July 9, 1850
Presidency: 1849-1850

Zachary Taylor's fame rested on his success as a frontier general and Indian fighter. In that role he demonstrated his ability to conduct fast-paced, fluid, opportunistic warfare, the sort of warfare at which the Artisan is most likely to excel. Like Andy Jackson, his predecessor twenty years earlier, Taylor was a good example of the frontier Artisan. His rough-hewn bluntness, his disregard for social niceties, his casual informality in dress and manner, and his ability to put up with great inconvenience and discomfort, all gave him the aura which his men applauded by giving him the nickname, "Old Rough and Ready."

While Jackson was a sometimes bitter and always contentious Operator, Taylor was a Player Artisan, at ease with himself and the world. He was shambling and shabby in his appearance, loud and profane and common in speech and action, but his loud and common demeanor could not obscure his natural affability and kindness or his frontier-style graciousness. One could make too much of his loud profanity; Artisans naturally prefer the vernacular, the language of impact. His unpretentious charm inevitably made one feel at ease in his company. Overall he was a very even-tempered and pleasant man, unaffected by his own successes, and in true Artisan fashion indifferent to pomp and immune to the disease of self-importance. Not even being selected as a presidential candidate could puff him up. When he was approached by a friend about the possibility of running for the highest office in the nation, Taylor's reply was a simple "Oh, stop your nonsense and drink your whiskey."[88]

At times his plain and rough manner made plausible the accusations that he was irresponsible and the rumors that he was a hopeless drunk. No less a light than Daniel Webster dismissed him as "a swearing, whiskey-drinking, frontier colonel."[89] In fact Taylor was happy to offer alcohol to his guests, but he himself didn't drink. His only vice seemed to be tobacco, usually chewing tobacco, since tobacco smoke upset his wife.

Overall it would have been difficult to dislike this pleasant, easy-going Artisan or to resist the spell of his relaxed, comfortable charisma. However one would have a very incomplete and inaccurate understanding of the man if one attended only to his easy affability. Taylor was after all a military man with a record of brilliant successes in frontier fighting. Of necessity he was capable of iron discipline and stern justice when it seemed necessary. He hung more than one man as a spy or a deserter during his time as a commanding officer. After a campaign he was capable of considerable generosity to those who had been his enemies, but during the heat of battle (whether political or military) stern

---

88 *Presidential Anecdotes*, 103.
89 *Presidential Anecdotes*, 103.

discipline and bold action were everything, for these were the ingredients of victory.

Taylor was also an unquestioning and fervid patriot, and where his own convictions were at issue he had an iron will. He found in his own beliefs no complexities to discuss, no difficult moral questions to be answered. Like Jackson before him and the other Artisans that followed him, his utilitarian style was concrete, down to earth, sensible, uncomplicated with fancy abstractions. What he believed, was so; nothing further was called for but to act. Shortly prior to the outbreak of the Civil War, for instance, he was approached by several Southern congressmen who asked him where he stood on the issue of Southern secession. The staunch patriot's angry reply was again in keeping with his Artisan predecessor General Jackson. Taylor retorted that if it were necessary to his execution of the law of the land, "he would take command of the army himself, and that, if they were taken in rebellion against the Union, he would hang them with less reluctance than he had hung deserters and spies in Mexico."[90]

In spite of his military successes Zach Taylor was not terribly bright except as a military tactician. He was not a planner, not even as a general, and strategy was a subject that seemed to escape him regularly. He frequently moved without bothering to formulate a clear plan of action or taking the trouble to establish adequate military intelligence about the terrain or the population ahead of him and his troops. He was weak in logistic work as well, moving his troops without adequate attention to his transportation or his supply lines, logistical matters whose importance would have been obvious to any Guardian quartermaster. Of necessity he improvised in combat, but he acted boldly, and displayed enough of the Artisan's tactical virtuosity that he was able to win battles. This combination of on-the-spot improvising and headlong boldness was of crucial importance to Taylor because his impetuous style of leadership led him headlong into battles that somehow just seemed to happen to him. He had less of Jackson's tactical cunning, the ability to shape the immediate course of events,

---

90 *Presidential Anecdotes,* 107. This sort of impetuous pronouncement bears resemblance to that of General Patton at the close of WW II when he said he was ready, willing, and able to go after his (erstwhile) Soviet allies to prevent WW III.

though he was gifted with a well-developed ability to respond to what was already happening and somehow to emerge victorious.

Like many candidates of the time, Taylor was not picked by the political machine because of his qualifications for the office, his convictions, or his statesmanlike qualities. He was selected primarily because he was a very popular figure, especially with the plain people of the country, and therefore a candidate with good prospects for winning an election. But as a candidate Taylor was a pesky problem for the machine politicians who managed his campaign. He proved himself to be as plain-spoken, as rough, and as ready for action as his nickname suggested, and his party advisors had great trouble corralling him and training him to speak with the caution that his presidential candidacy demanded. He spontaneously said the sorts of things that candidates shouldn't say (even admitting that he had never voted in an election), and he spoke without hesitation and without regret. Overall he went through his political campaign as he went through his military campaigns: it all seemed to "just happen to him" and he worked things around so that somehow he came out ahead in the end.[91]

One of the most pleasant things that "just happened to him" was his meeting with Margaret Smith. Young Zach was much taken with her when they met in 1809 and the bold, dashing lieutenant courteously pursued the shy young woman. In 1810, less than a year after their first meeting, they were married.

Margaret Smith Taylor (probably a Conservator Guardian) was very much in love with her husband and cheerfully followed him from place to place throughout his long military career, living without complaint in log cabins, tents, or whatever other accommodations offered themselves. Her initial shyness dissolved in time and she cheered up others (especially other military wives), saw to the comfort of her husband's soldiers, and with her energetic and gracious manner made everyone's life more agreeable. Though she was often ill and weak she continued to be a warm and hospitable hostess when she was able to. Slanderous

---

91 This sort of campaigning would never do in the latter part of the 20th century, of course, since all it takes to disqualify a candidate of any type of personality is one unguarded remark picked up by the ever present and ever vigilant media. But in Taylor's time a candidate could still manage a bit of bluster and brashness without fatal consequences to his campaign.

comments that described her as a rough, ill-mannered frontier illiterate were very wide of the mark, though she seems to have suffered these affronts with her usual good grace. For his part, Zachary Taylor spoke infrequently of her but seemed to love her and be happy with her.

Neither of the Taylors had any political interests. Margaret Taylor avoided such matters and Zach Taylor harbored what were at best rather ill-defined political views. He had never bothered to vote—not even in his own presidential election—and didn't even know what his party affiliation was. He reacted from his convictions, impulsively and naively, and the fact that he was ignorant of national issues and the political process did not discourage him from speaking out about them.

Nevertheless, Zachary Taylor was elected to the presidency in 1848 and took office in 1849. Like most Artisan Presidents, Taylor had little interest in the complexities of government policies and so made no effort to understand or implement them. When he stood for election he felt free to promise whatever his constituents wanted, much as did the vastly more clever Artisan, Lyndon Johnson, in the next century. He also restored the spoils system, in keeping with his hedonic nature, a system established by Andy Jackson earlier, but dismantled by the staunch Guardian, James Polk.

During his short time as President Taylor suffered from the acrimony and the insults to which an incumbent is likely to be subject even in the best of times. Though he took quite to heart the criticisms and the complaints of his political opponents, and felt he was being slandered and abused quite unjustly, forty years as a soldier had left their mark. In his usual fashion he damned well stood up to the assaults of the opposition and carried on with his own campaigns.

One of his presidential campaigns was for the admission of California and New Mexico to the Union as states which would decide for themselves whether they would permit slavery. Taylor had himself previously been a slave holder but, as we noted earlier, there could be no doubt about where his sentiments lay. He was an American and a patriot, and he was a military commander. If any rebellious state chose to try remove itself from the Union Taylor was again quite clear about what he would do: "I will command the army in person," he declared, "and hang any man taken in treason."[92] No self-respecting Artisan commander, after all, will put up with insubordination, let alone treason. Nor is he

---

92 *The American Presidents,* 112.

likely to stand on ceremony in punishing those who resort to either. (One might remember World War II's famous Artisan, General George Patton, who almost ended his military career by impulsively slapping a terrified soldier.)

One hot summer day in 1850 President Zachary Taylor, now in his mid-sixties, participated in the ceremony for laying the cornerstone of the new Washington Monument. To relieve himself from the effects of the heat, and despite the pleas of his personal physician, he consumed enormous quantities of iced milk, cold cherries, and pickled cucumbers. Shortly thereafter Taylor suffered a stroke and died of the effects of combined overexertion and overindulgence. The tough and impetuous, warm and unassuming frontier general had been President for only sixteen months. His last words were marvelously expressive of his Player character: "I regret nothing, but am sorry that I am about to leave my friends."[93]

Taylor's presidency was remarkable only in the sense that he was the first Player Artisan to occupy the White House. His tenure was so brief and his grasp of the reigns of government so loose, that he left no mark on the office or the nation.

Bibliography

Frost, J 1847   *The Life of Major General Zachary Taylor*
Hamilton, H 1941   *Zachary Taylor*
Howard, O 1892   *General Taylor*
Mckinley, S 1946   *Old Rough and Ready, the Life and Times of Zachary Taylor*
Nichols, E 1963   *Zach Taylor's Little Army*
Oyer, B 1946   *Zachary Taylor*
Prentiss, G 1850   *Eulogy on the Life and Character of General Zachary Taylor*
Scott, F 1935   *Old Rough and Ready on the Rio Grande*

---

93 *World Almanac of Presidential Facts*, 60.

Franklin Pierce

The marriage of pleasure and sorrow

Player
Born: November 23, 1804
Died: October 8, 1869
Presidency: 1853-1857

The Democratic party nominated Franklin Pierce to run for the presidency in 1852. It was an unfortunate choice both for Pierce and for the country. The slavery issue was becoming increasingly inflamed, the breakup of the United States loomed ever more likely, and the nation badly needed someone who could wield the power of national leadership during this terribly difficult time. But the newly-elected President Franklin Pierce showed no more strength in his handling of the issue, and probably less good judgment, than had his unsuccessful predecessor, Millard Fillmore.

Pierce's candidacy had come about (rather like that of James Polk's) because no one else could prevail at the Democratic party's nominating convention. His name didn't even appear in the Democratic convention's nomination process until the 35th ballot was taken, and the popular but uninspiring party politician still wasn't nominated until the 47th ballot. The exhaustion of the Democratic party delegates more than anything else carried the day for Pierce.

Franklin Pierce was a graceful and easygoing young man, hearty in manner and naturally gregarious, an outspoken Player Artisan. As is often the case with more playful Artisans, he had a reputation for enjoying the local taverns and for tippling considerably more than was good for him. In fact he was reputed to be drunk rather frequently, during which times he often made a fool of himself with his loud and undignified behavior. On one occasion, for instance, he and his friends were attending a play whose performance they so badly disrupted that they were ejected from the theater. Then, as if to wrap up their evening's festivities, Pierce and his comrades apparently began a street fight outside the theater.

But Pierce was an able young man who did remarkably well in college,[94] and who had good political connections and a smooth, personable style. After he graduated college he undertook law studies, passed the bar, and soon became an effective and successful trial lawyer. As usual the Artisan interested in law was better suited to trial law than other types of law, such as tax or business law. Trial law is a matter of contest and Artisans are likely to do well there because of their canny observation of the immediate and their skillfulness in tactical variation. So it was with Pierce. With his deft personal skills and his magnetic character he had a talent for handling juries.

Then when he moved into the political arena he displayed a naturally winning way with other politicians and a charisma with the voters. Pierce the Player was chary of scholarly or philosophical pursuits. Most of his political position seemed to come from his conservative, headstrong Artisan father, a man much in the mold of

---

94 He had done a senior Latin dissertation—written entirely in scholarly Latin—entitled "De Triumphis Romanorum" and had gone on to graduate third in his class from Bowdoin College in 1824.

Zach Taylor, but with a strong emphasis on states' rights. Franklin Pierce was thus a states' rights man, too, and so palatable to the South. Otherwise he had great trouble making up his mind about important issues unless there were a comfortable path to follow already marked out. The few powers of conciliation he did have were usually used to find the easiest course for himself, the path of least resistance. Coupled with his constant efforts to keep life pleasant, this pattern of weakness made him a docile character and a feeble President whom one historian succinctly characterized as a man of "mediocre talents, with a flighty mind, a defective education, and schooled to the toadying demanded by the Southerners."[95]

Pierce hoped, as did many during that time, that by focusing on the matter of states' rights rather than on slavery he could keep the support of the South and avoid offending the North. The issue would be a legal one this way, not ideological, a question of the legal relationship of the states with the federal government rather than the more dangerous question of slavery. Perhaps this at best questionable strategy was a natural one for the opportunistic Artisan lawyer, but even here his impetuous style and unexamined views dictated his actions.

He vigorously enforced the cruel and foolish fugitive slave laws which declared that an escaped slave could be pursued across state borders, all the way to Maine if necessary, and brought back forcibly to his owner. These laws had the horrid effect of making legal the forcible return to slavery of escaped slaves even if they had lived for decades in the North as respectable citizens, even if they were married and even if they had children. The cruelty of the laws and the violent anti-slavery sentiment of the Northern states led to more than one bloody confrontation between slave chasers and the former slaves' Northern protectors.

The violence of abolitionist sentiment was powerful and the legitimacy of the fugitive laws was equivocal. Pierce was still headstrong enough to insist on federal prosecution of the protectors of runaways. He wanted to use federal marshals and federal troops against northern abolitionists in order to help slave owners recover their "property," though cooler heads apparently counseled him that this

---

95 Rexford Tugwell, *How They Became President*, 173.

employment of Federal forces would be met with the most violent possible response.

In spite of his personal weaknesses, his administration might have proven itself to be of some value if Pierce had chosen a strong and wise Cabinet to advise and support him. True to character, however, he toadied to the southern powers and selected an undistinguished but strongly pro-slavery group of politicians for his Cabinet posts. By depriving himself of sound and thoughtful advisors he further weakened his prospects for leading effectively. Given all these handicaps there was not much to be expected of President Pierce except clumsy and ill-advised maneuver resulting in further deterioration of the nation's condition.

To complicate matters further, Pierce was an ardent expansionist. "Manifest destiny" beckoned invitingly and he saw the foreign territories to the south of the United States as ripe for the picking. "Our expansion," he exclaimed, "our position on the globe, render[s] the acquisition of certain possessions...eminently important for our protection." He did not make it clear which "certain possessions" he had in mind and from whom these possessions would protect us. But in typically optimistic Artisan fashion he made the cheerful but meaningless pronouncement that "the future is boundless" and proceeded with several foolish and fruitless operations to secure more territory for the United States.

The "certain possessions" he had in mind, including Cuba, would not only naturally be the provinces of the United states, he thought, but would also be natural and reasonably distant magnets for slavery. Their acquisition, he thought, might therefore help to dampen the heated slavery issue by drawing the conflict to the overseas south. Gambling that this approach would help soften the impact of the slavery issue, he pursued plans for new conquests eagerly. But he had little final success. He attempted, for instance, to foment a rebellion in Cuba against the island's Spanish rulers. When this ploy failed, and it failed miserably, he attempted to purchase Cuba from Spain outright. By this time however the Spanish were so disenchanted with his high-handed meddling that there was no hope of successful negotiation.[96]

---

96 Artisans in any kind of job are happiest when they are trouble-shooting. They will sometimes stir up trouble just so they can exercise their trouble-shooting skills. Pierce's creating a Cuban uproar is a possible case in point.

Pierce was never able to comprehend the power of the North's anti-slavery sentiment. He hated the abolitionist movement and saw its members as nothing more than reckless fanatics, and his own actions were consistently in accord with this remarkably shallow view. His clumsy interest in expansionist manifest destiny not only alienated Spanish and Mexican sentiment, it also brought him into conflict with the powerful abolitionist sentiment of the North, for whom further territories for slave holders would have been anathema. In general, he simply and rashly made a mess of things, adding to the nation's emotional upheaval rather than serving to ameliorate it.

It is one of the fascinations of temperament theory to see the relationship that sometimes develops between Artisan husbands and Guardian wives. One occasionally finds an otherwise wayward Artisan husband who is so devoted to his home-dominant Guardian wife that he seems to find pleasure in bending his impulsiveness to her wishes and emotions. This was apparently the situation with the Pierces. Jane Appleton Pierce was at first glance a shy and retiring woman. She was of frail constitution and easily upset but was tirelessly devoted to her husband and her children.

Devoutly religious, even puritanical, Jane Pierce insisted upon daily religious services and Bible readings and saying prayers at mealtimes. She hated the hurly-burly of public life and was also distressed by her husband's drinking and carousing.[97] During his first term as Congressman and then later when he was a Senator from New Hampshire, Franklin spent most of his time in the nation's capital. In the meantime Jane spent most of her time at home in Hillsborough, New Hampshire, with the children. She was stiff, very uncomfortable at social functions, and she despised Washington and hated its climate, which she seemed to feel adversely affected her tubercular constitution. She hated Franklin's life in politics. When he was nominated for the presidency she had not known he was being considered for nomination. When she heard the news of his selection she fainted dead away.

Nonetheless, and though Jane was a very serious person with no apparent sense of humor and no evidence of any good cheer whatsoever,

---

97 She had reason to. Pierce, for example, was arrested in 1855 after accidentally running down an old woman with his horse, which he had been riding rapidly and carelessly. (When it was realized that he was the President he was released.)

Franklin apparently remained devoted to her.[98] Early in their marriage and in response to her continuous appeals, he had resigned from the United States Senate to return to New Hampshire to practice law. But when the Mexican War broke out he volunteered for service and was commissioned a field officer. He had more elbow room, more opportunities for adventure during the war, and seemed both more reliable and happier than he had in many years. Hunger for stimulation and search for adventure, more urgent in Artisans than all others, can sometimes lure a domesticated Artisan from the warmth and comforts of his home to the perils and thrills of the open field. War is a powerful magnet to the dozing Artisan, and such it was to Pierce. But all good things must end, even the exhilarations of life in the field. Politics beckoned and Franklin responded, his wife's protests notwithstanding. Beyond the pleasures of action his performance in the field and his political connections served him well, and a few years later Pierce was elected to the presidency.

Even before he took office, however, the Pierces were visited with a tragic event which shadowed their days as long as they lived. Jane and Franklin had had three children, two of whom had died while still very young. Jane doted on the third, little Benjamin. Two months before Franklin's inauguration the Pierces were making a journey by train when their locomotive derailed and the passenger cars tumbled, one after the other, from the tracks. Franklin and Jane escaped with bruises, but their beloved Bennie was crushed under the wreckage of a passenger car. Jane Pierce never recovered from the tragedy; if she had been cheerless before, she was now and for the rest of her life little more than a grey, morose shadow. Now her hatred of her husband's career could find another expression: she informed him that she saw her son's death as a sacrifice demanded by God for Pierce's election to the presidency. She again refused to move to Washington, even to the White House. When

---

98 The marriage of cheerful Artisan to doleful Guardian is the most frequent of all marriages, no surprise given that the Artisan and Guardian combined comprise as much as 85% of the population. Such marriages offer strong mutual attraction and completion. Each has what the other does not have: the home-loving Guardian provides safe harbor for the wayward Artisan while the cheerful Artisan provides excitement and optimism for the worried and pessimistic Guardian. See Montgomery's *The Pygmalion Project, Volumes I and II*.

she did finally come to the capital she remained chronically depressed and her morose behavior became increasingly bizarre. For instance she would sometimes refuse to admit that little Bennie was dead and would write frequent notes to him.

Still, Franklin, in spite of his boisterous and impetuous ways, remained solicitous of his wife. He was endlessly patient with Jane, whom he saw as a tender, finer creature than his own coarse self. None of the other types appreciate the salving and nurturing attitudes of the Guardian as much as does the Artisan. Jane in turn continued to help keep him sober and persisted in trying to induce him to leave politics.

After four years in the White House, when he told her that he wanted to run for re-election to the presidency in 1856, she was terribly upset. She admitted later that she had prayed ardently for his defeat should he run again. Her prayers were answered in the most economical fashion: the Democrats did not renominate Franklin Pierce for the presidency. Pierce, with his love for the stimulation and excitement of political life, was terribly disappointed; a friend wrote of him after he had left office that, "My heart bleeds for him, for he is a gallant and generous spirit." Still, he observed further, Pierce was thoroughly overshadowed by the demands of the office.

When someone asked the heartbroken Pierce what he would do after leaving the presidency, he sighed and said, "There's nothing left...but to get drunk."[99] In this he was again a typical Artisan. The Artisans, and especially the Players, are far more likely to react to disappointment with self-indulgence.

Pierce did find a few other things to do besides drinking. After leaving office he persistently and nastily attacked Lincoln and the Union war effort, maintaining his campaign until he had no friends left. His Artisan intemperance, overwhelming the tactical good sense typical of Artisans, led him repeatedly to take stands which finally resulted in his complete rejection. For instance he made the repeated claim that the much-heralded Emancipation Proclamation was unconstitutional. He thereby showed himself to be one of the few people in the North sufficiently lacking in common sense that they could adamantly insist on such a stance about the proclamation.

---

99 *Presidential Anecdotes*, 116.

Jane Pierce died in 1863 and Franklin again took up his habit of heavy drinking. For the few remaining years of his life he lived in complete political eclipse, dying almost unnoticed and largely unmourned in 1869.

Bibliography

Bartlett, D 1857 · *The Life of General Franklin Pierce of New Hampshire*

Democratic Party, 1857 · *Sketches in the Lives of Franklin Pierce and William King*

Hawthorne, N 1970 · *The Life of Franklin Pierce*

Nichols, R 1958 · *Franklin Pierce, Young Hickory of the Granite Hills*

Sloan, I (ed) 1968 · *Franklin Pierce, 1804-1869: Documents, Bibliographical Aids*

James A. Garfield

"Sound and fury..."

Player
Born: November 19, 1831
Died: September 19, 1881
Presidency: 1881

James Garfield was a man whom many people found easy to like but difficult to respect. He was a spellbinding orator, exceptionally eloquent in his public addresses. Even as a young man he had that captivating, charismatic quality found so often among the Artisans. His physical appearance also served him well, for he stood a handsome and virile six feet tall in a day when the average height for men was about five feet eight inches. He had been strong and athletic all his life and was blessed with abundant energy, and his blond, blue-eyed attractiveness was complemented by the oratorical skills he honed so constantly and intently. Like those Artisans who practice their duelling skills daily, Garfield practiced his, though he replaced the gun and sword with flowery speech.[100]

Garfield's personal history was very attractive politically. He was his own Horatio Alger story, starting off as the youngest son of a poor widowed farm woman, working at all manner of odd jobs to earn money, leaving home to work on the Great Lakes as a sailor, then a canal boy guiding horses and mules along the Ohio Canal—all before he reached age eighteen. Thereafter he worked his way through college by tutoring in Latin and Greek and still managing to do well with his own studies. He even left college for a time to earn money to complete his degree by teaching school. From the menial position of seventeen year old canal boat boy he then went on to earn his college degree first at Hiram Eclectic Institute (now Hiram College) and then at Williams College. Then, when he was twenty-six he returned to Hiram, this time as its new president.

He had grown up with no father and had rebelled often against his mother's direction, but he remained for a time part of a close-knit rural religious community. The Disciples of Christ had formed their own community which, though strongly religious, was not so overbearing that young Garfield rebelled entirely. In fact he adapted so well that he even became a lay preacher noted for his marvelous oratorical skills. As one writer put it, James Garfield became "almost too popular for his own good."[101] There was some question about whether as a young man he knew the proper place for him to rest his head at night, and he later and somewhat ruefully described his childhood as "wild, chaotic, unrestrained."

Given his exciting boyhood and young manhood it is not surprising that the rather lofty life of a college president was too dull for Garfield.

---

100 When Artisans take up composition as their art they easily outdo the other types especially in screenplays, stage plays, musical scores, and poetry. This is not to say that other personalities cannot or do not compose works of art; it is only to say that the latter must work much harder to attain works of lesser artistry. See the film *Amadeus* for an explicit comparison of a virtuoso (Mozart) to a renowned but lackluster Guardian composer.

101 *Profiles and Portraits of American Presidents*, 194.

He described himself, after all, as a man who loved the idea of action when he was at rest and the idea of rest when he was active. So he entered politics, ran for and was elected to the Ohio State Senate in 1859. When the Civil War broke out two years later he took advantage of the event by helping raise a regiment from Hiram, being elected its colonel, and performing so fearlessly in the field that he became the youngest brigadier general in the army.[102] His popularity was so great by then that he was elected to Congress while still in uniform.

For another year he continued to serve in the army, but finally resigned his commission in 1863 to take his seat in the Congress. It was right at the midpoint of the Civil War, and though the timing seems politically awkward his glamorous reputation offset the awkwardness of the timing. Besides, it was said, Lincoln himself apparently asked him to do so; he could be a brave patriot in Congress as well as on the field of battle.

With all his energy and ambition and glamor Garfield seems to have had no strong political convictions. Such convictions are mere abstractions which, in the Artisan view at least, have little to do with immediate circumstances. Some weak men, like Pierce, may have had strong beliefs handed them when young, and these may pass for convictions. Others, like Garfield, seem to have been exposed to few strong beliefs, and found no value in hamstringing themselves with convictions later. Thus he had little of value to offer toward the resolution of the important issues of his day. Instead he generally presented himself in a way which seemed designed to win over the powerful while alienating as few as possible.

And he was good at it, glossy and smooth, though as a statesman he was completely without substance. James Garfield was an ambitious and charismatic political orator first, everything else second. He seemed to trust in nothing but his own ambitions and his own talents. He changed his positions easily as the tides of opinion and power changed, drifting from one point of view to another as political necessity dictated. As is

---

102 The distinction between courage and fearlessness is important. The person who is fearless is *without* fear, while the one who is courageous *has* fear, but stands firm despite it. A person who is fearless doesn't need courage. Fear comes from anticipating injury, defeat, or death, and Artisans are usually so caught up in exploiting the moment that they do not look ahead to the possibility of getting hurt.

sometimes the case with Artisans, he engaged in constant activity which was, to borrow Shakespeare's phrase, sound and fury signifying nothing—except to James Garfield. In fact when he was nominated for the presidency, twenty-five years after the Civil War ended, Garfield announced that only one act was required finally to restore harmony with the South: "that it shall be admitted, forever and forever more, that in the war for the Union, we were right and they were wrong." This is apparently as close as Garfield ever came to holding a firm political conviction or practicing thoughtful statesmanship!

Perhaps as a part of the legacy of his early upbringing in the Disciples of Christ community, Garfield seemed not to care much for the spoilsmanship of politics. On the other hand this single-mindedly ambitious politician accepted the wheeling and dealing as a necessary (and probably intriguing) part of his political life. He wanted to please everyone and offend no one, and the spoils system of politics, whether he liked it or not, was one device for doing so. Therefore he adapted to it well. And since political parties were necessary vehicles for political success he also made it a point to be a good party man. Thus his party, the Republicans, considered him to be a reliable and "safe" member. In their eyes he was a hack who did not aspire to real leadership, but only to the appearance of leadership.

Along with his interest in oratory and politics Garfield dabbled in poetry and the classics. But one finds no indication that his interest was other than passing. If he had a special love for these subjects it was for their practical applications rather than for any love of antiquity or the classics. He wrote passable verse himself, for instance, and would dazzle his friends with his versatility by simultaneously writing Latin with one hand and Greek with the other. His performance suggested more a love of showmanship than a love of learning, and though he claimed that he saw the value to the country of a well-educated population of voters, he did little to support a program to bring about such a population.

Garfield's marriage to Lucretia Randolph was a difficult one for them both, though not through any fault of hers. Even before marriage he had admired her because of her logical, precise, well-balanced mind. Yet after marriage he often found the rather withdrawn Rational "Crete" to be dull company for him. Lucretia had been raised in the same conservative small community of "God-fearing" Disciple of Christ churchgoers, and attended a Disciples seminary with Garfield. They shared almost identical cultural and religious backgrounds, and they did seem drawn to one another, yet James expressed strong and persistent doubts about the advisability and the durability of their relationship. The courtship was low key and quite lengthy and for many years after they married they spent little time together. James's political affairs continued to be almost the sole focus of his attention—with the possible exception of certain affairs of the heart about which Crete was to know nothing. (Fidelity is not the strongest point in the character structure of Artisans.)

After four years of marriage James considered that it was probably a mistake. He seems never quite to have gotten over the idea that he had been subtly pressured into marriage and of course Artisans don't do at all well with being coerced. Lucretia on the other hand seems to have loved him. Certainly it was she who most actively promoted the idea of marrying. She did not nag James in marriage, however. She was good with words, especially in writing, and she did often remind him of her love and admiration for him. Along with her own gift for powerful expression she displayed a talent for finding the admirable. She could write to James about himself, for instance, that "...when a man has a wife who holds him in large esteem, who knows that in him there is no pretense, nothing but the genuine,—then he has reason to believe in his own worth."[103] James read, he believed, and they married.

In marriage as in politics Garfield the Artisan was reluctant to commit himself to anything. It was Lucretia Garfield's continued expressions of love and admiration that maintained and strengthened their marriage. As the years passed, slowly, unsteadily, but surely they became increasingly content with each other. James was recurrently impressed with her devotion to him and was eventually astonished to find himself reciprocating her love. Then when children were born to them he found himself taking up the role of father quite energetically and apparently with great pleasure. Captured by the idea of parenthood, he became a doting father, an interested teacher, even a moral instructor for his children who could draw upon his background as a lay preacher in the Disciples of Christ.

---

103 *Profiles and Portraits of American Presidents*, 193.

Then on a vacation to Little Mountain (in his senatorial home in Ohio) he was taken with an impulse to become a gentleman farmer. Seeing a farm that appealed to him he immediately purchased it, and "Lawnfield" became the Garfields' home for the remaining years of his life. Finally James acknowledged to Crete that love between them had been slow in coming but had finally come and was there to stay.

It may be that Garfield, in spite of his Artisan's tactical virtuosity, would never have come to the presidency without his wife's counsel. Lucretia the Rational had the strategic sense, the long-term view that James would never have. His genial Player's style charmed others to his side but it was Lucretia's cooler judgments that he counted on to help him know who was worth keeping there and in what political directions they ought to travel.

She observed and passed judgment on the men he considered his friends and she moved about Washington in the informal but informative company of shops and shoppers, and there she collected political and social gossip. She gathered and gleaned and sent back to James the information and advice she saw as important to him, and he seems to have attended to it well. Especially important in their early years in Washington, she kept him from becoming too familiar with the powerful and monied people who so effectively seduced the Grant presidency into incompetence and dishonesty. As one observer wrote, Lucretia had "a strength of unswerving absolute rectitude her husband has not and never will have."[104]

The presidency of the United States, no matter how sweet it may be to win, is often a dubious honor. "My god, what is there in this office that a man should ever want to get into it?" cried Garfield about the presidency not long after taking office. He called it "the bleak mountain" as he became more and more familiar with its demands, some weighty but so many so trivial.[105] He didn't suffer the price of his ambition long, however, for he was President less than a year.

In 1881 the spoils system which he claimed to dislike but which had helped him achieve the presidency reached out for him. Garfield was shot and fatally wounded by a man who angrily claimed that he was

---

104 *Profiles and Portraits of American Presidents*, 196.
105 *Presidential Anecdotes*, 170.

being cheated of his rightful share of those political spoils. James Garfield lingered for eighty painful days before he finally died in September of 1881.

His treasured Crete lived on for another thirty-seven years. Not one to be a passive observer, she devoted herself to managing carefully her children's lives as they grew, and as long as she lived she declared insistently and proudly that she was still the wife of her beloved "General Garfield."

Bibliography

Bancroft, W 1901 — *McKinley, Garfield, Lincoln: Their Lives—Their Deeds—Their Deaths*

Brown, E 1881 — *The Life and Public Services of James A. Garfield*

Bundy, J 1880 — *The Life of General James A. Garfield*

Caldwell, R 1931 — *James A. Garfield, Party Chieftain*

Conwell, R 1880 — *The Life, Speeches and Public Services of James A. Garfield of Ohio*

Doenecke, J 1981 — *The Presidencies of James A. Garfield and Chester A. Arthur*

Feis, R 1963 — *Mollie Garfield in the White House*

Fuller, C 1887 — *Reminiscences of James A. Garfield*

Hope, E 1885 — *The New World Heroes, Lincoln and Garfield*

Leech, M 1978 — *The Garfield Orbit*

McClure, J 1881 — *General Garfield from the Log Cabin to the White House*

Mitchell, A 1881 — *James A. Garfield*

Peskin, A 1978 — *Garfield: a Biography*

Riddle, A 1880 — *The Life, Character and Public Services of Jas A. Garfield*

Ridpath, J 1882 — *The Life and Work of James A. Garfield*

Smith, T 1925 — *The Life and Letters of James Abram Garfield*

Taylor, J 1970 — *Garfield of Ohio, the Available Man*

Thayer, W 1880 — *From Log Cabin to the White House*

Wasson, W 1952 — *James A. Garfield: His Religion and Education*

Chester Alan Arthur

"Chet Arthur President of the United States? Good God!"

Player
Born: October 5, 1830
Died: November 18, 1886
Presidency: 1881-1885

"Good God!"

Such was the expression of disbelief and dismay that greeted Chester Alan Arthur's ascension to the presidency when the incumbent James Garfield died.[106] Vice-President Arthur, an influential and popular political boss from New York, had been a comfortable choice to pair with presidential candidate Garfield. Arthur was always in the political inner circle, always belonged to the right organizations, knew

---

106 *The American Presidents,* 180.

how to help out his friends, and had a knack for constantly making friends while generating few enemies. He was competent and charming and likeable, but he was still thought to be nothing more than a party hack. He would do as a Vice-President; anyone who could capture enough votes would. But no one—not even Chet Arthur—ever intended that he become President.

Chester Arthur was an easy-going Player Artisan, cut from the same cloth as his predecessor, Garfield, who also enjoyed the game of politics and power. Arthur was considered the very model of the political back-scratcher, good-naturedly and adeptly trading favors for payoffs of various sorts. A fastidious dresser with polished manners, always affable, he had neither the viciousness nor deviousness of many professional politicians. He was simply a Player who recognized the opportunities political power offered and who enjoyed indulging in them. Though he had proven a very able student and was a successful lawyer and a popular politician, everyone recognized that he was a totally unsuitable candidate for the presidency of a great nation.

But President James Garfield was killed by an assassin's bullet, and Vice-President Chet Arthur, the good-humored, back-slapping Player, was suddenly the President of the United States.

Perhaps it is true, as some have said, that the office itself sometimes reaches out to change those who occupy it. Arthur the machine politician, the spoilsman, the cheerful power broker, the completely unsuitable candidate, seemed to be transformed by the office into a different person. Though he had always been a reasonably honest politician (at least by the standards of the times) and a competent administrator, he was still a professional politician. He understood and enjoyed Washington's political give-and-take and appreciated the good living and pleasant socializing it offered. Some years earlier, in 1871, he had been appointed Collector of the Port of New York, a position which allowed him to make about a thousand political appointments of his own. The post provided him with a quick and convenient way to become modestly rich, and Arthur had no qualms about enjoying the advantages of the post. He kept the position until the Guardian President Rutherford Hayes forced him to resign in 1878 as a part of a political clean-up campaign.

But while President Garfield lay mortally wounded for those eighty days in 1881, Vice-President Arthur refused to accept any presidential duties. Then, when Garfield died, he stepped very reluctantly into the presidency and offered the world a different side of Chester Arthur than it had yet seen.

President Arthur was still reasonably honest and competent, but now he did a political about-face and surprised everyone who knew him by supporting Civil Service reform.[107] He thereby helped to destroy much of the utility of the system as a means of political payoffs, the most obvious example of the political spoils system. In this and other ways he disrupted Washington's system of payoffs and distressed the machine politicians who came to him seeking political favoritism. He also sponsored various committees, legislation, and international agreements to improve conditions in the United States and in the Western Hemisphere. Though not all his efforts were successful, most were recognized as aiming at goals that were fair, progressive and in support of the disadvantaged. Though the voters looked favorably on his work many people with considerable political power became disenchanted with their old friend Chet; as one disappointed machine politician said, "He isn't Chet Arthur anymore, he's the President."[108] Unexpectedly, this unlikely Player was demonstrating dignity befitting the office, and an unanticipated ability to live up to many of its demands.

But this apparent transformation of character wasn't a transformation at all. Of all the temperament types the Artisan is the most responsive to immediate circumstances and can adapt himself most quickly to change. Such apparent about-faces occurred with high frequency in the lawless West of the nineteenth century, where outlaw gunslingers, Artisans one and all, became incomparable lawmen bent on upholding the law to the death. None can compare with the Artisan in this kind of adaptability. Such "rising to the occasion" is the province of the Artisan because the Artisan sees "occasions" close up and in full color.

Perhaps we may have a glimpse of how Arthur saw this "occasion," his ascendancy to the presidency, by considering the comment he made

---

107 Just as a reformed criminal is often most adept at working with criminals, or a reformed addict is most effective in dealing with addicts, so Arthur the reformed spoilsman seemed to be adept at attacking the spoils system.

108 *Presidential Anecdotes*, 175.

to a friend in 1880. Arthur was being considered for the vice-presidential nomination and his friend and political boss Roscoe Conkling thought he should reject the nomination for the "meaningless" office. Arthur replied that "the office of Vice-President is a greater honor than I ever dreamed of attaining. A barren nomination would be a great honor."[109] In spite of his Player's genial ways, Chester Arthur still thought that the highest political offices in the land held some honor, and honor is coveted by Artisans as well as Guardians. Thus the presidency, once he was captured by it, inspired him to bring forth the best he had to offer. And the best, though it might not make him a Washington or a Lincoln, was good enough to earn him a decent share of honor and respect.

Chester Arthur would have enjoyed the White House more if it had come to him while his wife, Ellen Herndon Arthur, was still alive. As is frequently true of Artisans, Chet Arthur loved her but was often guilty of neglecting her in favor of his other pursuits. "Nell" Arthur, who was probably also an Artisan, was an accomplished and popular hostess, and the Arthurs had both enjoyed the good life, the entertainments, the socializing, and the affluence that came with his successes. Nonetheless she had complained often and angrily of his neglect of her in favor of his political cronies. When she died of pneumonia at age forty-two he was terribly remorseful about his neglect and heartbroken over his loss.

His love for Nell was no idle bit of romance or mere habitual fondness, though detractors were slow to understand that. When he assumed the presidency rumors were soon circulating that the widower Chet Arthur had a new love interest. After all, he had the picture of a woman in his rooms, and each day he placed fresh flowers in front of it, they said. This meant that the rumors about a new romance were true; only the identity of the new object of his affections remained to be ascertained. Washington's curiosity was feverishly high but the gossip soon stopped. Someone discovered that the picture before which he placed fresh flowers each day was a photograph of his beloved Nell.

Of course none of the President's sudden expression of dignity and integrity and constancy should suggest that Chester Arthur ceased to be a Player Artisan. Throughout his term of office he continued to be less than diligent in carrying out his duties, seldom did today what he could comfortably put off until tomorrow, and made it a point to enjoy thoroughly the social side of the office. He clearly continued to relish good living and pleasant society and he devoted himself to them after

---

109 *How They Became President,* 267.

the daily grind of his office. Indeed, he was known as something of a social lion. He also took it upon himself to refurbish the White House, hiring the famous Louis Tiffany to renovate the place, so that it became a bright, lively, social center with good food, good booze, and popular music.

Still, he wanted to look as if he was hard at work, he wanted to look presidential. So as he roamed the White House he usually carried with him a basket which was filled with official-looking documents, as if he couldn't quite shake loose of them. But in spite of his little pretences, his honest efforts and his social and political talents, Arthur was unable to hold the various factions of his party together or to win back the disaffected machine politicians. As a result, though he was a rather popular President, the Republican Party failed to nominate him for re-election in 1884.

It seems likely that Arthur wasn't terribly interested in continuing in office anyway. Though he expressed a desire to run again he doesn't seem to have tried very hard to force the issue of his re-nomination. If he had he might well have been nominated. But the Players are not as unshakeably competitive as the Operators, and Arthur had had his fill of the Office. So he did not try to capture the nomination, and after leaving office he returned to New York and took up his law practice again. Less than two years later he died, probably of kidney disease. It is likely that his high living seriously affected his health and led to a premature death.

Chester Alan Arthur left office, and this life, honored as one of the most unlikely, but far from the least able, of Presidents.

Bibliography

Brisbin, J 1880   *From Towpath to the White House*
Bronner, F *et al* 1948   *Chester Alan Arthur, Class of 1848*
Doenecke, J 1981   *The Presidencies of James A.. Garfield and Chester A. Arthur*
Howe, G 1935   *Chester A. Arthur, a Quarter Century of Machine Politics*
Reeves, T 1975   *Gentleman Boss: the Life of Chester Alan Arthur*
Smalley, E 1880   *The Republican Manual: Biographical Sketches of Garfield and Arthur*
Stoker, R 1965   *The Legacy of Arthur's Chester*
Wiegand, W 1983   *The Chester A. Arthur Conspiracy* (a novel)

Warren G. Harding

The bloviator misled

Player
Born: November 2, 1865
Died: August 2, 1923
Presidency: 1921-1923

Warren Harding was a good-looking, agreeable young man who knew how to enjoy himself without having to strain at it. Some friendly drinking, a few friendly games of pool, and plenty of friendly poker: these alone were almost sufficient for a rich, full life. These were what it took to be a successful bloviater, to use Harding's own term.

Of course if one wished to live the good life it was also necessary to avoid too much labor, but Warren Harding showed a natural talent for that. The young Harding did have a brief college career which he terminated after one semester. He also tried studying law and selling insurance, but neither was sufficiently alluring and they soon dropped out of his life. Warren Harding was also a very easygoing man and always willing to oblige a friend or acquaintance. His father once commented that it was a lucky thing Warren was not born a girl because he just couldn't say "no."[110]

To complete the picture of a man unlikely ever to rise far in the world, Harding's family background was not impressive, his home was shabby, his connections with influential people and his affiliations with the local church community were nil. In his meandering he bought out a bankrupt newspaper in Marion, Ohio with the help of a couple of friends (who soon gave the project up), and he did seem to enjoy being a newspaper publisher. It was especially pleasant since the paper also gave him a forum from which to provide properly—though quietly—compensated support for the Republican party, to which he had firmly and enthusiastically affixed himself.

Enter Florence Kling DeWolfe. Prior to the time Warren met and married Florence Kling there was clearly little likelihood that the pleasant wastrel, five years her junior, would amount to anything beyond a small-town newspaper publisher and local political functionary. Even the newspaper's future was economically questionable, and Harding's prospects remained dim. For some reason Mrs. Kling, divorced from her husband, became fascinated and perhaps infatuated with the charming and pleasant young Artisan. It has in fact been suggested that she courted him more actively than he did her. Harding was certainly a handsome young man after all, six feet tall with finely chiseled features, thick, dark hair, and a commanding voice. He was inveterately cheerful, a hail-fellow-well-met, though he did show the restlessness typical of the Artisan nature, which moved him to travel as often as he could manage.

William G. McAdoo, who served as Secretary of the Treasury under Woodrow Wilson, wrote of Harding that

> He was, as every one knows, soft and pliable and easily managed. The possessor of an adjustable conscience, which could be altered to fit every changing circumstance, Harding went through life with cheer and gusto, believing thoroughly that a man can get along very well if he can fool some of the people some of the time.[111]

---

110 *Presidential Anecdotes*, 231.
111 *Presidential Courage*, 177.

He demonstrated nicely the rather marked pliability of many Player Artisans. In this regard the Player sometimes stands in extreme contrast to the total self-willed immovability of the more blazing of the Operator Artisans such as Andy Jackson.

Harding's pleasant pliability didn't fool Florence Kling. No swooning romantic, she apparently knew well what she was getting into and upon their marriage Mrs. Florence Kling Harding moved swiftly. She had a child from her prior marriage but turned the task of raising the child over to her father. She took over her new husband's rather uncertain business affairs and managed them well. She paid careful attention to his and to her own public appearances and helped him embark on his political career. When he became too lethargic she prodded him. When he became embroiled in the results of his playfulness (including dalliances with other women) she shielded him. And throughout his life she fired his ambitions with the flames of her own furious, determined ambition.

Vigorous, defiant, sometimes ruthless and a life-long nonconformist, she chafed under the restrictions to which she was subjected as a woman. Warren was to be her way of ameliorating those restrictions, her pathway to higher status, more power, perhaps even First Lady. So imperious was her manner, so strong was her influence, and so intent was she to direct his path toward her goals that Harding called her "Duchess," and once remarked that his automobile was the only thing he possessed that the Duchess didn't have a wish to run.

It wasn't that Florence forced Warren against his will into a life of high political aspiration. He did want to join the company of successful politicians. He was eager to enjoy their advantaged life style and avail himself of their perquisites. He relished being a Senator and as one would expect of this obvious Player, he joined the senatorial fraternity cheerfully and charmingly. One politician who knew him well, George B. Christian, said that Harding really did not enjoy politics. When asked if Harding liked being a Senator, the politician replied, "No, he didn't like being a Senator, he liked being in the Senate."[112]

In office Harding dedicated himself to having a good time and to enhancing his own popularity, two tasks for which he was very well-

---

112 *Presidential Courage*, 177.

suited. Aside from these activities Warren continued to bloviate as frequently as possible. (Bloviate: a rustic word which means to sit around in easy-going and pleasant company, talking, laughing and generally amusing one's self.) Harding remembered people's names, carried out his party's orders without objection, played the senatorial game well, showed some ability to serve as peacemaker between various factions in the party, and became quite popular if not particularly respected. He refrained from criticizing Senators of either party, avoided taking a stand on doubtful measures that might cause difficulty for him, disliked engaging in serious discussion, spoke out as his party required, and was unavailable for voting almost half the time. One writer said of him that,

> If I had known him as a traveling salesman, a vaudeville actor, a nightclub entertainer, or a restaurant keeper, I should have liked him very much, I know, for I have had a strong liking for many men just like Harding who held those positions.[113]

But politics sometimes means peculiar choices, and in 1920 Warren Harding was nominated by the Republican Party as their candidate for the Presidency of the United States. (His vice-presidential running mate was Calvin Coolidge.)

Harding had no interest in the presidency and knew himself well enough that he found it difficult to take his nomination seriously. It was said that he remarked about his surprising nomination that "I feel like a man who goes in on a pair of eights and comes out with aces full."[114] (We see here again, by the way, the gifted use of the game analogy so typical of the more fluent Player Artisans.) All this aside, he was always popular, often eloquent, though never about anything of substance, and a good Republican. Above all, he was an electable candidate.

The Democrats and their very ill President, Woodrow Wilson, were in trouble. There was considerable bitterness in the country about a number of events tied to Wilson's administration and a natural wish to put the memory of the pain of the Great War behind it. On the other hand there was a certain euphoria, born of entering and winning a war, which continued well into the 1920s and lasted almost until the crash of

---

113 *Presidents I Have Known*, 333-334, quoted in *How They Became President*, 368.
114 *Presidential Campaigns*, 215.

1929. Harding with his call for a "return to normalcy" and his humorous, home-town, easy-going manner seemed a welcome change to wartime rigors in the wake of the austere, imperious, and conscience-stricken reign of Wilson, the supreme Monitor.

So to his considerable surprise and perhaps to his dismay, Warren G. Harding was elected President of the United States in 1920. It looked like he might serve as a sort of master of ceremonies over the "roaring '20s," a position for which he would be well-suited, though he seemed ill-suited for any other presidential duties. For it cannot be said that Harding rose to meet the challenges of the presidency, either politically or personally. He remained an easy-going man who enjoyed a good time and continued to hang around with as much pleasant company (both male and female) as he could. Though these were the days of Prohibition and alcohol was illegal, he still had access to a sufficient flow of alcohol to keep things moving nicely at his White House poker parties.

He also was active with a number of women; his famous affair with Nan Britton lasted many years and did not end when he reached the White House. It is said that Harding and she used the closet adjoining his office and that a number of other young women also became familiar with it during approximately the same period.[115] Harding had an unfortunate propensity for writing love letters to the various women with whom he became involved. Harry M. Daugherty, his friend and advisor, made enormous efforts to track down and destroy these missives when Harding was being groomed for the presidency, and earnestly enjoined him to avoid writing them when he was in the White House. (Several love letters to a woman back in Marion, Ohio were discovered a full forty years after Harding's death.)

Harding's administration was far from a successful one. Though he did make some effort to rise to the demands of the office no great issues were resolved, no significant steps forward were taken. There was massive corruption at all levels of his administration, many questionable political favors were done, and in general a self-serving political presidency rather than a statesman's presidency characterized Harding's years in office. Harding himself did not seem to be directly involved in the rampant dishonesty, nor did he profit from it. In fact, though he was

---

115 *Presidential Courage,* 173-174.

rarely able to resist requests of friends and colleagues for favors, he had no interest in or flair for political corruption. And though he was hardly a moral giant, it appears that the largely honest and good-hearted Harding was rather distressed by the enormous corruption uncovered in his administration. "I am not fit for this office and should never have been here," he commented in despair when confronted with the evidence of scandal.[116]

In 1923, two years into his term of office, he embarked on a good-will voyage to Alaska and parts west to escape the furor in Washington, to evade being associated with some of the worst of the scandal, and to restore public confidence in himself. Harding also started to comport himself in a more presidential fashion, resisting temptations and blandishments and avoiding most of the usual rounds of parties, poker, and drinking. But it was too late. His reputation and his administration were in tatters and there was nothing he could do about it.

On the return trip from Alaska Harding was stricken by what was probably a heart attack though he seemed to recover fairly well. A day or so later he came down with pneumonia, and finally, on August 2 he died of what may have been a blood clot reaching the brain. After only two years in office the easygoing Player Warren Harding, appalled by the scandals of his administration and muttering with dismay about being betrayed by his friends, was dead. Florence Harding, dismaying some but surprising very few, destroyed most of the records associated with her husband's presidency and as much of his correspondence as she could retrieve.

For Harding personally the presidency was a disaster. He didn't enjoy the job, he felt inescapably imprisoned by it, he knew he was overmatched by its demands. Even his wish to be well-loved by the people of the country (for he knew he could not be respected for his greatness) was frustrated as the ineptitude and dishonesty of his administration became known. Instead of living his simple, homey, well-lubricated Player's style of life, the unfortunate Player Warren G. Harding encountered tragedy: falling into bad company, he became President of the United States.

---

116 Alice Roosevelt Longworth, Teddy Roosevelt's daughter, agreed with him. She wrote that "Harding was not a bad man. He was just a slob." (From her *Crowded Hours,* quoted in *Presidential Anecdotes,* 231.)

Bibliography

Adams, S 1939	*Incredible Era: the Life and Times of Warren Gamaliel Harding*
Blythe, S 1923	*A Calm Review of a Calm Man*
Chappie, J 1944	*Life and Times of Warren G. Harding, our After-War President*
Downs, R 1970	*The Rise of Warren Gamaliel Harding*
Grieb, K 1976	*The Latin American Policy of Warren G. Harding*
Jenks, A 1928	*A Dead President Makes Answer to the President's Daughter*
Murray, R 1969	*The Harding Era: Warren G. Harding and his Administration*
Russell, F 1968	*The Shadow of Blooming Grove: Warren G. Harding in his Times*
Sinclair, A 1965	*The Available Man: The Life Behind the Masks of Warren Gamaliel Harding*
Trani, E 1977	*The Presidency of Warren G. Harding*

Ronald Reagan

The Entrepreneur's Advocate

Player
Born: February 6, 1911
Presidency: 1981-1989

Ronald Reagan presents the student of temperament with a difficult problem: he is the most recent ex-President, and he has been a controversial President. Passions still run high about what he has or has not done, and about how his deeds ought to be judged. He has been presented as a brilliant and courageous American Hero, and as a careless, dull-witted, easily-manipulated man who merely played the role of President as a mere actor.

Actor he was to be sure—the only professional actor to win the White House—but at the same time Reagan has been virtually unique among American Presidents in his enormously persuasive advocacy of restricted government and of maximum freedom for capitalist enterprise. Whether in political office or out, he has been *the entrepreneur's advocate* for more than forty years, and those who belittle his virtuosity as a speechmaker and his understanding of free-market economics will miss the man by a wide margin. Nonetheless, only two years have elapsed since he left the presidency, and for some the debate continues as passionately as ever. Care is required to write about Reagan, then, if we are to avoid becoming enmeshed in the controversy.[117]

The beginning was simple and pleasant enough. Reagan was born in Tampico, Illinois, a small town in which the traditional small town virtues still seemed paramount. His family shared, and in many respects were exemplars of, the traditional small town ethos that people should be self-reliant and charitable in deed and spirit, should look after themselves and, when necessary, look after one another. The consensus in Tampico was that the world (at least the world in and around Tampico) was a decent place in which to live, that friends and neighbors had good intentions, and that ill will had to be proven. Nelle Wilson Reagan, Ronald Reagan's mother, lived these values thoroughly. Though her own family was often in difficult straits, this enthusiastic, kind, and energetic woman (probably a Conservator Guardian) devoted a great deal of her time and energy to helping the less fortunate and the downright needy. She also advised her two sons, Neil and Dutch (Ronald), that it was their obligation to do likewise.

Reagan loved to read as a youngster and later commented that his early reading "left an abiding belief in the triumph of good over evil....There were heroes who lived by standards of morality and fair play."[118] His unshakeably optimistic faith in the triumph of virtue has stayed with him all his life. Indeed, Dutch Reagan projected this image of natural small-town decency in most of his best movie roles—it seems likely that he never really noticed the dark side of small town life (as it was portrayed, for instance, in his most successful film, *King's Row*). His optimism is one of the most obvious hallmarks of the Artisan

---

117 Because of Reagan's background in economics as well as his persuasive advocacy of free enterprise capitalism, this portrait pays considerably more attention to economics than do the other 39 essays.

118 *Reagan*, 19.

character, just as it is part of the message that he has delivered so effectively for so many years.

It was his father, John Edward Reagan, who nicknamed Ronald "Dutch," declaring when Ronald was born that he looked like a "little fat Dutchman." Jack Reagan was by career a shoe salesman, and an excellent one. He was also an impulsive Player Artisan who had what his Irish ancestors would have called "a powerful thirst"; he struggled with alcohol all his adult life. Nelle told the boys that they must be patient and tolerant about their father's difficulty, and she apparently demonstrated well how to maintain such a loving tolerance.

Dutch Reagan's father, impulsive Player that he was, still found time to demonstrate for his sons passionate and enduring interest in the rights and welfare of the working man and of blacks, Jews, and other minorities. Jack Reagan had a hatred of racial and religious prejudice of any kind and was not afraid to act on what he believed. Ronald recalls his father speaking of an occasion, a bitterly cold evening, when he had taken a hotel room, but then realized that the hotel discriminated against Jews. Jack Reagan refused to stay there; instead he walked out and spent a freezing night sleeping in his automobile.

Dutch's father was also, by the way, a great raconteur, with the Irishman's love of story-telling. As is often true of the more expressive Players, Jack Reagan could charm anyone with his stories when he had not had too much to drink, and the young Dutch learned a great deal about telling anecdotes from observing him. Whatever their difficulties might have been, the Reagans were self-sufficient and kindly people who loved their children and wanted the best for them. Neither parent had much schooling, but they both saw the value of education and both were eager for their two sons to attend college. Both older brother Neil and younger brother Ronald eventually did so, but it was not easy: the Great Depression had settled darkly over the country by the time they reached college age.

Neil Reagan remembers his growing up as marked by the family's constant struggle against poverty and the problem of his father's drinking. But Player Artisan Ronald remembers his childhood much more fondly than does his brother, referring to that time as "a rare Huck Finn idyll" in which he experienced all the joys of a happy childhood.[119]

---

119 *Where's the Rest of Me?*

As is usual with the Player Artisans, Dutch Reagan didn't seem to have any difficulty getting along with others. He fit in well when he wanted to. But he was by choice a quiet youngster and usually preferred to spend his time alone. Neil was by far the more gregarious of the two and would be found hanging around with the local gangs of kids. He was also the adventuresome brother, the one who could enjoy being a bit "bad." As for his brother Dutch, Neil once commented that "I don't think he ever saw the inside of a pool room!"[120] Perhaps not, for young Ronald loved stories about soldiers, athletes, even Presidents, who had started with nothing and became successful and respected, and he nourished and enriched these stories endlessly. He also loved tales of adventure and often used his precious solitude to close himself away from others where he could fight and win glorious battles with his toy soldiers. Pool rooms didn't offer enough room for adventures and heroes of such large scale. Reagan cheerfully acknowledged all this in a letter many years later, writing "I'm a sucker for hero worship."[121]

When Reagan graduated from high school he enrolled in Eureka College along with Margaret Cleaver, his first real girl friend and later, briefly, his fiancée. He was already a pleasant, well-mannered young man with handsome good looks. He also had a resonant and magnetic voice, a winning smile, proper and decent behavior, and no social flaws. Artisans, especially Player Artisans, are quick to catch on to what is considered seemly and decorous, the rites, rituals, and ceremonies of the local culture. Artisans will follow these quite unconsciously and spontaneously, not so much because they revere them as because they are so useful in getting them what they want. Reagan was a splendid Player in this regard.

Overall Ronald Reagan was growing up to be a very active, confident, and optimistic young man, and his winning style was already very well developed. But it was at Eureka College that he discovered something which became central to his life. It was there that Dutch Reagan discovered his talents for persuasive public speaking, his love of sports announcing, the excitement of political campaigning, and the heady experience of being on the receiving end of the cheers of the crowd. Further, although he had already had some minor experience

---

120 *Early Reagan*, 62.
121 *Reagan*, 18.

with amateur acting and had a taste for it as well, it was at Eureka that he first experienced the wonderful rush of excitement and self-confidence that Artisans often find in stage-acting. Having an impact and impressing others attracted him like a powerful magnet and he was thereafter happily captured in its intense field.

When he entered Eureka College the campus was in turmoil. Money was scarce and the college administration was planning certain cutbacks in its offerings. Many students believed that the integrity of the College's curriculum was endangered, and shortly after Reagan's arrival, a student strike forced a mediation meeting. Since freshman would be unaffected by the changes, the students wanted a freshman who could, as an uninvolved party, speak to the question of fairness. Reagan was selected, and Reagan spoke for them. He spoke eloquently, and he captured his listeners thoroughly. Later he commented about this occasion that "I discovered that night that an audience has a feel to it and, in the parlance of the theater, that audience and I were together."[122] He had also discovered something of his remarkable gift for face-to-face negotiation, the almost magical qualities of his voice and the remarkable appeal of his friendly and unassuming style. Not only could Dutch Reagan be a persuasive speaker, but he could win the warmth and admiration of individuals and crowds simply by "being himself"—and he loved it. And though he was delighted with his success he never became arrogant or self-important about it; in the egalitarian fashion of the Artisan (remember Kennedy's "band of brothers") he remained "Dutch" Reagan.

Nor did he forget the lessons he had learned from his parents about social issues. On the football team at Eureka he saw for himself something of the problems of racial discrimination, and he reacted to what he saw in the way his parents had demonstrated. The team, which included three black players, was travelling for a game to a town which happened to be near Reagan's home. When they tried to book rooms for the night the hotel would not admit the three black players. Dutch Reagan promptly took a leaf from his father's book: he got enough money from the coach to cover transportation costs, and he escorted the three black players to his own home. They were welcomed warmly by his parents and invited to spend the night.

---

122 *Reagan*, 35.

The young college student Dutch Reagan was a very competent athlete, and became a star swimmer and a first string football player. When he graduated from Eureka in 1932 he was able to combine his love of sports, his ability as a story-teller, and his flair for dramatics, by becoming a sports announcer. One of his early jobs was to reconstruct the plays in baseball games from written play-by-play accounts that came in continuously from the wire service. (Once, when the wire went dead for a short time, he was forced to ad-lib the "action" on the field, never letting the audience know he was making the game up as he went along.) This kind of job was hard work, but Reagan knew that his voice was a powerful asset and a natural gift, and he displayed his Artisan's flair for spontaneous and engaging commentary about subjects that interested him. However, during his time as an announcer in Des Moines, Iowa he learned another very valuable lesson: that failure to practice that which was not interesting to him—in this case, radio commercials—could be disastrous. In fact, he presented his commercials so poorly on the air that he lost his job. So he buckled down to work, practiced hard at his delivery, and was able eventually to regain his job. From that time forward rehearsal found its valued place in his professional tool kit.[123]

In 1937, after five years of sports announcing, Reagan took a gamble: he quit his secure announcing job and left for Hollywood. His optimism was again justified, and he was soon able to break into films. He was a good-looking, personable, cooperative, and pleasing young actor, willing to heed sound advice and work hard at his craft. Though he never quite became a top-ranked "star," he became a solid journeyman actor who eventually played in more than fifty films over a two-decade career. He easily remembered what he read (when it seemed important to him)[124] and learned as a very young actor how to

---

123 None of the other types, not even the Operator Artisans, is willing to spend the enormous amount of time required of the showman in perfecting an upcoming performance. The Player Artisan outstrips all others in this, the center of their lives: rehearsal. The Player Artisan Garfield, for instance, devoted enormous amounts of time to rehearsing his eloquent and moving speeches and even to writing simultaneously Greek with one hand and Latin with the other.

124 Reagan seems to be one of those fortunate individuals, usually Artisan characters, who possess what psychologists call eidetic imagery and what laymen call photographic memory. See Jaensch's *Eidetic Imagery*.

"become" his character. According to his first drama teacher, he *was* the character when it was time to perform. This was especially true when he played the role of the decent, clean-cut Midwesterner. To a considerable degree he had only to act like himself for these roles.

The political and social activist Reagan had not disappeared with the emergence of Reagan the actor. Shortly after he arrived in Hollywood, unhappy with actors' relations with the studios which hired them, Reagan joined the Screen Actors Guild. He soon emerged as an important figure in the Guild and eventually became its president, occupying that office for six years altogether. During that time he busily engaged himself on behalf of the Guild in various negotiations with the film studios. The work was interesting to him, he enjoyed it, and he did a good job with it. And that was sufficient; nobody loves negotiation like an Artisan, after all, and nobody is likely to be as good at it as a clever Artisan. The Artisan Lyndon Johnson is an outstanding example of the superlative negotiator, though Reagan's easy-going Player style is generally more palatable to others than Johnson's more high-handed Operator style.

In the late 1940s the anti-communist worries that began to sweep the country led to the notorious McCarthy hearings into the presumed subversive influence of communism in Hollywood. Reagan, as president of the Screen Actors Guild, was called upon to testify before the congressional committee, and here again showed his virtuosity in dealing face to face with people. From the beginning an ardent capitalist, he was untainted by communist affiliations. But many others in Hollywood had joined communist organizations at one time or another, having seen them as social activist groups without subversive intent. Most people dropped their affiliations when the questionable intentions of these groups became apparent to them. But having belonged at any time and for any reason to such groups was enough to make them highly suspect to the more fanatical anti-communists. They might then be "black-listed" by politically powerful fanatics such as McCarthy, and in Hollywood that could mean that they would be unable to find work, sometimes for years. Reagan had no connection with any such groups, his public stance was consistently patriotic, and he had his prodigious competence in dealing with disputants. He was able, therefore, to avoid the trap that so many others fell into: either challenging the committee (usually to the great misfortune of the challengers) or appeasing the congressional inquisition by testifying against friends and acquaintances. The keen Artisan observer and tactician Ronald Reagan came through the ordeal skillfully, and very likely learned much about political maneuvering from the experience.

It was at this time and because of these hearings that he met his future wife, Nancy Davis. He had married his first wife Jane Wyman in 1940, but they divorced in 1948.[125] Though distressed by the divorce, and though he agreed temporarily to play the part of the very eligible man-about-town, Reagan was said to have hated dating and the highly-publicized night life it entailed. On his second try at matrimony Reagan was to choose a mate much more suited to his temperament and character, a very stable Monitor Guardian.

For it happened that during the McCarthy hearings Nancy Davis, a young actress, was concerned about whether she would be under investigation by the fearsome congressional committee. She asked the Guild whether she was a likely target of the committee, and was informed that she was not. But she was also interested in meeting Ronald Reagan, so she asked for his personal assurance about the matter. Reagan agreed to check into it, and then got together with her to reassure her again. The relationship which developed from this meeting was extremely satisfying for them both, and about two years later, in 1952, they were married. At that moment she gladly surrendered her career and dedicated herself to being a wife and mother. "My life began when I got married," she said, and she has never entertained any doubts about her decision.

Nancy Reagan saw herself as her husband's comforter, the guardian of his privacy, his friend and companion, the one person who could provide him with the loving and comfortable home they both so much enjoyed. In these respects she took on a very traditional expression of what it is to be a wife, one not seen so clearly in the White House since the days of Mamie Eisenhower. But the Monitor Guardian Nancy

---

125 Wyman was a very versatile actress who had won an Oscar for her performance in *Johnny Belinda*. It must be said that marriages of this kind, between two talented, ambitious, and attention-getting Artisans, more often than not end in divorce. Indeed Hollywood is still notorious for its exciting, tempestuous, but often very brief romances between competing artists.

Reagan did not content herself merely with being the traditional "wife-and-mother" who is isolated from her husband's career. She was also "Ronnie's" resolute defender (quite literally his guardian) and in this role she could be like a mother lion protecting her cub: watchful, silent, and ready to attack if danger comes too close. "She was his protector and nurturer," said one writer, "whom he has sometimes called 'Mommie' and who can be cold, freezingly so, with people she sees making his life difficult."[126] In 1987, for instance, two years into Reagan's second term as President, his wife instigated the sacking of his long-time aide, Don Regan, who she believed did not sufficiently support and protect her husband. She and Regan had become bitterly disapproving of each other, even though Regan and her husband were on good terms. It says something of Nancy Reagan's influence on her husband that he agreed to the firing of someone he felt so close to.

The egalitarian Reagan was, after all, a man of great loyalty to his friends, and felt genuinely distressed about dispossessing anyone he knew and liked. Nancy Reagan's judgment about the people who surrounded her husband was apparently rather sound, and she was quite willing to make her opinions known. She has also been willing to work behind the scenes on her husband's behalf and even to change some aspects of her own personal style and habits. For example, she was initially seen by many as a social elitist, interested only in expensive clothing, expensive friends, and high society. This of course was quite out of keeping with Reagan's image as the honest middle-American fighting against waste and excess. She therefore agreed to doing what was necessary to shift her image to one more consistent with her husband's image and more widely acceptable to the voters.

She succeeded in doing so, of course, and included in her campaign active leadership in combatting the nation's drug problem. She was especially interested in influencing young people, and made numerous visits to schools and classrooms. When a young student once asked her what to do if someone offered him drugs, her immediate response was "Just say no!" Those three words have since become almost ubiquitous in anti-drug campaigns. Thus not only did Nancy Reagan become an

---

126 *Reagan,* 146. It is quite common for Artisan husbands to refer to their wives as "Mommie" or "Mother," especially when they have children, as if the usually Guardian wife is as much parent as spouse to the Artisan.

effective worker behind the scenes, she also became a Guardian of the public virtues and a political asset to her husband as well. Mike Deaver, who knew the Reagans very well, summarized her contributions nicely when he said that Nancy Reagan deserves as much credit for her husband's political success as anyone who has worked for or with him.

Reagan's years as a sports announcer and his unfailing wit stood him in good stead as he developed his skills as a public speaker.[127] When his film career began to flag Reagan got a job with General Electric Corporation as host to the *General Electric Theatre*, a television show, and spokesman for General Electric. In his junkets around the country he would on some days give as many as fourteen speeches, both to GE personnel and to local establishments and municipalities. The speeches were actually one basic speech, slightly modified to fit the locale, and was eventually dubbed "The Speech." The topic invariably was how indispensable free enterprise is for the health and welfare of America. During these "corporate years," as they were called, he came to be seen more and more as the champion of business and industry. He told the millions who listened to him how important it is to the nation that businesses be free to choose the means and ends of production and distribution. It is not so much, he said, that government *has* a problem, as it is that government *is* the problem. After all, it was free enterprise, he argued, that made America the wealthiest nation in history.

He apparently came to this belief in entrepreneurial freedom rather naturally—as an Artisan he was a born entrepreneur—but he also majored in economics in college, studying with particular care the work of Adam Smith and also the Austrian school of economics.[128] In any event, it would be his Artisan's virtuoso speech-making on the theme of free-enterprise that would take him all the way to the Governor's seat in

---

127 His wit was genuine, not merely the reciting of lines written by others (though at times, of course, he used such lines). Six months into his first term in the White House, for instance, he was shot by a would-be assassin. As he was being wheeled into the operating room of a nearby hospital he was still conscious and alert. He smiled somewhat painfully and quipped to the medical staff gathered round his guerney that "I hope all of you are good Republicans."

128 One of Reagan's biographers said of him that in earning his degree in economics he seemed to his instructors to have an instinct for economics, so that he was able to ponder even the most complicated treatises, including not only Adam Smith's *An Enquiry into the Nature and Causes of the Wealth of Nations*, but also the works of the Austrians Friedrich Hayek, Ludwig von Mises, Karl Menger, and Eugen Böhm-Barwick.

Sacramento, to the President's chair in Washington, and to lasting fame as "The Great Communicator." For when he spoke, the nation's entrepreneurs saw before them, at long last, an avowed enemy of big government. Here finally, they said, was someone who would slice the fat out of the monstrous Washington bureaucracy. Here, they thought, was someone who openly advocated the confinement of government to its one legitimate function—keeping the peace. If he were elected to the presidency he would get rid of all the inefficient bureaus in the government, along with thousands of federal bureaucrats. But that would not be all. Perhaps he would even get rid of the thousands of regulations and red tape that businessmen felt were increasingly strangling trade, for example, some of the 5,600 regulations that he said governed the steel industry.

His job would be to erase such restrictive regulations. Indeed, his eager followers began to anticipate massive deregulation throughout the business world, something in their view long overdue. After all government, he had said to them time and again, must "get off the backs of" American entrepreneurs so that they could get on with their business of making America more prosperous without bureaucratic interference. Furthermore, he said, the colossal waste of bureaucracy must be eliminated, and the Hoover and Grace Commissions had already described in detail just where the cuts could be made. Reagan, his supporters believed, would act on these recommendations.

Reagan entered the oval office with a disarmingly simple agenda consisting of three proposals: release the entrepreneur from government bondage; restrict the size and activity of the federal government; and get tough with the "evil empire," the Soviet Union. He had dwelt on all three of these themes for a long time, and we should of course not be surprised that his agenda was in keeping with his Artisan character. Reagan's championing of the entrepreneur is consistent with his Artisan's *laissez faire* nature. Second, the reduction in the power of government fits nicely with the individualistic style of his Artisan father, as well as with his own natural Artisan abhorrence for anything which might try to dominate him. And third, as Andy Jackson showed us, nothing is more characteristic of the Artisan than to respond aggressively to the challenge of an aggressor. Thus, believing that the Soviet Union's avowed aim was, in Khrushchev's famous words, to "bury" the United States, Reagan made his first priority the re-arming of America. What was needed, said Reagan, was an iron resolve to resist Soviet aggression supported by a large increase in defense spending.

Reagan's domestic agenda—freeing the American entrepreneur and reducing the size of government—met with mixed success. Some credited him with gains, especially in the economic sphere, such that Reagan's first two hundred days in office were compared favorably with Franklin Roosevelt's first one hundred days. Some even said that Reagan's policies (what came to be called "Reaganomics" by his critics) ushered in over a decade of prosperity, with reduced inflation, lowered interest rates, and flourishing enterprises creating millions of new jobs. However, in less than two years he had surrendered to the forces of big government. His own military spending strained the federal budget, and the federal bureaucracy, special interest groups, and the Congress fought with all their power his efforts to trim government control and spending on social programs. And to the bitter disappointment of many of his conservative supporters, Reagan capitulated, failing not only to cut government down to size; but failing even to stem the steady tide of its growth.[129] As a Player Artisan Reagan was a natural gambler, with the successful gambler's instinct for cutting his losses. He knew that when he didn't have the cards it was better to drop out and let the player with the stronger hand take the pot. A Rational or a Guardian with the same agenda might have tried to bluff the special interest groups, and might have lost everything. But Reagan, the tactically adept Artisan, backed off, especially from his early attacks on Medicare and Social Security. As a result he left the game with his popularity virtually intact and good naturedly shrugged his shoulders. As one commentator remarked, "it is doubtful whether any modern President compromised so often on so many major issues as Ronald Reagan did in the latter months of 1982."[130]

---

129 Indeed, in spite of his determined stance when he took office, Reagan rarely exercised the President's prerogative to veto legislation. This willingness to accommodate is probably more characteristic of the Player Artisan than of the Operator. The extremely aggressive Operators, Andrew Jackson, for instance, were willing to fight to the death over many issues, while the Players were rarely so fierce in their demeanor or their actions.

130 *Roosevelt to Reagan*, 257.

Reagan's handling of the Soviet Union was much more forceful, and apparently more successful. Early in his administration the President's critics faulted him for referring to the Soviet Union as the "evil empire," claiming that his language risked antagonizing the Russians unnecessarily. At the time, most politicians and civil servants were glossing over the Soviet Union's enslavement of its own people and its incursions into central Europe, Africa, the Arabian Peninsula, Central America, and Southeast Asia. Reagan, on the other hand, described Soviet wrongdoing in graphic detail, warning clearly of the Soviet's intent to dominate the world and of its enormous military build-up. And his dramatic verbal lashing of the Soviet Union set the stage for his efforts to strengthen the United States' military forces.

The extent of Reagan's success against the Soviets is for political scientists to determine, including what part if any his build-up of U.S. defenses played in the collapse of the "evil empire" during his second term. Whatever his role, Reagan's gamesmanship with the Soviets was remarkable. As the United States' military strength steadily increased, and as the Soviets increasingly worried about Reagan's Strategic Defense Initiative (dubbed "Star Wars"[131] by its critics), Reagan changed his tactics. Again to the consternation of his conservative supporters, the President gradually relaxed his stance and agreed to arms-control negotiations with the Soviets. Reagan apparently felt he had the winning hand in this game with the Soviets, believing that it was American strength, not American weakness, that had brought them to the conference table. But he also had a powerful bluff. The Soviets could not know just how far or how fast American military technology was developing, and so apparently fearing the worst they sought to keep their huge advantage in missile numbers with proposals for symmetrical bilateral disarmament. The Soviets also attempted their own bluff, making their disarmament contingent on the United States abandoning

---

131 Reagan, the irrepressible fan of the movies, probably pulled the expression "evil empire" from the movie *Star Wars*. He seemed to have a fascination with science fiction movies, in which the action tends to be plentiful and the distinction between good and evil is usually made quite clear.

its "Star Wars" research. But Reagan kept his nerve, and continued to promote the peaceful intention of SDI, even offering the technology to the Soviets for their own defense.[132] Eventually, of course, the Soviets softened many of their demands and the negotiations effected meaningful, indeed, historic cuts in the Soviet arsenal. In this hand with the Soviets Reagan played his cards masterfully, and many attribute to him the fact that Soviet hegemony has receded all over the world.

Reagan was certainly not the first Artisan to take a hand in presidential games, and most of the Operator Artisans were also high rollers. For instance the first of them, Andy Jackson, was gambling when he refused to renew the charter of the United States Bank, and of course he gambled continuously with his own life in his many duels. Then there was Teddy Roosevelt and his numerous ventures, and his nephew Franklin Roosevelt may have used the U.S. Pacific Fleet at Pearl Harbor in a gambit to trigger U.S. entry into World War II. Nor were John Kennedy and Lyndon Johnson averse to playing for high stakes, such as in the Cuban missile showdown and the micromanagement of the Viet Nam war. In this same way Reagan faced down the Soviets on the international table, while at home he played against the big-government, welfare-state hand that had been winning since Franklin Roosevelt's New Deal.

Reagan was involved in one other game, what seemed to be a low stakes game in Central America, but a game that eventually cost the Reagan administration dearly. The stakes were how money would be given to support Contra rebels fighting against the Soviet-installed Sandanista government in Nicaragua. Reagan gambled that he could circumvent a law passed by Congress that explicitly forbade him from supporting the Contras with government funds. Outflanking the Congress, he kept what he called the "freedom fighters" going for

---

132 Creating uncertainty in the Soviets by speaking repeatedly of "Star Wars" technology is a good example of what the social psychologists call "disinformation." As suggested before, see Watzlawick's *How Real is Real?* for a seminal analysis of the uses and abuses of disinformation in conflict situations. The Artisans are particularly adept at this tactic. For instance this was how John Kennedy outfoxed Khruschev in the Cuban missile crisis.

months with funds supplied by private entrepreneurs and by foreign governments. And for a long while the Congress could do nothing to stop the President—after all, he was breaking only the spirit of the law, something that Artisans rarely let stand in their way. To be sure, the Operator Artisan Teddy Roosevelt, who also played a game south of the border in Panama with both success and impunity, would have been proud of the skill shown by his Player cousin.

Of course, Reagan's gamble with Congress suddenly turned sour when it was discovered that money from arms sales to Iran was being channeled by his aids to the Contras. The so-called "Iran-Contra" affair exploded on the floor of Congress and in the news media, and when the dust settled several of the President's top advisors were facing trial for their part in the clandestine operation. Whether or not Reagan knew of the arms sales to Iran, or of the diversion of funds to the Contras, is still a subject of much controversy. We can only comment here that when Reagan left the presidency in 1989, when the final curtain rang down on this Player Artisan's greatest role, his fans still looked upon him fondly and enthusiastically. Artisans have a knack of landing on their feet, and the man his detractors called the "Teflon President" had managed to avoid being tarred by the same brush that was blackening the reputations of his aids. Indeed, he remains in the eyes of millions of Americans a great and noble leader.

The ultimate effect of Reagan's presidency will of course be debated for a long time. Some will insist that he is merely another President who not only failed to do what he said he would, but who was also of questionable integrity. Others will take a very different view. One admiring author has written, for example, that "the ultimate irony of the twentieth century may be that lasting world wide political revolution was accomplished not by Trotsky and the communists but by Reagan and the capitalists."[133]

Reagan has claimed a less exalted place for his presidency. "What I'd really like to do," he said, "is go down in history as the President who made Americans believe in themselves again."[134]

---

133 *Revolution*, 37.
134 *Reagan*, 320.

Bibliography

Anderson, J 1982	*Ronald Reagan*
Anderson, M 1988	*Revolution*
Armentano, D 1982	*Antitrust and Monopoly: Anatomy of a Policy Failure*
Barrett, L 1983	*Gambling with History: Ronald Reagan in the White House*
Boyarsky, B 1981	*Ronald Reagan, his Life and Rise to the Presidency*
Burris, A 1983	*A Liberty Primer*
Cannon, L 1982	*Reagan*
Cannon, L 1991	*President Reagan: The Role of a Lifetime*
Clark, T 1986	*Ronald Reagan's Economy*
Dackard, B 1985	*Agenda Control and Policy Success: Ronald Reagan and the 97th House*
Deaver, M 1987	*Behind the Scenes: The Author Talks with Ronald and Nancy Reagan*
Denton, R 1988	*The Primetime Presidency of Ronald Reagan*
Donaldson, S 1987	*Hold On Mr. President!*
Edwards, L 1980	*Ronald Reagan, a Political Biography*
Edwards, A 1987	*Early Reagan*
Feiffer, J 1988	*Ronald Reagan in Movie America: A Jules Feiffer Production*
Fitch, N 1982	*The Management Style of Ronald Reagan*
Flynt, L 1984	*The Secret Life of Ronald Reagan*
Friedman, M	*Free to Choose*
Friedman, D	*The Machinery of Freedom*
Greenhaw, W 1982	*Elephants in the Cottonfields: Ronald Reagan & the New Republican South*
Greenstain, F 1990	*Ronald Reagan—another Hidden-Hand Ike?*
Hazlitt, H	*Economics in One Lesson*
Hayek, F	*The Road to Serfdom*
Hobbs, C 1976	*Ronald Reagan's Call to Action*
Jinks, H 1986	*Ronald Reagan—Smile, Style, and Guile*
Leamar, L 1983	*Make-believe: the Story of Nancy and Ronald Reagan*
Laipold, I 1968	*Ronald Reagan, Governor and Statesman*
McClelland, D (ed) 1983	*Hollywood on Ronald Reagan: Friends and Enemies Discuss our President*
McGlothlin, D 1982	*Star to Guide Us*
Mervin, D 1990	*The Presidency and Ronald Reagan*
Minar, M 1986	*The Great Pacifier*

Mises, L	*The Anti-Capitalist Mentality*
Mises, L	*Liberalism*
Nozick, R 1974	*Anarchy, State, and Utopia*
Troxlar, W 1983	*Along Wit's Trail: The Humor and Wisdom of Ronald Reagan*
Reagan, R 1965	*Where's the Rest of me?: The Autobiography of Ronald Reagan*
Reagan, R 1968	*I Goofed; the Wise and Curious Sayings of Ronald Reagan*
Reagan, R 1983	*A Time for Choosing: The Speeches of Ronald Reagan*
Reagan, R 1984	*Ronald Reagan: In God I Trust*
Reagan R 1989	*Speaking My Mind*
Reisman, G	*The Government Against the Economy*
Simon, W 1978	*A Time for Truth*
Smith, A 1776	*The Wealth of Nations*
Smith, H et al 1980	*Reagan the Man, the President*
Schieffer, Gates 1989	*The Acting President*

A Backward Glance

The twelve Artisans who have been American Presidents divide themselves rather naturally into four groups. Andrew Jackson, Teddy Roosevelt, and Lyndon Johnson stand out as examples of *rough competitors* whom it was usually imprudent and sometimes even dangerous to cross. They would have their way no matter what, and when the occasion demanded it were quite reckless in their actions. Jackson's assaults on the eastern financial structure, Roosevelt's Panamanian adventure, and Johnson's blatant Congressional arm-twisting demonstrate their willingness to play rough.

Martin Van Buren, Franklin Roosevelt, and John Kennedy, on the other hand, were the *smooth operators*. They were consummate maneuverers who enjoyed the game as well as the result. Thus Van Buren was able to harmonize his loyalty to Jackson with his connection with Jefferson. Thus Roosevelt promoted aid to the Allies before the American entry into World War II. And thus John Kennedy reduced taxes without alienating his supporters.

Zachary Taylor, Franklin Pierce, Chester Arthur, and Warren Harding, on the other hand, were the *office players*. Taylor's "Oh, stop your nonsense and drink your whiskey" characterizes these men far more accurately than the thundering political pronouncements of a Jackson, Roosevelt, or Kennedy. Pierce and Harding were especially likely to appreciate Taylor's invitation, and though Arthur, and Taylor himself, were not especially noted for drinking, they both had a well-developed appreciation for having a good time. None of them were serious politicians in the sense of pursuing a presidential agenda, but instead preferred playing the role of President.

James Garfield and Ronald Reagan were the two Artisans who were *theatrical orators*. Garfield was the polished orator, the two-fisted scribbler writing poetry in Greek and Latin simultaneously, the man perpetually on stage. Reagan was also a "Great Communicator," the speechmaker forever intent on capturing his audience, impressing the crowd. Both men were consummate performing artists whose presentations were the highly polished result of endless hours of rehearsal.

Chapter Three

THE GUARDIANS

"The eternal rules of order and right which heaven itself has ordained."

Guardians who have been American Presidents

George Washington	1789-1797
James Monroe	1817-1825
William Henry Harrison	1841
John Tyler	1841-1845
James Polk	1845-1849
Millard Fillmore	1850-1853
James Buchanan	1857-1861
Andrew Johnson	1865-1869
Rutherford B. Hayes	1877-1881
Grover Cleveland	1885-1889, 1893-1897
Benjamin Harrison	1889-1893
William McKinley	1897-1901
William Howard Taft	1909-1913
Woodrow Wilson	1913-1921
Calvin Coolidge	1923-1929
Harry Truman	1945-1953
Richard Nixon	1969-1974
Gerald Ford	1974-1977
Jimmy Carter	1977-1981
George Bush	1989-

"The propitious smiles of Heaven can never be expected on a nation that disregards the eternal rules of order and right which heaven itself has ordained."

So spoke the Guardian George Washington in 1789, and so speaks the Guardian from time immemorial: heaven smiles on those who obey the divinely-ordained rules; all others must live, and should live, in fear and trembling. For, the consummate Guardian reminds us, "There is no Truth more thoroughly established than that there exists...an indissoluble union between virtue and happiness."[1]

His words were echoed fifty years later by another Guardian, William Henry Harrison: "Sound morals, religious liberty and a just sense of responsibility are essentially connected with all true...happiness."[2]

It is no coincidence that these two Guardians, separated by a half century, should speak so similarly. Guardians insist that the keys to honor and assets alike are respect for law and order, and for authority and tradition, caution in all things, and persistent attention to one's resources. Washington offered dramatic evidence of this. Before he was elected President of the United States, he led the rag-tag Continental army to victory over the well-trained and well-equipped British expeditionary force in America. To do this he had to keep his desperate little army together over a long period and under harsh conditions. Further, he had to avoid engaging the British army in open battle, or, if he did engage them, to do so only on his own terms. General Washington's abilities were not those of a battlefield general, and he was not inclined to engage in battle with the British. Instead the Guardian Washington executed steadfastly the less glamorous job of recruiting, clothing, feeding, arming, and providing shelter for his soldiers.

Washington avoided head-on battle most of the time, for he recognized that his task was to wear the British out, to let them exhaust themselves chasing after the constantly moving rebels. The British could not subdue the rebellion as long as Washington maintained his force, so that the very existence of the Continental Army was a victory.

Guardians with high intelligence tend to be the great logistical leaders. Logistical or quartermaster leadership consists in accumulating and preserving materiel, and seeing to it that authorized personnel receive that materiel at authorized times and places. Any distribution which is in any way *un*authorized simply will not do, and Guardians steadfastly refuse to be responsible for such distribution, and will even

---

1 From George ... To George, 91.
2 *From George ... To George*, 62.

forestall those who attempt it. Truman was at his best in his determined supplying of a prostrate Europe after World War II, just as Washington was at his best in his determined supplying of his disheveled army during the War of Independence.

Guardians also have a deep and abiding sense of responsibility to their family, business, church, country; in short, to any group they belong to. Whatever the group may be, it is theirs, they are connected with it, and they are bound to preserve and protect it. "The President of the United States is the steward of the nation's destiny," said the Guardian Jimmy Carter,[3] and stewardship means duty, obligation, loyalty—responsibility. Nor would they have it any other way, for as the Artisan must be free, the Guardian must be obligated.[4]

And Guardians take their obligations very seriously. "No President who performs his duty faithfully and conscientiously can have any leisure," insisted the Guardian James K. Polk.[5] The character of the Guardian often leads them to feel burdened, and sometimes Guardians become quite overburdened with worries and regrets. Perhaps their perspective of life so weighted down with responsibility is what prompted Hippocrates to dub them the "Melancholics." Nonetheless, they do seek out obligation, and to marry and start their own family is to become obligated in a fundamental and enduring way. Even very young Guardians are likely to presume that they will be (or at least should be) married and beget children, and they look forward to that time.[6] The Guardian relishes this sort of obligation, indeed even flourishes under its heavy weight. The notion of the "empty nest syndrome" probably applies most aptly to the Guardian whose children have grown and left and whose obligations—and opportunities for place and for appreciation—have all but disappeared.

As we said above, it is the quartermaster who collects, stores, and distributes materiel to those sanctioned to receive it, and this

---

3 *From George ... To George*, 10.

4 This is different than to be indebted, which is dishonorable. To be indebted means to have possession of something that belongs to someone else. To be obligated, which is honorable, means to have a responsibility to earn and then provide the other something of one's own.

5 *From George ... To George*, 4.

6 Stephen Montgomery's *The Pygmalion Project II: The Guardian* offers the novelist's and playwright's views on how Guardians act as spouses and parents.

quartermaster function is one which the Guardians understand well and at which they often excel. In every aspect of life Guardians work to see to it that those responsible do their job of providing needed supplies and equipment. More broadly, it is the Guardian's task to make sure that people do what they are supposed to do, what their duty calls upon them to do. "Liberty unregulated by law degenerates into anarchy," said Millard Fillmore,[7] and it is the Guardian's task to be certain that such degeneracy does not occur.

Thus Guardians quickly take note of the transgressions of others, whether they be sins of omission or of commission. Because they are not likely to remember when others do what they *should* do, they are quite likely to be unforgiving when others do what they should *not* do. They must learn to be careful about this propensity, for the righteous indignation of the outraged Guardian is something to behold.

Such indignation seems designed to evoke guilt and to inspire repentance. This makes sense since guilt is the abiding burden of the Guardians. Guilt, the Guardian assumes, will be equally burdensome when visited upon any wrongdoer. Surely pointing out his wrongs will move the guilty one to rectify his ways just as it moves the Guardian. Then, if the transgressor will express his heartfelt remorse and promise to change his ways, if he is truly repentant, all may be forgiven him.[8]

It is difficult for the Guardians to recognize that they are largely wasting their time trying to convert their Artisan, Idealist, and Rational brethren this way. It's not that the others are incapable of feeling guilty, but rather that they don't feel guilty about the same things that make Guardians feel guilty. Artisans feel guilty if they "chicken out," Rationals feel guilty if they become dependent, and Idealists feel guilty when they become malevolent or harbor ill-will. The Guardian suffers pangs of guilt upon being lazy or indigent, for idleness and impoverishment prevent them from nurturing properly those who deserve to be nurtured. Guardians recognize that the world is not as it should be; the wiser among them recognize the truth of George

---

7 *From George ... To George,* 20.

8 Though all may be forgiven, nothing will be forgotten. The Guardians cannot help remembering every debit, every slight, every wrongdoing, every falsehood. In moments of anger or hurt they are likely to drag all those prior sins out again and present them, one by one, to the guilty party, as if they were still fresh.

Washington's comment that, "We must bear up and make the best of mankind as they are, since we cannot have them as we wish."[9]

Of all the varieties of character, the Guardians will be most concerned—indeed, downright worried—about these matters of preservation and duty, of reward and punishment. This is not only because these matters are central to the Guardian, but also because they tend to be worried about *anything* that touches their lives. Just as the Artisans are the great optimists, assuming that somehow, no matter how bad things look, they will work out, so the Guardians are the great pessimists, sure that something will go wrong, sure that they must worry over everything, worried even that worrying won't help.

Like the Artisan, the Guardian is given to concreteness of expression. Guardians can also be just as impatient as the Artisan with "as-if's," "what-if's," and with those fictions, ideas, and theories which are merely imaginary rather than down-to-earth and sensible, and which (as we shall see) are so typical of the Rationals and Idealists. But, though they share the Artisan's focus on the concrete, Guardians are strongly opposed to the purely utilitarian viewpoint the Artisans take about concrete matters. In the Guardian's view no one has permission to do as he pleases just because it might work effectively. The Guardian believes fully that all actions must be judged by a tribunal, duly authorized by the community, to determine their compliance with moral and regulatory codes. In the absence of such judicious scrutiny there would inevitably be chaos and exploitation of the weak and innocent. The regulations and laws and standards, the "should's and should not's" found in every community, exist as an internalized "tribunal" by which every person can know whether his or her behavior is right or wrong.

For this reason George Washington favored an educated citizenry and proposed establishing a national university. He declared that, "Knowledge in every country is the surest basis of public happiness."[10] But what sort of knowledge? Listen to the words of the Guardian Harry Truman 150 years later:

---

9 *From George ... To George*, 53.
10 *From George ... To George*, 57.

The fundamental purpose of our educational system is to instill a moral code in the rising generation and create a citizenship which will be responsible for the welfare of the Nation.[11]

Through *sanctions*, through the judgments of the community, enculturation by education, and the sanctions of formal religion, everyone can cooperate, and everyone who deserves to can flourish. Let us all cooperate with one another in pursuit of common goals, says the Guardian, let us go by the book (the sanctions of established procedure) and thereby prevent anarchy and licentiousness. Sanctioned cooperation is the foundation of society and no society can survive without it. Or so the Guardian would have it.

As one might expect, even as very young children the Guardians are eager to learn of and participate in the rites, rituals, and ceremonies practiced by their elders. Their absorption in the traditional is apparent in the stereotypical stay-at-home Guardian wife, working to preserve the family home, raising (and enculturating) the children, and treasuring the anniversary cards, the little gifts, the flowers that her husband may bring her on special occasions. The Guardian husband, meanwhile, has his family's pictures at the office and in his wallet, and he has in his desk a stash of related memorabilia that he may feel both proud of and just a bit sheepish about showing others. "I believe that power must always be kept close to the individual," said the Guardian President George Bush, "close to the hands that raise the family and run the home."[12] The power of the presidency itself finds its legitimacy only in its association with the responsible family member.

Births, baptisms, weddings, anniversaries all become more important with the passing years, since each is a reminder of the stability and continuity made possible by respect for the traditional, established ways of duty, responsibility, and cooperation. At the traditional Thanksgiving or Christmas dinner, most likely to be hosted by a Guardian, it is the Guardian guest who will be found in the kitchen (or wherever else there is work going on) both before and after the meal,

---

11 *From George ... To George*, 59.
12 *From George ... To George*, 37.

assisting with preparation and cleanup. But if it is a Guardian who is hosting the traditional dinner, it is he or she who will be laboring over the logistics and insisting that the guests (including the Guardian guests) stay away from the work and enjoy themselves. And it is he or she who will feel offended if the guests do not enjoy themselves instead of helping, but who may also feel a bit put upon if a few guests don't at least observe the tradition of offering to help so they can be shooed away by their Guardian host.

The Guardians at work value the traditional entitlements of their position, treasure its perquisites and relish such physical markers of recognition as plaques, trophies, certificates, and awards. The office of the Guardian may be conspicuous for its large array of such objects. It is also likely to harbor the photographs of the ceremonies during which the awards were made, side by side with photographs of his or her family: spouse, children, grandchildren. The Guardians' interest in these matters makes them the easiest of the four temperaments to enculturate.

The leadership of Guardian Presidents is predominantly oriented to preservation of the nation's traditional institutions, laws, and organizations. Their concern with matters of membership, protocol, and duty are the natural reflection of this orientation. While Artisan Presidents are strongly *tactical*, Guardian Presidents are strongly *logistical*. That is, their leadership is also likely to focus on the properly sanctioned husbanding and disbursal of resources. All persons and agencies under the President's gaze (and the President himself, for that matter) will be expected to meet these responsibilities properly and will be expected to discharge their duties faithfully

Guardian Presidents can bring enormous determination to the Office when they think they are right (as they usually do). Harry Truman exemplified this Guardian characteristic nicely when he commented that: "Any politician with nerve and a program that is right can win in the face of the stiffest opposition."[13] George Washington, holding together his threadbare army, provided another excellent example of this kind of determined leadership, sustained chiefly by his Guardian character, his impressive moral stature, and his unswerving patriotism.

---

13 *From George ... To George*, 37.

responsibility with such thoroughness, that it is often difficult for them to satisfy their desire for appreciation. How to fit these together in a workable form is one of the life puzzles that probably confronts every Monitor at one time or another. Consider, for example, the plight of Monitor parents who find it necessary to punish their child but who at the same time want the child to appreciate their good intentions. The situation is very difficult for everyone involved, and sometimes the Monitor can only offer the somewhat forlorn promise so many of us have heard at one time or another: "This is for your own good; you'll thank me for it later."

The Conservator Guardians

Millard Fillmore	1850-1853
James Buchanan	1857-1861
William McKinley	1897-1901
William Howard Taft	1909-1913
Gerald Ford	1974-1977
George Bush	1989-

While the Monitors guard against deviance, the Conservators guard against another kind of danger: loss. While the Monitors are busy regulating, the Conservators are busy nurturing. We see again the "economics" of the Guardian, of course, but now with a focus on well-being rather than on husbanding, on rewarding rather than gathering. And while the Monitors direct, the Conservators habitually report; it is up to others to know what to do on the strength of the information the Conservators provide. Thus Conservators are likely to appear somewhat warmer in manner and to be noted for their generosity. Indeed, when they are unwilling or unable to be dutifully provident or protective, the Conservator Guardians are likely to be afflicted with a painful sense of guilt.

The Conservators' propensity for nurturing will at times run them afoul of their Monitor brethren. The Conservators may, against their better judgment, abandon some of the rules and regulations for the sake of nurturing. The Monitor President Harry Truman was not a man to forgive wrongdoing readily and had no compunction about seeing wrongdoers punished. The Conservator Gerry Ford, the also a Guardian, was a quite different man. The Conservator Ford was subjected to

outraged criticism—much of it probably from his Monitor colleagues–
when he used his presidential prerogative to pardon former President
Richard Nixon. Such an act of forgiveness would have been unthinkable
to a Monitor like Truman but it made good sense to Ford, whose
explanation was that he granted the pardon because he wished to "heal
the country," to spare it further injury and torment. His explanation
captures nicely the nurturing and protective orientation of the
Conservator in contrast to the regulatory orientation of the Monitor.

The Conservator's memory for wrongdoing is as long and as
thorough as that of the Monitor's, but the Conservator is far more likely
to excuse transgressions. Thus the Conservators may appear rather less
sure of themselves, or alternately, a little more flexible in their
judgments, than the Monitors. This is only appearance, however, for
their sense of right and wrong is as strong and stable as that of the
Monitors, and their memory for wrongdoings no less well-developed.
Indeed, their recall may cause them more discomfort than the Monitors'
causes them, for the Monitors are more free about taking action when
they feel wronged. William Howard Taft, a Conservator, was appalled
when his presidential predecessor and (presumed) friend, Teddy
Roosevelt, abandoned him because Taft would not pursue Roosevelt's
interests. Taft felt so betrayed that he prayed that his former friend
would be roundly defeated in the coming election. He noted in his
journal that he would never forget Roosevelt's betrayal "as long as he
lived."

Conservators are so good at nurturing that they are very likely to be
taken for granted, and this leaves them feeling very resentful. But they
feel far less able to speak out than the Monitors do, and they are likely to
try to manage their resentment in this quiet fashion—prayer and journal,
for example—at least for a while. They are even uncomfortable about
asking—some find it almost impossible to ask—for the little things they
want, for they seem to feel perpetually indebted, and cannot bear to
increase the size of the debt. The Conservators will eventually protest,
and vigorously, but even then they may not speak as pointedly or as
directively as the Monitors. "They are very nice people, unfortunately at
the price of stewing in their own juices in the face of ignominies."[16]

---

16 *Portraits in Temperament*, 55.

As we did for the Artisans, we now offer a visual summary of the facets of the Guardian character.

The Guardians

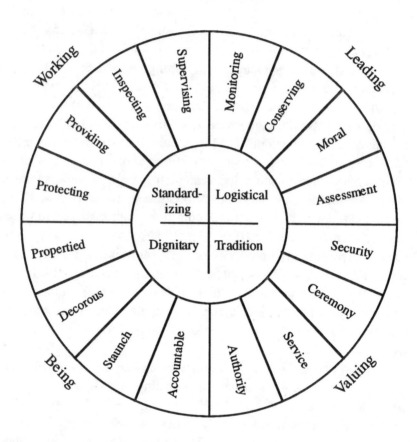

Extensive accounts of the Guardian character other than American Presidents can be found in Kretschmer's "melancholic," Adickes's "Traditional," Spränger's "Economic," and Keirsey's "Epimethean" and "Guardian" in their respective works. There are also many biographies of great individuals who were Guardians, such as those of General Omar Bradley, Queen Victoria, and Florence Nightingale. But in some respects novelists and playwrights seem to understand the Guardian character better than psychologists, and have captured well some of the more salient Guardian traits in countless fictional works. For a survey of the more dramatic portraits of Guardians in fiction the reader is advised to read Montgomery's studies of how Guardians interact with their Artisan, Rational, and Idealist mates.

The Guardian Presidents

Directing Guardians: The Monitors		Reporting Guardians: The Conservators	
1 George Washington	1789-1797	13 Millard Fillmore	1850-1853
5 James Monroe	1817-1825	15 James Buchanan	1857-1861
9 William H. Harrison	1841	25 William McKinley	1897-1901
10 John Tyler	1841-1845	27 William H. Taft	1909-1913
11 James Polk	1845-1849	38 Gerald R. Ford	1974-1977
17 Andrew Johnson	1865-1869	41 George Bush	1989-
19 Rutherford B. Hayes	1877-1881		
22 Grover Cleveland	1895-1889,		
24 Grover Cleveland	1893-1897		
23 Benjamin Harrison	1889-1893		
28 Woodrow Wilson	1913-1921		
30 Calvin Coolidge	1923-1929		
33 Harry Truman	1945-1953		
39 Jimmy Carter	1977-1981		

Non-fiction	Fiction
Studies in Psychosomatic Medicine (Alexander)	*Robinson Crusoe* (Defoe)
Please Understand Me (Keirsey)	*Ordinary People* (Guest)
Portraits of Temperament (Keirsey)	*Babbitt* (Lewis)
Physique and Character (Kretschmer)	*Death of a Salesman* (Miller)
The Pygmalion Project: Guardians (Montgomery)	*King Lear* (Shakespeare)
	The Hobbit (Tolkien)
The Pygmalion Project: Artisans (Montgomery)	*The Accidental Tourist* (Tyler)
	The Importance of Being Ernest (Wilde)
Types of Men (Spränger)	*Winds of War* (Wouk)

Directing Guardian Presidents: The Monitors

George Washington

"Integrity most pure..."

Monitor
Born: February 22, 1732
Died: December 14, 1799
Presidency: 1789-1797

Four of the United States' first six Presidents were Rationals. Though they are the least numerous of the temperaments, the Rationals also found their way in unexpected strength into almost every position of importance in the new nation. They were present in very high proportion among the writers of the Declaration of Independence, the framers of the Constitution, the government's earliest elected members and its representatives to other nations. In this way and in spite of their small numbers they occupied a remarkably influential position in early American history.

Against this background of strong Rational predominance it might be expected that the first person to be honored with the office of President of the United States also would be a Rational. But the man who was given this singular honor was not a Rational. Instead the person the founding fathers most trusted to stabilize the country's position, to manage its passions and to consolidate its gains was a Guardian.

The choice was an undisguised blessing. In fact, given the circumstances under which the first President would take office, it seems that no other choice was possible.

The American continent was rich with natural resources, and the colonists had always been vigorous and resourceful. The distance from England to the North American continent was great; the sea voyage took weeks and was at best risky. Over the decades the American colonists had of sheer necessity developed an independent and self-reliant spirit. The Americans, many more loyal to their own colonies than to the British Crown, had spent years gradually increasing their political and economic independence from the island Empire. Perhaps it was inevitable that they would eventually form a new nation fully independent of their British forbearers. And perhaps, given the spirit of the times, it was also inevitable that the new nation would embody a novel and daring experiment in political and social reform.

Finally, in 1775, discontent erupted into rebellion, and soon the rebellion was transformed into outright revolution. The Declaration of Independence was published, a new nation was declared into being, and the War of Independence began.

It was seven long years before the war ended and the new American nation was recognized by Great Britain. With the war over, the patriots and visionaries who had labored so long and risked so much to establish the new nation faced another struggle. This one was a struggle of vision and ideas, pride and passions, this time concerning the final, radical architecture of the new government. They had decided to divide the functions of government into a set of "checks and balances" to ensure that power could never be concentrated in the hands of a rapacious few. But how many divisions should there be so that there could be no take-over? Might not too much division destroy the effectiveness of the government? Should the legislature, charged with making policy and enacting law, be the predominant force in government? Or should it be the presidency, whose function was to enforce policy and laws but never to make them? How could we be certain that a powerful President would not establish a dictatorship by force of arms? What should be the relationship between the federal government and the individual states? Should there be a loose confederation of strongly independent entities, or a supergovernment overseeing weak individual governments?

Debate and then argument over these matters was in full swing long before the events of 1775. But they were very difficult issues; in fact they still are. Consensus was slow in coming and even then far from complete. Those struggling with the task were overall a brilliant group of men, and deeply dedicated to finding the best possible answers.

But they were also a turbulent group of very independent thinkers. The new government would embody the ideas of certain members while the hopes and visions of others would inevitably be discarded, and none of these dedicated and visionary men was likely to abandon his convictions easily. Pride was inevitably at risk, but so was their concern about the well-being of the new nation and its people. Some of these patriots would never be able to accept with equanimity having their views discarded.

These men did largely agree on one point: that their passionate disputes threatened the new nation with fatal disunity even before it could be fully born. Failure to achieve consensus would destroy the delicate political stability of the new nation and might easily mean the loss of that wondrous prize for which they had struggled so painfully and, for some, at such terrible cost. The first President of the United States must therefore be someone who could stand impartially aside from their arguments, and he had to be someone who had earned their trust and their loyalty. The man who would become the United States' first President must be someone with an unimpeachable reputation for integrity and honor, for patience and determination, for the impartial wisdom of Solomon. Fortunately there was at least one additional item upon which the men who shaped the early course of this country could agree: they knew just the person to take on the task.

With little hesitation they chose as the first President of the United States the highly respected Monitor Guardian, George Washington.

Washington was a military hero. As General of the fledgling Continental Army during the war for independence from Britain he had demonstrated great courage and stolid tenacity. Some had criticized him for being too cautious as a general, but his careful Guardian generalship was perfect for the military situation he faced. Washington knew from the beginning, as many did not, that the Continental Army was not an organization likely to win many military victories. He also understood that it was far more important to keep his army intact and in the field than it was to win exciting but indecisive victories. His Guardian's caution and logistical sense were perfect for the task.

Washington needed no elaborate strategy for fighting the British. Instead of waging many pitched battles or trying to outmaneuver the enemy, he traded space for time. He retreated when necessary in the face of a stronger enemy, he counterattacked against isolated British outposts or detachments where conditions promised success. He generally avoided major battles with his better trained and equipped enemy. Instead he harassed the edge of the British forces, withdrawing into the woods when they counterattacked. In this way he set out to make the conflict too wearisome and too expensive for the British, a war of supply lines (lengthy for the British, short for him) rather than one of large-scale, violent combats. His most significant victories came when he besieged the enemy, for instance, walling them up in New York City, until they withdrew. These sieges were essentially logistical, not tactical operations: the Monitor is best at battles of supply, not of maneuver.[17]

As we observed earlier, Washington's task was to avoid losing the conflict, which meant he had to maintain an army longer than his enemy was willing to keep paying for war. In understanding this and in succeeding so well at it, Washington demonstrated the special leadership of the Guardians: he was a superb logistical general, a superb quartermaster general. At the same time, and as is usually the case with Guardian leaders, he was not a very good tactical general. Most of the set-piece battles he undertook against the British went against the Continentals, even when initial conditions seemed favorable for them, and a good Artisan subordinate, an Andy Jackson, for example, would

---

17 He did surprise the Hessians at Trenton on the day after Christmas in 1775, and shortly thereafter he defeated the British at Princeton. But such tactical victories were rare for Washington.

have been a boon to him in these battles. But he had few such men and the conditions of the war required that his leadership avoid all glamor and hints of derring-do. It is no wonder that when he was nominated by John Adams for command of the new American Army in 1775 he declared to Patrick Henry that "This will be the commencement of the decline of my reputation."[18] The revolution itself faltered and almost collapsed during the first two years of war. During the winter of 1776 the Continental Army had shrunk in on itself until, in the severe winter of 1777, it was nothing but 5,000 cold and discouraged men freezing at Valley Forge.

In spite of the arduous difficulties he and his army faced, however, Washington's reputation was intact when hostilities ended. George Washington was a military hero, the nation's first. Of course he was much more than a military hero. He was also a serious, solid, rock-stable man, as are most Monitors. He possessed a solid reputation for unwavering patriotism, impeccable integrity and scrupulous honesty. He was also greatly respected for his unflappable common sense and for his unswerving moral courage. Abigail Adams lauded him for being "Polite with dignity, affable without familiarity, distant without haughtiness, grave without austerity, modest, wise, and good."[19] Thomas Jefferson also knew Washington well and wrote of him that

> his mind was great and powerful, without being of the very first order....As far as he saw, no judgment was ever sounder. It was slow in operation, being little aided by invention or imagination, but sure in conclusion.[20]

Jefferson offers a portrayal of some of the best of the Guardian character as he continues his description of Washington.

> Perhaps the strongest feature in his character was prudence, never acting until every circumstance, every consideration, was maturely weighted; refraining when he saw a doubt, but, when once decided, going through with his purpose whatever obstacles opposed. His integrity was most pure, his justice the most inflexible I have ever known, no motives of interest or consanguinity, of friendship or hatred, being able to bias his decision. [21]

---

18 *Presidential Anecdotes,* 9.
19 *Presidential Anecdotes,* 5.
20 Quoted in *The American Presidents,* 3.
21 Quoted in *The American Presidents,* 3.

Thus in the midst of the violence, frenzy, and despair which were part of the prolonged struggle for American independence, the Monitor George Washington was the very bedrock of calm deliberation, natural prudence and unyielding determination. Even the irascible Patrick Henry, volatile and quick to criticize, had commented earlier in Washington's career that "If you speak of solid information and sound judgment, Colonel Washington is undoubtedly the greatest man [present]."[22]

During the period of combat against the British, the Continental Congress, the only legitimate authority in the newly emerging United States, was often in near chaos. Differing factions and incompatible strategies abounded, finances were a disaster, and the country's mood often near despair. So desperate did the situation seem and so inept the Congress's leadership that some encouraged Washington to use his army and his reputation to take over the conduct of the government. In effect he was being asked to become a dictator. But his patriotism and honor could not abide such an action and he refused.

His deliberate, cautious concern for what was right was a welcome, indeed a necessary counterpoint to the intellectual lighting strokes of the Adamses, Jeffersons, and Madisons of the time. Unlike many of these august Rationals, Washington also had the good sense to listen to the opinions of others, especially when he didn't grasp the subtleties of an issue. He also had the patience to weigh carefully the opinions he heard and the determination to reach the most sound possible conclusion about the matter at hand. And finally he had the courage, then and only then, to pursue the course of action dictated by his own judgment.

It was much the same with him when he was a young man. Like most Guardians, Washington was quite ambitious, pursuing opportunities to improve his position wherever he could. His father died when he was eleven. His mother was a possessive, querulous woman, with little talent for managing the family plantation, and it was sinking slowly but hopelessly into debt. When he was sixteen he decided something had to be done, and so he broke out his father's old surveying equipment and became a surveyor's helper. Of course he worked hard and within a year was appointed the county surveyor.

---

22 *The American Presidents*, 8.

He now followed the example of his revered older brother, Lawrence, and applied for a position as adjutant in the Virginia militia. He was granted the appointment and not long thereafter was appointed a militia major. At nineteen he was a major and by twenty-three he was a colonel, in charge of the entire (though the admittedly small) Virginia state militia. While an officer the young Washington was involved in a number of the wilderness battles that befell the colonies in those years, and though he was never careless or reckless, he soon gained a reputation for being steady and fearless under fire. He took no special pride in this, however; he once commented that he could never understand how one could be a coward to begin with.

Washington was not a unique Guardian in his fearlessness. Guardian fearlessness isn't the reckless absence of fear of the Artisan, but Guardians can still be surprisingly bold in battle. A number of Guardian Presidents were military men and all seemed similarly fearless while most of them were cited for gallantry in leading their soldiers in the attack. Perhaps cowardice requires a vivid imagination that Washington and his Guardian successors simply did not possess or care to cultivate.

In any event, Washington's travels into the largely unsettled western regions of the colonies had their share of adventure, but he was not a seeker of adventure for its own sake. On the contrary, he was pursuing his own financial security. Security is of overwhelming importance to the Guardians; they never seem to feel they have found quite enough of it. Washington attempted to satisfy his hunger for ownership and security (which are much the same thing for the Guardians) by making investments in land. Even while exploring the western frontiers he was constantly on the lookout for land worth buying, and with his strong logistical sense he was astute in his purchases. Over the years he acquired considerable wealth through investment in land. In fact, at his death his holdings included 33,000 acres of land in five states, Washington, D. C., and the Northwest Territory. His total wealth—even before two centuries of inflation—was in excess of a half million dollars.

Washington was stiff and formal even while still a young man exploring the borderless West, and fighting savage battles. His severity of manner seemed very much a part of him and, as is sometimes the case with the Monitors, almost seemed to define him. Even so, he was not incapable of a bit of romantic involvement. When Colonel Washington, commander of the Virginia militia, met Martha Dandridge Custis in 1758 he was immediately taken with the spirited young widow and mother of two children. Washington somewhat impetuously, at least for him, undertook an immediate courtship. Martha Custis apparently reciprocated his interest from the very beginning; she and George were married in January of 1759, less than a year after their first meeting.

The high-spirited and independent widow Custis had a fairly sizable estate and some people rumored that Washington married her only for her money. The accusation, as one might expect, rankled him greatly and it seems unlikely that there could be much truth to it. Certainly Guardians are sensitive to matters of social station and financial condition, and they are likely to avoid marrying "beneath their station" in either respect. It is quite another matter, however, to suggest that they would marry only for money.

Further, Washington showed no interest in unearned financial gain. Though he had considerable opportunity to profit from his positions of General of the Army and later of President of the United States, during the years he commanded the Continental Army he served completely without pay. When he assumed the presidency he also announced that he preferred to serve without pay. He asked for reimbursement only for the considerable expenses he incurred during his period of service, just as he had as commanding general of the Army. He was doing his duty, after all, not trying to earn a living at government expense. Of course it was also equally in character for him to monitor scrupulously all his expenses and to report them to the Congress in minute detail in his requests for reimbursement. But these were payments he had earned, funds to which he was entitled; they were not an attempt to get something for nothing, an act which would have been abhorrent to the Monitor.

With or without her money, Martha Custis Washington was an attractive, cheerful, and amiable young Conservator Guardian. She apparently found her new husband a congenial and admirable man and, as Conservators usually will, she showed great affection and loyalty for him all her life. He returned both her affection and her loyalty in full measure, though in his letters to her we find his characteristic stiffness and formality: "I embrace the Opportunity to send a few words to one whose life is now inseparable from mine," he wrote on one occasion. "Since that happy hour when we made our Pledges to each other, my thoughts have been continually going to you as to another Self."

After their marriage, and especially after Washington became President, Martha Washington toned down her self-sufficient ways. She had been a widow responsible for managing a plantation and for raising her two children alone, and the ability of Guardians to handle such chores responsibly is something in which they can take enormous satisfaction. Once married to George, however, she turned her attention to establishing a respected and pleasant place for herself as wife to the ambitious young colonel. The admirable Conservator Martha was known for her graciousness and her invariably pleasant good nature. It was she alone who added some semblance of warmth and grace to the Washingtons' social events, not only through her own presence but also through her management of Mount Vernon, Washington's estate, inherited at the death of his brother.

Martha much preferred the pleasures of her home to the demands imposed by her husband's increasingly exalted position. Even the gracious Martha would occasionally complain about the constant public scrutiny and the occasional criticism to which his elevated status subjected them. With her husband, she looked forward constantly to the day when they could together settle down, peacefully and aristocratically bucolic, at Mount Vernon. Unfortunately that day was a long and difficult time coming. From the moment the revolution began until he was elected President the Washingtons were together only infrequently. The Revolutionary War had rampaged through the colonies for seven years and George was away from Martha much of that time. The Declaration of Independence was signed in 1776 and it was not until 1783 that the fighting was officially over.

The war was won, peace concluded, and recognition was tendered the United States by the nations of Europe. But even now there were major obstacles to a secure peace. The United States' first constitution was the Articles of Confederation, adopted in 1777, but not ratified until 1781. But the Articles were a very weak instrument upon which to found a nation. They established a "league of friendship" between the various colonies, now independent states. This approach made for a confederation that was far too loose and unruly to be able to survive.

There was no way to guarantee effective and unified action against the foreign attack. For that matter there was no way to guarantee that one state might not take up arms against another. Some way had to be found to bind together these loose-knit and wary states in spite of their extreme desire to protect their individual autonomy.

A Federal Constitutional Convention was called to deal with these difficult matters, but resistance and suspicion among the states was so great that there was a serious question about whether the Convention would occur. It was of the greatest importance that George Washington, weary and already fifty-five, agreed to serve as a delegate from Virginia and to preside over the Convention, which finally took place in the summer of 1787. Without the impressive endorsement for the Convention's efforts conferred by his presence it is improbable that the gathering would have been productive—if indeed the Convention had taken place at all.

With Washington's support (and that of the enormously respected Benjamin Franklin[23]) the Convention floor became a lively, productive and vital place. The men around him were mostly well-known to him and to each other. They were friends, patriots, they were veterans of the darkest days of the Revolution at Trenton, Yorktown, Monmouth. The atmosphere was intense, opinions were attacked vigorously and defended vigorously, but the work of designing a new constitution proceeded remarkably well. What is now the Constitution of the United States of America, that magnificent framework for the governing of the United States, was hammered out and adopted in place of the Articles of Confederation.

Then, with the work of the Convention successfully completed, Washington was elected to be the first President of the new United States under its new Constitution.

It was not his wish to become President. When he gave his inaugural address one observer commented that he seemed "grave almost to

---

23 Benjamin Franklin was eighty-seven at the time of the Constitutional Convention. His presence along with Washington's, gave legitimacy and weight to the proceedings. He was in ill health, and could not be an active participant. He did not offer any clear ideas about how the government should be structured, but was instead a conciliator, someone who could smooth over conflict and calm others. At the conclusion of the Convention he agreed to the new constitution, he said, "because I expect no better, and because I am not sure it is not the best."

sadness" throughout the speech.[24] Long before the war was over
Washington had expressed his ardent wish to retire permanently to his
home at Mount Vernon. He wanted very much to return to his wife, his
home and his farming. But he was now entreated by his fellows to serve
the nation further, to accept the responsibilities of the United States' first
President. The country, he was told, was in grave danger without him,
and Washington, the responsible Guardian, could not turn his back.
Guardians always have a difficult time warding off responsibility and
duty. Since their self-esteem rests so strongly on being accountable that
they can easily bury themselves under their demands.

Furthermore, the entreaties presented Washington were couched in
the kind of language he would be least able to resist. Alexander
Hamilton wrote to him rather elegantly that "every public and personal
consideration will demand from you an acquiescence in what will
certainly be the unanimous wish of your country."[25] But a Maryland
official wrote him with a much more devastating simplicity: "We
cannot, sir, do without you." Here is the soft spot in the Guardian's
armor: others need him and he is obligated to respond unselfishly to that
need. Living as he did among the likes of John Adams, James Madison,
and Thomas Jefferson, Washington could not dispute the importance of
what he had to offer. Very realistically, and with the Guardian's natural
pessimism, he feared what might happen if the inevitable dissension
among the brilliant and fiery Revolutionaries were not carefully
monitored. Thus the reluctant but concerned Guardian had little choice;
he must agree to become the first President of the United States. He
claimed no happiness about doing so. He wrote to a friend in 1879, "My
movements to the chair of Government will be accompanied by feelings
not unlike those of a culprit who is going to the place of his execution."

He must have felt honored by the appeals of his countrymen. He was
a Guardian after all, and Guardians have great respect for high status and
do naturally aspire to it. Washington was nonetheless a man of innate
modesty and, like Guardians everywhere, innate pessimism. The
prospect of failure in handling his obligations had to be terrifying to
him. To be a Guardian and to meet one's obligations, to satisfy one's

---

24 *Presidential Anecdotes*, 19.
25 *Presidential Campaigns*, 4.

accountability, is to be in touch with the source of self-esteem. Conversely, to be a Guardian and to fail in one's accountability is to touch the source of Guardian shame. Further, merely "getting the job done" will not satisfy this accountability. The end does not justify the means, success never justifies wrong action. One must observe the proper procedures and follow the established rules in meeting the demands of one's role and the proper way is seldom the easy way. Guardians typically pride themselves on their ability to do things the right way, the way they should be done, just as they take pride in seeing to it that others also do things the way they should be done. Again, the source of their self-esteem lies in their reliability.

Not surprisingly, then, Washington was known as "a stern administrator, strongly religious, a stickler for rules, and a strict military disciplinarian."[26] Performing these monitoring functions he was assured, he knew his job, he knew how things ought to be done. But when he stepped out of the monitoring role his confidence wavered. He was formal and stiff in his writing and a poor public speaker, clumsy and ungainly in his delivery, often trembling visibly as he spoke. He also lacked the scintillating conceptual talents and the rich background of theory possessed by many of the brilliant men around him. Washington recognized these shortcomings in himself and worried greatly about them. Though he held office for eight years he never found relief from his persistent fear that his countrymen would expect more from him than he could give them, that he might fail to meet all the obligations he had assumed by becoming President.

Guardians are acutely sensitive to matters of protocol and quickly master them even as children. As adults they naturally set about seeing to it that people conduct themselves in a manner proper to the occasion and to their position in the hierarchy. The aristocratic Washington was no different. During his terms of office Washington insisted upon the President being treated almost as royalty. He rode in an ornate carriage drawn by splendid white horses. He insisted on being treated rather like a European monarch and wanted the President addressed as "Excellency." Mrs. Washington was sometimes called "Lady Washington," and people did not shake hands with President

---

26 *Atlas of the Prsidents*, 12.

Washington, but they (and he) bowed to each other. He didn't seem to have any wish to exalt himself in all this. He seemed to derive little personal pleasure from the pomp and ceremony. Guardians are little given to the pursuit of pleasures, and the regal style he demanded was in his view simply proper to the dignity of the office of President.

Moreover, he was very concerned with how American dignitaries as well as representatives of foreign nations should conduct themselves around the President, what diplomatic protocols ought to be observed in the United States' dealings with other countries, and how to ensure that representatives of the American government would be treated with proper respect. He was also concerned with matters of protocol within the government of the United States. He was attentive to how the President and the Congress and the Supreme Court should function with each other, what sort of deference would be appropriate for the President, and where executive right and privilege should be safeguarded. He took it for granted that he was important by virtue of being President, and that it was his task to comport himself—and to see that others comported themselves—according to the office which it was his privilege and duty to occupy. Even so, it must be said, he was concerned with how the common people would react to such a regal atmosphere, for he never lost sight of the fact that the United States was a democracy. How to reconcile the demands of protocol with the democratic nature of the country was a problem he was never quite able to resolve for himself.

In short, Washington took on the responsibility for establishing the marks of legitimacy and setting the mold for the conduct of this radically new, still uncertain and experimental nation and government. Perhaps unwittingly and probably inevitably, Washington showed his Guardian colors in doing so. He molded the new government according to precepts with which he was already familiar and for which he had a natural respect: royalist, almost imperial patterns taken straight from the tradition of European monarchy.

In 1793, at the end of his four year term of office, the danger of fatal disunity still had not dissipated. Some issues had been settled but new and important ones were arising and there still seemed a real and immediate danger of national collapse. Washington understandably remained concerned about the possibility of national disaster; his fellow citizens entreated him to accept a second term of office, duty again conscripted him to his country's service, and he reluctantly agreed to serve four more years as President. The weight of his duties and obligations as President was enormous. He had to settle down the Hotspurs at home and he had to try, through cautious diplomacy, to keep the British at bay. He established the Departments of the Treasury, State, and War, oversaw the adoption of the Bill of Rights, and of course had the somewhat more edifying task of working out the fundamental protocols for the new government.

Though he accomplished a great deal he was often depressed about the heavy burden he carried. He was also frequently, indeed almost constantly, concerned about his health, and was often depressed about being kept so long from his Virginia home. He hated spending so much time away from the wife that he loved and being deprived of the quiet pursuits natural to his tastes and his patrician background. It was not until after eight years as commander of the Continental Army, various public duties thereafter, and another eight years as President that he was finally able to retire in 1797 to Mount Vernon, his beloved Virginia plantation. There at last he could resume his life as a gentleman farmer and take up again the peaceful study of agriculture, which was for him that occupation which "has ever been the most favorite amusement of my life."

Perhaps only a Guardian such as George Washington could find agriculture a "favorite amusement." Perhaps even more than most Guardians he seems to have been born already serious and to have grown up already concerned. His prevailing mood was worry, which was punctuated by brief periods of excitement and enthusiasm, but almost never by serenity. The rather serious business of agriculture might, for such a man, become an "amusement," perhaps along side finding new land in which to invest.

Washington did have a lighter side. He liked a little light flirting with attractive women, though never in an improper fashion or degree. He enjoyed cards, fox hunting, horse-racing and the theater. He is said to have had an earthy sense of humor, though traces of it are not easily found. One example which has been cited in many places is the time he was sitting at dinner when the fireplace, located behind him, got too hot. When he wanted to move away, someone said merrily that a general should be able to stand fire. Yes, Washington replied, but it doesn't look good if he receives it from behind.

Another example: during the Constitutional Convention one member moved that the nation's standing army be limited to five thousand men. When Washington heard this proposal he remarked that this would be acceptable to him as long "as the convention agreed to an amendment prohibiting armies from invading the United States with more than three thousand troops."[27]

Lighter side notwithstanding, Washington clearly differed from the Rational firebrands around him in his devotion to common sense and in his lack of interest in abstract or scholarly pursuits. Never an enthusiastic reader, even in his later years he read books only if doing so served a concrete purpose. He loved farming, of course, and his devotion to it was so widely recognized that in his later years he was known affectionately as "Farmer Washington." As we would expect, much of his library concerned itself with farming; very little had anything to do with philosophy or politics.

As is often the case with Monitors, he was very aware of the personal costs of the duties he had undertaken, and was not above complaining about those costs. While still General of the beleaguered Continental army, for example, on one occasion he reached for his glasses in order to read a document to his staff and commented, "Gentlemen, you will permit me to put on my spectacles, for I have not only grown grey, but almost blind in the service of my countrymen."[28] His correspondence to the Continental Congress during the Revolutionary War is full of requests for more arms and money, but it is also replete with complaints about the Congress's neglect of him and his army: failure to provide logistical support in the form of weapons, ammunition, food, clothing, those items so important to the Monitor. And he continued to complain, not only about the Congress but about the cost to his health of his unending struggle with both the British and the Congress. The Guardian under stress may keep silent for a long while, but will eventually become far better than most at registering complaints. When the time comes those complaints will be issued

---

27 *One Night Stands with American History*, 40.
28 *A Pocket History of the United States*, 83.

loudly, clearly, and frequently. This may be rather unpleasant for those in range of the complaint, but it is likely that before the complaints begin the Guardian will have made a greater and more conscientious effort to manage the troublesome situation than anyone else.

George Washington shared with many Guardians, perhaps especially the Monitors, a tendency to be something of a hypochondriac. He frequently expressed concern about a variety of diseases, ailments, and infirmities which he might have contracted. His comment that he was going blind in the service of his country was merely one such complaint. When he felt especially depressed he spoke readily of death as if it were an immediate threat. As most Guardians will, however, he fought against ill health, both real and imagined, with the same patient stoicism he displayed against the British. He was not entirely unrealistic in being concerned about his health, by the way. He had been subject to a number of major illnesses in his life including, according to one researcher,"tuberculosis, smallpox, removal of a 'bone-deep tumor' from his thigh, frequent attacks of pneumonia and other respiratory diseases, tooth decay and extractions and the famous ill-fitting wooden dentures."[29]

Whether or not he was too stiff and formal, a complainer or a hypochondriac, one still sees in George Washington some of the very best of the Monitor Guardian character: solid and stable dependability and unswerving loyalty to the institutions with which he associates himself; a strong sense of integrity and fierce tenacity when sure of the rightness of his cause; and long and laborious effort to satisfy obligations from which he granted himself no reprieve. As one usually critical historian described him,

> Of all the statesmen in American history, Washington has most conspicuously the characteristics of simplicity, steadfastness, integrity, and absolute devotion to his country to such a degree that they dominate all his other traits.[30]

One cannot imagine these fine—and accurate—words of praise being written about any other character type than the Guardian. But one also finds foibles in the person of George Washington, and his foibles no

---

29 *Presidential Courage*, 31.
30 *How They Became President*, 23.

less than his virtues are those of the Guardian. Nathaniel Hawthorne, for instance, knew Washington well. Though he admired Washington greatly even Hawthorne couldn't resist a wry comment about Washington's stuffy hauteur:

> Did anybody ever see Washington nude? It is inconceivable. He had no nakedness, but I imagine he was born with his clothes on, and his hair powdered, and made a stately bow on his first appearance in the world.[31]

Washington, like many quiet Monitor Guardians, was stiffly formal, with little knack for personal, relaxed socializing. He offered none of the conversational ease or amicability of his wife Martha, a more open and amiable Conservator. Instead when he hosted a social occasion he presented a rather stately, chilly ceremony and an awkward formality. His entertainments were "precise, elegantly set, and of a dullness that overpowered Martha's gentle efforts."[32]

Although Monitors are not alone in this characteristic, they can indeed be marvelously stuffy. Listen for the victory of propriety over grace, in Washington's terse reprimand of a latecomer to one of his "entertainments": "We are obliged to be punctual here. My cook never asks whether the company has arrived, but whether the hour has."[33] Or consider the experience of Gouverneur Morris, one of the signers of the Declaration of Independence. Morris was a flamboyant, flagrant Artisan, a man who enjoyed making his presence felt, sometimes in the most outrageous ways. But even he could not unbend Washington's stiff reserve. Arriving at one of the formal receptions offered by that august Guardian, Morris laid a friendly hand on his host's shoulder. Washington had put his hand out to greet Morris but as soon as Morris touched his shoulder the indignant Washington "withdrew his hand, stepped suddenly back, fixed his eye on Morris with an angry frown, until the latter retreated, abashed, and sought refuge in the crowd."[34]

Though Washington himself may have been loved and revered, his parties were not.

George Washington, first President of the United States, left office in 1797. In 1796, a few months before stepping down, he made his

---

31 Quoted in *Presidential Anecdotes*, 4.
32 *Profiles and Portraits of American Presidents*, 39.
33 *Presidential Anecdotes*, 20.
34 *Presidential Anecdotes*, 4.

famous Farewell Address. In it he offered some sound Guardian advice, stressing the importance of avoiding political entanglements with foreign nations, exhorting us that unswerving loyalty to the Constitution should be "sacredly obligatory upon all," and reminding us that "virtue and morality" were the absolutely necessary wellspring of good government. A short while later in a more private communication he wrote that "I feel myself eased of a load of public care. I hope to spend the remainder of my days in cultivating the affections of good men, and in the practice of the domestic virtues."[35] At Mount Vernon he was finally able to do so for a few precious years, living in quiet honor and in the cultivation of his "most favorite amusement."

In Washington's case as in few others, his own countrymen seemed to comprehend and appreciate widely what he had made possible. Without his patient steadiness, his stoic stubbornness, and his considerable ability at maintaining the Continental Army under the most difficult logistical conditions, the Army would have fallen quickly either to the British or to the natural elements, and the nation still struggling for birth would have died with it.

Without the legitimacy and importance his very presence gave it, the Constitutional Convention of 1787 might well have collapsed. The disunity, the confusion, and the disputes between the various states already distressing the new nation would probably have persisted. The United States might well have disintegrated into a patchwork of minor nations-states, subject to threat from each other and domination by larger nations from across the sea.

Finally, without Washington's presidency, the crucial eight years of stability his presence conferred might have been proven impossible to find elsewhere. Washington's eight year tenure of office bought desperately-needed time for revolutionaries such as Jefferson, Adams, Hamilton, and Madison to hammer out enough of their differences under Washington's watchful eye to ensure that the new nation was stabilized even without his steadying hand.

George Washington, the austere, aristocratic gentleman farmer, stalwart exemplar of Guardian integrity, common sense and selfless service, died on December 14, 1799. "I die hard, but I am not afraid to

---

35 *Presidential Anecdotes,* 16.

go," he said near the end. "Let me go quietly. I cannot last long." With these words he courteously dismissed the doctors who were attending him and shortly thereafter he died.[36] The gracious Martha Washington lived three years longer than her husband. She was seventy-one years old when she died in 1802. She was widely loved and respected and her passing was greatly mourned.

Bibliography

Bancroft, A 1882	*The Life of George Washington*
Boynton, E 1909	*The General Orders of George Washington, Commander-in-Chief of the Army of the Revolution*
Corry, J 1812	*The Life of General George Washington*
Cunliffe, M 10958	*George Washington, Man and Monument*
McLaughlin, R 1912	*Washington and Lincoln, Leaders of the Nation in the Constitutional Eras*
Fitzpatrick, J 1933	*George Washington Himself; a Commonsense Biography*
Ford, H 1918	*Washington and his Colleagues: A Chronicle of the Rise and Fall of Federalism*
Kingston, J 1813	*The Life of General George Washington*
Lowe, J 1807	*The Life of General George Washington: Proposals*
Van Dyke, P 1931	*George Washington, the Son of his Country, 1732-1735*
Washington, G 1800	*The Last Will and Testament of General George Washington*
Weems, M 1932	*An Anecdote Concerning the Cherry-Tree and George Washington*
Woodward, W 1926	*George Washington, the Image and the Man*
Wrong, G 1921	*Washington and his Comrades in Arms; a Chronicle of the War of Independence*

---

36 *Presidential Courage,* 34.

James Monroe

The last of the cocked hats

Monitor
Born: April 28, 1758
Died: July 4, 1831
Presidency: 1817-1825

The year was 1816; the United States was thirty-seven years old. After George Washington the people of the United States had elected three consecutive Rational Presidents, had already endured bloody episodes with France and Spain, and had gone through its second war with England. Now the most immediate pressures had abated, and there was time to salve the nation's wounds and to consolidate its very significant gains. The atmosphere in the year 1816 was bright and warm with peace and prosperity and good feeling. James Monroe, Secretary of

State at the time of the election, was the favorite of the highly respected Thomas Jefferson and James Madison, and was easily elected to the presidency. Now was the time for the last of the Revolutionary Presidents, the last representative of that extraordinary group of men who had been directly involved in the formulation of the Declaration of Independence, the agonies of the Revolutionary War, the creation of a new nation, of a new Constitution, and of a new government.

James Monroe did not present the image of a great revolutionary hero. He was tall and plain and rather awkward in appearance. Though his behavior was formal and well-starched, he was always gentle and courteous and, as one observer noted, "not displeasing to the ladies."

> A bust of him shows a clean firm jaw, a cleft chin, a pleasant mobile mouth, a prominent nose, and deeply hollowed eyes. It is the head of a responsible, thoughtful, but agreeable young man, sure of himself and ready for an important place in the world.[37]

Monroe like Madison before him was something of a throwback to Revolutionary days. He was one of the few men who still wore the traditional knee britches and long hose, and he was the last President to wear the old-fashioned tricorne hat, a habit that won him the sobriquet, "the Last of the Cocked Hats." Monroe was fond of recalling his Revolutionary background, and certainly he had a background worthy of remembering. He quit college when the Revolutionary War broke out, joined the Continental Army and was soon commissioned a lieutenant. He participated in Washington's famous attack across the Delaware River on the bitterly cold Christmas Day of 1776 when the Continentals surprised and defeated the Hessian mercenaries. He was with Washington's Continental Army during its long retreat and desperate encampment in the fall and the terrible winter of 1777.[38] He was at that time not yet nineteen years old and already a veteran of some of the worst days of the Revolutionary War.

When the war ended, the Guardian Monroe settled down to a career in politics. He was fortunate to become a protege of Thomas Jefferson.

---

37 *How They Became President,* 68.

38 He had been wounded in the attack on Trenton, apparently suffering a severed artery which he was fortunate to have attended quickly by a doctor. Many others were less fortunate than Monroe and died of wounds less menacing than his. Proper medical help was in terribly short supply in Washington's army, as it was in all armies of the period.

He studied law under Jefferson's guidance and with Jefferson's sponsorship won election to the Virginia state legislature. As is so often the case with Guardians who enter political life, it is likely that Monroe chose that path because of its promise of high status, its badges of rank and responsibility and, especially in Monroe's case, the opportunity it offered him to continue to make a contribution to his nation. He was after all very much a patriot even if the war was long since ended.

Though politics was a fitting way for Monroe to continue in the service of his country, there is a question about how far he would have risen in the political world without the sponsorship of Thomas Jefferson and James Madison. In spite of his rather colorful history Monroe seemed to be a rather commonplace person, lacking any special qualities that would persuade his fellow citizens to vote for him. His manner of dress was obviously reactionary, and he had no distinctive brilliance or charm, no noteworthy wit or charisma. In short he seemed to be a quite unremarkable man who in no way resembled, for instance, the brilliant Jefferson or the noble Washington.

Also unlike his Monitor predecessor Washington, Monroe had strongly egalitarian convictions, insisting that everyone, regardless of rank, should be treated with "friendly, republican, and unassuming manners."[39] Egalitarianism is not especially common in the Guardian, who has a temperamentally given respect for hierarchy and authority. Monroe's egalitarianism may have been in part a reflection of Thomas Jefferson's intellectual leadership. Jefferson had a powerful faith in the ability of the average citizen to choose and to act wisely, and Monroe's egalitarian stance was in part a reflection of the temper of the times, but was also something adopted almost whole cloth from his friend and mentor Jefferson.

Not that Monroe was a gullible man, or one easily persuaded to unfamiliar views. This Monitor, like most of his kind, was always steady and careful in his actions. Like Washington before him he wouldn't be stampeded into hurried judgments or rash actions by anyone or anything. Monroe had, as John Quincy Adams later wrote, "a mind sound in its ultimate judgments, and firm in its final conclusions." One can hardly avoid noticing the similarity of Adams' description of the Monitor

---

39 *The Life of James Monroe*, 286, quoted in *Presidential Anecdotes*, 50.

Monroe with Thomas Jefferson's earlier description of the Monitor George Washington: "As far as he saw, no judgment was ever sounder. It was slow in operation, being little aided by invention or imagination, but sure in conclusion."

The Constitutional Convention of 1787 was one situation in which Monroe's measured steadiness and sound judgment were of extraordinary importance. The country's original constitution, the Articles of Confederation, was a painfully defective document and in 1787 a new convention of representatives of the states was called to remedy the problem. An alternative Constitution was hammered out to replace the Articles at the Constitutional Convention and the new document had great appeal for most of the delegates. The delegation included some very intelligent and articulate men, men who strongly approved of the new instrument, but the wary James Monroe fought vigorously against its adoption. He was convinced, as were several others, that the proposed Constitution as it stood would enable the government to undermine the rights of citizens, and perhaps eventually destroy their freedom. It was not until Monroe was assured that a Bill of Rights would be added to the Constitution to prevent such abuse that he relinquished his opposition to it.

Monroe was not the only person to resist adoption. A solitary stand would be most unusual in a Guardian, and he took his cue initially from others who were concerned about the potential dangers of the document. Nonetheless, once alerted, he attended to the various arguments for and against the document and worked out in his own terms which of them was most sound, much as the Monitor Washington did before him. Every citizen of the United States has reason to be grateful for Monroe's careful Guardian common sense and his immovable Guardian determination, for the Bill of Rights has been crucial to the survival of political freedom in this country.

Neither Washington nor Monroe was noted for flashing imagination or ingenuity; these are not the special strengths of the Guardian. Both were greatly respected instead for their extraordinary prudence, their impeccable fairness, and their unhurried deliberation. Monroe, for example, was initially opposed to a strongly centralized federal government. Like Jefferson, he believed that power should be left as much as possible in the hands of the people and their local governments.

Yet during his two terms as President five new states were added to the Union, the long shadow of civil war was cast by the addition of Missouri as a slave-holding state, and the extraordinary expansion of the country, its prosperity, and its sectional rivalries led him to the opinion that a more centralized government was desirable. Though his viewpoint about this fundamental matter had changed his reputation did not suffer; no one would accuse James Monroe of perfidy or waywardness, for Monroe, like Washington, had earned a reputation as a thoroughly honorable and respectable man. As his friend Thomas Jefferson wrote of him, he was a man "whose soul might be turned wrong side outward without discovering a blemish to the world."[40]

Both Guardians, Washington and Monroe, were keenly sensitive to matters of protocol. Monroe shared the "republican" sentiments of the unassuming Rational Jefferson, but understood far better than Jefferson the importance of custom and tradition. Monroe was appointed the United States' Minister to England in 1803. Thereupon he sailed to London to represent the new government at the English court. Soon after his arrival he attended a formal court dinner with other foreign diplomats only to find himself seated at the table in a quite lowly position. Monroe became greatly angered, almost speechless about the implied insult. "James Monroe doesn't care where he eats his dinner," he later declared. "But to find the American minister put at the bottom of the table between two little principalities no bigger than my farm in Albemarle made me mad."[41] Monroe's comment is a nice juxtaposition of the Rational Jefferson's egalitarian influence, "James Monroe doesn't care where he eats his dinner," and the Guardian Monroe's natural sensitivity to matters of protocol, to the proper placement of "the American minister."

Monroe's indignation was not assuaged until the powerful Russian minister, who sitting in a highly placed position near the head of the table, caught Monroe's eye and offered a toast to the President of the United States. It's just as well the Russian was so considerate. Monroe did have something of a temper and could be rather easily aroused to indignation. Indeed he and Alexander Hamilton came within a hair's

40 Quoted in *The American Presidents*, 50.
41 *The Life of James Monroe*, 286, quoted in *Presidential Anecdotes*, 50.

breath of fighting a duel when the angry Hamilton accused him—unwarrantedly and, for a Monitor, nearly unforgivably—of lying. Only the intercession of a third party prevented Monroe from offering a challenge that might have ended in the death of one or both men.

It was of course inevitable that people would compare Monroe with his four presidential predecessors. Perhaps partly because he simply was not an extraordinary man, or perhaps simply because he was being compared with an extraordinary group, James Monroe did not seem to register very favorably. His contemporaries saw him as plain and modest, a decent and sincere person who was free of any guile or insincerity. He was admirable in these respects, but to most observers he was still a rather dull, conventional man, slow and unoriginal and lacking in polish. His conservative sagacity, his sensible prudence, was quite undramatic, as is so often the case with the strengths of the Guardians, and its value to the country was little recognized or appreciated.

It may be surprising to some that Monroe was such a close friend of Thomas Jefferson and James Madison since he was in so many respects so different from them. Jefferson's wide-ranging, restless, and astonishing Rational intellect provided a constant spark for their association, while Madison's more carefully disciplined and scholarly Rational manner kept their discourses on track. Monroe the Guardian lawyer became the rock-ribbed stabilizing influence for the other two. Slower in conceptual thought, less facile in formulating principles, he was nevertheless solid in his thinking and persistent in his views, a man who could provide a grounding realism that the Rationals left to their own devices might frequently have lacked.

Jefferson and Madison were rather like the fictional heroes, Mycroft and Sherlock Holmes. Monroe then served as Dr. Watson: a less scintillating, but utterly dependable man without whom the others might have fallen victim to the vagaries of their own flashing intellects. But the comparison breaks down in that each of the three assumed the preeminent position in the nation's history; none was locked into an unchanging public role. Jefferson was the oldest of the three, Madison eight years younger, Monroe the youngest by seven years. Each took his turn as President, in succession by age, oldest to youngest. Throughout their successive presidencies each provided support for the others.

Monroe may have achieved the presidency in part because of his long and faithful association with people such as Jefferson and Madison. But, typical Guardian, he also earned the position by virtue of his own earnest hard work and his diligent commitment to public service. Over the years following Valley Forge he studied law at William and Mary, was elected to the Virginia Assembly, to the Continental Congress, then was again elected to the Virginia Assembly, then to the new United States Senate. He was appointed by President Washington as Minister to France and to England, then elected Governor of Virginia. Later sent by President Jefferson on a mission to France, he returned and was elected again to the Virginia Assembly, then again elected Governor of Virginia. He resigned the governorship to become President Madison's Secretary of State, and subsequently had added to his duties those of the Secretary of War as well. All this service was provided, all these positions filled by one man in the course of only three decades.

Many Guardian Presidents have "worked their way up through the ranks" in this way. Guardians very often affiliate themselves with some institution while young and work their way up the hierarchy. In Monroe's case four successive Presidents found constant and essential work for him to do until he became President himself almost as a function of increasing seniority. As is often true of Guardians, he did not need flair or dash. Instead he stood out as a persistent model of loyalty, probity and patience. To borrow from the brokerage firm commercial so widely-seen in the late 1980s, the Guardians often seem to come to the presidency "the old-fashioned way; they earn it!" Monroe's determination to make the best use of his personal resources served him well, even when those Guardian resources might not have been as impressive, and certainly not as flashy, as those of many of the people around him.

Monroe was pleased to have come to the presidency but he was still imbued with Jefferson's "republican" sentiment. The office was what was important, after all, and the man who held it was merely its custodian. Thus a European diplomat visiting the White House during Monroe's presidency discovered a man in a side room sitting at a desk writing in old and sloppy clothing, an ink-stained vest, and a tired pair of slippers. The diplomat, accustomed to European ways, was appalled that such a dishevelled clerk should be found in the White House; he was even more appalled to discover later that the "dishevelled clerk" was President Monroe! Again the influence of Thomas Jefferson may have been at work here, for Jefferson was almost notorious for the informality of his appearance, even as President. Guardians usually have sufficient concern for the badges of office (even clothing) that they would not want to take a chance on being discovered in such attire.

Elizabeth Kortright Monroe presented quite a different appearance than did her unobtrusive, unbending, and unostentatious husband. She was a strikingly beautiful woman who looked much younger than her years. Her easy youthful beauty even caused offense to certain envious Washingtonians; some people are readily offended when they don't wish to admit envy. She was as self-contained as her husband but more regal, elegant, and reserved in manner. She was also a rather independent woman, not ready to bow to the expectations about the role of a President's wife. She had been plagued with illness for many years and was concerned about her health. She was also determined to maintain her own privacy and her freedom of movement. She went out of her way therefore to avoid the extremely busy social life of her predecessors. There would be no political fence-mending by Elizabeth Monroe in the exuberant Dolley Madison style, no effort to court the favor of the public and politicians for her husband's sake.[42]

James's own reticence coupled with Elizabeth's adamant refusal to "fit in" properly did nothing to help his presidency. In different times his lack of fire and his wife's refusal to play Washington's social games might have been fatal to his ambitions. But Monroe was popular with the respected old guard and as one of Monroe's contemporaries observed, this quiet, good and friendly man "had the zealous support of nobody, and he was exempt from the hostility of everybody."[43] Furthermore, times were good, the Federalists, his political opposition, was withering away for lack of a common cause and for eight years the country was prosperous and at peace. When Monroe ran for his second term he was unopposed. One elector cast his vote for John Quincy

---

42 Relatively little is known about Elizabeth Monroe. Her independent turn of mind is clear, but whether she was an Artisan or a Rational is not. Her illness, which persisted for many years, had an effect on her performance as a presidential wife, but the amount of influence on her behavior is impossible to determine.

43 Rufus King, quoted in *Presidential Campaigns*, 30.

Adams; the others all voted for Monroe. James Monroe survived nicely as President for two quiet terms and missed by that one electoral vote being the second man (the first being George Washington) to be elected unanimously to the presidency.

Although the nation continued to prosper, Monroe like his presidential predecessors, chose not to run for a third term. He had conducted his administration in the same fashion that he conducted his life: it was solid, honorable, responsible, courageous when necessary, filled with significant events but still rather quiet overall. His administration was conducted honorably and he could leave it behind with dignity.

The presidency was a place of honor and service for Monroe as it had been for his four predecessors. It was a place for public service, not an opportunity for self-aggrandizement. The office of President did not pay well; Washington did well financially because of his and his wife's property. Adams and Madison did less well, and Jefferson had run up heavy debts in the service of his country which plagued him for the rest of his life. Monroe too had contracted numerous debts over the years and the presidency did nothing to help him reduce them. After leaving office he was eventually forced to sell his home in order to meet his obligations. James Monroe, fifth President of the United States, died quietly a few years later in New York in the home of his son-in-law, little more than an impoverished and neglected patriot.

Bibliography

Adams, J. Q. 1850   *The Lives of James Madison and James Monroe*
Ammon, H 1971   *James Monroe: the Quest for National Identity*
Bond, B 1907   *The Monroe Mission to France, 1794-1796*
Cresson, W 1946   *James Monroe*
Cullum, G 1870   *In Memory of Colonel James Monroe*
Duval, M 1982   *James Monroe: An Appreciation*
Gilman, D 1911   *James Monroe*
Noonan, J 1977   *The Antelope: The Ordeal of Recaptured Africans*
Morgan, G 1921   *The Life of James Monroe*
Wilmerding, L 1960   *James Monroe, Public Claimant*

William Henry Harrison

"Tippecanoe..."

Monitor
Born: February 9, 1793
Died: April 4, 1841
Presidency: 1841

At age sixty-eight William Henry Harrison was the oldest man ever to become President, a distinction he didn't lose until the election of Ronald Reagan at age sixty-nine. Harrison still holds the dubious distinction of having had the shortest presidency on record: just one month.

His election to the presidency was the culmination of a long career of military and civil service, but his presidential campaign also included a great deal of judicious political nonsense. During the presidential campaign of 1840 Harrison was portrayed as a humble farmer raised in a log cabin who climbed to success through his own industry to become a famous general as well as a politician. He was thus offered to the voters as a latter-day Andy Jackson, a plain, honest man of the people and a military hero of the same stripe as the popular Jackson.

The association of the stolid, Monitor Guardian Harrison with the hell-for-leather Artisan Andy Jackson was a rather foolish one except that it seemed to work well with a populace that did not have an opportunity to see Harrison up close. Harrison's appeal to "the plain man" in the campaign was an important factor in his defeat of the more aristocratic Martin Van Buren. In fact it was crucial, for neither he nor his party offered much else in the way of a campaign except this image and considerable hoopla.

Though it was effective against Van Buren, the populist imagery was quite false. Harrison was plain enough, though perhaps only in terms of his talents, and he was a general, though with two exceptions an undistinguished one. He grew up in a well-to-do family, studied medicine for a while, but at his father's behest quit to join the army. He was an educated man of moderate wealth who lived as a country gentleman on his 2000 acre property near Cincinnati, Ohio. He had been commissioned an officer in the military, he was in and out of the army a couple of times, appointed secretary of the Northwest Territory by President Adams, and elected briefly to office as a delegate from the Territory. He was then appointed Governor to the new Indiana Territory, appointed to fill a vacancy in Congress (and lost a re-election campaign), was elected to the U. S. Senate, and then appointed Minister to Colombia. Finally, prior to campaigning for the presidency, Harrison served for about seven years in the undistinguished position of Hamilton County Clerk for the court of common pleas. As he moved from position to position, Harrison was willing to settle for whatever office was available if he couldn't have the office in which he was currently interested. With a few exceptions, that is, the history of the purportedly hell-for-leather Harrison showed him to be an undistinguished career bureaucrat, reliable but mundane.

Perhaps he was unfair to himself in his willingness to settle for whatever office was available. He had shown some genuine administrative talent and responsibility as Governor of the Indiana Territory. In this office he provided the Indians of the Territory medical assistance including inoculation against smallpox, offered them significant educational opportunities, and forbade the sale of liquor to the tribes. His policies were constructive enough that he was able to negotiate a treaty with the Indians in the area which gave large tracts of territory to white settlers there. In short he was an able administrator who showed some of the best of the Guardian's talents while he was Governor of the Territory.

None of this ensured that he would be a likeable person. Unlike his Guardian predecessor James Monroe, whether Harrison's star happened to be rising or setting he managed to be somewhat officious. As Guardians usually are, he was acutely aware of social position and desirous of improving his own place in the political hierarchy. His manner was the manner of career bureaucrats everywhere, and in general he managed to show the less pleasant side of the Guardian style.

Nonetheless, as General Harrison he had achieved a military victory against the incendiary Indian chief Tecumseh at the Tippecanoe River in 1811. Though the battle was relatively small, only seven or eight hundred combatants participating on each side, its consequences were considered quite important. Then in the War of 1812 he managed a victory against a mixed force of British and Indians. These two victories eventually propelled Harrison into the public eye and eventually helped make him a likely presidential candidate. The battle at the Tippecanoe River was famous and was the subject of considerable ballyhoo by his political backers. The presence of John Tyler as Harrison's vice-presidential running mate in the 1840 presidential campaign gave rise to the catchy, though hardly meaningful election slogan, "Tippecanoe and Tyler too." The slogan is one of the few memorable events in Harrison's political career.

William Harrison had married Anna Symmes in 1775. She was a cheerful, vigorous woman, a pleasant hostess, a conscientious schoolteacher, and an able partner to Harrison in the development of their Ohio farm. Probably a Conservator Guardian, she was a churchgoing woman who enjoyed inviting the entire church congregation to dine right after services on Sunday mornings. Anna Symmes Harrison warmly supported her husband's ambitions and was proud of his accomplishments, though she was doubtful about the wisdom of his seeking the presidency. William was often away vigorously pursuing his uneven career in the world of politics, but apparently the Harrison's marriage was a satisfying one anyway.

Harrison was a bluff and honest man in spite of his tendency to pretentiousness. It was not difficult to portray him as the possessor of rugged strength and heroic firmness, but public relations campaigns can do only so much. The public imagination was not set aflame by what it saw in Harrison and at election time people weren't so much voting for him as finding that they could find no good reason for voting against him. This was in part due to his campaign managers' efforts, for they had instructed Harrison to do and say as little as possible during the campaign. It was a task in which he succeeded admirably. It was also important to his campaign that he do so. Though honest and respectable, and though he had his moment of administrative worthiness in Indiana, he was also a professional political office-holder. As with many such professionals, his chief talent seemed to be to follow directions and to avoid taking stands that could damage his public image.[44]

Tragically, one of Harrison's few failures to follow directions proved to be fatal. After he won the election of 1840 Harrison insisted on writing his own inaugural address. The speech was a very long and rambling affair, and Daniel Webster (one of the movers and shakers of Harrison's party) labored for many hours to make the speech more presentable. But the speech meandered for almost two hours and dwelt at length on Roman history and Roman proconsuls. (There seemed to be many of these even though Webster had in his editing "already killed a dozen Roman consuls dead as smelts.") Inauguration day in January of 1841 was very cold and rainy, but the sixty-seven year old Harrison rode bare-headed on a splendid white horse to his inauguration and gave his two-hour speech anyway. He came down with a cold a few days later and the cold quickly developed into pneumonia.

Harrison died on April 4, 1841, victim of pneumonia, hepatitis, and septicemia. He might have survived the pneumonia if it had not been complicated by the hepatitis and septicemia, which were probably acquired through the questionable ministrations of his physicians. (Among other measures, these gentlemen insisted on prescribing brandy and opium to him and on feeding him emetics and cathartics in spite of his severe colitis and raging diarrhea.) The energetic, gracious, and charming Anna Harrison, who appears to have been by and large as undistinguished as her husband, outlived him by some twenty years. She died in 1864 at the age of eighty-nine.

---

44 Nonetheless, in spite of his political involvements Harrison never bothered to cast a vote until he was nominated for the presidency. Rather atypically for a Monitor, he even bragged about the omission. Perhaps the failure to vote simply didn't seem very important to him. It wasn't, after all, part of his job description.

William Henry Harrison, like George Washington (and of course James Monroe), was a Monitor Guardian through and through. But the differences between the Monitor Washington and the Monitor Harrison are marvelous to behold: one stately and dignified, the other status-seeking and self-important; one caring deeply about his country, the other caring primarily about his own career; one wise, the other ambitious; one thoughtfully deliberate, the other a party professional who knew only how to follow directions; one who will be remembered as long as the United States exists, the other who will be vaguely remembered only because of a catchy campaign slogan.

Of course there are also parallels: both showed the stolid, persistent, hard-working style of the Monitor. Both were known to be decent, honest, and straightforward men. Both were sensitive to matters of personal reputation and social position. Both married Guardians who were pleasant, cheerful, and gracious women whose personal warmth helped to sustain happy marriages. Had he lived, William Henry Harrison might have shown himself to be made of more remarkable stuff than his earlier career demonstrated, but it must be said that there appears to be little likelihood of such a turnabout. He seems destined always to have been an honest, ambitious, manageable mediocrity.

Perhaps one might best guess at what sort of President Harrison would have been by noting that while as a military officer he was recognized for his ability to command decisively, which Monitors do well, while having little idea of what his commands were finally supposed to accomplish. Again Harrison is unexceptional in this. Except in matters of routine or logistics, this failure to be clear about desired outcomes is the weakness most likely to be displayed by the Monitor in command. One thing is certain, however: for the student of temperament there is in the comparison of Harrison with Washington an excellent example of the diversity to be found among people who share the same temperament.

Bibliography

Burr, S 1840   *The Life and Times of William Henry Harrison*
Cleaves, S 1939   *Old Tippecanoe: William Henry Harrison and his Times*
Goebel, D 1974   *William Henry Harrison*: a *Political Biography*

John Tyler

"...and Tyler too"

Monitor
Born: March 29, 1790
Died: January 18,1862
Presidency: 1841-1845

John Tyler seemed to be a trustworthy party man, solid, dependable, honest, even if he was also obstinate and crusty at times. He was selected as William Henry Harrison's vice-presidential running mate in the campaign of 1840 because he was a good compromise candidate. Harrison was a Northerner whose appeal was largely in the North, while Tyler was a Southerner who favored states' rights and who might attract the Southern vote. Harrison and Tyler, "Tippecanoe and Tyler too," were both Monitors and offered the party bosses a pairing of reasonably attractive, predictable, and manageable candidates. At least the bosses hoped so; Tyler was more of a question mark than they could be quite comfortable with. But after all he was only slated for the vice-presidency; he would get votes for Harrison and he would not be a problem in the lesser office.

Harrison and Tyler did win the election of 1840, but Harrison died only a month later. His death was a powerful shock to the nation, for no President had died in office before. It was especially upsetting since no procedure had yet been established to determine presidential succession in the event of the President's death or disability. The party politicians around him had been trying to manage Tyler ever since Harrison had fallen ill, and Tyler complied reasonably well during Harrison's illness. But when Harrison died no one was quite sure what to do next. No one, that is, except the tall, slender John Tyler. Without regard to the wishes of his political managers he boldly assumed for himself all the powers of the presidency just as if he had been elected to the office. Handed an official document to sign, Tyler noted that the words "Acting President" had been written below the space for his signature. He picked up his pen, obliterated the word "Acting" with a bold stroke and signed his name to the document. That was that; John Tyler was the President of the United States.

The death of President Harrison followed immediately by Vice-President Tyler's assumption of the office of the President was a shock to the party politicians. They had not expected Harrison to die, of course. They had also hoped that Tyler would under any circumstances remain a good party man. They knew that he could be stubborn, but they hadn't imagined that he would be so completely unmanageable. To some degree they had judged their man rightly; Tyler the Monitor was certainly not given to precipitous action. As with any Guardian, whether Monitor or Conservator, he knew his place in the party hierarchy and he certainly had respect for the voice of authority. If Harrison's death had been sudden his actions would probably have been determined by the wishes of his political mentors and bosses.

But Tyler had already had a month to think about what would happen if Harrison's illness should end in death; his action when the President died was far from off-the-cuff or the result of a simple impulse to act. His decision was rooted in prolonged worry over what he should do if Harrison did not recover. He had had a month to work out the rightness of his conclusions and, as a friend of his once commented, "When he thinks he is right he is obstinate as a bull, and no power on earth can move him."[45]

The cynical party leaders had confused Tyler's consistent and cooperative manner with an absence of backbone. Now the party's power brokers discovered that the new President was not merely a dependable party hack. John Tyler's dependability and forthright honesty were a two-edged sword which was now swinging the other way. The power brokers really should have known better.

After all, Tyler was opposed to almost everything Harrison advocated. In spite of his bureaucratic leanings he was also a man who stood staunchly by his own moral principles. Guardians acting vigorously from their sense of moral rightness (and moral indignation) can be resolute to the point of rigidity, and Tyler was a classic example of this sort of Monitor intransigence. Earlier in his career, after winning a seat in the United States Senate, for instance, he was given firm instructions by his own state Democratic party bosses to support a resolution that he considered unconstitutional. Rather than give such support he resigned the Senate, abandoned his own political party and joined the Whig party. In fact his unwillingness to compromise alienated him more and more from the political mainstream, and he might well never have survived politically if his states' rights leanings hadn't made him an attractive vice-presidential candidate.

Even though he was not pleasing to most party politicians, he had some popularity with the voters. He became so well recognized as a man who acted from his own moral principles rather than from what was expeditious that he was given the nickname "Honest John" Tyler. And yet, so severe was his party's disenchantment with him after he assumed the presidency, that it completely abandoned him. Tyler was for the remainder of his term known as "the President without a party."

In spite of the serious miscalculations of his party's politicians, John Tyler was never a mystery. He favored a very strict interpretation of the Constitution. He insisted adamantly that the powers of the federal government should be severely restricted so that only to those clearly

---

45 Quoted in *The American Presidents*, 23.

given in the Constitution were permitted it. He had never made any effort to hide this simple, straightforward but extreme conservatism, but then Guardians have great difficulty trying to hide their point of view anyway. For them it's not "just a point of view" after all, and Tyler was usually quite outspoken about his. At his best he was patient, calm and dignified, but he could often be quite tactless in his speech and often downright offensive in his manner.

For a time the impact of his blunt and even harsh manner was softened by the presence of his wife, Letitia Christian Tyler. But this quiet and retiring, pleasant and courteous Guardian had a stroke in 1838 that left her virtually bedridden. She died in 1842, about a year after her husband assumed the presidency, the first woman to die while her husband was President. Tyler felt her loss terribly and there were many who worried that he would never recover from the blow. Yet only eighteen months later the country was astonished to witness the marriage of the widower President John Tyler and Miss Julia Gardiner, a popular and vivacious beauty known as "the Rose of Long Island."

Julia Gardiner Tyler was an Artisan of great charm and exuberance who was thirty years younger than her new husband. Nonetheless the energetic and impetuous Julia Tyler was remarkably happy with him. She was his most ardent supporter and she saw him as a great man who was gifted with unending statesmanlike wisdom and presence. She also gloried in the role of First Lady, conducting herself in an almost regal fashion during her time in the White House and generally enjoying herself immensely. Though some considered her rather too regal (some newspapers rather nastily dubbed her "Lady Presidentess"), all agreed that she was a charming hostess of irresistible good cheer. Tyler held her in great affection and seemed entranced by her almost magical buoyancy. He never ceased to enjoy the unabashed pleasure his "Fairy Girl" took in her role.

Despite Julia Tyler's enthusiastic attempts to help him on the social front John Tyler's administration was a very difficult one and rather unproductive. To be sure, his problems arose partly because of his tendency to alienate everyone in sight through his own unbending behavior. Not only did he refuse to sponsor actions that seemed illegal to him, but this Monitor had no hesitation vetoing Congressional bills, one right after the other, if they did not fit his ideas of Constitutionality.

Popularity mattered not at all; when he vetoed bills calling for the establishment of a new United States Bank and when he also vetoed a bill calling for higher tariffs, both very popular pieces of legislation, outraged mobs surged through the streets outside the White House, screaming, hurling stones, and burning Tyler in effigy. His response was to arm the While House staff and calmly await the departure of the crowds.

Though he was a very strict conservative in the matter of federal power, and though he was very literal and stringent in his interpretation of the Constitution, he was still an ardent expansionist. He thought that the United States should annex Texas (or "re-annex" it; there was some claim that it was once part of the United States), though, as Thomas Jefferson had discovered, the Constitution made no provision for such an action. The problem he faced was that he wanted Texas admitted as a slave state, and the North would not permit such an action. There was little that could generate more hatred more quickly than the slavery issue, and Tyler's support for the Texas-slave state idea was politically deadly and personally dangerous.

It was not merely Tyler's actions that made his administration so troubled. The times were becoming increasingly troubled as well, and chief among the Tyler's difficulties was exactly this issue of slavery. The practice was being savagely attacked by the North and ardently and angrily defended by the South. The argument was raging so violently that murder was not uncommon. It had also become inextricably intertwined with the question of what the inherent rights of the states were as against the constitutional powers of the federal government. Either issue without the other might, just barely, have been manageable. But the two intertwined were impossible and the horrors of Civil War were less than twenty years away. In spite of his own convictions Tyler worked persistently to help the two factions reach some accommodation with one another. But Monitors are rarely good negotiators; their strengths lie elsewhere. The issue was also a most difficult one, and Tyler failed completely to remove the growing malignancy.

Tyler the Monitor was far from the best man for the job. The political climate called for a man of a very different stamp. Either a Rational with a more strategic, long-term vision, or someone with the Idealist's diplomatic leadership style, or even (at least for temporary respite) a cool, easy-going Artisan would have been more appropriate. Tyler's efforts betrayed his outspoken and stubborn style, his obstinacy, and his complete unwillingness to accommodate. His efforts consisted too much of authoritarian demands, and he finally became both isolated and detested. When time came for the presidential campaign of 1844 his party declined to nominate him. The Whig's nomination went instead to another Monitor, James K. Polk.

Still, Tyler was unstinting in his efforts to subdue the terrible animosity gradually consuming the country. After leaving office he continued his work to reconcile the Northern and Southern factions, and even organized and led a Peace Convention of border states. But it was no use; the dispute between North and South was becoming more bitter and more bloody and it seemed that nothing could stop it.

When most of the Southern states finally seceded in 1861 he accepted political office with the newborn Confederate States of America. John Tyler was still a Southerner at heart, and he and Julia moved to Richmond, Virginia so he could take up his new duties. But in 1862, before he could participate actively in the Confederate government, he died of a stroke.

Two years later, though the war was still being fiercely fought (it was then 1864) Julia Tyler moved from the Virginia to New York. There she continued to work politically for the Southern cause, amidst extreme controversy and, in that bastion of Northern sentiment, even some danger to herself. Julia Tyler lived until 1889, eventually moving back to Richmond, Virginia. There, twenty-seven years after her obstinate husband passed away, and in the same hotel which witnessed his death, the vivacious "Rose of Long Island" passed away.

Bibliography

Abell, A 1843	*Life of John Tyler, President of the United States*
Chidsey, D 1978	*And Tyler Too*
Gordon, A 1916	*Monument to John Tyler*
Lambert, O 1936	*Presidential Politics in the United States, 1841-1844*
Merk, F 1971	*Fruits of Propaganda in the Tyler Administration*
Moran, R 1954	*A Whig Embattled: The Presidency under John Tyler*
Fraser, H 1936	*Democracy in the Making: The Jackson-Tyler Era*
Seager, R 1963	*And Tyler too: A Biography of John and Julia Gardiner Tyler*

James Knox Polk

The marriage of duty and ambition

Monitor
Born: November 2, 1795
Died: June 15, 1849
Presidency: 1845-1849

The Texan Sam Houston once remarked of James Polk that the only thing wrong with him was that he drank too much water.[46]

Houston's caricature of Polk was rather accurate. Both James Knox Polk, the stiff, stern Methodist and his wife Sarah, the strict Presbyterian, were remarkably upright and gave very little indication that they were interested in any of life's little amusements. They were

---

46 *The American Presidents*, 102.

also incredibly conscientious. Indeed, they were probably the most hard-working couple ever to occupy the White House. They were invariably resentful of any time lost from their duties and worked hard to avoid being pulled away from their work. When state occasions demanded that they attend formal events they would often appear briefly and then make up for the "lost" time by disappearing as soon as possible to return to their duties, continuing to work until long after their guests had left. So conscientious were James and Sarah Polk about their self-imposed schedule that during the entire four years of Polk's presidency the couple spent a total of only three days away from the White House. James and Sarah Polk are magnificent examples of the Monitor tendency to schedule their procedures and stick to their schedules no matter what.

The hard-working President could lay claim to few friends and seemed to have little interest in establishing or maintaining friendships. In fact his stoic manner was tinged with a certain bitter character. He apparently felt that he had started life at a social disadvantage (though his circumstances were not especially difficult), and he was angry about that and resolute about rising to the top. Those who might want to be friendly with him found it very difficult because of his cold and forbidding demeanor and his lack of humor and warmth. However, though the seclusive Polk did not seek the company of others, flatly and plainly preferring to spend his time alone, he did mix when it was important to do so. He had chosen politics as his career, and since politics was his choice, he followed its course and met its demands, social and otherwise, diligently and patiently. But he hardly did so with charm or flair. In fact he had been elected Governor of Tennessee in 1839 but his stiffness and that of his wife cost him so much popularity that he failed to be re-elected in 1841 and failed again in 1843.

Though he would never be described as either charming or brilliant, Polk was still an effective, ambitious, enormously hard-working Democratic party loyalist. He was studiously precise and careful in his speech and actions, and he made it a point to acquire a huge storehouse of information about topics relevant to his political career. It was typical of his approach that he managed to have more facts at hand about anything being discussed than did anyone else involved in the discussion. In this uninspired but determined way he drove himself throughout his life, studying and working, studying and working. The

Rational John Quincy Adams, hardly a model of grace and charm himself, once wrote of Polk as speaker that

> He has no wit, no literature, no point of argument, no gracefulness of delivery, no philosophy, no pathos, no felicitous impromptus; nothing that can constitute an orator, but confidence, fluency, and labor.[47]

He captured Polk well: certainly confidence, but more especially, labor was the hallmark of James Polk, the industrious Monitor.

Polk had driven himself since he was a schoolboy. He studied harder and longer than anyone else, he avoided socializing, he showed no signs of imagination or human empathy. When he was eventually admitted to the bar he proved to be so assiduous that he soon had a reputation as an able lawyer and developed a solid clientele. Politically, as one might expect, Polk was a very good party man. He followed the orders of his party's leadership well and built up credit with them slowly and carefully over the years. He took on unpopular tasks and executed them diligently, even when they might seem to put him at a disadvantage. In this way he gradually obligated the party to him and thereby he made the most of his somewhat indifferent abilities. It was important that he do what he could to gain the party's indebtedness, since he was considered at best an uninspiring candidate, little more than a career politician of unquestioned loyalty and great persistence.

Uninspiring or not, Polk's diligent loyalty to his party (including his loyalty to the still influential Andy Jackson) paid off. In 1844 the party's presidential nominating convention was still deadlocked after eight ballots. John Tyler, the incumbent, had been abandoned and neither of the alternative candidates, one of whom was ex-President Martin Van Buren, could prevail. The party needed a compromise candidate and Polk, almost by accident and to everyone's surprise, was selected. So unlikely a candidate was he that when the news of his selection was transmitted over Samuel Morse's new invention, the telegraph, the recipient of the message decided that there must be something wrong with the machine. But Polk and the Democrats won the following national election. The margin of victory was extremely small, however, and due as much to the dissent within the opposition Whig party as to the Democrats' strength or Polk's appeal.

---

47 Quoted in *The American Presidents*, 102.

The United States in those days, still confined to the eastern part of the continent, could look beyond its western borders and see enormous stretches of land waiting to be settled or to be brought under the flag of the United States. The Monitor James Polk was an especially ardent advocate of the popular idea that it was the United States' "manifest destiny" to control all of the North American continent. Keeping in mind George Washington's frontier land purchases, and recalling that Guardians have a powerful hunger for ownership, it should not be difficult to imagine the impact on this patriotic Monitor of the idea that his country's destiny was to "own" an entire continent. "manifest destiny" was popular in his party, and in fact his stand for the annexation of Texas helped him get elected, as did his loyalty to Andy Jackson, who was also eager for the acquisition.

As usual Polk's overwhelming determination and sheer hard work made him as good as his ambitions. The way having been smoothed to some degree by his Monitor predecessor John Tyler, Polk presided over the occupation of Texas, the "re-occupation" of Oregon, and the flagrantly expansionist war with Mexico, the outcome of which included the acquisition of what is now the southwestern United States, including California, Arizona, Colorado, Nevada, New Mexico, Utah, and part of Wyoming.[48] It apparently mattered little to Polk that he was (with justice) accused of starting the war with Mexico, for by the end of his term of office the United States encompassed half again as much of the continent as it had on the day he was elected.

The United States accrued more territory during Polk's presidency than during the tenure of any other President in American history. True to his Monitor character and humorless personal style, Polk was not graceful in bringing all this about. After a bit of warlike drum-banging ("54° 40' or fight!") Polk backed down and negotiated peacefully with Great Britain for the Oregon Territory. The Mexican operation, as was noted even at the time, was little more than theft. Legitimized theft, of course; but it brought no honor to the United States or its government.

Polk's successful expansionism carried a dreadful toxin. The addition of more territory to the Union meant that pro-slavery and anti-slavery forces had more to fight over. They had dangerously more to

---

48 Not every American approved of Polk's behavior. Young Lieutenant Ulysses Grant, who served in the Mexican War, called it "the most unjust ever waged by a stronger against a weaker nation," and Abraham Lincoln opposed it vigorously during his one term in Congress.

gain or to lose, for neither faction could allow the other the political upper hand that control of the extensive new territories would ensure. Polk himself was a slave owner and had only a limited sense of the incredible emotional significance of the issue.

Concrete expansion he could understand; Manifest Destiny, the physical expansion of the United States was a clear-cut matter to him. But he could not see the significance of what he dismissively labelled the "abstract question" of slavery, and he could not predict that his remarkable success in territorial acquisition would promote a terrible intensification of the dispute over slavery. There should be no problem, he thought, for there was no likelihood that any territories acquired from Mexico would ever support slavery. Therefore, he proclaimed, those who concerned themselves with the matter were "not only mischievous but wicked."

Some Monitors, especially the more reclusive of them, often show little indication of warmth or sympathy, and Polk was clearly no exception. He seemed almost totally unable to enjoy most people and disregarded most of the pleasant pastimes that life offers. Apparently he didn't even miss them, nor did he have any compunctions about denying them to others. During the four years James and Sarah Polk occupied the White House, for instance, dancing disappeared, alcohol was forbidden, and card-playing was banished from the place by the humorless and upright couple.

Sarah Childress Polk, nine years younger than her husband, was a striking, handsome woman. She was an ambitious one as well; when James proposed to her she made her acceptance conditional on his agreement to run for political office. He agreed and was successful in his bid for elective office. Sarah and James then married and were ever after political partners as well as husband and wife. Sarah Polk had a persistent and significant influence on James's political career. Certainly she was often his eyes and ears in the political world and apparently his trusted advisor as well. Well-educated and well-read, Sarah Polk was well-respected as First Lady for her perceptiveness and her determination. Sarah, like James, was unwaveringly industrious. Once she had prompted James's decision to pursue a political career she aligned her own aspirations with his cold ambition and sense of duty. And, like him, she carried through with unswerving resolution.

Sarah Polk was an interesting study in contrasts. When she was a young woman others considered her to be rather high-spirited and more independent than a lady ought to be. Later she reversed course and became quite religious in the conventional sense. The Sabbath, for example, she came to see as holy, and business was not to be conducted on that day. It was apparently also at her instigation that so many of life's most pleasant vices were excluded from the White House. Throughout her life she would defer publicly to her husband, even stating her own opinions with a preliminary "Mr. Polk believes...." Before long it was well understood that she might be stating her own strong and independent position as well as her husband's. Though she always presented herself as a respectful spouse and proper wife, she also made lifelong friendships with some of the most unconventional and outspoken, and therefore some of the most questionable, women of her time. But her leavening of the unconventional did not alter the fact that her life paralleled her husband's very closely. Though she was a capable and industrious hostess who could even manage to be reasonably pleasant during James's life, she fell back into her own grim seclusiveness after his death and died a determined recluse.

In spite of his accomplishments James Polk was not a popular President. Even those who knew him well couldn't warm to him; his cold and suspicious nature, his extreme isolation, and his laborious and demanding style could not win him friends or garner popular support. He exacerbated the problems his curt manner generated by eliminating much of the spoils system, the rewarding the party faithful with offices or other favors for which they might have no qualification except they had worked for the party. Like many others, Polk saw the system as wrong, even immoral, recognizing that it often rewarded partisan party activity, including political corruption and toadyism, with government office and power.

Andy Jackson had fostered the system and Van Buren, Harrison, and Taylor had allowed it to persist. Its elimination meant that Polk's own party could not provide some of the political patronage it was expected to. Polk made himself especially unpopular by eliminating, if not all spoilsmanship, at least its worst excesses. He doubtless would have eliminated every vestige of the practice if he could have; he was a Monitor's Monitor, even more rigidly upright than his Guardian predecessors had been. Popularity be hanged; what was *right* was at issue. Popularity had never been one of Polk's goals anyway. Since he was interested in only one term as President he paid it no heed after he reached office. In spite of his lack of popularity, and unlike most Presidents, he could find satisfaction in having accomplished most of the goals he had in mind when he assumed the presidency. This was no trivial accomplishment, by the way, for Polk had so many goals that he was known as "the short man with the long program."

But the personal cost of success was high. Ambition and duty left no time for taking care of one's self; there was work to be done after all, and "Polk the Plodder," the stolid Monitor, would personally see to its doing, despite any self-damaging consequences. The Monitor had his duty to attend to, even if, as seemed to be the case with Polk, he hated being the President. Polk himself once declared about the office that "I have had enough of it, Heaven knows! I have had all the honor there is in the place and...responsibilities enough to kill any man."[49] Still there could be no appeal from the demands of duty and ambition, nor would such appeal be sought even at the cost of life itself.

When he left the White House Polk had aged terribly. Exhausted, suffering great pain from chronic diarrhea, and feverishly struggling for breath, he died on June 15, 1849, less than fifteen weeks after leaving the presidency. At the end he said to his wife, his life's love and his life's partner, "I love you Sarah, for all eternity, I love you."[50]

He was only fifty-three.

Bibliography

Bergeron, P 1987	*The Presidency of James K. Polk*
Bowers, C 1954	*Making Democracy a Reality; Jefferson, Jackson, and Polk*
Chase, L 1850	*History of the Polk Administration*
Jenkins, J 1850	*James Knox Polk*
McCormac, E 1922	*James K. Polk, a Political Biography*
McCoy, C 1960	*Polk and the Presidency*
Mitchell, S	*Four Legends about President Polk*
Morrel, M 1949	*"Young Hickory," the Life and Times of President James K. Polk*
Nelson, A 1988	*Secret Agents: President Polk and the Search for Peace with Mexico*
Sellers, C 1957	*James K. Polk, Jacksonian, 1795-1843*
Sellers, C 1966	*James K. Polk, Continentalist, 1843-1846*

---

49 *The Presidency*, 81. It must be confessed that Guardians are given to complaining, sometimes frequently and vigorously, of their burdens. But they secretly covet burdens, and some of them manage to get themselves overburdened, the weight of their burdens taken as the measure of their value to others.

50 *World Almanac of Presidential Facts*, 57.

Andrew Johnson

The impeachment of decency

Monitor
Born: December 29, 1808
Died: July 31, 1875
Presidency: 1865-1869

Abraham Lincoln was re-elected President in 1864 in the midst of the Civil War. His running mate for the vice-presidency was the outspoken Andrew Johnson, selected because his ties with the South were likely to help Lincoln attract voters with Southern sympathies. Then, only six weeks after his second inauguration, Lincoln was assassinated. Andrew Johnson was suddenly President of the United States.

It was a tragic way to come to office and Andrew Johnson deserved better. He was an honorable and indomitable man of unquestionable moral integrity. And though he was an irascible man with little humor or patience, he fought tirelessly for the course of moderation in an era of violent and vengeful passions.

Johnson was raised in poverty and was totally illiterate until he was in his teens. The only United States President never to go to school, Johnson was apprenticed to a tailor in Raleigh, North Carolina. After some sort of scrape with the tailor when he was sixteen Johnson ran off and established his own tailor shop in Greenboro Tennessee. There he met Eliza McCardle, who was later to become his wife. The connection between Andrew and Eliza was apparently immediate. They sought each other out from the very beginning and marriage was only a matter of time.

Andrew Johnson was a capable man, of necessity self-educated, though with the able assistance of his future wife. He was energetic in everything he did and he worked to develop dynamic oratorical skills. In fact, though he had never attended school he sharpened his skills by participating in student debates at nearby colleges. Perhaps because of his impoverished and low-born beginnings, the Monitor Andrew Johnson had a profound thirst for recognition and an overpowering ambition to better himself. His unending drive for self-improvement—and of course for improving his position—began early. He tried to teach himself to read, he developed a persistent habit of digging out information to add to his supply of data at every opportunity, he even undertook a relentless study of grammar books. The energetic young Guardian quickly became recognized for his remarkable industry, his friendly, direct and open dealings with people, and his responsible, honest, and forthright manner.

When still a young man he was already a person of firm and outspoken convictions and it was not difficult for his friends and neighbors to persuade him that he ought to run for local political office. He did run for alderman, won the contest, and immediately and vigorously set to work to bring about worthwhile reforms in town affairs. In the next election he was the people's choice for mayor. Then came Tennessee's state legislature where the earnest Monitor was the first to reach his desk each day and the most diligent about searching out the facts about issues coming before the legislature. In this step-by-step fashion Andrew Johnson, by dint of his ambition, his hard work, and his reputation for energetic honesty, eventually became the most powerful politician in Tennessee. He also found a place in the United States House of Representatives, the Governorship of Tennessee, and the United States Senate.

Johnson welcomed the recognition he received as a legislator and he responded enthusiastically to the cheering crowds he encountered as a political speaker. But his memory of the unceasing poverty of his early life and his awareness of his relative lack of education were a source of constant embarrassment for him. He never forgot his own beginnings and he persistently went out of his way to identify himself with the working people, the small farmers and the poor of the country, and to represent himself as their spokesman. He always claimed fiercely (and some thought ostentatiously) that he was proud of being a tailor; until he went to Washington as a Congressman he continued to make his own clothes. Making his own clothes was economical for him, and Johnson was especially fierce in his Monitor's appreciation of resource management.

It was a good political move as well, for it helped him maintain his stance as the working man's advocate. Making his own clothing also has the resonance of a "poor but proud" stance which seemed very much a part of the man, a feisty pride which served in place of the dignity which could never be his through culture or wealth.

Andrew Johnson was indeed feisty. Perhaps in compensation for his own early lowly estate Johnson had a tendency to strike out scornfully against the more privileged. Privilege by itself was enough to make one a target of Johnson's invective; Some of his contemporaries in fact saw him merely as a mean, malicious man, rigid and dogmatic. He was quite closed to any reconsideration of his opinions, and his opinions were cast in unsophisticated good-bad, right-wrong terms. Writes one biographer, "Having gone through the agony of decision-making, Johnson's narrow mind snapped shut." Thus,

> He never acquired the breadth and suppleness of mind that formal training might have developed. Complex problems frustrated him, and he sought refuge from them in general rules to govern all situations.[51]

Johnson had "general rules" which applied to money as well as to politics. His rules were not legal codes but rather of handy maxims and standard operating procedures. Thus the general rule for money was that

---

51 *The Impeachment and Trial of Andrew Johnson,* 3.

it should never be wasted ("waste not, want not"), and that it should be spent, especially by others, only after a full, even tortured justification of the expenditure ("look after the pennies and the dollars will look after themselves"). He was tight-fisted even with federal money. He once voted against providing funds to repave the badly deteriorating streets of Washington on the grounds that to do so would be unconstitutional. The Monitor's orientation to the gathering and husbanding of resources becomes painfully obvious when carried to these remarkable lengths.

Whatever his shortcomings, Andrew Johnson's behavior exemplified the Monitor's orientation both to being accountable and to demanding accountability of others, as well as his tireless determination to elevate his status without sacrificing his sense of honesty and responsibility. His behavior also showed the Guardian's proclivity to preserve and protect the institutions and traditions of the past, and in Johnson's instance, fortunately, this included the United States itself. Granted that he was bitter about his own difficult path, and granted that he could be savage in his public reflections on those more privileged, still it seems almost beyond belief that a man of such outspoken integrity would have been accused of being a traitor and a drunkard, and that the Guardian Andrew Johnson would become the only American President ever to be impeached.

The unfair rumor that Johnson was a drunk, for instance, stemmed from a single painfully public incident. On the day of Lincoln's inauguration Johnson was not feeling well and wanted to avoid the inaugural ceremony altogether. If he missed the ceremony it might have been misunderstood by the public, however, and so he was encouraged to drink a little alcohol to ameliorate his discomfort. But Johnson rarely drank and the combination of illness and alcohol for a man unaccustomed to either led to his undeniable intoxication. Though this was the only reported instance of drunkenness in Johnson's career, in the hands of his unsavory political enemies it was enough to sully his reputation permanently.

The matter of his impeachment for traitorous activity is more complicated. Part of the explanation for its occurrence is to be found in the temper of the times. Johnson was a man who preached moderation at a moment in history when almost everywhere tempers had become inflamed, first over the issue of slavery, and later over the question of how the vanquished South should be treated. Before the war broke out Johnson, a Senator and then Governor of Tennessee, had worked exceptionally hard to prevent secession. He had stumped tirelessly in the South, campaigning against the widespread and popular calls for secession and for the far less popular course of moderation and conciliation.

That a Southern politician would take this politically risky course is noteworthy, especially since he was also putting his life at risk when he did so. But in spite of the risk Johnson went ahead anyway. He really thought he might help prevent secession and he bitterly denounced the few Southern aristocrats whom he held, with some justification, responsible for persuading the untutored mass of Southerners to accept secession.

His efforts in the 1850s to heal the frightful breach between North and South failed, of course, and the Civil War followed. Succeeding to the presidency after the death of Lincoln, Andrew Johnson was again a spokesman for moderation after the collapse of the Confederacy a few months later. This time he spoke out for moderate treatment of the defeated rebellious states, and as he had in the pre-war South, he was again speaking against powerful popular sentiment. Not only did many powerful people feel that the South deserved punishment, but others also realized that the prostrate South offered an opportunity for quick riches if one were willing to act quickly and ruthlessly. Many exploiters (the "carpetbaggers") did just that under the protection of the North's military occupation of the Southern states.

Johnson continued his tactless ways in the White House and of course did not fit in well with the relatively urbane Washington society. He was loudly and publicly intolerant of the corruption and the other scandals which were associated with the military occupation. No man for half-measures when angry, he attacked many of these opportunists with his usual energy and pugnacity. He declared these men, some of whom were in fact former allies, to be "bloodsuckers who have been fattening upon the country." Energetic Monitor that he was, he was rather naive about the subtle and devious maneuvering to be found in politics at the national level, and naturally preferred bluntness to subtlety. Because of this he was never able to be an effective or even a well-received leader in the nation's capital.

His forthright manner was not simple ignorance of course. His personal hero was the frontiersman Andy Jackson, to whom many compared him in later years. As Jackson sometimes did, he even carried with him, and on several occasions drew, a loaded revolver. Johnson probably would have used it if necessary, with regret but with effectiveness. His violent attacks on the widespread postwar villainy along with his pursuit of a policy of political moderation and fairness won him few friends and made him many enemies during those rancorous days.

Equally important in the matter of his impeachment, however, Johnson summarily dismissed his Secretary of War, Edwin M. Stanton.

Stanton, a holdover from Lincoln's cabinet, was collaborating with a group of congressmen (the "Radical Republicans") that promoted a viciously punitive and self-aggrandizing policy for the treatment of the Southern states. Stanton exercised a great deal of political power, and even Lincoln had to deal with him carefully, but Johnson chose to throw him out him anyway. The former Secretary of War had many political allies, a strong position in Washington, and a vengeful nature, and he did not take Johnson's dismissal lightly.

To complicate Johnson's position, the Radical Republicans saw Johnson's dismissal of Stanton as an assault on its own control over the presidency. The Congress hated the idea of a strong presidency, and had enacted a peculiar piece of legislation called the Tenure of Office Act. This Act gave Congress some say-so over the President's choice of appointees to his cabinet. In fact the President was not supposed to fire anyone from his own cabinet without congressional approval. But this is what Johnson had done and Congress was not going to sit idly by and allow him to diminish its influence.

Along with his stubborn and incendiary behavior Johnson was also a man who did not know how to gather allies around him, or did not care to try. Thus he was not only an aggressive man, but a defiant and isolated man as well. He would not give ground when challenged and rarely looked around for help even when the most elementary wisdom demanded he do so. So there he stood, an inviting, in fact an almost irresistible target for an angry Congress. He stood alone, an outspoken champion of unpopular positions, a man with few allies struggling vigorously against broadly-based corruption.

And he had pushed his opponents too far by firing one of the most powerful politicians in the country. Johnson made a big and obvious target, and a rather easy one in those times of high passion, smoldering hatred, and greedy ambition. Stanton and his allies were able to move the Congress to accuse Johnson of high crimes and misdemeanors, and in due course Andrew Johnson was impeached.

To accuse Johnson of impeachable offences was little short of ludicrous, an exercise in the wielding of political power rather than in the application of juridical wisdom. The trial was clearly a political rather than a legal matter. Even so, Johnson refused to use his own political influence, by now rather meager, to affect the outcome of his trial; he thought it would be unethical to do so. Throughout the proceedings he was, predictably, defiant and unwilling to compromise. On one occasion he was in fact offered a compromise as an alternative to the impeachment. His response was to explode, "I know I am right and I am damned if I do not adhere to it!"[52]

Politics is a tricky and sometimes nasty game. Though the arguments against him were at best questionable he survived the impeachment proceedings by only one vote. Yet when it was all over he still displayed his immovably upright attitude: "It is not a victory for myself," he said, "but for the Constitution and the Country."[53]

His remark was at least partially correct. This was the first impeachment of a President in the nation's history, and there were some who wondered if the Constitutional process was sturdy enough to withstand such a one-sided and underhanded assault on a President as had been made on Johnson. In the end it was, of course. The spirit and intent of the Constitution did prevail, however marginally. But Andrew Johnson's reputation and career were in tatters.

Throughout the grim ordeal one person never lost faith in him or doubted the rightness of his position: his wife, Eliza McCardle Johnson. The young tailor Andrew and Eliza McCardle had met when he was seventeen and she sixteen. She helped him learn to read and write and became not only his wife, but also his closest friend and ally. They were by their own declaration simple country folks not up to the social life of Washington—and not interested in trying to be. Eliza Johnson (who was a rather reclusive Guardian) rarely presented herself in public, preferring to spend her time alone knitting and sewing and being visited by her

---

52 *The Impeachment and Trial of Andrew Johnson*, 13.
53 *The Impeachment and Trial of Andrew Johnson*, 201.

grandchildren. She was seen so seldom by Washington society that one newspaper referred to her as "the almost mythical" First Lady. She loved Andrew and respected him greatly, as he did her. During the prolonged tribulation of the impeachment process he turned to her constantly, seeking her comfort and her advice. All through that three-month struggle her comfort was never failing and her advice always the same: "Do what you think is right." Justice would prevail, she was sure, and in the case of Johnson's impeachment her faith was finally vindicated.

Whatever criticism might have been levelled against Johnson as a President, Mr. and Mrs. Johnson as occupants of the White House were, as would be expected, impeccable. They quickly earned a reputation for irreproachable behavior and demonstrated an admirable interest in taking care of and improving the place. Their Guardian orientation made itself known as strongly in this regard as it did everywhere else in their lives.

This said, it is still the case that no matter how responsible they may be, and no matter how satisfying or solid their marital relationship, there is no guarantee that any couple's children will flourish. In the case of the Johnsons, for example, it appears that all their sons were heavy drinkers who proved to be far from responsible citizens. Even so, in spite of his well-deserved reputation for dissolute behavior, when Johnson reached the White House he made one of his sons his presidential aide. Johnson apparently hoped that the responsible position would bring his son to his senses, as it would likely do for almost any Guardian. But the young man, apparently a hell-raising Artisan, rewarded his father by continuing his usual pattern of drunken and disgraceful behavior.

The Johnsons extended themselves mightily and probably unreasonably on behalf of their wayward children. This is often true of Guardian parents with wayward offspring, and as frequently happens to such parents, they paid for it heavily. The Johnsons' unwise attempts to help their sons by appointing them to office became another painful smirch on Andrew Johnson's reputation. The Guardians often seem to have difficulty realizing when it is time to stop trying to help, especially where their own children are concerned. Like the Johnsons, they may keep themselves entrapped for years in agonized efforts to help wayward offspring who show no indication that they wish to be helped—except perhaps by parental financing of their wayward activities. Non-Guardian relatives and friends of such delinquent children will eventually become disgusted and step back, leaving the recalcitrants to sink or swim. The Guardians often cannot seem to allow themselves this course and their painful efforts may continue for a lifetime. They are, if anyone is, the world's most hardy and perennial rescuers.

But the damage done by the Johnsons in their efforts to help their sons was incidental. At the close of Johnson's term of office in 1868 his party refused to nominate him for the presidency; he was being abandoned. Johnson wouldn't lie down and die however; in 1874 the career politician re-entered active political life to run for the United States Senate. It is little short of amazing that, in spite of the terrible pounding his reputation had taken while he was President, he was elected to the Senate. Sadly, he died of a stroke only five months later. (He had taken the floor to speak only once after his election and used the occasion to deliver a vitriolic attack on one of his enemies.) Eliza Johnson, his faithful and loving companion for so may years, died only a year later.

Andrew Johnson was buried with his personal, much-used copy of the Constitution beneath his head as a pillow and the American flag draped over his body as a blanket. It seems a fitting arrangement for the dedicated Guardian who, in his outspoken and stubborn way, loved his country so loyally and worked so hard to protect it and to help it heal its wounds.

Bibliography

Beale, H 1930 — *The Critical Year: a Study of Andrew Johnson and Reconstruction*

Benedict, M 1973 — *The Impeachment and Trial of Andrew Johnson*

Bowers, C 1929 — *The Tragic Era: the Revolution after Lincoln*

Brabson, F 1972 — *Andrew Johnson: a Life in Pursuit of the Right Course, 1808-1875*

Castel, A 1979 — *The Presidency of Andrew Johnson*

Jones, J 1901 — *Life of Andrew Johnson, Seventeenth President of the United States*

Mantell, M 1973 — *Johnson, Grant, and the Politics of Reconstruction*

McKitrick, E 1969 — *Andrew Johnson; a Profile*

Severn, B 1956 — *In Lincoln's Footsteps: The Life of Andrew Johnson*

Steele, R 1968 — *The First President Johnson: the Three Lives of the Seventeenth President*

Stryker, L 1929 — *Andrew Johnson, a Study in Courage*

Trefousse, H 1989 — *Andrew Johnson, a Biography*

Winston, R 1928 — *Andrew Johnson, Plebeian and Patriot*

Rutherford B. Hayes

A respectable place for a respectable man

Monitor
Born: November 4, 1822
Died: January 17, 1893
Presidency: 1877-1881

Rutherford Birchard Hayes was prouder of having been a soldier during the Civil War than of having been Governor of Ohio or President of the United States. He had a great deal of enthusiasm for life in the field, was considered a capable and courageous officer by his superiors, and was popular with his troops. A major in the 23rd Ohio Volunteers, Hayes was right at the front of several intense battles. Though he was several times wounded in action he refused to allow his wounds to remove him from the action. General Grant himself once went so far as to praise Hayes for his "conspicuous gallantry" and Hayes's courage and fortitude were such that he eventually rose to the rank of brevet major general. But his tenure as a Union officer in the Civil War seems to have been the one period in his life that could be characterized as exciting, or during which Hayes himself could be called colorful. Perhaps this is part of the reason that even years later he loved being called "General Hayes."

As a young man Hayes was rather ordinary. He had his unswerving ambition, his solid and dependable character, a good education on which to build. He had as well some facility with oratory, but he recognized that if anything at all stood out about him it was only his extraordinary drive to improve himself. For example he decided to undertake a prolonged course of difficult reading during which would immerse himself in material that he considered to be "useful, instructive, and solid." He also kept a diary in which he could record his observations and decisions. Note the Monitor's plan for self-improvement with respect to the matter of alcohol:

> I am a sincere but not extreme or violent friend of the temperance cause. I mean to prepare myself to speak on this subject by accumulating and arranging in my memory as many interesting facts, arguments, and statistics as I can; also by jotting down my own ideas on the subject as they occur to me.[54]

He was thought by his friends to be rather colorless and stuffy, though still a decent man, solid, lackluster and very upright. So upright that some people claimed that he had never sowed any wild oats in his life simply because he never in his life had any wild oats to sow. He was impeccable, deliberate, reserved and conservative, steady and good-natured, and remarkably determined once he made up his mind.

In spite of his military successes Rutherford Hayes appeared more the stereotype of the small businessman than he did a potential President. Like the small businessman, he was dutifully conservative, with his feet firmly on the ground, and reluctant to accept suggestions for change. Though he tried to be outgoing and pleasant, he seemed ill at ease with the back-slapping bonhomie so common to the political style of his time. One nickname he bore was "Granny Hayes." Still, he was a good party man who voted the party line and managed to stay on the

---

54 Quoted from Hayes's diary in *How They Became President*, 240.

popular side of most issues. In most matters he conformed with the party position with reasonable equanimity so that in spite of his somewhat nondescript qualifications he managed to be elected Governor of Ohio three times. Then, in the very close race of 1876, he was elected President of the United States.

How close the race was is indicated by the fact that his Democratic opponent, Samuel Tilden, received more votes (popular and electoral) than did Hayes. It appears that Tilden should have been the nineteenth President of the United States. But Republican claims of dishonesty and ballot fixing, followed by some complicated political deal-making between the Democratic and Republican party bosses, led to Hayes being proclaimed President. But the final proclamation was widely recognized as the result of political back-room maneuvering, and though he was an honest and conscientious man Hayes's administration never overcame the stigma of the election. His was therefore a far less potent presidency than it might otherwise have been.

Rutherford Hayes's wife was cut from the same respectable cloth. Lucy Webb Hayes was a serious-minded person and very religious as well. Like her husband, she was a college graduate with a degree from Wesleyan Women's College, a Methodist institution. Married in 1852, they made a sober—and sobering—pair, Rutherford so upright and Lucy so straight-laced. When they eventually reached the White House the Hayes refused to serve alcohol there. Profanity and tobacco also disappeared from the place, and morning hymn-singing became standard. It was not just hard liquor that was banished from the White House; even wine disappeared. Lucy Hayes was given credit for what was widely seen as the awful deed and acquired the sobriquet "Lemonade Lucy."

It is likely however that Hayes himself was responsible for the decision. That this rather stern and moralistic Monitor would have taken such a step is not difficult to believe. Even the austere Lucy Hayes was more gracious and pleasant than her husband. Her religious convictions were firm, but this certainly didn't prevent her from being a pleasant and considerate person. She was apparently a Conservator and the Conservator Guardians often add a degree of warmth to relationships likely to be wanting with the Monitor Guardians. Her fondness for sponsoring ceremonies such as weddings and baptisms, for example, gave her a chance to add a more friendly and personal touch to Hayes's presidency. No doubt due to Lucy's influence, the Hayes's family quarters, even with Rutherford in attendance (he did seem to relax a little with Lucy), were considered "cheerful and folksy as a quilting bee."[55]

Hayes's formality and gravity were not just a reflection of his exalted view of his position, nor were they some politically-inspired attempt to look dignified. They were merely the Monitor, Rutherford B. Hayes. He seems always to have been serious and earnest. Even as a young man studying law he studied himself to uncover faults and found in himself what he considered many serious ones. "Trifling remarks, boyish conduct, etc., are among my crying sins. Mend, mend!" he entered into his diary. Later, upon pondering the works of Aristotle, part of that curriculum of "useful, instructive, and solid" reading, he commented somewhat cryptically that "virtue is defined to be mediocrity, of which either extreme is vice." It is difficult to decipher what he meant by this entry. Perhaps he had been reading about the splendid Greek principle of the Golden Mean and had failed to distinguish between balance or proportion and the merely mediocre. In Hayes's case, perhaps, a little learning was indeed a dangerous thing.

But he was not interested in "a little learning." When he was twenty-nine he made this entry in his diary:

> I feel that I have read too much light reading, too little that is useful, instructive, solid, of late. I must give up my mental habits; become more energetic by tough reading. Let my lightest for a time be biographies and miscellanies such as the statesmen of Cromwell's time.[56]

Though Hayes was not a colorful President, and though he has not captured the interest of biographers, he has had an important influence on our nation's history. He was, for example, one of the first United States Presidents to challenge seriously the idea that the President should be merely the executor of Congress's wishes. Jackson operated as if he owned the government, though this was before the Congress was as powerful as it subsequently became. Lincoln had also preceded Hayes as

---

55 *Profiles and Portraits of American Presidents*, 189.
56 Quoted from Hayes's diary in *How They Became President*, 241.

a powerful decision maker and an unabashed formulator of policy. But Lincoln felt forced into the role by the peculiar circumstances of the time and acted without making an issue of the matter. The bull-headed Andrew Johnson also acted independently when he fired Stanton and thereby disregarded the Tenure of Office Act. But Rutherford Hayes was more deliberate about his assertion of executive power: he saw the President's role as that of chief policy-maker as well as chief executive officer. He had no sympathy for the idea that the President should merely carry out the wishes of the Congress.

Hayes also proved to be an able administrator, supporting extensive and needed reforms in the civil service system, and doing what he could to dismantle the political spoils system. The cloud under which he had taken office mitigated his effectiveness. But the corrupt civil service system and the blatant spoilsmanship of party politicians had become so debased by Hayes's time that they were matters of public shame. In spite of his weak position he managed to see to the passage of a number of reforms, thereby pleasing many outraged voters even while disgruntling many of his less conscientious political associates.

Among the disgruntled was future President Chester Arthur. Hayes fired him from the lucrative office Arthur had acquired as his share of prior political spoils. Hayes had to take on the powerful Senator Roscoe Conkling when he went after Arthur (along with two other Conkling appointees). It took an eighteen-month struggle for Hayes to dislodge the spoilsmen. Victory was expensive, however; in the process he cost himself most of his party support, for he was no longer behaving as a good party man. It could be said that his most significant political failure was that he proved to be an honest man. "In a period of national corruption, his brief term as President shone like a beacon in the dark," and this sin the party bosses would not tolerate.[57]

Still, it is worth noting that the spirit of the times was strongly for reform. Hayes was not deliberately throwing away his political future when he did his stern political monitoring. Hayes and the party did hope to stay on the crest of the wave of popularity they had generated by taking a reform stance. The cost may have been high, but the rewards could be even higher.

---

57 *Atlas of the Presidents*, 50.

Not all Hayes's presidential actions were as salutary. Part of the deal that the bosses had made in awarding the presidency to Hayes was that he would end the Union Army's occupation of the Southern states. It was a step sorely needed if the country was to claim convincingly that the war was truly over and the nation truly reunited. It was also in keeping with Hayes's opinion that the Southern states should be treated with leniency, even if not with total forgiveness. Unfortunately the withdrawal of Federal troops also meant that there were no anti-slavery or pro-civil rights advocates in places of authority in the South. Although Hayes could not know it at the time, the withdrawal of Federal authority from the South destroyed the possibility of Black equality there for almost a century.

When his first term of office came near to its end Hayes decided not to run again. The decision was probably strongly influenced by his recognition that his own party was not interested in having him do so. For his own part Hayes was glad to be done with what he called "this life of bondage, responsibility, and toil."[58] After leaving the White House in 1881 he and Lucy Hayes led a peaceful, comfortable, and unremarkable existence, doing good works for charities, enjoying the honors of an ex-President, and gradually sinking into a happy obscurity. Lucy Hayes died of a stroke in 1889, and Rutherford Hayes died four years later.

Hayes rarely gave evidence of reflecting on the course he had taken in life, but on one occasion he did note that he recognized the sober quality of that course. "In avoiding the appearance of evil," he wrote, "I am not sure but I have sometimes unnecessarily deprived myself and others of innocent enjoyment."[59] It is not difficult to discern a certain sadness in these words. He was a Monitor, after all, but the General was still a man who knew something of excitement and gallantry and the lustrous pursuit of honor on the field of battle. Finally the Monitor Rutherford B. Hayes concluded that it was all worthwhile. Perhaps his own words in this regard provide his most fitting epitaph and speak to us of his typically Guardian desire:

---

58 Quoted in *Presidential Anecdotes*, 166 from *Diary and Letters of Rutherford B. Hayes*, III, 557.

59 *Presidential Anecdotes*, 156.

Without any extraordinary success, without that sort of success which makes men giddy sometimes, I have nevertheless found what I sought: a respectable place. Good![60]

Bibliography

Banard, H 1954   *Rutherford B Hayes, and his America*
Davison, K 1972   *The Presidency of Rutherford B Hayes*
Eckenrode, H 1963   *Rutherford B Hayes: Statesman of Reunion*
Burgess, J 1916   *The Administration of President Hayes*
Howells, W 1876   *Sketch of the Life and Character of Rutherford B Hayes*
Williams, C 1924   *Diary and Letters of Rutherford B. Hayes*

---

60 *How They Became President*, 241.

Grover Cleveland

The rule of obstinacy

Monitor
Born: March 18, 1837
Died: June 24, 1908
Presidency: 1885-1889, 1893-1897

Stephen Grover Cleveland was a man who knew how to say "no." During his two terms in office he issued more than six hundred vetoes, four hundred and thirteen of them in his first term alone. This was more than the combined vetoes of all the twenty-one Presidents before him and more than any other President except Franklin D. Roosevelt.

Cleveland was quite proud of his record. It was the continuation of a pattern begun during his tenure as Mayor of Buffalo, New York. He had there been dubbed "the Veto Mayor" as he turned down measure after measure proposed by the corrupt politicians of that city. Once he had achieved the presidency Cleveland took great pleasure in using the veto to put a stop not just to corruption, but also to eliminate as much as he could of the legislative "foolishness" of the Congress. He thereby continued the struggle undertaken earlier by Rutherford B. Hayes to make the White House something other than a rubber stamp for the Congress, which it had been, with rare exceptions, for most of the country's history.

Cleveland was a very large but handsome man whose bearing exuded dignity and power (and whose girth led his youngest relatives to call him "Uncle Jumbo"). He spoke, said Governor La Follette, with "splendid diction and rather lofty eloquence." But, added La Follette in a telling afterthought about the Monitor Cleveland, "I do not remember a suggestion of humor."[61]

It has been written that Cleveland was the only man since George Washington to have achieved the presidency through sheer character alone. Cleveland was also one of those rarities in American politics: a man who was elected to office (in 1884), defeated in his campaign for re-election (in 1888), and then re-elected to the same office (in 1892). If we accept the association with Washington then it should not surprise us that both men were Guardians. They were both Monitors whose utter commitment to duty and whose integrity were indisputably above reproach.

The famous statement that "public office is a public trust" is attributed to Grover Cleveland and reflects the accountability in which Guardians take so much pride. Though it is a paraphrase of his own words, it summarizes his view beautifully, and he persistently lived up to the demands of his own Guardian credo. Considered to be the hardest working man in Washington, he often stayed at his desk until 3 a.m. plowing through his day's work, firmly resolved that he would get it all done. His industriousness was such that his life could be encompassed by the observation that "he eats and works, eats and works, and works and eats." Grover Cleveland modeled almost too well the stubbornly duty-bound character of the Monitor Guardian, the moral, no-nonsense, hard-working, and totally incorruptible caretaker and overseer.[62]

---

61 Quoted in *The Presidency*, 200.

62 He never drew the line at unpleasant tasks, especially where saving money was concerned. While sheriff of Erie County, New York, for instance, Cleveland personally hung two men: he affixed the ropes, put on the blindfolds, and pulled the lever which opened the trap door. Thereby he saved the county the cost of hiring a hangman.

Guardians are not nearly as adept at delegating responsibility as they are at accepting it. Industry has its limits, but Cleveland rarely seemed to recognize them. It was his friend Samuel Tilden who remarked that Cleveland would rather do something badly for himself than to have someone else do it well. Nonetheless, in a time of many notorious politicians and few honest ones, it is well for Cleveland's political career that he was such a conspicuous example of honesty, determination, and industry. There seemed little else to recommend him for the presidency. He was not above being pompous and self-righteous at times, and quite capable of occasional irascibility. His personal style was serious and conventional, weighty, and rather long-winded, and he struck many people as being more a statesman than a politician. Others thought that his natural probity and gravity, his honesty and persistence, and his traditional perspective recommended him more for a judgeship than for elective political office.

Cleveland had served in the Civil War and was promoted to lieutenant when his work came to the attention of his commanding officer, Rutherford B. Hayes. Hayes had taken note of the remarkable skill Cleveland showed in foraging for supplies for his unit. Of course a Guardian who is busy collecting supplies can be quite resourceful and he will be far less negative than the Guardian who is attempting to safeguard them. But in either case he will be watchful and quick to act when he sees the opportunity to gain more supplies or to prevent those already collected from being wasted upon undeserving persons or projects.

With his forthright Guardian conservatism, Grover Cleveland was a popular President throughout most of his time in office. During the course of his political career his absolute refusal to become a party hack became well-known and admired by the public even if it was resented by the professional politicians of his day. Like the illustrious George Washington, Cleveland could not be blackmailed or compromised by anyone, and like Washington he would neither give nor receive favors. This sort of political independence and constancy is likely to make one many enemies in a very brief period of time, especially for a man who is already fighting widespread corruption and special privilege. Cleveland might not have minded making some of those enemies, however, since they included some of the most self-serving and the least honorable men in American politics. In fact it was said of him that people loved him for the enemies he made.

However much he might devote his life to the legitimate rewards of honest hard work done conscientiously, perfection evades the Guardian just as it evades us all. Even Grover Cleveland could fall from grace. At one time Cleveland had an affair of some duration from which, it was claimed, there was born an illegitimate child. Cleveland kept the affair secret but still took good financial care of the child and the mother, one Maria Halpern. But the existence of the Cleveland-Halpern affair was discovered, and so of course was the child. When Cleveland ran for the presidency his political opponents hoped to impugn Cleveland's most important asset, his character. One tasteless ploy they offered was the jingle, "Ma, ma, where's my pa? Gone to the White House, ha ha ha!"

But once again Cleveland's stubborn honesty prevailed over political expediency. When the facts were made known during the election campaign Cleveland insisted with quiet simplicity that the full truth be told. Though there was ample opportunity for him to use similar tactics against his opponent, a man with a long history of such transgressions, Cleveland refused to make use of it. Instead he went ahead with a clear and forthright admission of the Halpern affair. The record showed that he had readily assumed the responsibility for the child's education and upbringing, though it was never determined that he was actually the father. He never explicitly acknowledged paternity, but he was otherwise so quick to acknowledge the affair and take responsibility for the child's future that the public voted him into office as "Honest Grover," and some even called him "Grover the Good."

It is comforting to know that even the upright "Grover the Good," at least as a young man, could engage in a little social drinking and some friendly social singing, some sociable card gaming and the occasional fishing trip with friends. It is almost endearing, gazing upon this mighty incarnation of bleak duty and principled honesty, to know also that Cleveland could enormously enjoy his food and his precious beer throughout his life. Guardians, however virtuous, are rarely mortifiers of the flesh, and Cleveland's continual indulgence gave him a rather portly figure. But such was his reputation that in Cleveland's case it seemed to be considered an indication that he was a man of solid and statesmanlike substance rather than a victim of overindulgence.

Cleveland especially enjoyed his beer, so it was painful for him to admit to a friend that they were drinking entirely too much of the brew. They decided to restrict their beer intake severely: they would allow themselves a paltry four glasses of beer per sitting. But they had trouble staying within the limits of this cruelly diminished ration. Then in a moment of inspiration they realized that they could relabel their very large beer tankards "glasses." They discovered that their rationing campaign worked far better after this minor adjustment in terminology. Cleveland also loved to go fishing, but his father had told him when he was a boy that fishing on Sunday was sinful. Cleveland certainly did not want to be sinful, so Sunday fishing was abandoned. But, Cleveland later pointed out, "he never said anything about draw poker." Finding permission in this paternal oversight, Grover Cleveland managed some fishing during the weeks, and found his Sunday poker games an adequate and innocent substitute for the sin of Sunday fishing.[63]

As is so often the case with Monitors, Cleveland was not industrious and conscientious simply because he loved his work. Duty is not to be confused with pleasure, after all, nor conscientiousness with satisfaction. Far from it; so distressing did Cleveland find his work in the White House that he was the first President to buy a separate residence to give himself the opportunity to be away from what he called the "cursed constant grind" of the day's work. And when he was defeated in his campaign for re-election in 1888 he claimed that there was no happier person in the United States than he. He could not turn his back on responsibility, but he could still be pleased if the electorate *deprived* him of it for a while.

Perhaps he looked forward not only to escaping the burden of political office in 1888, but also to having more time for his delightful young wife, Frances Folsom Cleveland. Some years before he came to the presidency Grover Cleveland had agreed to assume the duties of guardian for Frances Folsom, the young daughter of his friend and former law partner, Oscar Folsom. When Folsom died young Frances became Cleveland's ward.

But the relationship was more than protector and protected. When she reached college age Cleveland requested of her mother that he be

---

63 *Presidential Anecdotes,* 178.

allowed to court the young lady. Permission was granted, though the courtship was done by mail, and when Frances reached her majority Grover proposed. She had responded favorably to the courtship and now she accepted his proposal, and to the great delight of the American public Frances Folsom and Grover Cleveland were married. The year was 1886; she was twenty-one and he was forty-nine, already serving his first term as President of the United States.

It was a happy marriage for both of them. Frances Folsom Cleveland was a cheerful, poised, attractive woman as well as an affectionate wife, and Cleveland's love for her never wavered. But he was still a stuffy traditionalist, and in spite of his affection for her his opinion of her rightful position as a woman could have caused problems for someone less gracious and cheerful than Frances. A good wife, he wrote in a magazine article, is "a woman who loves her husband and her country with no desire to run either."[64] He didn't want his new wife called by any special titles, or treated in special ways, since he didn't want her getting any "notions" into her head. Monitor Guardians are probably more reluctant than any other kind of temperament to praise others. They are not selfish with praise, but are often concerned that the one praised will "get uppity" and "take on airs," or in some other way let the praise get the better of them. Cleveland had exactly this concern about his young wife.

Cleveland also thought it was not a wife's place to decide or even to have opinions on matters of finance or public policy. He was, in our current idiom, a male chauvinist. Nonetheless when it came to matters of dress or manners or of raising their two children, there is no question that Frances Cleveland's opinion was the one that counted. And in spite of Cleveland's wish to shelter her from political life she became an important factor in his career. So popular did she become that when Grover Cleveland ran for office in 1892 Frances Cleveland's picture was given a more prominent position on many campaign posters than his. He disapproved of the public scrutiny to which his wife was exposed and Frances Cleveland herself detested it.

But that would be in 1892, and there was a blow the Clevelands would have to absorb before that victorious campaign. At the end of his first term Cleveland sought re-election in the campaign of 1888. He was at a disadvantage in that campaign, for he did not campaign at all; he

---

64 "Woman's Mission and Woman's Clubs," *Ladies' Home Journal,* May 1905. Quoted in *Presidential Wives,* 167.

believed it was improper for an incumbent President to do so. Still he managed to win a larger popular vote than his opponent, Benjamin Harrison. But Harrison captured more electoral votes and therefore won the presidency. The election was still close and Cleveland would have won had he not lost the decisive New York electoral votes. These were lost to him due to the machinations of the Tammany Hall political bosses who never forgave him for being so incorruptible.

But Harrison was the new President and Grover and Frances had to bid farewell to the White House. Frances Cleveland had always enjoyed the White House and when the Clevelands left she cautioned its staff to take good care of the furniture; the Clevelands, she said, would be back in four years. Her prediction proved accurate: the Clevelands returned four years later and Mrs. Cleveland returned to her position as one of the most popular first ladies the White House has ever known.

If Grover Cleveland had a truly major fault it is to be found in his narrow approach to issues. He was a President whose action was typically "against": he was against corruption, against waste, against immorality. But he was not a man who had much vision of what could be, and he seldom worked *for* anything. Early in his second term in office, for example, there occurred the financial Panic of 1893, which was followed throughout the United States by widespread unemployment and the terrible and prolonged misery associated with it. So difficult was the Panic that only the Great Depression four decades later overshadowed this appalling period. But Cleveland was unable to comprehend the social and economic realities of his time. He was in fact totally baffled by the complaints which reached his ears about the misery in which so many people found themselves. Through his own ignorance as well as his tendency to say "no" rather than to have a goal about which to say "yes," he failed to take any constructive action. Perhaps his failure to witness firsthand the suffering that so many people were enduring kept him from being able to apprehend the full impact of its grinding misery.

The ability and the intention to maintain traditions and customs is of course better developed in the Guardian than in any other character structure. But difficulty in envisioning the possible, such as divergent or non-traditional courses of action, is perhaps their greatest shortcoming. Cleveland was a strong supporter of a gold standard, of the rule that all paper money be backed by gold held in reserve by the federal government. But federal reserves had dwindled to almost nothing by 1896, and Cleveland's administration therefore contracted with the incredibly wealthy J. P. Morgan for a loan to the government. Morgan received federal bonds in return, upon which he soon made a very healthy profit. Cleveland, unwilling to depart from the rules he had already established, made Morgan even more money.

In spite of the difficulties and dangers involved, and typical of the Monitors, Cleveland had remained wedded to custom and divorced from strategic planning. The continuation of the terrible economic conditions of the times and Cleveland's failure to respond to them with some show of compassionate concern, or with any sign of creative or long-range vision, was immensely damaging to his popularity—especially since he had inadvertently enriched the detested J. P. Morgan. Cleveland finished his second term of office one of the most unpopular men in the country.

His failure to recognize the full extent of the nation's problems was in part born of a problem of his own. It was discovered early in 1893 just after his re-election that he had cancer of the mouth. The condition was serious, even life-threatening, and he was very concerned about the impact of such news on the public. He was afraid that if the truth were known it would be interpreted to mean he was dying, and "if word gets around that I'm 'dying' the country is dead, too."[65] Therefore he and his closest staff undertook in secret an operation to remove the cancer.

It was a difficult undertaking at best; there was a good chance that the anesthetic procedures of the time would kill him even if the operation or the cancer did not. Nevertheless Cleveland was very calm about the event, very stolid throughout the painful ordeal, and apparently maintained his equanimity during his abbreviated recuperation. The operation was performed in secrecy, and several days of recuperation were stolen on a boat isolated out on the Potomac River. The plan worked; even his wife thought Cleveland was on a vacation and the secret was maintained for two decades before it was finally and accidentally disclosed. Nevertheless rumors began to circulate that the President was ill, though where they originated was never determined. In

---

65 *Presidential Courage,* 16.

spite of his pain Cleveland managed to make public appearances and dispel the gossip. The ordeal must have been terrible.[66]

At the end of Cleveland's second term of office he retired rather than run again for office. It was just as well; the nation would not relish being reminded further of how difficult the last few years had been, and many thought Cleveland should have acted more vigorously to end the depression. Even so, time has softened the judgments made about him. While the painful economic realities of his second term in office have been all but forgotten, the memory of his indomitably honest character has lived after him.

After he left the White House Cleveland's physical condition gradually weakened. In 1908, at the age of sevennty-one, he died. His last words were a perfect representation of the life of this most conscientious Guardian: "I have tried so hard to do right."

Frances Folsom Cleveland remarried in 1913 and lived quietly until 1947 when she died at the age of eighty-four.

Bibliography

McElroy, R 1923   *Grover Cleveland, the Man and the Statesman*
Hensel, W 1888   *Life and Public Services of Grover Cleveland*
Merrill, H 1957   *Grover Cleveland and the Democratic Party*
Gillis, J 1897   *The Hawaiian Incident*
Ford, H 1921   *The Cleveland Era: a Chronicle of the New Order of Politics*
Hollingsworth, J 1963   *The Whirligig of Politics: the Democracy of Cleveland and Bryan*
Nevins, A 1932   *Grover Cleveland: a Study in Courage*
Tugwell, R 1968   *Grover Cleveland*

---

[66] After his operation Cleveland was "fitted with an artificial jaw so that he could speak intelligibly." (*Congressional Quarterly's Guide to the Presidency*, 378.)

Benjamin Harrison

An iceberg in the White House

Monitor
Born: August 20, 1833
Died: March 13, 1901
Presidency: 1889-1893

Benjamin Harrison was the grandson of President William Henry
Harrison and great-grandson of (and named for) a signer of the
Declaration of Independence. He was a Monitor, as was George
Washington, but had not the nobility, the energy, or the personal
grandeur of the country's first President. If Washington was the
Guardian made noble, Harrison was the Guardian made inconsequential.
The difference was made obvious even physically: Washington was an
imposing six feet, two inches tall; Harrison was five foot six.

Harrison was a cautious, unimaginative man. He had a sense of integrity and responsibility, but as President was content to let Congress run things, as so many Guardian Presidents before him had been. He was dignified and polished in his manner, calm and cool to the point of being downright frigid with anyone outside his family or his small circle of close friends. He was also a minor military hero, having shown himself to be a brave and fiery leader and a firm disciplinarian during the Civil War.

His fiery leadership and his firm discipline, however, were not in evidence while he held political office. Quite the contrary, he was known as something of a solemn, impersonal, and imperturbable cold fish. One man who knew him said speaking with him was like "talking to a hitching post,"[67] and another reported that he had a handshake "like a wilted petunia."[68] Even his election campaign managed to reflect his colorless, frosty quality. Like Harrison himself it was a carefully managed political affair, polite, sober, and uninspiring.

Harrison from time to time made an effort to behave in a warm and friendly fashion, but he never acquired the skill. After each attempt he seemed to feel more and more defeated, and eventually he abandoned the effort. He had practiced a great deal to become a good orator and could be quite effective when there was some distance between him and his audience. But his chilly reserve was so pronounced that his political backers struggled desperately to keep him from talking to people face to face. During a whistle-stop train campaign, for instance, after Harrison delivered a typically rousing speech from the platform of the train one of his managers would immediately give the signal to start the engine. In this way the managers could ensure that Harrison and his audience wouldn't be able to get too close to one another.

As a politician Harrison had always been a loyal party member and the party bosses thought of him only as a political hack, a rubber stamp useful for legitimizing the interests of the politicians who put him in office. This was however a somewhat limited view of Benjamin Harrison. He might be naive about the stealthy secrecy and squalid chicanery of many of the career politicians, but his Monitor's crusty

---

67 *1001 Things Everyone Should Know about American History,* 131.
68 *Presidential Anecdotes,* 183.

incorruptibility ensured that he would never intentionally be part of their schemes. Though he was not an active or astute President he was always a coolly and steadfastly honest one, and when he saw that what he was being told to do was tainted he felt quite free to refuse. In fact his honesty became legendary in much the same fashion as did that of his predecessor, "Honest Grover" Cleveland. His administration was largely an honorable one chiefly because Harrison refused to countenance anything else.

Benjamin Harrison's home life was overall as plain and uneventful as his public life. He did not give parties, he avoided glamorous dinners, he showed no interest in the pursuit of worldly pleasures. Only as a family man and among a few close friends did he become warm and genial. At home he and his family were always orderly and routine in their behavior and at no time were they known to depart from their established patterns of daily life.

His wife, Caroline Scott Harrison, had many of the social qualities that he knew were not his. She was bright, pretty, charming, and ebullient. In spite of being raised by a staunchly conservative Presbyterian minister she was an enthusiastic dancer, had a great fondness for music and painting, and proved to be a cheerfully terrible housekeeper. Apparently an outgoing Player Artisan, she loved needlework, painted watercolors, was a fine pianist, raised flowers in profusion, and delighted in socializing. Though her active life would not suggest it, she was physically somewhat frail, and in stature she was rather small, which made her a good match for "Little Ben."

Benjamin always saw her as quite frail even if she herself didn't. After she and Ben had become secretly engaged she became quite ill, possibly from overwork. Benjamin, good Guardian that he was, became frantic about her health and insisted on rescuing her. He decided that her twin careers of both teaching and nursing were too much for her. Overwork was contributing, he was sure, to the dreadful physical problems that their prolonged and secret engagement must be causing her. Therefore, and in spite of the great financial difficulties involved, he persuaded her to marry him without further delay. The marriage followed quickly and the young lawyer Harrison (the year was 1853 and he was still not twenty-one) struggled with considerable difficulty to make ends meet.

Their financial struggles and domestic bliss were interrupted eight years later by the Civil War. Upon its outbreak Benjamin raised a regiment of infantry, the Indiana Volunteers, for the Union Army. He considered himself a patriot so he also served as a lieutenant in the Volunteers. The Governor of Indiana appointed him major and Harrison soon became the regiment's commanding officer. He studied hard and conscientiously, and learned the job of commanding officer of a regiment of infantry reasonably well, while his cold and stern manner helped him control the men of the regiment. But Ben's heart was still at home and while he was away with his regiment his letters to Caroline were full of love and constant requests for more and more of the little, concrete details about her everyday life. "Your daily domestic life I feel to be a part of my life and I love to know every little event of it...."[69] In spite of his homesickness and loneliness he was known as a good soldier and a fine officer, brave and energetic and dependable.

After the war ended Ben returned to his law career and developed an interest in politics. He was always concerned about providing a good home for his family and did increasingly well in this regard, but in the early days of their marriage Carrie resented the long hours he devoted to the task. As he became gradually more successful he enjoyed moving his family to larger and more opulent houses; the Guardian's need for ownership seemed well-developed in him.

It seems likely that Carrie, though she enjoyed the fruits of his success, found the routine of life with Ben a bit suffocating. She had a way of finding interesting projects and little adventures with which to amuse herself, however, and she was always able to persuade her husband that they were just the sort of thing anyone in her position would be expected to do. For his part, he was interested in helping her find more ways to occupy herself, whether doing charity work, painting, playing the piano, or even sponsoring forbidden dancing lessons (it was a moralistic community) in her own home for the Harrison children and their little friends.

In the meantime Harrison continued his steady climb up the political ladder. He was Reporter of Decisions of the Indiana Supreme court, Member of the Mississippi River Commission, defeated in a campaign

---

69 *Presidential Wives,* 179.

for governor of Indiana, elected to the United States Senate, and finally the Republican Party's candidate for the presidency. He was successful in the presidential campaign only because he won more electoral votes than his opponent, Grover Cleveland. Cleveland had gathered 100,000 more popular votes than had Harrison but they were not enough to give him victory in New York. The local political machine successfully denied Cleveland these electoral votes and their loss was enough to tip the scales in favor of Harrison.

Benjamin Harrison's position as President was a bit unsteady because of the manner of his election, but once comfortably in possession of the White House Carrie Harrison was quite at home. She managed cheerfully to keep a host of carpenters, plumbers, and various other workmen busy for two full years modernizing the somewhat dilapidated structure. Not only did she enthusiastically oversee the renovation of the White House; she also started the White House's now famous china collection, including in it a set of china of her own design, and became one of the founders of the Daughters of the American Revolution.

Overall Harrison's family life seems to have been satisfying to him. Perhaps in the long run it was of greater importance to him than the presidency itself. Harrison seems to have been more interested in providing a pleasant and secure home for his family than he was in being a politician anyway. But Carrie Harrison contracted tuberculosis, fell into lingering illness in 1891, and died in 1892. It was an election year and Harrison had restricted his campaign appearances to be with his wife. His opponent, the popular and honorable Grover Cleveland, curtailed his own electioneering in recognition of Harrison's situation. Cleveland won the election anyway, and became for the second time President of the United States.

Harrison left office and, unhappy with living alone, married Mary Scott Dimmick, Carrie Harrison's widowed niece, four years later in 1896. "A home is life's essential to me," said this withdrawn Guardian by way of explanation to his family, "and it must be the old home." But his children strongly resented the new marriage and snubbed him and his new wife. His pleas for them to accept the second marriage were unheeded during the remaining five years of his life.

Benjamin Harrison died of pneumonia in 1901; Mary Dimmick Harrison lived until 1948. Harrison's Guardian character is perhaps best summed up in the words of two modern historians: "He was free from scandal and his regime was an honest one. Harrison's career is as uninspiring as the man himself."[70]

Bibliography

Northrop, H 1888   *The Life and Public Services of General Benjamin Harrison*
Sievers, H 1952   *Benjamin Harrison*
Wallace, L 1888   *Life of General Ben Harrison*

---

[70] *Pictorial History of American Presidents*, 188.

Woodrow Wilson

The magnificent purpose and the hand of God

Monitor
Born: December 28, 1856
Died: February 3, 1924
Presidency 1913-1921

During Dwight Eisenhower's presidency there hung in the White House a picture of Thomas Woodrow Wilson, holding a book and staring over his glasses directly at the observer. Eisenhower once commented that he did not like the picture because every time he looked at it he thought Wilson was about to come to life and correct his grammar.[71]

It was a fitting fantasy; Wilson was regarded by many as a dedicated scholar and a skillful speaker, a tireless writer of books and essays on

---

71 *Among Those Present*, 183.

government and history, and an extremely popular college lecturer. He was also the first Southerner to win the presidency since before the Civil War. Born in Virginia, he lived in Atlanta, Georgia as a small child. There he saw some of the war's devastation, but was apparently not strongly affected by it. Probably the powerful and loving presence of his father softened whatever impact the tragic scenes of the war might have had.

"Tommy" Wilson (he later abandoned his first name) adored his father, and sought to be like him. The Reverend Joseph Wilson was an energetic pastor, a powerful orator, and a man who loved and used words with remarkable effectiveness. Wanting his son to follow his path in the ministry, Joseph Wilson taught Tommy with endless patience and good humor, playing word games, sharing word exercises, instilling in the youngster every verbal skill he could. As long as he lived the Reverend Wilson was his son's personal preceptor and inspiration. "Study manner, dearest Tommie, as much as matter," he once wrote. "Sentences ought to resemble bullets—that is, be compact and rapid, and prepared to make clean holes."[72] Woodrow did all he could to follow his father's advice, and eventually became considered by many to be one of the most powerful orators the presidency has known. (Even memorizing the speeches of famous figures from history, which he would then practice giving in front of a mirror.)

Woodrow's start in the academic world was hesitant, for he did not attend public school until he was thirteen, having been tutored until that time by his capable father. He began his college career in 1873 at Davidson College, but after one year he returned home, apparently physically ill. He pursued his studies at home, again under his father's tutelage, and then entered the College of New Jersey (later Princeton University), and graduated in 1879, in the top third of his class.

Among his extracurricular activities at Princeton were the school's debating society and its student newspaper, both of which fit nicely with his interests. He had early decided that his job was to be "a statesman," to guide the world and shape its beliefs and behaviors by means of his oratory. He wanted to be the American Gladstone, the staunch and sober Guardian prime minister of England. Gladstone's speeches were among

---

72 *Presidential Courage*, 134-135.

those Wilson studied most thoroughly. His life was to be a political life, and since law was the gateway to politics, he would study law. So he enrolled in the University of Virginia law school, and though he soon concluded that the details of law were "as monotonous as hash," he studied assiduously and later passed his bar exam with high marks. He subsequently opened a law office, a partnership with a friend from school, but it produced not a single client, and of course no income for him, and he again returned home to his parents.

But still, his interest was not in law itself. Those "subjects whose study delight me," and which fit with his aspirations, were government, constitutional history, economics, and international law. Enrolling in the graduate school at Johns Hopkins University, he studied these as devotedly as he had studied law, but now he brought a powerful interest with him, and was soon trying his hand at writing about them as well. He had already begun writing a book which would eventually be titled *Congressional Government*, and in 1889 he published a textbook on comparative government called *The State*. (In 1902 he would also have published his five-volume *History of the American People*.) Though most of this work was neither original nor especially scholarly, it "revealed a lively intellect, a conviction that moral purpose must infuse politics if it is to achieve right ends, and a profoundly conservative attitude toward political and social change."[73] The books were well-received, but his success only made more keen his desire "to take an active, if possible a leading, part in public life, and strike out for myself, if I had the ability, a *statesman's* career.[74]

But one must earn a living, and he had become engaged. Before becoming a professional "statesman," he took a position at the new Bryn Mawr College outside Philadelphia. Then, in 1885, he married Ellen Louise Axson, a winsome young lady who is said to have loved art and literature, and to be unusually attractive and warm. In 1890 he was offered a teaching position at Princeton University, and over the next few years held professorships of history and political science, political economy, and jurisprudence.

His courses were popular, his writing was respected, his oratory was persuasive, and he soon occupied a strong position among his colleagues at Princeton. In 1890, a mere two years after accepting a position at the

---

73 *Woodrow Wilson*, 26.
74 *Woodrow Wilson*, 23.

politically unsettled university he was offered, and he accepted, its presidency. Once appointed president of Princeton, Wilson overhauled the curriculum: students were to achieve a "general education" as undergraduates, and put off specialization until graduate school. He thereby turned Princeton into a "liberal arts" college, quite in contrast to the technology schools, such as MIT and CalTech, that prospered despite the conversion of one college after another to the Princeton model. In the service of the liberal arts plan he hired no less than fifty tutors, called "preceptors," each of whom was to shepherd his quota of students through their four years of undergraduate work, duplicating the European preceptor system and allowing the University to monitor the actions of each student. In this Wilson showed both his Guardian's attraction to the traditional, "tried and true," and the Monitor's inevitable interest in (quite literally) monitoring the behavior of others. (Wilson, the preacher's son, even made church attendance mandatory for all students.)

Wilson provided a turning point for the American colleges by giving them a model to use in place of the growing technological pragmatism advocated by American pragmatists such as philosophers John Dewey and William James. Whether or not this turning away from technological training to appreciation of the "humanities" was desirable is still hotly debated in the colleges across America. All the same Wilson is the man that turned the tide, and the turn away from specialty to generality was in keeping with Wilson's Monitor character. Technology is the province of Rationals, not Guardians, who tend to seek out standard procedures rather than technological procedures. These reforms frequently brought him into sharp and persistent—and public—conflict with the University's trustees and with some powerful alumni.

The battles caught the eye of some New Jersey Democratic party politicians. They contacted him and, without much difficulty, persuaded him to run for the office of Governor in 1910. He won easily but initially showed himself to be an indifferent machine politician. Instead of going along with the political machine which had elected him, he remained consistent with the campaign promises which helped get him elected, and pushed through the state legislature several political reform bills. Wilson was riding a crest of "progressive" sentiment, (which fit well with his Guardian bent for honest and orderly government) and the bosses could forget their annoyance with the very popular Governor. Two years later the Democratic national convention nominated Wilson as their presidential candidate, and in November of 1912 Wilson won the nation's highest office. In only three years he had gone from university professor to President of the United States.

The times were favorable for an outsider with probity to catch the public's eye, and the incumbent Taft and the agitated Teddy Roosevelt had quarrelled and hopelessly split the Republican Party. Nonetheless, Wilson's election was still quite an accomplishment for the rather stiff Monitor, whose habits impressed most people as unpleasantly distant and cold. Many people, for instance, were understandably offended by Wilson's habit of taking off his spectacles and polishing them while they were talking to him. One writer commented that Wilson's handshake was "like a ten-cent pickled mackerel in brown paper."[75] Newspapers called him "the long-haired bookworm of a President." And while the outspoken Artisan Andrew Jackson might be "Andy" to the crowds, and the outspoken Artisan Theodore Roosevelt might be "Teddy," the Monitor Thomas Woodrow Wilson would never be "Tom" or "Woody."

His victory was made more surprising by the fact that the aloof, judgmental Wilson had originally been something of an arch-conservative. His performance as Governor of New Jersey was a striking about-face, for it presented him as a progressive political reformer, and many observers saw this remarkable turnabout as nothing but a cynical political ploy. Given his lack of charisma and his questionable change of political position, it is unlikely that Wilson could have won in the campaign of 1912 if the Republicans had not quarrelled among themselves. (In fact he garnered only 42% of the vote, the remaining 58% split among Roosevelt, Taft, and other minor contenders.)

In the aftermath of victory it became apparent that, whatever his shortcomings, simple cynicism was not one of them. President-elect Wilson coolly announced to the political bosses who had worked so hard for his election that he owed them nothing. His election, he declared, was ordained by God. The many who had labored so long and intensely during his campaign were the instruments of divine will and nothing

---

75 *Presidential Anecdotes*, 218.

more. Fortunately for his political future, he gradually softened his stance—slightly—and learned to cooperate—a little—with other politicians. But his initial repudiation of his campaign bosses pointed to one of the most salient facets of this Guardian's character: he was a moralistic, staunchly conservative, literal-minded Presbyterian, the Calvinist son of a Calvinist minister, a believer that Jesus Christ and His teachings were the model and the guide for the behavior of individuals and nations. And his faith was simple, not an intellectual faith, or a faith that allowed for questions.

> For Wilson faith was the way of life. Maturity found his faith unshaken by the theological storms of the late nineteenth century. He did not fit into any particular mold. Historical criticism and the evolutionary hypothesis, which he readily accepted, only strengthened his belief in revelation and the truth of scriptures.[76]

And now he was President; in his own eyes he had become what he had intended to be since he was a young man: a "Christian statesman." It is no wonder that he tended to be inflexible and intolerant and that he looked with pity upon those who disagreed with him. After all, he said, "I know they are wrong."

Wilson's leadership style was largely consistent with this view. He assumed that the President should be the nation's moral voice and political guide, and that proposing new legislation was the President's prerogative and duty. He insisted upon a strong leadership role, and was the first President to deliver a personal message to Congress since John Adams more than one hundred years earlier. He proposed and fought for legislation with dogged and sometimes irascible determination.

Wilson may have cast himself as a political liberal, but his views of women were in general traditional and condescending: women should be wives, and as wives they should center their interest on the home and family. Biology, he seemed to believe, limited their suitability for other roles, even though their intellects might in some cases be admirable. Still, Wilson could admire and be enchanted by women who were attractive, lively, and intelligent, and Ellen Axson whom he had married in 1885, was one such woman. Outside his role as "Christian statesman," she was the centerpiece of his life, his friend, confidante, and even his

---

76 *Woodrow Wilson*, 27.

trusted advisor. He found in her presence a liveliness and warmth that otherwise was largely missing from him, just as he delighted in their three children, with whom he could unbend enough to play contentedly. But Ellen Wilson died of Bright's disease and tuberculosis of the kidneys in 1914. It was during Wilson's first term as President, and he was so heartbroken and lost that for a time he was barely able to conduct the business of government.

But less that a year after Ellen Wilson's death, Woodrow Wilson proposed marriage to a forty-three year-old widow he had met only a few months earlier, Edith Bolling Galt. He had met her in March, 1915, and only a few months later proposed, affectionately calling her "Little Girl," and proclaiming that he was desperately in love. In his letters to Edith Galt the otherwise cold, austere Wilson complained of the "lifetime of loneliness" that he had experienced since Ellen Wilson's death, he begged Edith Galt to marry him, and when she refused him he took to his bed, offering an extraordinarily pitiful picture of dejection.

It wasn't the first time such a thing happened, for Wilson was subject to periods of despondency and worry, some of which closely followed remarkable successes. These episodes could be quite lengthy, and the total time devoted to them is an impressive 95 months: almost eight years, of headache, indigestion, exhaustion, despondency and worry. This phenomenon is more likely to be found in the Guardian than in the other temperaments. Even so, most Guardians, if they do show such problems, will have only one or two episodes of such apparently unwarranted distress, and these will not last long. Wilson, in contrast, was distressed for no apparent reason for months on end, beginning in early childhood and extending until his death.

In any event, the rather elegant and independent-minded Edith Galt finally succumbed to his importuning and agreed to marry him. Their wedding was in December, 1915 and then in 1916, with Edith Wilson beside him, he ran for re-election and won.

Woodrow trusted Edith completely in matters of health, rather in the way that a good and dutiful child might, and as time passed he trusted her more and more with his political problems as well. In fact her position in his life was very similar to that of Ellen Wilson: she was his friend, confidante, and trusted advisor. Unlike Ellen Wilson, who was probably an Idealist, Edith Wilson was possibly a Rational. But, like her predecessor, Edith Wilson was very devoted to Wilson, saw him as a truly great man, and she worked to protect him and enhance his political position in whatever ways she could. She was an enduringly important figure in his life and, as events transpired, she became an important figure in the history of the nation. When they married World War I was raging, and by the time it ended the desperately important matter of a workable European peace would be at issue. She was to have a part, however unobtrusive, in how it was resolved.

During the early part of the war, public sentiment was divided roughly into three camps. Some thought the United States should go to war to support the Allied nations against the Central Powers, that is to say, Germany, Austria-Hungary, and their allies. Another camp thought that we should support the German side. By far the largest camp wanted the United States to remain firmly neutral, and only gradually did the sentiment for entry into the war on the Allied side come to dominate. Wilson's own position shifted rather like that of the public: initially, he wanted neutrality, though with a bias toward certain kinds of support for the Allies. "The example of America must be the example not merely of peace because it will not fight, but of peace because peace is the healing and elevating influence of the world, and strife is not," he declared. "There is such a thing as a man being too proud to fight."[77] Only gradually and reluctantly did he favor armed intervention on the Allied side. The sinking by a German submarine of the passenger ship *Lusitania*, with the loss of 124 American lives, was one of a number of events which finally provoked a declaration of war against Germany, and when Germany failed to show an interest in working for a mediated peace, Wilson finally cried to Congress for the need for "Force, Force to the utmost, force without stint or limit, the righteous and triumphant Force which shall make right the law of the world, and cast every selfish dominion down in the dust."[78] The moralistic Guardian orator at his most exalted!

Of course his style showed itself clearly in less exalted ways as well. In a speech to soldiers preparing to go overseas he said, "Let it be your pride, therefore, to show all men everywhere not only what good soldiers you are, but also what good men you are, keeping yourselves fit and straight in everything, and pure and clean through and through."[79] His tone is at times reminiscent of a later Monitor President, Jimmy Carter.

---

77 *Woodrow Wilson*, 95.

78 *Woodrow Wilson*, 131.

79 *Woodrow Wilson*, 117.

Though Wilson was said to have a powerful intellect he also seemed to have a frail body. In his youth he suffered from a variety of complaints which included nausea, constipation, indigestion, headaches, poor eyesight, and allergies. He could work with remarkable energy and intensity, but his health seemed always to remain fragile and uncertain. As indicated above, he occasionally found it necessary to take time away from his work to recuperate from various ailments, and there are thirteen instances of this, some of them lasting as long as eighteen months. But his difficulties were not going to halt his campaign to rescue the League of Nations. In 1919, having failed to persuade the Congress to vote to join the League, the angry and desperate Wilson decided to go over the legislature's head: he would go directly to the American people. He was still, after all, a very powerful orator, and he thought that if he campaigned hard enough he could win over the people and thereby move the Congress.

So he set off on a cross-country tour, speaking to the gathered crowds day after day, trying to shape public opinion in favor of membership in the League. But he was already in ill health and the physical strain of the campaign was too much for him. He suffered such severe exhaustion that he had to call off the remainder of the campaign. Three days after returning to the White House he suffered a stroke, and for months thereafter he was an invalid, almost mortally ill.

At the advice of his physician, Edith Wilson took upon herself the task of monitoring his contacts with others. She it was who decided who would see her ailing husband. She it was who decided what matters would be brought to his attention, and what aspects of these matters would be considered. Though the presidency almost ceased to function during the period of his illness, she was an important source of advice and recommendations, and her judgment was apparently good enough that her husband gave it considerable weight.

In spite of the severity of his illness he was obsessed about how long it would be before he could start walking again, how long before he could regain his powers and resume his campaign. "The soldiers in the trenches did not turn back because of the danger," he said, "and I cannot turn back from my task of making the League of Nations an established fact."[80] But he was too ill, and he never regained his former vigor. His frailties had finally rendered him permanently unable to exert his old authority.

---

80 *Presidential Courage*, 155.

Woodrow Wilson will probably be remembered best for his Fourteen Point plan for the settlement of World War I, and his support for the League of Nations, the abortive precursor to the United Nations. The League was not his idea, but it fit so well with his conception of a world lived according to Christian principles that he made its establishment part of his Fourteen Point plan. He struggled laboriously for its adoption in Europe and the United States, but gaining acceptance for it was a difficult task. The immanent European victors, chiefly Great Britain, France, and Italy, were determined to punish and weaken the Central Powers, Germany and its allies, and to exact for themselves whatever other advantages they might from the collapse of their enemies.

When he arrived at the peace treaty meeting being held at Versailles, France, Wilson refused the stance of the thoughtful negotiator; instead he sounded more like a pompous Christian missionary preaching to the heathen Europeans, and the war-weary and cynical perspective of the Europeans had little common ground with Wilson's stiff righteousness.[81] He was drawn into lengthy and detailed negotiations about many items of the settlement, both large and small, and he did his best to preserve intact his original fourteen points. Nonetheless, he did sign the Versailles Treaty whose provisions, in spite of his efforts, were so galling to the losers, especially to Germany, that the seeds of a second world war were planted while the horrors of the first were fresh in Europe's mind.

Could Wilson have forced Clemenceau and Lloyd George to agree to a more reasonable treaty? He had the muscle, his critics said; why did he not use it? Why did he let Britain, France, and Italy make off with the spoils of war while he was claiming that the treaty was "a ninety-nine percent insurance against war," that it insured "absolute justice," and that it constituted "the incomparable consummation of the hopes of mankind?" Wilson must have known that the Treaty of Versailles was no such thing. Yet, on his 1919 journey through the country in support of the League of Nations, each time Wilson spoke to audiences the Versailles Treaty became an increasingly perfect work until in Cheyenne, Wyoming on September 24 he said of it that:

> It is the most remarkable document...in human history...a complete reversal of the processes of government which had gone on throughout

---

81 France's Georges Clemenceau commented wryly about Wilson's Fourteen Points that even God, "le bon Dieu," presented mankind with only ten.

practically the whole history of mankind....It is a people's peace...so much of a people's peace that in every portion of its settlement every thought of aggrandizement, of territorial or political aggrandizement on the part of the Great Powers was brushed aside...by their own representatives....They did not claim a single piece of territory.[82]

Perhaps he believed the Treaty was a temporary expedient which would soon be replaced by the League of Nations. He knew the European powers would not accept the proposal for a League without it, but it can also be argued that Wilson's Guardian character had something to do with his claims for the Treaty. He was naive about the ways of the Artisan politicians and failed to appreciate fully the animosity which existed between the various European powers. It appears that he was to an important degree out-maneuvered by those wily foxes, Clemenceau of France, Orlando of Italy, and Lloyd George of England, as often happens to non-Artisans in their dealings with Artisans.[83]

But Wilson believed the League of Nations still offered a promise of a just peace, one that would correct the decidedly unjust Treaty of Versailles, and Wilson came home eager to persuade the Congress to vote for joining the League. Unfortunately he became embroiled in an angry feud with the powerful Senator Henry Cabot Lodge. Lodge sought compromises to ensure that League membership would not mean abandoning any of the United States' freedom of action, while Wilson, convinced that Lodge was without principles of any kind, and sure that the League of Nations fit with God's design, refused to compromise. The consequence of his refusal to bend was that he failed to get adequate political support for the League from Congress. Thus the inspiring vision of a League of Nations was lost to the vengefulness and self-serving interests of some men, and the unbending arrogance of others, like Wilson, its strongest supporter, who could be absolutely foolish in his high-minded stubbornness.

The League of Nations was eventually established, to be sure, but the Congress stoutly refused to vote the United States into the League. Because of the failure of the United States to join, the League of Nations

---

82 Quoted in *Thomas Woodrow Wilson: A Psychological Study,* 289.

83 The treaty was, if anything, the opposite of what he said it was. Perhaps Wilson could not live with the terrible contradiction of having advocated in the strongest terms a just peace and then capitulating to the tactics of the European politicos. His dream of being the "Christian statesman" may have disappeared in the negotiations at Versailles, along with the hope for world peace.

remained a political weakling throughout its brief life. Less than twenty years later Hitler could begin his destruction on the continent with no organized resistance from the European community until it was much too late.

It was during this time that Wilson had the stroke that immobilized him for months, and when Edith Wilson became so important. Wilson was too impaired to run for a third term of office the following year. His party selected James Cox, who was defeated in the presidential election by the Player Artisan Warren Harding. But for his efforts on behalf of the League of Nations Woodrow Wilson was awarded the Nobel Peace Prize.

He died four years later, on a Sunday morning, deaf, nearly blind, able to speak and move only with assistance. "The machinery is worn out," he said; "I am ready." His dear Edith Galt Wilson lived an active public life until her death 37 years later, in 1961.

Bibliography

Baker, R 1927-39	*Woodrow Wilson: Life and Letters*
Bailey, T 1944	*Woodrow Wilson and the Lost Peace*
Bailey, T 1945	*Woodrow Wilson and the Great Betrayal*
Baruch, B 1960	*The Public Years*
Bell, H 1945	*Woodrow Wilson and the People*
Blum, J 1956	*Woodrow Wilson and the Politics of Morality*
Blum, J 1951	*Joe Tumulty and the Wilson Era*
Freud, S, Bullitt W 1967	*Thomas Woodrow Wilson*
Garraty, J 1956	*Woodrow Wilson*
Grayson, C 1960	*Woodrow Wilson: An Intimate Memoire*
Hoover, H 1958	*The Ordeal of Woodrow Wilson*
Kerney, J 1926	*The Political Education of Woodrow Wilson*
Lawrence, D 1924	*The True Story of Woodrow Wilson*
Link, A 1947	*Wilson: The Road to the White House*
Link, A 1953	*Woodrow Wilson*
Link, A 1971	*The Higher Realism of Woodrow Wilson*
Martin, L 1958	*Peace Without Victory: Woodrow Wilson and the British Liberals*
Tillman, S 1919	*Anglo-American Relations at the Paris Peace Conference*
Seymor, C (ed) 1926-28	*The Intimate Papers of Colonel House*
Walworth, A 1958	*Woodrow Wilson*
Wilson, E 1938	*My Memoir*

Calvin Coolidge

An extraordinary ordinary man

Monitor
Born: August 4, 1872
Died: January 5, 1933
Presidency: 1923-1929

John Calvin Coolidge was Vice-President under President Warren Harding. When Harding died in office in 1923 Coolidge completed his term and then was elected to the presidency in his own right in the campaign of 1924. It wasn't much of a contest; as the incumbent, he was the natural choice for his own party, the Republicans, and the Democrats were busy fighting among themselves. The Republican nominating convention and the election campaign were unusually dull.

The apathy was fitting, for Coolidge himself seemed to be a study in resolute colorlessness. He was taciturn to the point of caricature, hardheaded and stubborn whether his mouth was open or closed, and focused entirely on the conventional and traditional values, on orderly labor, and on unswerving honesty.

The jovial and erratic Harding, Coolidge's Player Artisan predecessor, had been at the head of an administration marked by carelessness, ineptitude, and graft. Though he was Harding's Vice-President, Coolidge was never associated in the public's mind with the excesses of the Harding administration. On the contrary, the newly sworn in President Coolidge was heartily applauded when one of his first steps was to see to the prosecution of the worst offenders, which included some highly-placed officials in Harding's administration. Aside from this, however, Calvin Coolidge (he had dropped the "John" from his name as a boy) conducted a presidency that was remarkably inactive and lackluster.

None of this was a surprise to those who knew him. Even as a child Calvin Coolidge was resolutely conscientious and trustworthy, though he would never have been described as either brilliant or fired with initiative. He always followed instructions thoroughly, and in everything he undertook, no matter how trivial, he was doggedly persistent. His father once characterized the young Calvin by commenting that the lad could extract more maple syrup from a maple tree than anyone else he had ever seen. Of course once one knows Coolidge is a Monitor there is nothing remarkable in all this, for Monitors rarely overlook a detail in anything they undertake, supervise, or inspect.

Other than a quiet and slight humor, Coolidge never developed any discernible sense of play. Nor did he show any appreciation of beauty, or indulge in romance, profligacy, or boisterousness. He seemed never to have had the time or the inclination to behave in these frivolous ways. Instead he became a man who didn't waste time, didn't waste energy, and didn't waste money. He didn't waste words either, and "Silent Cal's" taciturnity became so legendary that one commentator later noted that "on the rare occasions that he opened his mouth, moths flew out."[84]

Coolidge hated meeting people and being in the public eye and he never pushed himself to the front or tried to show off. He preferred instead to attend conscientiously to the task at hand and to go about his

---

84 *Meet Calvin Coolidge*, 6.

business patiently and quietly until it was finished. Like a Horatio Alger hero, he started at the bottom, worked his way patiently upward one step at a time, and kept going, making no waves and leaving hardly a ripple, until he reached the top.

As a young man he practiced law in Northampton, Massachusetts and was elected to the City Council there. He was later elected City Solicitor, became the court clerk, and was then elected to the General Court of Massachusetts. Next he became Mayor of Northampton, then he was elected to the Massachusetts Senate, then to the presidency of the state Senate. Next came the position of Lieutenant Governor of Massachusetts, and finally the Governorship. In 1919, during his term as Governor, the Boston police walked out on strike. But Coolidge made his famous declaration that the strike was illegal: "There is no right to strike against the public safety by anybody, anywhere, anytime." His strong position brought him national recognition and helped set the stage for his accession to the vice-presidency. Patiently, carefully, slowly but steadily he worked his way upward until, in 1920, he was the Republican nomination for Vice-President of the United States.

When President Harding died, Coolidge completed Harding's term of office. Then of course it seemed quite sensible for him to run for the presidency himself. It was almost equally sensible that the campaign would be routine, humdrum, even boring—and successful. Once Coolidge had taken steps to clean up the mess made by Harding's administration, the country seemed to be in pretty good shape. Even if the hedonic Harding was not corrupt, his cronies certainly were. Coolidge was by contrast so honest, hard-working, and low key that the voters readily looked upon him with relief and approval.

Coolidge was an almost perfect caricature of the least sociable of the Monitors. He was born and raised in small-town New England, and the combination of soft-spoken Monitor and hard-soiled New Englander made an almost perfect antithesis to the jovial corruption of a big-city Player like Harding. Though it is a combination of temperament and background hardly likely to lead to wild displays of spontaneity, Coolidge was not merely a sour curmudgeon. He seemed to be a remarkably serene man who was quite comfortable with his own natural unobtrusive simplicity and not at all disturbed by his own lack of fire or brilliance.

Perhaps it was the serenity that comes with knowing so thoroughly what one ought to do and what one's aspirations are that one need rarely question one's actions. (Guardians only rarely make themselves the an object of their own scrutiny, while Rationals and especially Idealists seem to be observing themselves most of the time.) The Guardian Coolidge was following a course that had, in a small town way, been modeled by his father. And he was pursuing the sort of goal that was both desired by his father and natural to his Guardian character. A paraphrase of Coolidge's serenity might in part be "Right is right, wrong is wrong. I, like anyone who cares to, know the difference. I also know what I want and I will keep working until I get it."

If as some have suggested Calvin Coolidge possessed a certain earthy wisdom, it would be of this kind: a way of operating that has emerged from the bedrock of traditional goals and methods, and has met with success and approval. "I suppose that I am not very good copy," he once said calmly; "the usual and ordinary man is not the source of very much news."[85] But that was part of his attractiveness at the time: his "usual and ordinary" uprightness and common sense were very welcome to a country which had been visited by excesses of everything except uprightness and common sense.

Perhaps the man is being painted a bit too bleakly. It must be admitted that Calvin Coolidge did have a quiet, almost unnoticeable sense of humor. He enjoyed delivering little quips, always with his head turned away from the listener. Having made his comment he would check out of the corner of his eye to see if the listener had caught the joke. In fact this was so much his style that he became noted for his pithy, almost stealthy humor. Very dry and very understated, it used as few words as possible. One had to be alert to catch it, but the humor was there.

Once, for example, when the Treasury Department's messenger arrived at the White House to deliver Coolidge's first presidential paycheck to him, the messenger made something of a ceremony out of it, added a certain number of "ruffles and flourishes" to the delivery. Coolidge, silent and unmoving, allowed the messenger to complete his ceremony. Then he responded simply, "Call again."

---

85 *Meet Calvin Coolidge*, 8.

One of the most famous of the "Silent Cal" stories, which we can only hope is more than apocryphal, goes as follows:

> He once attended a formal dinner at which a female guest sat down beside him and gushed that she had bet some friends of hers that she could get him to say more than two words to her. Coolidge stared at her in silence for a few moments. "You lose" he responded, and addressed himself to his dinner.[86]

Another: during the 1924 election campaign one of his publicists asked him for a photograph of himself. The man making the request admitted he already had one, but that it had been taken back when Coolidge was Lieutenant Governor of Massachusetts. "I don't see what you want another for," snapped Coolidge. "I'm using the same face."[87]

His wife, Grace Goodhue Coolidge, made a marvelous contrast to the crusty Calvin. She was full of vigorous good health and the joy of living; in fact no one could seem more different from Silent Cal than this warm, gracious, and spontaneous creature. Probably an Idealist, and touched with just a bit of high spirited rebellion, Grace Coolidge loved to try out whatever was new. Because of this many considered her somewhat peculiar, but Cal Coolidge loved her as much as he ever loved anyone or anything, though he was embarrassed about showing it; Guardians generally regard it as unseemly to display spousal affection in public. Coolidge found great enjoyment in her buoyant animation and he would, somewhat secretly, buy her handsome and elaborate clothing which he delighted in seeing her wear. His indulgence in this bit of whimsy was apparently unique; there was no other area in his life in which the tight-lipped and tight-fisted Coolidge was given to whimsey or extravagance. Perhaps only an enthusiastic Idealist could have elicited from Coolidge this rare departure from his normal style.

Grace Coolidge had earned a Bachelor's degree and after leaving school had worked for several years teaching the deaf. She apparently took her involvement with this humane task quite seriously; even after she quit teaching she remained involved in one way or another in education and training for the hearing impaired. But in spite of her education and professional competence, and though he loved her, the conservative and autocratic Calvin Coolidge did not consider her an equal. He could be very critical and impatient in monitoring her actions

---

86 *Presidential Anecdotes*, 240-241.
87 *Presidential Campaigns*, 221.

and would at times restrain her actions quite unreasonably. He never discussed with her matters of politics, business, or profession.

Nor would he allow her to be content with her own expertise, whether concerned with cooking, her general fund of knowledge, her professional education, or even her recreational interests. When he heard that she had taken up horseback riding, for instance, he discouraged her from continuing. "I think," he said, "you will find that you will get along at this job [being First Lady] fully as well if you do not try anything new."[88] Hidebound traditionalist that he was, he meant it. But Mrs. Coolidge, with her ability to adapt gracefully to the demands of her position, quickly rose to celebrity status in her own right. She became recognized as an extraordinarily gracious and popular First Lady, and her schedule became as full as the President's. There is little question that her constant activity and immense popularity helped Coolidge in the election of 1924.

Nor was Grace otherwise helpless under her husband's balefully judgmental eye. If she wished to she could usually and with little difficulty subvert Cal's very traditional stance. The Coolidges often teased each other playfully in the way that only equals can, and in spite of Cal's carping and directing they seemed to have an understanding about their relationship so that it was the source of considerable happiness for both of them. Calvin acknowledged her marvelous impact on others (and on him) when he wrote to his father in his usual laconic style, "She is wonderfully popular here. I don't know what I would do without her."[89] The fortunate Coolidge had an inkling of just how lucky he was to have captured one of those rare and saintly Idealists, even while Franklin Roosevelt was failing, as we shall soon see, to appreciate his own Idealist, Eleanor.

But Coolidge's public behavior was always reserved and taciturn and he was not going to be demonstrative of his appreciation—or of anything else—where others might notice. The public had a good deal of fun with his taciturn manner, so that when he died the sharp-tongued author Dorothy Parker could ask, "How can they tell?" [90] Even when Coolidge decided to step out of politics he made his announcement with no fanfare and with no elaboration. In 1927 when it was again time for the presidential election campaign Coolidge, in his usual clipped

---

88 *Meet Calvin Coolidge*, 70.
89 *Presidential Wives*, 260.
90 Quoted in *Presidential Anecdotes*, 235, from *Try and Stop Me*, Bennett Cerf, 1944.

fashion, announced "I do not choose to run for President in 1928." Period.

He was, as always, as good as his few words. Thus it fell to his successor, Herbert Hoover, to try to deal with the terrible events that transpired only a year after Coolidge left office. Coolidge was fortunate enough to escape being associated with the disaster now known as the Great Depression; his reputation was essentially intact even after the Depression descended over the country.

Though he did step down before the Great Depression, Coolidge's presidency is not generally considered a successful one. He did not seem to grasp the nature of the economic difficulties the nation was encountering. He and his administration were strongly and perhaps somewhat blindly oriented to satisfying business interests. This meant ignoring the demands of both factory and agricultural workers, but Coolidge believed that the focus on the needs of business was the best way to preserve a healthy national economy. Other groups such as the workers would naturally profit from the nations's economic health, so they need not be an immediate concern. It was Coolidge after all who said that "the business of America is business," and who assumed that business knew how to take care of itself.

Coolidge viewed liberal (which in his eyes included labor-oriented) politics with deep suspicion and would not listen to the protests that issued from that area. One need only hold firm to what was already working, he believed; that would be enough. Stay with the tried and true and the traditional values and don't tamper. Coolidge also resisted fostering an active Executive branch; in this he was something of a throwback to the "weak" Presidents of the nineteenth century who saw themselves primarily as executors of the will of the Congress. Still, the conservative Coolidge had no reluctance to veto Congress's wishes if they seemed extravagant or wasteful. There would be no "weakness" of that sort with this Monitor!

Thus by belief and by preference, by training and temperament, Coolidge was able neither to see nor to make preparations for the enormous economic difficulties about to envelop the United States and Europe. We should note however that this is very mild criticism. Very few anticipated the coming economic collapse. Most people, even when the Great Depression was already wrecking countless lives, failed to recognize how deep it was and how long it would last.

Coolidge wrote an autobiography after he left office. His writing also shows little indication of introspection or analysis of human motives, his own or others. The book is a rather concrete and straightforward recounting of fact after fact, beginning at the beginning and ending at the end. That "step backward" of introspection, the commentary upon one's own life that helps make an autobiography intriguing, is absent. His writing carries no more suggestion that events may have complex or hidden roots that did his administration; both are completely consistent with his character.

After he left office Calvin and Grace Coolidge lived in relative seclusion. He did some law practice and wrote articles for various magazines, and even wrote a newspaper column for a time. It was during this time that he wrote his autobiography in which he included a tribute to Grace. Coming from the pen of taciturn and cool Calvin Coolidge it is touching: "For almost a quarter of a century she has borne with my infirmities and I have rejoiced in her graces."[91]

Coolidge died in 1933, apparently of a coronary thrombosis. His death came only four years after he left office. Grace Coolidge lived an active and productive life until 1957 when her great natural vitality finally ebbed away.

Bibliography

Carpenter, E 1925	*The Boyhood Days of President Calvin Coolidge*
Coolidge, C 1929	*The Autobiography of Calvin Coolidge*
Fuess, C 1940	*Calvin Coolidge, the Man from Vermont*
Gilfond, D 1932	*The Rise of Saint Calvin: Merry Highlights on the Career of Mr. Coolidge*
Green, H 1924	*The Life of Calvin Coolidge*
Kinsley, E 1924	*Calvin Coolidge, Vermonter*
Lathem, E (ed) 1960	*Meet Calvin Coolidge*
McCoy, D 1967	*Calvin Coolidge: the Quiet President*
Phillips, H 1940	*Calvin Coolidge, 1872-1933*
Roberts, K 1924	*Concentrated New England: a Sketch of Calvin Coolidge*
Rogers,C 1928	*The Legend of Calvin Coolidge*
Washburn, R 1924	*Calvin Coolidge, his First Biography*
Waterhouse, J 1984	*Calvin Coolidge Meets Charles Edward Garman*
White, W 1925	*Calvin Coolidge, the Man Who is President*
White,W 1938	*A Puritan in Babylon, the Story of Calvin Coolidge*
Woods, R 1924	*The Preparation of Calvin Coolidge: an Interpretation*

91 *Presidential Wives,* 264.

Harry Truman

"The buck stops here."

Monitor
Born: May 8, 1884
Died: December 26, 1972
Presidency: 1945-1953

Franklin Roosevelt was elected to the White House for a third term in 1944, but he was far more ill than most people suspected. His new Vice-President was Harry Truman, a career Congressman from Independence Missouri. Roosevelt died only three months after beginning his third term and Truman was horrified suddenly to find himself President of the United States. When he was told what had happened he whispered, "I'm not big enough for the job. I'm not big enough."[92] If he was not big enough at that moment then there is no question that by the time he left office in 1953 Harry Truman had grown enormously.

It isn't difficult to find similarities between Truman and his Artisan predecessor Roosevelt. They were both vigorous and active men. They both exhibited extraordinary determination. Both were politicians who loved their involvement with the people and the affairs of state. They were both gifted with the ability to grasp the essence of immediate situations but were less gifted in their ability to make sense of abstract issues. And both had great and usually unyielding faith (sometimes misplaced) in their own opinions.

The differences between the two were also great and these differences help us grasp the fundamental distinction between the Artisan and the Guardian. Roosevelt was charismatic, as the Artisans often are; Truman was in comparison rather colorless (except for the color his feisty determination lent him). Roosevelt was smooth and sleek in his handling of people and issues, as the tactically astute Artisans so often are; Truman was either unpretentiously cooperative, or as feisty as an angry banty rooster, as is often true of the Monitors. Like most Artisans, Roosevelt loved action for the sake of action; like most Guardians, Truman loved it because it was what enabled him to do what he should be doing.

Roosevelt knew he had his own presidency; it was his tool. Truman was the custodian of an office that could never "belong to" anybody. Roosevelt had the Artisan's love of a challenge; Truman took on burdens to satisfy his Guardian's sense of right and duty. Roosevelt was naturally good at maneuvering people and issues and could abandon either immediately when it suited his purposes. Truman despised dishonesty and was persistently loyal to his friends and associates (unless they violated his sense of right and wrong or deliberately failed in their duty). Roosevelt lived in an Artisan's world of expediency, maneuver, winning, and losing; Truman lived in a Guardian's world of duty, loyalty, responsibility, right and wrong. Roosevelt was devious and ingenious for the fun of it, as well as for utilitarian reasons; Truman preferred to be straightforward and sensible both by choice and in order to accomplish his ends.

---

92 Quoted from the *Boston Globe*, July 10, 1983 in *Roosevelt to Reagan*, 36.

Soon after he became President, the Monitor Harry Truman emphasized an essential difference between himself and the Artisan FDR with the declaration that

> I want to keep my feet on the ground; I don't want any experiments; the American people have been through a lot of experiments and they want a rest from experiments.[93]

There had been far more than enough "New Deal" programs set up during Roosevelt's tenure and Truman believed that few of them had done more than apply cosmetics to the ravages of the Great Depression. Only the advent of the war had shaken the country loose from its economic difficulties, and then only at the cost of huge government debts. Truman had seen enough fiddling around with the economy. It was foolish, it was wasteful, it was finally immoral, and Truman wanted no more of it. He modified Roosevelt's New Deal extensively and transformed it into his own plan (which, among other things, would guarantee every American a job) and labelled it with the wonderfully Guardian rubric, the "Fair Deal."

Harry Truman was just sixty years old when he was sworn into office on April 12, 1945. He had enormous energy and he probably was second only to Polk in how hard and long he worked. He rose every day at 5:30 in the morning and usually took a swim or went for a walk of a mile or two before he got around to breakfast. After breakfast he went straight to the day's work and continued persistently, usually late into the evening, long after everyone else had gone home. He followed this routine day after day without ever showing signs of stress or of overwork. By his own account he was fresher at the end of these long days than he was at the beginning. The office of the President, he claimed, "is an all day and nearly all night job. Just between you and me and the gatepost, I like it."[94]

A comparison of the Guardian and the Artisan shows a difference in how they view the needs of other people. Roosevelt, for instance, is said to have operated from the premise that what people really needed was "freedom from want" of such things as food, clothing, shelter, transportation, and jobs, with as few obstacles as possible standing in the

---

93 *Harry Truman and the Crisis Presidency*, 120.
94 *The Presidential Character*, 278.

way of getting them (Roosevelt's famous "four freedoms"). One could expect individuals who have been given such freedom to find effective ways to take advantage of it. Government need only prime the pump and individual initiative would take over from there. People, in Roosevelt's view, were Artisans, and they wanted what all Artisans wanted, what Roosevelt himself wanted: the opportunity to adventure, to act boldly, to impact, to win.

In contrast, Truman seemed to see a need for a great deal of deliberate, careful cooperative effort on everyone's part. Free-flowing individual initiative, though valuable and even necessary, could never be enough and certainly should not be encouraged if it meant opposing the community's standards. The world was not and should not be a place of adventurers and entrepreneurs, but rather of stable institutions and, most importantly, families and their members. Life was not a mere exercise in unfettered individuality, but at root a cooperative enterprise with its own rules and regulations, rights and wrongs, always sanctioned and approved.

Perhaps one of the most massive exemplifications of Truman's character is to be found in the Marshall Plan. This remarkably ambitious program for the economic recovery of Europe after the close of the Second World War was masterminded by Truman's Secretary of State George C. Marshall. Much of the population of war-impoverished Europe was on the edge of starvation in 1945. The Marshall Plan proposed economic aid on a scale which had never been seen before (nor has anything like it been seen since), and which no one had ever before dreamed of offering to recent allies and recent enemies alike. The plan was adopted and by 1952 the United States had assisted European economic recovery to the tune of some thirteen billion dollars. It was a remarkably successful application of principled generosity. The chief requirement for the receipt of Marshall Plan aid was merely that recipients must cooperate with each other in improving their general well-being (and that they avoid allowing Communists into positions of power or influence).

George Marshall was an Organizer Rational, a brilliant strategist and planner, who had been a powerful part of Roosevelt's and then Truman's administration. During the war Marshall had become the highest-ranking general in the United States Army. He was responsible for overseeing and coordinating the entire United States war effort, including constant consideration of the nation's relationships with its allies. Though Truman could have taken credit for his subordinate's post-war plan he insisted that General Marshall's name be used instead. Here was a program which exemplified in a gigantic way the Guardian's viewpoint. Charitable behavior, after all, is necessary to the Guardian's self-respect. How wonderful if it can be offered to responsible people ready to take care of themselves. Such people are then accountable for getting back on their own feet and becoming respectable and contributing members of the community again.

This was exactly the vision, the long-term strategy in which the Marshall Plan was rooted. Marshall devised his plan from a different perspective and somewhat different considerations, however, and Truman probably did not fully grasp the enormity of what Marshall proposed. The strategist, after all, can peer into the distant future and search the wide horizons in a way that the Guardian cannot. Perhaps Truman's recognition of the terrible plight of the people of Europe in the years immediately following World War II would not have been so immediate or Marshall's arguments so persuasive had Truman not served in France during the First World War where he could see for himself the effects of such a conflagration.

Perhaps his experience in Europe also influenced his decision to rebuild Japan. Whatever his reasons, he turned the job of refashioning and revitalizing that defeated nation over to General Douglas MacArthur. Truman gave the famous general a free hand, and if it is to MacArthur's credit that he did his work so well, it is to Truman's that he allowed the general, whom neither he nor his predecessor Roosevelt had trusted or liked, to proceed. The results were worth the discomfort, however, for Japan was quickly transformed into a democratic and industrial nation whose economic recovery, like that of Western Europe, was little short of miraculous.

Truman's Monitor orientation is clear not only in his approach to offering aid to responsible others, but also in his approach to post-war relationships with the Soviet Union and in his later handling of the Korean conflict. From the time the Second World War was nearing its end the Soviets under Josef Stalin were making a powerful effort to take possession of as much European territory as possible. Their ambitions certainly and especially included Germany, whom the Soviets saw as a traditional and powerful enemy. Stalin wanted Germany brought to its knees and kept there forever. If this could be done Germany would never again be a threat to Soviet security or Soviet ambitions.

Perhaps Stalin was especially concerned with the impact of the Marshall plan on the economic revival of this dangerous enemy. Berlin, the capital of Germany, was occupied by the Soviets and by the forces of all the major Western allies, France, Great Britain, and the United States. But the city is in northeastern Germany, and this placed it solidly in the heart of Soviet-occupied territory. Western communications of all kinds necessarily passed through Soviet-occupied terrain and were therefore under the control of the Soviet military. Stalin used the Soviet military to try isolate Berlin from the West and thereby to starve the Western allies out of the city.

Harry Truman, however, was a stubborn Missouri Monitor. He was not going to be cowed by any such high-handed, dishonorable, selfish, and downright pushy behavior. A Monitor like Truman, who grew up in a hard-working farming community, might be especially sensitive to the loss of supply. He might well be expected to act on the principle that when you're pushed, you plant your feet firmly and push back! And Truman did exactly that. He insisted that the city remain in the hands of the French, the British, and the Americans and that it would be continuously and properly supplied, regardless of Soviet wishes. But he did not want to risk starting a third world war by trying to resupply the city by land. Thus came about the famous "Berlin airlift" in which an entire major city was for the first time in history continuously supplied for a prolonged period of time by air transport and only by air transport. The airlift was in fact continued for some eleven months, cargo being flown into the isolated city on a twenty-four hour schedule.

Soviet fighters planes tried to discourage the effort by engaging in provocative maneuvers against Allied cargo planes bringing in supplies. The Allies countered by adding fighter escorts to the supply missions, thereby daring the Soviets to hazard more. Stalin had two alternatives: drop the attempt to gain total control of Berlin, or risk a shooting war with the West. In the face of the Allies' (and this certainly means Truman's) staunch and stolid persistence, the Soviets backed down. Berlin remained in the Soviet-dominated east for four more decades, of course, but the Western presence was never again subjected to this sort of threat. Furthermore, the United States and the major non-Communist countries of Europe formed the North Atlantic Treaty Organization as a joint protection against Soviet encroachment. NATO still exists today, outstaying the Soviet's own response, the recently-dissolved Warsaw Pact alliance.

Stalin didn't know Truman well. If he had, he might have recognized that it is simply very bad strategy to try to beat a man like Truman, a logistically intelligent Monitor, by playing games—however light or serious—with supplies.

Truman's Monitor point of view, with its roots in a turn of the century small-town upbringing, was naturally very down-to-earth. It was oriented first to home and family and right and wrong, broadening only gradually into concerns about the world at large, and about matters of moral complexity. Given an issue that had tangible consequences and a set of guiding rules which he could reference confidently he could quickly decide what ought to be done to his own satisfaction. Then having made his decision Truman could pursue his decision vigorously; only rarely would he need to reconsider matters. Quite thoroughly a Guardian, Truman generally saw matters concretely. For him matters were to be decided by observation rather than imagination. Abstract goals, by definition mere concepts, were neither of interest to him nor particularly easy for him to consider. When he could work with perceivable events, when he was faced with decisions about tangible problems, he could address himself to them with considerable success.

Truman's support for the Marshall Plan and his handling of the Berlin airlift are good cases in point: he knew what was right; his feisty spirit was aroused; the decisions seemed clear. The rest was simple: determined, persistent follow-through. In the same way the "Truman Doctrine," which declared Greece and Turkey to be under the protection of the United States, and Truman's strong support for the formation of the North Atlantic Treaty Organization (NATO) exemplify his determination to defend what he saw as right.

Though the initial decision was more difficult, the same comments otherwise apply to his actions when communist-controlled North Korea invaded American-backed South Korea in 1950. He was able quickly to secure the sanction of the United Nations for his decision to send more American troops into South Korea. He also went to work quickly to mobilize individual countries' support. The defense of Korea (and punitive invasion of North Korea) finally involved the military of the United States, Great Britain, and a host of smaller nations.

General Douglas MacArthur was the enormously popular military commander of the United Nations forces in Korea. He was considered a great war leader, and he had done a remarkable job of transforming the entire governmental structure of Japan after World War II. But he was also an arrogant man, one whom Franklin Roosevelt had considered extremely dangerous, and in the familiar Rational fashion he had set himself up as a master of foreign policy—sometimes in direct opposition to President Truman's decisions. Of special importance was that while Truman wanted to contain the conflict on the Korean peninsula, MacArthur wanted to expand United Nations strategy by bombing China, which had sent large numbers of troops (all "volunteers") into the conflict. There was even some indication that MacArthur would favor the use of nuclear weapons against China to force a victory. After some sparring and half-hearted attempts at negotiation, nothing had changed: Truman was still avoiding direct conflict with China, MacArthur was still speaking out for direct and violent action against China. The conflict between the two men could not, in Truman's opinion, be permitted to go on. It was direct insubordination by an American military man to his Commander in Chief, the President of the United States. It was dangerous to the conduct of the government; it was wrong for any military man, and Truman the ex-artilleryman knew it; it was intolerable. In April of 1951 Harry Truman relieved MacArthur of his command.

It was an act that required considerable political courage. MacArthur was so popular (many people saw him as almost a military savior) that his dismissal resulted in a furor. There was even an effort to impeach Truman, and the storm still had not blown completely away when Truman retired from office in January of 1953. But it was an act that should have been almost predictable. The feisty, unyielding Monitor would not back down for Marshall Stalin, and there was really no reason for presuming he would permit what he saw as MacArthur's assault against the American presidency. Only political expedience could restrain him, and mere expedience had its limits.

With more abstract issues, with concerns less tangible in their implications or less well-defined by the rule book, however, Truman needed more time and more energy to work his way through to an acceptable solution. Complex or ethically ambiguous issues require more than consideration of the immediately relevant facts or appeal to the usual regulations or codes of conduct. They demand attention and time, the balancing of multiple variables. Unfortunately a President is rarely given the luxury of extensive time, and the result of time pressures on a Guardian President may be that he will rush to execute decisions made on the basis of the facts and rules already at hand. The Guardians' long suit is in maintenance, in keeping things stable. Their short suit is in differential analysis, which invokes a myriad of possible actions and consequences. It is quite uncharacteristic of Guardians such as Truman to complicate deliberately their understanding of the situations in which they find themselves.

Thus when the atomic bomb became available as a weapon in 1945, Truman's decision to use it was not a difficult one. Abstract arguments about the ethics of such an act or about its potential long-range impact could be ignored, if they were ever noticed to begin with. The simple fact was that American lives, perhaps hundreds of thousands of them, were at stake. The Japanese were being intransigent about acknowledging that their cause was lost. They refused all overtures for bringing the war to an end. To Truman it was stupid and callous of them, unforgivably stubborn and wantonly destructive. Furthermore, U. S. bombing raids were killing thousands of Japanese civilians already, and thousands more would continue to die as long as the conflict continued. In the face of these simple and frustrating facts Truman could decide rather quickly to drop the atomic bomb on Japan. To do so might bring a quick end to the Second World War and save those hundreds of thousands of American lives. Furthermore, if one included civilian lives in one's calculations, then the number of lives saved, Japanese and American, might be in the millions. No moral complexity here, no meandering thoughts about unforseeable futures or unspeakable ethics. The task was clear, the morality obvious.

The decisions Truman had to make during the war and after would have been of monumental significance for any man. It is remarkable that a man like Harry Truman would, overall, be able to confront them so well. He was, after all, a small-town man at heart. He had been born into a hard-working farming family in the modest, rural, rather provincial world of Independence, Missouri, only three decades after the Civil War ended. He wore glasses even as a child so most sports were considered too rough for him. He used his time instead to read; American history was one of his favorite subjects and he amassed a wealth of information on the subject.

He was also a hard worker. By the time he was twenty-two he had been a railroad gang timekeeper, a mail clerk at a local newspaper, a bank clerk and a bookkeeper, all good Monitor jobs, and had been a page at the Democratic National Convention in 1906 (where he heard William Jennings Bryan speak). For the next eleven years, until he was thirty-three, he led a more settled life helping his grandmother run her farm. He had developed an interest in politics rather early but didn't become involved until his father died in 1914. Truman, now age thirty, was given his father's job, county road inspector, a kind of political patronage. The following year he was appointed postmaster of the local town, handled his responsibilities conscientiously and energetically, and gradually became well known in local political circles. He was soon recognized as a man who knew everyone and could look into (that is, monitor) everything going on around him. Consistent with both his temperament and his cultural background, he also became known as a down-to-earth, honest and responsible politician who understood and safeguarded the needs of his constituency.

These characteristics and his ability to fit into the local political machinery (he had become a career politician by then) eventually led him to the United States Senate and the seat he occupied there from 1934 until he was elected Vice-President in 1944. Truman was an honest man but he was also a loyal party politician, and his loyalty is a part of what helped him into the Senate. But the political machine that had helped him get his start was corrupt. As the evidence of its wrongdoing began to grow, Truman the conscientious Monitor realized he could no longer align himself with it, and once in the Senate he led an investigation that uncovered many of the Pendergast gang's corrupt dealings. He also led the "Truman Committee" during the Second World War, whose purpose was to examine the efficiency of defense production. This was of course a classic Monitor function, which Truman carried out with great thoroughness and great fairness, rather than turning it into a political game. By the time he ran for re-election he was sufficiently well-recognized for his honest and conscientious work that his former association with the corrupt political machine couldn't hurt him.

Harry Truman was happy in the Senate. His secure position in this political family and his success in looking after his constituents back home contented him. He had some aspirations for the presidency, but these were tempered by the satisfaction he found in his place in the Senate. He was a good, hard-working Democrat and he had the grass-roots common sense of the vaunted "common man," who is typically a Guardian. He was an advocate of a populist, grass-roots democracy consistent with his small-town heritage. He largely approved of and followed the Democratic party line during his first term of office, and in general Harry Truman found no difficulty being a good party man.

Then in 1944 he was unsettled to find himself selected by Franklin Roosevelt as his vice-presidential running mate. As usually happens, Truman's selection for the vice-presidency was more a matter of managing political necessity than of picking out the most able and qualified candidate. The current Vice-President, Henry Wallace, had made himself too unpopular to run for re-election. Truman on the other hand had made few enemies and could bring into the Democratic camp voters who might otherwise vote against Roosevelt. In essence, Truman might not be inspiring, but he was steady and predictable, no one could really object to him, and he would pull some of the voters who objected to Roosevelt. Truman was the man Roosevelt's campaign needed.

Truman was reluctant to accept the nomination. He was happy in the Senate and pleased with his work there. The story has been told that he agreed to run only after Roosevelt advised, "Tell Harry the country needs him." This was too much for Truman; his wavering disappeared under the force of the appeal to duty. The story exactly parallels the way in which the reluctant Monitor Guardian George Washington was induced to accept nomination. Though it may be apocryphal it describes perfectly the hard-working and conscientious Guardian.

Truman accepted the nomination, the campaign was successful, FDR was again elected President, and Harry Truman was the country's new Vice-President. Then, only eighty-two days after the election, Roosevelt was dead and Harry Truman was President of the United States.

During his time in office he gained a great deal more certainty about the scope of his own abilities. He ceased to be the man who worried that "I'm not big enough for the job. I'm not big enough." He became again the cocky scrapper who knew when he was right and who was able and willing to fight for what he believed in. When he ran for election to the presidency in 1948 he could stand up at the Democratic nominating convention and confidently predict victory over the Republicans in the coming presidential election "because they're wrong and we're right!"

Whether as small-town politician, United States Congressman, Vice-President or President, Harry Truman was extremely gregarious. He was always at home with people and he greatly enjoyed the constant social contact his busy political life demanded.

In his fondness for contact with people he stood in strong contrast to his wife, Elizabeth Wallace ("Bess") Truman. Bess Truman was also a Monitor Guardian, but unlike her husband she was very self-contained, quiet and taciturn except when she was within the confines of her own family. She guarded her privacy jealously and only rarely involved herself with the social world of Washington and its political demands. Apparently she had something of a horror of embarrassing herself and her husband; she lived constantly with the fear of making a mistake or otherwise showing herself less favorably than she might wish to—or than she ought to.

There were other differences between Bess and Harry Truman. Bess Wallace grew up in the same area that Harry Truman did but was much better off financially and socially as a youngster. While Harry was working on his family's farm and trying to keep it from going deeper into debt, Bess was attending finishing school with other young ladies of relatively affluent families. Her family later fell on financial hard times and was not able to survive as well as did the Trumans, and Bess Wallace's father committed suicide. Bess held her reactions inside, remaining silent, grim-faced and clench-fisted throughout the night he died. Then and there she decided that if she married she would share her whole life with her husband; he would never have to feel alone, as she believed her father had, in either his difficulties or his triumphs.

Harry Truman said later that he fell in love with Bess Wallace when they were still children. But while he had wanted to marry her from a very early age Bess took fifteen years to make up her mind about him. He later said he didn't mind; he was convinced all the rest of his life that she had been worth the wait. He loved her unreservedly and appreciated and trusted her judgment and her taste. They got along extremely well together, two Monitors sharing the same social background who understood how marriage was supposed to be and who also happened to be fond of each other.

Their happiness with each other didn't prevent Bess from getting rather stern with Harry at times. He was a bit hotheaded and would occasionally threaten to do something rash to someone who had offended him. Bess had a strong sense of decorum and at such times could be quite put out with Harry's bad manners. On at least one occasion Bess is said to have led him with a firm grip on his ear, back into their hotel room when she decided that his temper rendered him temporarily unfit to be out in public. Harry's salty language sometimes showed up in public. More than once he declared someone to be "an S.O.B." who ought to "go to hell," and he announced during Richard Nixon's first presidential campaign that anyone who voted for Nixon also "ought to go to hell." After such occasions the White House would later resonate to Bess's irritated reproach, "You didn't have to say that!"

During Harry Truman's election campaign against Thomas E. Dewey in 1948, Mrs. Truman had joined in with the

> small group of advisers which met every night to plan the next day's strategy. She also went over her husband's speeches with him, saw that he ate properly and got enough rest, and supplied ailing reporters with aspirin and sewed buttons on coats for people on Truman's staff.[95]

When Truman became President he continued to talk with her quite freely about matters of politics and matters of state, and he apparently appreciated hearing her opinions about these things. It is likely that his conversations with her did at times influence his decisions, for he had learned early in their marriage that he could not only love her, but that he could also count on her. He and a friend opened a haberdashery after he left the army at the end of World War I. Bess took on the bookkeeping, planned the advertising, and handled the inventory. But times were bad and in spite of their tremendous efforts the business failed. The Trumans could have declared bankruptcy and thereby escaped many of the financial obligations the business had incurred, but debts are, after all, almost holy to Guardians and contracts of any kind are matters of sacred honor. The Trumans, rather than declaring bankruptcy, worked instead to pay off all the debts the business had incurred.

Mrs. Truman's sense of propriety was certainly not confined to matters of morality and financial obligation, of course. She also had strong opinions about what was and was not "ladylike," and she was resolved to adhere to her understandings in this area. Being a good wife, mother, and household manager were certainly a part of "being a lady"; working at a salaried job definitely was not. Personal privacy was another matter with which a lady properly concerned herself and this is another reason Bess Truman protected her privacy assiduously. Though she accompanied her husband on his political campaigns (as a lady

---

95 *Presidential Wives*, 322.

might), she refused to speak to reporters or to bring any sort of publicity to herself (for a lady should not). "A woman's place in public," she told a friend, "is to sit beside her husband, be silent, and be sure her hat is on straight."[96]

She contributed endlessly behind the scenes to her husband's success and well-being. Though her perspective about a woman's (or a lady's) place may seem dated or even objectionable in some quarters today, one must recognize that in terms of her own traditional Guardian values and those of her husband she was a complete success. She did well the things she intended to do, including being a mother and a wife and serving as a valued partner and advisor to her husband. During his presidency she also managed the White House with quiet and admirable efficiency, another task for which her Monitor character helped prepare her.

In general, Harry Truman was a vigorous and straightforward man of his word in a time of change and complexity. He had great and sometimes righteous determination, a love for and fascination with details, and he was impatient with sloppy or lazy people who failed to perform as they should. He also naturally respected and lived by the traditional values, the traditional ways of doing things which he saw as so essential to the well-being of the country he loved. Being President meant for him working hard and talking straight, and he gained a great deal of satisfaction from doing both. He was the quintessential Monitor who understood that being accountable is the gateway to self-esteem. It was the Monitor Truman, after all, who had the famous sign in the President's office, "The buck stops here."

Truman enjoyed being President, but he recognized that even the presidency has its limitations. Monitor that he was, he could ruefully reflect that "I sit here all day trying to persuade people to do the things they ought to have sense enough to do without my persuading them. That's all the powers of the President amount to." He had been embroiled in a wide variety of conflicts during his two terms of office, including his efforts to get civil rights legislation passed, to desegregate the armed forces, to provide more money for economic recovery, to fight post-war inflation, and to deal with the vicious Senator Joseph McCarthy (including McCarthy's claim that Truman had "lost" China

---

96 *Presidential Wives*, 316.

by refusing to give increased support to Chiang Kai-Shek's corrupt regime). The final blow was the discovery of corruption in his own administration. In March of 1952 he announced that he would not run for re-election. Instead he backed the nomination of Democrat Adlai Stevenson, who campaigned against the Republicans' Dwight Eisenhower. During the election campaign Truman commented that if Dwight Eisenhower won the election the former general would be less than thrilled about what would come next.

> He'll sit here, and he'll say, 'Do this! Do that!' And nothing will happen," he said. "Poor Ike—it won't be a bit like the Army. He'll find it very frustrating.[97]

The Trumans retired to their home in Independence, Missouri after Eisenhower won the election. Harry, energetic and peppery as ever, stayed active until his health failed him. It was a full decade after he left the White House, while he was campaigning for John Kennedy, that he made the famous remark that Nixon voters ought to go to hell. Bess Truman maintained her vigor too, and continued to monitor her husband as she always had. When she heard about Harry's comment she called him and told him that if he couldn't talk more politely than that he "ought to come right home."[98]

Harry Truman died in 1972 at age eighty-nine. Bess lived on for another ten years. She was ninety-seven when she died.

Some have said that Harry Truman was at best a mediocre President. Others have suggested that he was close to greatness. The argument continued for several decades, during which time sentiment seems to have shifted in Truman's favor. It is perhaps the usual cost of being a Guardian President to be seen as pedestrian by one's contemporaries. Only in retrospect is the value of the Guardian's down-to-earth judgment and well-developed common sense likely to become appreciated. The Guardian President will never be seen as flashy or glamorous and his statesmanship is rarely dramatic. There is little glamour but there is the possibility of great honor in the behavior of the Guardian who says as Harry Truman did, "The only thing I ever do worry about is to be sure that where I'm responsible the job is properly done."[99]

---

97 Quoted in *Presidential Power*, 281.
98 *Presidential Wives*, 324.
99 *Plain Speaking*, 36.

Bibliography

Bolte, C 1970	*Give 'em Hell, Harry: A Documentary Drama of the Truman White House Years*
Cochran, B 1973	*Harry Truman and the Crisis Presidency*
Donovan, R 1977	*Conflict and Crisis: The Presidency of Harry S. Truman*
Druks, H 1966	*Harry S. Truman and the Russians*
Ferrell, R 1983	*Harry S. Truman and the Modern American Presidency*
Gosnell, H 1980	*Truman's Crises: A Political Biography of Harry S. Truman*
Hamby, A 1973	*Beyond the New Deal: Harry S. Truman and American Liberalism*
Levantrosser, W (ed) 1986	*Harry S. Truman: The Man from Independence*
Haynes, R 1973	*The Awesome Power: Harry S. Truman as Commander in Chief*
Hedley, J 1979	*Harry S. Truman: The 'Little' Man from Missouri*
Hersey, J 1980	*Aspects of the Presidency*
Maddox, R 1988	*From War to Cold War: The Education of Harry S. Truman*
McCoy, D 1984	*The Presidency of Harry S. Truman*
Miller, M 1974	*Plain Speaking: An Oral Biography of Harry S. Truman*
Pemberton, W 1989	*Harry S. Truman: Fair Dealer and Cold Warrior*
Powell, E 1948	*Tom's Boy Harry: The Story of Harry Truman's Connection with the Pendergast Machine*
Robbins, C 1979	*Last of his Kind: An Informal Portrait of Harry S. Truman*
Roberts, A 1985	*Brother Truman: The Masonic Life and Philosophy of Harry S. Truman*
Steinberg A 1962	*The Man from Missouri: The Life and Times of Harry S. Truman*
Truman, H 1980	*The Autobiography of Harry S. Truman*
Truman, H 1966	*Good Ol' Harry: The Wit And Wisdom of Harry S. Truman*
Truman, H 1955	*The Memoirs of Harry S. Truman*

Richard Milhous Nixon

"...lethally anxious about his place and future."

Monitor
Born: January 9, 1913
Presidency: 1969-1974

Richard Nixon is the only United States President to resign from the office. His resignation came in the midst of a firestorm of accusation and condemnation such as no other President has endured, and during a time of national turmoil more intense than any since the Civil War. Yet today, nearly two decades after his presidency, Richard Nixon has emerged from what might have been total defeat and complete obscurity to become something of an elder statesman. To write about Richard Nixon is necessarily to write against this background of accusation and condemnation, defense and applause, a background that is enriched by some further allegation or exposition almost monthly. We the authors do not wish either to add to the controversy or to try to resolve it. As with the thirty-nine other Presidents we seek only to demonstrate the power of the temperament and character model. We leave it to the historians to pass judgment on the man and his doings and concern ourselves only with how those doings reveal his character unfolding from his temperament.

Richard Milhous Nixon was born into a small Quaker community in Yorba Linda, California, when the area was still rural, chiefly citrus groves and undeveloped land lying on the outskirts of Los Angeles. Quakers are typically considered to be reserved and strict, though still gentle and loving. Richard Nixon's mother, Hannah Nixon, was loving in her own fashion, and loyal to him all his life. But she was also gently demanding of her children, in the manner of a "saint," as some people (including Richard) described her. And though she did not punish physically, it has been reported, her way with words made physical punishment eminently preferable to being the subject of one of her quiet corrective lectures. Richard's father, Frank Nixon, was probably an outgoing Operator Artisan. Frank Nixon has been described as sometimes genial and fun-loving, but also sometimes as bitter and hateful, a man whose discipline of his children occasionally frightened those who witnessed it.

Times were hard when Richard was a boy, and the Nixons did not flourish financially. Everyone in the family worked diligently, and the youthful Richard was no exception. Whether in the lemon groves, his father's gas station, or at school, Richard was a tireless, uncomplaining worker. In fact he reminds us of another young Monitor, the stolid, thorough Calvin Coolidge, of whom his father reported that he could get more maple syrup from a maple tree than anyone else he had ever known.

Young Richard Nixon survived two close brushes with death, and his mother sometimes described his survival as "miraculous." But his two brothers were not so fortunate. Arthur, his younger brother, died when Richard was twelve, and his oldest brother, Harold, died after a five-year struggle with tuberculosis, when Richard was twenty. (Another brother, Donald, was born when Hanna Nixon was in her forties and Richard already a young man.)

As is so often the case with the Monitor Guardians Nixon was noted for his serious and sober manner, in elementary school and high school, at Whittier College, where he earned a degree in history in 1934, and at Duke University, where he earned his law degree in 1937. Upon completing the degree he tried to find a job with a prestigious law firm in the East. But he was unsuccessful, and he settled for working in Whittier, where he and his family were already known. It was here that he met and, in 1940, married Thelma "Pat" Ryan. When World War II broke out at the end of 1940 Nixon was commissioned into the Navy. He served in the Pacific, chiefly as a supply officer.

When the war ended in 1945 a group of local Republicans in the Whittier area were desperately searching for someone to run against the incumbent United States Representative, Jerry Voorhis, a man too "liberal" for their tastes. The more conservative lawyer and soon to be released Naval officer Richard Nixon looked better to them than anyone else they could find to oppose the able Voorhis, so they invited Nixon to consult with them about campaigning in the 1946 election.

Nixon did not hesitate, for here was a chance to distinguish himself. He met with his sponsors and immediately began preparing his plans to do battle with Voorhis.

Nixon won the election, and then won re-election to the House in 1948. In 1950 he challenged Helen Gahagan Douglas for her Senate seat and won again. He became known in the Senate as an aggressively anti-communist Senator and a very competent professional politician. He established his political credentials so well that in 1952 Dwight Eisenhower, running for President, accepted him as his vice-presidential running mate. Though Nixon's career continued to be stormy, and in spite of allegations of wrong-doing that shadowed his career even while he was Vice-President, Eisenhower kept him on the ticket for the 1956 election.

Thus by 1960 Richard Nixon had eight years of vice-presidential experience under President Eisenhower. He was therefore the natural candidate for the Republicans, and had also established a reputation as a capable man in the area of international relations. But in the campaign of 1960 Nixon could not capture the voters' favor, even as an incumbent Vice-President. The charming and dashing Operator John Kennedy, was simply too charismatic for the dour Monitor, Richard Nixon. A year later, having returned to California, Nixon ran for state Governor, but experienced another stinging defeat at the hands of Pat Brown. So galled was he in his disappointment about the California failure that when it was time to concede to Brown he made his bitter announcement to the assembled press that he was removing himself from politics, and that "you won't have Nixon to kick around any more." It seemed that his political career was over. He was now merely a defeated Vice-President who could not win office even in his own state.

But Nixon's determination to put himself in the highest office of the land asserted itself. Through five years of slow, careful and patient rebuilding, Nixon re-established his political strength and increased his hold on the apparatus of the Republican Party. In 1968 he was selected for a second time as the Republican candidate for the presidency, he ran, and he won. From what seemed almost total obscurity Richard Nixon had risen to become President of the United States.

In spite of his successful bid for the presidency, Nixon was never free of his critics' claim that he was amoral, ruthless, even vicious. Nonetheless there is far more to Richard Nixon the Monitor Guardian than the mere caricature of a darkly ambitious and ruthless politician. First, he is clearly a remarkably thorough and determined Monitor. Second, he is a polished orator and a champion debater. Third, he was able to make use of the help of the clever Henry Kissinger to exploit opportunities for improved relations with both mainland China and the U.S.S.R. and to arrange several important treaties with foreign nations.

Looking at Nixon through the lens of temperament theory we are immediately struck by his resemblance to another Monitor Guardian, Woodrow Wilson, whom he admired and sought to emulate. Both Richard Nixon and Woodrow Wilson were tremendously ambitious; both were very intelligent schedulers; both were given to perpetual anxiety about their status; both avoided personal confrontations; both were loners; both trusted no one, or they trusted the wrong people; both were finally outmaneuvered by clever Artisans. Like Wilson, Nixon could finally not sustain himself in office; his abilities, though considerable, proved less than his ambitions, which were enormous.

Though he has always pursued public recognition, Richard Nixon has never been outgoing, an easy man to know, or a person possessing either charisma or the gift of laughter. He operates with a serious, business-like, even stiff demeanor, with few traces of humor or of relaxation, and he perseveres until he succeeds. He succeeded in becoming a recognized and even respected campus figure, for instance, in high school and college, but he was never greatly liked or, for that matter, disliked. Instead he was the (young) man with a mission, in steady pursuit of his goals. Except when among a few close friends he was talkative only for a specific purpose: to persuade, to induce, to impress or sway someone for the sake of his own agenda. Always there was the desire to get a place for himself in the hierarchy, as high in the hierarchy as possible.

Perhaps nothing better captures Richard Nixon's determination than his behavior with the Whittier College football team. He wanted earnestly to be a member of the team, but his relatively poor physical coordination coupled with his small size (he weighed about 150 pounds then) kept him from being a first or even a second string player. But he suited up, he practiced, and he sat on the bench, game after game for four years. During practice sessions he was, in effect, a living "practice dummy," whose light weight and indifferent physical prowess made him a painfully easy target. But he would not quit, he would not succumb to pain or embarrassment or humiliation: he was a member of the team and he would maintain that prized membership, no matter what. (He was put into a few games for a few plays if Whittier's win or loss was already assured, and his appearance on the field became the occasion for sympathetic cheers from the stands.)

Nixon's early political campaigns were battles which included deliberate and very damaging distortions of his opponents' characters and records, among them inflammatory accusations that they were communists or communist sympathizers. His critics offer these campaigns (especially those against Jerry Voorhis in 1946 and Helen Douglas in 1950) as the prototypes for his political career, portraying him as a ruthless politician willing to engage in dishonorable tactics in order to win. But however much his tactics may have offended some observers, he (and most of his supporters) did not seem to have any difficulty justifying their use. After all, as he quite accurately commented, he was not the only elected official ever to resort to them, and this was apparently a sufficient justification for their employment. Many Guardians are not reluctant to say that in business and politics "it's a dog-eat-dog" world, or "it's nothing personal, just business."

Nixon has clearly placed himself among this group of Guardians, and his campaigns strongly reflect it.[100]

Nixon's campaigns have usually been quite effective, but often rather heavy-handed. Unfortunately, as in the case of Helen Douglas, they were sometimes executed so thoroughly that his opponents were not merely defeated, but politically ruined. His political campaigns, like his preparations for debate, were carefully listed, studiously rehearsed, and deliberately executed. He loved the details of campaigning, including working out the list of places to be visited during the campaign, and the times when the visits would take place. In this he was again the typical Monitor, with his interest in listing and scheduling.

Though he was an effective political campaigner, Nixon has never been very good at the *art* of persuasion. Like most Guardians, and far different from the natural, fluid, opportunistic style of outspoken Artisans like Ronald Reagan, Lyndon Johnson, or John Kennedy, Nixon was very deliberate, and sometimes ponderous in his efforts. He was an outstanding college debater, but consistent with his training and experience in debate, and consistent with his Monitor character, he prefers to write out and thoroughly, repetitively rehearse his arguments, rather than reacting opportunistically or spontaneously, in a more Artisan manner.

Indeed, repetition seems to have been a way of political life with him, a trait not unusual in Guardians, though in Nixon's case the trait was very pronounced. He views everything that concerns him with a watchful and evaluative eye, acts out a prepared role which seems to him to fit the situation, and then weighs and measures each element of his performance. From his evaluation he can then devise further "scenarios" or "scripts" in order to schedule himself to act more effectively in the next go-round.

He could be quite adept in such performances, just as he could be quite inept, even embarrassingly so, when he was apparently trying to be spontaneous and casual. Often uncomfortable in casual conversation, he

---

100 "Of course I knew Jerry Voorhis wasn't a communist....The important thing is to win. You're just being naive." So responded the victorious Nixon to a Voorhis aide who angrily accused him of lying. (The quote is taken from *Richard Nixon*, page 171.)

reportedly had trouble reading his audiences, and his personal style sometimes "was an embarrassing blend of the slick and the corny."[101]

> He was an uncomfortable host...disappearing from time to time, only to return and urge guests to have another drink, with a vigorous show at being friendly. Being a host did not come easy for him.[102]

Furthermore he is reported to have no special interest in camaraderie. One observer noted that when he was in Congress "Richard Nixon was never one of the boys, never enjoyed the smoke-filled rooms which sustained the Irish around Kennedy or the loyalists around Johnson. Such an atmosphere bored him."[103] He was cautiously task oriented, scheduled down to the last minute, and so could not spare even moments for such frivolity. As another commentator wrote of Nixon, "Show him the rules, and he will play your game, no matter what, and beat you at it. Because with him it is not a game."[104] His social interest, like that of many other Guardians, is carefully scheduled series of interactions toward higher status. With his life-long climb up the social ladder he could not spare any time for nonsense; the road to prestige and power lay in making sure of the favor of the party and of the voters.

Once in office, Nixon's conservative stance seemed to shift. He did not attempt (as many thought he would) to dismantle the Democrats' welfare programs; if anything he reinforced them. Instead of decreasing taxes as expected, he actually increased them. Then, in order to increase revenues further, he took back the tax credits that were designed to favor business enterprises. But what shocked the conservatives, and especially the capitalists among them, was that he froze the prices that businesses were allowed to charge their clients and customers. To make matters worse, in the eyes of some at least, Nixon also froze the pay that employers were to give to their employees for their services.

Regardless of political commitments, this regulation of wages and prices was quite in keeping with Nixon's Monitor Guardian character. After all, inflation was out of hand and depression threatened. What *can*

---

101 *Roosevelt to Reagan*, 109.
102 *Among Those Present*, 26.
103 *Among Those Present*, 23.
104 *Nixon Agonistes*, 160.

go wrong of course *will*, so best to take no chances. Best to reign in the entrepreneurs and tell them how to run their businesses. Otherwise they will charge gouging prices and pay as little in wages as possible, and thereby make matters worse. Nixon eventually suspended his wage and price control measures, of course, but imposed them once again during his second term in office. In all this Nixon seemed to have a remarkably strong interest in monitoring the actions of anyone and everything which might come under the scrutiny of the federal government, and to bring more and more of the flow of daily life under that scrutiny.

In spite of his activity in domestic matters, the domain in which he most aspired to be honored was the domain of foreign relations, and in this he has had—and continues to have—remarkable success. His behavior in this area is interesting. He campaigned, after all, as a staunchly anti-communist, conservative candidate, while his presidential actions looked like those of a liberal politician seeking a rapprochement with the communist world. He had made a name for himself as a communist hunter, with the scalps of Gerry Voorhis, Helen Douglas, and Alger Hiss secured to his belt. But as President and Vice-President, if he could increase the possibilities for world peace, he would be that much closer to the goal of being, even more than his hero, Woodrow Wilson, a great statesman. And to some degree he succeeded. Nixon it was who (with the painful exception of Viet Nam) managed to work out arrangements that gave the United States a more honorable place in the world community, and especially it was Nixon who negotiated the Strategic Arms Limitation Treaty (SALT) with Russia and who managed to negotiate a tripartite relationship between the United States, China, and the USSR, nations between whom there was much ill will, and which had been brandishing nuclear weapons for some time.

These feats of diplomacy required several years of rather delicate, sensitive, and secretive maneuvering, in which Nixon was ably assisted by the peripatetic Henry Kissinger from Harvard. Nixon the persistent politician had teamed up with Kissinger, the wily tactician whom he could turn loose to maneuver—or so he thought. Operators are difficult to control at the best of times, and Nixon probably underestimated Kissinger's wiliness.

Nonetheless Nixon had considerable success in the arena of foreign relations, and we can only speculate about what would have happened if

Nixon had not been drawn into the Watergate matter. Management of the sequelae to the break-in was fundamentally a tactical matter (leaving aside the matters of law and ethics for the moment) in which Nixon allowed himself to become enmeshed. In this respect his political downfall may have been the consequence of trying to direct a fluid tactical action, which also involved significant violations of the law. For in doing so he involved himself, at great risk, in the conduct of the kind of tactical maneuvering for which he, like most Guardians, could claim little talent. Unfortunately for Nixon, most of his immediate subordinates were either Guardians whose tactical prowess was no better than his, or Artisans, sharply focused on their own interests, and who could maneuver with remarkable agility through the ambiguities and complexities of the coverup.

As these pages are being finished, a new and apparently thorough exploration of the Watergate matter has just been published. If *Silent Coup* is to be believed, Nixon was drawn, almost unaware, into the illegal efforts to obscure the connection of the Watergate break-in with important personnel in Nixon's administration. Once he was entrapped by those who were using him to protect their own interests, the mire became deeper and deeper, and soon Nixon could not extricate himself. Appearances were deceiving, the authors claim, heroes became villains, and villains became heroes. Others escaped with minor damage to themselves, or with whole skins, but Nixon could not.

This reference to *Silent Coup* is meant neither to exonerate nor to condemn Richard Nixon. But it does help make sense of events from the perspective of temperament. For instance, Nixon's enormous Guardian ambition for high office was accompanied by a powerful fear of losing it. (As one of his biographers put it, he was "lethally anxious about his place and future."[105]) Many bright and ambitious Guardians seem never able to satisfy their hunger to belong, or achieve a sufficient place of honor. Just as the Rationals hunger always for greater achievement and aspire to more wizardry, so the Guardians hunger after more security and aspire to greater prestige. So as Nixon became more entangled in the tricky and dangerous Watergate matter, he became enormously anxious about his political future. With so much at stake, and since Guardians

---

105 *Silent Coup*, xiv.

naturally worry more than any other temperament to begin with, it is no wonder that Nixon eventually became nearly disabled by his worrying.

Best, therefore, to keep a wary eye on those who might betray the cause. But what if one's most trusted confidants are those most likely to betray?

Two of those confidants, Robert Haldeman and John Ehrlichman were both Eagle Scouts and Christian Science devotees, teetotallers, and extremely loyal to Nixon. Both were probably Monitor Guardians, just as Nixon was, and they took it upon themselves to monitor others' access to the President. Apparently they too were somewhat ruthless, but their own ambitions could be realized through Nixon's success, and their loyalties were clear.

But General Al Haig and Professor Henry Kissinger were something else again: Operator Artisans, brilliant tacticians, something the Guardians Nixon, Haldeman, and Ehrlichman could never be. Nixon seemed both to admire them and to fear them, and it is likely that he wanted to be able to pass for one of them when he was in their company, to be able to mimic their style and their skills. The two of them were much of what Nixon was not: articulate, adventurous, fearless, and smooth. But Nixon rarely questioned whether he had them securely tethered, and apparently his failure to do so was fatal to his aspirations, for certain of his subordinates were apparently quite willing to bring him down in order to protect themselves and their interests.

Haig, for example is reported in *Silent Coup* to have remained loyal to the Joint Chiefs of Staff, and to have kept them fully informed of Nixon's every move. Nixon erred in counting on Haig's loyalty to him. But this is not unusual, for all of us are subject to misunderstanding the direction and strength of loyalty. It differs with character. Guardian loyalty, for instance, is *up and down* the hierarchy whereas Artisan loyalty is independent of the hierarchy, given only to their "buddies." Artisans are insubordinate in their very nature and this is something Guardians cannot understand. The fraternal Artisans are instinctively egalitarian, their loyalty *sideways and across* rather than up and down. Nixon must have naturally assumed that Kissinger and Haig would be just as loyal as Haldeman and Ehrlichman. After all, as he the Guardian saw it, his office *entitled* him to their loyalty. But, it appears, this isn't the way *they* saw it.

Of course Richard Nixon's ordeal was not his alone; his family was also caught up in the agony of 1974. His daughters, Tricia and Julie, each suffered through the Watergate troubles, but probably the most poignant example of the price of both his successes and his failures is to be found in his wife, Pat Nixon.

Catherine Thelma "Pat" Ryan, probably an outgoing Idealist, was a cheerful and charming young woman in 1938, a teacher at Whittier High School with a lively and sunny disposition, admired and greatly liked by everyone, friends, colleagues, and students. The young lawyer Richard Nixon was so taken with her that he predicted their marriage the same evening they met. It took him two years of work, and Pat Ryan was at first not very interested in him, but she finally accepted his proposal. They were married in 1940. From that time on Pat Ryan Nixon, who had an interest in amateur theatricals and who had even played a few bit parts in movies, had a new role to play: she was the wife of an ambitious Monitor politician operating with a grim determination to succeed.

Though she rarely complained about her new life, her friends noticed that much of her good cheer, liveliness, and spontaneity gradually disappeared. Her manner became increasingly stiff and tense, she adopted a formal and practiced self-presentation, she became the professional wife of a professional politician. It is as if she developed her own equivalents of the self-monitoring, practiced self-presentation that her husband naturally displayed. Pat Nixon's tense, stilted demeanor came to stand out starkly from her manner prior to marriage, just as Richard Nixon's impetuous proposal of marriage stands in stark contrast to the deliberate and self-controlled way he lives the rest of his life.

Richard Nixon, like most Monitors, was not demonstrative of affection in public, and even the most minimal touching or affectionate glances in his wife's direction were notable by their absence. Pat Nixon has never acknowledged any disquiet about this absence of most of the usual public tokens of affection, and has stood loyally by him through both his successes and his failures. Most of those who have written about her seem to have great admiration and affection for her, and often betray a sense of sadness for a woman whom they have seen as a tragic heroine on the national scene. One observer wrote, for instance, that her public presence during Nixon's days in office showed "a stoic weariness and tired sweetness, that, to some who followed her, was close to tear-provoking."[106]

It is apparent that Nixon's actions during his first term bore profitable fruit, for in spite of the violent upheavals that had wracked the country during his first administration, Nixon won a second term of office by a landslide. But the matter of the Watergate break-in and cover-up would not disappear. More evidence of wrong-doing at high levels of government appeared, one piece at a time, and finally Nixon's administration could not withstand the intense and revealing inquiry. By early August, 1974 Richard Nixon's impeachment was being debated on national television, and was soon recommended by the House Judiciary Committee. For the second time in American history, it seemed, the President of the United States would be brought to trial by the United States Senate. Nixon's prospects for success in that trial appeared even less than those of Andrew Johnson in 1868, who survived the impeachment process by only one vote.

The stress the embattled Nixon was under was enormous, and some feared that he was no longer capable of rational action, and therefore was a danger to the country. Certainly his physical well-being was deteriorating, and this alone might lead to a crisis, as Eisenhower's illnesses had done only a few years earlier, and as Nixon's hero, Wilson's stroke had done five decades earlier. There was a great deal of concern in many quarters about what would happen next, and some worried that the United States might lose even the semblance of a properly functioning government at any moment. Finally George Bush, head of the Republican National Committee, always a strong supporter of Richard Nixon, but now concerned about the unraveling of the Republican Party itself, wrote the President a letter saying that he saw no alternative to Nixon's resignation from office.

On August 8, 1974, in the midst of this enormous controversy, threatened with impeachment, and with the people of the country savagely divided, Nixon announced his resignation from the presidency. One day later, at noon of August 9, Richard Milhous Nixon stepped down from the presidency of the United States, to be succeeded by Vice-President Gerald Ford. Finally, after all his striving, his ambitions were defeated, and he retreated into a tainted obscurity.

---

106 *TRB*, 342.

But not quite "finally" after all. As we said at the beginning, Nixon's ambition and his patient persistence are enormous. From obscurity the fallen politician has risen again, now being regarded by some as Richard Nixon the elder statesman, and especially as Richard Nixon the expert in foreign relations. The Monitor Nixon, with his tremendous ambition, unrelenting drive, and enduring patience might again have turned what seemed a total defeat into victory.

Bibliography

Brodie, F 1981	*Richard Nixon: The Shaping of his Character*
Colodny & Gettlin 1991	*Silent Coup: The Removal of a President*
Craft, J 1972	*The Chinese Difference*
De Toledano, R 1969	*One Man Alone: Richard Nixon*
Eisenhower, J 1986	*Pat Nixon*
Evan & Novack 1971	*Nixon in the White House*
Frost, D 1978	*"I Gave them a Sword:" Behind the Scenes of the Nixon Interviews*
Harris, M 1964	*Mark the Glove Boy, or the last Days of Richard Nixon*
Mazlish, B 1972	*In Search of Nixon: a Psychohistorical Inquiry*
Miller, R 1972	*The New Economics of Richard Nixon*
Morris, R 1990	*Richard Millhous Nixon: The Rise of an American Politician*
Nixon, R 1980	*The Real War*
Nixon, R 1982	*Leaders*
Nixon, R 1988	*1999: Victory without War*
Parmet, H 1990	*Richard Nixon and his America*
Schulte, R (ed) 1978	*The Young Nixon: an Oral Inquiry*
Spalding, H 1972	*The Nixon Nobody Knows*
Strong, R 1980	*Bureaucracy, Statesmanship, and Arms Control: the SALT I Negotiations*
Wicker, T 1991	*One of Us: Richard Nixon and the American Dream*
Wills, G 1969	*Nixon Agonistes*
Woodstone, A 1972	*Nixon's Head*

Jimmy Carter

The outsider

Monitor
Born: October 1, 1924
Presidency: 1977-1981

"I will never lie to you," promised Jimmy Carter in his 1976 campaign for the presidency of the United States. With this rather strange but appealing promise Jimmy Carter presented himself to the public as an honest man who could stand in admirable contrast to the deceptive and self-seeking insiders dominating Washington. He positioned himself as the above-board outsider who owed nothing to the capital's political insiders; he was the stranger to Washington who could represent the whole of the people against waste, Watergate, and the other cynical and corrupt dealings of Washington's power elite.

And his positioning struck a nerve; Jimmy Carter promised the voters an openness and integrity in government which they badly wanted and he promised them a straightforward competence which many felt had been missing from Washington for far too long. "Jimmy who?" (as his opponents initially referred to him) was the unknown underdog, the untainted outsider; he was the plain man from Plains, Georgia.

Yet many puzzled observers have described Jimmy Carter as a persistent study in contradiction. In one moment he could be friendly and unpretentious, in the next, inapproachable, aloof, and superior. He absorbed himself in a wealth of isolated facts but he claimed to be interested in the broad picture. He could be described as gentle and self-effacing, but he was also described as possessing a steely, even ruthless determination. He was filled with cold-blooded ambition; he was a loving, born-again Christian. He was stiff, reserved, impossible to know; he was gracious and open, easy to befriend. He was warm and hospitable; he was distant and calculating.

Photographs of Jimmy Carter hold a striking contrast. The mouth so often displays that warm, winning smile he's had since childhood; but the brow is permanently furrowed, the eyes distant, cool, searching. The mystery seems etched into his face. Such mystery, such confusion and contradiction, are not what one would expect to find when studying Jimmy Carter. After all, Carter was a Monitor, and the Guardians, whether Monitor or Conservator, generally offer us a comforting clarity and consistency. Puzzles and contradictions are rarely found in them. The Conservators William Howard Taft and Gerald R. Ford, for example were excellent and consistent exemplifications of the Conservator style and George Washington and Harry Truman were clearly Monitors and were both wonderfully consistent examples of the Monitor.

Of course Jimmy Carter did not see himself as mysterious (Guardians never do), but merely as a man who had many sides. "I am a farmer, an engineer, a businessman, a planner, a scientist and a Christian," he declared.[107] A clear and concrete self-portrayal, and in that respect worthy of a Guardian. It may be a bit difficult to understand how he managed to string together all these labels into one coherent

---

107 *I'll Never Lie to You*, 30.

identity, but such stringing together of the disparate is almost characteristic of him. In fact if one rearranges the labels chronologically (and adds the label "politician") one would have an approximate capsule history of Carter's adult life. He was in rough sequence a farmer, a businessman, and a Naval officer. And within the constraints of his naval commission he was an "engineer," in that he did take several courses in physics and engineering. Then upon leaving the navy he became a businessman, then a politician, a "born again" Christian, and along the way a self-appointed "planner." Having played each of these roles, Carter maintained his identification with each. Thus by the time he reached the presidency he could label himself a Christian politician businessman engineer farmer scientist.

He often made fond reference to his simple small-town beginnings and his family heritage with its tradition of stolid independence. His forbearers, he said, "...were honest people, but they never have been willing to be pushed around."[108] They were also hard workers, and like them Carter was extraordinarily hard-working. He was also very good at detail work, very punctual, and carefully self-disciplined in every regard. In this much, at least, there is no confusion or contradiction.

There can also be no confusion or uncertainty about another Carter characteristic: he was extraordinarily ambitious. Early on in his political career he lost an election. His initial response was despair but he soon translated it into a promise which became almost a sacred litany: "I do not intend to lose again." Though it finds a softer voice his staunchness may remind us of the previous Monitor President, Harry Truman.

As is typical of the Guardians, Carter had a powerful sense of connection with his family. He and his wife both love children and loved raising their own. Carter also saw himself as a good Christian family man and he took pride in that role. Family and religion were all pre-eminent parts of Jimmy Carter's life. As a close observer of the Washington scene, wrote, "religion fused with family in the spiritual and emotional grounding of the man."[109] Indeed these matters did seem to be "fused," and not always in a fashion that comforted others. So intense was his sense of partnership with his wife Rosalynn, for example, that he

---

108 *Jimmy Carter: The Man and the Myth*, 30.
109 *Roosevelt to Reagan*, 241-242.

often had her sit in on Cabinet meetings; at times she apparently had a significant impact on his presidential decisions. Carter even had his young daughter Amy present at certain state dinners, as if the presidency could be treated as a family affair as much as a political one. Unfortunately very few others seem to agree with this view of state dinners, especially those guests who were partnered with Amy, who might devote most of her dinner time to reading a book.

This combining of family and politics caused difficulty in more places than Washington. Shortly after his election he sent Rosalynn Carter in his place on a good-will tour of South America and the tour was nearly a failure before it began. Mrs. Carter was not well-received initially; her presence rather than her husband's was taken by many to be a slight. Her South American hosts, not noted for their feminist leanings to begin with, wondered aloud to her how the mere wife of an elected official could presume to present herself as the representative of the government of the United States. Her response was clear and accurate: no one is closer to the President, she said, and therefore no one could present the views of the President better than she. It was not an entirely satisfactory response for many listeners, but Rosalynn Carter's determined and pleasant tact made her trip fairly successful anyway.

On first meeting Carter seemed to fit the image of the unassuming, gracious Southern family man, friendly and hospitable. "He was the most unpretentious politician I had ever encountered," wrote one Washington observer. "He carried his own hanging bag. He slept in the homes of supporters instead of hotels. He was a Christian who kept yearning for a country 'filled with love.'"[110] Another commentator wrote that "Some people who knew him much better than I said he had no real friends [and yet] he does have a great friendliness. His particular mix of modesty, warmth and courtesy could be completely winning."[111] But Carter was after all a rather soft-spoken Monitor. One would expect him to be a bit cool rather than spontaneously warm. Easy warmth would be much more natural to a Conservator like William Howard Taft or William McKinley, than to Monitors like George Washington or Benjamin Harrison for example.

---

110 *Hold On Mr. President!*, 76-77.
111 *Roosevelt to Reagan*, 8.

And, this writer continues, unsettling dissonances were evident: Carter, for instance, was in spite of his warm and hospitable manner "quite capable of making very cold, calculating decisions."[112] A stern Carter critic, who was in 1979 the editor and publisher of the San Francisco Examiner, resolved the matter of Carter's inconsistencies quite easily by calling him "one of the three or four phoniest men I ever met." He wrote further that Carter seemed to him to be quite ruthless. "I don't think," he said of Carter, "he has any human warmth in him." [113] An old acquaintance of Carter's commented that he was "...a very seductive personality." He could warm up to you very quickly and, apparently, very sincerely. But later, when you are totally unprepared for the switch, "you reach a point with Jimmy where you suddenly found you hit wall...and you're totally not expecting it. The feeling seems to be that you one day find that you seem to be dancing a tune—with him playing the fiddle—and you're the only one doing the dance."[114] Here is a description which may begin to portray something central about Jimmy Carter: the contest between his hard-edged determination to climb the ladder of social position on the one hand, and his commitment to Christian grace and charity, on the other.

Carter often seems quite naturally modest, as can be seen in his difficulty understanding how pleased people were to accept his invitations to come to the White House. But even with his modesty "a very cool self-esteem in Jimmy Carter left him skeptical that he would learn much from these big shots that would be helpful in his work."[115] Overall, then, in spite of his warm and gentle initial embrace, the observer must be prepared for the "other" Jimmy Carter, the Carter that Vice-President Walter Mondale called "Iron Ass Jimmy." This is the Carter who after sounding sincerely warm and gracious, could still suddenly comment about his political opponent, "I'll whip his ass!"

There is still more: Carter was a successful student and a successful businessman, his Georgia governorship was considered to be generally (even if only modestly) successful, and he proved to be a capable political campaigner. Yet he has been rated by many as one of the

---

112 *Hold On Mr. President!*, 76-77.
113 *Jimmy Carter: The Man and the Myth*, 23.
114 *Jimmy Carter: In search of the Great White House*, 74-75.
115 *Roosevelt to Reagan*, 212.

United States' least effective Chief Executives. He is the clean desk executive who claimed to enjoy taking charge and solving problems and who campaigned on the promise not only of an open and honest government, but of a competent and efficient one. Yet he was also the man who in April of 1978, less than a year and a half after taking office, was considered in a national Lou Harris poll to be quite incompetent. (He received a painfully low 33% approval rating in that national poll. Only the Watergate-tainted Richard Nixon, with 27%, had ever scored lower.)

Carter's abilities had certainly served him well enough up to the time he reached the presidency. As a youngster he always did well in school without showing signs of struggle. Even in junior college and at the Naval Academy at Annapolis, he never found it necessary to study more than the average student. He finished among the top sixty students in a class of more than 800 and after graduation he was able to grasp the knowledge required in his role as the engineering officer on a modern and complex naval vessel. He was also able to put the family business back on a sound footing when he returned to it from the Navy, though it must be acknowledged that he had a great deal of valuable help from his wife Rosalynn.

One part of the explanation of his success is his unfailing memory for facts. As is usually true of bright Guardians, Carter was a sponge for concrete information. He could very quickly and apparently permanently master great masses of factual material, including material of the statistical and technical kind. Annapolis, like West Point, is an information curriculum; it requires absorbing great masses of facts rather than demanding highly original thinking (which is likely, in fact, to be discouraged). Guardians tend to do well with this kind of curriculum, just as the other temperaments tend to struggle with it. Carter's success as an engineering officer can probably be explained in the same way: most successful military officers learn quite early to "go by the book." They find that there is a rote procedure to follow, they learn to follow it, and they recognize early that departure from routine is likely to get them into trouble. To the degree that the demands of Carter's "engineering" required that he operate this way the special talent of the Guardian for amassing facts and adhering to prescribed procedures was his ally.

Carter, of course, would argue that his abilities were not confined to rote memory. He claimed certain capabilities that we would be more likely to find in the Rational than in the Guardian. Especially in the realm of technology and engineering, for instance, he claimed comprehension of the functional implications of the facts and figures he acquired, and he claimed further to have a genuine interest in those implications. Even as President he was said to be well enough informed in several advanced technologies that he could ask worthwhile and probing questions about them. He also said he had a genuine curiosity about such phenomena as the Mount St. Helen's eruption and the astronomical phenomenon of "black holes."

But, it must be said, it is not unusual for Monitors to say of themselves that they have these interests. In fact most Monitors do so. And the claim is quite legitimate in the sense that they are interested in adding to their storehouse of facts, but they seldom recognize that this is very different from the Rational's "engineering" or "science." The Rational's interest is a matter of systematic differentiation, while the Guardian's is maintenance of standard operations. Carter's "clean desk executive" style was similarly a matter of making lists rather than establishing contexts and priorities. His tendency was to go down the list, starting with "A" and finishing with "Z" rather than establishing priorities based on desired outcomes. Following plans and making lists is quite different from exercising logic, and Carter operated as if he did not clearly recognize the difference.

Related to this was what an observer called "an odd lack of sense of history. In Carter's immense storehouse of factual information there must have been plenty of history packed away; yet it never seemed a steady presence in his thinking."[116] The storehouse of historical facts was almost surely there; what was *not* there was a sense of historical context within which the facts could be connected with one another.

Whatever may be true about his interests Carter was successful in business. In 1953 his father died, and because of the business difficulties the family suddenly found itself in, Carter regretfully resigned his naval commission and returned to Plains. He studied the business assiduously, worked extremely hard, and put in long, long days of heavy labor to save it. Over the next several years he did well enough that the business became successful and began almost to run itself. He even found time to

---

116 *Roosevelt to Reagan*, 233.

be a scoutmaster and to teach occasionally in the local Sunday school, both avocations coveted by the Guardian.

When he was in the Navy Carter had dreams of rising to the top; he could even entertain the idea of becoming the Chief of Naval Operations, the highest position a Naval officer can attain. Now he was no longer a Navy man, but there was another route for his ambition: he could pursue his long-time interest in a political career. His pursuit was vigorous and careful and after some preliminary political skirmishing he won election to the Georgia State Senate. Then when it appeared he could run a worthwhile race for the state's governorship he shifted his target. He ran for that more exalted office twice, losing his first campaign and winning the second.

Whether in the Navy, in business or in politics, however, and whatever his personal skills and talents may have been, Jimmy Carter had another very important asset that cannot be overlooked: his able, energetic, and supportive wife Rosalynn.

Eleanor Rosalynn Smith, like Jimmy, grew up in Plains, Georgia, and she and Jimmy Carter had known each other distantly most of their lives. Rosalynn, also a Monitor Guardian, was always "a good girl." She was obedient, she dutifully studied and did well in school, and she apparently enjoyed doing so. She loved her parents, and especially she dearly loved and admired her father and flourished under her parents' care. Then when she was thirteen Rosalynn's father died after a long struggle with leukemia. "He thought I could do anything," Rosalynn reflected later. "I could do anything except keep my father alive."[117] She felt terribly responsible and very guilty over his death. She couldn't help thinking that her own religious faith must have been too weak or that her own behavior in some way must have failed to measure up (not an unusual response for a young Guardian). And though she continued to do well with work and school, and though she re-entered the social world of her peers, she was many years recovering from the tragedy. Regardless of the adequacy of her adjustment, she said later, "my childhood really ended at that moment."[118]

Jimmy's life and Rosalynn's drifted away from each other. Eventually Jimmy went away to Annapolis and then, on a trip home, he rediscovered her. This time he found himself drawn to her and very soon began to court her. There was an affinity between the two, the courtship

---

117 *Jimmy Carter: The Man and the Myth*, 262.
118 *Jimmy Carter: The Man and the Myth*, 262.

went well, and after some initial uncertainty she agreed to marry him. They were married on July 7, 1946. She was only nineteen and he only twenty-one.

Rosalynn, like Jimmy, wanted very much to get past the isolated rural world into which she had been born. She was very pleased when they moved to the more cosmopolitan East Coast. Rosalynn also discovered the heavy and constant demands that go with being a Navy wife. The Carters soon had three sons, Jimmy was away much of the time, and Rosalynn was responsible for single-handedly taking care of all the demands of the household and the children and, occasionally, her husband. She was "the total wife and mother"[119] and found that she truly loved it. She was out on her own learning to be an effective manager, deciding what had to be done, how it had to be done, and then doing it. Then when Jimmy was able to be at home they satisfied their persistent desire to broaden their small-town horizons as much as possible. Together they studied courses in "The Great Books," they studied classical music (they would spend a portion of Jimmy's meager pay on classical records for the purpose), they memorized Shakespeare, and they pursued other areas of knowledge in which they felt their rural upbringing had been deficient.

But most of their time for self-improvement disappeared when Jimmy left the Navy to return to Plains. Jimmy's father had died, the family's business had gradually lost its profitability, and Jimmy went to work to restore it to health. The Carter family business included peanut farming and warehousing, and running a large cotton gin. Rosalynn helped to restore order to these business's financial ledgers, and gradually proved to be highly competent in handling their operation. She took over more and more as manager as Jimmy became increasingly involved in political life. And she flourished. "I loved it," she declared. And here we witness one of the chief delights of the Guardian: "To make all those books balance? I liked it better than anything I've ever

---

119 *Jimmy Carter: The Man and the Myth*, 263.

done."[120] Nothing is as satisfying to the Guardian as finding the sums of debits and credits to be the same, whatever is being accounted.

Rosalynn was also very active when her husband invested himself into politics. She went out on the campaign trail for him in 1976, following one crowded travel itinerary while he followed another. Jimmy was very little known and he needed as much exposure as he could get, and by following separate routes they were able to contact twice as many people. When Rosalynn Carter eventually became First Lady she was as busy as ever. She was still collaborating with her husband, but now she had an agenda of her own as well: mental health programs, support for the mentally retarded, ERA ratification, help for the aging, and a campaign to promote local voluntarism. So busy was this energetic Guardian, so well-regarded did she become in her own right, and so influential in her pursuit of her humanitarian (and strongly Guardian) causes that she was compared by some to Eleanor Roosevelt. No wonder she once commented that "I've never had time for friends.... I've always worked too hard. Besides, I never was one for coffee klatches."[121]

Rosalynn Carter learned to handle well the inevitable criticism political families are naturally subject to. "I had already learned from more than a decade of political life that I was going to be criticized no matter what I did," she once said, "so I might as well be criticized for something I wanted to do."[122] During her husband's presidential campaign one reporter noted her unbreakable strength, and dubbed her the "steel magnolia blossom."[123] The name stuck, though it was truncated to "The Steel Magnolia." (Insofar as it honors her strength, it is fitting; if it suggests to anyone a lack of caring or compassion, it has been misunderstood.)

But again, in spite of Rosalynn, and in spite of his own massive, rock-solid ambition, well-developed business sense, campaigning skills, superb memory, and reasonable administrative experience, most observers do not appraise Jimmy Carter's presidency highly. If one accepts that his administration was unsuccessful, how does one account for that lack of success? Can the study of character offer us anything

---

120 *Presidential Wives*, 439.
121 *Jimmy Carter: In search of the Great White House*, 73.
122 *A Ford, Not a Lincoln*, 304.
123 Judy Klemesrud of the *New York Times*.

here? And is there a relationship between his alleged failure and the puzzling contradictions in his behavior?

One important clue to the puzzle of Jimmy Carter may be found hidden directly in the center of his highly effective presidential campaign tactics: his presentation of himself as the outsider. His campaign ploy was rooted in something which may be more true than he realized. He loved Plains and he loved his family. When he left Plains for Annapolis he found no adequate substitute home in the service. In fact he was considered a rather self-centered isolate by his fellow Midshipman. His church and his family came first, but church and family were far away; and though his fellows and his friendships were at hand, fellows and friendships came a distant second.

When Jimmy Carter graduated Annapolis and he and Rosalynn Smith were married the new Ensign Carter received his first duty assignment. Though Rosalynn was apparently more outgoing than Jimmy, and though the Carters developed a circle of friends, they were still a couple who were never easy to know. Jimmy continued his reserved ways, didn't mix easily with his colleagues aboard ship, and didn't usually seem interested in trying to. He was a pleasant, smiling, supportive officer with the crew of the submarine he served on, always willing to help and to tutor ambitious enlisted men. But he was still not at home nor did he seem to feel he was among friends. Any group of men who must serve in close proximity soon develop a reputation, are noted for particular mannerisms, habits. They inevitably become heir to a series of anecdotes about their adventures, misadventures, and foibles. In the Navy these inevitable anecdotes are called sea stories. Yet, as one officer who served with him was startled to realize, "there are no sea stories about Jimmy Carter."[124] Jimmy Carter continued to be aloof, reserved, the loner.

There was no change when he finally reached Washington. Carter continued to be the reserved and aloof outsider who declined consistently to develop personal friendships or to forge political alliances there. "He still had no close Congressional friendships after he had won the Democratic nomination and then the election," and "far more revealing, he still had none four years later."[125] Instead his closest

---

124 *Jimmy Carter: The Man and the Myth*, 62.
125 *Roosevelt to Reagan*, 238.

advisors tended to be the people whom he knew from his time in Georgia politics. But these too were outsiders with no significant national political experience, and it showed. Knowledgeable Washingtonians "groaned at his clunky outsider's ineptitude, but abominated most of all the failures of his handpicked insiders." So unpopular and so "clunky" was this group of Carter aides that it eventually became known as the "Georgia Mafia."

> It might also be said that Carter was from-but-not-of-the Navy....He was from but certainly not of the governor's fraternity, where he was considered a self-centered loner. Even in his fourth year as President, Carter seemed not part of Washington, still the outsider....As to where Carter was truly of, I would say his church and his family.[126]

To be an outsider and isolate is one thing, but to couple it with enormous political ambition and almost blind determination is quite another. To combine these in a Guardian is perhaps most troublesome of all, for the Guardian, whether Conservator or Monitor, counts on custom and convention to guide him. The more ambitious he becomes the more he may unwittingly trap himself into a rigid dependence upon what he already knows, regardless of how appropriate it is to new circumstances. The facts he had on hand and the routines or procedures with which he was already familiar would therefore largely determine his actions. In Carter's administration this pattern led to what one writer called his "zigzag tendency" in policy and execution. There was little in the way of an overarching strategy to guide him; as different facts came to his attention he would make use of different procedures.

Carter's ambition was this sort of double-edged sword. Even as a child he was hard-working and enterprising, a "good boy" who did largely what he was supposed to, who didn't smoke or fight or get into much trouble. Quite the contrary; he seemed determined to be "the best" at everything from a very early age. By the time he was six he was already industriously picking peanuts from his family's farm, boiling, packaging, and wheeling them into town to sell, a nickel a bag. Even at that early age he kept his money tucked away, had it all accounted for, and kept working to amass more of it. He hated to lose at anything in which he participated. He wanted to hit a home run every time he came to bat, he wanted to win all the debates he participated in while on his

---

126 *Roosevelt to Reagan*, 240-241.

high school debating team, always he wanted to win, to be the best of anyone. Even before he went to junior college he had already set his sights on Annapolis, which carried prestige and opened important doors, especially in the pre-war rural South. He had already announced to his friends that his ultimate target was the governorship of Georgia.

In spite of his ambition he did not win any particular prominence as a leader at Annapolis or stand out in any way that made him especially memorable. He continued to be the ever-smiling nice guy, not the best and far from the worst overall. He could still be characterized by his nice grin, his intense competitiveness, on occasion his immovable stubbornness and always his persistent striving to get ahead. The consensus of his fellows: "he was capable but not marked for greatness."[127]

Clearly, Jimmy Carter never had the charismatic quality most likely to be found in the Artisan. His success would not come from being able to inspire others or even to charm them for long. The Monitor was a rather stiff and awkward speaker and when he tried to speak inspirationally his efforts sounded preachy at best. If this ambitious man was to attain the presidency his major suit had to be the Guardian's greatest strengths: long, hard, persistent work and careful management of his resources, political and otherwise. These strengths Jimmy Carter had in plenty. Long, hard work, certainly. In business, in the Georgia Senate, and in his political campaigning he was well known as a very hard worker. He arrived early and stayed late, and he rarely took time for the occasional party-time camaraderie so often indulged in by legislators or campaigners when they could break free from the day's political demands. In this he was a quintessential hard-working, conscientious Guardian.

He also had his persistence. In 1966, after he had lost in his first campaign for Governor of Georgia, his sister Ruth Stapleton talked with him earnestly about her own Christian beliefs. Carter was so strongly moved by her words that he soon became a "born-again Christian." But, he made it clear, he would not give up his political aspirations even for his fundamentalist Christianity. Furthermore, his defeat in the gubernatorial race left him more doggedly intent than ever about

---

127 *Jimmy Carter: In search of the Great White House*, 53.

succeeding in the political arena. "I did not intend to lose again." If persistence made a difference then there was nothing that could stand in the way of Jimmy Carter's ambitions.

But more is required than persistent ambition, especially when one positions oneself as the nation's hope for honest and effective government. And here Carter began to run into trouble, even before the election. He had a "penchant for hyperbole," as one writer put it, a way of exaggerating the significance of certain aspects of his character or his history, of stretching these matters beyond their proper limits. He once made the astonishing claim, for instance, that he had read and understood Tolstoy's massive *War and Peace* at the age of twelve and that it was one of his favorite books. His political aspirations probably exacerbated this sometimes unfortunate penchant, for of course a campaigning politician must look good. But trying too hard to look good—and getting caught at it—can leave one looking bad.

On other occasions he characterized himself as a "nuclear physicist," apparently drawing on his experience as a precommissioning officer on a nuclear submarine and a semester of graduate nuclear physics courses at Union College. It was apparently only his experience as the engineering officer aboard ship that justified for him his claim that he was "an engineer" of any kind, whether or not "nuclear." And though his ranking at Annapolis certainly did not warrant it, he had tried while there for a very prestigious Rhodes scholarship. He later claimed to a syndicated columnist that he had been a finalist for the highly coveted award though he apparently never came close to that position. In much the same fashion, he declared that he had "voluntarily served in two wars," though during one (World War II) he was still at Annapolis, and during the other (the Korean War) he was safely stationed on the East Coast of the United States. Technically the claim was true; but it carried just beneath the surface an implication of heroism which would be difficult to support.

In spite of his grasp of detail and his ability to campaign effectively, Jimmy Carter often showed how the Guardian's strengths, improperly utilized, can become weaknesses. For instance, his excellent memory for facts and figures is offset by his failure to move from the specific to the general, to comprehend the relevance (or irrelevance) of the dazzling array of facts he has acquired. He "didn't seem to recognize instinctively when ideas are in collision, when two sets of facts cannot be equally pertinent," wrote one observer,[128] nor did he always see the relevance of one piece of information with another. He was not likely to note, for instance, that economic conditions in West Germany (which he might have studied in detail last week) might be connected to the political well-being of the rest of Europe (about which he might be studying today.)

A former Pentagon official once characterized James Schlesinger as interested in the big picture, "a forest man," while Harold Brown, Carter's Secretary of Defense was "a tree man," someone with a much narrower vision. And Carter? "My God," the official groaned, "he was a leaf man!"[129] Thus Carter's vast storehouse of facts did not seem to have any implications for action. Instead the facts were squirreled away, sometimes only showing up again to support some platitude that Carter was offering.

Jimmy Carter was clearly a Guardian President; thus he was very strongly and very naturally concrete in his calculations. He had a penchant for isolated facts and standard operating procedures rather than for interrelated concepts and strategic intentions.

The "zigzag" behavior mentioned in reference to his political behavior was also to be found in his personal behavior. It has already been noted, for instance, that Carter's warmth toward others "can be turned on and off like a spigot" without apparent reason.[130] Yet, though one is reminded of that description of Carter as "one of the three or four phoniest men I ever met," it seems very unlikely that Carter was simply and deliberately trying to fool the people around him. It makes more sense that Carter

> operates at two very different levels, with missing links between the two. One is the level of high principles, noble yet sometimes fuzzy. The other is the level of daily pragmatic politics, flexible (almost dazzlingly so) and minutely detailed....When there is nothing between disembodied, if appealing, goals, and the level of daily execution, an outside observer all too easily gets the impression of watching a rudderless ship.[131]

---

128 *Roosevelt to Reagan*, 235.
129 *Roosevelt to Reagan*, 235.
130 *Jimmy Carter: In search of the Great White House*, 497.
131 *James Earl Carter, The Man and the Myth*, 28.

In the case of a Guardian this impression is most likely to emerge if the usual routines are not made use of. There is at that point neither policy nor procedure, but only moment-by-moment improvising, and this is about as far from the Guardian's strengths as one can go.

Carter's use of his Bible-belt morality tended to get him into trouble too. When his homey approach failed to produce results he fell back on what was more natural to him: he became moralistic while still trying to clothe himself in a stance of humility. Apparently Carter's born-again Christianity was quite genuine. He really did speak sincerely when he said that we should honor the same high moral standards "in our home, our office, or our government."[132] But the rituals of religion, so absorbing for the Guardian, are insufficient for the presidency. The moral code is easier spoken (and has been spoken by countless people before) than it is enacted. Carter's "missing links" are obvious and it is in trying to turn his moral policy into daily operations that he consistently ran into extreme difficulty.

Perhaps the final blow was that he acted as if morality, helping, caring, and belonging are things that he could bring about by proclamation, by following the rules and by exhorting others to do likewise. It is interesting that this approach is the fundamental approach of the Guardian parent: exhortations to walk in the paths of righteousness, and indignation, even outrage, when exhortation is not sufficient. One is also reminded of his assertions that he is a "Christian-businessman-farmer-" etc., as if to say the word is to generate the fact, to act properly is to be proper, to exhort is to inspire.

Finally Jimmy Carter was in reality what he had proclaimed himself to be: an outsider. He was inexperienced with the demands and accommodations which are an inevitable part of holding national political office. Thus he could naively propose to have his Cabinet meetings open to the press, which meant that there would be no opportunity for private discussion of political or international affairs. Yet even though it seemed to fit so well with his campaign to restore the people's trust in government, he was soon dissuaded from acting on this remarkably impractical notion. He could begin his presidency with an announcement of an "open" administration in which each member of his

---

132 *Jimmy Carter: In search of the Great White House*, 477.

staff could speak honestly for him or herself without regard for political repercussions. Another fine-sounding idea, but it quickly led to heated disputes and disrupted staff relationships so much that political fratricide seemed inevitable. Carter soon stepped in and had a meeting with his people in which he announced grimly that no further infighting would be tolerated. The "open" administration was at an end. The outsider could not forge alliances, could not understand others' disenchantment with him, could not comprehend their failure to give him approval for his accomplishments and his sincerity, could not really be "one of us." He could only, through his virtue and accomplishment, stand above and away from us, the Outsider.

Carter seemed unable to comprehend the nature of the public's gradual loss of confidence in him and liking for him. A reporter close to the White House offers a poignant glimpse of Jimmy Carter the man and his inability to comprehend what had gone wrong. "Carter only once asked me a head-on political question, and it was such an engaging one that I couldn't resist. I should take my time, but would I please think about why I didn't like him."[133] A more gregarious Artisan in Carter's place would probably have adapted very quickly to the new environment, and would have found all the most interesting ways to play with the new rules and enjoy the new opportunities. The upright and stand-offish Guardian Jimmy Carter steadfastly refused—or was unable—to adapt. The outsider Carter was too stubborn, too committed to his own rhetoric, too ignorant of the sophisticated ways of national politics to do so or to wish to do so. "Always so goddamned right, and righteous....If you happened to agree with him, he thought you were one of God's chosen tribe—but if you didn't, you were automatically in league with the devil himself," bitterly reflected one of his adversaries.[134] In the same fashion, Carter

> felt morally superior to Congress. He was elected by all the people; he saw the individual representative or Senator as vulnerable to special interests...lacking the President's commitment to the welfare of the nation itself.[135]

No wonder that Jimmy Carter's self-proclaimed love for others and his efforts to display Christian humility failed him. Carrying his own

---

133 *Roosevelt to Reagan*, 20.
134 Quoted in *Dasher: the Roots and Rising of Jimmy Carter*, 328.
135 *Roosevelt to Reagan*, 239.

luggage even as President, his informal and "homey" cardigan sweater, his fireside chats ultimately failed to convince people of his Christian goodness. They also failed to distract people from how poorly things seemed to be going with him at the helm. Intended to show everyone (including himself) that he was "one of us," his chats instead were more like parodies of genuine human contact, "clunky" imitations of genuine human belonging.

Perhaps this was the final flaw in Jimmy Carter's presidency: that he could never make best use of his own native abilities to address the problems he was so eager to solve. He so much wanted to analyze and understand and resolve what he thought were important problems, not realizing that analysis was the least of his abilities. He would not allow others to do analysis, to point out relevance, to establish context; he insisted on doing all these things himself. He tried to develop successful strategies by amassing more facts. He didn't comprehend that this was very different from placing fewer facts strategically on a conceptual map to discover their overall relationship to a difficulty. Carter was a man who had to be better at almost everything than anyone else. The facts had to be his, the conclusions his own, the decisions on his authority, on the authority of his facts. Finally the presidency of Jimmy Carter fell victim to the demands of his vaulting ambition, to his pretense, to his piecemeal thinking, to his strongly entrenched rural Guardian perspective.

It was not long before these weaknesses and gaffes, many of them rooted in his ignorance of the way national politics was conducted, began to pile up in the minds of the press and public. When Carter ran for office against Reagan in 1980 the economy was severely troubled, inflation was painfully high; some of his own appointees to high national office had been forced for various reasons to resign; American hostages were still being held by Iran; and the surprise rescue attempt across the Iranian desert had succeeded in doing nothing but killing eight American soldiers and embarrassing Carter's administration. Even the Panama Canal was "lost" to the United States.[136] Carter's clean-desk

---

136 No matter the claim that every President since Lyndon Johnson had been trying to negotiate an acceptable transfer of the Canal to Panama. Carter, to the great relief of those who believed a violent confrontation with Latin America was brewing over the Canal, succeeded in completing the unpleasant task. To the many who believed the situation to be far less ominous, Carter thereby became the man who "gave away the Panama Canal" to an untrustworthy group.

approach was no longer a sign of efficiency. To many voters it had become instead the signature of a narrowly-focused man who paid too much attention to the commas and not enough to the meanings, who was more adept at being precise and orderly than he was at thinking things through.

In spite of the claims of his detractors, not every move Jimmy Carter made was an error, nor was his every instinct misplaced. For example, Representative Henry J. Hyde of Illinois commented about Carter's successful work at Camp David during which he brought together the bitter enemies Anwar Sadat of Egypt and Menachem Begin of Israel. These two men, with Carter's persistent and resolute mediation, were able to talk about the possibility of ending the dangerous hostility then rampant between their nations. "After Camp David," wrote Hyde, "it was possible to think that unending conflict between Israel and its neighbors was not a given, like the sun rising in the east. These were not mean accomplishments. In fact, they were great accomplishments. And they were Carter's accomplishments as much as any man's."[137]

Perhaps it should be enough for any person to have played such a vital part in lessening the chances of more Arab-Israeli conflagrations and, through them, the likelihood of a third world war. The job is clearly not finished, but Jimmy Carter, whatever his strengths and weaknesses, began it well.

Bibliography

Carter, H 1978	*Cousin Beadie and Cousin Hot: My Life with the Carter Family of Plains Georgia*
Glad, B 1980	*Jimmy Carter: In search of the Great White House*
Lasky, V 1979	*Jimmy Carter: The Man and the Myth*
Mazlish, B 1979	*Jimmy Carter: A Character Portrait*
Meyer, P 1978	*James Earl Carter, The Man and the Myth*
Schram, M 1977	*Running for President, 1976: the Carter Campaign*
Shoup, L 1980	*The Carter Presidency and Beyond*
Stroud, K 1977	*How Jimmy Won: the Victory Campaign from Plains to the White House*
Turner, R 1976	*I'll Never Lie to You, Jimmy Carter in His Own Words*
Wooten, J 1978	*Dasher: the Roots and Rising of Jimmy Carter*

---

137 *Los Angeles. Times,* February 2, 1989.

Reporter Guardian Presidents: The Conservators

Millard Fillmore

The second -hand President

Conservator
Born: January 7, 1800
Died: March 8, 1874
Presidency: 1850-1853

In the campaign of 1848 presidential candidate Zachary Taylor, a Westerner, was being typecast by his party's strategists as a robust, rough-hewn frontiersman. That image would capture many votes, but the party now needed someone to run for the vice-presidency who could capture the (presumably) more sedate and civilized Easterners, someone who would provide a more cultured image.

Millard Fillmore was just the man. He was a New York lawyer, he was good looking, he was conservative and temperate in his views, he had the dignified appearance, even if not the substance, of a statesman, and his manner had an easy, pleasant warmth to it that easily made him friends. He was not politically ambitious; he had initially run for public office only because friends talked him into it. He would therefore be no threat to the professional party men. Fillmore was thus an easy selection; no one voiced much concern about the choice. The office of Vice-President was not considered to be of great importance anyway, for nothing seemed to have been learned from President Harrison's death in office less than a decade earlier.

Then, when President Zachary Taylor died after only sixteen months in office the pleasant, temperate, but rather ineffectual Millard Fillmore suddenly found himself President of the United States. This unexpected turn of events may have been a more painful shock to Fillmore than it would have been for most men. He was after all a man who had lacked confidence in himself and in his abilities all his life; he usually saw himself as just barely up to the demands of his work. To become the President might be a horrible test of his modest abilities.

The discouraging appraisal he had of his abilities was apparently widely shared by those who knew him. Though he was a soft-spoken and persuasive advocate, no one ever accused him of having a scintillating mind. And though he could offer gentle wisdom in counsel and would stand firmly for what he truly believed, no one would have considered him sagacious. In fact he has been described as "second-hand, commonplace, mediocre, undistinguished."[138]

Fillmore was reasonably successful in the profession of law, though his success came about by virtue of his dogged persistence, probably aided by his handsome and distinguished appearance, rather than by virtue of a fine legal mind. Fillmore was simply a solemn, handsome, mediocre Conservator Guardian, not a man of ideas or a charismatic mover of people or events. His solemn demeanor eventually earned him the nickname "Father Fillmore." It was a term of gentle mockery, but it apparently expressed no real hostility. Fillmore did not seem to be a man about whom people could bother to work up much anger.

Perhaps the generally unfavorable appraisal of his abilities was not as troublesome to Millard Fillmore as it might have been. Fillmore had a loving, intelligent, witty, and knowledgeable wife, Abigail Powers Fillmore, whom he loved intensely. Conservators find great importance

---

138 *Presidential Anecdotes*, 110.

in a strong and loving family relationship and great satisfaction in the warm acceptance and approval of those around them. Fillmore was a typical Conservator in this regard. Millard's beloved Abigail loved him, encouraged him, and advised him right from the very beginning of their relationship all through their stay in the White House. Love and approval such as hers, and even guidance properly offered, can help make tolerable for the Conservator situations that might otherwise be terribly dispiriting.

Fillmore had come from a family with nine children and few financial resources. As was customary in such cases he left school early to learn a trade. After struggling for several years at various jobs, among them woodcutting and tailor's apprentice, he decided to better his situation by returning to school. Thus he found himself in a country schoolhouse with a teacher who at eighteen was only two years older than he. Fillmore became so enamored of his teacher, Abigail Powers, that he began a courtship that lasted for eight years before it culminated in marriage. Not that Miss Powers was resisting his advances all that time; on the contrary, she was apparently quite taken with him. It was rather the demands of his work and the troublesome state of their finances that led them to delay their marriage for those eight long years.

The marriage was worth the wait. Time never diminished his love for her and after they married he was as enamored with her as he was before. Even after years of marriage he would not destroy the little notes she sometimes sent him, but held onto them as keepsakes. She remained his beloved wife, his lover, his friend and his mentor through all the years of their marriage.

Abigail (who was probably a Rational) was fascinated with learning all her life. She was an insatiable reader to whom Millard habitually brought stacks of books when he returned from his various trips. It was Abigail Fillmore who established the White House library, for the place had been barren of all but the occasional book during its entire existence. Abigail was also a fine and witty conversationalist when among friends, though she was otherwise an extreme recluse. She so consistently turned down invitations to the capital's social events, in fact, that Washington society finally ceased even to bother to send them to her.

The Fillmores' marriage demonstrated a happy complementarity: the warmth and constancy of the Conservator Millard coupled with the intellectual curiosity and thoughtful counsel of the Rational Abigail. Her counsel could be humorous as well as appropriate. The story is told that on a visit to England Millard was to be presented with an honorary degree by Oxford University. Aware of the inadequacy of his own rustic education, he confessed to Abigail his terror of being embarrassed by his political opponents for accepting such a degree. It was apparently she who helped him work out his courteous and humorous refusal of the degree which, as was customary in those times, was written in Latin. "No man," he commented in the refusal, "should accept a degree he cannot read."

Even with Abigail's counsel Millard was unable to avoid being swallowed up in the turbulence of the times. He maintained a moderate and conciliatory stance, and signed into law the Compromise of 1850, which attempted to defuse the explosive slavery issue. But the Compromise included legislation which permitted the forcible return of runaway slaves to their owners, even if the former slaves were living in Northern states. This legislation was detested by most Northerners, and it cost Fillmore most of his Northern political support. The Conservator Fillmore was a sympathetic and charitable man, as Conservators generally seem to be, but in spite of his earnest wish to improve the matters he managed to make many such wrong moves, or to offset the right moves with contradictory ones. His lackluster efforts made himself sufficiently unpopular that he was not nominated by his party for re-election in 1852.

Fillmore seems not to have been too distraught about stepping down. After leaving office in 1853 he was for a while content being honorary chancellor of the University of Buffalo, serving as chairman of several civic committees, taking leadership in charitable affairs, and standing at the top of various social lists. For a Guardian such as Fillmore these rewards for his service were almost ideal. They brought him some sense of honor, dignity, public acknowledgment of his special position. He tried again later for the presidency, but it is doubtful that his heart was in the effort. It appears that he was responding chiefly to the urgings of several small and scattered factions who could not find a more suitable candidate.

Millard's beloved Abigail died of pneumonia in the same year that he left office. Fillmore did later marry again, this time a woman some

thirteen years younger than he. He lived on for another two decades in
quiet obscurity and died in 1874, his passing largely unremarked.

Bibliography

Barre, W 1856   *The Life and Public Services of Millard Fillmore*
Chamberlain, I 1856   *Biography of Millard Fillmore*
Dix, D 1975   *The Lady and the President: the Letters of*
                         Dorothea Dix and Millard Fillmore
Farrell, J 1971   *Zachary Taylor 1784-1850, Millard Fillmore*
                         1800-1874
Fillmore, M 1958   *The Early Life of Millard Fillmore*
Garrison, W 1874   *Fillmore and Sumner*
Griffis, W 1915   *Millard Fillmore, Constructivist Statesman,*
                         Defender of the Constitution
Grayson, B 1981   *The Unknown President: the Administration of*
                         President Millard Fillmore
Rayback, R 1959   *Millard Fillmore, Biography of a President*
Smith, E 1988   *The Presidency of Zachary Taylor and Millard*
                         Fillmore

James Buchanan

"I am the last President of the United States"

Conservator
Born: April 23, 1791
Died: June 1, 1868
Presidency: 1857-1861

James Buchanan was a professional politician, durable and reasonably competent, at least until he reached the presidency. Beginning with the administration of John Quincy Adams and including his tenure as President, he held political office of one kind or another for forty-six years. His positions included stints in both the House of Representatives and the Senate and appointments as Secretary of State, Minister to Great Britain, and Minister to Russia. He held office for so long that some called him "Old Public Functionary."

Buchanan seemed to be a gentleman of the old school: distinguished in appearance, courtly and urbane in manner. He wore an old-fashioned standing collar with a stiff white choker, but was otherwise faultlessly attired and managed overall to present the picture of the well-to-do confirmed bachelor. Buchanan was affable and unostentatious, and displayed a warm and pleasant informality which helped make him quite popular. Though his tastes were considered refined he was also celebrated for being a world-class professional drinker. He once wrote to the business that supplied alcohol for him that he wanted no further pint bottles. "Pints are very inconvenient in this house," he said, "as the article is not used in such small quantities."[139] When he became President, White House functions took on a considerably more festive and gracious air than they had for some time.

Not that Buchanan was an irresponsible drunk or a wastrel. Courteous and affable he might be and a heavy drinker as well, but beneath the affability and the drinking he seemed always to be calm, cool, and watchful. Even during his heaviest drinking he rarely gave any indication of being inebriated; he didn't become a noisy celebrant but remained serious, even dour. His affability was well known and seemed quite genuine, but it was plainly not all there was to the man.

Buchanan enjoyed his active social life but he was no stranger to hard work. As a young man he had labored assiduously in school and continued to do so in his later study of law. Though he was not considered especially bright he tended to do well because he worked harder and longer and more conscientiously than others did. He was characterized as a "grind" while a student at Dickinson College but he didn't like the label. Apparently he tried to dispel the image by allowing some of his more boisterous classmates to lead him astray. It must have been a tall order for everyone involved; by his own admission Buchanan had no natural talent for raucous noise or dissipation. Nonetheless he did succeed in getting himself expelled from college for disorderly conduct. This pronounced success was considerably more than Buchanan had intended, so he pleaded his case, got himself readmitted, and work hard enough that he graduated as an honor student.

While attending Dickinson Buchanan became greatly impressed by the college's dean, a man known as "The Blessed Peacemaker." The dean was described by an acquaintance as "vain, formal, solemn, and precise; yet withal kindly and gentle, always eager to settle disputes without force and solve problems by a calm and pleasant meeting of the

---

139 Quoted in *President James Buchanan: A Biography*, 275.

minds."[140] Buchanan evidently admired the man a great deal. Perhaps he even tried to model himself after the dean, for the same words could have been applied to him in his own later life.

After leaving college Buchanan took up the practice of law. He was so successful in winning court cases and lived so frugally during those early adult years that he gradually became independently wealthy. Then while still in his twenties he entered the political world. Just as he had in other arenas he went to work and laboriously and carefully moved up the Democratic Party's political ladder. He was a volunteer in the War of 1812, a member of the Pennsylvania legislature and then the United States Congress; he was Andrew Jackson's Minister to Russia, a U. S. senator, Polk's Secretary of State and Minister to Britain. Though he had aspirations to the presidency it seemed that they would never be fulfilled, for he was not highly regarded by his party except as a hard-working, moderately competent, but unremarkable party man.

But in 1855 the Democrats found their own party's President Franklin Pierce to be unworthy of renomination and it occurred to the party bosses that James Buchanan might serve as a good replacement. He was available, he was cooperative, he was experienced, and he had done nothing to make himself objectionable. As one writer put it, he was "colorless and safe."[141]

Unobjectionable, cooperative, "colorless and safe": it was almost as if something were missing in the man; even in person he seemed only partly present. His affable informality made him easy to approach and his graceful and charming manner gave people the feeling that they were really in intimate contact with him when they spoke. But in retrospect they would realize that Buchanan had kept a cool distance between them and himself. Buchanan himself had been fundamentally untouched by the contact; it was only his attentive and mannerly way that gave the impression that he was sensitive to their concerns. In the same vein, formal dinners in the White House showed a Buchanan who was affable and who could offer friendly and entertaining anecdotes. But more watchful observers would note that he was essentially cool beneath his affable manner.

Perhaps his personal life was conducted similarly. This would help account for the tragic outcome of his relationship with Annie Caroline Coleman. He and Annie Coleman had become engaged in 1819 though

---

140 *President James Buchanan: A biography*, 12.
141 *Battle Cry of Freedom: The Civil War Era*, 136.

the relationship between the twenty-eight year old lawyer and Miss Coleman was not especially warm. Her family considered Buchanan to be beneath them socially and her brothers apparently circulated the rumor that James was being unfaithful to her. The distraught Annie broke off their engagement and died shortly thereafter, apparently of an overdose of laudanum.

Laudanum was an opiate derivative favored by ladies of the time as a calming agent and sleeping potion. Miss Coleman may have taken too much in an effort to calm herself at bedtime, but the Colemans accused Buchanan of being her de facto murderer and would not even permit him to attend her funeral. Buchanan was deeply shaken and depressed by the affair and vowed never to marry. He was as good as his word; he is the only United States President never to have married. There are varied opinions about whether he ever engaged in serious flirtations thereafter. Some writers claim he did, others say no, and a few even suggest that he might have been actively homosexual.

Whatever the facts of the Coleman tragedy, Buchanan's professional life seems to have been untouched by it. Buchanan the politician continued to present himself as a strong man who was certain in his thoughts and actions—and a cooperative party member. He was said to have the ability to offer clear and logical argument, he claimed a strong confidence in reason and self-restraint, and he seemed wary of the passions of the moment. Some observers noted that watching him work was like watching a chess player, not unlike Martin Van Buren: cool, calculating, keeping his own counsel.

But Buchanan's "cool calculation" was not the calculation of a Rational such as Dwight Eisenhower. It was rather the cautious exercise of the ambition of a rather pessimistic Monitor whose facade was of confident strength, but whose spirit was concern and worry. The *planning* of the Rational, rooted in skepticism, should never be confused with the pessimistic *accounting* of the Guardian. Buchanan's "calculation" was literally that; he was extremely careful about recording and balancing his own income and expenditures. The youthful Monitor James Buchanan had learned well the importance of good records by watching his father, a successful small businessman. So well did the young Guardian learn that in later life Buchanan once refused a check for more than $15,000 because it contained a ten-cent error. In good Guardian form, Buchanan insisted on paying his bills down to the very penny and would not allow even trivial oversights to pass uncorrected. From early on he kept ledgers in which he carefully recorded the coming and going of every cent that he earned or spent, including even the cost of pins and of his suspender buttons.

Even the dour Monitor James Polk once observed of Buchanan that he was capable enough, but added that he was "in small matters without judgment and sometimes acts like an old maid."[142] It was a surprising comment to make about the man whom Polk had appointed his Secretary of State and his minister to Britain. Andy Jackson had made Buchanan his minister to Russia. Buchanan did have favors due him, and neither Polk nor Jackson could set him aside. But Jackson once declared that he had sent Buchanan to Russia because "It was as far as I could send him out of my sight, and where he could do the least harm!"[143]

Buchanan's caution and conventionality kept him close to his party's doctrine and wishes. He responded to these reasonably well, and had he stayed in the Congress instead of reaching the presidency he might have been known to history as a competent if undistinguished legislator. But his aspiration for the honor and majesty of the presidency and his desire for his party's recognition led him from the relative anonymity which had served him so well into the maelstrom of the pre-Civil War presidency.

In keeping with the instructions of his party managers, Buchanan dealt with the ordeal of the 1856 presidential campaign by saying little and committing himself to less. His name became known, but Buchanan himself remained effectively anonymous. His campaign managers handled most of the work and distributed the campaign promises. (One observer wryly commented during the campaign that "There is no such person running as James Buchanan. He is dead of lockjaw.")[144] The strategy of silence worked well enough for campaigning.

But there is an old military dictum, probably made up by an Artisan, from which Buchanan as President might have profited: a poor plan, energetically pursued, is better than a good plan followed timidly. Unfortunately the timorous and unimaginative Buchanan hid behind timid actions and legalistic justifications, both for his actions and for his frequent avoidance of action. He may have had a vision of himself in the role of "The Blessed Peacemaker" whose skills would allow the country to live at peace, but he just didn't have what it took to close the ever-

---

142 *Presidential Anecdotes*, 118.
143 *Presidential Anecdotes*, 118.
144 *Presidential Campaigns*, 98.

widening breach between North and South. He lacked the diplomatic talent of the Idealist, the tactical skills of the Artisan and the strategic sense of the Rational. Furthermore he was allied with a party so slanted in its views toward slavery that there was no hope that he could even pretend to be a "blessed peacemaker." His Guardian's logistical and maintenance competencies, so handy in other circumstances, would not do for the crisis under which Buchanan was being buried.

Even Buchanan's own Guardian strengths were largely useless to him, for when he took office he became even more uncertain and cautious than before. He made careful plans but failed consistently to translate them into effective action. He proposed legislation but was not politically strong enough to see it passed. He discussed political strategy but left it to others to try to implement it. He usually avoided taking a strong stance about important issues since doing so might lead to even worse political brawls in an already inflamed situation. He advised an increase in the sizes of the army and navy, but could not convince; he advised the construction of a transcontinental railway but could not persuade. When Confederate troops fired on a Union ship (this was before either side had committed to full-scale combat) he failed to respond. So pronounced became his pattern of avoiding or ineptly pursuing sustained action that Buchanan has been condemned by one writer as nothing more than "a hopeless ditherer."[145]

But in fairness to Buchanan it must be recognized that the nation had for decades been split into increasingly angry and more desperate slavery and anti-slavery factions. His problems were further complicated by the still-unsettled and immediately significant debate over the limits of the authority of the national government. Was not the federal government, in its involvement in the question of slavery, trying to usurp the states' rights to self-determination? Or was it merely executing the guarantees presented by the Constitution? How much power, after all, should the federal government have over the individual states, and in what matters? The arguments over these issues became more bitter with the admission of each new state to the Union, for each admission threatened to establish a new precedent of the greatest importance. The passions aroused resulted in many small armed rebellions and not a few murders. Some of the most notorious of these activities provided American history with the tragic label, "Bleeding Kansas." Kansas was the killing ground for both sides of the guerrilla warfare between Kansas

---

145 *How They Became President,* 182.

abolitionists and pro-slavery factions from neighboring Missouri. James Buchanan was not the man to master such turmoil; perhaps by then no human could have been.

President Buchanan believed that slavery was evil, but, demonstrating the dark pessimism (and perhaps the accompanying fatalism) of the Guardian, he also thought it irremediable. He also believed, however, that the Abolitionist movement was responsible for the nation's troubles. But rather than take vigorous action against either side, he took the very conservative position—and the one preferred by the Congress—that the federal government had only those powers specifically and explicitly given it by the Constitution. This interpretation meant that the office of President was much less powerful than it could have been otherwise. In fact, in this view of the powers of the government, it really didn't matter what the President believed anyway, and Buchanan finally went so far as to claim that he lacked the constitutional right to make use of federal force to maintain good public order.

Buchanan did try to persuade each of the factions to choose the course of moderation. He wanted desperately to appeal to the use collaboration and self-restraint rather than force and to be able to encourage measures that would quiet the storm. Unfortunately he proved to be inept as a tactical, strategic, and diplomatic leader, and a pliant servant of the Southern faction as well—and therefore of pro-slavery and pro-states' rights. Thus his measures to reconcile North and South were inevitably timid, presented halfheartedly, and finally unacceptable to both factions. Eventually frozen into helpless inaction and watching the country disintegrate around him, James Buchanan could only lament "I am the last President of the United States."

In his last message to Congress—when it was much too late— Buchanan finally stood with uncharacteristic firmness (perhaps because he had nothing left to lose) for the assertion that no state had the right to secede from the Union. He declared forthrightly and in the face of his Southern supporters that to allow secession was to destroy the country. And one final time he appealed for moderation. But he was still incapable of the kind of leadership the situation called for and he had lost whatever political support he might once have been able to muster. No one had confidence in him any longer nor any interest in offering him further political support.

As a final sad note, Buchanan's administration became recognized as one of the most corrupt in the nation's history. Though Buchanan himself apparently did not profit from the corruption (nor would one expect the Guardian to do so), he was unable to correct the widespread and rampant dishonesty and in fact showed little interest in doing so. At the end of his term of office in 1860 Buchanan had become so unpopular that he was not renominated by his own party, but by then it must have seemed no great loss to him. He said himself that he was eager to leave behind the office that was for him a "crown of thorns" and he commented to his successor, Abraham Lincoln, that "If you are as happy in entering the White House as I shall feel on returning to Wheatland [his country estate in Pennsylvania] you are a happy man indeed."[146]

The following administrations, both Lincoln's and Johnson's, excoriated Buchanan mercilessly after he left office. It seemed that they wanted to hold him personally responsible for fomenting or at least for permitting the Civil War to occur. But the assaults on the hapless man were somewhat unjust and most unkind. The conventional and partisan-shaped solutions of the unimaginative and uncertain bureaucrat James Buchanan were insufficient to manage these difficult issues and the passionate intensity of their advocates.

After his retirement Buchanan wrote a typically dignified, restrained, and rather dull autobiography of his political life in which he attempted to defend his views and restore his reputation. The book was published in 1866 and less than enticingly entitled *Mr. Buchanan's Administration of the Eve of the Rebellion*. As did so many things associated with his presidency, the book failed.

James Buchanan died in 1868 at his home in Wheatland and was buried in nearby Lancaster, Pennsylvania.

Bibliography

Auchenampaugh, P 1965   *James Buchanan and His Cabinet on the Eve of Secession*

Buchanan, J 1946   *The Diary of a Public Man*

Curtis, G 1969   *Life of James Buchanan, Fifteenth President of the United States*

Horton, R 1971   *The Life and Public Services of James Buchanan*

Klein, P 1962   *President James Buchanan: A biography*

Smith, E 1975   *The Presidency of James Buchanan*

---

146 *Presidential Anecdotes*, 120.

William McKinley

The murder of decency

Conservator
Born: January 29, 1843
Died: September 14, 1901
Presidency: 1897-1901

If Benjamin Harrison was as cold as an Indiana winter, William McKinley could only profit by comparison, for he was as warm and gracious as a summer breeze. He stood in remarkable contrast to Harrison, displaying a gentle kindness that could encompass and soothe the most irritable of men. Both Harrison and McKinley were Guardians, and the contrast between them highlights especially nicely the difference between the extreme Monitor and the extreme Conservator. Add to this the contrast between the seclusiveness of Harrison and the gregariousness of McKinley and the difference shows up even more clearly.

McKinley was noted for his great charm, his remarkable tact, and his inexhaustible personal warmth. Along with these attributes, not unusual in the Conservator Guardian, he also had a dignity and a powerful sense of decency and moral constancy which never seemed to leave him. "He had such a good heart that the right thing to do always occurred to him," commented an admiring William Howard Taft. Like so many American Presidents, McKinley had served in the Civil War. When he was honorably discharged from his regiment at the war's end, he was said to be "the only man in the regiment who had completed his hitch without ever having uttered a profanity, gotten drunk, or lost his virginity."[147]

In spite of his character and perhaps because of it many professional politicians saw McKinley only as a party hack, a man fit to be only the instrument of others' policies. His warm, gentle, and responsive demeanor could mislead those who did not watch closely. Nation Magazine, for instance, described him as "the mildest-mannered President that ever suffered long and was kind in the White House," and went on to comment that McKinley had little more to offer than a "flabby good nature." Theodore Roosevelt, a blazing Operator Artisan, apparently had trouble gauging Conservators. His later troubles with William Taft indicated this, as did his acid and inaccurate comment that "McKinley has a chocolate-eclair backbone."

Those who leveled such criticisms at McKinley failed to recognize the strength and rock-hard staunchness which underlay his deceptively gentle appearance. Others have seen him more accurately. "He was a man of great power because he was absolutely indifferent to credit. His manner was gracious and responsive, but his great desire as an office holder was to get the job done." And another comment: "He cared nothing about the credit, but McKinley always had his way." Furthermore, he imbued the office of President "with a dignity that became almost imperial." Hardly the marks of a man possessed of only a "flabby good nature" or a backbone of a chocolate eclair.[148]

---

147 *Presidential Courage,* 170.
148 All three comments found in *The Presidency of William McKinley,* 9.

He had a remarkable memory for names and faces which, he said, just came naturally to him, as it does to most Conservators. This characteristic makes them good salespeople; they really do know something about the person to whom they're selling. The same is true in politics of course; the Conservators really do know something about the people they're talking to. Even in the rough and tumble of political debate the Conservator McKinley was admired for his temperate and reasonable attitude, his personable style and his general kindliness.

Many said he was a little too serious to allow one to be completely comfortable around him, but this was for most people their chief criticism of him. Speaker of the House Tom Reed, used to the antagonism of partisan politics and wondering at the good will that surrounded McKinley, once complained that "My opponents in Congress go at me tooth and nail, but they always apologize to William when they are going to call him names."[149] Another congressman, once stormed into President McKinley's office in a rage only to emerge a few minutes later with a smile. He looked around at the men who had accompanied him and declared, "I don't know a blamed word he said, but it's all all right boys."

McKinley was a fine example of the Conservator in more than his ability to soothe upset politicians. When the Civil War broke out, the eighteen year-old McKinley volunteered for service in the Union Army and found himself in the regiment of future President Rutherford B. Hayes. He was shortly appointed commissary sergeant which means that he was the regiment's chief cook. This splendid Conservator distinguished himself by managing to serve a hot meal to the soldiers of his regiment while they were under fire, a feat almost unheard of in that war (or most others for that matter).

McKinley's career moved relatively well from that time on. He was later promoted through the ranks to the officer corps and ended his brief military career as a major. He had become well-recognized in that short period of time not only for his resourcefulness but for his repeated acts of bravery in combat. After leaving the army he read law, launched a legal practice, married Ida Saxon in 1871, and six years later was elected to the House of Representatives. He was then elected Governor of Ohio

---

149 *Presidential Anecdotes*, 188.

and the year his term expired, 1896, he ran for and was elected President of the United States. He had become a popular, energetic, and remarkably successful career politician.

At the time McKinley assumed the presidency there was already developing a powerful outcry over Spain's colonial policies in the Americas and especially in Cuba. There was some good reason for the indignation against Spain, for it treated the people of Cuba contemptuously and cruelly. The fires of outrage were also being fueled by a jingoist press and a number of politicians, including the influential Teddy Roosevelt. McKinley was not eager to embark on a warlike adventure, however, and did what he could to ward off the move. "I have been through one war," he said. "I have seen the dead pile up and I do not want to see another." He was vilified for his anti-war stance, mocked, even burned in effigy, and the impetuous Teddy Roosevelt went so far as to call him a white-livered coward.[150]

Then in February of 1898 an American warship, the *Maine*, blew up mysteriously in Havana Harbor. The press published rumors that the Spanish had done the deed. American anger was white-hot, and two months later, in spite of his reluctance, McKinley knew that his party might be split over the issue and that his own political future was at stake. Further, he had begun to realize that there might be worthwhile territorial gains for the United States if the war was concluded successfully. He gave in and moved for war, and even when he received word that Spain was eager to make concessions to keep the peace, he let events take their by now inevitable course. Congress declared war, the Spanish-American War began, and United States forces attacked Spanish forces in the Caribbean and in the Pacific. The Spanish military and naval establishments were at that time quite inept (though to tell the truth the United States was not much better off) and only four months later the American flag flew over Cuba, Puerto Rico, and the Philippines. To wrap up the territorial package, McKinley also recommended that the United States annex the Hawaiian Islands.

In spite of the turmoil associated with his presidency William McKinley's political life was in some respects far easier than his personal life. Ida Saxon had been a bright, effervescent young woman

---

150 The irrepressible Artisan Teddy Roosevelt, at that time Secretary of the Navy, had already sent United States naval vessels to the Far East, with instructions to attack the Spanish fleet in the Philippines as soon as war broke out.

when Major McKinley discovered her and began to court her. She found
him to be all she could wish for and became absorbed in the handsome
and promising young lawyer. Marriage would be difficult financially,
but McKinley believed that if he worked hard in the practice of law he
could manage it. Ida Saxon agreed and the two were married in 1871. In
spite of financial difficulty the McKinleys were quite happy for the first
two years of their marriage, which was blessed by a baby daughter.

But Ida McKinley became seriously ill during the latter part of her
second pregnancy. Adding to her illness were the death of her mother
and then the death of the McKinleys' infant daughter five months later.
She never seemed to recover from the twin tragedies, and soon thereafter
their older daughter died as well. Ida began acting strangely; the
attending physicians called her behavior "petit mal epilepsy," and later
the diagnosis was expanded to include grand mal epilepsy. She also
developed headaches so severe that the weight of her own hair was more
than she could bear, so she had her hair cut off. She would on occasion
sit in her darkened room, moaning to herself and acting as if she were
rocking a baby. As time went by she seemed less and less able to care
for herself and became more and more fretfully dependent upon
William.

William McKinley paid his wife remarkably solicitous attention,
well beyond what most people would consider reasonable. He was
terribly anxious and concerned for her well-being, especially on social
occasions, which she insisted on participating despite her difficulties.
Her "attacks" were usually signalled by a sudden sucking in of air
through her pursed lips and this signal would give McKinley time to
spirit her away. He could then look after her in a quiet part of the White
House until the episode passed. He didn't always see this as necessary,
however. If he thought that the attack would be a brief petit mal episode
he would "whip out a damask napkin and drape it over her head and
allow her to sit there sometimes grunting, drooling, or smacking her lips,
until the attack had passed."[151] Once the napkin was in place McKinley
would continue the conversation which had been occurring as if nothing
untoward were happening. Sometimes he did so with a pleading look on
his face which spoke volumes to those present. Then when the attack

---

151 *Presidential Courage*, 123.

was over he could remove the napkin and dinner would continue as if nothing had happened.

McKinley's solicitude was not something noted only when he reached the White House. It was already becoming legendary when he was Governor of Ohio in 1891. Each day he would walk across the street to his office in the State Capitol, stop on the steps before entering the building, and wave his hat to his wife. And each day, precisely at three no matter what he was doing, he stopped his work to signal her with his handkerchief from his office and wait for her to respond from her rooms across the street. Even his one real diversion, cigar smoking, he indulged only away from home because Ida objected to the odor. He still managed to find ample time, apparently, for he was said to smoke twenty cigars a day.

Over the years McKinley studied epilepsy and became something of an expert on the subject insofar as the confused theorizing about the disorder made any claim of expertise possible. In consequence he also became his wife's best, most knowledgeable and most competent nurse. William fed her, soothed her, and nursed her day and night. He spent hours holding hands with her in a darkened room since Ida could not tolerate the light; he devoted hours to reading poetry to her because she liked the sound of his voice; he gave hours to gentle massage of her tortured head. Though she in return was often ill-tempered and ill-mannered and probably one of the most demanding invalids in American political history, she did love him and saw him as a "dear, good man." And although Ida became more and more demanding as time passed, William in his turn seemed to love her more each year.

Meanwhile, the country was doing well. Other than the quick and glorious Spanish-American war and a few worries about inflation, things had been pleasantly quiet in the United States and the nation was riding on a wave of prosperity. Add to this the success and the popularity of the war against Spain with its easy and dramatic victories and it is understandable that the Republican President William McKinley again found tremendous popularity. The Democrats could find no persuasive issues to present and the presidential campaign of 1900 was rather quiet. Little new was to be noted during the desultory campaign except the emergence of the enthusiastic and charismatic Teddy Roosevelt as McKinley's vice-presidential running mate. McKinley was easily re-elected for a second term.

He was also put in place for a murderer's bullets.

On September 6, 1901 he was shot twice and fatally wounded by an assassin. As we described in the opening chapter, this humane man, this fine exemplar of much of the best of the provident Conservator, was true to type even in his own dying. As the outraged crowd surrounded and subdued the young man who had shot him, McKinley cried out to protect his assassin from them, and then earnestly implored his friend and advisor, George Cortelyou, to be careful about how he told Ida about the shooting.

He struggled against the bullet's damage for eight days, but died on September 14, 1901. At the end he whispered to his wife, "Good-by all, good-by. It is God's way. His will be done." Again stricken with tragedy, the unhappy Ida McKinley lived on for another half dozen years, dying in 1907 at age sixty.

Bibliography

Dobson, J 1988   *Reticent Expansionism: The Foreign Policy of William McKinley*
Gould, L 1980   *The Presidency of William McKinley*
Gould, L 1982   *The Spanish-American War and President McKinley*
Halstead, M 1901   *The Illustrious Life of William McKinley, our Martyred President*
Hay, J   *On William McKinley*
Heald, E 1964   *The William McKinley Story*
Leech, M 1959   *In the Days of McKinley*
McClure, A 1901   *The Authentic Life of William McKinley [and] a Life Sketch of Theodore Roosevelt*
Morgan, H 1963   *McKinley and His America*
Olcott, C 1916   *William McKinley*
Spielman, W 1954   *William McKinley, Stalwart Republican, a Biographical Study*

William Howard Taft

A step in the right direction

Conservator
Born: September 15, 1857
Died: March 8,1930
Presidency: 1909-1913

It is fascinating and at times almost frightening to see how thoroughly people can misread each other. Consider the case of Teddy Roosevelt and William Howard Taft. Chosen by the energetic and outgoing Roosevelt to be his successor, Taft in just a couple years became so hated by TR that he formed his own political party, the Progressive or "Bull Moose" party, to battle Taft's re-election.

There was certainly no intent on Taft's part to betray Roosevelt. He was in fact initially eager to follow TR's lead. It was just that William Howard Taft had a mind of his own, political ideas of his own and a strong sense of personal honor. These not only led him away from strict adherence to Teddy Roosevelt's interests, but eventually brought him into sharp and irreconcilable conflict with them—and with Roosevelt. Neither Roosevelt nor Taft understood how badly they had misunderstood each other.

Beyond the difficult but reasonably straightforward matter of very different political orientations, there was another difference, much more profound and absolutely certain to lead to difficulty: Roosevelt the hell-for-leather Artisan had hand-picked a sober-sided Guardian to be his political heir.

It was of course an impossible choice.

The choice seemed quite sound at the time; certainly there were numerous superficial similarities between the two men. They were both affable, both reputed to be decent men, both (largely) above-board and hard-working, both quite bright, both energetically and honestly concerned with the well-being of their country. Roosevelt and Taft were physically big men as well, powerfully built and capable of vigorous physical expression. Roosevelt had pursued an athletic life and Taft as a young man had done well at both boxing and wrestling. Furthermore, Taft had a warm relationship with TR and, like many Conservators, he had a difficult time saying no to people he liked.

Taft had reached his prominent public position by virtue of political appointment rather than by the slugfests and maneuvering of elective politics. He therefore had little firsthand experience of the practices of professional politicians. In his relative innocence Taft could usually be counted upon to cooperate with the professionals and to acquiesce to their requests for (presumably) legitimate political favors and political appointments. To Roosevelt and his people it looked as if Taft's election would ensure a comfortable continuation of the Roosevelt administration. Only a few names would be changed.[152]

The differences between the two were striking, however, even if Roosevelt underestimated their importance. TR the Artisan was daring, action-hungry, eager to make changes, to effect events and have an impact on people. Taft the Guardian was careful, conservative,

---

152 So close was their relationship considered to be that there was a joke widely repeated that "TAFT" stood for "Take Advice From Teddy."

judicious, concerned with discharging his responsibilities properly. TR found exhilaration in political office, had a charismatic power to move people, was joyously responsive to opportunity. Taft had little charisma; instead he was a bit stuffy in his appearance, he felt burdened by the demands of the presidency (as Guardians typically do), and he was concerned about the possibility of any President gathering too much power.

Whereas Roosevelt could be counted on to make changes if for no other reason than that change was exciting, Taft was dedicated to a tradition of institutional stability and legal precedents whose demands had to be satisfied before he would consider action. While TR was vigorously active by choice, Taft was by choice placidly quiet—except of course when duty called or protocol demanded.

While the Artisan TR devoted himself to adventuring, Taft the Guardian preferred to devote himself to the study and teaching of law and to being a good judge. And as both a teacher (he taught law at Yale) and a judge Taft preferred to understand and adhere to the received wisdom of the legal tradition rather than to try to break new ground with his interpretations. While Roosevelt saw the law as an instrument to be used in pursuit of his own enterprises, Taft so respected legal precedents that he would readily surrender his own wishes to their requirements. His respectability was also of enormous importance to him. Appointed as U. S. Collector of Revenue, for instance, Taft realized within a year that he was likely to be compromised by the position no matter what his intentions were. He so feared having his reputation tainted that he resigned the position.[153] Roosevelt was also a man of honor, but "respectability" was never an issue for this Artisan.

Each of these differences is paradigmatic of the distinctions between Artisan and Guardian. Just as the Artisan Teddy Roosevelt was the quintessential Player, the Guardian Taft was a magnificent Conservator. But to underscore their differences even further note that Taft had no particular interest in being President. Even his presidential campaign was not of his own choosing, but was devised and conducted by TR's people. Roosevelt could move Taft to action by appealing to his sense of duty and obligation, and it was only through this sort of appeal that TR

---

153 *William Howard Taft*, 12.

was able to secure Taft's reluctant agreement to run for office. Then when the campaign began Taft was told he had to campaign hard; he was obligated to those who had nominated him and were supporting him. Now he was drawn into the trap: he was running for an office in which he had little interest but he campaigned hard because he felt obligated to do so. "I am not much of a politician," he said, "but I feel very deeply the responsibility that I have upon me now as a candidate."[154]

It was well known that one could play not only upon Taft's sense of obligation and duty, but also upon his strong desire for friendly, warm, and amicable relationships with others. Those who knew him knew that he was a kindly and open man and that they could count on his generosity, his honesty, and his forthrightness. They could also count on him to work hard and long, no matter how onerous the task, if his sense of obligation required it of him. He did not accept the position of Governor General of the Philippine Islands in 1900 because he wanted it, but because he was persuaded to see it as a duty he owed his friends and his party. Secretary of War Elihu Root pointed out to Taft that he had enjoyed something of a free ride thus far; his positions had come by appointment, not by sweat.

> Now his country needed him. It was a kind of parting of the ways. He could continue sitting on the bench in a humdrum, mediocre way or he could do something that would be a real test, requiring effort and struggle.[155]

It may be that TR's people, more accustomed to the maneuvering of the professional Artisans, were fooled by Taft's easygoing and open Conservator style. Taft had great affection for and loyalty to his friends, and he could be cajoled by them, but in spite of his amicable ways he was no doormat. He was an able man in the field of law and he had his own ambitions in that domain. Thus it was understood that the appointments he so reluctantly accepted would not be exercises in duty alone, but would also be stepping stones to his own ultimate ambition.

---

154 *William Howard Taft*, 58.

155 *How They Became President*, 331. It is interesting that Tugwell saw Root's ploy as a challenge or dare rather than as an appeal to duty and conscience. If Root was as able as history portrays him, he appealed to the Guardian Taft's sense of *duty*. Challenges are best reserved for ensnaring Artisans.

As it happened, Taft's time in the Philippines was gratifying for him and very beneficial for the Philippine people. First, he was meeting an obligation which he felt the United States had taken on when it took the Philippines from Spain in the Spanish-American War. Next, he was bringing traditional American organization to the islands, something badly needed. Third, as Governor General of the Philippines he proved to be a very able administrator. Finally, the Philippine people could see that he was genuinely working in their interest. After suffering under Spanish despotism and putting up with the almost imperial Governorship of Arthur MacArthur, they genuinely appreciated Taft's openhanded efforts and became quite fond of the big American. Taft the Conservator of course enjoyed their recognition of his efforts and their appreciation of his benevolent intentions.

Taft's ultimate aspiration was not to be the President of the United States; William Howard Taft aspired to nothing less than a seat on the Supreme Court of the United States. The position combined his wish for status with his enduring interest in duty, service, and the laws of the land. There were the focus of both his ambition and his interests, as the wonderfully Guardian titles of two books he wrote indicate: *Four Aspects of Civic Duty*, published in 1906, and *Ethics in Service*, published in 1915.

Clearly Taft's preference to be a Supreme Court Justice rather than the President made sense, given his Guardian character. Though he was a warm and bright and honest man, he had little (in fact none) of the powerful charisma of a Teddy Roosevelt. The rather seclusive Taft had a talent for forgetting names and saying the wrong thing at the wrong time and, unlike most Conservators, he could rarely remember to wave to or look at the crowds which cheered him as he passed by. Though he was certainly capable of hard work, he also had a facility for dozing off at inopportune times, including Cabinet meetings and White House dinners. It is said that he once dozed off at a funeral service while sitting in full view in the front row.

Furthermore, the high level of activity, both mental and physical, which characterizes most presidencies was almost beyond him. He was rather lethargic and quite large and ponderous, and had been since childhood. His great size meant that it was a great deal of work for him to move about. He weighed between 300 and 350 pounds, little of his weight being muscle in his later years, and he was therefore a natural and almost defenseless target for quips and stories. For example it was once said of him that he was so polite that on a street car he would get up from his seat and give it to three women. The story is also told that he once cabled Secretary Root from the Philippines that he had gone horseback riding and felt fine. Root is supposed to have cabled back, "How is the horse?"[156]

William Howard Taft offered a lot of material for conversation, though little enough of it seemed presidential. Helen Herron Taft, on the other hand, was quite another matter.

Helen Herron was a very ambitious woman. Even as a young girl Helen ("Nellie" to those close to her) wanted more independence for herself and more respect from others than the feminine roles usual to her day allowed. Probably an Organizer Rational, she was also strongly drawn to the intellectual life. She established in her home in Cincinnati a "salon" in the European fashion, a place at which intellectuals would gather to discuss serious or recondite matters. Though she had several interested male friends, Helen Herron kept them all at proper arm's length. She abjured romance as a weakness and once wrote in her diary that she saw love without intellectual friendship as "that fatal idealization which is so blind and, to me, so contemptible."

Her choice of William Howard Taft as a husband was apparently a choice of the heart, but was also clearly influenced by her recognition that he was intellectually able and that he might—especially with her guidance—have a worthy future. In fact it is probably Helen Taft who was chiefly responsible for William's entry into elective politics. Roosevelt offered his friend Taft a position on the Supreme Court, something the latter wanted very much, while Taft was still Philippine Governor General. Taft turned down the offer. The Conservator refused this greatly-desired appointment partly because his work in the Philippines was not yet finished, and he couldn't feel right about abandoning it, but also because Nellie Taft decided the Court was not the right position for him politically. She had bigger things in mind for him and she insisted that he refuse the offer. Later, when he was later offered the position of Secretary of War, she bade him accept it. After

---

156 *Presidential Anecdotes*, 215.

all, she wrote, "it was in line with the kind of work I wanted my husband to do, the kind of career I wanted for him and expected him to have."[157]

When William Taft assumed the presidency Helen Taft was not one to sit back, obscured by her husband's ample shadow. She signalled this immediately when she took the unprecedented step of riding back to the White House with her husband after his inauguration, something no first lady had ever done before. Mrs. Taft also energetically took over and revamped the management of the White House. She busied herself with a number of other projects, including a modest beautification project for Washington's Potomac Speedway. (Washington's famous cherry trees, a gift from the Mayor of Tokyo, came from this project.) In one of her less popular moves Helen Taft went so far as to keep a cow which fed on the White House lawn to ensure that there would be fresh milk available each morning. Rationals often have an almost complete disregard for tradition and protocol, and Helen Taft demonstrated this disregard many times, including her ride with her husband from the inauguration and the use of the family cow.

Nellie Taft sat in on many of her husband's conferences, advised him on political matters, and at times intruded herself into political discussions in a way unlikely to endear her to anyone. She was sometimes more than a little too vigorous, a little too innovative, a little too unwilling to recognize that the "Wife of the President" was not a recognized political office. It is ironic that shortly after Will took office Nellie suffered a stroke which severely impaired her ability to speak. There is some likelihood that the intense pressure under which she put herself was partially responsible for the stroke. Be that as it may, Helen Taft's will was unbreakable, as always. For more than a year she devoted herself to learning to speak all over again. Though her recovery was good she never again engaged in the vigorous routine she had previously followed. Still, some is better than none. Her disability almost broke Will Taft's heart and he was unreservedly delighted to see her recovering. As she regained her strength he wrote with happy contentment to his brother that "She is quite disposed to sit as a pope and direct me as of yore."[158]

---

157 From her *Recollections*, quoted in *Profiles and Portraits of American Presidents*, 262.

158 *Presidential Wives*, 213.

As already mentioned, Taft's disagreements with Roosevelt became so pronounced that Roosevelt ran against him in the election campaign of 1912, splitting the Republican Party to which they both belonged. Taft was puzzled and hurt by Roosevelt's disaffection and never understood why his sponsor had betrayed him. "I have a sense of wrong in the attitude of Theodore Roosevelt toward me which I doubt if I can ever get over," he wrote. He stood aghast at what he saw as "the hypocrisy, the insincerity, the selfishness, the monumental egotism" of his former friend Roosevelt.

This brief notation portrayed several fundamental Guardian themes. Here are claims of betrayal and hurt, the assertion of inability to forgive, and pointed charges of terrible wrongdoing: dishonesty, selfishness, egotism. Taft's doubt that he could "get over it" is especially believable, coming as it did from the pen of this very sensitive Conservator. Taft, like all Guardians, held in eternal memory every instance of others' wrongdoing to him, however slight. Guardians one and all naturally keep a detailed accounting of social transactions in the same manner and with the same diligence that they track financial transactions. It is the distinguishing characteristic of the Guardian, whether Monitor or Conservator.

Taft, Roosevelt, and the divided Republican Party could not withstand the assaults of the Democrats in the presidential campaign of 1912. The Democratic candidate Woodrow Wilson won easily against the incumbent Taft, whose defeat was caused as much by Roosevelt's "Bull Moose" campaign as by the Democrats. Still Taft was in his own terms something of a victor: he was so bitter about Roosevelt's turnabout that he hoped that if he, Taft, could not win, Wilson would. Taft had the bittersweet pleasure of witnessing Wilson's victory and then the richer satisfaction of being appointed a professor of law at Yale University. Helen's wishes notwithstanding, Will could finally and happily comment that "I am now in a respectable profession. I hope to live and die a professor."[159]

In 1921 Taft was finally appointed Chief Justice of the United States by his old friend (and now President) Warren G. Harding. William Howard Taft had finally realized his highest ambition. Once he reached

---

159 *William Howard Taft*, 111.

the Supreme Court the less than overwhelming President proved himself to be an honorable and respectable and relentlessly hard-working jurist. Even so, his Conservator's natural interest in cooperation found an interesting but characteristic expression while he served on the Court: during his time on the Bench he never once wrote a dissenting opinion to the majority decisions of the Court. "I would not think," he wrote of the absence of such opinions, "of opposing the views of my brethren if there is a majority against my own."[160]

He and Nellie Taft, the latter's ambitions apparently reasonably satisfied, found their years out of the public eye of elective politics both pleasant and satisfying. But William's gradually deteriorating health forced him to resign from the Supreme Court in 1930, and he died a few months later. Helen Taft lived until 1943, long enough to see her children become successful and to look with deep suspicion on Franklin Roosevelt's New Deal, the work of another hated Roosevelt and another Artisan.

Bibliography

Anderson, D 1973	*William Howard Taft: A Conservative's Conception of the Presidency*
Anderson, J 1981	*William Howard Taft, an Intimate History*
Burton, D 1986	*William Howard Taft: In the Public Service*
Colletta, P 1973	*The Presidency of William Howard Taft*
Duffy, H 1930	*William Howard Taft*
Haley, P 1970	*Revolution and Intervention: The Diplomacy of Taft and Wilson with Mexico*
Manners, W 1969	*TR and Will; a Friendship that Split the Republican Party*
Mason, A 1965	*William Howard Taft: Chief Justice*
Minger, R 1975	*William Howard Taft and the United States Foreign Policy*
Pringle, H 1939	*The Life and Times of William Howard Taft, a Biography*
Scholes, W 1970	*The Foreign Policy of the Taft Administration*

---

160 *The American Presidents,* 236.

Gerald R. Ford

"I am disgustingly sane."

Conservator
Born: July 14, 1913
Presidency: 1974-1977

When Richard Nixon resigned his presidency the reigns of power were turned over to Vice-President Gerry Ford, a man whom many people saw as a simple and unremarkable plodder, a pleasant and decent man who seemed to have little to offer except his pleasant decency.

The nature of Ford's ascendancy to the presidency was unparalleled in American history. When Richard Nixon was elected President his vice presidential running mate was Spiro Agnew. Agnew was forced to resign the vice-presidency because of massive scandals which eventually surrounded him (the proximate cause of his resignation being charges of income tax evasion). Nixon sought someone to replace Agnew about whose honesty there could be no question—and about whose loyalty Nixon would have no question. Nixon nominated Ford to become the new Vice-President and in December of 1973 Ford was confirmed for the office by the Congress. Then, on August 9, 1974, President Nixon himself resigned and Gerry Ford, the unlikely and what his wife Betty termed the accidental Vice-President suddenly became the unlikely and accidental President of the United States.

When Ford assumed the executive office he became the object of the intense and constant scrutiny to which any President is subjected. Because of the peculiarity of his route to the White House he may have been the object of more intense—and less generous—scrutiny than most. Gracefully acknowledging the oddness of his situation he said when he assumed the presidency, "I am acutely aware that you have not elected me President by your ballots. So I ask you to confirm me as your President with your prayers....I am indebted to no man, and only to one woman—my dear wife—as I begin this very difficult job." In these few words one can read much of the heart and the mind, the character, of the Conservator Gerald R. Ford.

Gerald Ford Jr. was the adopted son of Gerald Rudolph Ford. Ford had married the boy's mother, Dorothy King, and at the same time adopted her son, Leslie King, and gave Leslie his own name; Leslie became Gerald Junior. Young Gerald was athletic, a big, well-built youngster who became a successful player on his high school football team and later attended the University of Michigan partially on the strength of a football scholarship. He was a good player, winning recognition in the East-West football game of 1935 and the College All-Stars game later that year. He even received invitations to try out for both the Detroit Lions and the Green Bay Packers. In both high school and college he had pursued his studies diligently and managed to maintain a high "B" average.

The "B" average was a problem. Gerald Ford wanted to attend Yale law school and most of the students there were Phi Beta Kappas. But Ford pled his case and managed to win a trial placement; he would be allowed to take a few courses and see how it went. Given his chance Ford saw to it that it went well enough: while still working as a coach he succeeded in handling the courses, and was admitted to a full program. He received his law degree in 1941, graduating in the upper third of his class.

Ford was then admitted to the Michigan bar and entered practice in Grand Rapids, Michigan. His legal career was short lived, however, for when war broke out at the end of 1941 Gerry Ford volunteered for military service. He was given a naval commission and spent the next four years in the Navy. He left the Navy in 1946 when the war ended with the rank of Lieutenant Commander and resumed his practice of law.

Ford had been interested in politics for some time. When he returned to Grand Rapids, with the help of family and friends he took the plunge and became active in the local political scene. From minor political activity he quickly graduated to a campaign for a seat in the House of Representatives. His incumbent opponent had become increasingly unpopular and Ford's energetic, hard-working, and disarmingly honest campaign was successful. His Conservator's honesty in the campaign was engaging: when asked about issues about which he didn't know much he candidly replied that he didn't know but would find out. From that time in 1949 until he was sworn in as Vice-President, Ford was re-elected to the House of Representatives in every election for 24 years. He turned down the chance to run for the Senate and his increasing seniority in the House eventually led him to what was his ultimate political goal, Speaker of the House of Representatives.

Throughout his years in the House Gerald Ford's reputation for honesty and diligence was impeccable. Even after a quarter century in the Congress, Ford was still the Eagle Scout he had labored so hard to become as a boy, patiently, persistently working to earn merit badge after merit badge until he achieved his Eagle status. (The Boy Scouts, by the way, with its emphasis on honesty, loyalty, and duty, and with its many badges of achievement and multiple rungs on the ladder of hierarchy, must have been put together by a Guardian.) With comforting predictability Ford's conservative political orientation continued to be carefully, and almost always mildly, to the right of center. He was in essence an honorable and palatable conservative Representative for the people of Michigan's Fifth District. He was a successful career politician and, after twenty-four years, almost an institution himself.

After he took the presidential oath of office things did not go as well for him. He was still quite physically active, and though he was sixty-one years old at the time he kept himself in good physical condition. He played golf and tennis and found time for skiing and swimming even while he occupied the presidency. But the national press did not focus on this aspect of the new President; it chose instead to seek out and report the occasional gaffes that anyone can be found making if he is observed long enough. Ford was soon characterized as an awkward and clumsy bumpkin who could be counted upon to stumble, bump his head, or drop or spill or break things, or otherwise entertain the news-hungry press by embarrassing himself.

It must be granted that to some extent he earned this unflattering attention. He was well coordinated and unquestionably able and experienced on the public scene, but he did have more than his share of awkward moments. He seemed to stumble and spill things more than one would expect, his speeches were typically rather flat, lacking any dynamism, and he could claim no particular charisma. He recognized this himself. "I'm a Ford, not a Lincoln," he once said, "My addresses will never be as eloquent."[161] To make matters worse he committed some verbal gaffes from which he had considerable trouble recovering. Perhaps the worst of these was his stunning assertion that Eastern Europe was not dominated by the Soviets, which all his efforts to cover gracefully only made more visible. (He also had the misfortune to comment publicly that "if Lincoln were alive today he'd roll over in his grave."[162])

Perhaps the final blow to Ford's presidential future came within a month of his taking office. Ford used his presidential powers to grant Richard Nixon full pardon for whatever transgressions (as yet undetermined) the former President may have committed. He thereby alienated and even enraged a large numbers of politicians and voters. Some people speculated that a deal might have been struck between the two men before Nixon resigned. The presidency, in this view, was Ford's payoff for rescuing Nixon. This seemed likely to some because Ford had taken his action without consulting Congress, his own advisors, or anyone else in the government or in his party. The pardon was his own personal decision. To make matters worse for himself politically, he also offered a conditional amnesty to the draft resistors

---

161 *Jerry Ford, Up Close,* 3.
162 *Presidential Anecdotes,* 335.

who had avoided service in the Viet Nam conflict. According to the terms of the amnesty these people would be forgiven their illegal evasion if they would perform two years' low-paid public service. But this act of Ford's was seen as an insult by those many had supported the Viet Nam action, and especially by those who had fought there.

Throughout the rest of Ford's tenure the country was gripped by a severe recession. Simultaneously, inflation pushed prices violently upward, and Ford was able neither to draft a program acceptable to the Congress nor to stop most of Congress's efforts (many of which were in his view ill-advised) to solve these problems. Even his foreign policy efforts, which were largely continuations of Nixon's efforts to increase the prospects for world peace, seemed to work out poorly. It appeared to many that Ford's ability to handle the demands of the presidency was, as some had feared, at best questionable.

But Gerald Ford was neither a foolish man nor an incompetent as President. Though his self-presentation was often awkward, though he did not present a charismatic manner, and though many considered him little more than a faithful party man for years, he was still the man who held a job while competing with top notch scholars at Yale law school and still managed to graduate in the top third of his class. Nor was he a man easily fooled by others. He usually demonstrated an acute "down to earth" perceptiveness about people he met and about matters brought before him, and most of his decisions have proven over the years to be remarkably sensible.

Ford was also a kindly President and one whom most people would probably describe as quite healthy psychologically as well as physically. As he himself put it on a several occasions, he is "disgustingly sane" and "the first Eagle Scout President of the United States." Even in high school he managed to be a successful high school athlete and a serious student and still be voted the most popular high school senior. Then as later he was calm and rather easy-going, with a pleasant disposition, conscientious, and hard-working. Then as later he was loyal to his friends and associates and seemed instinctively to give people the benefit of the doubt—at least initially.

In all these respects he is a fine example of a well-adjusted Conservator.

He is also a fine example of the Guardians in that though he was inclined to give people the benefit of the doubt he was quite able to turn his back on those who had proven that they were not deserving. For instance he stood steadfastly by Spiro Agnew during the initial stages of the latter's difficulties and even at the cost of some of his own popularity. But when he realized that Agnew had lied to him repeatedly while looking him straight in the eye, Ford abandoned the man without hesitation.

Gerry Ford was sure enough of himself that he could appreciate and applaud the talents and successes of others, as he demonstrated with the good relationship he was able to establish with the brilliant Artisan Henry Kissinger. He resented the fun that was poked at him, and especially the comments about his lack of intellectual ability. Lyndon Johnson once commented that Ford had "played too much football with his helmet off." (The Artisan Johnson never did respect Ford. Johnson apparently thought he could manipulate Ford too easily to respect him and, true to his Artisan nature, was certain that those easily manipulated are stupid.) Even so Ford showed a remarkable ability to take all the criticism in stride and to respond to it in a measured way.

The Wall Street Journal, for instance, once commented that Ford was "a pleasant but plodding wheel horse who often speaks and apparently thinks in cliches."[163] Ford responded to the comment in a way that reflects his character well and with dignity: "I'd rather be plodding and get something done," he replied, "than have charisma and accomplish nothing."[164] Perhaps, considering what many regarded as Lyndon Johnson's rough and tumble political maneuvering, Ford might also have said that he'd rather do something right, slowly and carefully, than do something wrong, speedily and carelessly.

Ford's integrity, personal and political, was impeccable. As a member of the House of Representatives he compiled one of the best attendance records of anyone in the House. He did not avoid controversial votes but stayed true to his conviction that Congressmen were elected to represent. That meant they were there to vote and to have their votes stand as matters of public record. His unyielding

---

163 *George Bush*, quoted in *A Ford, Not a Lincoln*, 4.
164 *Jerry Ford, Up Close*, 188.

firmness in this respect is so well recognized that was dubbed by his congressional colleagues as "the Gentle Tiger." He was also widely known as a man whose word could be trusted absolutely. So well established was his integrity that one of his political opponents once acknowledged that "You'd have to catch Gerry Ford smuggling heroin into the country to make the people in Grand Rapids think he was dishonest."[165]

Certainly Gerry Ford, like anyone else, had limitations. He was able to follow through quite competently on policies he inherited, including the difficult matter of the new detente with the Soviets. But he was neither an innovator nor a person to offer up new visions of the future or new strategies for achieving them. As one biographer commented, "Imagination: there was a lack. In Gerald it was like an appendix, a little used facility. He much preferred facts."[166] In this regard he again shows the concrete style of his Guardian character quite clearly. And, it must be admitted, even Gerry Ford didn't always live up to his own code of conduct. Ford has acknowledged that he committed one presidential act of which he was ashamed: when standing for election to the presidency in 1976 he agreed to placate the conservative wing of his own party by dumping his own Vice-President, Nelson Rockefeller. He never fully forgave himself for that act of disloyalty.[167]

Ford, like most Conservators (and unlike most Monitors) was not good at laying down the law. His geniality and his sensitivity to others' wishes made it difficult for him to manage his own staff with the firmness that is sometimes called for. He was also very reluctant to dismiss people, even when their work was less than satisfactory. And he certainly did not have the "killer instinct" that sometimes makes the difference in a hard battle. There was none of Lyndon Johnson's "fox on a leash" or Eisenhower's steely, impersonal resolution and dispassionate organizational genius. There was instead the openness and lack of complexity of a warm, patient, conscientious man, and with it at least a certain illusion of vulnerability that one sometimes sees in the Conservator.

---

165 *Jerry Ford, Up Close*, 152.
166 *Jerry Ford, Up Close*, 206.
167 *Roosevelt to Reagan*, 145.

Vulnerability or no, Gerry Ford still had what it took to pursue a successful career in politics for a quarter of a century and to be a partner in an enduringly successful marriage. Gerald Ford married Elizabeth (Betty) Bloomer Warren in 1948. Though Betty Ford was unprepared for the demands of her new position as wife of a professional politician she showed a noteworthy ability to adapt to those demands. Betty Warren might have had an immediate vision of things to come when Gerry, having been delayed by a political appearance, arrived late for their wedding. She adapted to the demands and delays of her husband's career and she was able to keep pace with them. She did what a politician's wife had to, she looked after her relationship with Gerry, and she raised their four children successfully and often alone, but the stress she felt was unavoidable. It couldn't be easy for her and there were times when she complained of her husband's frequent absences from the family. Their marriage endured even so, and in spite of the stress and the separations there is no doubt that Gerry and Betty Ford were devoted to each other and to their children.

Ford's political life was usually his first priority, but his wife was not shunted aside or treated as a mere detail of his life. In the presidency he was frank in his acknowledgment that his wife's opinions carried considerable weight with him and that they had been influential in the enormously important matter of Nixon's pardon. He showed an appreciation of and connection with his wife that many of his presidential predecessors never demonstrated during their entire tenure.

But then few of his predecessors were Conservators.

Betty Ford, probably another Conservator Guardian, was a very active First Lady. Though she was involved in a number of different projects she used her position especially to campaign for passage of the equal rights amendment. With a refreshing and sometimes unsettling candor she also spoke out about many subjects rarely discussed by previous First Ladies, including her family, her opinions about child-raising, the still risky issue of equal rights for women, and eventually her own surgery for breast cancer. Her openness about these topics and her genuinely forthright way of presenting herself endeared her to the press and eventually to much of the American public. Combined with her natural energy and ebullience they offered an appealing picture of both the First Lady and her family, one which was certainly helpful to her husband during his difficult tenure.

Conservator Guardians are usually fine hosts and the Fords were no exception. They were a comfortable and appealing couple even in the White House. They enjoyed entertaining and displayed a natural warmth which was in marked contrast to the stiff formality of their predecessors. They seemed to want the executive mansion to be like a home, not a monument, and they succeeded without impairing the dignity appropriate to the place. The White House became a much warmer and happier place during their tenure than it had been for quite some time. But the stresses associated with her husband's role had taken their toll on Betty Ford. One wrenching April evening a year after leaving the White House in 1977, her husband and their children got together with a couple of professional advisors and confronted her. They persuaded her to acknowledge that she was heavily dependent on medication and alcohol and that she needed assistance. Then, having done so, they supported her in getting the treatment she needed for her difficulties. One outcome of that painful experience was her founding of the nationally recognized Betty Ford Centers.

Everything about Gerry Ford confirms his Conservator temperament: his warmth, his loyalty, his hard-working and conscientious honesty, his devotion to his family even in the face of the demands on his time and energy of his political career. His wish to "heal the nation" quickly of the damage done by the Nixon controversy, his concern that the controversy was "tearing the country to pieces" and his concern for Nixon's own physical and emotional health, his attempts to resolve the problem of the numerous Viet Nam period draft evaders: all these are demonstrations of the Conservator perspective.

It is difficult to imagine that Ford could have made his decision to pardon former President Nixon without recognizing the severe political penalty he might visit upon himself. There was an element of sacrifice in that act which perhaps has not been sufficiently acknowledged. It was in fact just the sort of sacrifice the Conservator is more likely to make than is any other temperament. To the degree that he recognized the cost of providing the presidential pardon and amnesty, and weighed it against the healing effect they could nevertheless have on the nation at large, Gerald Ford showed us the unselfish charity of which the Conservator is so capable. Its cost for him may have been nothing less than his own election, two years later, to the presidency of the United States.

But the outcome for Ford has been far from bleak. In an interview in January 1989 the irrepressible Betty Ford offered a portrayal of success where it most counts for the Conservator. "My most important role is the role of wife, mother and grandmother," she said, "and I treasure that above all else. I try to put consideration of my husband's needs first, although I don't think he always thinks that. But after forty years we have the best years of our lives right now."[168]

Bibliography

Coward, M 1974	*Jerry Ford, Up Close*
Lankevich, G (ed) 1977	*Gerald R. Ford, 1913—: Chronology, Documents, Bibliographical Aids*
Ford, G 1979	*A Time to Heal: the Autobiography of Gerald R Ford*
Hersey, J 1980	*Aspects of the Presidency*
Mollenhoff, C 1976	*The Man who Pardoned Nixon*
Reeves, R 1975	*A Ford, Not a Lincoln*
Schapsmeier, E 1989	*Gerald R. Ford's Date with Destiny: a Political Biography*
TerHorst, J 1979	*Gerald Ford and the Future of the Presidency*
Thompson, K (ed) 1988	*The Ford Presidency: 22 Intimate Perspectives of Gerald R. Ford*

---

168 *Los Angeles Times*, Jan 18, 1989.

George Herbert Walker Bush

"Mr. Have Half"

Conservator
Born: June 14, 1924
Presidency: 1989-

As this is being written, George Bush is entering the third year of his presidency. Since he took office in January, 1989, the United States has invaded Panama and imprisoned Panama's president Manuel Noriega on charges of drug trafficking; it has encouraged vigorous anti-drug action in Colombia and in South America in general; it has extended aid to governments taking such action; and it has, in company with other members of the United Nations coalition, demolished the armed forces of Iraq. Since throwing Iraq out of Kuwait the United States has provided food, clothing, shelter, and medical supplies to Kurdish refugees within the borders of Iraq itself, it has extended the zone declared safe for refugees, and it has commanded the Iraqi government to stop harassing them.

No one who knew the young George Bush would have predicted for him such a conflict-torn future. Since early childhood he has been cheerful and even-tempered, someone who dearly enjoys the company of others, and who, like many Conservators, so spontaneously shares anything he has that as a child he was nick-named "Have-half." (Remember that the Conservators, in contrast to their Monitor cousins, are more the providers and protectors than the supervisors and inspectors.) Besides being unusually provident little George was also unusually dependable about doing household chores and cleaning up after himself. When, for example, he went fishing and caught a fish he would clean it immediately, an unpleasant task even for an adult. Only then would he display his catch to family and friends.

Even as an adult Bush's manner is so kind, cheerful, and generous that, as one acquaintance in Kennebunkport, Maine (the Bush family's primary residence) put it, "if Bush were running for sainthood in this area he'd make it unopposed."[169]

Bush was born to privilege. Prescott Bush, his father, had done very well in the financial world and the family was well-off. George Bush was fortunate in another regard as well: his early life seems to have been pleasant, his parents supportive, his family happy and stable. His religious upbringing was conventional, and done with overtones of duty, though hardly in an unpleasant fashion. His father, for example, would read from the Bible every day before breakfast, and the whole family attended church each Sunday (though there might be occasional exemptions from attendance to allow for special events).

George's father, a Monitor Guardian, "was a towering man who invited no argument and brandished a belt to punish his children."[170] Even today George says of his father that he was "pretty scary." (It is not at all unusual for Guardian children reared by Monitor Guardian parents to fear them and later to regard such strict and punitive upbringing as the proper way to rear children. In contrast however it is quite usual for Artisan children to rebel against such parents and later to

---

169 *George Bush*, 12.
170 *Flight of the Avenger: George Bush at War*, 21.

get even in some manner. Rational offspring of such parents often steer clear of them later, and have as little to do with them as possible.)

Perhaps because of his father's encouragement George became rather proficient in several sports, but especially in tennis, which he began practicing when he was six or seven. Interested in sports from this early age he became an avid fan of big-league baseball, and in this interest displayed a trait typical of the Guardian: he could recall, apparently with ease, an enormous amount of data about his heroes, big-league baseball players. Later he said "I knew the average of every batter and pitcher in the various leagues."

Young George attended Andover, a private school with predominantly wealthy students from the east coast, and proved to be an industrious student, a fine athlete, and a cheerful and friendly youth whom both students and teachers liked. While at Andover he became President of Senior Class, Chairman of Student Deacons, President of Greeks, Captain of the baseball and soccer teams, a member of varsity basketball team, and manager of the basketball and baseball teams.[171] He was on the editorial board of the school newspaper; a member of the Society of Inquiry, an on-campus religious organization; he was Deputy Housemaster, and he occupied other positions as well. And all the while, as part of the fabric of his life, his inherently provident nature was shaped by Andover and home to an almost upper-class British sense of the importance of noblesse oblige, the obligation of the privileged to render public service, to give to one's community a significant portion of one's time, energy, and resources. The budding Guardian seemed bent on knowing everybody on campus, on taking charge of most proceedings, and on being of service in every possible way.

By the time he completed Andover, Bush had reason to be gratified with his life. He had become a young man endowed with great energy and exceptional athletic skill, good academic talent, a pleasing physical appearance, and the winning warmth so characteristic of gregarious Conservators. His family was very well-off, his parents were loving, and

---

171 Of all the characters, the provident Conservators, especially those coming from warm, stable, and nurturing homes, tend to be most liked by their classmates and the most perfectly adapted to the school environment. Even their teachers prefer them to all other students because they support their teachers and tranquilize their classmates.

his brothers and sister good to be with. And now he was earning the social recognition and position so important to Guardians.

But he learned early, and being a Guardian he learned well, that his life was not meant to be an unfettered vacation. Prescott Bush had made a good deal of money and moved in the privileged circles of Wall Street insiders, but he, and his wife Dorothy, also worked to instill traditional social and moral values in his children. Kindness, courtesy, honesty, thrift, and so on were all taught, and Prescott and Dorothy Bush also demonstrated them in their own behavior. Dorothy Bush also seemed to have a very strong competitive streak, and George Bush was apparently powerfully influenced by it. He had not only his father's modeling of public service, but his mother's focus on winning. That focus was important to him, for, as his wife Barbara said years later, "His father had enormous influence on him, and his mother had ten times more."[172]

World War II broke out in December, 1941. When he turned eighteen six months later, Bush immediately enlisted in the Navy. Before the tremendous American victory at the Battle of Midway, the Navy required two years of college for naval aviation training. After Midway the Navy decided to step up their pilot training program, and to permit prospects with only a high school diploma to enter. Bush became an aviation cadet on August 6, 1942.

Only those who went through it can fully appreciate the thrills and terrors of the naval pilot training program. The training was gruelling, demanding, fraught with peril, and costly in personnel and materiel, for the Navy deemed it imprudent to waste the program on any but the very best candidates. The "wash-out" rate was awesome and frightening to the cadets, who knew that any mistake or hesitation or lapse of will would result in instant dismissal from the program. Fear of failure dogged the steps of every cadet no matter how tough and brave he may have been in his previous career.[173]

George Bush showed that he had the toughness and the determination to make it through the eight-month pilot training program,

---

172 *George Bush*, 212.
173 Some of the quality and spirit if not the sheer quantity of the rigors of pre-flight training was captured in the recent film, *An Officer and a Gentleman*. Flight training itself, however, was infinitely more challenging and terrifying than pre-flight training, that is for cadets other than Artisans.

though he was said not to be a natural pilot. He had to work hard to avoid skidding, yawing, and losing orientation during loops, snap rolls, and the other violent maneuvers required of Naval pilots. On the other hand radio and blind flying, bombing and straffing were reportedly no special problem for him. Aerobatics and deflection gunnery are managed "by the seat of one's pants," being an art done gracefully only by Artisan pilots. As a bomber pilot, away from the Artisan maneuvering, the Guardian Bush is said to have done very well, even permitting himself the "flat hatting" (flying low and fast to harass motorists and boaters) that most Naval Aviators surreptitiously practiced upon their return from some combat exercise out over the Atlantic.

But Bush's trials were not over and done with, for his air group was put aboard an aircraft carrier and dispatched to the Pacific Theater of operations. During his tour of duty he was shot down twice while flying combat missions, the second time with the loss of his two crew members. Pulled from the ocean by a submarine assigned rescue duty, he was unable to transfer back to his carrier for a month, after which he was given leave. He cut his leave time short, however, to return to his squadron. He said later that he felt honor-bound to do so. Typical of the Guardian, Bush equated honor with duty, where an Artisan in the same situation is more likely to equate it with daring.

Both the period of pilot training and combat were dangerous. Making it through training, even before combat experience, convinced every naval pilot that he was special; he would take pride his achievement for the rest of his life, and he would never again doubt whether he had the right stuff. In spite of his gentle public manner, George Bush showed that he has what it takes.

George Bush and Barbara Pierce, sweethearts since George's Andover days, married in January 1945, two weeks after he was transferred back to the United States. In the fall of that year the young pilot (he was now twenty-one) entered Yale and, with many other veterans, took an accelerated two-and-a-half-year program and earned his bachelor's degree in economics. The domain of economics, especially its business applications such as accounting, banking, and investment, is clearly very attractive to Guardians. Their interest most can be seen from an early age. While other types, if they get into economics at all, do so much later in their lives and only after sampling other avenues, Guardians head right for it in their youth, as if by instinct.

As usual, he worked very hard and conscientiously, and did well academically. Meanwhile he had played on the varsity baseball team, and was team captain during his senior year; he played soccer, and was a strong swimmer, golfer, and tennis player. And to round out his schedule he also did volunteer work for the United Negro College Fund.

He graduated in 1948, and the Bushes moved to Texas, where he went to work at International Derrick and Equipment Company. George Bush had entered the oil industry, which was now beginning what proved to be an enormous boom. His move was probably helped by his father; George was hardly abandoning his family or his family's Eastern connections. This would have been very unlike a Guardian.

Bush started his new career doing odd jobs and minor maintenance work while he learned the business. As we would expect, he proved to be a hard working, thorough employee who worked strenuously and lived frugally. (Bush, like most Guardians, and unlike most Artisans, is the natural saver.) Later he was assigned the job of selling drilling parts, and did well in this face-to-face work, where personality means so much and a handshake is a contract.[174] After two and a half years of progress within the company, he joined several young entrepreneurs intent upon going out on their own in the speculative but often lucrative world of oil prospecting. He did fairly well investing capital in exploring and drilling for oil, buying and selling drilling options, and so forth. But, as one would expect of a Guardian, he eventually moved away from the high-risk entrepreneurial end of the business, and into the more stable business of leasing and selling oil equipment to others. Along the way his sense of public service continued, and he and Barbara campaigned for better hospitals, schools, and museums for Midland, the town where they now lived, and he still found time to coach Little League baseball.

In spite of the pleasant, cheery cast to their lives, their time in Texas also included a tragedy: in spite of their frantic efforts to save her, they lost their daughter, Robin, to leukemia. She was only three years old.

But the Bushes had gradually become financially secure in their own right, and George began to involve himself in politics. He campaigned

---

174 Decades of research show that the gregarious Conservators are far and away the best circuit salesmen. This is because they take a personal interest in each of their customers and remember most details of their customers' home lives, which they learn from their lengthy chats with those customers.

locally for Dwight Eisenhower in 1952 and 1956, and was eventually elected Chairman of the Harris County (Texas) Republican party. He was neither a performer, nor a spell-binding orator, nor a Texan; personal charisma did not get him elected. Instead, his election signifies recognition of his industrious and effective efforts to knit together a fractious local Republican party, a demanding, time-and patience-consuming task.

In 1964 he won his district's Republican nomination for the United States Senate, but was defeated in the general election by the incumbent Democrat, who called attention to his support for Barry Goldwater and the war in Viet Nam. To his dismay, these positions cast Bush as a very conservative Republican, and in 1965 he began to avow his own more naturally moderate attitudes. "I took some far right positions to get elected. I hope I never do it again," he said ruefully to a friend.[175] He ran again in 1966, this time for the House of Representatives, and, with some help from Richard Nixon and Jerry Ford, he won. Now, after almost two decades in Texas, Bush was on his way to Washington, D. C. Of great importance to him, of course, was that with him came his wife and their five children.

Bush served two cheerful and energetic terms in the house, during which his attendance was nearly perfect. In his first year, when new congressmen are supposed to be seen and not heard, he introduced an ethics bill dealing with financial disclosure, another bill concerned with pollution, voted for a fair housing bill which caused him great difficulties back home, and continued his shift away from support for the Viet Nam war. He ran for re-election in 1968, and won. Then in 1970 President Nixon encouraged him to run for the Senate, but in spite of Nixon's support he lost. The President then offered Bush the position of ambassador to the United Nations, which Bush accepted gladly, and in December 1970 he went to work at the United Nations in his outgoing Conservator's vigorous, thorough, and friendly fashion. His warmth and endless energy and his enthusiasm for working with people face to face served him well there.

But only two years later President Nixon asked him to abandon his U.N. post to become head of the Republican National Committee. The

---

175 *George Bush*, 91.

Watergate incident was becoming more troublesome all the time, and as Chairman of the Republican National Committee Bush supported Nixon strongly, and avowed his innocence persistently. Later, as more of the facts emerged, and Nixon's involvement became undeniable, Bush worked to maintain the integrity of the Republican party. Though Nixon's aides, Haldeman, Erlichman and Colson intended Bush to be their "point man in a counterattack against investigators leading the Watergate charge,"[176] he refused. "Jugular politics—going for the opposition's throat—wasn't my style," he once said. "When competition gets cutthroat, everybody loses,"[177] and he didn't want any part of such cutthroat politics, nor did he want the Republican party used to such ends.

Bush remained loyal to the Republican party and as loyal as he could manage to the President. But the evidence against Nixon was massive, and Bush could only take the position that the party and the President were separate and the Republican National Committee was not responsible for the President's behavior. Even so, he still resisted criticizing Nixon, and remained civil throughout the ordeal. On August 7, 1974, Republican National Committee chairman Bush finally wrote to Nixon urging him to resign, but still expressing his gratitude for the support the President had given him over the years.

When Nixon stepped down the new President, Jerry Ford, offered Bush the post of Ambassador to either Great Britain or France. Bush instead requested the People's Republic of China, and was appointed Chief of the United States Liaison Office there. It was not a highly influential position at the time, and more a position for gradually cultivating relationships with the Chinese than a substantive political position. When there were substantive matters to be dealt with, Henry Kissinger handled them, and without much regard to Liaison Chief George Bush or his feelings.

Then, in November of 1975, Ford decided to ask Bush to become the Director of the CIA. The intelligence organization had been severely criticized for its policies and procedures, and Bush's chief job was to restore respectability to the agency's image, to repair its damaged

---

176 *Looking Forward,* 46.
177 *George Bush,* 82.

morale, and to buttress its integrity. Henry Kissinger sent him a telegram which suggests that Kissinger knew his man well. In fact the letter is reminiscent of the requests made to the Guardian George Washington almost two hundred years earlier. It reads in part, "The president asks that you consent to his nominating you as the new Director of the Central Intelligence Agency....The President feels your appointment to be greatly in the national interest and very much hopes that you will accept. Your dedication to national service has been unremitting, and I join the President in hoping that you accept this new challenge in the service of your country."[178] The appeal of the letter to duty and public service, would be very powerful to a Conservator Guardian like Bush, and Bush agreed to take over the leadership of the CIA. He remained at that post until he was removed by Jimmy Carter when Carter took over the White House in 1979.

Bush went back to private industry in Texas where he was a well-paid consultant, and continued his pattern of doing public service work. Then in 1979 he made another attempt at elective office, campaigning against Ronald Reagan for the Republican nomination. But Reagan's Artisan style overshadowed his own decisively. Reagan won the Republican nomination, and then offered Bush the vice-presidential spot in the Republican ticket. Bush accepted it without hesitation, the Republicans won the national election, and Bush served as President Ronald Reagan's Vice-President for eight years.

In his 1988 campaign for the presidency against Governor Michael Dukakis of Massachusetts, Bush struggled with an image which one commentator described as "wimp, wasp, weenie. Every woman's first husband. Bland conformist."[179] Bush's "read my lips" slogan was apparently designed to make him look tougher, but coming from this pleasant Conservator, it was of questionable utility. The promise to which it was attached, "no new taxes," was probably far more important in securing his election. The "wimp" image is a significant distortion of Bush's character, but it is interesting because it became most notable during his contest with Dukakis. Governor Dukakis was also a Guardian, but a Monitor Guardian rather than a Conservator. One can discern the

---

178 *George Bush*, 148.
179 *Washington Post*, Outlook section, July 10, 1988, article by Curt Surplee.

differences between the two men—and between the Conservator and Monitor Guardians—in the scribbled reflections of an observer of their television debate:

> Bush's overall performance, though marred by error and small slips of the tongue, is more lively, humorous and warm. Dukakis seems to glare, bore in like a street fighter and talk with the metallic speed of a professional auctioneer. Though tougher than Bush and effective in making debating points, his icy demeanor leaves a bitter aftertaste. [180]

Errors or not, bland conformist or not, George Bush was elected and took office in January 1989. "Every woman's first husband," the "wimp" was President of the United States. Some feared that he would be merely the weak and (because of the Iran-Contra scandal) tainted shadow of Ronald Reagan, while others, especially of a strongly conservative stamp, counted on him to be just that.

But as soon as he took over Reagan's job in 1989, Bush abandoned the former President's agenda. His defection was a real shock to those who expected that he would be Reagan's dutiful conservative echo. But Bush was a remarkably industrious Guardian, not an easy-going Artisan, and a look at presidential history suggests that Bush's disaffection was all but inevitable. Guardian Vice-Presidents have succeeded Artisan presidential partners four times, and in every instance they have abandoned their predecessors' agenda.

Vice-President Taft, for instance, a Guardian who respected the laws above almost everything else, succeeded Teddy Roosevelt, an Artisan who used the laws to gain his own ends. Taft so obviously abandoned Roosevelt's agenda that in the following election campaign the outraged Roosevelt ran against his well-meaning successor. The same turning away occurred in the case of Calvin Coolidge, a stalwart Guardian who believed in doing nothing that was not legitimate, and very little that was, when he succeeded the Artisan Harding, who naturally did whatever he enjoyed, and little he didn't. The third instance of the discontinuity of Artisan and Guardian administrations was Harry Truman's. Try as he might, the stubborn Guardian moralist could not remain a firm disciple of Franklin Roosevelt, the wily Artisan utilitarian, and the "philosophy" of FDR's New Deal quickly gave way to Truman's own.

---

180 Green's on-the-spot notes to himself about the Bush-Dukakis debate in September 1989. In *George Bush*, 236.

Now Bush has provided the fourth instance of the Guardian former Vice-President abandoning the path traveled by his Artisan presidential predecessor. The Reagan administration seems to have operated much the way FDR's did, at least in that big government got bigger and the actions sponsored by the executive office were often secretive. Reagan's Grenada raid, for example, was kept from the public, the press, and the Congress, until it was already under way, and the same sort of stealthy maneuvering became apparent when Reagan's administration tried to bypass the Congress in the Iran-Contra matter. This way of dealing with matters is alien to George Bush.

In fact George Bush reminds us of two other straightforward and remarkably aboveboard Conservators, Jerry Ford and William McKinley, both of whom were noted for their warmth and gracious manner and both of whom avoided deviousness and hated conflict. And as in Bush's case, their warmth and kindliness hardly tell the whole story. Jerry Ford's nickname in Congress was "the Gentle Tiger;" McKinley was familiar with the bloodshed of the Civil War and fought to avoid a repetition; George Bush was a decorated Navy combat pilot who fought, and was twice shot down, during World War II.

The Conservators are usually very nice people, but their pleasantness should never be confused with weakness. When they decide that they *must* fight, especially when their moral outrage is triggered, they can fight very well indeed. Perhaps one more instance is in order, for it seems in some respects a kind of rehearsal for Bush's presidency.

In 1982 Miami was inundated with drug trafficking and President Reagan created the South Florida Task Force, with Vice-President Bush in charge. Bush went to work, his Task Force providing more jail space, judges, and courtrooms; more prosecutors, more FBI agents, Customs agents, and IRS and DEA agents; and a permanent U.S. Attorney and more military assistance to oversee the country's borders. This extensive action was taken as a model for drug interdiction and suppression by President Reagan, who converted the task force into the National Narcotics Border Interdiction System. Bush was appointed Chairman of the new NNBIS, and his talent at working with people of various agencies helped to break down turf-war-barriers to effective interdiction. This massive use of resources, coupled with his strength in working with others, has become almost a hallmark of Bush's presidency.

When United States forces landed in Panama, it looked initially rather like Reagan's Grenada adventure. The Panama incursion was also a raid rather than a campaign, and it too was launched in secrecy. But we should note that Panama was essentially a *moral* and *legal* affair, a punitive expedition designed to bring a malefactor (Manuel Noriega) to justice, and as a head-on assault on international drug smuggling. Once the invasion was under way and the occupation of parts of Panama and the surrender of Noriega complete, Bush pressed to have matters conducted according to all applicable laws, so that even the ruthless Noriega is being accorded a lawyer and his case is being handled with scrupulous attention to matters of law.

If Bush's Panamanian expedition was remarkable, his enterprise in the Persian Gulf, the war with Iraq, was astonishing. Even so, Bush did not want it to be simply a military adventure. The Conservator Bush is no adventurer, and he worked carefully to minimize risk. He gained United Nations sanction for the operation, he wooed two dozen or so other nations into cooperating with the United States, and he courted world opinion at every opportunity. Not content with this considerable international approval, the effective Guardian was able to induce several other nations to underwrite a portion of the cost of the conflict. Thereby he tried to minimize the economic risks of the conflict. Only after amassing a great deal of agreement from other nations did Bush turn to the United States Congress to ask for its approval. The Congress could no longer pass the buck. The House and Senate had to debate the matter in the glaring light of the world's scrutiny. They had to consent openly to Bush's project, or block it openly and in so doing isolate themselves from the largest segment of public opinion. He thereby minimized the political risks involved in the project.

Characteristically, the Guardian Bush undertook the operation with considerable openness. There was no suggestion of tactical or clandestine behavior, and in this regard his operations contrast sharply with some of President Reagan's. He first established an economic campaign, a blockade. Meanwhile he carefully prepared for stronger action by a deliberate and massive buildup of military force in the Gulf region. Recognizing that the embargo was not sufficient, he then moved to armed attack. But the attack was conducted by air, and was a logistical campaign rather than a war of maneuver. The effort was to bring massive resources to bear to eliminate the enemy's lesser resources. Thereby, it was hoped, the Iraqis' will and ability to resist would be broken—or at least severely damaged. Only after this arduous preparation was complete would the ground action begin in earnest.

It was a classic example of Guardian planning: careful, cautious, logistical, and almost ponderous in its attention to the economics of warfare. Bush managed it rather openly, and with typical Guardian caution, attention to very complete preparation, and according to a typically Guardian timetable. Indeed, one of the announcements that resonated time after time through the military briefings from the Gulf was, "the campaign is proceeding according to schedule." (The *really* good news came in the form of comments that "We are ahead of schedule.")

The following editorial conveys some sense of Bush's Conservator orientation. No one would expect to find such a passage written about a military action orchestrated by the adventurous Player Artisan, Ronald Reagan:

> An America resigned to war went to war, knowing it was necessary but not welcoming it....America was not driven into this conflict lightly. If ever a political leader had gone down the list of preconditions for a just war, seeking alternatives short of rewarding the aggressor, it was George Bush. Hussein would not budge one inch.
>
> In the end, President Bush has managed this whole complicated process brilliantly. He formed and led an international coalition. He retained and built popular support at home. He carried enough bipartisan support in Congress. He gave appropriate leeway and support to America's military planners and our fighting men and women. They all deserve our thanks and prayers.[181]

Bush was also viewed by many Europeans as a man of moderation, strength, and statesmanlike determination. Consider the following opinions compiled by a Los Angeles Times reporter:

> Former French President Valery Giscard d'Estaing was so full of praise for Bush he could hardly contain himself. "A great President who has erased the shameful stain of Vietnam," he declared...."The performance of George Bush has been remarkable," said Giscard

---

181 Mortimer Zuckerman, *U. S. News and World Report,* January 28, 1991. © 1991 U.S. News and World Report.

Polling experts and political analysts cite several reasons for Bush's positive image—firmness and clearness of purpose through the crisis; willingness to consult his allies and take their advice, and modesty in victory.

"Before the outbreak of war," said Pierre Giacometti, director of political studies with the French BVA polling agency, "the image of George Bush was mixed." But after the war began, the image changed to one of strength. "He knew how to manage a very, very serious crisis. His image was very strong. Even among [French] voters who are by nature extremely hostile, such as the Communists, more than 50% were favorable. That has never been seen before."

One admiring diplomat in Paris said, "Bush understands what other American Presidents have not. What works here is personal contact, not power plays."

The most tempting comparison is with Bush's immediate predecessor, Reagan. Although Reagan was popular in Europe, he was not necessarily taken seriously. He was considered a good President for a country populated, in the mocking words of columnist d'Ormesson, by "gum-chewers, cowboys and overgrown children."[182]

So George Bush can present a very strong image. But, as one expects of such an outgoing Conservator, he makes friends easily, too, and keeps them well. He has that great memory for names, to which he long ago added the habit of writing gracious notes to people with whom he is dealing, especially if for the first time. And no one who has followed his climb to the presidency is likely to forget his call for "a kinder, gentler nation." He seeks consensus, enjoys liking and being liked, but when pushed hard enough, or when made morally indignant enough, he can generate a Desert Storm.

Like his Conservator friend and predecessor, Jerry Ford, George Bush deserves the name "Gentle Tiger." The combination of peacefulness and menace the name conveys is ignored at one's own risk. Even so, Conservators have little of what is called "the killer instinct," and Bush may eventually be criticized more for terminating hostilities as soon as hie did in the Gulf than he will be for anything else he has done. Some will argue that there is too much of the "gentle" and not enough of the "tiger." The historians will have to struggle with the question of how valid such criticism may be. For the student of temperament, however, the evolution of the combination of Bush's powerful determination and his Conservator warmth may be a matter of enormous interest.

---

182 *The L. A. Times*, Saturday, March 2, 1991. By Rone Tempest, *Times* Staff Writer.

Bibliography

Arndt, R 1987   *Profiles of the Candidates, George Bush*
Barnes, J 1988   *The Comeback Trail: George Bush*
Barnes, J 1987   *Out on his Own*
Brady, K (ed) 1989   *The Wit and Wisdom of George Bush*
Cohen, R 1989   "Lonely runner" in *National Journal* vol. 21,
                         no. 17, April
Gold, V 1987   *Looking Forward, George Bush*
Green, F 1989   *George Bush: an Intimate Portrait*
King, N 1980   *George Bush, a Biography*
Mullins, K 1991   *The Procedural Presidency of George Bush*
Solomon, B 1990   *Vulnerable to Events: George Bush's First Year
                         in the Presidency*
Wiese, A 1979   *George Bush*

A Backward Glance

The government of the United States was designed to prevent even the possibility of despotism. The President was merely to enforce the laws established by the Legislature. Some might think that none are better equipped to do this than the Monitor Guardians, and the toughest of them might seem the most suitable. There were three of these *tough and unyielding supervisors:* John Tyler, firmly grasping the reigns of government as they fell from the dead President Harrison's hands and in spite of the consternation of his political managers; Andrew Johnson with his loaded pistols, touring the border states, and later refusing to back down in the face of Congressional impeachment proceedings; and Harry Truman waging an almost personal war with Stalin over the isolation of Berlin, and firing the immensely popular Douglas MacArthur.

Though they were also capable of toughness, there are three Presidents whose manner is more accurately characterized as *burdened inspectors*. They took onto their shoulders innumerable responsibilities and struggled unceasingly to meet the demands of those burdens they so readily assumed. Washington's efforts extended over more than two decades of struggle, of which Valley Forge was only one small part. Monroe's equally lengthy and equally strenuous career of public service, often under harsh circumstances (remember, he too was at Valley Forge) is another example. James Polk ("Polk the Plodder") literally worked himself into an early grave discharging his remarkably ambitious and taxing responsibilities.

Grover Cleveland, Rutherford Hayes, Woodrow Wilson, and Jimmy Carter were also hard workers, as we would expect of any Monitor. But they also had a way of being *righteous moralists* about their work that marks them out from their Monitor brethren. Cleveland, the great naysayer, found considerable righteous satisfaction in vetoing so many pieces of legislation, just as he appears to have found a certain righteous satisfaction in personally hanging criminals when he was still a sheriff. Rutherford ("Granny") Hayes had no compunctions about removing liquor, dancing, and festivity of almost any sort from the White House during his tenure, and it was he who wrote with satisfaction, "I have found what I sought: a respectable place." Jimmy Carter's righteous judgments could make him a very hard-eyed customer, even while his smile remained fixed in place, just as his pronouncements could sound like sermons even while he spoke from a presidential pulpit.

Calvin Coolidge was a cool and distant man who preferred to stay away from the public and to execute his duties as quietly and unostentatiously as possible. He had no special liking for people and if he was not ungracious about meeting with them, he could never be considered warm. For this reason he may be named one of the *cool and distant officials*. Even more aloof than Coolidge was Benjamin Harrison, the man whose handshake was said to be reminiscent of a "wilted petunia." And William Henry Harrison, though not so impersonal as Benjamin, was also noted for his standoffishness. Richard Nixon, with his stilted demeanor and his penchant for isolating himself in the oval office is yet another example of the cool and distant official. These men's administrations were characterized by hard work and burden, but even more by the cold and aloof demeanor of the Monitor functionary who has risen to the top and disappeared behind his badge of office.

There is a remarkable contrast between the cold and distant Coolidge and the Harrisons, on the one hand, and the Conservator Presidents on the other, every one of whom was a gentle, courteous, and kindly man who managed to combine successfully his civility with his ambition. Thus they are not only civil servants, but also *gentle protectors*. Millard Fillmore's benevolent service was most in evidence after his presidency when he became a leader in charitable affairs. James Buchanan attempted desperately to subdue the angry forces of dissent tearing at the country by becoming a presidential "Blessed Peacemaker." William Taft was perhaps too solicitous at times; when he was on the Supreme Court he commented that he would not dream of writing a dissenting opinion, thereby opposing the views of his fellow Justices. Gerald Ford in pardoning Nixon sought to protect the nation from being torn apart, and he did such things in such a firm but his gentle manner that he was known in the House of Representatives as "the Gentle Tiger."

The other three Conservators may be regarded as the *kindly providers*. Millard Fillmore's benevolent service was most in evidence after his presidency when he became a leader in charitable affairs. So considerate was William McKinley that during the Civil War he managed the remarkable feat of providing hot meals to the men of his regiment even when they were under fire, and whose political opponents in Congress (after he became President) would "always apologize to William when they are going to call him names." And George Bush made an indelible impression on the American public when he campaigned for "a kinder, gentler" government, thereby establishing (however unwittingly) his provident Conservator character for all to see.

Chapter Four

THE RATIONALS

"I have sworn on the alter of God eternal hostility against every form of tyranny of the mind of man."

Rationals who have been American Presidents

John Adams	1797-1801
Thomas Jefferson	1801-1809
James Madison	1809-1817
John Quincy Adams	1825-1829
Abraham Lincoln	1861-1865
Ulysses S. Grant	1869-1877
Herbert Hoover	1929-1933
Dwight D. Eisenhower	1953-1961

"Tell General McClellan that if he does not intend to use the Army I should like to borrow it for a while."

So spoke the frustrated Rational President Abraham Lincoln. During the Civil War he was President of the United States and therefore Commander-in-Chief of the Union armies. But he was initially saddled with generals, like the timid George McClellan, that were fitted for neither strategic nor tactical command. McClellan was extremely able at provisioning the Northern forces under his command, but was also a man who would not move his beautifully equipped army out of its safe encampment.

On the other hand the Confederates were well-equipped with tactical virtuosos, including Beauregard, Bragg, Early, Hill, Jackson, Longstreet, Stuart, and Johnston. The Union, though it must have had many budding tacticians (the cavalry officers Phil Sheridan and George Armstrong

Custer serve as two notable examples), did not for whatever reason allow them to rise to more than company command. The command of regiments, brigades, corps, and armies seem to have been given mainly to quartermaster type leaders.

Each of these was in turn put in command of the Union armies, but none of them had enough strategic or tactical leadership to avoid humiliating defeat at the hands of the Confederates. Lincoln had already contrived a war machine vastly superior to that of the Confederacy, but still he had no one suitable to run it. It wasn't until he found another strategically-oriented Rational, in the person of Ulysses S. Grant, that he had the commander he needed.

With Grant's victory at Vicksburg, Lincoln knew he had found his man. He gave Grant command of the Army of the Cumberland and loosed him upon the Confederates. "The miracle of Missionary Ridge" and the wresting of Tennessee from the South were quickly accomplished, most gratifying results for an overburdened Commander-in-Chief. Lincoln then gave Grant command of all the Union armies and told him that he did not want to know what Grant planned to do with them. The General-in-Chief Grant would fight the southern Confederates, and the Commander-in-Chief would fight the northern bureaucrats and politicians.

Here was a division of labor between two analytic geniuses: the one the Rational political engineer, the other the Rational military organizer.[1] Why this collaboration of two Rationals should have proven so powerful is not difficult to understand. Even more important than the advantage they had in relative strengths of the opposing armies, the collaboration brought together two able strategists at a time when the greatest deficit the North faced was of talented strategists in positions of high command.

Rationals with great systemic analysis intelligence are equipped even in youth with the highly developed organizing and engineering skills that make them capable strategic leaders. This strategic leadership consists in conceiving remote ends, and then designing long-range plans, (including back-up contingency plans) and using the "high tech means" of their time to accomplish those ends. Strategic leadership also pursues the quest for maximum effect for minimum effort. Ill-defined goals and

---

1 See *Grant Takes Command* by Bruce Catton.

obsolete technology, or great effort for little result, will not suffice for the Rational leader.

General Dwight Eisenhower was given the job of managing the Allied invasion of Europe in 1944. He had to put together the leadership of several armies. He had to work out a plan of attack that promised success, and that would be acceptable to all the Allies involved. He needed to oversee an array of contingency plans, based on differences in weather conditions, tide levels in the English Channel, enemy troop dispositions ashore, and so forth. (And even with all factors considered, including predictions of the weather by the "high-tech" meteorology of the day, there was still enough uncertainty about conditions on the French coast that he postponed giving the go-ahead until the last possible moment before the invasion was due to begin.)

Thomas Jefferson exerted his systemic abilities in ways that were usually far less warlike. He was, for instance, a chief author of the Virginia constitution, and an important architect of the Declaration of Independence. He also devised the architecture of the University of Virginia, and the architecture of its course of instruction as well. He designed a naval strategy to manage the British embargo in the early 1800s and a political strategy for initiating action against the Tripolitan pirates. Each of these endeavors stands out clearly from the logistical leadership of the Guardian or the tactical leadership of the Artisan.

Those of the Rational temperament seek knowhow, and they will continue relentlessly their efforts to understand, by stealing from the gods if necessary, or by forcing from nature her most hidden secrets. About 1600 the Rational Sir Francis Bacon declared that knowledge is power and demanded that nature be "put to the rack," where her secrets could be torn from her by scientific experimentation. In doing so he set the Rational goal of Western experimental science for the next 400 years.

The Rationals are guided, indeed driven, in this undertaking by a special demand: that they *be able to*. Thus their interest in power over nature, the ability to understand and potentially to shape the universe itself. But life is not all nuclear physics, and the Rationals want to be able to understand and control anything in their lives that seems important to them. It doesn't matter whether the task be to design an airplane or a workbench, a theory or a patio, whether to build a cyclotron or a business, whether to run a company, a meeting, or a computer. Whatever it is, if it is significant in the Rationals' lives, they must be able to master it: they must know that they could take charge of it if they had to. Above all, and in whatever domain seems important to them, the Rationals must be *competent*. Over their lifetimes the Rationals tend to accrue to themselves a repertoire of competencies which become the basis of their self-esteem.

To be able to is to become increasingly autonomous, and the Rationals constantly seek greater and greater autonomy. Their self-respect is rooted in their autonomy, just as their self-esteem is rooted in their competency. The self-respecting Rational rejects dependency in any form and wants to be free of all constraints to efficient action.

To be incompetent, which is ultimately to lack autonomy, is abhorrent to them and it is their special curse that no one is more self-critical, more ruthlessly demanding of their own behavior. However well they have done something in the past, that performance offers them no laurel with which they can finally rest content. It is merely a benchmark for determining their success in future performances. To rise above that benchmark is to succeed; to fall short of it is to fail. Thus the Rationals must achieve, and achieve again, always at a higher level of accomplishment, never able to rest content with their accomplishments.

The Rationals are born to technology. In the past they were the magicians, the seekers after the philosopher's stone, the alchemists. Rationals are those who experiment, who ignore traditional views in their search for more elegant, more powerful models of understanding and control. They are also found among those who apply knowledge as a technological device. They may, for instance, become computer programmers, electronics engineers, or inventors. The Rational Abraham Lincoln, for example, constantly tinkered with mechanical objects (including his son's toys, which he occasionally wrecked in the process), and had an invention registered in the U. S. Patent Office. When the Civil War began he gathered information on how to conduct military campaigns, and he took special pleasure in trying out new weapons and examining all the latest technology of warfare.[2]

The Rationals are not driven to achieve for the sake of achievement, however. It is not the accomplishment itself that counts, but rather the

---

2 Many Guardians go into engineering too, but while the Guardians are drawn more to civil engineering, and become builders of the solid, time-tested artifacts, the Rationals prefer to press for the new, the ingenious, the inventive. While the Guardians are designing and building roads and dams the Rationals will be designing and building space shuttles and microchips. The structure of each of the temperaments leads them to center their efforts in these directions, so different but so necessary.

ability to accomplish: again, competency. Thus Rationals may over a lifetime collect a considerable set of skills, few of which are ever employed extensively. In this respect they are quite unlike the Artisans, who also become skillful. For the Artisans, skills are opportunities for action and have no meaning if they are not used, while for the Rationals skills are competencies to be held in reserve, to be employed either for practice (to improve their competency) or of necessity (because the skill is actually needed).

Their fate is continuous self-appraisal, for increasing their competence is the source of their self-esteem. Even from an early age they will be demanding more of themselves, taking their "competency temperature" every hour on the hour. Yesterday's achievements will not suffice for today and the yesterday's *high* in performance becomes today's *standard* of performance. Anything less than the new standard is judged as failure; the Rationals' hunger for greater achievement presses them constantly, and all their lives. Rationals mostly skate on the very edge of failure since they will not allow themselves any regression, even now and then, to lower their constantly escalating standards.

Learning, knowing, and understanding drive the Rationals all their lives. As children Rationals will be more persistent in asking parents or teachers why or how something works than will children of any other temperament. (For the Rationals, by the way, these terms are almost identical; "why" finally means "how.") Even when they receive what they consider a coherent answer—which is seldom the case—they will inevitably and automatically maintain a certain skepticism until they have checked the answer out for themselves.

Rationals cannot help noticing problems, whether in logic or understanding, that life presents them. Whether the problem is a riddle in the newspaper or speculation about the nature of astronomy's "black holes," Rationals will try to apply their knowledge to a resolution of those problems. If they don't happen to notice a problem they will set problems for themselves as a way of checking the adequacy of their understanding and of exercising their abilities. In fact this propensity justifies calling the Rationals "the Problem Seeking Personality."[3]

Rationals have great confidence in themselves as long as they sense in themselves a strong will. The self-confident Rationals rely upon an

---

3 *Portraits of Temperament*, 67, 78.

iron will to see them through even the most difficult situations. Emotional excess is likely to be seen as self-indulgent or weak, and though they may allow such indulgence to others, they rarely permit it to themselves.

Others' emotional and personal problems may sometimes have some intrigue for Rationals, by the way. Rationals will initially understand them as failure to apply self-discipline, or problems of inaccurate or incomplete knowledge, or of faulty logic. Such problems should therefore surrender to a little careful investigation and logical analysis. But most Rationals soon lose interest in personal problems; their fellow humans are likely to seem hopelessly irrational about their difficulties, and they thereby surrender any right to a solution—and probably annoy the Rational as well. Similarly, Rationals typically hate to discuss their own personal problems, since they want to treat them logically and independently, only to find that some of them threaten to exhaust the capabilities of logic or will, and therefore are seen as demoralizing.

Rationals are naturally and inevitably the reasoners and they are prone to equate reason with intelligence. Rationals love intelligence— verbal intelligence at least—just as they hate foolishness and stupidity, especially in themselves. When Thomas Jefferson designed the University of Virginia he wrote that it "will be based upon the illimitable freedom of the human mind, for here we are not afraid to follow truth wherever it may lead, nor tolerate error so long as reason is left free to combat it."[4] By "truth" he clearly meant something that could be adduced by "the human mind," that marvelous utilizer of words, and in this he was typically Rational. Rationals have a great fondness for words, and insist on precision in their use. The power of language fascinates them and they recognize language as the single most powerful tool available to human beings. "Reasoning," in fact, is the act of constructing consistent and comprehensive sentences. Thus in language, as in life, the Rationals want nothing inserted that doesn't logically belong, and nothing left out that is logically required.

Paralleling his previous thought, Jefferson also wrote that "error of opinion may be tolerated where reason is left free to combat it."[5] And again he speaks for the Rationals, though especially for the Engineer Rationals. Given that he does so, it is not difficult to see that the most

---

4 *From George ... To George*, 57.
5 *From George ... To George*, 22.

influential philosophers in the Western world, Plato, Aristotle, Descartes, Kant, Husserl, and Cassirer, for example, are invariably Rationals. Each of these men could be found examining the conceptual structures of other Rationals and subjecting them to the most intensely logical scrutiny imaginable, seeking to perfect them or to abandon them.

Not that Rationals want to be "intellectuals." They recognize instantly the difference between the raw power of intelligence and the pretension of intellectualism. In fact they will probably see "the intellectual" as a mere dilettante, who only pose as knowledgeable. But if they happen to be intellectually able, then the structures of their ideas tend to be careful, logical, precise—and utilitarian, even if utilitarian in a visionary sense. The Constitution of the United States was powerfully influenced by such Rationals as Thomas Jefferson and James Madison, "the Father of the Constitution." In fact it was written almost entirely by Rationals. It was crafted in the mind, brought to life in thought, carefully organized in logical argumentation so that it could reliably house the guiding philosophy of a nation for centuries to come.

The Constitution was meant to be something that worked well, and to this end the conventions of the past were ignored, unless they appeared to be useful. Rationals are naturally disinterested in tradition and custom, and it is no surprise that they abandoned without hesitation those customs in favor of more workable operations. Even when the Rationals participate in the conventional, they tend to do so somewhat halfheartedly, and never seem to learn to do these things spontaneously. (Unfortunately certain others, especially Guardians and Idealists, believe that no one could fail to learn the essential social niceties, and are likely to believe that the Rationals are uncaring, and this can of course cause relationship problems.)

The Rationals are the "big picture" temperament. They focus their attention on overarching issues, long-term goals, and general principles, rather than on immediate details or established routines. For example, Sherman Adams pointed out that the Rational Dwight Eisenhower "focused his mind completely on the big and important aspects of the questions we discussed, shutting out with a strongly self-disciplined firmness the smaller and petty side issues."[6] Eisenhower also knew when it was important to pay attention to details, and he could be scrupulous and painstaking about them. In this regard he demonstrated a concern for particulars that Rationals tend to develop only slowly.

---

6 Quoted in *The Presidential Character*, 158.

The demand the Rational places on himself for competence is not confined to matters of physics, logic, or philosophical inquiry: it can apply to almost anything the Rational happens to be doing. If one observes a Rational playing tennis or golf, or throwing a ball or a Frisbee, for instance, one is likely to discover that he is not as much playing as practicing to become better at whatever he is doing. In this way recreation often, even usually, becomes a demand for increased competence and a laboratory for skill development. Just as the Artisan's "practice" is absorbing because it is doing, the Rational's "doing" is absorbing because it is practice.

Rationals are often rather serious and just as often aloof, even arrogant in manner. But their serious mien is not the worried seriousness of the Guardian, or some poorly-hidden unhappiness. It is the thoughtful, absorbed, no-nonsense style of the born scientist or technologist. There may be great satisfaction in the research or problem-solving in which the Rationals are engaged (and they are always engaged in some project), but that satisfaction is rarely obvious to others.

Good scientists will manage their behavior carefully so that they do not inadvertently disturb their own inquiry or contaminate their experimental results. They must be quite self-conscious in this regard. The Rationals are prone to examine and control themselves in much the same way, at times as thoroughly as they examine and control any other natural phenomenon, even if without noting the sometimes remarkable extent of their self-control. The Rational's prevailing mood of calmness must have been what Hippocrates had in mind when he named the Rational temperament "phlegmatic." And in fact most Rational presidents usually remained calm in times of conflict, whether political or military.[7] Their systems analytic consciousness lends itself to an objective self-presentation that underscores the Rational's innate distrust of anything but logic and of controlled observation and imagination, a distrust that makes them more skeptical than anyone else. Rationals have their doubts about almost everything proposed to them.

> The true rule in determining to embrace anything is not whether it has any evil in it; but whether it has more evil than good. There are few things wholly evil or wholly good. Almost everything, especially of governmental policy, is an inseparable compound of the two.[8]

---

7 As will be seen, the Adamses, father and son, are exceptions to this rule of thumb.
8 *From George ... To George*, 22.

These words of Abraham Lincoln point up the Rational's systemic, rather than doctrinaire, thinking, and demonstrate the natural *skepticism* of the Rational's analytic consciousness. Projects and means and ends, observations and conclusions, the Rationals know, will contain errors and mistakes at every turn. Rationals are therefore rarely surprised when things go awry. With rare exceptions, this approach naturally produces carefully qualified communications. Rationals speak in terms of possibilities, probabilities, and assumptions, rather than universally-acknowledged facts or truths. They understand the world, and speak of it, in terms of coordinates, dimensions, conditions, contingencies, sectors, and intersections. Their coordinate maps enable the brain to stay on target and avoid getting lost in the myriad ideas that sometimes flood the Rational consciousness.

The leadership talents of the Rationals are the strategic talents. That is, Rationals have a talent for *engineering*, for devising powerful instruments. They also have a talent for *organizing* people and resources, for fashioning them into those powerful instruments. In doing so they will look naturally to the distant horizons rather than to the step, or even the several steps, immediately in front of them. Thomas Jefferson demonstrated this sort of vision when he said in 1811 that "the last hope of human liberty in this world rests on us."[9] Lincoln did the same when he said in 1861, at the beginning of the Civil War, that "The struggle of today is not altogether for today—it is for a vast future also."[10]

Their vision is often grand (we leave aside the question of whether it is wise), and their orientation is utilitarian. Thus Rational Presidents are usually impatient with political pettiness or with anything that pulls them from their vision for the execution of their projects.

The Organizer Rationals

John Adams	1797-1801
John Quincy Adams	1825-1829
Ulysses S. Grant	1869-1877
Herbert Hoover	1929-1933
Dwight D. Eisenhower	1953-1961

---

9 *From George ... To George*, 19.
10 *From George ... To George*, 131.

The directive Rationals, with their penchant for organizing what they regard as efficient means to pursue their always well-defined ends, are called the "Organizers." Both the Organizer and the Engineer Rationals are born to science, technology, and philosophy. Both are constantly in search of more elegant, more powerful models of understanding and control. But the Organizer Rationals, unlike the Engineers, are often seen as "take charge" people. The Organizers have no special love of taking charge. It's just that they focus so sharply on the outcomes of their activities and they have such a clear sense of the relationship of means and ends that they cannot *not* step in and give direction when they see wasteful or inefficient action. They focus sharply and very single-mindedly on their ever-present projects, rather like a flashlight whose beam is very narrow but very intense and stable. Anything within the circle of light is brightly illuminated and stays illuminated, all else is in darkness and stays in darkness. Only when the project is complete does the narrow beam of the Organizer's focus move on or broaden out.

The Organizers may as a result find themselves "taking over" rather frequently; in comparison to their rigorously logical approach, other people seem to be absurdly inattentive and aimless. When they do take over their almost exclusive attention to the project at hand makes them less than attentive to the sensitivities of those around them. In fact it is not unreasonable to call them "the Field Marshals" in recognition of their penchant for taking powerful but impersonal charge of everything related to projects which interest them.

Though they can become very intensely involved in their projects the Organizers will still keep themselves in careful emotional check. Self-management is as natural to them as project management, and they will avoid what they consider too much enthusiasm or excitement. Emotional excess, after all, can interfere with their precise analysis of means and ends and their careful oversight of the project and its progress. The Organizers also will refuse to concern themselves with matters they cannot control, since it would be merely wasting energy to do so. Instead they will keep themselves tightly-focused where their efforts will be most productive.

This pattern is not a matter of a simple preference. The Organizers *must* exercise this sort of will-power over themselves; they must keep themselves oriented to plans and goals. The publicly smiling, easy-going President Eisenhower was in fact a highly self-disciplined, carefully self-monitored Field Marshall, figuratively and literally. Similarly, if Organizers have contracted with themselves or with anyone else to do something, they *must* keep the covenant; to fail to keep their word is to visit shame upon themselves. Not that breaking their word is in itself so terrible; granted that it may be undesirable, but the shame arises for another reason. Shame for the Organizer Rationals is the natural consequence of having managed themselves so poorly that they could fail, and thereby break their word, in the first place. For the Rational, failure is the ultimate indication of incompetence, and incompetence is the ultimate sin.

The Engineer Rationals

Thomas Jefferson	1801-1809
James Madison	1809-1817
Abraham Lincoln	1861-1865

The reporter Rationals are called the "Engineers" because of their penchant for engineering inventions and models. The Engineer Rationals, unlike the Organizers, typically do not take charge of enterprises. They can do so (with considerable reluctance) if they must, but the Engineers are neither leaders nor followers. Instead they are forever pursuing their own intensely personal vision, always embarked on their own private project. Because of this the Engineer Rationals are as likely to see others as inconveniences as they are to see them as resources. For the Engineer the best course would be simply to ignore others, though of course it is seldom possible.

Engineers are also unlike the Organizers in that they find it difficult to concentrate on one thing to the exclusion of all others. They don't have any difficulty in concentrating; they are very good at it. It's just that they are curious about many things and they recognize that pursuing one subject means abandoning, at least for the moment, the pursuit of all others. Because of this, when Engineers stay with one subject or one project for long periods they will soon nag themselves; they recognize that their attention to the subject means they are missing out on the opportunity to satisfy their curiosity about some other subject. The single-minded style of the Organizer John Adams differed radically from the style of the Engineer Thomas Jefferson, with his extraordinarily wide range of interests. Adams's entire life was devoted to the study of government and law, especially constitutional law. Jefferson, on the other hand, was a writer, an inventor, a lawyer, a philologist, a political scientist, an educator, a behavioral scientist. He was the architect for the University of Virginia and for his own home, Monticello. He studied a half dozen languages, some mathematics and philosophy, and in his spare time he also managed to become a respectable violinist. (This is only a partial listing of his accomplishments.) Adams and Jefferson show dramatically the difference in focus of the two types of Rational character.

The Engineers are fascinated with the enigmatic, the paradoxical, and the inexplicable. They are especially intrigued with complex problems or puzzles, and will use puzzles to keep their ingenuity honed, rather like a cat sharpening its claws on a particularly attractive piece of furniture. Puzzles, especially logical puzzles, are almost irresistible to them, and they will sometimes put aside the work they need to get done in order to tackle for a while some especially intriguing conundrum.

The converse of this is that Engineers are not very good at small talk. Chit chat is not demanding and therefore not interesting. It is usually drawn out and merely redundant, rather than complex, and this makes it merely enervating to the Engineer. At times Engineers may wonder why others waste their time and breath on what is, to them, such a pointless and dull activity. Conversation, after all, is the opportunity to learn, to exercise one's abilities, to increase one's proficiency in some manner, and to find a conversational partner who equally enjoys the exercise is a rare delight for the Engineer, as it is, to some lesser degree, for the Organizers. Jefferson was an excellent example of this, for he was considered a fine conversationalist, in the style of the elegant philosophical *salons* of Europe, but not where simple small-talk was concerned. John Adams again stands in marked contrast, as he was usually far too preoccupied with his projects to bother with anything that required as much give and take as a friendly conversation.

We offer now, as we have for the other temperaments, a visual summary of the Rationals, their abilities, leadership style, values, and favored self-definition.

The Rationals

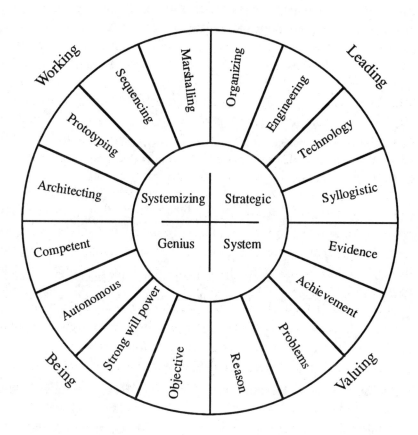

For those who may wish to read further about the Rational character, Kretschmer's "anesthetic" type, Adickes's "Agnostic" type, Spränger's "Theoretic" type, and Keirsey's "Promethean" and "Rational" types collectively offer the full range of Rational traits of character. A few novelists and playwrights have understood the Rational quite well, and so have captured their more salient traits in fictional works. Ayn Rand, for instance, presents some interesting variations in the behavior of Rational characters including that of some female heroines. But by far the best work depicting the Rational character, trait by trait, revealed in action over a long career, is C. S. Forester's ten volume saga of Horatio Hornblower, an officer in the British Navy during the Napoleonic wars. Of course, biographies of Rationals abound, for the list of philosophers and scientists that have been portrayed as Rational characters is long indeed. Locke, Hume, Descartes, and Kant, Galileo, Kepler, Einstein, Tesla, and Newton are but a few examples.

Non-fiction	Fiction
Tesla (Cheney)	*Pride and Prejudice* (Austen)
Einstein (Clark)	*Horatio Hornblower* (10 volumes,
Please Understand Me (Keirsey)	Forester)
Portraits of Temperament (Keirsey)	*The American* (James)
Physique and Character (Kretschmer)	*Moby Dick* (Melville)
Types of Men (Spränger)	*Atlas Shrugged* (Rand)
	The Fountainhead (Rand)
	Pygmalion (Shaw)
	To the Lighthouse (Woolf)

Now let us look more closely at the Rational Presidents. The first of them was the far-sighted but intemperate and irascible Organizer, John Adams.

The Rational Presidents

The Directive Rationals: The Organizers		The Reporter Rationals: The Engineers	
2 John Adams	1797-1801	3 Thomas Jefferson	1801-1809
6 John Quincy Adams	1825-1829	4 James Madison	1809-1817
18 Ulysses S. Grant	1869-1877	16 Abraham Lincoln	1861-1865
31 Herbert Hoover	1929-1933		
34 Dwight Eisenhower	1953-1961		

Directive Rational Presidents: The Organizers

John Adams

The "Atlas of Independence"

Organizer
Born: October 30, 1735
Died: July 4, 1826
Presidency: 1797-1801

The newborn United States of America had eight years of single-minded, cautious consolidation under the highly polished maintenance skills of the Guardian President, George Washington. His capable stewardship of the infant nation completed, Washington retired to his beloved Mount Vernon. The United States was secure enough to look again to its vision for the future.

It elected as its second President John Adams of Massachusetts. Adams was an intellectual firebrand, for eight years Vice-President and minister to France under Washington and one of the primary figures in the Revolution. Along with James Madison, he was one of the most influential figures in the framing of the new Constitution, and in the establishment of the United States and its government. His active commitment to the nation was so intense, so single-minded and finally so important to its cause that he was called by some "The Atlas of Independence." In this John Adams was a typical Organizer: single-minded, vision fixed always on his goal, tightly focused on central issues, and impatient with inefficiency and irrelevancies of any kind.

Like Washington, Adams was a patrician, an aristocrat; not so much a man of the people as a man for the people. But Adams the soft-spoken Directive Rational stands in clear and remarkable contrast with Washington the Monitor Guardian, in spite of their shared patrician backgrounds and their powerful commitments to the new country. Adams was a scholar, a life-long student of political science. He was also an able writer on the theory of government whose knowledge of the theory and practice of government was probably greater than any other man who has ever occupied the presidency. Of course his intense and wide-ranging scholarship in this area differentiated him from the more concrete "Farmer Washington," but the differences do not end there.

Those who knew him knew that Adams the scholar, scientist, and political pragmatist was a very learned man. They could hardly avoid noting, sometimes with great discomfort, that he was also vain, obstinate, and suspicious, a man whose outbursts of temper were set off by a hair trigger. John Adams was outspoken and tactless, sharp-tongued and disputatious. He was habitually sarcastic in speech and contemptuous in manner of those he saw as his inferiors—which meant almost everyone. Thomas Paine's "Common Sense," for instance, a very influential, in fact rabble-rousing call to rebellion, was quite valuable to Adams' revolutionary cause. Nonetheless Adams once described Paine's most powerful work as nothing but "a poor, ignorant, malicious, shortsighted, crapulous mass." Alexander Hamilton fared no better in Adams' commentaries. In a fit of anger Adams proclaimed Hamilton to be no more than "the bastard brat of a Scotch peddler."[11] To make matters worse, Adams was unwilling to do anything to soften the impact of his contentious manner, or to reconcile himself with those he offended.

---

11 *Presidential Anecdotes*, 26.

Adams' intemperance created many unnecessary enemies, people with whom he could have been friendly. Instead of allies he generated a plague of enemies with whom he was absolutely unwilling to be conciliatory. Even when his temper was under control his stern and patrician manner alienated him from most people anyway, leaving the impression, often quite justified, that he was looking down on them. Thomas Jefferson once wrote that Adams was "distrustful, obstinate, excessively vain, and takes no counsel from anyone."

Rationals do find it difficult to hide their contempt for those around them whose intelligence is not the intelligence of the Rational. This is most especially true of them when they are very bright, and it is especially noticeable if, like Adams, they are especially concerned with expanding and honing their own intelligence. They do not consider the forms of intelligence characteristic of the other temperaments[12] to be worthy of their attention, much less their respect.

So consistently disdainful, stiff, and distant did he appear that any departure from this demeanor was a surprise. Thus on one occasion then-President Adams was to turn over a few shovelfuls of dirt as a part of what we would call today a ground-breaking ceremony. Since it was a hot day he removed his coat before proceeding. As his coat came off he was astonished to hear applause coming from the people witnessing the ceremony. The crowd was applauding Adams' simple, homely gesture of removing his coat!

Though he could be quite arrogant Adams was not blind to the competencies of other Rationals. He and Thomas Jefferson were asked by the Continental Congress in June of 1776 to write the document which later we came to know as the Declaration of Independence. Adams insisted that Jefferson should write it, not he. Most of the reasons he gave were politically astute, but two of them also reflected his recognition of the personal side of the matter and his frank admiration of Jefferson's ability. "I am obnoxious, suspected, and unpopular," he said to Jefferson. "You are very much otherwise [and] you can write ten times better than I can."[13]

---

12 We mean here the Guardian's logistical-maintenance intelligence, the Artisan's variation-tactical intelligence, and the Idealist' diplomatic-integrating intelligence. Keirsey's *Temperament* will define these thoroughly.

13 *Presidential Anecdotes,* 36.

More often, however, Adams seemed to observers as genuinely puzzled (when not annoyed) by the behavior of men of lesser intellect or of less aspiration. Further, his own rigidly held principles came before any affiliation with any person, as is typical for the Rationals, and few men and fewer motives could conform to his principles. Political parties had already begun to emerge on the scene, the Monitor Washington was already warning against their excesses, and the Rational Adams already held them in contempt. Even the Federalists, his own political party, could not escape his scorn. He was indebted to them for his election, but because he was of the opinion that the Federalist party was much less principled than he, Adams was contemptuous of them and usually refused to collaborate with them.

Rationals usually respect the process of law though they may hold in contempt most sets of particular laws they encounter, and Adams was a rather typical Rational in this regard. In the eyes of Rationals such as he, laws must be carefully written statements of *principle*, rather than mere chronicles of precedent. This viewpoint stands in clear contrast with the Guardian perspective in which laws are regulations concerning *procedure*. Laws define how we are to conduct ourselves; these definitions of conduct are for the Guardians the essence of law. Not so, say the Rationals. Laws are policy statements, rooted in principle, and regulations are drafted merely to enable application of policies to real situations. Customs, traditions, procedures, accepted practices—these follow rather than precede the formulation of laws. Individual laws are likely to be trivial, impertinent, and, as often as not, contradictory to the *law* they are presumed to execute. For the Rational the abstract principle is the important issue. The Rational asks if a given law is coherently and comprehensively written. If it is not, then rewrite it. If it is, then apply it. But apply it only if the occasion for its application arises as a matter of principle.

It was John Adams who, in keeping with his profound respect for the abstract process of law (not just "the laws," a mere set of regulations), defended in court the British officer and six British soldiers involved in the infamous Boston Massacre. He certainly had no sympathy with the British cause; he was among the first to declare that total independence from Britain, rather than mere redress of grievances, should be the colonies' goal. Nor did he adopt a popular position in undertaking the defense; quite the contrary. It was rather his respect for the process of law, however unpopular its application might be in this instance, that led him to take their defense. It was perfectly clear to Adams that the murderous actions of these soldiers, however detestable their justifications, must not be the occasion for abandoning the process of law.

Adams was not thoughtful about explaining or patient about having to explain principles to others. He said what he had to say and if others didn't comprehend, then so much the worse for them. It was important to Adams, as it is to all Rationals, that ideas be stated logically and clearly. Logic is for the Rational neither more nor less than the rules of self-consistent sentence construction. Given this definition of logic, scratch a Rational and find a logician, however little a given Rational has studied the writings of those who proclaim themselves logicians. If the precisely formed sentences of the Rational are not understood, it is the fault of the listener, not the speaker, the failure of the reader, not of the writer. Unfortunately, as often happened with Adams, this sometimes means that accuracy overtakes comprehensibility, and the Rational's desire to explain is overtaken by impatience and scornful intolerance.

Because of his angry and scornful impatience Adams often failed to persuade others of the value of his ideas. Unfortunately, though not unusually for an Organizer, he often compounded his difficulties by acting as if others' understanding was irrelevant anyway, and the manner in which he did so was of course often curt and extremely offensive. Benjamin Franklin knew John Adams well and summarized Adams' heedlessly outrageous side nicely when he wrote that Adams was "always an honest man, often a wise one, but sometimes, and in some things, absolutely out of his senses."[14]

Franklin was commenting on Adams' conspicuous lack of interest either in being diplomatic with others or in observing the traditional civilities, regardless of the status or power of the other. Rationals are largely indifferent to status, whether in the form of rank or repute. Indeed, they are more than indifferent; they discount rank and status absolutely. Only relevant and coherent statements count, only logical

14 *Presidential Anecdotes*, 25.

coherence. The status of the speaker therefore carries not one ounce of weight. (Rationals would probably be willing to converse with Lucifer himself if he has something useful to say.)

Artisans and Rationals have in common that they are utilitarian in their choice of actions. They do not like to do, indeed they will not do, useless things. They typically refuse to do useless things even when such useless conduct might win them the approval of others, and the more intelligent and aggressive they are, the more ruthless their rejection of pointless action undertaken merely to appear cooperative. John Adams was a Rational and he was highly intelligent and quite aggressive. It is little wonder that he was so impatient with social nicety for its own sake.

In spite of his difficult and unbending nature, and unlike George Washington, Adams wanted to become President so badly that he ran against Washington in the second presidential election in 1792. It was an almost hopeless undertaking because of Washington's enormous popularity and Adams was of course defeated. Upon hearing of his defeat in the election Adams turned to his wife and exclaimed, "Damn 'em! Damn 'em! You see that an elective government will not do!"[15] Later the frustrated Adams declared about the vice-presidency (to which he was automatically elected by virtue of running second to Washington), "My country has in its wisdom contrived for me the most insignificant office that ever the invention of man contrived or his imagination conceived."[16]

The same opinion of the vice presidency has been expressed many times since by frustrated men holding the office, though rarely with the intensity or eloquence of the tempestuous John Adams. It was, we believe, Mark Twain who said there were once two brothers, one of who went to sea and the other who became Vice-President. Neither of them, added Twain, was ever heard from again. The inherently subordinate position of the vice presidency has never been a satisfying place for the Organizer, who is the Directive Rational and who is naturally drawn to taking charge of events. It was terribly galling for Adams to have to let events meander inefficiently and wastefully toward—or away from— desirable outcomes. But, as Adams also noted about his position as

---

15 *Presidential Anecdotes*, 6.
16 *Presidential Anecdotes*, 4.

Vice-President, "Today I am nothing, but tomorrow I may be everything." Tomorrow he might not have to permit unfocused and wasted action.

Recall again that Artisans and Rationals have their utilitarian orientation in common. But the utilitarianism of each differs fundamentally. The Artisan is concretely utilitarian, the Rational, abstractly utilitarian. While an Artisan President such as Andrew Jackson insists upon being *practical* in his actions, the Rational President, in this case John Adams, requires himself to be *pragmatic* in his actions. The practical man gets the job done any way he can, "quick and dirty" as he is wont to say. What the action costs doesn't usually enter into the equation. Artisans do not bother with equations anyway. They prefer to shoot from the hip, fly by the seat of the pants, and correct on the basis of what happens next.

But the equation is central in the pragmatist's consciousness. He tries to get the job done in very precise ways, ways that are gauged more in terms of their efficiency than their efficacy. While the Artisan fires for effect before "zeroing in," so to speak, the Rational fires for effect only after pinpointing his target through precise analysis. Adams was a true pragmatist; he preferred economy of action, precise outcomes, and no tomfoolery (politicking, for instance) in the process of governing. It never seemed to dawn on the single-minded Organizer that a little politicking might be annoying for the moment, but would over the long haul allow for even more efficient action.

Distaste for tradition, pragmatic criteria for deciding on a course of action, weighing and balancing effort and results, a respect for the rational, which is to say, the carefully and logically thought-out: all these characterized the Rational John Adams. Especially did they come together for him in the creation of the Constitution of the United States. Here was a document that was not the mere extension of tradition but was rather the reasoned product of rational discourse. Here was a document whose guidelines were the expression of a strategy for maintaining all of what was most valuable for the body politic. Here, he believed, was rational creation that worked, and worked with elegance. Its operation, he declared, "has equaled the most sanguine expectations of its friends, and from an habitual attention to it, satisfaction in its administration, and delight in its effects upon the peace, order, prosperity, and happiness of the nation I have acquired an habitual attachment to it and veneration for it. What other form of government, indeed, can so well deserve our esteem and love?"

The Constitution was for Adams a very important safe harbor in the midst of a dangerously irrational world. Adams not only rejected custom regularly, but he also had a strong distrust of the passions of the people. His "rejection" by the electorate in 1792 (which re-elected Washington to the presidency) did nothing to soften his distrust. He therefore spoke of a strong central government, one which could operate on behalf of the people, but which would be largely unimpeded by them. He thereby evinced a preference for a more European model of government in which the government would go about its business and elections would be held rarely and only by special request rather than as a routine matter of the calendar.

Adams also advised that the American President be treated with the respectful ceremony with which monarchs were treated. Such treatment, he believed, would underscore that separation between the President and the people which seemed to him to be so useful and perhaps even necessary to successful government. He further believed that titles and politically inspired elegance were essential to a strong government, and suggested that the president should be called "His Highness the President of the United States and protector of their Liberties." Unlike the Guardians, however, his interest was only in the utility of such appointments; he did not have the orientation to tradition and convention that, for example, Washington had. (As we shall see, the perspective of Adams, the Directive Rational, also stood in contrast to that of Jefferson the Engineer Rational, whose faith in the electorate was enormous and whose wish to take charge was therefore far less pronounced.)

Adams' unbending arrogance, though it made his life (not to mention the lives of those around him) much more difficult than it might otherwise have been, had its occasional advantages. A noteworthy example of this: for various reasons war had been brewing between the United States and France, its recent ally against Great Britain. The French, now under Napoleon, were showing an imperious disregard for American sovereignty. By 1798 war appeared inevitable, especially in view of the fact that there were numerous sea battles already taking place between French and American warships. The Americans were winning these battles rather regularly and a formal declaration of war against France was being widely and enthusiastically encouraged. War is after all always more attractive when one's own side seems to be winning.

But John Adams the strategist recognized that such a war was unnecessary and might eventually become disastrous. Coupling his analysis with his innate distrust of popular passions, he determined to fight the will of most of the population of the United States to prevent matters from worsening. To be sure, when Adams took the conflict over from Washington he made war-like gestures toward the French. But then, having beefed up the army, and particularly the navy, he shifted his position and was able to negotiate, from a position of greater strength, an acceptable resolution of the difficulties.

But his party and much of the nation hated to give up on what might have been a stirring war. As usual, he waged his struggle under a full head of highly pragmatic and principled steam, but almost alone. And as usual he did so with little regard to the matter of his own personal or political popularity. In the end he prevailed; more moderate courses of action were found, and a bloody and expensive war was avoided. But here was another action he had taken against the wishes of a large segment of his own Federalist Party. Many Federalists, including the very influential Alexander Hamilton (that "bastard brat of a Scotch peddler"), never forgave him. The presidential election campaign which followed in 1800 was very closely fought, and the lack of support from the Federalists cost Adams a second term in office.

Pride and political power are perilous partners. They may lead one quickly into byways that betray one's highest vision, and of course even a high-minded Rational can lose his perspective at times. Adams, it must be said, looked benignly upon the notorious Alien and Sedition Acts of 1798. These Acts required first, that an alien must live in the United States for fourteen years (rather than the previously mandated five) before he could become a citizen; second, that the President could order any alien out of the country for a period of two years for any reason; third, that in time of war the President could deport or imprison any alien for as long as he deemed desirable; and fourth, that it was a "high misdemeanor" to conspire against any law or even to criticize a public officer.

Clearly these laws, and especially the last mentioned, callously violated the spirit of the Constitution. They not only invited suppression of freedom of speech and created a group of legally disenfranchised persons, they also put into the hands of individuals in the Federal government a frightening measure of power. What is more, they allowed the President to become under certain circumstances a de facto dictator, with almost absolute control over the press, over opposition political figures, and even (if he were sufficiently unprincipled) over the government as a whole. There was the likelihood that a strong President could use these laws to shift the balance of power from the States to the Federal government, perhaps so focusing power in the hands of the few that tyranny would be the inevitable outcome. In practice the government would then have resembled the government of the Soviet Union under Stalin.

Adams' frustrated and intemperate pride was partly at the root of his support for the Alien and Sedition Acts. So were his distrust of the unlettered masses and his hatred of his powerful political opponents, the Democratic-Republicans. And though these considerations might not do him honor, it should be recognized that he was also moved by a genuine love and concern for the United States. He wished desperately to strengthen the federal government against what he saw as dangerous and destructive divisiveness which he feared might destroy the still fragile nation.

Fortunately his concern for the nation proved excessive and his efforts and those of the Federalists to support the Alien and Sedition Acts failed. The Acts were vehemently opposed by James Madison and Thomas Jefferson, both Engineer rather than Organizer Rationals, and by many other thoughtful people. They were in fact finally abandoned entirely. It might be noted, by the way, that George Washington did not speak out against the Alien and Sedition Acts. From his inherently conservative Guardian's perspective they were desirable measures. They would, he thought, help provide a strong and stable central government. His concern with the nation's stability seemed to blind him to whatever defects he might otherwise have found in the Acts.

Adams' public life was a persistent display of arrogant brilliance and willful fire, stubborn principle and impatient intolerance, genius and sarcasm, suspicion and obstinacy. His private life shows, if not a complete reversal, at least a softening of these behaviors. His wife, Abigail Smith Adams, could even go so far as to describe him as "the tenderest husband and father." Clearly he was at home a far cry from the arrogant, tactless, obstinate man that the public world saw. For his part John saw Abigail, who was his equal in wit and intelligence, as his "dearest friend." He was not a man comfortable with tender language; Rationals never are. Still, the letters he and Abigail exchanged convey a depth of love and mutual respect which is rarely found in any couple.

Perhaps their prolonged separations helped to prevent some of the everyday wear and tear that living with each other daily might have entailed. They were married in 1764 and from the beginning John was gone much of the time. He earned his living then as an itinerant lawyer, hungry for achievement and determined to improve his competencies as quickly and efficiently as possible. When he became involved in the resistance to Great Britain in 1765 his political activities required even more frequent separations. The travails of the Revolutionary War, his service to the Continental Congresses, and then his diplomatic service in Europe until 1784 were a burden for Abigail. As she herself put it, she felt that she was a widow for much of her married life. She finally joined John in London in 1784, just after the end of the War, where John was serving as the first United States Minister to Great Britain. (The Revolutionary War was ended and the sovereignty of the United States had been recognized by the British in the Treaty of Paris of 1783.) From 1784 until the end of Abigail's life in 1818 the Adamses were at last able to be together.

Abigail Adams apparently was very much like her husband. Also possessed of a Rational temperament and character, she was a highly capable manager and organizer and was skillful enough gradually to improve the Adamses' somewhat tenuous financial condition. She was also a sharp political observer and John respected greatly her acumen and welcomed her advice. She and John shared a keen appreciation for the lessons of history, as Rationals so often do; Rationals will search out history related to their own enterprises as a way of ensuring that they will not have to repeat the blunders of their predecessors. Abigail and John also shared a rather dry sense of humor, the often rapier-like wit that Rationals enjoy honing and displaying. (Rational humor is usually ironic rather than slapstick, by the way. They may enjoy slapstick, but they specialize in irony.)

Though the Adamses also had very similar political views, Abigail could still surprise him occasionally, as she did when she protested quite outspokenly about the role of women in politics, and indeed their role in general. She once wrote a lengthy letter to John requesting that he and his fellow designers of government "remember the ladies." She continued only slightly tongue-in-cheek, that it was well known that the male sex is naturally tyrannical, and that if the men failed to consider the rights of women, they would foment a rebellion of their own! It was a warm and humorous reminder to her loving husband, but not one easy to forget. She would probably be an energetic advocate of women's rights if she were alive today, and her energy, intelligence and wit would make her a powerful one.

Abigail's egalitarian political views and John's (to the extent he had them) were not mere intellectual exercises. The Adamses, for example, owned two slaves when they were first married. But a few years later they became convinced that slavery was incompatible with the principles for which the Revolutionary War was being fought and they therefore freed both their slaves. They did have black servants (who were not slaves), one of whom Abigail later enrolled in a local school. She also took it upon herself to teach him to read and write. When an acquaintance objected to her actions she heatedly replied that the boy was as much a free man as anyone else. Further, "merely because his Face is Black, is he to be denied instruction, how is he to be qualified to procure a livelihood? Is this the Christian principle of doing to others as we would have others do to us?"[17]

Of course most of the changes which influenced the Adamses' lives were happening elsewhere as well. When George Washington was elected to the presidency in 1789 the nation's capital was established in New York, and Washington was sworn into office in New York City. By the time John Adams assumed the presidency in 1797 the capital had been moved to Philadelphia in Pennsylvania. Washington, District of Columbia, was already designated to be the nation's permanent capital. But it was at that moment still a distasteful conglomerate of mud and mosquitoes, enervating humidity and unfinished shacks. Washington, D.C. was not occupied by the government until near the end of Adams' term, the autumn of 1800. When the Adamses moved in the White House was still incomplete, and the irreverent Abigail seemed to find some wry pleasure in writing about hanging her laundry to dry in the

17 *Presidential Wives*, 26.

large but still unfinished "audience room" there. In this less than elegant environment Adams completed his term as President.

Though he was eager to serve a second term he was narrowly defeated in his bid for re-election by Thomas Jefferson. American election campaigns were already taking on some of their least savory characteristics and supporters of both candidates engaged in a vicious trading of insults that might have gotten them jailed today. Jefferson, for instance, was called an atheist, an anarchist, a coward, and trickster, and his supporters were described as "cut-throats who walk in rags and sleep amidst filth and vermin."[18] But what was probably the political final straw for Adams was his support for the Alien and Sedition Acts, which so many found abhorrent.

Adams and Jefferson apparently managed to stay on good personal terms through the campaign. But strong philosophical and political differences including the dispute over the Alien and Sedition Acts, and Adams' condemnation of the French revolution (which Jefferson ardently supported) eventually led them to break off contact with each other. Abigail Adams made an effort several years later to reopen communications with Jefferson, but their brief correspondence broke down quickly because of the heated feelings the two men still had about their political differences. (It seems, then as now, that political differences are readily transformed into personal differences.) In 1816 John Adams finally extended what might be seen as the Rational's olive branch. He presented it in terms that ought to be well understood as a peace offering by another Rational (even if others might be less certain of its peaceful intent). "You and I," he wrote to Jefferson, "ought not to die before We have explained ourselves to each other."[19]

But that gesture of peace was to come much later, when both Adams and Jefferson had completed their tenures as President. In 1801, outraged over having lost the election, John Adams left Washington without bothering to attend Jefferson's inauguration ceremony. This disregard of the niceties of the most important political transition in the nation makes him almost unique in the history of American Presidents. The only other President who failed to attend his successor's inauguration was another intemperate Organizer Rational, John Adams' son, John Quincy Adams.

---

18 *Presidential Campaigns*, 8.
19 Letter to Thomas Jefferson dated September 10, 1816, quoted in *Thomas Jefferson: An Intimate History*, 598.

After leaving office John and Abigail Adams lived relatively quietly and, as was the case with many of our early ex-Presidents, they lived under some financial constraint. The financial advantages of high political office were relatively few at that time and the men who were our first Presidents, dutiful Guardians and visionary Rationals, were unwilling to try for financial gain from their position. At any time during his long political career Adams could have improved his financial position simply by leaving the government and returning to the practice of law. But he did not, and though he was much poorer for the decision, the country was far richer. Adams lived for another quarter century during which time he had the satisfaction of seeing his son John Quincy Adams elected to the presidency. Abigail Adams, beloved Rational partner and "Friend", died at age seventy-three, in 1818. John Adams, Controller Rational, intolerant firebrand, enormously able scholar, and steadfast, unyielding American patriot, died on July 4, 1826. He was ninety years old. His death came, as did that of Thomas Jefferson, fifty years to the day after the signing of the Declaration of Independence.

He was a patriot and a fighter to the end. His last words were "It Is the glorious Fourth of July!" and then "Jefferson still lives." He did not know that he had outlived his respected enemy and revered friend by three full hours.

Bibliography

Adams, C 1968	*The Life of John Adams*
Adams, J 1961	*Diary and Autobiography of John Adams*
Adams, J 1973	*John Adams; an Autobiography in His Own Words*
Allison, J 1966	*Adams and Jefferson: the Story of a Friendship*
Bowen, C 1950	*John Adams and the American Revolution*
Brown, R 1975	*The Presidency of John Adams*
Chinard, C 1933	*Honest John Adams*
Dauer, M 1953	*The Adams Federalists*
Haraszti, Z 1952	*John Adams and the Prophets of Progress*
Howe, J 1966	*The Changing Political Thought of John Adams*
Hutson, J 1980	*John Adams and the Diplomacy of the American Revolution*
Kurtz, S 1957	*The Presidency of John Adams; the Collapse of Federalism*
Levin, P 1987	*Abigail Adams: A Biography*
Oliver, A 1967	*Portraits of John and Abigail Adams*
Peterson, M 1976	*Adams and Jefferson: A Revolutionary Dialogue*
Shaw, P 1976	*The Character of John Adams*
Walsh, C 1915	*The Political Science of John Adams*

John Qunicy Adams

The arrogant aristocrat revisited

Organizer
Born: July 11, 1967
Died: February 23, 1848
Presidency: 1825-1829

James Monroe had been President during what became known as "the era of good feeling." But good times and good feelings don't last forever. In 1824 the United States was neither at war nor immediately threatened with war, but if international relations were not demanding constant attention, there were complex, painful domestic issues pressing on the country's rawest nerves. The South and the East were vying intensely with one another for political and economic supremacy. Now the West was joining the struggle, a much more powerful faction since Jefferson's purchase of the Louisiana Territory. The struggle went beyond simple economics: it began to focus sharply on the terrible and demanding question of slavery. The ideological arguments surrounding the question were becoming increasingly strident and increasingly polarized. The country needed a leader who was intelligent, experienced, and skillful in negotiating difficult matters, someone farsighted enough to see the danger in easy but ultimately unworkable solutions to the nation's difficulties.

It seemed that the need had been met, for John Quincy Adams, an Organizer Rational, was elected to succeed James Monroe. The aristocratic Adams was the son of former President John Adams, and one might have hoped he was a more even-tempered and diplomatic man than his father. Perhaps he might share some of the tempered strength of the Rational James Madison. John Quincy Adams was after all a learned man, educated in Paris, Leyden, and at Harvard. As a child he learned to speak six languages including Greek and Latin. He was an admirer of careful philosophical thought who treasured books, especially the classics. So much did he appreciate such books that he once wrote that "to live without having a Cicero and a Tacitus at hand seems to me as if it was a privation of one of my limbs."[20] In 1805 he became Boyleston Professor of Rhetoric and Oratory at Harvard College, and had acquired the nickname "Old Man Eloquent." He was a published poet whose verse had been collected in a volume called, somewhat forbiddingly, *Poems of Religion and Society*. Perhaps this thoughtful, learned, intelligent Rational scholar would have subdued whatever acid irascibility he might have acquired from his Rational father.

It was not to be so. It was painfully apparent that John Quincy Adams was his father's son in more than just intelligence and scholarship. In fact he managed to be even more stuffy, hard-edged, coldly immovable and hotly contemptuous than the irascible and difficult John Adams. One observer once described him as "doggedly and systematically repulsive."[21] Furthermore, the younger Adams was much like his father in that he seem to have no interest in modifying any of these unfortunate qualities. He once commented:

---

20 *The American Presidents*, 58.
21 *Presidential Wives*, 58.

I am a man of reserved, cold, austere and forbidding manners, my political adversaries say, a gloomy misanthropist, and my personal enemies, an unsocial savage. With a knowledge of the actual defect in my character, I have not the pliability to reform it.[22]

He had confessed his shortcomings and announced his decision that there was nothing to be done about them, though his confession was not a confession of guilt. More accurately it was an acknowledgment of traits of character which seemed to him to be unworthy of his further attention or concern. Thus Adams was like all Rationals in his response to personal criticism: he could silence his critics by condemning himself even more roundly than they did and then he could shrug his shoulders in contemptuous dismissal of those critics. No wonder that he could be charming and witty with intimates but still seem to most people (and that included most of his admirers) to be as "hard as a piece of granite and cold as a lump of ice."[23]

His personal "defects" notwithstanding, the brilliant and intellectually resourceful Adams was still a highly experienced and very able statesman. He shared his father's tremendous public spirit, he was farsighted, resolute, and courageous in pursuit of the nation's good, and he was honest and steadfast in his dealings with others. In all these ways the younger Adams was a splendid choice for the country's First Statesman. But like his acerbic Organizer Rational father he was haughty, brusque, opinionated, and ill-tempered, a man who could easily fly into a rage in the presence of stupidity or incompetence, or when his plans were thwarted by others' foolishness. Pragmatic and thoughtful he might be, but Adams was still painfully deficient in the Rational self-discipline the nation had been so fortunate to find in the Engineer Rational Madison. Like so many Rationals, John Quincy Adams would not force himself to make the tactical moves so natural to the Artisans.

But he had even less in common with the Guardians. And as usual, he refused to accommodate to those different from him and thereby greatly increased his own difficulties. Guardians look to tradition (which is standard operating procedure sanctified by time) for guidelines about how to behave. Rationals are largely oblivious to tradition, and when they happen to notice tradition they will look upon it as totally irrelevant

---

22 *The American Presidents*, 58.
23 *The American Presidents*, 58.

to their pursuits. There is more than a hint of contempt, even if amused contempt in this Rational view of tradition, and Guardians are likely to take note of that fact.

As the government settled down into a workable routine it also became more infused with the Guardians necessary to carry on its daily functioning. The progression from unstable innovation to stabilized and routine Guardianship is typical of the history of almost any institution. But Adams would not bow to this important fact; he would not bend his efforts to satisfy the demands of tradition, and he made enemies because of this arrogance.

Rationals are not typically hostile to traditions, by the way. They will tolerate them more or less graciously on special occasions such as weddings, funerals, and the like. It is when there is work to be done that the Rationals become offended by the existence of such customary actions. The Rationals' search is for maximum output from a minimum input, for much progress following little expenditure, so what they see as the inefficient hand-me-down methods typically used by Guardians will not do. One must first figure out where to go, and only then, how to get there, by the shortest route of course, with all obstacles and risks taken into consideration.

Traditions, customs, and standard operating procedures are objectionable, for they neglect the question of "where" and so cannot satisfy the Rational's criteria for selecting means and methods, the "how." Thus, when there is important work to be done, traditions are to be brushed aside. John Quincy Adams shared the blind spot of his father before him, and of so many impatient Rationals before and since. He did not recognize that a little gracious tradition-invoking might make for the most efficient route he had available to his goals, even though it might not be the most direct.

Circumstances did not help to soften John Quincy Adams' manner. When he ran for President in 1824 one of Adams' two chief opponents was the hero of New Orleans, General Andrew Jackson. Jackson (who was running for the presidency for the first time) actually received the largest popular and electoral college votes of the three major candidates. But no candidate had a majority of the electoral vote, and a majority of electoral votes is a requirement for election to the presidency. The election was therefore turned over to the House of Representatives, as the Constitution requires in such cases, and the House chose John Quincy Adams rather than Andrew Jackson.

Adams had prevailed in spite of his lack of personal popularity, but Jackson's supporters were outraged. They were sure that some sort of deal had been made and that Adams had in fact stolen the election from their candidate. Adams himself was extremely angry that the election had to be decided in this unpalatable way; the contest had been fierce and his victory was painfully equivocal. Even as the winner he was bitter and such a winner is not likely to show himself at his best. In Adams' case, facing the even more bitter opposition of Jackson's angry supporters for the next four years, he tended to show himself at his not inconsiderable worst.

Were it not for his bitingly cold reserve, his brooding anger, and his episodic fulminations, John Quincy Adams might have come as close as any President ever has to being that caricature of the Rational, the thinking robot. A Washington woman who had the chance to read some of his letters caught something of this when she pronounced them the work of "a bookworm and abstracted student." Someone had once called him a "poor stick of a shy man" and the characterization was striking, for Adams didn't seem to live in the warm, personal world occupied by most people. His was a different sort of world entirely, with the lifelong reserve and stiffness of manner so natural to the more soft-spoken Rationals. He was coldly reserved and ungracious in public, a man who "treated individuals as if they were issues instead of warm-blooded, sensitive human beings."[24] Simply by being his natural acerbic self he managed to alienate and often to make active enemies of people who might otherwise have become good friends or powerful supporters.

Adams' manner was not a display of mere arrogance—though he was capable of remarkable arrogance. It was also his own expression of the Rational style, an impersonal, dispassionate, pursuit of dry precision in all things. Just as he had no patience with tradition he also had none for sentiment and the niceties of cooperation so important to Guardians and Idealists, no matter whether the cooperation was personal or international. In both cases the question was one of strategy, and the criterion for acceptability was efficiency. For example, bandits and

---

24 *Profiles and Portraits of American Presidents*, 59.

troublemakers of various kinds were fond of making forays into the United States from Mexico and Florida, then a Spanish possession. These predators would then high-tail back over the border to the safety of foreign territory. General Andy Jackson in typical Artisan style had high-handedly undertaken military expeditions of his own into Mexico and Florida to eliminate the problem. His incursions were of course in violation of international law; in fact they constituted a small-scale invasion of a foreign country.

But Adams did not object strongly to Jackson's violations. He recognized that in the long view Florida had to become a possession of the United States; as long as Spain or any other foreign power possessed it Florida would always threaten this country. Jackson was rough, even murderous in his pursuit, but he got the job done; the borders were made secure. As one historian noted, "If Jackson was rough and even murderous in his conquest, he got it done. This essential Adams respected."[25] Of course Adams was like most Rationals in this regard: he respected Jackson's practical and effective methods of getting the job done. Like Jackson himself, Adams put effectiveness before and above cooperativeness and it is this utilitarian insistence upon doing things that work that Rationals have in common with Artisans.

Unlike the Artisans, however, Adams took the long view—the strategic view—about the United States' relationships with European powers, and he acted with cold and calculated firmness there as well. His support of Jackson's incursions was not merely a matter of doing what worked for the moment. Adams knew that Florida and indeed any part of Latin America could become a staging area for future aggression against the United States, and he wanted to serve notice to the world that the United States would not tolerate such a thing.

Good Organizer that he was, he took action to realize his project. While James Monroe was President John Quincy Adams had formulated the policy declaration that became known as the Monroe Doctrine. Generated almost entirely by Adams, the doctrine was that the European powers were forbidden to seek political or military footholds anywhere in Latin America. Any troublemaking in South America by European powers would be dealt with immediately and decisively by the forces of

---

25 *How They Became President*, 84.

the United States. In effect, Latin America was off-limits to everyone except the United States! The iron determination conveyed by the Doctrine was typically Adams, just as the strategic mentality which formulated it was typically Rational.

Like his father, Adams was a man of great experience and unassailable integrity in matters of politics and economics. In recognition of his many years of thoughtful and impeccable service as minister to Prussia, Russia, the Netherlands, Portugal, and Great Britain, George Washington once pronounced him the most valuable man the United States had in Europe. But Adams was largely untouched by such praise. Like all Rationals, he remained quite unassuming about his own personal position even though he was widely admired and praised for his considerable ability and integrity.

In fact Rationals don't do well with praise; they are usually rather puzzled by it. It seems peculiar to them that someone unqualified to praise their competence would attempt to do so, and they consider almost everyone unqualified. Those few people the Rationals are likely to consider qualified are of course other Rationals, but it rarely occurs to Rationals (especially the Organizers) to praise anyone. Thus Rationals find themselves in the unpleasant position of receiving praise only from those they consider unqualified to give it. Not that they often need praise. They are their own most qualified (and harshest) judges anyway.

Though they judge their competency harshly, Rationals will seek out the most powerful positions they can to help them accomplish their projects as if they had all the confidence in the world. Thus, once having achieved the presidency, Adams proposed a national university, promoted government-sponsored scientific expeditions, weather stations, and astronomical observatories, and later helped in the founding of the Smithsonian Institute. His proposals of course demonstrate beautifully the Rational's interest in learning, in analysis and technology, as a pathway to enhanced power. He also requested funds for a much expanded system of roads and canals to facilitate communication within the national borders. Though he was defeated in most of these proposals by the vengeful Jacksonians, he did manage to coerce both the Congress and Spain into the purchase of troublesome Florida from The Spanish.

Like his directive father, John Quincy Adams was interested in expanding the powers of the President. As we noted early, this interest in a strong Executive branch seems to be frequent among the Organizer Rationals. They are not especially power-hungry; they merely want to get the job done—as long, of course, as it's the job they've decided to get done. John Quincy Adams struggled arduously and bitterly to push through the legislature his own programs because he saw them as good for the country, not because they offered him personal gain or party advantage. When the United States was the subject at hand President Adams persistently refused to consider party lines or personal friendship or advantage in his decisions.

This of course meant no "quid pro quo" in his dealings with others; John Quincy Adams was not a man to stoop to political bargaining with anybody. Like his father, he put what he saw as the good of the nation above the good of everything and everybody, including himself and the party which had elected him. Like his father, he refused to credit the necessity for collaboration between the three branches of government. And as in his father's case others recognized that his behavior was highly principled, and whether they liked him or not both his friends and his enemies admired his courage and integrity.

But one can finally be vanquished as thoroughly by frustrated admirers as by angry enemies. As one historian noted,

> he was so extreme in his rejection of compromise with his principles
> that he was considered by contemporary party men to be very nearly a
> fool—and this in spite of his vast learning, his ripe wisdom, and his
> wide experience.[26]

The political price was high. Congress was already troubled with great animosity between several of its members. Adams himself was partly responsible for additional divisiveness since his excessive high-handedness and stubborn integrity made life difficult for his supporters in the Congress, and as a result he had very little support for his ambitious programs. His presidency was thus largely ineffectual from the start and he had to settle for being the United States' second single-term President. Perhaps John Quincy Adams should have been able to predict these outcomes. His father, after all, had been the country's first single-term President.

Adams' coldness and inexhaustible arrogance cost him personally as well politically. They were not confined only to his public or political life; his wife Louisa and his children also knew them first-hand.

---

26 *How They Became President*, 83.

John Quincy Adams had married Louisa Catherine Johnson in 1797. Paul Boller described her as "a prize catch: bright, charming, witty, attractive, and well-educated."[27] After their marriage Louisa Adams was able to soften the impact of his uncompromising demeanor, and this was important to his political success. As time passed John depended upon Louisa more and more to look after the social demands of his career and she in turn responded energetically. At one stage of his career she undertook an arduous and exhausting campaign of daily visits to the wives of influential politicians. She had little time and less energy for herself or her family after these visits, but John didn't usually seem to notice. True to his usual form he developed the habit of providing her each morning with a stack of cards indicating the people whom he wished her to visit. There was no question of consulting her about the agenda; he would merely give her the itinerary. Louisa would then begin her daily trek, openly charming to all, privately dismayed and resentful of her husband's offhand treatment of her.

She did her best nonetheless, and throughout John Quincy's long public career she also organized the very proper and elegant parties and lively entertainments that his position demanded. In other ways, as opportunity presented itself, she did what she could to offset the most unfortunate results of her husband's arrogant impatience.

Unfortunately John Quincy Adams was as arrogant in his appraisal of most women as he was in his appraisal of most men. It was his view that Louisa was a woman and therefore could not be expected to understand affairs of state, political matters, or scientific pursuits. He discouraged her from the study of astronomy, for instance, a subject which interested her greatly, on the grounds that it would be too difficult for her. On another occasion he bought a gift for her: a book on the diseases of the mind, perhaps delivering an unspoken but pointed message to a woman who would have pretensions to being as intellectually able as a man. At best he looked upon her pursuit of scientific or political knowledge with tolerant disdain. Apparently he would have had little patience with the notion that a woman could be just as bright, and just as much a Rational, as a man.

Louisa Adams felt a perpetual resentment about the intellectual imprisonment her marriage to John had imposed upon her. She had a

27 *Presidential Wives*, 54.

European education (her parents lived in London during her childhood; indeed, she was born in England) and her teacher was an able woman who was persuaded that women were the intellectual equals of men. The contrast of this perspective with John Quincy Adams' could hardly have been more striking. Also, over the years she had a dozen pregnancies, of which seven resulted in miscarriages. Her health was often frail as a result, and John was frequently gone during her crises in health. Her feeling about her unfortunate position is reflected plainly enough in the comment she once made that "hanging and marriage were very much alike."[28] She held John accountable for some of her difficulties and she once told her oldest son that the Adams men made poor husbands. Her complaints were warranted, for there is no question that John Quincy Adams underestimated her intelligence and abilities seriously and was remarkably insensitive to her feelings and desires.

Still, as is sometimes the case with men whose experiences of love and affection are the most austere and reserved, Adams could easily be touched by others' expressions of admiration and friendship–if he deemed them worthy judges. When he found himself in company that could appreciate his gifts and tolerate his manner he could be a lively and entertaining conversationalist, witty and knowledgeable. Perhaps there were other compensations that even John Quincy Adams could offer his wife and children. Unfortunately relatively little seems to have been recorded of the more considerate and compassionate side of Adams' character. When reading about him one is left with the imperious and impersonal image of "King John the Second," as his political enemies sometimes called him.

In spite of his unpopularity and the activity of his political enemies, Adams thought he might still win re-election when his term of office expired. But the election campaign of 1828 presented him with a new political phenomenon. It was a campaign that had little relevance to his areas of his strength: matters of statesmanship, rationality, knowledge, research. Instead the charismatic Andrew Jackson was running again for the presidency, politicking the masses, his supporters crying out for "democracy" rather than aristocracy, for power in the hands of the common man rather than an aristocratic President. However

---

28 Quoted in *Presidential Wives*, 55.

unrealistically or unwisely, the cry was raised for a man of the people rather than one above the people. But John Quincy Adams, in the fashion of the past and in keeping with his own stubborn principles, stood aloof from the vigorous campaigning of Jackson's crowd. It was simple, he said: if the people wanted him they would elect him.

The people elected Andrew Jackson.

Though Adams lost the presidency to Andy Jackson, he remained active in government for the remaining twenty years of his life. In spite of his imperious nature he was still enormously respected. Thus two years after leaving the presidency he was elected by an overwhelming majority to the House of Representatives, where he remained until his death 17 years later.

During these later years he and Louisa found more common ground and developed a more satisfying affection and respect for each other. They were both drawn gradually into the anti-slavery movement, and John Quincy Adams eventually became impressed also with the matter of women's place in American society. In fact he became something of a sympathizer with the feminist movement of his times. Perhaps this was partially because of the eloquent letters of his own mother, Abigail Adams, whose writings he and Louisa read and catalogued after her death. Abigail Adams wrote with tasteful eloquence but she was capable of some very feisty commentary. It was she, remember, who had written to her husband John Adams about the unfortunate place of women in their society and had half-jokingly threatened him that he might find a new revolution on his hands if the place of women did not become a more respected one.

John Quincy Adams was elected time and again to the House of Representatives. Then in 1848 he had a heart attack and died on the floor of the House. It was almost to be expected that he would die pursuing matters of government, still trying to meet the rigorous standard he had set for himself. Years earlier this cold, intelligent, obstinate, and isolated Rational, all his life unwilling to meet half way any who disagreed with him, had recorded these words in his diary: "If I cannot hope to give satisfaction to my country, I am at least determined to have the approbation of my own reflections."[29]

---

29 *The American Presidents*, 60.

Bibliography

Adams, J. Q. 1981	*Diary of John Quincy Adams*
Bemis, S 1956	*John Quincy Adams and the Union*
Bemis, S 1956	*John Quincy Adams and the Foundations of American Foreign Policy*
Clark, B 1932	*John Quincy Adams, "Old Man Eloquent"*
Ford, W (ed) 1968	*Writings of John Quincy Adams*
Hargreaves, M 1985	*The Presidency of John Quincy Adams*
Hecht, M 1972	*John Quincy Adams; a Personal History of an Independent Man*
LaFeber, W (ed) 1965	*John Quincy Adams and American Continental Empire*
Lipsky, G 1950	*John Quincy Adams, his Theory and Ideas*
Morse, J 1985	*John Quincy Adams*
Noonan, J 1977	*The Antelope: the Ordeal of the Recaptured Africans*
Oliver, A 1970	*Portraits of John Quincy Adams and his Wife*
Quincy, J 1858	*Memoir of the Life of John Quincy Adams*
Richards, L 1956	*The Life and Times of Congressman John Quincy Adams*
Shepherd, J 1980	*Cannibals of the Heart: a Personal Biography of Louisa Catherine and John Quincy Adams*

Ulysses S. Grant

"I kept right on"

Organizer
Born: April 27, 1822
Died: July 23, 1885
Presidency: 1869-1877

Hiram Ulysses Grant was another man who reached the presidency by virtue of his success as a leader of warriors. He was credited with being the North's preeminent military leader during the Civil War, the general who finally led the Union forces to victory over the Confederacy. The reputation seems warranted; without him the war might have dragged on for much longer and its conclusion might have been much less favorable to the North.

When the young Hiram Grant arrived at West Point he discovered that his name had been entered into the record as "Ulysses S. Grant." He never succeeded in getting the error corrected, but this was no special bother; he didn't care for his name anyway. Whatever his name, Grant seemed an unlikely candidate for West Point and an even more unlikely candidate for future greatness. He was always a shy, quiet, awkward youth, thought to be dull at best and most probably stupid. The young Ulysses was the frequent butt of local humor. He made an easy mark since he never seemed able to counter the painful jibes of his neighbors in Georgetown, Ohio. Nowadays he would probably be called a "nerd"; then he was simply "Useless."

When Grant embarked on his trip for West Point nothing had changed; even to strangers he looked dull and listless, an ignorant farmer. "A more unpromising boy never entered the Military Academy," said William Tecumseh Sherman, a fourth year cadet at the time.[30] Grant was not at all surprised to be still the uncertain, ill-dressed, awkward bumpkin in others' eyes. He largely agreed with the view and he fully expected to be again the butt of the jokes and tricks of his peers. (In their youth Rationals often expect to be misunderstood and disliked by others, and will be surprised when others understand them and like them. Some Rationals carry this expectation to the grave.)

The directive Organizer Rationals, talkative or not, are not usually so shy and self-effacing; it almost seems that life trained Grant to be so. His mother, Hannah Simpson Grant, was apparently a rather careless mother, perhaps plainly uncaring. She is reported to have once watched, doing nothing, while her little boy Ulysses played under the hooves of a team of horses. According to the story she didn't even bother to warn the youngster of his danger. In fact Hannah Grant seems to have done little to nurture or protect young Ulysses at any point in his growing up. She was to all appearances a serious, even grim woman. No one ever remembered her laughing and Ulysses said he had never seen her cry. "No one played cards in Hannah Grant's house, and no one danced or played music there either."[31] The emotional impoverishment in which he grew up must have been extraordinary. As he left for the military academy hundreds of miles away, Grant stopped off at his neighbors to say good-bye. Their farewell to him was tearful, and the astonished

---

30 *Generals*, 53.
31 *Generals*, 25.

young Grant exclaimed, "Why, you must be sorry I'm going. They didn't cry at our house."[32]

It was Grant's father Jesse, a tanner, who insisted that he attend West Point. An education at the Military Academy at West Point was at that time considered to be a foundation for maintaining one's social status or even improving it. The elder Grant was certainly interested in matters of social status. In fact he was something of a loudmouth who enjoyed bragging about Ulysses, whether the boy liked it or not—which the shy, awkward lad clearly did not. The consequence was that both father and son stood out as objects of ridicule for their neighbors.

Ulysses had no wish to enter the military, but he was not opposed to the idea either. "I really had no objection to going to West Point," he later wrote, "except that I had a very exalted idea of the acquirements necessary to get through. I did not believe I possessed them, and could not bear the idea of failing."[33] In any event he found that he disliked the Academy, hated the regimentation which is so much a part of military training, and discovered that even with earnest application he couldn't learn to march in cadence.

Military training institutions are possessed of and by an endless sequence of routine procedures whose functions have been largely forgotten, carried out largely because they are traditional, and those most likely to relish such posts are those who appreciate tradition and are willing to work to uphold it. Cadet Grant, Rational to the core, did not fit into this beehive of tradition any better than he fit into the mindless routine of the small town. In both places he went underground: his body did what was required, but most of his attention was elsewhere most of the time. He discovered that he needed to go over his studies only a few times. He would quickly grasp them well enough to give a creditable performance when he was tested, and that was sufficient for him. He had nothing to prove with his studies and saw no need to be a hard-working student.

On the contrary, he was overall a sloppy and indifferent cadet who excelled only in mathematics and map-reading, almost as if he were offering a preview of the strategic abilities which would be so useful for

---

32 *Generals*, 30.
33 *Generals*, 29.

high command. Grant was also an excellent horseman from an early age, though he apparently had very little training in horsemanship. His specialty was breaking colts, something he did extremely well. In spite of his indifferent effort and appearance, he graduated successfully in 1843 and was duly commissioned a lieutenant in the United States Army. But the army was still not a prime interest of his. It was still merely a stepping stone, for even after graduation from West Point he still had a notion of some day becoming a teacher of mathematics in some college.

When the war with Mexico began in 1848 young Lieutenant Grant was with the invading American army. He showed considerable bravery, was twice cited for gallantry, and found some incidental success as an officer in the field. (Typically, he played down his own role, claiming that the danger from the short-range muskets of the day was trivial. He had commented in 1846 about them that "A man might fire at you all day without your finding it out."[34]) He gradually came into his own in the military, becoming more open, more cheerful, more energetic and self-confident. But the war was relatively brief and its ending meant a return to routine and boredom.

But there was still excitement in Grant's life: he could now return to St. Louis, his former posting, and Miss Julia Dent.

Grant first met Julia Dent after his graduation from West Point. He was immediately intrigued with her and courted her intently. He did not have to work hard to win her affections; apparently Ulysses and Julia fell in love almost immediately and agreed quite early that they would marry. Their marriage was delayed primarily by the exigencies of his military service. When the war with Mexico ended Ulysses returned to St. Louis for Julia; they were wed and moved to his new posting in New York. But the time in New York was brief; Grant was soon transferred to deadly dull frontier outposts in California and Oregon. The separation his new posting meant was terribly difficult for them both, for they hated being away from one another. Yet the hazards of travel to the West, Julia's pregnancy, and the couple's severe financial difficulties made it impractical for her to join him.

Nor was Grant being merely overcautious in his decision to keep his wife in the East. Travel to the West in those days could be done most

---

34 *One Night Stands with American History*, 39-40.

safely and quickly by sailing to the eastern coast of the Isthmus of Panama, crossing overland to its western shore, and then sailing up the coast to California. Grant had seen first hand the persistent mismanagement of men and resources at the Isthmus and the many unnecessary deaths among military and civilians that resulted. He was terribly embittered by the stupidity he saw and very fearful of subjecting Julia and their child to the lethal dangers of the journey. But he suffered greatly from loneliness and boredom in his isolated posts and worried about his family's precarious financial situation as well.

Grant made several attempts to earn additional money to supplement his army pay but was unsuccessful. He also began (apparently) to engage in sporadic bouts of heavy drinking, riding his horse wildly down the main street, and generally blowing off his anger, frustration, and melancholy. His erratic behavior attracted enough attention that he was finally asked to resign his commission. (To be "asked to resign one's commission" is the military equivalent of being fired.)

Many stories have been told of Grant's alcoholic binges, by the way, but there is a legitimate question about whether many of these binges ever happened. Apparently Grant actually drank relatively little, but his body's response to alcohol was dramatically out of proportion to what he drank. Grant was himself concerned about the impact of alcohol on his behavior and by and large avoided it. Even so, when he was separated from Julia or when he did not need to be alert, he would occasionally, and quite deliberately, get drunk. His forays into the bottle gave him an enduring—and overblown—reputation as a persistent and heavy drinker.

In any event, after his resignation from the army Grant again found himself nothing more than a plain and taciturn civilian, unpretentious in manner and unimposing in appearance. In addition he showed a marked inability to earn a decent living for himself and his family. The Organizers, the directive Rationals, are frequently poor in conducting ordinary social and business transactions. They question traditional manners, regulations, and procedures or are typically almost oblivious of them, and therefore manage to do all the "wrong" things, Grant had a way of consistently doing the wrong things in business: he loaned money when he couldn't really spare it; he didn't press to have the loans repaid; in fact, he kept books poorly enough that he couldn't always be sure who owed him what. On the other hand he was scrupulously honest about money he owed others. He unfailingly repaid his debts even when it might take him a considerable period of time to do so. He tried farming and failed, supplemented his efforts by selling firewood, took a menial job collecting rents and managed to do poorly in all these endeavors. Finally he took a job clerking in the leather goods store owned by his younger brothers.

Even in the leather-goods store Grant distinguished himself only by his indifferent performance. Rather than staying in the front of the store and talking with customers, as was the practice, he preferred to hide out back and read. He didn't even like to wait on customers, let alone pass the time of day with them. When he did wait on them he rarely knew the price of the materials he was selling and sometimes sold items for considerably less than their established price.

Rationals such as Grant are rarely accomplished at rambling discussions of food, clothing, shelter, transportation, and recreation. In essence, they are poor at the small talk and gossip typically found in rural stores and sidewalk gatherings of townspeople. Rationals are typically at a loss as to what to say in such situations, so they absent themselves to read or ponder complexities. But of course they deprive themselves thereby of opportunities to observe how others manage the normal flow of everyday conversation, and they cannot comprehend how people can do this sort of thing for hours on end.

So while others were passing the time of day Grant was reading. Of course he read the way Rationals typically read: with an avid search for knowledge, collecting a large fund of information in many different categories. This is the distinguishing characteristic of the Rationals, this thirst for knowledge; it is a trait that abides throughout the full span of their lives. They must continuously learn the useful things, the technology of living, that will prepare them for upcoming challenges to their competence.

Grant was chary of letting others know of his learning. If they found out some of them might want to talk with him about books or, even worse, they might ridicule him for putting on airs. People did not find out how well-read he was; they saw only what they considered the shy, impractical, irresponsible dreamer, a failure who was plainly not at all bright. No one recognized that behind that bumbling exterior was a very able and very active brain. The "hard time" he served in commerce was a painful period for Grant, a time which he and his family lived with only marginal success and little satisfaction. With the likelihood that things would never get better, the shy Organizer's old nickname, "Useless," did seem fitting for him.

He was sustained during this time by his love for Julia Grant and for his children. Though far from beautiful (she was, for example, somewhat cross-eyed), Julia Grant was even so a charming and affectionate woman with a flair for the warmly dramatic. Probably an Idealist, Julia Grant wrote about her life as if she were looking back at it through a lovely haze, sweetly scented with magnolia blossoms. She had been raised in much better economic conditions than those she had to endure during the early years of her marriage to Ulysses. But her early years were far less a reflection of the genteel South than she portrays them, just as her own family home was much less than the warm and rather opulent world she recalls so fondly in her memoirs. Most of her life with "Ulyss" was much more difficult than the days of her youth, but her reminiscences are far from the unrealistic nostalgia of a woman who regrets her current circumstances. She seems never to have regretted her marriage to "Ulyss"; she lived through the difficult times with him with equanimity and only occasionally did she flare up or show impatience toward him. She was during the bad times his center, his compass, the one person in the world who seemed to make it all worth while for him.

So they endured, he in his taciturn way, she with her warm, outgoing flair. They lived in remarkable harmony with one another, their mutual fondness obvious and unchangeable. Even in their later years they would find opportunities to wander off together, talking and holding hands affectionately. Even her physical defects were thoroughly acceptable to him; he was in fact shocked when, near the end of his first term as President, Julia told Ulysses that she planned to get an operation which would fix the problem of her slightly crossed eye. As far as he was concerned, he told her, it was not necessary. He met her and fell in love with her the way she was, he protested. And anyway, he continued, he was not such a handsome fellow himself.

Of course there is only so much a wife, no matter how much she is loved, can do to unbend an uneasy, incommunicative Rational husband.

He continued to be his uncomfortable and taciturn self in social situations, even with Julia present to smooth the way. While Ulysses was still an army officer they were expected to attend various dinners and balls. On these festive occasions Julia could dance away the evening with various other officers in attendance while her husband made it a point, as she put it, to "hold down a seat all evening."[35] It was not mere reticence at work of course. Rationals like Grant usually show little interest in dancing. It is to them just one more annoying ritual, making no more sense than countless other rituals. The quieter Rationals are likely to wonder why most other people seem to enjoy it.

Julia on the other hand loved the social whirl and when the Grants finally reached the White House the she found herself in her element. Unlike many presidential wives she gloried in her position and in her husband's fame. Thus when Grant after two terms in office turned down the opportunity to run for a third term she was extremely disappointed. She was a strong woman and there were times when the Grants tested the strength of their wills against one another. Sometimes she won; sometimes he did. He stuck to his decision not to run for a third term. In this he was clearly the winner.

But in 1860 the small-town ex-army nonentity "Useless" Grant could have had no idea that such fame would come to him. He was still the quiet, unassuming, dull hard worker for whom financial matters never seemed to turn out right. Then in 1861 the explosive issues of slavery and states' rights finally detonated. The South was up in arms; most of the southern states (those which had not already done so months earlier) seceded from the United States and declared themselves to be a separate nation, the Confederate States of America. A shooting war broke out and men began to die as the Confederates assaulted Federal military bases located in Southern territory. The four-year agony of the Civil War had begun.

Ex-army officer Ulysses Grant immediately sought an officer's commission. After a suitable bureaucratic delay he did receive his commission and was given command of a regiment of Union volunteers. Initially his job was merely to hold them in safety and whip them into some semblance of a military formation, but it was not long before he was called upon to lead the regiment into combat. A Confederate unit of

---

35 *Generals* 102.

unknown size and strength was approaching his own base; his job was to meet them, attack them and turn them back. He wrote later of what happened when he led his force out to repel the Confederates. His regiment marched down the road toward the enemy, encamped straight ahead. As he approached the Confederate camp he found that he was absolutely terrified. But, he wrote later in a memoir that characterized his tactical approach, "I had not the moral courage to halt and consider what to do; I kept right on."

It is worth noting again the distinction between being courageous and being fearless. The Artisans are distinguished by fearlessness, the Rationals by courageousness. Grant advanced while fearful; that shows courage. Artisans are not usually fearful; they are absorbed in looking for immediate opportunities to win and don't have time to consider the awful consequences which might arise. (Churchill's Dardanelles campaign in World War I is a prime example of this kind of approach.) Thus they are fearless, for it is not clear to them that there is anything to fear. Rationals on the other hand are usually fearful because they can, indeed must, imagine the possible outcomes of their actions, including the most horrible of them. Artisans observe immediacies, Rationals imagine possibilities. The Rational Grant usually anticipated outcomes rather than noticed moment-by-moment opportunities. His strategic skills were therefore far superior to his tactical skills, but he would also have to have courage in abundance. He would have to "keep right on."

When Grant lead his newly-formed regiment against the Confederate invaders he reached the Confederate encampment and found that the enemy had abandoned it hastily. Grant suddenly realized that his enemy had as much reason to fear him as he had to fear them. Somehow this hadn't occurred to him before and this new recognition, he later wrote, made the critical difference for him as a war leader. From that point on, though he was always apprehensive before a battle, he never again experienced the terror of that first encounter.

His autobiography makes interesting reading not just for historians, by the way, but also for those interested in temperament. Grant shows an extremely terse use of language and this particular reminiscence is a good example of his dry, tightly controlled, even self-effacing writing style. Note for example his comment, "I had not the moral courage to halt and consider what to do; I kept right on." It would hardly be possible to write more tersely of such an important event. This compact style characterized Grant's writings all his life, whether he was writing his memoirs or issuing orders, and is not unlike the eloquent terseness of his Commander in Chief, the Rational Abraham Lincoln.

Though Ulysses Grant hated the violence and bloodshed of battle he seemed finally to come to life in the face of its demands. The war seemed to pour vitality into him even as it tore the life from so many other men. During the initial period of hostilities Grant was constantly busy, thinking, planning, writing out his clear and concise orders, offering encouragement, issuing commands, almost jaunty in his demeanor. Though his dress and manner continued to be rather off-hand and even sloppy (Rational commanders in any war and any of nation are usually reluctant to observe the "spit and polish" of military decorum), his plans and his orders were clear and crisp and far-sighted. This brilliant Organizer, this superbly directive Rational had at last found his niche.

As the war wore on Grant quickly rose in rank, partly because of his own obvious strategic good sense and partly because of widespread incompetence in the Union Army's officer corps. Though like most Rationals he never stood out as a brilliant tactician, he seemed to understand the broad strategy of the war in terms of both its military and its political goals. In spite of an early opinion that the war would be quite brief, his own observations soon convinced him that it was likely to continue for a very long time. The North's dreams of rapid victory and quick glory, he decided, were to be terribly disappointed.

Grant responded to this recognition by becoming a more ruthless and more grimly determined strategic leader. With his remarkable ability to see the larger picture he understood that the war would be won not by a few clever battlefield maneuvers, but by prolonged and bloody pressure on the enemy. The north had many more men than the south and its casualties could be made up fairly readily while those of the Confederacy could not. Grant saw the long term implications of this situation. He took the battle to the Confederates whenever he saw the chance to gain a strategic advantage and fought them stubbornly until they withdrew or surrendered.

It was a heartbreaking strategy and a terrible one for a man who so hated bloodshed that he refused even go game hunting.[36] Rationals, whether directive or nondirective, see neither honor nor glory in

---

[36] Rational warriors contrast sharply with Artisan warriors in this respect too. The latter are often avid hunters and weapons masters. The former either never hunt or, if they do, soon tire of the sport and end up even repelled by it.

bloodshed and find no satisfaction in it. They are never thrilled, as are their utilitarian cousins the Artisans, by skirmishes or warfare. But there was iron behind Grant's casual and sloppy dress and manner. He insisted on fighting almost every battle to the bitter and bloody end, grinding down the enemy forces until they were helpless or exhausted. It was Ulysses Grant who became famous for having said "I propose to fight it out on this line if it takes all summer."[37] The statement has become a symbol of grim, unyielding determination, and as such it characterizes Grant extremely well. His usual facial expression fit equally well, for Grant was said to wear an expression on his face which indicated that he was considering driving his head through a brick wall, and that he did not intend to be prevented from doing so.

Many people were appalled by the horrendous casualties that his units endured in the execution of this strategy. Some bitterly suggested that the initials in U. S. Grant's name stood for "unconditional surrender." In those days the suggestion was not complimentary; instead it indicated instead an ignoble viciousness. Some even called him "Grant the Butcher." But, as Grant recognized it would be, the cost to the South was proportionally far greater than to the North in terms of both men and resources. Grant would have preferred to win by maneuver rather than by pitched battle, but by one of the ironies of history, late in the war Confederate General Robert E. Lee kept blocking Grant's maneuvers, while Grant blocked his. Each sought to win by outmaneuvering the other rather than spilling blood, and Lee did as much through his stubborn and wasteful persistence to spill southern blood as did Grant "the Butcher." Grant pursued this strategy only as long as he considered it necessary. After the successful battle of Missionary Ridge in 1863 the Southern heartland was accessible, and Grant sought territorial gains that would cripple the South rather than seeking only the bloody attrition of the battlefield. But history has been kinder to Lee who is still, in spite of his role in the battles in the Wilderness and at Gettysburg, considered a gentleman and a brilliant war leader.

President Lincoln, another Rational with his own strongly-developed strategic sense, appreciated Grant's determination to fight and his string of successes. Lincoln throughout most of the war was cursed

---

37 *Presidential Anecdotes,* 155.

with a batch of generals who seemed more concerned with winning newspaper headlines to enhance their reputations than with winning battles with the enemy. Lincoln once responded to criticism of Grant by the simple but heartfelt comment that "I cannot spare this man—he fights."

Grant wrote later that "One of my superstitions had always been when I started to go anywhere or do anything, not to turn back, or stop until the thing intended was accomplished."[38] Even when he was still a young man he would never turn around to return to a house he had walked past. Instead he would find a different way to work his way back, even if it meant going around a block. As a Civil War commander Grant was similarly resistant to retreating or retracing his steps. Lincoln also noticed this characteristic and once commented happily that "when General Grant once gets in possession of a place he seems to hang onto it as if he had inherited it."[39]

General Grant seemed to have an almost unerring sense of the best strategy for a given situation and a remarkable ability to give complex orders for executing that strategy simply and clearly. His tactics might have been coarse rather than clever, but they were in the service of overall plans that were sometimes novel and often daring. His final decisions were clearheaded, made with a utilitarian detachment, and his communications about them were clear and incisive. He was typical of the Organizers in his particular single-mindedness which screened out everything irrelevant to the task at hand, focusing with laser-like sharpness on his own goals and plans. When it was time for important decisions, and while his subordinates discussed what course of action would be best, Grant sat quietly and without commenting made up his own mind as if unaware that the others were present.

Grant's single-mindedness was a very important aspect of his military talents. The Union army had learned to live in a rather unseemly anxiety about what the Confederate General Robert E. Lee and his famous Army of Virginia would do next. Speculations about what Lee's next move would be were a constant distraction to Grant's staff, as they were to so many others. Grant finally became exasperated by the

---

38 *Presidential Anecdotes*, 62.
39 *Presidential Anecdotes*, 155.

worrying of his officers. Unwilling to be cowed by anyone, Grant declared to his subordinates that "I am heartily tired of hearing what Lee is going to do. Go back to your command, and try to think what we are going to do ourselves."[40]

Grant possessed a confident reliance on his own ability that was almost absolute and had a tenacity so fierce that it might make a bulldog whimper. Though it usually served him well that stubborn tenacity could at times be costly for him precisely because it was so single-minded and unyielding. Of course this propensity for focusing very tightly on one's own plans is always a potential weakness in the Organizer. Grant's sharp and narrow focus meant that he didn't always pay sufficient attention to the possible actions of his foes. This was troublesome when his enemies had a good tactical sense, as some of the Confederate generals did.

At the outset of the war the Confederates put their regiments and armies under the command of Artisan generals, most of whom were very capable tacticians, especially in cavalry and artillery operations. Unfortunately for the Union, the command of regiments and divisions was mainly in the hands of Guardian generals, commanders suited more for logistics than for strategy and tactics. It appears that a large proportion of Southern graduates of West Point were Artisans, perhaps because the military still had a glamorous patina there while in the north it was seen more as a career or profession. The result was that the Confederacy was at the outset far better equipped to win battles in the field. However, though his enemies could sometimes surprise Grant, even then they could rarely defeat his plans.

His hard-won victories seemed to afford Grant little pleasure. After accepting General Lee's surrender at Appomattox Courthouse, an event that effectively signalled the end of the Civil War, he refused to engage in any victory celebrations while on Southern soil. He felt no personal triumph, nor did he want to add to the distress already inflicted on the land, on Robert E. Lee, or on the brave and loyal soldiers of Lee's Army of Northern Virginia. Many of Lee's officers, after all, had been Grant's friends and colleagues before the war. When he saw them after the surrender at Appomattox he immediately urged them to resume their friendships with him. In spite of the prolonged suffering of the war

---

40 *Battle Cry of Freedom*, 726.

Grant showed neither a conqueror's glee nor any vindictiveness toward his recent enemy. There was a dirty, bloody job to do, he did it, and it was finished. There was no glory in death, no honor in murder. Enough.

Ulysses Grant was not a political creature. He didn't vote in a national election until he voted for James Buchanan against John Frémont. (He gave his reason for voting very tersely: "I knew Frémont.") He did not try to present himself in an ostentatious manner nor did he care about what was fashionable. When he agreed to be the Radical Republican party candidate for President in 1868 he refused to campaign and didn't bother to answer questions about his policies. He had spent most of his time as a Union general dressed carelessly in the uniform of a private, and none of his unpretentious informality changed after he became President Grant. As a matter of fact, because of his informal style he was rarely recognized as a man of importance. The story is told of the time Grant raced his vehicle down a Washington street. He was stopped and cited by a police officer, William West, who failed to recognize the President. Grant paid the $20 fine and, like a good superior officer recognizing a worthy subordinate, sent a letter of commendation for West's personnel file.

Whatever Grant's success in warfare, he did not seem to be able to make use of his strategic talents in the White House. The very habits that helped make him a great soldier later helped make him a poor chief executive. After his election he appointed many friends and relatives to office, as a war leader might appoint aides-de-camp. This infuriated the party bosses, who wanted to dispense patronage to those to whom the party owed favors. Grant similarly made appointments to his Cabinet without consulting the party bosses, but his judgment of good Cabinet members was less trustworthy than his judgment of military men. Further, as he ignored the party bosses, they in turn operated behind his back, and the spoils system returned to a vigorous liveliness.

Galling political scandals dogged him throughout his tenure and historians have frequently considered him a failure as President. Though Grant himself was a man of impeccable honesty he was clearly not a good judge of others' integrity or judgment. Grant would have been a more successful President if he had been as effective at spotting and recruiting good subordinates as he had been as a Union general. But he was not, and he was also almost blithely ignorant of the nature and demands of the office.

As is often the case with Rationals, wide-ranging issues seemed interesting and accessible to him in a way that the minutiae of day-to-day administration do not. The intricacies of moment-by-moment political maneuvering have no fascination for the Rational when compared to the overall status of the nation or its relationships with other nations. But, with his natural eye for executive machinery, Grant did try to persuade Congress to pass civil service reforms and to eliminate the spoils system his own administration exemplified so well. He failed, however, and he has absorbed much of the blame for the corruption and incompetence which flourished during his eight years as President. He commented tersely about the debacle in 1876, when he wrote, "It was my fortune or misfortune to be called to the Chief Magistracy without any prior political training."[41]

Some claim that Ulysses and Julia Grant were rather awed, almost hypnotized, by the famous, the rich, and the powerful people they met while Grant was President. The Grants moved in circles of wealth and power which had been unknown to them previously, and Grant's naiveté about people was no ally of his during this time. Indeed, he managed to lose almost all his own carefully built up financial resources by entrusting them to others who ultimately proved to be incompetent or dishonest or both. Grant could splendidly manage the straightforward relationships of men in uniform and in battle; he could not handle, nor did he ever seem to fully comprehend, the deviousness of politicians or of political and financial opportunists. Rationals, as a rule, do not make good politicians, and Grant was no exception.

Grant saw the office of President as an executive rather than as a legislative post. In this view, widely held in Grant's time, the President was not so much a leader or policy maker as he was the simple executor of the laws created by the Congress. Thus Grant took a rather unassertive stance (except in foreign policy) and his overall impact was feeble. One can only wonder what his place in history might have been had he taken a more activist view of the presidency. He might then have more closely resembled another Organizer general, Douglas MacArthur, who almost single-handedly changed Japan from the shambles of a defeated feudal state into what became a thriving democracy.[42] If Grant

---

41 From his autobiography, quoted in *From George ... To George*, 5.
42 The Rational General MacArthur, in fact, tore a page from history's book by personally handwriting Japan's constitution, much in the fashion of the Rational

had seen political leadership rather than administration of others' policies as his chief function, history might have considered him very differently.

As was so often the case with the Grants, when he left office they found themselves in serious financial difficulty. Grant also made the terrible discovery that he was dying of cancer. He was very worried about what would happen to his family so he agreed to write his autobiography in the hope that the book would sell well enough to provide for his family after his death. He was assisted in the financial end of the project by Samuel Clemens ("Mark Twain") who respected both Grant and his ability to write.

Grant wrote the autobiography slowly, carefully, articulately, in his usual terse and tightly controlled language. Though his pain was increasingly intense as time passed, he would not permit it to interfere with his work. He was determined to finish the book, no matter what. And finally the book was finished, only a few days before he died. Some thought that he simply refused to die until the book was finished. The project kept him alive and when it was done Grant had met his final challenge. He could at last let go.

Ulysses Grant died on July 23, 1885. He was sixty-three years old. The unassuming military hero and abiding financial failure would have been enormously pleased to know that sales of his autobiography ultimately earned a half-million dollars for his beloved wife and family.

Bibliography

Anderson, N & D 1988   *The Generals: Ulysses S. Grant & Robert E. Lee*
Arnold, M 1968   *General Grant. With a Rejoinder by Mark Twain*
Badeau, A 1887   *Grant in Peace: From Appomattox to Mount McGregor*
Badeau, A 1887   *The Vagabond*
Barber, J 1985   *U S Grant: the Man and the Image*
Catton, B 1969   *Grant Takes Command*
Childs, G 1885   *Recollections of General Grant*

---

founding fathers of the United States. (See *An American Caesar* by William Manchester.)

Church, W 1897   *Ulysses S. Grant and the Period of National Preservation and Reconstruction*

Clemens, S 1959   *The Autobiography of Mark Twain*

Conger, A 1931   *The Rise of U. S. Grant*

Dana, C 1868   *The Life of Ulysses S. Grant, General of the Armies of the United States*

Fuller, J 1957   *Grant and Lee: A Study of Personality and Generalship*

Garland, H 1898   *Ulysses S. Grant: His Life and Character*

Goldhurst, R 1978   *Many are the Hearts: The Agony and the Triumph of Ulysses S. Grant*

Grant, J 1925   *In the Days of My Father, General Grant*

Grant, J 1975   *Personal Memoirs of Julia Dent Grant*

Grant, U 1885   *Personal Memoirs of U. S. Grant*

Grant, U 1969   *Ulysses S. Grant, Warrior and Statesman*

Hesseltine, W 1935   *Ulysses S. Grant, Politician*

King, C 1914   *The True Ulysses S. Grant*

Lewis, L 1950   *Captain Sam Grant*

McCartney, C 1953   *Grant and His Generals*

Mantell, M 1973   *Johnson, Grant, and the Politics of Reconstruction*

Martin, A 1951   *After the White House*

Thomas, H 1961   *Ulysses S. Grant*

McCormick, R 1934   *Ulysses S. Grant: The Great American Soldier*

McWhiney, G 1964   *Grant, Lee, Lincoln and the Radicals: Essays on Civil War Leadership*

Porter, H 1897   *Campaigning with Grant*

Richardson, A 1902   *A Personal History of Ulysses S. Grant*

Ross, I 1959   *The General's Wife: The Life of Mrs. Ulysses S. Grant*

Sheridan, P 1888   *Personal Memoirs of P. H. Sheridan, General, United States Army*

Smith, G 1984   *Lee and Grant, a Dual Biography*

Thayer, W 1887   *From Tannery to the White House: The Life of Ulysses S. Grant*

Wister, O 1901   *Ulysses S. Grant*

Herbert Hoover

The "Great Engineer"

Organizer
Born: August 10, 1874
Died: October 20, 1964
Presidency: 1929-1933

Herbert Clarke Hoover was born into a Quaker family in West Branch, Iowa. His parents died early in his life and he was raised by his Quaker relatives in a warm and nurturing community. He worked hard all his life, beginning as a child with weeding vegetables and killing potato bugs for pocket money, eventually delivering papers, managing a laundry, and doing a variety of other odd jobs to get through college. He worked so much as a teen, in fact, that he had difficulty preparing himself for college. But with extra work he succeeded, and attended Stanford University. There he studied mechanical engineering and graduated as a mining engineer. After graduation he continued his industrious work pattern and in a relatively short time developed a reputation for being a brilliant engineer and a masterful organizer and administrator. In 1898, only three years after graduation, he traveled to China to fill the position of chief engineer for the Chinese Imperial Bureau of Mines.

After resigning his position with the Imperial Bureau of Mines Hoover traveled to London and set up his own highly successful engineering firm. Eventually his work as a mining consultant carried him all over the world, and during his travels he developed an expertise in working not just with the tools of his trade, but also with governments and their agencies.

Hoover's organizational abilities were remarkable, and along with his knowledge of government operations eventually led him to considerable success as an international organizer of various public agencies. He was chairman of the American Relief Committee in London in 1914, during which time he helped Americans isolated behind the closed borders of the warring European nations to escape back to the United States. Then he became chairman of the Commission for Relief in Belgium during World War I, doing a brilliant job of organizing relief (especially bringing in food) to a population of ten million people. He was appointed United States food administrator in 1917, chairman of the Supreme Economic Council in Paris in 1919, of the European Relief Council in 1920, and Secretary of Commerce in 1921. His accomplishments were so highly admired, and his reputation so impeccable that, even though he had no professional political experience, the Republican Party nominated him for the presidency in 1928. He was easily elected on the strength of his reputation and on the strength of his campaign slogan, "two chickens in every pot and a car in every garage." The sound of the rhetoric sounds quaint now, perhaps, but in 1928 times were good and the slogan was more a celebration of the nation's apparent prosperity as it was a promise to be kept.

Thus the Great Engineer, as Hoover became known, won election to the presidency. He had risen to the world's most powerful office by virtue of his skillfulness, his energy, his intelligence, and his ability to plan, organize, and execute great and complex undertakings. Even after he left the presidency his strategic leadership and organizational intelligence were in great demand. Truman appointed this veteran Organizer the Coordinator of the European Food Program after World War II, then Chairman of the Commission on Organization of the Executive Branch in 1947, and finally, in 1955, Hoover was appointed Chairman of the Commission on Administrative Reform.

It was a remarkable record for a man whose presidency has been widely considered a failure.

Herbert Hoover was an austere man, and as is often the case with directive Rationals, somewhat blunt and tactless in conversation. He had little sense of humor or spirit of playfulness; he was shy, found crowds distasteful, was terrified of public speaking, and he intensely disliked what he considered superficial social contacts. He was given neither to what he regarded as trivial pursuits nor to small talk. Typical of Rationals in general and the more directive Organizers in particular, his will to productive action forbade him to waste time, and social chatter was, almost by definition, time-wasting. As is also common with Rationals, Hoover was also plain in his dress and completely disinterested in matters of style or fashion.

Public acclaim was also of only mild interest to him except when it promised to help him accomplish his purposes. Thus when he returned to the United States after completing the Belgian Relief project, his success was being wildly ballyhooed and his return enthusiastically celebrated, but Hoover's response was to act as if it were nothing more than an irritating encroachment on his privacy. This is a typically Rational response to praise or adulation, due more to a difficulty in handling approbation (and criticism) than to a dislike of it. Almost everybody, including the Rational, enjoys receiving praise, but the Rational is much more uncomfortable than others are about how to go about accepting it.

Hoover might be shy and even oblivious to the social niceties, but in his areas of expertise, engineering and organizing, he was bold and innovative. He was a pioneer of new approaches and, being a Rational, he was always eager to learn more. Though he had a great hunger for new technological knowledge, his hunger for knowledge was not confined to technology. He was fascinated by the classics for instance, especially the classics in economics, engineering and metallurgy. He was interested in the social sciences as possible vehicles for the rational, scientific resolution of human problems. He also found time to learn several languages, including a smattering of Mandarin Chinese. Like so many Rationals, he was driven by an unquenchable thirst for learning.

Hoover was a little grandiose about the powers of his own intellect. He saw his ability to reason as aligned with a greater Reason, which Reason he apparently saw as essential to human progress. He was seldom willing to consider that he might be in error about anything important, and he usually had cause to be confident. He could discriminate between the essentials of a matter and the trivial; he was confident in his own judgments; and, his judgments once made, he could turn over to subordinates the task of accomplishing what those judgments dictated. He would allow his subordinates the necessary freedom of action to get the job done while he himself concentrated on the matter of problem analysis and solution strategies.

Hoover, then, was a classic Rational: technologically bold, hungry for knowledge, disinterested in social custom or nicety except when there was purpose to be served by attending to them. Here is the organizational utilitarian, directing the actions of all around him toward maximum progress for minimum effort and cost. He was driven by an unquenchable lust for learning, for extending his repertoire of competencies, eternally studying, and forever testing his abilities. He sought out problems to solve, he found their solutions, he was naturally attuned to the power of reason. Also, and unlike some of his less patient Organizer predecessors, Hoover had the good judgment to recognize the value of self-restraint, thoughtful negotiation, the importance of bridling the passions, the cultivation of calmness and patience.

Perhaps partly because of his Quaker upbringing Hoover was also responsive to humanitarian issues, though such issues are perhaps more in the province of the Guardian and Idealist. The public service commissions he undertook over the years and the energy he brought to their accomplishment are ample evidence of his concern. As well known for his humanitarian interest as he was for his organizational competence, he had brought his calm and efficient style to an arena that stretched from war-tormented Belgium to the flooded anguish of the Mississippi valley.

Whether he was working on a relief mission, or serving as a mining consultant, or occupying the White House, Hoover still found time to entertain guests. His "entertaining" was a matter of business, a requirement of his position, but it was also something he could genuinely enjoy. After all, even his (and of course his wife Lou Hoover's) social evenings were likely to be filled with the most interesting people. By the way: their list of "interesting people" was not likely to include politicians. The Hoovers preferred interesting people, which is to say people from whom they could learn new things, hear new points of view.

> An evening's guests might count an eminent statesman or financier, but it was likely to include also a prospector fresh from the Klondike, a writer or painter, a railroad man from India, a Quaker acquaintance from back home. But always there were people, always there was lively talk and the friction of clashing views.[43]

Herbert Hoover's wife, Lou Henry Hoover, was a fascinating and highly accomplished woman in her own right and a Rational character very much like her husband. Demonstrating the Rational's passion for the sciences, she earned a degree in geology from Stanford, the only woman majoring in the subject, and earned a teaching degree as well. Herbert's marriage proposal to Lou was a singularly dispassionate one, as is sometimes the case among Rationals. He had been offered the opportunity to go to China to take the position of chief engineer for the Chinese government, he said, and he would accept the job if she would marry him and accompany him. She did; he did.

She and "Bertie" learned enough Mandarin Chinese during their time in China to speak with each other privately when others were present. Lou Hoover was the real linguist of the pair. She spoke five languages, and it was she who kept Herbert Hoover's linguistic skills current. She even embarked with her husband on a translation of a book written on mining techniques in 1556. It was titled *De Re Metallica* and was composed in late Latin Vulgate, a very difficult variant of Latin. The work may have been very interesting and engaging but it was not done in a whimsical or half-hearted fashion. The Hoovers cross-indexed their own translation of the book with previous German and French translations in order to be as accurate as possible. They also performed laboratory experiments derived from their own translation in order to check its accuracy. In this project Lou Hoover was the chief translator, her language skills being greater than her husband's. The translation was good enough that she eventually received a professional award for it.

Lou Hoover was very active with or without Herbert Hoover's company. This energetic Rational had a pronounced interest in far more

---

43 *Herbert Hoover*, 59.

athletic pursuits than were common to women of her time, including camping, hiking, and horseback riding. She also found time to support a variety of worthwhile causes of her own as well as speaking out (as Rational women are more and more likely to do) for more autonomy for women. Rationals find their self-respect tied closely to the degree of independence they can maintain, and Lou Hoover was quick to encourage American women to increase their own autonomy. They ought to take on business and professional careers for themselves, she said, rather than confining themselves to the "lazy" and dependent life of wife and mother. Though she was outspoken about the causes she supported, and though she was certainly a model for the independence she encouraged women to seek, Lou Hoover was also typically Rational in her reluctance to speak of her own many accomplishments.

As her husband began his campaign for the presidency in 1928, times were good. The Republican Coolidge had decided not to run again and the well-respected Republican Hoover was his natural successor. In his 1928 campaign Hoover had announced that "the poorhouse is vanishing among us" and his declaration was not mere oratory. Hoover had a deep distaste for emotional oration and when he made his announcement he was merely echoing the popular view. The nation was an immensely strong economic machine whose strength would inevitably wipe out poverty altogether.

Hoover was not a man to engage in the politics of backslapping, wheeling and dealing, or electioneering by rabble rousing. In his campaign he consistently made appeal to reason and only rarely—and rather gently—to emotion. He understood the power of emotion in political persuasion; he had seen enough of politics in his life to understand it well. But he wasn't good at using emotional ploys and couldn't bring himself to cultivate the distasteful skill of doing so. Cheap partisan politics, demagoguery, dirty campaigning were disgusting and unnerving to him. But the future was assured, optimism was everywhere, and the "final triumph over poverty" was near. Herbert Hoover, Coolidge's respected successor, didn't need political wheeling and dealing or mindless oratory to become the easy victor of the 1928 election campaign.

Hoover took office in March of 1929. Seven months later the stock market began its incredible collapse and within a year the country's economy was suffocating under the impact of what proved to be the decade-long Great Depression, the worst depression ever experienced by the United States. It certainly was not Hoover's actions which brought the Depression down onto the country, but none of his presidential actions prevented the depression from devouring more and more of the country's wealth and well-being. Like most other knowledgeable people, Hoover did not believe that matters could become as bad as they did in fact become. Further, he was very concerned about the possibility of the federal government becoming big and powerful if it were given the responsibility for managing the crisis. He wanted to see plans and organizations set up on the local level, the sorts of organizations with which he had so much expertise, and in which he had so much faith. And he did see to the establishment of such organizations, but it seemed that these measures were mostly too little too late. Further, he believed that the Congress was closer to the people that the President could hope to be, and it was with the Congress that the responsibility for action really lay. And though he might want to press the Congress to act, he was hesitant about doing so. "The constitutional division of powers is the bastion of our liberties and was not designed as a battleground to display the prowess of Presidents. They just have to work with the material that God—and the voters—have given them."[44] Broad government relief programs would be not only unconstitutional, he believed, but by their nature and the nature of government, they would be "beyond the competence of the national government."[45] But many held him responsible for worsening conditions. If he didn't cause the Depression, they said, he could at least have done something more to alleviate it. As it was, nothing seemed to help much; men left their families to try to find work somewhere, anywhere; makeshift camps of unemployed men seeking jobs began to appear all over the country; and so bitterly was Hoover reviled that such camps were called "Hoovervilles."

The economic disaster dragged on into the election year of 1932. Hoover ran for re-election, this time against the charismatic Democrat Franklin Delano Roosevelt. The dour Hoover was the last President to write all his own speeches. He thought them through, constructed them with precision, edited them for logical consistency, and delivered them with academic solemnity. But no matter how coherent and comprehensive their construction, they were dry and dreary affairs, especially over the radio. Given the troubled times Hoover could not stand on his administration's successes, and his Rational speeches were no competition for the rousing orations the Artisan Roosevelt offered.

---

44 Quoted in *Congressional Quarterly's Guide to the Presidency*, 112.
45 *Congressional Quarterly's Guide to the Presidency*, 112.

In the best of times the Rational has great difficulty holding his own against the Artisan in political campaigning. The Artisan appeals to desires, and the Rational to principles. In Hoover's case the times were bad, his principled comments sounded hollow, and there was an urgent desire in America for the country's return to a normal economic life. The magnificently charismatic Franklin Roosevelt easily took the White House away from the frustrated and preoccupied Hoover. The Great Engineer, earlier so admired for his administrative genius and his humanitarian drive, had now become unalterably, though rather unfairly, associated with the Great Depression. Though he lived for two decades more, and though his organizational skills were again used to contribute much more to the public good, his name is still linked inseparably with that tragic time.

Bibliography

Barber, W 1985 · *From New Era to New Deal: Herbert Hoover*
Best, G 1983 · *Herbert Hoover, the Postpresidential Years*
Best, G 1975 · *The Politics of American Individualism: Herbert Hoover in Transition*
Burner, D 1978 · *Herbert Hoover: A Public Life*
Fausold, M 1985 · *The Presidency of Herbert Hoover*
Hinshaw, D 1950 · *Herbert Hoover, American Quaker*
Hoff-Wilson, J 1975 · *Herbert Hoover, Forgotten Progressive*
Irwin, W 1928 · *Herbert Hoover, a Reminiscent Biography*
Krog, C (ed) 1984 · *Herbert Hoover and the Republican Era: a Reconsideration*
Lloyd, D 1972 · *Aggressive Introvert: a Study of Herbert Hoover*
Lochner, L 1960 · *Herbert Hoover and Germany*
Lyons, E 1948 · *Herbert Hoover*
McGee, D 1959 · *Herbert Hoover: Engineer, Humanitarian, Statesman*
Nash, G 1983 · *The Life of Herbert Hoover: the Engineer, 1974-1914*
Nash, L (ed) 1987 · *Understanding Herbert Hoover: Ten Perspectives*
Robinson, E 1975 · *Herbert Hoover, President of the United States*
Smith, R 1984 · *An Uncommon Man: the Triumph of Herbert Hoover*
Warren, H 1959 · *Herbert Hoover and the Great Depression*
Weissman, B 1974 · *Herbert Hoover and the Famine Relief to Soviet Russia*
Wilbur, R 1937 · *The Hoover Policies*
Wilson, C 1968 · *Herbert Hoover: a Challenge for Today*

Dwight David Eisenhower

"A soldier's pack..."

Organizer
Born: October 14, 1880
Died: March 28, 1969
Presidency: 1953-1961

Dwight David Eisenhower and Douglas MacArthur were the most successful American generals of World War II. While MacArthur (along with the United States Navy) was responsible for much of the Allied war effort in the Pacific, Dwight Eisenhower organized and oversaw the Allied war effort in Europe. Every general of every Allied army in Africa and Western Europe eventually worked under his command while he was the Commander of the Supreme Headquarters, Allied Expeditionary Force (SHAEF). Eisenhower was responsible for the planning and execution of the North African campaign, the landings in

Sicily and Italy, the Normandy landings and those in southern France in 1944, and for the overall conduct of the war in Europe until it came to an end in 1945. His success in this huge undertaking was the primary source of his reputation as a great political and military leader. He retired from the military in 1948 and became President of Columbia University for two years. Then in 1950 he assumed another military command, Commander of all NATO forces in Europe. In 1952, after years of being urged to run for the presidency he agreed to do so, was elected by a landslide, and four years later ran and was again elected by an overwhelming vote.

Dwight Eisenhower, the man who was so widely recognized as a great military hero had never fought in a battle. He had never been a commander in the field, the on-the-spot leader of soldiers going into battle. His military brilliance was demonstrated at a higher level of command than the level of the weapons-carrying warrior. His hallmarks were strategic competence, organizational brilliance, political sagacity, and endless patience.

This distinction, military commander as warrior versus military commander as organizer, points out clearly the difference between the Artisan tacticians such as General George "Old Blood and Guts" Patton or Erwin "The Desert Fox" Rommel and the strategist Rationals such as Eisenhower and MacArthur. The Artisans could be counted upon to exploit brilliantly opportunity wherever they found it. The latter might be rather slow and awkward in the same situation. The on-the-scene brilliance and the charismatic quality of the Artisan generals in fact can make the Rational generals seem rather stodgy and uninteresting. But it would be the strategist with his long-range, broad view events who would most likely bring about the opportunities for the Artisan tactician to exploit. This difference in style is one reason the Artisans frequently acquire colorful nicknames like "Blood and Guts" or "Desert Fox," while the Rationals so seldom do. (Eisenhower was called "Ike," of course, but the name is quite colorless, and certainly neither warlike nor inspiring in comparison to the nicknames of his Artisan subordinate and his Artisan enemy.)

Those who remember the eight years Dwight Eisenhower was President will probably recall rather vividly two images of Eisenhower: "Ike," the political candidate with his cheery grin, so wide and so friendly, and Eisenhower the President, playing a leisurely game of golf. These images gave many the impression that Dwight Eisenhower was a genial, outgoing man who never really did much while he was President. In fact some commentators of that time saw his presidency as a very passive one, but the image was quite inaccurate. Dwight Eisenhower was extraordinarily determined and hard-working, quite incapable of being lazy or passive. "A soldier's pack is not so heavy a burden as a prisoner's chains," he once said,[46] and also warned that "A people that values its privileges above its principles soon loses both."[47] These were not the words of a self-indulgent man, nor of a man unwilling to take action when he thought the time was right.

Born in Denison, Texas and raised mostly in Abilene, Kansas, he had a background rooted firmly in the Midwestern tradition of hard work and solid character. His father was hard-working but never quite as successful as many others, and almost of necessity his mother was a provident and hard-working woman. She taught her sons the value of planning ahead, of being economical, and of working hard. This early training had its impact on the young man. Early on Dwight Eisenhower decided to work to put his brother through college and then, in order to attend college himself, to go to the Military Academy where admission was by appointment and tuition was free.

Like the earlier Rational war hero, Ulysses S. Grant, Ike was not interested in military life as such. West Point was chiefly the only economically feasible route to getting a college education. When it was time for his graduation from the Point in 1915 and his commission as a second lieutenant, Eisenhower had some decisions to make. While most young men in his position were already sure of their career, the quiet, reserved young Rational spent three long and thoughtful days deciding on his course of action. His plan, he wrote in his journal, was to perform every duty given him in the Army to the best of his ability and to do his best to make a creditable record, no matter what the nature of the duty.

This steady, deliberate program of self-management was not just a reflection of his Rational character; it was also a realistic representation of what it would take to survive in a peacetime army where promotions

---

46 *From George ... To George*, page 97.
47 *From George ... To George*, page 54.

came slowly. It also gave a clear indication of the long-range planning and the self-management so typical of the Rational. Though the words Eisenhower used in the above quotation might remind one of the solid and stable approach typical of the Guardian character, it should be noted that the young man took three days to arrive at his decision. It is most unlikely that there would have been any three-day rumination for a Guardian in Eisenhower's position; indeed there would probably have been no decision over which the Guardian would ruminate. Eisenhower's deliberately adopted course is what most Guardians would naturally, unquestioningly, in fact almost inevitably, find themselves doing.

Eisenhower's successes were not the result of mere stolid routine however. During his career as a junior officer and as a staff officer he demonstrated an unusual talent for devising plans and marshalling forces. He was commander of a tank training post in Virginia, executive officer of Camp Gaillard in the Panama Canal Zone, mastered the course of instruction at the army's Command and General Staff School, graduating first of the 275 officers taking the course in 1926. He becoming well-enough respected that in 1935 General MacArthur took him on as his aide where he organized the Philippine Military Academy. From that time on he moved in the ranks of the army's upper echelons, planning strategies, organizing resources, and showed himself to be remarkably gifted in these activities.

Throughout his career he was promoted to higher rank well ahead of schedule. Promotion in the armed forces tends to be as much a matter of time and seniority as of talent or competence, but Eisenhower was one of the fairly rare individuals whose competence was enough to break down the traditional pattern. As is often the case with the Organizer, Eisenhower seemed to be able to recognize and then focus on major issues and to leave to trusted subordinates the management of less important matters. As Sherman Adams later commented about him, Eisenhower "focused his mind completely on the big and important aspects of the questions we discussed, shutting out with a strongly self-disciplined firmness the smaller and petty side issues."[48]

His ability to marshal forces combined with his talent for planning generated some very powerful effects: sound campaigns, military and

---

48 Quoted in *The Presidential Character*, 158.

other, with well-implemented chains of command; duties and functions interlocked in just the right way to support the campaign; and personnel carefully selected to fit into the command structures. As Sherman Adams later noted, Eisenhower's peculiarly Rational talent was later demonstrated in his leadership of the White House as well as in his work as a military leader.

> In managing the office of the Presidency, Eisenhower was highly effective. He left the office stronger, as an institution, than he found it. He extended and systematized the staff support that had taken shape during the Roosevelt and Truman administrations. Like a good military man, he had a strong sense of order and a readiness to delegate, and he liked clean-looking lines of authority.[49]

In fact his success in reworking the organization of the Executive Branch was partly responsible for his administration's quiet appearance. A well-organized and well-managed office just may not look busy to an outsider. As in the case of so much of Eisenhower's work, the result was smoothly coherent and globally comprehensive rather than flashy and ostentatious.

Rationals don't merely plan and manage external events, however. They will also plan for and manage their own behavior, often including their own feelings and thoughts. They will typically observe their behavior, coolly and mercilessly pass judgment on it, and systematically modify it in the direction of increased control and competency. Rationals typically begin this task in youth and continue it for life. Like most Rationals Ike was automatically and sternly in charge of himself, as this poignant entry taken from his personal memoirs indicates:

> My father was buried today. I've shut off all business and visitors for thirty minutes—to have that much time by myself to think of him....My only regret is that it was always so difficult to let him know the great depth of my affection for him.[50]

Contrast this highly disciplined approach with that of a Thomas Jefferson, whose ability to manage himself seemed so less well developed, and who seemed to suffer the various trials of his life so much more intensely. Perhaps it is usually the case that the Rational who cannot manage himself well is destined either to withdraw from life or to suffer exceptionally.

---

49 *Roosevelt to Reagan*, 55.
50 *Eisenhower: Portrait*, 112.

In the solitude that Eisenhower invoked for himself, no matter how briefly, we may discern his strong need for privacy. He disliked the public clamor and its intrusion into his private world in spite of cheerful and breezy grin he so readily donned for the crowds. Enormously popular he may have been; this could not keep him from commenting, "You know, once in a while I get to the point, with everybody staring at me, where I want to go back indoors and pull down the curtain."[51] But his self control was marvelous; he was his own manager, his own disciplinarian, his own chief executive officer. He endured the largely unwelcome tumult, friendly wave never faltering, warm grin intact.

Dwight Eisenhower's remarkable success was not a function of his personal self-control (though he did manage himself beautifully most of the time), or of his Rational planning and executive abilities alone. Unlike most of the Rationals that had occupied the White House, Dwight Eisenhower had a well-developed ability to work with people. He could be patient yet persuasive, tactful yet dominant. He could formulate his own opinions and still listen thoughtfully to opposing views; he could disagree with his subordinates' views and still work to reconcile them with what needed to be done.

During the Second World War he was of enormous help to the Allies in his ability to work effectively with strong-willed and impulsive Artisans like General Patton, and British Prime Minister Winston Churchill, and the equally strong-willed Guardians, British General Bernard Montgomery and the inimitable Frenchman, General Charles De Gaulle. These men could drive people to fits of anger and frustration, but Eisenhower had developed his principles of leadership over his years in the service and stayed with them scrupulously. No matter what the provocation he was almost invariably able to apply his principles to his own behavior. "You don't lead by hitting people over the head," he once said. Leadership is a matter of "persuasion, and conciliation, and education, and patience. It's long, slow, tough work. That's the only kind of leadership I know or will believe in, or will practice."[52]

The public Eisenhower was characteristically very charming, sporting his amiable manner and wide, warm grin. He showed the world

---

51 *The Presidential Character*, 154.
52 *Presidential Anecdotes*, 293.

a "sunny, sky-blue temperament,"[53] enormous patience, and seemingly irrepressible good cheer. Like most Rationals the unpretentious "Ike" had little patience with pomp and no respect for pomposity. He made much of being a Kansas farm boy and usually spoke in a disarmingly simple and down-to-earth manner. In his simplicity of speech he was much like his Civil War counterpart, U. S. Grant, another Rational who was preeminent in winning a war and who was then drafted to the presidency.

Underneath Ike's "sunny, sky-blue" exterior was a very tense man, especially when there was unfinished business at hand. This is quite typical for Rationals. They may be placid as a mountain lake when they are certain that all that can be done has been done, but they will be roiled as a stormy sea when they are not certain that all useful actions have been taken, all contingencies anticipated. Eisenhower was a standout in this regard, a world-class worrywart. For instance, during the final days before the Allied invasion of Normandy in 1944, he

> went over and over his battle plan. He spent hours alone in his tent, checking every calculation he had made, taking everything that could possibly go wrong into account—and decided to stick to his plan. But he was worried.[54]

Observers would occasionally notice the serious and at times brooding man underneath the cheerful mask. This was probably never more true than during his command of SHAEF, but Eisenhower's intense, thoughtful preoccupation was not something confined to military matters. It extended to how he dealt with almost all of the decisions he made or plans he set into motion, and as is so often true of the Rationals, even to his recreation. He was constantly working on his golf game when he found time for golf, constantly studying poker when he had time to play, carefully and studiously devoting himself to drawing and studying architectural plans, all this concentrated effort as a matter of recreation. The Rational character never permits resting on one's laurels, even in matters of recreation. To learn is always the objective.

There could be no question that Ike's patience was a learned characteristic more than a natural one, and that his soft and pleasant exterior clothed lightly a mind and will of steel. His temper was almost

---

53 *Presidential Anecdotes*, 292.
54 *Past Forgetting*, 214.

always held in check, but sometimes he lost control of it. Sloppy execution of important work would at times produce an awe-inspiring explosion of anger, and at such times his voice and words were not those of the mild Kansas farm boy but rather the stunning invective of the enraged career military man. Many people will resort to such outbursts when language fails them. Eisenhower was not one of them however. He had a gift for language and a love of it, a natural recognition of the impact of words, both spoken and written.

He commented once that the grandiose General MacArthur had gained a reputation as a silver-tongued speaker when he was in the Philippines. And who wrote MacArthur's speeches then? "I did," said Eisenhower. He wrote many of his own speeches as well, and went over the drafts of every speech, whether he had written it himself or not, focusing his attention for very long periods on every word, every phrase, on matters of grammar and sentence structure, on style and clarity. When he was a commander smaller matters and operations could be left to trusted subordinates. But in the matter of language and its uses Eisenhower considered every detail, large and small. Words were clearly too important, and Ike's skill with language too refined, for him to allow sloppiness or error in his speeches.

In spite of his service to MacArthur, Eisenhower would always avoid high-flown and grandiose statements in his own speeches. He much preferred precise and careful statements, analytic rather than grandiloquent, precise rather than flowery. Nevertheless, Eisenhower as President had a reputation for speaking in an ambiguous, even bumbling fashion at times. The reputation was well-deserved. It was also deliberately earned; Eisenhower the politician and diplomat understood the uses of ambiguity very well. When he spoke he always knew "exactly what he planned to say and what he intended to avoid saying by employing vague and evasive language."[55] Just as he could be coolly logical and analytic when he wished, he could also be masterfully incomprehensible and long-winded when it served his purpose. "Don't worry," he once said to an aide about a topic that might come up at a press conference, and about which he didn't want to commit himself, "If that question comes up, I'll just confuse them."[56]

---

55 *Presidential Anecdotes*, 296.
56 *Presidential Anecdotes*, 297.

He wanted under most circumstances to express himself clearly and succinctly, of course, regardless of the opinions of others. When he first ran for the presidency he made the comment that:

> The people who listen to me want to know what I think, not what I think about what someone else thinks. This is all I have to offer. If the people believe in what I say and do, nothing else matters and they will vote for me. If they don't, there's nothing I can do about it.[57]

One cannot help but be reminded of his famous Rational forbearer, Abraham Lincoln, who understood language so well, and who so often spoke in a similarly straightforward and simple vein and who made a very similar comment.

It must have been rather painful for him to sacrifice coherence and clarity this way; to be vague in language is to run counter to one's Rational character. But one cannot be surprised that he did so well. Beneath the casual, relaxed surface one finds always Eisenhower's Rational self-management, always the calculation of effects, always the attention to goals and strategies before his own wishes are considered. Always the Rational, living almost in the third person, as if he himself were another device to be managed. Notice the dispassionate firmness with which he described, after experiencing a heart attack during his first term as President, how he would conduct himself if he were re-elected to the presidency. During his second term he would undertake, he said, "a regime of ordered work activity, interspersed with regular amounts of exercise, recreation, and rest."[58] Orderly, planned, systematic.

Mamie Doud Eisenhower was in many respects an excellent choice for the wife of a career military man. It is difficult not to compare her with her Guardian predecessor, Bess Truman. She was, like Bess Truman, raised in relative comfort and attended a young ladies' finishing school, although in Mamie's case only for a year. Her personal style and interests were reminiscent of Mrs. Truman's, though Mamie seemed to engage in fewer intellectual pursuits. Both these Guardian wives excelled in family and household management. Both had a sense of lady-like behavior that precluded them from adopting more

---

57 *Ordeal of Power*, 27.
58 *Presidential Campaigns*, 291.

vigorously political or public roles. Both were naturally interested in matters of home and family; both understood the importance of taking proper care of the social demands imposed by their husbands' position.

Both were also willing to, and even desirous of, presenting themselves as women standing in the shadows of their husbands. In Mamie Eisenhower's case the wifely role was played out in a more flowery fashion than Mrs. Truman's and with a deliberate disregard for the "intellectual" side of events. Mrs. Eisenhower was an outspoken Conservator, demonstrating more sociability and warmth than did Bess Truman, the soft-spoken Monitor. As often happens, the Conservator Mamie Eisenhower also showed a fondness for pink and pretty "cuteness" that the more restrained Monitor Bess Truman did not. Dwight Eisenhower was of course a Kansas farm boy and a Rational, which meant that he would be rather slow to acquire the social graces which are of some importance to the career military officer. The Conservator Mamie Eisenhower, naturally attentive to these graces, proved to be very important in helping him develop his skillfulness with them.

The gossip was that Mamie Eisenhower had a drinking problem. She was observed at times to stagger as she walked, even to have an assortment of bumps and bruises from walking into things, to have some equilibrium problems, and to sleep late many mornings and these events were taken to be evidence of her drinking. She claimed that she suffered from an acute ear condition that seriously disturbed her equilibrium. The evidence suggests that her explanation of her occasionally awkward movements is the true one. Her physical difficulty may also account for her habit for staying in bed much later than one would otherwise expect.

Her time in the White House could not have been very easy for her. Her habit of rising late, coupled with the poorly-founded rumors that she had a drinking problem, and the rumors (true, as it happened) that her husband was having an affair with Kay Summersby, an Englishwoman who was his aide while he was in England, were all painful for her.[59]

---

59 The rumors were well-founded. Ike apparently considered divorcing Mamie for a time near the end of the war.

Yet she bore up stoically with very little indication of distress or anger toward Ike or toward the press. It was an admirable and gracious performance for which she deserves considerable recognition. Of course the reviews were far from all negative. Mamie's show of having no intellectual curiosity, no political savvy, and in fact few interests outside the home was well-received. It was even celebrated by the media as a demonstration of traditional American values. The public Mamie may have also been a fairly accurate portrait of the private Mamie as well; it seems that her interests were largely as they appeared to be.

Regardless of one's opinions about appropriate roles for women, it is difficult not to admire her inherent strength and the stability she brought to the Eisenhowers' many years of marriage. Not only did she succeed in the difficult role of army wife with its constant demands, dislocations and separations; not only did she do so with what appears to have been genuine emotional resilience and good grace; but she also managed to handle in the same fashion the assaults of the press and of rumor-mongers on those matters which must have been most important to her: her marriage and her character and reputation.

Though they were very different in character the Eisenhowers were in many respects fine representatives of the conscientious and conservative heartland of early twentieth-century America. They were both decent people, largely without meanness or rancor. At their core they were populists who believed in the goodness of people and their right, as well as the right of nations, to responsible self-determination. Eisenhower himself was opposed to pettiness, to spitefulness, to militarism, and to colonialism. He worked constantly for a world at peace in spite of, and perhaps because of, his military background and temperament. While Artisan commanders such as Patton and Halsey loved war, Rational commanders like MacArthur, Marshall, and Eisenhower hated it and would have it banished from the human scene.

Eisenhower rarely paid close attention to details; that was not his style. Nor did he occupy himself with domestic affairs the way he did with international affairs. Thus he allowed the noxious and destructive Senator Joe McCarthy to go on with his notorious Communist witch-hunts for a considerable period of time when he might have stepped in and crippled the Senator's influence much sooner than he finally did. As in the case of Rational Presidents before him, Eisenhower was also sensitive to the importance of how the office of the President was understood. He personally held it in very high esteem and did not want it to become a mere political device. Further, he saw it as an instrument of international policy formation, and he did not want it sullied by internal bickering. This was an important part of his resistance to taking on McCarthy. He once commented to his brother about the McCarthy situation that "I will not get into a pissing contest with that skunk."[60]

He was no politician, and in fact he considered, much as the early Presidents had, that the Office should remain above politics. He felt much the same way about being a career soldier, and in fact never cast a vote until he was fifty-eight years old. But in some internal matters he was a much more active president than in, for example, the McCarthy matter. He took the dramatic step of ordering the army into Little Rock, Arkansas, for example, to help with school integration there when the local and state governments refused to follow the Supreme Court's guidelines for school desegregation.

International matters made a larger demand on his attention. The strategist helped find an end to the Korean conflict, promoted establishment of SEATO, the Southeast Asia Treaty Organization, undertook with Canada the construction of the St. Lawrence Seaway, and offered an "Atoms for Peace" plan, finally endorsed by sixty-two nations, for the peaceful development and use of atomic energy. He also broke off relations with Cuba when Castro seized United States property on the island and failed to negotiate an "open skies" agreement with the Soviet Union. But overall this gifted strategist was able to leave office after two terms with the nation in good economic condition and the world, if not fully at peace, at least neither in flames nor threatening to explode.

Eisenhower was not physically well during his years in the White House. He experienced three major illnesses during that time which

---

60 *Congressional Quarterly's Guide to the Presidency,* 118.

seriously threatened his ability to act competently as President. He finally died on March 28, 1969, eight years after leaving office, of the effects of severe and prolonged arteriosclerosis. Near the end he commented to his wife that "we've had a wonderful life together." Just before he died he said to his son John, "Be good to Mamie."[61] For her part, Mamie Eisenhower lived for another ten years. It was difficult, for when she died, she said, "the light went out of my life."[62] For those ten rather lonely years she never stopped thinking about the famous man who was always, whatever he might be to others, her own quietly loving husband.

Bibliography

Burk, R 1986	*Dwight D. Eisenhower, Hero and Politician*
Donovan, R 1956	*Eisenhower: the Inside Story*
Eisenhower, D	*Crusade in Europe*
Ewald, W 1981	*Eisenhower the President: Crucial Days, 1951-1960*
Killian, J 1977	*Sputnik, Scientists, and Eisenhower*
Lyon, P 1974	*Eisenhower: Portrait of a Hero*
Norton, P 1979	*Eisenhower and Little Rock*
Pusey, M 1956	*Eisenhower, the President*
Rowe, R 1976	*The Eisenhower Administration and the Recession of 1957-58*
Smith, W 1956	*Eisenhower's Six Great Decisions: Europe, 1944-1945*
Welch, R 1963	*The Politician*

---

61 *Presidential Wives*, 347.
62 *Presidential Wives*, 347.

Reporter Rational Presidents: The Engineers

Thomas Jefferson

The Glorious Enigma

Engineer
Born: April 13, 1743
Died: July 4, 1826
Presidency: 1801-1809

The United States' first two Presidents, George Washington and John Adams, were remarkable men, the former was earthy and prudent, the latter fiery and luminous. But if these two were extraordinary then the third President of the United States was astonishing. Thomas Jefferson was a multifaceted genius who demonstrated all his life an insatiable curiosity, constant restlessness and enormous energy. The curiosity was to be expected of course; all Rationals are instinctively curious, and they search unceasingly for problems, enigmas, paradoxes, puzzles. But Jefferson's turbulent curiosity and his inventiveness were immense.

He had an unending fascination with philosophy, political and economic theory, architecture, inventions, science and technology. He single-handedly designed and founded the University of Virginia, was the architect for his own home, Monticello, and for the homes of a number of his friends; he also studied a half dozen languages, some mathematics, astronomy, surveying, botany and zoology, and became successful as a lawyer, farmer, philosopher, political scientist, writer, scientist, musician, and inventor. In his spare time he also managed to become a respectable violinist. He was also the holder of several patents and, along with his other activities, found time to devise a folding chair, a dumbwaiter, swivel chair, pedometer, and a lazy Susan.

He was, like most Rationals, deeply interested in technology. The introduction of phosphorus matches fired his curiosity, and he was intrigued by the first experiments with balloons large enough to carry men. When in France he noted the new European means of mass production of firearms, including the novel notion of interchangeable parts for these weapons. And along with his other inventions he also developed a small printing press.

In his college years at William and Mary he studied philosophy, the literary classics and mathematics, and the law. He was deeply engrossed in his studies and could at any time, as one of his classmate recalled, "tear himself away from his dearest friends and fly to his studies." Even in college his thinking was characterized by a terrible intensity, by great complexity, and by remarkable precision. Jefferson was not just a Rational; he was a brilliant Rational. He was able to master almost anything to which he turned his mind and almost automatically (and without any ambition to become a politician) he became a legislator, a Governor, a Congressman, a diplomat, the Secretary of State, Vice-President, and President of the United States. So outstanding were his abilities that almost a century and a half later President John F. Kennedy, hosting a White House dinner for a group of Nobel Prize winners, described that remarkable group as "the most distinguished gathering of talents ever assembled in the Executive Mansion except for when Jefferson dined there alone."[63]

---

63 *The American Presidents*, 38.

Fortunately for the United States, Jefferson was as passionately dedicated to the new nation as were his presidential precursors, Washington and Adams. His remarkable gifts were brought to bear in pursuit of a United States that would focus first, last, and always on the well-being and independence of its ordinary citizens, who were the true heirs of the virtues of good government. Jefferson believed this very strongly, and the aristocratic Washington and Adams must have had mixed emotions upon hearing his comment that "kings are the servants, not the proprietors of the people."[64]

Consistent with his convictions, Jefferson undertook the practice of law in 1767 (he was only twenty-three at the time), served in the Virginia colonial legislature, was a member of Virginia's delegation to the Continental Congress, wrote the Declaration of Independence, was Governor of Virginia during the revolution, diplomatic Minister to France after the war, Secretary of State under Washington, Vice-President under John Adams, and finally President of the United States.

Thomas Jefferson was a man of striking contrasts. In spite of his busy public life the apparent contradictions in his makeup have always escaped clear and simple portraiture. Quoting Henry Adams, one of Jefferson's biographers remarked that all our early Presidents except for Jefferson can be drawn with a few broad strokes of the brush. "But the master of Monticello, with his shifting lights and shades, nuances and translucencies, defies even the finest pencil."[65]

That he was enigmatic to his observers, then and now, owes itself in important part to his temperament. Jefferson was a Rational, and the Rationals are complex creatures. But more to the point, he was a Rational Engineer, one of only three who have become Presidents of the United States. (The other two were James Madison and Abraham Lincoln, neither of whom could be considered straightforward in the organization of their character.)

The Organizer Rationals, such as John Adams, are directors, ordering people about without a second thought, though without the least interest in "dominating" or lording it over others. Recall John Adams: his preference for giving directives rather than giving

---

64 See *A Summary View of the Rights of British America, 1774.*
65 *The Hero in America,* 149.

information was pronounced, as one would expect of an energetic Organizer. Jefferson the Engineer Rational, on the other hand, was not in the least directive. He naturally and comfortably informed others; giving directives was much less comfortable. When he did give directions it was only after much thought and rumination—perhaps too much rumination at times. Engineer Rationals are usually discontent and even uncomfortable when circumstances force them to command.

Still, though they give information willingly, and even irrepressibly at times, Engineer Rationals are difficult to know well. The soft-spoken but eloquent Thomas Jefferson was easy to know as an acquaintance but, like all Engineers, almost impossible to know intimately. He preferred conversation to action, but the conversation was about ideas, concepts, abstractions, not small talk about himself.

Jefferson's thinking had a terrible intensity and he guarded his private world carefully so that others rarely had access to it. Yet he longed for friends and, at least in his youth, found some time to enjoy a reasonably outgoing and cheerful social life. Though he was profoundly discreet about his own personal world he enjoyed lengthy conversations about abstract and complex ideas and was considered one of the best conversationalists of his time. He usually showed a calm and even manner but some people considered that he was at times held prisoner by his own dark and brooding thoughts. There were times, as when his wife died, when this thoughtful, and self-controlled Engineer seemed to have been captured by the most agonizing despair imaginable. In all this, except perhaps for the remarkable intensity of his reactions and the brilliance of his thinking, he was a typical Engineer Rational.

In spite of his glowing intelligence and constant activity Jefferson had a reputation among some for being hopelessly lazy. John Adams complained vigorously about this from time to time. From the perspective of an Organizer like Adams, Jefferson might indeed look lazy or at least wasteful of time and effort. Jefferson was not an Organizer Rational; he was an Engineer Rational. He preferred learning to leading, reporting to commanding, suggesting to directing, open inquiry to final certainty. Taking public action, giving commands, exerting control, "making it happen" were never his preference except when his most strongly held beliefs were at stake. Even with his remarkable command of language he seemed to dislike public speaking.

To write an essay or a book, however, or quietly to design a building, write a declaration, a constitution, or to consult with others similarly occupied—these were the modes of involvement most favored by him and most natural to him. Perhaps there were those who saw these activities as somehow the frivolous behaviors of a "lazy" man. But had they been able to observe the furious pace and endless complexity of his thought they would have stood astonished at the enormous activity of Jefferson's mind.

Jefferson further demonstrates nicely the distinction between the Organizer Rational and the Engineer Rational in the wide range of his interests and in the frequent shifts of his focus from one interest to another. One does not find here the single-mindedness of the Organizer, the persistent fixed focus on a project or interest until it is complete. Consider for example the history of his book, *Notes on the State of Virginia*. He began the book merely as a set of replies to questions posed by a European friend about Virginia. As he wrote Jefferson expanded his replies—including in his notes other matters which he wanted to address—until a full-fledged book had emerged. In it Jefferson spoke to a very wide diversity of topics, making observations and rendering judgments, some of which, by the way, were controversial and a few quite inflammatory. Overall the book was intelligent, informed, and entertaining and is still interesting and readable today.

When he sent the manuscript to friends in France in 1781, however, Jefferson declared that it was "very imperfect." Though several of his friends thought it quite good and begged him to publish, he refused to do anything more with it for four years, as other matters drew his attention. In this Jefferson was typical of the Engineer Rationals: to spend years designing and building something only to regard it as irretrievably flawed and certainly not worthy of replication and distribution. Besides, Rationals hate to do anything over again. They are certain that there are other, far more interesting and intriguing problems that demand their analysis.

Thus it was four years later, only after he had extensively "corrected" and (almost inevitably) enlarged the book, that he finally agreed to publish *Notes on the State of Virginia*. But there were conditions to be met: the publication run was to be of only 200 copies, he insisted, and in spite of his corrections and other improvements, he required that his name would not appear on the title page. There is here no hint of the megalomania one sometimes suspects in the Organizer (again, such as John Adams). Instead the quintessential Engineer emerges: often so sure in his beliefs, yet so uncertain about his competence to translate them into the spoken or (especially) the written word. So impassioned in the midst of his certainty, so hesitant about his certainties when even one step removed from them.

The Rational Jefferson's love of learning, and therefore of books, was monumental. His home was destroyed by a fire in 1770. When he heard the news the first question he asked was whether his books had been saved. Years later the same deep love of books led him to replace from his own extensive collection the books lost when a fire devastated the Library of Congress's book collection. He then immediately and enthusiastically set about rebuilding his own collection until it was again a superior library of the best books. Rationals have an almost irrepressible penchant for (joyfully) replacing lost or obsolete capabilities with "state of the art" procedures and equipment. Witness the current frenzy with which countless Rationals pursue the computer technology that continuously threatens to outdistance them. One can imagine with sympathy an exhausted twentieth century Thomas Jefferson trying to keep abreast of advances in all the pure and applied sciences at once. Perhaps it was fortunate for him that in his time books were the embodiment of technology.

In spite of his many talents Jefferson was not the sort of man one expects to become a hero. He was brilliant but not always practical in the application of his brilliance. He was a visionary but not of the combative kind who aggressively tears from the world the fulfillment of the vision. He was ardent in his beliefs, but he was not ordinarily a forceful figure. And regardless of his magnificent intellect Jefferson showed clearly that he was far from a proficient tactician under conditions of war.

In 1779-1780 Jefferson was Governor of Virginia. The Revolutionary War was still in full sway and a British force landed on a nearby piece of Virginia coast. At this critical moment Governor Jefferson optimistically underestimated the strength of the British and so was slow and haphazard about establishing a defense. He had already failed to provide adequate numbers of men and arms for the general defense of Virginia and overall did a very poor job of marshalling and deploying his resources the way (for instance) a Monitor like Washington or an Organizer like John Adams might have. He similarly failed to seize favorable opportunities for combat the way an Artisan such as the later President Andy Jackson might have. At one point he heard that the British were approaching in force and, it is said in some quarters, he simply took off for distant vistas until the military threat passed. He was not a very good man for dealing with crises that demanded immediate action on the basis of insufficient data; his tactical and logistical talents fell far short of his strategic capabilities.

In fact Thomas Jefferson was, all things considered, a rather gentle, somewhat withdrawn man, a patrician scholar rather than a fiery revolutionary. He was passionate in his beliefs about government but rarely chose aggressive pursuit of them. He was at heart a soft-spoken, book-loving, reflective Virginia aristocrat. His highly public life as revolutionary leader, statesman, powerful political figure, and finally President, was not so much the result of any ambition of Jefferson's for a public life as it was the result of the entreaties of his friends and colleagues. His interests and his colleagues inevitably required of him much public involvement and his own passionate beliefs and vision thrust him along that path. Even when he agreed to run for the presidency it was not a matter of personal ambition but rather because rather his urgent desire to prevent the ambitious and unprincipled Aaron Burr from assuming power. The Fates time and again conspired against the gentle patrician Rational's desire for a contemplative life and dragged him, almost kicking and screaming, into the public eye.

Though he had a typically Rational faith in logic and reason and in what they could accomplish, he was always uncertain about his own individual performance. In spite of his enormous accomplishments he tended to judge himself somewhat harshly. One of his admiring biographers wrote of him that "He measured himself against his own ideal rather than against the performance of others."[66] She recognized in her own terms the Rational's problem: one's own best performance becomes merely the criterion of acceptability. Failure to perform as well as or better than one ever has is just that: failure. What others say about

---

66 Fawn Brodie, *Thomas Jefferson: An Intimate History*, 185.

what one has done, no matter how flattering, is of only incidental interest, and the more enthusiastic they become about one's performance the more they prove themselves to be untrustworthy judges.

The matter does not improve as the Rational becomes more competent. Rationals who become more and more able as a result of the constant exercise of their abilities, also become more critical of themselves, and hold themselves to ever higher standards of performance. In the end they may reach the absurd point where they view their own outstanding performances, performances which may far outstrip the work of their peers, as fatally flawed and unworthy of use or notice. (We may recall again Jefferson's doubts about his *Notes on the State of Virginia*.)

Rationals may have a sense of what is important—and what makes it important—that is quite different from those around them. For instance Jefferson's participation in the events surrounding the Revolutionary War, and in the establishment of the United States, was unusually important, and it was certainly a great honor for him to be only the third man entrusted with the presidency of the newborn United States. But it was not for these contributions and attainments that the retiring Engineer wanted finally to be remembered. Matters of the intellect were what counted. He was more proud of his part in writing the Declaration of Independence than of having been President. Rationals, after all, take no pride in being elected or appointed to office. Indeed, the epitaph he wanted inscribed on his tombstone read:

> Here was buried Thomas Jefferson, Author of the Declaration of American Independence, of the Statute of Virginia for Religious Freedom, and Father of the University of Virginia.

As noted, his career of public service was nevertheless very extensive, and it was capped by his assumption of the presidency in 1801, making him the first President to be inaugurated in the nation's new capital, Washington, District of Columbia.

At the time Washington was still little more than a village of muddy streets, inadequate housing, and very few amenities, and in some respects the setting was in keeping with Jefferson's own style. As is typical of the Engineer Rationals, he usually dressed quite carelessly. He was so oblivious to the niceties of traditional decorum, protocol, and personal appearance, that while President he once greeted a British minister in his slippers and dressing gown.

Even when he remembered matters of decorum there was no guarantee that he would attend to them properly. Rationals may accommodate to custom at times but they rarely do so in a genuinely cooperative manner. Instead they are likely to do so rather grudgingly, merely to avoid even greater annoyance. Jefferson seemed to represent the Engineers well in this regard, and since he stood more than six feet, two inches tall he must have been a daunting sight for the pompous British diplomat when he appeared in his unexpected attire.

It was not mere obliviousness or carelessness which occasioned Jefferson's informal style, nor a simple annoyance with custom and protocol (though the Rationals are typically rather disdainful of decorum). As a matter of principle Jefferson deliberately had abolished the aristocratic trappings which had already begun to grow up around the presidency. During his administration such titles of honor as "Excellency" preferred by the traditionalist George Washington were abandoned, along with much of the pomp that Washington and Adams had insisted upon. Jefferson was rather effective in this regard, for since his time the only title of honor regularly accorded the President of the United States is the simple, straightforward "Mr. President."

Jefferson was in much sympathy with the ideals of the French Revolution and its vision of an egalitarian, sage, self-determining populace. The vision was still fresh in those times; the national fragmentation, the severe disruption of law and order, and the remarkable viciousness which attended France's revolution had not yet impressed themselves upon him. Jefferson still held his strong faith in the consent of the governed rather than in autocratic executive control, a faith which put him at odds with both John Adams and Alexander Hamilton. The idea of the self-governing citizen of the self-governing nation was deeply rooted in him. It was the concept of "the free man" neither bowing to another nor wishing to be bowed to, but standing independently and proudly on his own.

Jefferson was among the large number of men at the Constitutional Convention in 1787 who were concerned about the possible abuse of the powers of the new American government. During the Convention he had written to his friend James Madison that "A Bill of Rights is what the people are entitled to against every government on earth, general or particular, and what no just government should refuse or rest on inference." Thus it was partly through Jefferson's urgings that the Bill of Rights was eventually included in the new Constitution. He was greatly concerned about the possibility that the power of the government could be usurped. Because of that he was determined that the President should not be a one-man authority, making and enforcing policy in some kingly isolation. The President should be largely subservient to the Congress, Jefferson insisted, which would presumably be more closely in touch with the people and more readily controlled by the people. (His friend Madison, usually so astute about such matters, had thought that the central government would always be too weak for such a Bill to be necessary!)

Jefferson, consistent with his Engineer's outlook, saw more clearly than his predecessors the distinction between the executive and the legislative function and the importance of keeping the distinction clear. The function of the executive, he declared, was to execute laws laid down by legislators, not to make up laws on his own. John Adams, even though a Rational, was an Organizer Rational. He seemed less willing to acknowledge the distinction between legislator and chief executive, and would have preferred to keep more power in his own hands so he could get things done more efficiently. Rationals are zealous in making and noting distinctions, and Jefferson and Adams do not differ in this. Where they differ is in their willingness to abide by the distinction. (The directive types of any kind, whether Artisan, Guardian, Rational, or Idealist, have a hard time relinquishing powers once acquired; the nondirective types do not.)

The importance to Jefferson of the idea that "the best government is that which governs least"[67] can be understood, in part at least, as a natural reflection of his Engineer style. Partly from this orientation also arose his belief in the value of an educated populace which could exercise the rational powers of the mind in its own best interest. The Rational Jefferson attached enormous importance to the mind and its powers. On the Jefferson Memorial Monument in Washington are inscribed the words "I have sworn on the altar of God eternal hostility against every form of tyranny to the mind of man." In these words the

---

67 Though often attributed to Jefferson, it was actually written by one John L. O'Sullivan, in the Introduction to *The United States Magazine and Democratic Review* (1837). O'Sullivan is also the man who wrote of the United States that it is "our manifest destiny to overspread the continent allotted by Providence for the free development of our yearly multiplying millions" (*The United States Magazine and Democratic Review*, 1845).

focus is on the most fundamental tyranny: the tyranny of the mind, against which all else must fail.

Outside his circle of friends and admirers Jefferson's political views were not everywhere applauded; Jefferson and Aaron Burr campaigned against one another and against the incumbent John Adams for the presidency in 1800 and the contest was so close that there was no winner. The election was therefore and according to Constitutional law turned over to the House of Representatives. Even there it took a week-long struggle and thirty-six separate votes before Jefferson was declared the winner. Aaron Burr, receiving the second-highest number of votes, had to settle for the vice-presidency; Adams lost out entirely.

So difficult, divisive and prolonged had been the election that some questioned whether the country could survive another such struggle. There were nightmarish predictions that various states would call out their militias to enforce the electors' choices, that others might call out their own militias to repudiate those same choices, great fears that war would erupt between the states if the election were sufficiently heated and indecisive, and that the new nation might be consumed in a political conflagration.[68]

Whatever the difficulty of the struggle, the outcome was exceptionally fortunate for the United States, for one remarkable consequence of Thomas Jefferson's presidency was the purchase of the Louisiana Territory from Napoleonic France in 1803. Napoleon was having troubles of his own in Europe and decided to dispose of the Territory though he recognized it was quite valuable. Though the cost to the United States was a mere $15,000,000, the Louisiana Purchase doubled the size of the country and not incidentally incorporated within the its boundaries a huge portion of the world's greatest farmland.[69] Jefferson appreciated that the purchase constituted a great real estate bargain, but Rationals are rarely acquisitive in the way that Guardians such as Washington are. At that time there was for Jefferson an even more compelling reason for the purchase: it removed France from our doorstep, thereby obviating our reliance on the British fleet to protect the nation from a perpetual French threat.

The matter of the purchase was an interesting one for Jefferson, for there was no Constitutional provision for the acquisition of foreign

---

68 The Twelfth Amendment to the Constitution was a direct outcome of this worrisome situation.

69 One Robert R. Livingston and future President James Monroe negotiated the details of the purchase with Napoleon Bonaparte.

territory. Even more dubiously from a Constitutional standpoint, Jefferson negotiated the deal without prior Congressional approval. Jefferson, though he was a strong advocate of limiting the powers of the government, admitted that he "stretched the Constitution till it cracked" in order to justify the acquisition. His action was an excellent example of the Engineer's ingenuity in circumventing rules and regulations while still, so he could argue, operating within the intent of those rules and regulations (given that the Constitution did not really specify that he could or could not take the action he wished to).

The Engineer Rationals, if they are forthright, will occasionally admit to a certain delight in getting around any regulations which they see as well-meant but ill-advised. By the way, for better or for worse, this activity is likely to include most regulations at one time or another. Rationals see most regulations as the work of a committee of incompetents whose efforts are supposed to implement laws but often seem to get in the way instead. The Rational appreciates the law and has no patience with regulations which fail to express the intent of the law properly—or with the committees which formulate those regulations.

Of course Jefferson didn't take his action cavalierly; the matter was much too important for that. On the one hand there was no question about the value to the United States of the Purchase. On the other, to arrogate that kind of power to the executive branch of government was something that Jefferson had always thought to be quite dangerous. He struggled hard with the issue before deciding on the action and we can be certain that the struggle was a considerable one. The Engineer is more sensitive than any other type to the tricky process of the weighing and balancing of principles and options and, especially on the way to an important decision, are much more likely than others to fall victim to agonized "on the one hand and on the other hand" arguments. They will worry and ponder and complicate the issue at hand until it seems totally undecidable, and then, somehow, decide.

So President Jefferson weighed principle against principle and finally, somehow, decided. By virtue of his stretch of Federal authority, the United States, which formerly had as its western boundary the Mississippi River, was now bounded by a zigzagging line running from present-day Louisiana northwest all the way to the western boundary of Montana.[70]

---

70 While in the Virginia legislature Jefferson, though a slave owner himself, had campaigned hard for legislation which would permanently abolish slavery. His bill

Not all Jefferson's actions were so fortunate in their consequences. His own personal life, for instance, was far less satisfying. In fact it was visited with tragedy in a way that his public life, even with all its failures and triumphs, never was. Other temperaments often stereotype Rationals as overly concerned with logic, devoid of loving feelings, empathy, or compassion. They may describe the Rationals as dispassionate and hollow human beings who are so preoccupied with theory and analysis that they miss out on what is most important in life. Thomas Jefferson's life shows clearly the inaccuracy of that image of the Rational. Though the depth of feeling of which the Rational is capable has already been hinted at in John and Abigail Adams' relationship, it becomes poignantly apparent in Jefferson.

Jefferson loved his wife, Martha Wayles Jefferson very greatly. But she died in 1782 while the War for Independence still raged. She was only thirty-three years old. The terrible and prolonged grief Jefferson experienced after her death was extraordinary. For the four final months of her illness he was with her constantly. He rarely left her side; instead he sat with her, talked with her and read to her late into the night. His daughter Patsy later recalled that when Martha Jefferson finally died Jefferson would not leave her room. He finally had to be led away from his dead wife's bed, and so violent was his emotion and so great his grief that he finally passed out. He was unconscious for so long that his family began to fear that he would not survive. When he did revive and for three weeks thereafter he would not even leave his room. He stayed there and paced back and forth almost incessantly, day and night, sleeping only when he became physically exhausted. When finally he did leave his room he would do little but ramble across the countryside, occasionally subject to wrenching outbursts of grief.

The death of his wife was not his only personal loss, though it was the most obvious. His intense involvement with the affairs of the country thwarted him in his wish for a quiet, scholarly life in the peaceful Virginia countryside. The affairs of state had cost him precious time with his wife. Death also claimed four of his six children while they were still quite young. He also lost much of the joy and solace of

---

failed to carry by only one vote. That one vote may have radically changed the future of the United States: witrhout slavery Virginia might not have seceded a half century later. If there had been a secession the Virginian general, Robert E. Lee, would have been a Northern general rather than Southern. Further, Ulysses Grant might never have become President, and even Abraham Lincoln might have lived out his life.

watching his two remaining daughters grow up. When he had the older of the two remaining daughters brought to him in Europe, she came almost as a stranger. She had, after all, been cared for by others during most of her early life while Jefferson served abroad.

One reads in Jefferson's letters to her his poignant attempt to be a father to his daughters. Many of them are letters of instruction which he offers as a loving and concerned father might offer them. But his injunctions sound stiff and false, and his language is so stilted, that the letters read more like those of a stuffy schoolmaster than of a loving father. Never go out without a bonnet, he instructed his younger daughter, for the unshielded sun would make her ugly, and she would be less lovable.

He didn't seem able to keep a warm contact with his cherished daughter, and his writings certainly didn't help. Rationals are typically not "warm" writers to begin with, and they *must* say things "just so," especially when they write. Their documents often have a rather pedantic cast because of this, for Rationals are uncompromising on this issue of how sentences are to be constructed. To say things in some other manner, after the fashion of Idealists or Guardians or Artisans, will not do. Sentences must be self-consistent and that is all there is to it. Their ability to communicate emotional matters is usually impaired because of this; their naturally pedantic style appears to negate whatever emotional expression they manage. A little girl would see the instruction clearly; she would be unlikely to feel the love being expressed thereby.

Jefferson never remarried, though he did at one point become extremely infatuated with a Maria Cosway, a woman with whom he became acquainted while on a diplomatic mission to France. Unfortunately Mme Cosway was already married. The tortures of passion with which Jefferson was afflicted in this hopeless situation are painfully apparent in his "Dialogue between My Head and My Heart," a letter he wrote in October of 1786 to Mme Cosway. It demonstrates not only Jefferson's undeniable eloquence as a writer but also the deliberate and sometimes agonizing self-scrutiny of which the Rational is capable.

The letter, some four thousand words long, describes a "dialogue" between his mercilessly logical utilitarian mind (the "Head") and his wretchedly disappointed emotional side, in love with passion and in love with love (the "Heart"). Displaying masterfully the "on the one hand but on the other hand" struggle so familiar to the Engineer Rational, the Dialogue is elegantly constructed and carefully disciplined. It offers an analysis, both dramatic and carefully reasoned, of almost the entirety of the tortured relationship of human intellect and emotion, and especially of Jefferson's agonized struggle to reconcile the two. For such a Rational as Jefferson, it would seem, even one's suffering should be expressed impeccably.[71]

Through the loss of his wife, his long and painful separations from his children, the deaths of two of them and his estrangement from the third, and the passionate and painful absorption with Mme Cosway, Jefferson continued to serve the Revolution and the new nation. Then in 1801 he was elected to the presidency. In 1804 when he again ran for the presidency the opposition could not overcome his great popularity and Jefferson was re-elected to office, this time in a satisfying landslide. When his second term of office neared its end he decided that he would not run for a third term. He stepped down from the presidency in 1809, making room for his long-time friend and successor, James Madison.

For the remaining seventeen years of his life Jefferson lived at his beloved Monticello. It was during this time that he founded the University of Virginia. He designed its buildings and curriculum, he employed the academic staff, and acted in the role of the president of the university, seeing the school finally opened to students one year before his death. During these same years, however, the remnants of his family, his in-laws, his friends and a few opportunistic hangers-on all managed to avail themselves of Jefferson's hospitality and of his rather limited resources. He was admired by many, and he enjoyed at least a few members of his family, though not all. There were more than a few self-interested louts in the crowd but Jefferson also enjoyed many friendships in these latter days. But he was able to luxuriate in all this only rarely, for he had gone severely into debt over the years and was constantly struggling to manage his obligations. He fretted, almost constantly and with good reason, over whether he would be able to keep Monticello from his debtors' grasp.

In fact he was able to keep Monticello until he died, but three years later his family sold the lovely home to satisfy the creditors. Jefferson's beloved home fell into terrible disrepair over the following years, until about one hundred years later it was purchased and extensively

---

71 Those interested in acquainting themselves with what lies behind the calm exterior of the Rational personality might read the Horatio Hornblower novels by the Rational author, C. S. Forester. The novelist Forester far outdoes the psychologist in this series, for few works in the English language offer so revealing and consistently accurate a portrait of the emotions, desires, and thoughts of the Rationals.

refurbished. As in the cases of John Adams and James Madison, the United States had failed to treat its former President well.

His health gradually failed and on the night of July the third, 1826, Thomas Jefferson lay dying. He and John Adams had both been determined to live to see the fiftieth anniversary of the signing of the Declaration of Independence, and Jefferson several times lifted his head from his pillow to ask, "This is the Fourth?" His friend Nicholas Trist was sitting with him, and finally didn't have the heart to tell him the time had not yet come. When a little before midnight Trist nodded that at last it was the Fourth, Jefferson breathed "Ah!" and sank back with a look of satisfaction. He died the following day, July the fourth, 1826, the fiftieth anniversary he had been so intent upon witnessing.

Thomas Jefferson had lived to see a new nation born, two wars fought in its defense, its life stabilized and secured, and its boundaries enormously extended. He had taken a very personal and very powerful part in all these events. He must have been, in spite of his Rational's self-criticism and self-doubts, immensely proud.

Bibliography

Benson, C R. 1971	*Thomas Jefferson as Social Scientist*
Binger, C 1970	*Thomas Jefferson: A Well Tempered Mind*
Bowers, C 1925	*Jefferson and Hamilton*
Brodie, F 1974	*Thomas Jefferson: An Intimate History*
Cohen, I B. 1980	*Thomas Jefferson and the Sciences*
Chinard, G 1929	*Thomas Jefferson, the Apostle of Americanism*
Dumbauld, E. 1978	*Thomas Jefferson and the Law*
Friedman, M 1980	*Free to Choose*
Huddleston, E 1982	*Thomas Jefferson: A Reference Guide*
Hirst, F 1926	*Life and Letters of Thomas Jefferson*
Miller, C 1988	*Jefferson and Nature*
Nock, A 1926	*Jefferson*
Padover, S 1942	*Jefferson*
Peterson, M 1970	*Thomas Jefferson and the New Nation*
Parton, J 1874	*The Life of Thomas Jefferson*
Randall, H 1858	*The Life of Thomas Jefferson*
Schachner, N 1951	*Thomas Jefferson, A Biography*
Spivak, B 1979	*Jefferson's English Crisis*
Stewart, R 1978	*The Half-way Pacifist*

James Madison

The Well-Tempered Scholar

Engineer
Born: March 16, 1751
Died: June 28, 1836
Presidency: 1809-1817

Thomas Jefferson served two terms as President, and like Washington before him decided that two terms of its "splendid misery" were quite enough for any man. He was eager to return to a life of study and to have his old friend, the gentle and scholarly James Madison, succeed him in the White House. There was little opposition to his choice and "Little Jemmy" Madison, who stood about five feet, five inches tall and weighed in the neighborhood of 100 pounds, won the presidential election of 1808 handily, and was sworn into office in early 1809. Though he was pleased to have become President, Madison intensely disliked the ceremony and celebration that attended his inauguration. He was quick to announce to a friend his reaction to the gala inaugural ball: he would rather be in bed.[72]

Another quiet, privacy-loving Engineer Rational had taken the helm of the ship of state.

The differences between Madison and his Rational predecessors are interesting. As we have seen, John Adams was an Organizer Rational, a very directive Rational who was also short-tempered and impatient. Like a sharp-edged sword of poorly tempered steel he was hard and cutting, but dangerous to himself as well as to his foes. Jefferson the Engineer Rational had a reporting, nondirective style, and was more scintillating yet delicate in his communications. If the Organizer Adams was a saber, a heavy slashing powerful blade, the Engineer Jefferson was a foil, flexible, slender, graceful, but breakable if bent too far.

The Engineer James Madison was made of the same steel as his Rational predecessors, but he seemed to have been built more sturdily and was far better tempered. Madison's strength was more reliable, his structure was more durable, and he had a balance and steadiness that both Adams and Jefferson lacked. James Madison seemed to have welded together the wide-ranging thoughtfulness of the informative Engineer with the single-mindedness steadiness of the directive Organizer in a way that neither of his Rational predecessors had been able to. Eventually this remarkably even-tempered and scholarly Engineer became recognized as one of the most far-sighted, conscientious, patient, and fair-minded men ever to be President of the United States. His Rational characteristics were apparent not only during his presidency, but also, and perhaps more importantly, during the Constitutional Convention of 1787. Madison was considered a shy man, but he was forceful speaker on the rather infrequent occasions that he chose to be. He was an energetic revolutionary, and of strong opinion about how the new government ought to be shaped, but he usually kept his own counsel during the Convention proceedings. When he did speak, however, he contributed a great deal.

One is likely to notice this trait even among youthful Reporter Rationals. They tend, even while young, to use speech only at opportune

---

72 *Presidential Anecdotes*, 47.

times; otherwise they simply keep their own counsel. Engineer Rationals carefully sculpt their speech and speak at the precise moment speaking will do the most good. Madison's scholarship and his precision in speech made it almost inevitable that he would be recognized in this circle of very able men as a sage political consultant. Today he is known as one of the chief architects of the Constitution, and in fact has become known as "The Father of the Constitution."

From the point of view of temperament this is no surprise. Architecture of every kind is the forte of the Rational, especially the Engineer Rational. Designing a home or a university campus (as in Jefferson's case) is not so different from designing a constitution or a government (as in Madison's).[73] In either endeavor the Engineer Rational is best suited by temperament to do the job, whatever strengths or deficiencies he might have otherwise.

It was also Madison who argued most persuasively that the new nation have a strong central government with three clearly defined branches, executive, legislative, and judicial, demonstrating his extremely high intelligence in structural and functional analysis. This absolutely fundamental structure of governmental functions exists today with only the slightest variations from the design presented in Madison's original and carefully thought out proposal. Madison was also one of the three men who wrote the Federalist Papers (the other two were Alexander Hamilton and John Jay), among the best known and most thoughtful discussions of government to be found in American history. He was the chief author of the Bill of Rights and for years had been a persistent advocate (along with Thomas Jefferson) for legislation to separate church and state, an idea that seemed radical to many in those times.

It says something of his architectural talent that, though he was the chief author of the Bill of Rights, he was not its strongest supporter. In fact Madison made a rare error with his prediction that the Federal government could never become strong enough to need the restraints the Bill imposed on it. The Constitution did not need a Bill of Rights, he thought, to keep the central government under control. In fact it was

---

73 Madison, while only in his twenties, also helped to draft a new constitution for Virginia, and the constitution was so successful that it became a model for other colonies.

Thomas Jefferson who had encouraged the Bill. He wanted additional assurance that the proposed central government could not become dangerously strong. Even so, once he had agreed to help with the task the industrious and determined Madison took on the laborious, gruelling, and in his words, "nauseous project" of writing a Bill that would be agreeable to all the parties.

This even-tempered and quiet disposition made him, on the surface, a different sort of Rational than the intense John Adams and the brooding Thomas Jefferson. Not that Madison was a cheery bon vivant or an open and friendly man, for all of his evenness of disposition. He was well known for his serious, dour manner and his archaic and solemn dress. His attire was old-fashioned, at least two decades out of date; he consistently dressed in black clothing, and he presented overall a rather strange and quite stuffy appearance. Madison looked, said one observer, like a schoolmaster going to a funeral. The attire of Rationals is rarely fashionable, for it is an exceptional Rational who pays enough attention to what others are wearing to emulate them. If he does so it is usually only to avoid bringing undue notice to himself. It is likely that Madison did not dress as he did to send messages about himself. It is unlikely that he gave the matter any thought at all.

Madison reminds us that it is dangerous to presume that even-tempered is the same as languid or lethargic. In debate he was powerful and energetic. He had many debates with the excitable Alexander Hamilton, also a very potent speaker, and Madison frequently walked away with the honors.[74] Madison was concerned, however, about becoming too carried away by the strength of his convictions. His concern was apparently rather well-founded. Thus at the Constitutional Convention he made a request of a friend who sat by him during the proceedings. If Madison became too excited while standing to address the assembly his friend was to tug on his coat tails. Later during a Convention debate Madison spoke out at great and fiery length; he was very excited indeed, but his friend did not signal him. After finally

---

[74] Hamilton, John Adams' "bastard brat of a Scotch peddler," was not given to gentle speech himself. He once said of Madison that "Mr. Madison, cooperating with Mr. Jefferson, is at the head of a faction...subversive of the principles of good government and dangerous to the Union, peace, and happiness of the country." (Quoted in *The American Presidents: Biographies of the Chief Executives*, 40.)

sitting down almost exhausted he asked his friend why the man had not tugged at his coat tails as he had agreed to. His friend, having been intimidated by Madison's passionate manner, replied with the simple and earnest comment, "I would rather have laid a finger on the lighting!"[75]

Even those otherwise soft-spoken Rationals can get carried away, then, when it comes to defending or promoting a prototype they have carefully and laboriously designed and built, or when a principle they argue for is attacked.

Later, when the Constitution and the country were established, Madison ran for Congress and easily won a seat. When Washington stepped down and John Adams became President, Madison, with some sense of relief, retired from Congress. But later the Alien and Sedition Acts were passed, and Madison wrote the Virginia Resolution which denounced them. He even ran again for public office, winning election to the Virginia state legislature, to give himself a stronger forum from which to fight the Acts. He served there from 1799 to 1800, and helped materially in bringing down the pernicious Alien and Sedition Acts.

Though he was the mastermind of the work of the Constitutional Convention, Madison still preferred the architect's role to that of the executive, the role of designer to than that of director. He was by disposition a scholar all his life; from the time he was a boy he loved to study and to learn, and by the time he was twelve he could already read and write Greek, Latin and Spanish. Whatever he studied he wanted to master, and the route to mastery was to understand the subject as thoroughly as possible. So compelling was his hunger for learning that as an undergraduate at Princeton he undertook the project of eliminating sleep from his daily life so he would not waste time sleeping which could be better spent studying. He attended Princeton, and there completed the four-year course in two years, though he exhausted himself in the process. His physical constitution was never strong thereafter, and some argue that his energetic pursuit of learning permanently impaired his health.

Madison always preferred the private and studious life to the life of a public figure. He was fascinated with his scholarly pursuits and he had

---

75 *Presidential Anecdotes*, 45.

no wish to take time away from them to deal with people. Even after he reached the presidency Madison could be found at his desk in the middle of the night, working on matters which were not yet complete or writing his notes to himself. Even as President he preferred to be placed as inconspicuously as possible at formal dinners, so he could avoid playing the host, or conversing with the guests. Like most Rationals, he found maintaining conversation about what seemed to be mere trivia quite difficult, and not in the least enjoyable.

Madison was extremely knowledgeable, but he was also quite willing to work long and assiduously to accomplish his purposes, as one might suspect, given his attempts to dispense with sleep as a young man. Rationals often show a trait that might be called "obsessive overlearning." We will find it in almost all Rationals, whether Organizers or Engineers, but in Madison's case the trait was so much in evidence as to be his most distinguishing characteristic. It was a happy circumstance for American history that Madison would become obsessed with preparations for drafting its Constitution. Of all the delegates attending the Constitutional Convention in Philadelphia, it was James Madison who arrived ten days early in order to prepare for it. Similarly, it was James Madison who devoted himself to taking exhaustive notes throughout the proceedings, and who then wrote them up, night after night. His notes covered more than six hundred painstakingly written pages, and we owe to Madison's exhausting private labor most of our knowledge of the events leading to the creation of our Constitution. ("Private" the work was; the notes were kept secret until after his death in 1836.)

James Madison was very studious and hard-working, then, and a very private man and a shy one as well. But like a later Engineer Rational, Abraham Lincoln, Madison did have a stock of amusing and earthy anecdotes. When he was among close friends he could relax enough to share them, and at such times he displayed the pleasant ability to poke gentle fun at himself. Engineer Rationals seem especially good at laughing at themselves, by the way. It seems to be the obverse of their penchant for severe self-criticism that they can look with an amused ruefulness upon their own multitudinous defects. With his friends Madison was a charming and witty conversationalist, though his comments tended to center chiefly on history, politics, and the technology of government.

Given Madison's shyness and all the work in which he was involved over the years, it is something of a wonder that he ever found the time and opportunity for marriage. When he did marry it was not until he was forty-three, though his marriage to Dolley Payne Todd, who was only twenty-five at the time, was a fortunate one. Dolley Madison, probably an Artisan, was a strikingly attractive and pleasant woman, energetic and of a sunny disposition, who had a genuine and unaffected liking for people of all sorts. She was already married and widowed when she and Madison met. Her husband and one of her two children had died in a yellow fever epidemic. In spite of the tragedy Dolley Todd's ebullience was irrepressible. Madison was instantly taken with her and after an intensively conducted four-month courtship James persuaded Dolley to marry him.

James did have some important help in his campaign for her hand. George and Martha Washington intervened on his behalf, strongly encouraging Dolley to make the match with the respected Virginia Congressman. Dolley recognized that James was not only brilliant, but that he was also a man of great personal stature in spite of his small physical size. She captured both Madison's aspects when she termed him, as so many did, "the great little Madison," and throughout their marriage she always referred to him as "Mr. Madison" or just "Madison." No other nicknames were ever used for him, by the way. Rationals, perhaps especially the more seclusive Rationals, only rarely receive intimate or affectionate nicknames. Even Madison's sobriquet "little Jemmy" was held in reserve to be brought out and dusted off for use only in Madison's political campaigns.

The Madisons' marriage of forty years was a remarkably happy one. Dolley Madison had no interest in politics or policies but she did go out of her way, enthusiastically and with great charm, to offer the best social backdrop possible for her husband's presidency. She was his cheerful supporter and his political fence-mender, not only to help him, but also because she very much enjoyed her life as First Lady. With her unfailing good nature and social grace, her good taste and her striking Paris gowns, she was herself enormously liked and admired. She was also the perfect complement to her soft-spoken Rational husband who even began to look a bit less like a man going to a funeral. He even took to doing a little dancing and obviously flourished in his relationship with his delightful wife.

Perhaps partially because of Dolley's popularity, James Madison had been re-elected for a second term of office in 1812. But it was not to be an easy presidency, for the times were very troubled for the United States. The British were struggling on land and at sea with Napoleon and were seeking advantage wherever they could. Their behavior was offensively high-handed, especially on the high seas, and Americans were becoming increasingly angry and vengeful. Spain, allied with Britain, was hardly friendly to the United States, and American relations with France were at best uncertain. The country was isolated politically even more than it was geographically, but the American public built up a warlike fury against the British. In fact the predominant sentiment was in favor of going to war against both Britain and Spain. Perhaps, some thought, the United States could push the British out of Canada and shove Spain out of the American west. Thus the flames of injured patriotism were made to burn even more invitingly by the prospect of adding great tracts of land to the nation's domain.

But Madison knew that the United States was still militarily weak and resisted the public war cry for some time. But his scholarship was much greater than his ability to maneuver against the immediate political pressures of the time. Here was an architect of government, a strategist, who had to act the part of the tactician, a part he was ill-equipped to play. He could not chart a clear course through the various practical and emotional cross currents surging at that moment, and eventually he gave in: war was declared against Great Britain. The initially popular but unnecessary and tragic conflict which became known as the War of 1812—and which was rather unjustly called "Mr. Madison's War" by some—became unpopular rather quickly. With only the occasional exception the United States military proved itself to be remarkably inept, and the poorly-prepared Americans managed to get themselves roundly defeated in most of their encounters with the better armed and more experienced British. Indeed the invaders seemed at times to roam the American coast with all the freedom of holiday vacationers.

The conflict had dragged on for two painful and pointless years when, in 1814, the British landed a force of soldiers in Maryland. The sizeable body of troops soon moved against Washington, now the nation's capital. The American force charged with defending the city failed miserably (and by now rather predictably) to impede the British force. After absorbing a few casualties in minor skirmishes the Americans turned tail and ran and in the panic which swept over Washington most of the capital's population that was in a position to do so left town as quickly as possible.

Dolley Madison was in Washington at the time, waiting for word from James about where to rendezvous with him. Word was late in coming, but, unlike most of those around her, she refused to panic and run. Instead she loaded a cart with some of the most valuable papers, paintings, books, silver and china to be found in the Executive Mansion. (The list of valuables included the famous Gilbert Stuart portrait of George Washington, the painting that most of us stared at as school children.) Not until she was reasonably satisfied with the collection of national treasures she had collected did she leave. She was one of the last important people to depart the nation's capital; the British soldiers arrived quite soon thereafter. In fact it is said that some of them helped themselves to her last meal, which was still warm when they arrived. The British occupied Washington briefly but found little reason for remaining; Washington had no military or economic value but was merely a political symbol. So they settled for burning down a considerable portion of the city and departed leisurely.

When the British departed James Madison returned to Washington, and Dolley Madison was ready to join him. As soon as her husband sent word that she could return she did so, and was thereby one of the last notables to leave and among the first to return. Word that she was coming back preceded her, and many people who had remained during the brief British occupation lined the streets to cheer her. Dolley Madison was now not merely an incredibly popular hostess and fashion-setter; she was a national heroine.

In spite of the terrific furor and the many political complications which surrounded the War of 1812, the outcome of this questionable conflict was trivial except for two things. One was that many men, British and American, died needlessly. The second was that Andrew Jackson won the Battle of New Orleans, one of the few American victories on land, and thereby became a national hero. The hell-for-leather Andy Jackson had unwittingly put himself in line for the presidency.

James Madison retired from national life at the end of his term of office in 1816. He live another twenty years, outliving the other Founding Fathers by five years. His retirement left him far more free to pursue a scholarly and contemplative life, to discourse with friends, and to enjoy the presence of his vivacious and charming wife, who survived him by some thirteen years.

Unfortunately, the Madisons' finances were not in good condition, and when James died Dolley was left destitute. In a rare act of respect and compassion, the Congress bought from her Madison's notes on the events transpiring at the Constitutional Convention. Dolley Madison continued for years to be the most brilliant star over the capital. In spite of her diminshed financial resources, her cheerful and gracious domination of Washington society finally extended over almost a half-century.

Bibliography

Alley, R (ed) 1985   *James Madison on Religious Liberty*
Brant, I 1961   *James Madison, Commander in Chief 1812-1836*
Brant,I 1968   *James Madison and American Nationalism*
Brant, I 1970   *The Fourth President: a Life of James Madison*
Burns, E 1938   *James Madison, Philosopher of the Constitution*
Gay, S 1898   *James Madison*
Hunt, G 1968   *The Life of James Madison*
Ketcham, R 1971   *James Madison: a Biography*
Kock, A 1964   *Jefferson and Madison: the Great Collaboration*
Koch, A 1966   *Advice to my Country*
McCoy, D 1989   *The Last of the Fathers: James Madison and the Republican Legacy*
Moore, V 1979   *The Madisons: a Biography*
Peterson, M (ed) 1974   *James Madison, a Biography in his Own Words*
Rutland, R 1987   *James Madison: the Founding Father*
Rutland, R 1990   *The Presidency of James Madison*
Shultz, H 1970   *James Madison*
Smith, J 1963   *The Plot to Steal Florida*

Abraham Lincoln

The mountain, the sea, the star

Engineer
Born: February 12, 1809
Died: April 15, 1865
presidency: 1861-1865

Of all the men ever to be President of the United States, Abraham Lincoln was perhaps the greatest, not just as President, but as a human being. As one studies the Presidents one cannot read about Lincoln without being struck with a sense of wonder: wonder at his grace and kindness, at his suffering and unyielding resolve, at his personal grandeur and finally at the simple humanity of this remarkable man. Lincoln was a towering figure. He stood six feet four inches tall and weighed a spare 180 pounds, and looked even taller and thinner when his lanky figure was topped with his famous stovepipe hat. It is fitting that Lincoln would be so imposing physically, for he is clearly one of the most towering of figures in our nation's history.

It is easy to be caught up in the quiet grandeur of the man, however, and we must avoid doing so here. Too much of him, including his temperament, is obscured if we gaze too raptly upon his greatness. Abraham Lincoln was a flesh-and-blood human being, and one must recognize his humanity in order finally to appreciate his greatness.

Like Thomas Jefferson, his Engineer Rational predecessor, Abraham Lincoln is a study in contrasts. He was slow to initiate conversation but always easy to be around. He guarded his private world with a profound reticence, yet people found his informal ways warm and open. He was unostentatious, unaffected, in manner, yet almost everyone who knew him called him "Mr. Lincoln." Even his wife addressed him, albeit affectionately, this way. He was a very serious and very earnest man. Yet he leavened his approach to matters both light and weighty with a wonderful sense of humor. He was beloved of many but there were few who could claim to be part of his inner circle and perhaps no one who was his confidant. He was a brilliant man whose speech was deceptively simple and earthy. He was a mild-mannered backwoods politician who had one of the shrewdest minds ever to grace American politics.

Some were fooled by his easygoing, earthy graciousness. They thought he was a rather simple creature whose plain and simple speech betrayed a plain and simple mind. They were greatly mistaken: Abraham Lincoln was always a canny, calculating Rational, cool and complex by nature. He was thoughtful about the most mundane issues, and earnestly and exhaustively studious about the important ones. Lincoln always took his time arriving at decisions. He was an Engineer Rational, after all, and premature judgment was abhorrent to him.

Lincoln apparently became interested rather early in politics. Naturally he brought the same thoughtful attention to his own political ambitions and behavior that he brought to everything else. He studied assiduously the impact of every move he made, both the moves that were successful and the moves that failed. When he spoke to people he tuned in as keenly as possible to their reactions and he constantly experimented with ways of speaking persuasively. For example the homely, folksy style was already rather natural to him, but he developed it quite deliberately and used it very effectively. It made a sharp and welcome contrast to the aristocratic and self-important posturing of many of his legal and political contemporaries. Similarly, he was well known for poking fun at himself and even this, though it too was natural to him, was in part a product of his strategy.

He had an ability to chat and joke with almost anyone with a genuine warmth that many tried to imitate but few could carry off. No matter how he was provoked Lincoln seemed able to stay in the role he had developed for himself without the slightest appearance of labor or artifice. Overall he recognized his strengths and weaknesses, and he used his knowledge to knit a public image which combined simplicity and honesty and an analytic brilliance that was at once studied and natural. In principle his accomplishment is not difficult to understand. He had observed and managed himself carefully, and what he presented himself to be was in fact who he was, though now sharpened and trained to fit the political goals he had set for himself.

> He quite certainly gave the most earnest and exhaustive study to every move he made. His calculations were pondered and tried in anticipation; he consulted everyone who could give him help; he never neglected a possibility; he worked and strained and, if necessary, bargained and begged for every grain.[76]

It is not unusual at all for the Rational to develop a social role that he dons like a piece of clothing when interacting with others. This is especially true of the Engineers. They, like the Organizers, tend to be preoccupied from an early age with abstractions of various kinds—theories, schematics, principles, categories—so that social development tends to lag and customary social pastimes and manners are not easily mastered. Even if they are acquired these customary social patterns are enacted awkwardly and self-consciously even while they are becoming perfectly natural to people of other temperaments. Youthful Rationals are constrained to devise a social role for themselves so they won't be seen as having absolutely no social grace. If such a self-constructed role doesn't enable them to fit smoothly into the social swim, it at least rescues them from the role of hopeless misfit. They gradually become seen as a bit odd but acceptable. Lincoln's political development reminds one very much of this deliberate "self" construction.

---

76 *How They Became President*, 190.

None of this should suggest that Lincoln was a mere showman or a shallow or callous fraud. He was an ambitious man of course, and cool, deliberate, and far-sighted in the way he advanced his ambitions. But his ambition never (so far as research reveals) led him to act dishonestly or in a way which demeaned or took unfair advantage of others. In fact, in spite of his brilliance even as a young lawyer Lincoln "did not do well with causes in which he did not believe, or which seemed to him to have little merit."[77] Even Rexford Tugwell, a writer who seldom finds virtue in our Presidents, wrote of Lincoln that through some incomprehensible process "...he came out in the end, on the issues most difficult for all politicians of his time, at solutions not only expedient but right—so right that, once started, they seemed to have the persuasive power of the simplest axiom."[78] It does not seem too much to claim that a determined, knowledgeable person of unbendable integrity who happened also to possess great strategic brilliance might accomplish just this.

Nor did Lincoln try to adopt and develop the slick demagoguery and oratorical devices so often found in politicians of the day. These tricks, more interesting to the Artisan, were of no interest to him. His speaking was instead a slow, deliberate monotone, his voice was high-pitched, and his speeches simple and concise. No bombast, no flowers, and no redundancy. His famous Gettysburg Address is a marvelous example of his ability to bring into sharp focus what is most central, as were his speeches during the famous debates with Stephen A. Douglas in 1854 about the future place of slavery in the United States. These are splendid examples of carefully crafted eloquence. They were marked by a disarming and persuasive simplicity that masked the painfully thorough analysis Lincoln had given the issues. What the listener hears comes forth with Tugwell's "persuasive power of the simplest axiom."

Of course Lincoln's Rational character wasn't confined merely to the world of politics. As a young man he was fascinated with technology of all sorts. He tried to invent a steam-driven plow and he developed and patented a design for riverboat flotation chambers. He studied patents on firearms, and even while President he was known to dismantle his son Tad's mechanical toys in order to understand their workings better.

---

77 *The American Presidents*, 140.
78 *How They Became President*, 191-192.

In spite of his remarkable reasoning powers, and as is often the case with the Engineers, his everyday habits could be the despair of those who worked with him. The tall stovepipe hat which Lincoln made famous, riding so obviously above his already tall frame, was not intended only to keep his head warm. It was also his traveling filing cabinet. In it were kept important notes and letters and daily reminders—those that hadn't been lost on his desk. Of course there was always the danger that some item of greater or lesser importance would be lost in his somewhat haphazard filing system. In 1859, for example, he was cleaning out a desk he had used for some years. In one drawer he discovered some seeds, relics of his Congressional days. The seeds had been put there long ago and forgotten, and finally had begun to sprout in the dirt that had gradually accumulated in one corner.[79]

His management style might seem unsystematic, his dress careless, and his style almost too plain and informal. But his remarkable analytic skills could never be ignored; he could find his way to the very heart of any matter and lift it out for all to see. Even the jokes and anecdotes for which he was famous were characterized by the way they focused unerringly and powerfully on a point he wanted to make. There were even times when he didn't need to use speech at all to make his point for he did not let his gift for language run away with him. He once commented to a friend that it was "better to remain silent and let people suspect you are a fool than to open your mouth and remove all doubt." On another occasion, while he was still a young lawyer, two farmers approached him about a dispute over the boundary between their farms. Lincoln warned them that going to court would cost them enormously both in court costs and in ill-will that might persist for generations. The farmers nevertheless stubbornly refused to see reason. Then to their amazement young lawyer Lincoln locked them together in his office and, without another word, went off to lunch. When they realized what Lincoln had done the two farmers started to laugh. Lawyer Lincoln returned later to find that the two farmers had settled the matter amicably.

Lincoln was once challenged to a duel by a certain James Shields. Since Shields was the challenger Lincoln was entitled to choose the

---

79 *The Hero in America*, 239.

weapon the duelists would use. After some thought he chose the ancient long sword, a huge weapon some six feet in length suited best to medieval knights and requiring considerable strength to wield. Shields took a look at the six foot four inch Lincoln with his long arms swinging that awe-inspiring weapon and hastily reconsidered his position. He called off the duel and he and Lincoln had no trouble working out a mutually satisfactory compromise.[80]

As is often the case with Rationals, Lincoln was largely oblivious to the conventions and formalities that attend social station. He could pay attention when he had to; witness the matter of the duel. But ordinarily these conventions and formalities and the usual privileges of rank or status meant little to him. Even when he was President he seemed genuinely uncomfortable with privilege and with pomp (and pomposity) of any kind. Though he valued the powers of the presidency, it was chiefly because of what they might allow him to accomplish. Otherwise he had no interest in rank and position and showed little patience with those who were preoccupied with such things. Even his physical appearance,[81] his great height, his dusty shoes, his poorly-fitting clothes, especially the famous stovepipe hat, which became something of a trademark, were of little concern to him except to the degree that he fashioned them into his political image.

Lincoln is considered a great President, but greatness is most assuredly not a matter of temperament. Greatness is not found in one's style or habits. It is found in the way one's style and habits are used to face up to difficult situations and trying circumstances. Lincoln was both a skillful politician and among the most honest of our political leaders, and his career is noteworthy for his resistance to dishonest political

---

80 His ingenious turn of mind is obvious in many such anecdotes, which express the quintessential Lincoln: the startling twist, the softening humor, applied powerfully but with no attempt to harm. In the days when dueling was legal, many Artisans practiced with sword and pistol for endless hours, and took advantage of every opportunity to show their fearlessness and skillfulness by duelling. Many Guardians, Rationals, and Idealists, forced to "protect their honor," fell easy victim to duel-hungry virtuosos; it was rarely that anyone could use the code to outwit his opponent as did Lincoln in this episode.

81 His slightly peculiar physical appearance may not have been the result of mere sartorial neglect. It has been speculated that Lincoln was afflicted with "Marfan's syndrome," a rare genetic disorder which includes "heart and eye problems, poor skeletal growth, and spidery, somewhat uncoordinated legs" from all of which, it is claimed, Lincoln suffered. See *Presidential Courage*, 91.

practice. His appeals were to the intelligence of the people rather than to their ignorance, to the generosity of the electorate rather than its venality. In spite of the extraordinary trials to which he was put he never wavered in these matters. But one can imagine that another Rational, struggling with the same circumstances, might have been less gracious and high-minded. We need only recall the Adamses for examples of lofty vision gone astray.

Lincoln's use of anecdotes and jokes tells us something of his profound understanding of and compassion for other people. He used parables in the way that religious teachers have always used them: to make a point about an important issue in a way that was compact, powerful, almost irresistible in its impact. He used his stories to cut to the heart of an issue, to sidestep polemic and to avoid tortuous logical excursions. He told jokes to soften a blow, to gentle an angry man, to brighten a saddened mother, even to assuage his own anger or sadness. As he recovered from highly infectious smallpox, for example, the much badgered President Lincoln announced how pleased he was that finally he had something he could give to everybody.

If we are to take Lincoln's measure we must finally observe him in the context of those twin horrors, slavery and the Civil War. It seems undeniable that in another time and place Lincoln would have been less noted by history. As it happened, Abraham Lincoln was caught at the nexus of the disarray of his own political party, the frightening, decades-long struggle over the question of slavery, and finally the terrible holocaust of the Civil War. The United States almost died as a nation then, and Lincoln was one of the most important factors in keeping the still-young nation alive. It is a part of what makes him magnificent that these crises strengthened rather than weakened him, brought forth his resolve and his compassion rather than hopelessness or vengefulness. During the four year agony of the conflict he never uttered a vindictive word against the people of the South, and even as the Union armies were winning their last victories he proposed to pay the South handsomely for the freedom of its slaves. During the darkest days of the conflict, in the face of an almost unbroken string of military defeats and the persistent ineptitude of his general staff, he told an acquaintance, "I expect to maintain this contest until successful, or til I die."[82]

---

82 Keirsey in *Please Understand Me*, erred in saying that Lincoln was a Guardian. Lincoln's frequent fits of depression during the war mislead the author. All four types

Lincoln was anxious above all to weld the country together again, not by capturing enemy cities, but by capturing the thoughts and the feelings of the people of the southern states. He was early convinced that the Union absolutely must be preserved, no matter what the cost. Its survival was important not only for the people of this country, he believed, but for the people of all nations. He believed strongly that the United States provided a model of a new, viable and excellent form of democratic government. He was very concerned that its collapse would discourage other countries from engaging in similar political experiments. Thus preservation of the Union was not important only for the American continent, said Lincoln; it mattered for the world.

> This issue embraces more than the fate of these United States. It presents to the whole family of man, the question, whether a constitutional republic, or a democracy...can or cannot, maintain its territorial integrity, against its own domestic foes.[83]

The evolution of Lincoln's position about slavery, though not well documented by Lincoln himself, shows the struggle he had with his own cultural heritage. He was raised in Kentucky where slavery was an accepted part of his early life. The moral problems slavery posed were no more pressing for him as a child than were the political dilemmas arising from its existence. Only after a long period of painful introspection did Lincoln embrace the position which now seems so logical, that blacks had the same entitlement as whites and that these entitlements must be granted to them as soon as possible. Lincoln also came finally to the recognition that slavery was, in its very nature, immoral, and that one could never rationally claim otherwise.

Lincoln finally declared slavery "an unqualified evil to the negro, the white man, and the State" whose existence made plausible the charge that the United States was a government of hypocrites.[84] Yet, he continued, the abolitionists with their strident calls for the destruction of slavery only endangered the Union and made worse the evils of slavery. Lincoln himself could offer no practical plan for the removal of this evil, he confessed; he could only counsel patience, assuming that slavery would eventually die out because of its moral and economic unfitness.

---

of personality get depressed on occasion, but only the Guardians can be said to *use* their depression to manage their relationships with others.

83 *The Collected Works of Abraham Lincoln*, IV, 439,426, cited in *Battle Cry of Freedom: The Civil War Era*

84 He did this during the Lincoln-Douglas debates in October of 1854.

"Just as an afflicted man hides away a wen or a cancer, which he dares not cut out at once, lest he bleed to death; with the promise, nevertheless, that the cutting may begin at the end of a given time," so would the nation eventually rid itself of slavery.[85] Thus even in dealing with this "unqualified evil" Lincoln attempted the path of reason and moderation. Typical of his Engineer Rational nature, he concluded by presenting his careful analysis of the alternatives he saw and noting that none of them seemed to promise any hope of genuine satisfaction for the slaves, their slave holders, or the nation.

Lincoln clearly wanted to find a peaceful solution to the issue of slavery. But he found, as had his predecessors, that none was available. In spite of all his painful analysis, in spite of his deep commitment to the American experiment in government, despite his agonies over the problem of slavery, he could find no course of action which would resolve both the moral and the political issues. He declared with remarkable forthrightness that "I surely will not blame [the southern slave holders] for not doing what I should not know how to do myself. If all earthly power were given me, I should not know what to do, as to the existing institution."

His declaration was politically effective but it was no mere polemic; Lincoln spoke the simple and painful truth. Indeed, it would not have been in keeping with his Rational character to say or even imply that he knew how to do something when in fact he did not. Even when a Rational such as Lincoln suspects a solution is at hand he will doubt it until it proves itself in action; indeed, the Rationals are more likely to express doubt about possible solutions, even their own, than is any other temperament. But this sort of disclosure of doubt is always politically risky, and Lincoln's straightforward statement led one newspaper to characterize him as "poor Lincoln, honest, hesitating, drifting, feeble-minded Lincoln: patriotic buffoon."[86]

The South, of course, finally took matters into its own hands. Secession and war made the emancipation of slaves, if not universally welcomed, at least politically possible. It must have been with a puzzling mixture of deep sadness over the circumstances and deep relief

---

85 This passage is also from the Lincoln-Douglas debates. Its accuracy may be judged by the fact that in 1861 only three countries in the Western Hemisphere still maintained slavery: Cuba, Brazil, and the United States.

86 *The Hero in America*, 243.

at the resolution of his own uncertainty that this Engineer Rational found the slave owners themselves forcing a course of action which would result in the abolition of slavery. It was an unreasonable course for the South to take, but these were terribly unreasonable times. In fact Lincoln's election was the straw that broke the back of Southern opposition to secession. His moderation and his Northern roots were too much for the ardent and arrogant Southerners; thus the event which led most directly to secession was Abraham Lincoln's victory in the election of 1860.

So, it appeared, the Union was broken, and the United States was reduced to little more than half its former size and strength, and another, antagonistic country snarling restlessly at its belly.

Lincoln the Engineer Rational might have been expected to restrain his use of the powers of government. In fact he was predisposed to restrain himself, just as the Engineer Jefferson was. But when he was faced with Southern secession he acted boldly and vigorously. When the crisis of the Civil War finally broke, when the American experiment was mortally threatened, the non-directive Rational Lincoln became ceaselessly active and persistently commanding. There is no indication that he ever enjoyed this more directive style but, like the Engineer Jefferson before him, the issues he faced were immense and so he "stretched the Constitution till it cracked" in pursuit of the nation's well-being. Lincoln saw the alternative to this presumption of power the likelihood of the United States collapsing. In the face of this danger, he later said, the President *must* act to preserve the Nation, whether or not the laws of the land sanctioned his actions. To the Rational, of course, rules are only rules, and if they are likely to hinder fatally, then they must be disregarded. And the Union *must* be preserved, and no rule would prevent him from acting to preserve it.

Congress was on its break and would be slow to reconvene, and Lincoln needed to act fast. He also needed the authority to act, so with the Congress recessed he immediately assumed the powers of the commander-in-chief of the nation's military. This was an ill-defined set of powers conferred on the President by the Constitution, which Lincoln claimed gave him special executive powers not otherwise available to a President. Using these "war powers," as he called them, he did not wait for the Congress to reconvene (in fact he acted to postpone the event) but instead proceeded to create a national army out of the state militias, as well as calling a further 40,000 volunteers into military service, a number which seemed enormous at the time. He declared a blockade of Southern ports, he spent Treasury funds for purposes which had not been properly authorized by the Congress, he suspended habeas corpus, which meant that he could detain thousands of suspected Southern sympathizers without showing legal cause, he coerced the Supreme Court, and in other respects, said his critics, he behaved as if the Constitution did not exist.

Here was no thoughtful, nondirective Engineer Rational debating "on the one hand, on the other hand." Here was the unavoidable call to action, and here one sees clearly the willingness of the Rational to circumvent rules, regulations, and precedents in the interest of effective action. Here too, of course, we see in Lincoln's assumption of the presidential "war powers" at least the vague appearance of staying within the recognized rules, regulations, and precedents.

There are many stories told of Lincoln's intercession on behalf of soldiers and their families during the war. Many soldiers were conscripted who simply could not understand the concept of desertion, for instance. When there was a family emergency or when the crops needed to be harvested, they would merely walk away from the army to go do the work that they always did on such occasions. Of course they were usually caught and not a few were brought before courts martial and sentenced to die. Many mothers and wives and sisters came to Lincoln about a son or husband or brother caught in such predicaments. Our Presidents were far more accessible then, and Lincoln especially accessible, and many of these women came away from their meeting with the President holding a pardon, granted by Lincoln on only the strength of their version of the story—and their tears. He could instantly and without a thought dismiss rules and regulations if they did not lead to desirable results, or if they impeded worthy results, whether the issue was saving a nation, saving time, or saving a mother's child.

He was of course vigorously criticized for his high-handed and unruly behavior by some of the press, other politicians, and disgruntled citizens, but he seemed remarkably unaffected by the criticism. Again, the Rationals recognize no one's right to criticize them, not even their superiors, unless the Rationals themselves decide to grant them license to do so. Lincoln would be less affected by criticism simply because of this, but it is likely that his own long-range concern for the nation and the place of the great national experiment on the world stage were also important. These concerns were so enormous that personal concerns are likely to disappear in their presence. Lincoln had the Rational's long-range view and part of his personal grandeur may be found in the degree to which he was gripped by the grandeur of his own vision for the nation and the world.

Perhaps his equanimity can also be accounted for by his trust in the final rationality of the human mind. Lincoln believed that ideas, not passions, were the lifeblood of the mind, and that over the long haul ideas would endure while the passions of the moment would pass away. "The [old] South is to be destroyed and replaced by new propositions and ideas," he once said. "New propositions and ideas," his natural Rational's hope: new ideas, new ways of thinking, new foundations for rationally organizing life in place of "clarion calls" or "demands" or polemics of the passions.[87]

And so he persisted throughout the years of war, attending only to what was expedient for the good of the country as a whole—which finally must include the rebellious southern states—and for his own political success, which he saw, quite accurately, as necessary for the country. Through all the turmoil he showed an absence of bitterness and malice toward his angry and often vicious detractors which is unmatched by any other American President. "If the end brings me out all right what is said against me won't amount to anything" he once told his secretary, John G. Nicolay. "If the end brings me out wrong, ten angels swearing I was right would make no difference."[88]

The ends he had in mind were, first, the preservation of the Union, and then, the abolition of slavery. It seems something of a miracle that Lincoln managed to bring the Civil War to a successful conclusion, return the Southern states to the Union, and emancipate the slaves. He managed all this while being violently vilified, hated by many, a politician whose political offices had been only three: Postmaster in

---

87 *Battle Cry of Freedom*, 558.

88 *The Hero in America*, 243. The Rational's relative invulnerability to criticism is again evident here. He knew what he wanted; he knew how he intended to get it; and he trusted his own thinking about the matter. Little else mattered.

New Salem, Illinois, Member, of the Illinois General Assembly, and a Member of the U. S. House of Representatives.

Abraham Lincoln has been written of and admired and praised endlessly since his death in 1865. His wife, Mary Todd Lincoln on the other hand, has fared far less well in the history books. She has been variously characterized as a madwoman, a shrew, a liar, and cheat. Some have it that she was a poor wife to Lincoln and an unwelcome burden to him, and Lincoln's one-time law partner William Herndon maintained that Lincoln's one true love was Ann Rutledge. Rutledge died when she and Lincoln were still young, and Herndon would have us believe that Lincoln's marriage to Mary Todd was an unfortunate mistake. Rutledge's death from malaria means that we can never know what the real facts were or what would have happened between her and Lincoln had she lived. Lincoln is also said later to have proposed marriage to a Mary Owen who, the story goes, promptly turned him down. Lincoln lacked those little things, those personal niceties, Mary Owen said, "which make up the chain of a woman's happiness."[89] In the case of Lincoln the abstracted Rational she was in certain respects unquestionably correct.

The facts seem to be less dramatic and these renditions of the Lincolns' relationship do not do justice to it or to Mary Todd Lincoln. William Herndon, an Artisan, and Mary Lincoln, probably an Idealist, had taken a dislike to each other years before Abraham Lincoln's death. Herndon's reports about the Lincolns' marriage came only after Lincoln's death and are highly suspect assaults upon the largely defenseless and somewhat unpopular widow. Less jaundiced reports comment that the young Mary Todd, raised as a traditional southern belle, was "a girl with everything that her peers envied: liveliness, charm, good taste, and if not beauty at least a special vivaciousness that made her seem pretty and pert."[90]

Even in their later years, when youth was no longer a natural ally, Abraham and Mary Lincoln seemed to love each other quietly and strongly and to share a great love for their four children. He was a calm, affectionate, gentle husband and a rather laissez-faire father. Tad, their

89 *World Almanac of Presidential Facts*, 76.
90 *Presidential Courage*, 80-81.

youngest son, was thought to be spoiled and was known by some in the White House as "the little tyrant." Lincoln loved the boy a great deal and did nothing to curb his rambunctious "tyranny." In this he resembled most Engineer Rational fathers, who tend to adhere to a hands-off policy in raising their children. He would step in only when he decided it was absolutely necessary, and such a decision could be rather long in coming. (The wives of Engineer Rationals will at times feel quite frustrated with their slowness to act, though their is no note taken of this in Mary Lincoln's case.)

Mary Lincoln was a person of a much more dramatic bent than her husband. She was after all an outgoing and energetic Idealist and an effusively doting mother. Her extravagant devotion to her children did little to endear her to others, and she had an inclination to "put on airs." She wanted, for instance, to be addressed not as "Mrs. Lincoln" but as "Madame President," and this sort of thing made her more difficult for many people to accept. Lincoln apparently looked with tolerant fondness on most of her behavior. In fact the assertion that he did not love her or that he found her merely a burden just doesn't seem to correspond with what was directly observed by those who knew the Lincolns.

This is not to deny that Mary Lincoln could be difficult to get along with; she could be quite difficult. Along with her penchant for protesting vigorously about others' behavior, she also had a penchant for spending remarkably large sums of money on herself and on the White House. Over time she incurred large debts with various Washington merchants that she was neither very prompt nor very gracious about repaying.

As time passed she struggled more and more to maintain herself, but with less and less success. It was not just her financial well-being that was at risk; it was also her emotional well being. Gradually she became more temperamental, more given to anger, even explosively angry on occasion, and at times terribly jealous of attentions paid by other women to her husband; some might say she was delusional about the matter. She worsened matters for herself and her husband by becoming more outspokenly and heedlessly caustic with others until she had finally alienated herself from almost everyone except her own family. Why her behavior should have become so extreme has never been made clear. Some have suggested that her eventual emotional disarray was the result of general paresis (though there is no evidence for this). Others consider that it was the natural consequence of a difficult life that finally overwhelmed this rather delicately-balanced woman.

In fact Mary Todd's life had never been especially easy. Her mother had died when she was only six. Her father remarried a year later and Mary and her sisters quickly decided that they hated the new stepmother. For her part, the rather supercilious stepmother eventually returned the favor. So things continued, and Mary Todd later summarized her childhood quite simply as "desolate." Though her life greatly improved after she met and married Lincoln, her young husband was busy and distracted in the fashion of Rationals everywhere (he was a surveyor, postmaster, and law student), and was therefore often not with her the way his more outgoing wife would have liked. Their life together remained difficult for various reasons, and only sporadically could Mary Lincoln claim to be genuinely content. She found that finances were a persistent problem, her husband's busy schedule and inevitable preoccupations left her feeling restless and ignored, and she was demeaned by the tightly-knit society of Washington D. C. and deprived (at least in her opinion) of the recognition due the President's wife.

To add to her difficulties, one of their sons, Willie, died of typhoid in 1862. Three years later her husband was murdered as she sat next to him in Ford Theater. Abraham Lincoln was shot in the head on April 14, 1865 by John Wilkes Booth. He was taken to a hotel across the street from the theater, but he died an hour later, without regaining consciousness.

The years still remaining to Mary Lincoln after his death were difficult and at times terribly painful. Her beloved Tad died six years after her husband. He was only eighteen. She never recovered from the effects of multiple stresses and tragedies; so erratic did her behavior become that her remaining son, Robert, eventually had her committed to a mental hospital.[91] She brought suit and had a competency hearing (the record of which reads rather like a criminal proceeding). She won and was released from the hospital and used the limited funds she could gather together to travel in Europe. Even there, however, she was a target for sometimes vicious gossip. Most of her remaining years were spent traveling, but her efforts to regain her peace of mind were apparently unsuccessful. She died in 1882, seventeen lonely and painful years after her husband's assassination.

---

91 Robert Todd Lincoln later became Secretary of War under President Garfield.

She was widowed by the fierce struggle over slavery and states' rights just as surely as were tens of thousands of other American women. Though it was terrible in its own right, her tragedy has found its way into history only because of the greatness of her husband. Since Abraham Lincoln's death, thousands, perhaps millions of words have been spoken and written about him. Yet, it would appear,

> there is no new thing to be said about Lincoln. There is no new thing to be said of the mountains, or of the sea, or of the stars... But to the mountains and sea and stars men turn forever in unwearied homage. And thus with Lincoln. For he was a mountain in grandeur of soul, he was a sea in deep undervoice of mystic loneliness, he was a star in steadfast purity of purpose and service. And he abides.[92]

Bibliography

Baringer, W 1949   *Lincoln's Vandalia, a Pioneer Portrait*
Barton, W 1928   *Abraham Lincoln and Walt Whitman*
Barton, W 1931   *Abraham Lincoln, American*
Binns, H 1927   *The Life of Abraham Lincoln*
Bollinger, J 1944   *Lincoln, Statesman and Logician*
Brooks, E 1896   *The True Story of Abraham Lincoln, the American*
Brown, F 1913   *The Every-Day Life of Abraham Lincoln*
Dodge, G 1965   *Personal Recollections of President Lincoln, General Grant, and General Sherman*
Donald, D 1956   *Lincoln Reconsidered: Essays on the Civil War Era*
Eggleston, P 1922   *Lincoln in New England*
Frank, J 1961   *Lincoln as a Lawyer*
Gore, J 1921   *The Boyhood of Abraham Lincoln*
Grierson, F 1948   *The Valley of Shadows*
Halsted, M 1960   *Fire the Salute! Abe Lincoln is Nominated*
Hertz, E 1926   *Great Emancipator a Politician and Proud of it*
Hertz, E 1986   *Lincoln Talks: An Oral Biography*
Lincoln, A 1952-55   *The Collected Works of Abraham Lincoln*
Nicolay, J 1914   *Abraham Lincoln: a History*
Ostenorf, L 1959   *Mr. Lincoln Came to Dayton*
Sandburg, C 1954   *Abraham Lincoln; The Prairie Years & the War Years*
Shutes, M 1957   *Lincoln's Emotional Life*
Slicer, T 1909   *From Poet to Premier: Poe, Lincoln, Holmes, Darwin, Tennyson, Gladstone*

---

92 Quoted in *Abraham Lincoln; The Prairie Years and the War Years*, viii.

A Backward Glance

The Organizers John Adams and John Quincy Adams were both *resolute strategists*. They were naturally preoccupied with the overall picture and the long haul, and each assumed that those who were not were misguided certainly, and fools probably. When in 1798 it appeared that the whole nation had roused itself to war against France, John Adams faced down almost the entire nation, resisted a declaration of war, and carefully arranged matters so that an advantageous peace could be wrought. His son, John Quincy Adams, was a chip off the old block, but managed to be even more high handed and strong-minded than his father. His strong-willed style is especially evident in the Monroe Doctrine, which Adams largely created, and which aggressively declared the political affairs of all the Americas out of bounds to the rest of the world—other than the United States. (His support for Jackson's invasion of Florida was another mark of this pragmatic willfulness.)

Ulysses Grant, Herbert Hoover, and Dwight Eisenhower were what we might call the *executor organizers*. They were men all well-experienced in exercising the authority of high command, and had demonstrated their skill at marshalling and wielding vast forces, whether of men or of materiel. None of them was politically minded and each in his own way eschewed the powers that the electorate urged them to use. They were relatively inactive, and were in fact criticized by some for their passivity. Their passivity was the result both of their disinterest in politics and of seeing their presidencies more in terms of the 19th century tradition of the executive President, than in terms of the 20th century tradition of policy leadership. The apparent passivity of the executor Presidents was a principled inactivity: each man sought to guard the division of powers the framers of the Constitution worked so carefully to ensure.

Thomas Jefferson, James Madison, and Abraham Lincoln were the *architectural engineers*, each constructing instruments of enormous value to the nation. Jefferson and Madison were among the chief architects of national unity, while Lincoln, with all the force he could command, restored the unity of the sundered nation. Though they did not pursue power for its own sake, these pragmatists, when the purpose seemed great enough, could wield power with surgical precision. The Constitution, the Louisiana Purchase, and the reunification of the United States, along with Polk's conquests, are among the most significant achievements of any American President.

Chapter Five

THE IDEALISTS

"Some leader must appear who can put into words the inspiration of belief in the dignity of man and the value of the human individual."

There have been no Idealist Presidents. Why this should be so is open to many explanations, of which the most likely concerns the matter of power. The political arena is above all a place of power, and Idealists find the pursuit of power inimical to what they see as their mission in life: personal fulfillment and the fulfillment of persons. When they see power they do not covet it, when they have the opportunity they do not seek it, when it is offered them they will not accept it. Even so, we will shortly consider at length two very famous Idealists whose presence and whose work (in the case of the Idealist it is often hard to separate the two) were quite effective and at times almost messianic. We will thereby complete the map of temperament, and this should highlight more completely the characters of those men who have been American Presidents.

In common usage the word "idealist" indicates a person who cherishes noble aims and lofty precepts. The idealist is believed to understand and value things as they could be rather than simply as they are, who naturally focuses more on the potential than the actual, on *becoming*, to which *being* is only a bridge.

In this respect, as in all other facets of temperament, the Idealists are the opposites of the Artisans. By far the most important opposition of the Idealists and Artisans is in what they stand willing and able to do, that is, in their values and abilities. Where Artisans are prepared to and want to make artistic changes in concrete things, Idealists are prepared to and want to assist individual human beings in the unfolding of their potential character. Where Artisans have an instrumental agenda, Idealists have a personal agenda. Where Artisans are prone to exploit, Idealists are prone to help. While Artisans fashion inanimate actualities, Idealists inspire animate possibilities. Artisans harmonize thing to thing, Idealists self to self.

On the other hand, the Idealists and the Guardians are much alike in one essential way: both are *moralizing* characters. Each looks to approval, permission to legitimize their actions before they look for utility. But while the Guardian looks to the community and its institutions, its laws and religions and traditions for authorization, the Idealist looks for moral sanction in a very different place. The Idealist's moral sanctions come from the personal and individual rather than the social and institutional. The voice within, the *spirit* of the rule rather than its *letter*; the voice of another unique person, rather than the voice of social authority; one's understanding of the ethical life, not one's understanding of regulatory strictures: it is to these that the Idealist turns for moral sanction.

Idealists also have a special talent for *personalizing,* for nurturing and promoting individual growth. That is to say, they are naturally able at coaching, counseling, and conciliating others, at helping people uncover what is hidden to them about themselves. Their special talents are most obvious when they are in a relationship in which they are *helping* someone who in their view needs it. Relationships that involve teaching or healing are clear instances, and so Idealists are likely to seek out occupations in which there are such opportunities for teaching or healing. They are often found in occupations that involve coaching and counseling those seeking guidance; conciliating the despondent and despairing; and helping people realize their latent possibilities. This often means the mental health professions, where they tend to be the most "humanistic" of mental health workers, those most interested in "growth" models of counseling and psychotherapy rather than the more usual corrective and remedial models. The "human potential movement" of which the encounter groups were a manifestation, was chiefly the creation of people like Carl Rogers, Eric Fromm, and Abraham Maslow, all of whom were Idealists. In its time it served to inspire interest in the pursuit of personal potential. Now it has largely passed away except in the world of the Idealist, who has always pursued its goals and will doubtless continue to do so.[1]

Their talent for individualizing and personalizing shows up so early in the life of many Idealists that we may presume they're born that way: born to become enthusiastic and capable individualizers. As they grow and begin to work with others—client, pupil, patient—they maintain constant rapport with the other's experience. They empathize: they follow each expression of that person; they become intuitively engaged and involved. It is this deep rapport with others that makes them extraordinary mentors and outstanding personal advocates.

The Idealists have an overriding concern with what they sometimes call "the Self." It is not that they are self-centered, self-serving, or self-ish, mind you; they focus on the Self of others as surely as on their own. But whether their own or another's, they are *centered* on the Self, focused on it, concentrated on it, committed to it. And the Self upon which they focus is not like the self that non-Idealists imagine when they use the word; the Idealist's Self has a capital "S." It is a *part* of the Idealist, not all of him or her. It is not merely a label that reminds us of ourselves, but it is a special part or aspect of the person. It is a kind of super-self, an inner self, a core of being, perhaps not unlike the "soul" or "spirit" of old. Idealists naturally seek to develop this extraordinarily important inner core of being, and find great satisfaction in being midwife to its development in others.[2]

Though Idealists live by the rules, their rules are ethical rather than regulatory. Violation of ethical rules injures what may be called the "ethos of the Self." That is, when some action violates a person's "soul" or "spirit," then that act is unethical; any act that thwarts or blocks the spiritual evolution of the person, that keeps a person from "becoming,"

---

1 The most famous existentialists, Buber, Kierkegaard, Heidegger, Merleau-Ponty, and Sartre, were all Idealists. It was their essays on being and becoming that gave rise to the post-war encounter group movement, which movement came to full fruition in the 1960s. Abraham Maslow's *Motivation and Personality* presented his seminal thesis concerning the hierarchy of motives, in which the motive for self-actualization was held to be the highest aim of mankind.

2 Alfred Adler called it the "Virtual Self," Carl Jung called it the "Archetypal Self," while Sigmund Freud referred to it as the "Superego," and Carl Rogers as the "Inner Self." Each in his own way regarded the self as part and therefore not all of the person.

is evil. Conversely, the good is that which enables growth. Good facilitates the realization of Self, evil forestalls it. In this absorption in the transcendent in human beings, the Idealists are inherently transcendentalists; the rest of us are earthbound physicalists. In a word, the Idealists are metaphysicians, one and all.

Idealists have a powerful and ever-present conscience which warns them whenever they are about to do injury to their own or another's becoming. In fact, whether it be a matter of the Soul or Self, or of one's more mundane life, the Idealists have a fierce aversion to cruelty and exploitation. It matters not whether the cruelty or exploitation is against them or against others; when they witness it they are deeply troubled and cry out against it.

As the preceding intimates, the Idealists are the most benevolent of all the types. They wish to be of goodwill to all, even their enemies, and they will suppress their feelings of enmity as best they can. The Guardian's propriety and the Rational's autonomy are virtues for the Idealists to cultivate as well, of course. But they are not nearly as significant as goodwill, for to the Idealist benevolence is the greatest virtue, malevolence the greatest vice.

Each year in the early summer people gather at the famous Mission in Capistrano, California, to be among those who spot the year's first returning swallow. The idea is that the appearance of that first swallow signals the beginning of summer. One must be wary, for the weather does not always heed the flight of the swallow, and "a single swallow does not a summer make." But for Idealists that single swallow does; the tiniest *sign* of a thing indicates that thing. Idealists have a charming habit of taking part for whole in this fashion, identifying the part with the whole. Their conception of the possible is inductive rather than deductive; they are the ones most likely to take the famous "inductive leap," that leap of faith they call "intuition," and in which they have the most profound trust.

Nor will their intuition lead them to the trivial. For the Idealists everything is meaningful, and Idealists focus on the meaning of events, believing that life is rich with meanings waiting to be unveiled, full of portents calling out to be discovered, events pregnant with significance. The Idealist is naturally drawn to uncovering that meaning, to understanding the "real" significance of events, a significance which is always obscured and which can only be brought forth by interpretation. Events may hint at love and hope; they may insinuate fear and despair, but whatever the Idealists may find revealed in them, the one thing they are not likely to find is triviality.

This same perspective applies to their images of themselves. Everybody has a self image, a way they want to see themselves to be seen by others. But Idealists are devoted to their self-image to a degree other types of character are not. This is a way of saying that they are more self-conscious, more aware of themselves as objects of scrutiny and sanction than others. From early on in their lives they seem to grant to others in their circle the right to pass judgment on them, while other types, especially the Rationals, reserve that right almost exclusively to themselves. And the Idealists take these judgments very seriously. Yet, in spite of their self-consciousness, they must behave with genuineness, which for the Idealist means with honesty and spontaneity.

Even a joking reference to their lapses in genuineness may occasion a quick and irate response. Their genuineness, their integrity, their authenticity, is the foundation of the Idealists' self-esteem. If they violate their own code of ethics by being phony or fake or sham, they suffer shame and will feel like hiding themselves away. Since they tend to escalate their standards of authenticity rather than to compromise with life as others may do, their need to be genuine at all times and everywhere makes it very difficult for them to avoid loss of self-esteem. Because of this, if they were not praised and encouraged as children to be true to themselves and were punished or criticized for their strange ways, then they have problems maintaining high self-esteem as adults.

Theirs is a dilemma. Desperate to please, yet fiercely guarding their integrity, they must skate on a razor's edge: reality on one side and integrity on the other. But since their sense of integrity is more important to them than their sense of reality, integrity stays and reality goes. Of all the temperaments, it is the Idealists that are quickest to give up their reality in favor of their integrity. Without integrity there is no self-esteem, and without self-esteem their is no unified Self.

Beyond the matter of their current authenticity, there is always at issue for the Idealist the fundamental question, "Who am I?" This is not a conscious inquiry on their part, but something beyond everyday awareness, lived out unspoken. And beckoning irresistibly, almost hypnotically, is a further question: "Who am I meant to become?" Realizing one's true identity is the Holy Grail of the Idealist, but the quest itself, however arduous, is also holy. "As [the Idealist] seeks self-actualization in identity and unity, he is aware that this is a life-long process, an ideal toward being and becoming a final, finished self."[3]

But Idealists will not find themselves no matter how long they search. And they certainly will not allow themselves to be found out by others. For each of them is a divided self, the evil in them split off from the good; the evil is not allowed to exist in the same Self as the good.[4] Otherwise, to disclose one's self fully would mean allowing this evil to be seen. Further, do not make the mistake of telling Idealists you understand them perfectly. They are for themselves alone to understand. No one else, no matter how intimate, may enter into the inner sanctum. They insist that they want and need a soul mate, someone to whom they can bare their inner self. But even the soul mate is disallowed entry, for in the inner sanctum, they fear, is every evil the Idealist has ever committed and forgotten. Not even the Idealists allow themselves to view this collection of evils. Thus the Idealists must present themselves as mysterious persons, never to be known completely and finally, either by themselves or by others.

The thought and speech of Idealists are intriguing. They involve the constant use of metaphor and of what is called "word magic." Word magic refers to the ancient idea that speech has the ability to make things happen; "saying makes it so." Our speaking and thinking, the Idealist will admonish us, produce results in the world around us, so we must be careful (even very careful) about what we think and say. There have been many books based on this way of comprehending language, for example, *The Magic of Believing* and *The Power of Positive Thinking*. This way of understanding thought and language can be found even in very young Idealists, when their use of language is still in its early stages of development. It is not something learned, then, but an inherent facet of the Idealist temperament.[5]

---

3 *Please Understand Me*, 66

4 R. D. Laing's brilliant work *The Divided Self* shows how Idealists abused as children may divide themselves into a "real" self and a "false" self. They then let others see only the false self and keep the real self inside and out of harm's way.

5 See *Temperament: Graces and Foibles of Human Conduct*, by David Keirsey, and *The Pygmalion Project, Volume III: The Idealist*, by Stephen Montgomery.

Idealists will often endow people and things alike with membership and attributes from alien realms. Idealists say that you are an Angel, I, a Demon. It isn't that you act *like* an Angel, you *are* one. And I don't merely *copy* some Demon, I *am* one. This fellow is a snake, that one, a pussy cat. It isn't that this fellow acts *like* a snake, he *is* one, totally, unconditionally. The other fellow doesn't have some of the attributes of a pussy cat, but he *is* one. And the dawn greets us, and the sun smiles at us. Similarly a corporation is grasping, a morning is without luster, a winter without cheer.

Just as Idealists speak in metaphors which lose their metaphorical property, they also speak in hyperbole which loses its hyperbolic property. They are *totally* distressed, *completely* disgusted, *perfectly* delighted, *absolutely* thrilled. They often exaggerate in this fashion, and will even finally avoid gradation altogether. Things are not "slightly" or "in some degree" or "in a manner of speaking" or "preponderantly" so; rather, things are either "altogether" or "not at all." The reality of which the Idealist speaks does not exist in a matter of degree.

Even so, the Idealists show an exceptional sensitivity to hints, suggestions, and meaningful details others are likely to overlook. Their extraordinary sensitivity to nuance makes the Idealists the best fitted of all the types to "read between the lines." They often say what we're going to say before we say it, or at least after we've spoken only the first word or two. In short, they take note of the world with a subtlety and a search for meaning that fills even the most mundane object or utterance with profound significance. When William Blake wrote of seeing the world "in a grain of sand" he was unknowingly describing the style of the Idealists.

Finally, then, the global style of the Idealists govern their world view in a manner enabling them—and at times condemning them—to create a very romantic and even mystical world. Their orientation to the "not visible" and the "not yet" makes the Idealists the most difficult of all the temperaments for others to understand, and the Idealist's style of communication, with its emphasis on symbols, emotional nuance and "intuition," doesn't make the task any easier.

At the same time it is a style in which the *act* of communication itself is intensely important, often more important than what is communicated. Idealists, after all, hunger for relationship, and their hunger is never assuaged. Their relationship hunger requires them to seek daily reassurances that the relationship is still intact, without rift or tear. Thus they find great satisfaction in their relationships when they are going well and become very distressed when they are not. To the Idealists, life is nothing without shared experiences and shared meanings. And because they are so responsive to the emotional condition of those around them, so sensitive to the emotional nuance of any communication, they cannot help responding with distress to the distress of the others in their relationships. Nor would Idealists wish it to be different, for at its very best, communication is so rich that consciousness itself seems to be shared.

Nonetheless, those close to an Idealist must be prepared to find themselves at times on a rather mysterious (though benign) emotional roller coaster. They must also be prepared to be thrown off balance by the meanings Idealists assign to events. For every comment they make, no matter how they try to ensure that it isn't taken personally by the Idealist, will be taken personally by the Idealist. And if they declare that they would like to discuss something impersonally, that declaration itself will probably be taken personally by the Idealist.

Idealists, after all, cannot *not* be personal, even if they try—which is rarely indeed. They can become totally absorbed in communing with one person, and they are simply not interested, not for very long at least, in things other than particular persons. Nor can they be objective. They are subjective in the very act of trying to be objective. After all, their relationships with others are beyond everything else their treasures. "Their hunger is not centered on things but people....They are not content with abstractions; they seek relationships. Their need does not ground to action; it vibrates with interaction."[6]

Given their benevolence, their desire to help, and the importance of their relationships, it is inevitable that sympathetic rapport with others is enormously important. They need it and they hunger for it. Their desire for rapport must be assuaged each day, else the Idealists waste away.[7]

Idealists naturally assume that they understand others and it can be a shock to discover that they do not. They will probably feel quite distressed unless they can regain the feeling that they do understand. They also take for granted that they are themselves being understood by others and are likely to feel hurt and disappointed if they discover that they are not, for they are sure that mutual understanding is the basis for all cooperative and satisfying relationships.

---

6 *Please Understand Me*, 66

7 The strength of this need may be related to strong and early imprinting of the nesting instinct in the Idealists, Advocates and Mentors alike, and to weak and late imprinting of territoriality, herding, and hunting.

The Idealists are the diplomatic leaders. Their leadership differs from that of the tactical, logistic, and strategic leadership of the other temperaments in that Idealists whose ability to individualize is well-developed, are skillful in mentoring and advocating, in using their own person as a positively transformative bridge between conflicting factions. They interpret each faction's communications in such a way that the positive elements are highlighted and the negatives are lost in translation, the possibilities for cooperation are magnified, and the obstacles minimized. Along the way both parties are likely to feel more thoroughly understood and much more richly accepted. In their diplomacy the Idealists may inspire both factions toward increased harmony, increased cooperation and benevolence, usually accomplishing this quietly, and always, warmly.

The leadership of the Idealist appears early, for in family matters Idealists naturally foster reciprocity and intimacy among members. They are the arbiters of family ethics and as such they are the family conscience. In this respect, no matter where they may be in the pecking order, and even when a tyrant is titular head, the Idealist still leads ethically.[8] Elizabeth Barrett Browning managed her tyrannical father this way, and so-called *anorexia nervosa* provides a striking, and more general instance of an Idealist adolescent dominating her entire family by the simple act of self-starvation.[9]

The Mentor Idealists

Recall the distinction between directing and reporting. Directive Idealists, the Mentors, quite comfortably, smoothly, and spontaneously, are prone to tell others what to do. This contrasts with the reporting Idealists, who direct others reluctantly, apologetically, and uncomfortably. On the other hand the Advocates, being reporter Idealists, are comfortable telling others what they feel others want to know, and they do so quite spontaneously. The Mentors, conversely, are

---

8 By the way, those interested in social psychology might wish to see the seminal work of Schelderup-Ebbe on the concept of "the pecking order" in man and animal. Especially they should see Robert Ardrey's definitive essay on dominance in groups titled *The Social Contract*.

9 See *Self-Starvation* and *Family Games* by Mara Selvini Palazzoli. Students and colleagues of the present authors in practice as psychotherapists consistently report finding cases of anorexia nervosa *only* in young Idealists.

reluctant to give information to others, and when they do, it is with apparent deliberation and awareness of purpose. So the Advocates are quick to inform and slow to command, while Mentors are quick to command and slow to inform.

Mentors are by far the best "mind-readers." They have an astonishing sensitivity to the emotional signals given by others in their relationships. They notice the most subtle of clues, and in this regard they are certainly the most talented of the types in divining what others have on their minds. More accurately however, they are not reading minds, but interpreting clues, and the interpretations they make may or may not be on the mark. It is remarkable, however, how often their attributions are close to dead center, especially when they are acting in their natural role of helper.

Not only are the Mentors the best mind-readers, but they are also the best spontaneous mimes. Indeed, their capacity for becoming attuned with others is so well developed that they may become too identified with others, taking on the other's gestures, mannerisms, and even their goals, occasionally at the expense of their own. This is especially true of their behavior with people whom they admire or prize.[10]

The Mentor diplomat will tell the disputants what they "need" to do (while the Advocate diplomat will offer useful information), and without hesitation or apology. This is not because they are arrogant or bossy, but rather that they simply recognize what "needs" to happen. It is then quite natural to let the other know what that is. Nor is it likely to occur to the Mentors that the other might not want to do as they've been told. After all, the Mentors' benevolence is beyond question. They are not just warm and caring teachers, but benevolently powerful, almost irresistible teachers as well, potent inspirational leaders, extremely energetic social agents, powerful and empathic counselors and therapists.[11]

---

10 Indeed, there is a certain danger of "losing one's self" through this penchant for attuning themselves with the other. One of the authors has worked in his therapeutic counseling practice with Mentors who have lost track of themselves in just this way. It is a price the Mentors sometimes pay for satisfying their hunger for rapport.

11 The masterful psychotherapist Virginia Satir, for example, was for three decades an outstanding example of the compassionate and inspiring Mentor. Her energy, her intense contact with others, her constant and profoundly empathic involvement with them exemplify beautifully the leadership style of the Mentor.

The Advocate Idealists

Much of what has been said of the Mentors applies as well to the Advocates. They too feel a powerful hunger for relationship, rapport, harmony, and authenticity. They too (and they especially) dislike deception and abhor exploitation. Fakery and sham are profoundly disturbing to the Advocate and ill-will intolerable. Like the Mentors the Advocates are remarkably perceptive and can usually see through fakery with amazing accuracy.[12]

The Advocates' constant self-scrutiny makes their own lapses in authenticity painfully apparent to them. They also naturally assume that others have the same highly developed ability to discover sham that they do, and thus the Advocates can't help feeling that others must also be able to see their (the Advocates') lapses too. Because of this they are the most self-conscious of all types. They are after all committed irreversibly to the ethical life, to "what is good and right,"[13] and when they violate their own high ethical standards they are painfully subject to shame.

The Advocates are probably the most interested in cooperative and harmonious relationships, and often the most talented of all the types in building and maintaining them. Because of this they can be wonderful at diplomacy, sometimes proving to be dedicated and effective peace-makers even between apparently implacable adversaries. "Conciliation, pacification, facilitation—these manners of sustaining smooth and productive interactions are near and dear to the heart of every one of them."[14] Their natural faculty for generating cooperative and supportive relationships is often apparent even when they are children. Even at an early age the Advocates are likely to be recognized as the most overtly helpful and caring of all the types. This is so characteristic of them that they tend to be seen by others in the family "almost as saints."[15]

Advocates are not comfortable with being thrust into a leadership role, especially on a permanent basis. They prefer instead to collaborate and to let others take the lead whenever possible, though their own enthusiasms may at times thrust them briefly into the leader's position.

---

12 There is an exception to this: the Idealists are rather easily taken in by the Artisans. They trust their intuitions so completely that those who know how to influence those intuitions (especially by using just the right sorts of words) find them to be remarkably easy to exploit.

13 *Portraits of Temperament*, 101

14 *Please Understand Me*, 100

15 *Please Understand Me*, 105

(This is a preference, by the way, and certainly doesn't suggest any lack of the ability to be effective leaders when they need to be.) They are capable of great loyalty when they are given any reasonable justification for loyalty, and they are extremely supportive of those to whom they are loyal.

As we have with the other three temperaments, we offer a visual summary of the Idealists, their abilities, leadership style, values, and favored self-definition.

The Idealists

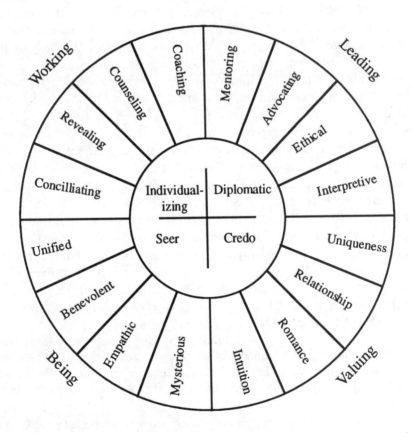

For those who would like to read further about Idealists, Adickes's "Doctrinal" type, Kretschmer's "Hyperesthetic" type, Spränger's "Religious" type, and Keirsey's "Apollonian" and "Idealist" types collectively present the full range of Idealist traits of character.

Biographies are also an excellent source of Idealist characterizations, although such individuals are not as easy to identify in biography as are the Rationals and Artisans. Idealist novelists and poets especially have been the subjects of study by biographers. For example, such writers as Henry James, D. H. Lawrence, Ann Morrow Lindberg, and Emily Brontë have been portrayed as Idealists by biographers. There are also the life stories of religious leaders such as Luther and Calvin, and political leaders such as Mohandas Gandhi and Eleanor Roosevelt. Finally, novelists, playwrights, and screen writers are quite aware of the Idealist character, perhaps more than are biographers and psychologists, so that there are countless fictional studies of the social interactions that typify the Idealist characters. Montgomery's account of the Idealists' morals and manners in relation to their mates may prove especially rewarding reading for those who are or have such a mate.

Non-fiction	**Fiction**
Please Understand Me (Keirsey)	*Jane Eyre* (Brontë)
Portraits of Temperament (Keirsey)	*Don Quixote* (Cervantes)
Physique and Character (Kretschmer)	*Lord Jim* (Conrad)
The Pygmalion Project: Idealists (Montgomery)	*A Passage to India* (Forster)
Types of Men (Spränger)	*The French Lieutenant's Woman* (Fowles)
	Siddhartha (Hesse)
	A Doll House (Ibsen)
	Hamlet (Shakespeare)
	Saint Joan (Shaw)
	The Glass Menagerie (Williams)

We will round out our survey of temperament with a look at two fascinating Idealists: the engaging Eleanor Roosevelt, wife of the Artisan Franklin Roosevelt, and the remarkable ethical and political leader, Mohandas K. Gandhi.

Two Idealists

Eleanor Roosevelt

"Something with me craved to be an individual."

Born October 11, 1884
Died November 7, 1962

> People aren't "made" by themselves or by anyone else: they are
> released to be what they always were but had never known they
> were.[16]

When he wrote these words Archibald MacLeish had in mind the
life of Anna Eleanor Roosevelt. To find another well-known life which
exemplifies MacLeish's words as well as Eleanor Roosevelt's we might
have to look back several centuries to another woman of the Idealist
temperament, France's famous martyr, Joan of Arc. That young woman

---

16 Prefatory comments to *The Eleanor Roosevelt Story*,

rose suddenly from peasant obscurity, became recognized as an inspirational military leader, and was considered by many to be a living saint. She accomplished this in a matter of only a few years and then died, burned at the stake, still a young woman.

Like the Maid of Orleans, the young Eleanor Roosevelt seemed a most unlikely candidate for fame; there was certainly nothing about Eleanor that suggested that an American President would some day honor her with the title, "First Lady of the World." Eleanor Roosevelt lived for almost seven decades, and her ascendancy was slow and measured. She never led men in battle, and like all Idealists, she abhorred strife of any kind and hated war. She was not martyred to a cause, she did not inspire crowds with her speech, she never wore the badge of any high office. Nonetheless it is possible that her fame will persist as long as that of the revered French peasant girl; certainly she will be admired by far more people than many American Presidents will be.

Eleanor Roosevelt was born in New York City in 1884. Her parents, Elliott Roosevelt and Anna Hall Roosevelt, were of an old and fashionable family and reasonably well-to-do (though they had some difficulty preserving their modest wealth). Eleanor was a niece of Theodore Roosevelt and a distant cousin of Franklin Delano Roosevelt, who would later become her husband. (In fact her "Uncle Ted," Theodore Roosevelt, was President of the United States at the time of her marriage to Franklin and gave her away at their wedding.)

Eleanor grew up cloaked in the stilted remnants of the Victorian age, which persisted longer in conservative monied circles in the United States than it did in Great Britain. In spite of her enterprising family young Eleanor seemed destined to become another fashionable post-Victorian woman whose life would consist of her "coming out," becoming engaged and then married, bearing children—though doing little to raise them—and remaining properly useless except for providing fashionable support for fashionable causes.

Eleanor's mother Anna, a beautiful but rather distant figure, apparently tried to be a properly warm mother. But she was an upright, conventionally-trained woman, probably a Monitor Guardian, with a strong Victorian bent. In spite of her wishes she was unable to close the gap (if she ever recognized it) between herself and little Eleanor, the remarkably different Idealist she was raising. On the other hand Eleanor's father, Elliott Roosevelt, was a Player Artisan, full of fun and frivolity. He loved Eleanor, his "Little Nell," and she adored him. Her memories of him were always rather selective. "With my father I was perfectly happy," she wrote. "He was the center of my world....I never doubted that I stood first in his heart."[17]

Her mother died of diphtheria when Eleanor was eight, as did her brother Elliott. Though these deaths were tragic it was really the death of her father Elliott, the high-living, affectionate, charming but very erratic Artisan, that affected her most strongly. The troublesome Elliott, the black sheep of the family, died of a riding accident when she was ten, and in later years she wrote about the event as if she had never really recovered from his death.

The ten-year-old Eleanor, now orphaned, was given over to the safe-keeping of her mother's mother, "G'ma" Mary Ludlow. Grandmother Ludlow was rather imperious though not unkind, better suited to the protocols of correct child-raising than she was to the loving nurturing an orphaned child. "G'ma" understood Victorian manners and mores, and Eleanor was to learn to be a proper young woman. She would eventually "come out," become engaged, marry, bear children, and so on.

The young Idealist grew up orphaned and isolated and afraid much of the time. She tried to fit in and (in the language of temperament theory) to become a good Guardian, for this is apparently almost all the modeling she saw. She could scarcely model herself after her father Elliot or her uncle Theodore, after all, both fiery Artisans and her opposite in every major dimension of temperament. Even as an adult she spoke often about "duty" and about the great satisfaction to be found in "being needed."

Her cousin Corinne once said of Eleanor's childhood that "It was the grimmest childhood I had ever known. Who did she have? Nobody."[18] The image may be a bit overdrawn, for young Eleanor did have good food and lodgings and treatment which was reasonable, even if less than compassionate. Yet Corinne had a point: for an Idealist such

---

17 *The Autobiography of Eleanor Roosevelt*, 5-6
18 *Without Precedent*, 4

as Eleanor to grow up isolated from emotional contact, not to be known personally, not to have empathic ties with her family, must have been close to traumatic for her.

In the autumn of 1899, when Eleanor was fifteen, Grandmother Ludlow felt it was time to send her off to school, and selected Allenwood for her. This school was run by a French educator, Mlle. Marie Souvestre, already known to and respected by the Ludlows. Allenwood had been transplanted from France and was located just outside London, and Eleanor made the transatlantic crossing in considerable trepidation. But when the young girl arrived Mlle. Souvestre was immediately taken with her, and Eleanor soon became one of Mlle Souvestre's favorites. A former classmate of Eleanor's remembered her vividly during an interview by the London Daily Mail in 1942.

> I remember the day she arrived at the school, she was so very much more grown up than we were, and at her first meal, when we hardly dared open our mouths, she sat opposite Mlle. Souvestre, chatting away in French.

The expression "chatting away" may convey a false image of light-hearted and light-headed talkativeness which would be quite wide of the mark. In spite of her self-deprecating memoirs about her schooling, Eleanor's fellow students recognized immediately that she was not just more "grown up," but also a person concerned with more weighty issues than those which typically occupy the attention of young girls. In the same interview her former classmate commented that Eleanor "once confided to me that all she wished for was to do something useful: that was her main object."[19] Despite her seriousness, she was very popular with the other girls at Allenwood. Her cousin Corinne said later, apparently with good reason, that she was "beloved by everybody," a comment most likely to be heard about the Idealists, with their noteworthy empathy and sense of diplomacy.

Thus Eleanor's time at Allenwood was marked not only by the work of a competent educator, but by a degree of personal acceptance she had known only rarely in her young life. The experience was marvelous for her, and she flourished, becoming a remarkably more self-

---

19 *Love, Eleanor: Eleanor Roosevelt and her Friends,* 27

confident young woman by Christmas of that year. "I really marvel now at my confidence and independence," she wrote later, "for I was totally without fear in this new phase of my life."[20] To be without fear and to believe that the world was predictable and benign delighted her, for "this was the first time in my life that my fears left me. If I lived up to the rules and told the truth, there was nothing to fear."[21]

Unfortunately Eleanor was at Allenwood for only a year. She then returned to New York for her "coming out" season as was proper for her and the other young ladies of her age and class. This season of her introduction to society as a young woman was both inevitable and very painful. She was shy, and she knew almost no one her own age. She knew that her looks and manner were not going to attract much attention, and she did not know the niceties of the parties and dances which became her agonizing lot. "I knew I was the first girl in my mother's family who was not a belle and, though I never acknowledged it to any of them at that time, I was deeply ashamed."[22] Being so sensitive to others' (especially family) expectations is especially characteristic of the Idealists, and Eleanor was no exception in this respect.

Perhaps her sensitivity left her insufficiently appreciative of her own physical attractiveness. Her teeth were too strong and her chin too weak for her ever to be a classic beauty. But pictures of her as a young woman show her to be considerably more attractive than she apparently saw herself. She had soft, rather large and engaging eyes. She also had a graceful carriage enhanced by intense study of the dance. And she had a tall, willowy, build that gave her a pleasing but fragile appearance which belied her great vitality and robust constitution. She must have been more attractive than she described herself, for it is quite unlikely that she would otherwise have attracted the attention of the dashing and popular Franklin Roosevelt, a very distant cousin.

Eleanor Roosevelt somehow made it through the arduous coming out season and took her uncertain place in New York society. Then in

---

20 *The Autobiography of Eleanor Roosevelt*, 25

21 *The Autobiography of Eleanor Roosevelt*, 24. The Idealists, more than any other character, may undergo this sort of transformation when they are warmly accepted by others. This is perhaps one of the chief reasons that the psychologist Carl Rogers, another Idealist, so strongly stressed the therapeutic importance of "unconditional positive regard."

22 *The Autobiography of Eleanor Roosevelt*, 37

1903 with some young friends in the newly established Junior League, the nineteen year old Eleanor began doing charity work with children in the tenements of New York City where she would teach calisthenics and "fancy dancing" (an interesting choice for a young woman who claimed to be terribly awkward in dance). She did this several times a week and her warm and gracious manner quickly made her popular with the children and their parents. It was certainly not unknown for young ladies of her social class to undertake such "charitable works," so Eleanor's involvement was not especially noteworthy.

Even so, Eleanor did take them more to heart than many of her peers. She saw first hand the difficult conditions under which so many workers labored and the impact of those conditions on the workers' children. Soon she became interested in the work of the National Consumers League, another volunteer group which investigated and worked for the improvement of the condition of the poor working class. Thus the altruistic calling so compelling for the Idealist emerged early in Eleanor's adult life.

While working with the tenement children Eleanor would occasionally be accompanied by the urbane and charming Franklin Roosevelt. Franklin had been drawn to her and had been courting her for some time, and when he finally proposed marriage the nineteen year old Eleanor accepted gladly.

> I had a great curiosity about life and a desire to participate in every experience that might be the lot of a woman. There seemed to me to be a necessity for hurry; without rhyme or reason I felt the urge to be a part of the stream of life, and so...it seemed entirely natural and I never even thought that we were both young and inexperienced.[23]

Eleanor and Franklin were married on Saint Patrick's Day, March 17, 1905. They had picked the date because Uncle Ted (President Theodore Roosevelt) would be in New York to attend the Saint Patrick's Day parade and would therefore be available to give his niece away. The wedding was held at Grandmother Ludlow's home and came off nicely. But when the very popular President went into Mrs. Ludlow's library immediately after the ceremony for refreshments, the entire wedding party followed him. The newlyweds were left quite alone at their own wedding until they too went into the library. Franklin, Eleanor's Artisan

---

[23] *The Autobiography of Eleanor Roosevelt,* 41

groom, may have been mightily impressed by this turn of events. Certainly he was a man who loved to have an impact.

The newlyweds went to Europe for their honeymoon. Franklin added spice to their travels by his bargain-hunting for items in which he had a special interest. Eleanor recalled with some bemusement how sharp a bargainer her new husband was even when he did not understand the language being used in the bargaining. She on the other hand bargained very poorly, in her case partly because she did understand the language. The problem was that when talking with merchants she listened to their sales pitches as if they were speaking the gospel truth; Idealists such as Eleanor are credulous in their expectations and therefore the most easily hoodwinked of all the types.

Franklin on the other hand, an optimistic, exploitative Artisan, understood the game and found great satisfaction in being able to outmaneuver the sellers. Overall the honeymoon was exciting and great fun for the young couple. Franklin was a wonderful Artisan, after all, and one should expect no less. But by the time the honeymoon was ended Eleanor was ready to fit smoothly into the role of "a conventional, quiet young society matron."[24]

The price of her "privileged" position in society was high for her. She had been trained to be a proper matron, with the rather extreme limits on what behaviors would be considered acceptable. But she knew nothing about preparing a meal for herself and her husband or about how to handle most other of the simple but essential demands of domestic life, and so was almost helpless in these matters. She soon became pregnant and realized that she also knew next to nothing about raising children. Her own childhood experience was not especially useful to her; both her mother and her grandmother had been rather distant and impersonal and were therefore far from the best models for an inexperienced Idealist mother.

In addition Sara Roosevelt, Franklin's mother, was a cool, strong-willed woman who had put most of her life's interest and energy into her children and who kept it there even after they had grown up. She and Franklin had a very strong connection and Eleanor Roosevelt's place with them could not be a comfortable one. Sara never approved of her

---

[24] *The Autobiography of Eleanor Roosevelt*, 55

daughter-in-law and apparently tried to discourage the marriage. For years after the marriage she dominated Eleanor Roosevelt's household—and Eleanor—in a high-handed, imperious manner. (It is said, for instance, that she once told Eleanor's young children that "she bore you but I'm your mother.") Eleanor struggled to fit in as she thought she should, but it was very difficult for her.

> ...I remember that a few weeks after we moved into the new house on East 65th Street I sat in front of my dressing table and wept, and when my bewildered young husband asked me what on earth was the matter with me, I said I did not like to live in a house which was not in any way mine, one that I had done nothing about and which did not represent the way I wanted to live.[25]

Franklin, Artisan that he was, could not project himself into her outlook and so couldn't understand the difficulty and somewhat impatiently told her she should pull herself together. As always in those days (it was 1908) Eleanor tried to do what her training called for. She later gave a glimpse, typically understated, of what can happen when Idealists try to live as they "should," thereby sacrificing the source of their self-esteem (authenticity) and their quest for their identity for the illusion of rapport.

> I pulled myself together and realized that I was acting like a little fool, but there was a good deal of truth in what I had said, for I was not developing any individual taste or initiative. I was simply absorbing the personalities of those about me and letting their tastes and interests dominate me.[26]

"Absorbing the personalities of those about me": the threat here is not just inauthenticity, but of the loss of one's identity itself. To confuse herself with others would have meant to lose her sense of self, and nothing could be more disturbing to an Idealist. The practical problems of life with Franklin were overshadowed by the distressing difficulty of maintaining her own sense of identity.

The struggles with Sara Roosevelt continued, sotto voce, until Franklin plunged headlong into the world of elective politics. In 1910 he ran for the office of New York State Assemblyman from Dutchess County and surprised many veteran observers by winning. He and

---

25 *The Autobiography of Eleanor Roosevelt*, 61
26 *The Autobiography of Eleanor Roosevelt*, 61

Eleanor then moved to Albany, the state capital, where Eleanor had her own special reason to celebrate her husband's success. Now she would be living on her own, with no one immediately at hand to help her—and dominate her. "I had to stand on my own feet now and I wanted to be independent. I was beginning to realize that something within me craved to be an individual."[27]

A remark such as this reveals the remarkable difference between Idealists and the other types of character. "To be an individual," as she put it, is taken for granted by other types so that the phrase merely puzzles them when they encounter it, while for the Idealists whether or not they are individuals is always a question, and a question that is never fully answered. Is seems a certainty that none of the forty Presidents ever wondered who he was, and certainly never went "in search of himself." Certainly her husband hadn't the foggiest notion of what on earth she meant to do in her search for self.

Now that Franklin and Eleanor were securely in Albany, his mother would visit the new residence of the couple, but she always returned to Hyde Park rather than staying. Eleanor announced that she felt as though someone has taken a ton of bricks off her. But still the young woman lived under the "compulsion" (as she later called it) of her early Guardian training, tied to duty above pleasure or joy or wishes of her own. Sometimes, she reminisced, "I almost forgot that there was such a thing as wanting anything."[28]

In 1913 Franklin was appointed Assistant Secretary of the Navy. Eleanor dutifully became very busy fulfilling the almost endless routine of social demands her husband's new position called for. Rationals and Artisans resist and can easily ignore the rituals that attend high office, but not an Idealist, especially one so inspired by devotion and driven by assumed duty as was Eleanor. She also had to hold together a household which now included three small children, Anna, James, and Elliott. (Franklin would be born in 1914 and John in 1916. There had been an earlier child named Franklin who was born in 1909 but died when only a few months old.)

Her life was complicated by the additional burden imposed by the outbreak of World War I in 1914 (though the United States didn't

---

27 *The Autobiography of Eleanor Roosevelt*, 65
28 *The Autobiography of Eleanor Roosevelt*, 66

declare war until April of 1917). She eventually found herself involved not just in the normal duties of a politician's wife, but also trying to take care of her own family, coordinating the Union Station canteen for soldiers en route to training, and speaking at numerous patriotic rallies. She was also involving herself in various Red Cross activities and overseeing knitting rooms established at the Navy Department, where volunteers knitted sweaters and other garments for soldiers and sailors. Here was an Idealist with an unusually powerful sense of commitment.

Especially noteworthy, for such activities became almost her hallmark in the following years, were her benevolent visits with wounded soldiers and sailors. Good will is the source of self respect for Idealists, and even in 1917 she was already showing her immense willingness to involve herself with others on a very personal level. She kept herself constantly busy by visiting the wounded, writing to their families, going out of her already crowded way to help in sometimes small and sometimes large but always compassionate ways.

One of the most important of her visits was to St. Elizabeth's Hospital in late 1917. The Navy Department had taken over a block of buildings there for "shell-shocked" marines and sailors and the block was already filled with the human wreckage of the European conflict. Eleanor was horrified by what she saw: "Poor demented creatures, with apparently very little attention being paid them, gazing from behind bars or walking up and down on enclosed porches."[29] The patients wandered aimlessly around the wards whose doors were tightly locked. The hospitalized servicemen were largely neglected, some were in pitiable emotional condition, and available resources for housing and rehabilitating them were meager. Her benevolent attitude toward these "war neurosis" victims stands in very sharp contrast with that of General Patton, an Artisan virtuoso of battle tactics, who slapped a hospitalized soldier suffering from "battle fatigue." Patton, seeing the wounded men in the same ward, ordered the attendants to "get this coward out of the presence of these noble men." Eleanor Roosevelt's heart went out to those who might have felt Patton's fist, and this difference between the two illustrates how deep is the gulf in every major dimension of character between the Artisans and Idealists.

---

29 *The Autobiography of Eleanor Roosevelt*, 92

Eleanor's visit to St. Elizabeth's was important because it was the first time in her life that she took a vigorous role in bringing about a political remedy to a social problem. She prodded the Secretary of the Interior (who was ultimately responsible for St. Elizabeth's) to go over and see for himself what was happening. Then she kept after him until he persuaded the Congress to increase appropriations for the hospital. She also hounded the Red Cross into providing a recreation room for the patients and coaxed $500 from the Colonial Dames with which to begin an occupational therapy program. Along with these political and organizational activities she also offered her own quiet and personal help, trying one way or another to help with many of the problems the patients and their families faced, or simply being there to talk in her warm and pleasant way with the patients. "My son always loved to see you come in," one mother wrote to her later. "You always brought a ray of sunshine."[30]

Eleanor Roosevelt had become, suddenly and unexpectedly, a vigorous political activist, powered by her own personal values rather than by her training about what properly bred young women should do. It is remarkable, but entirely characteristic of the Idealists, that she managed this transformation without the least sacrifice of her own personal, warm, compassionate style.

Indeed, she was able to make the transition because her natural Idealist style values above all else in decision making the role of "personal" observation. Idealists resist instruction from any external source, and because she was so powerfully touched by the suffering of others her visitations would have been especially memorable to her. Her many inspection trips (including those into the dark interiors of West Virginia coal mines) came out of her understanding of the importance of first-hand observation as well as her natural inclination to contact and acknowledge people personally as individuals. Her activism was thus rooted in a very personal way of understanding events. In these respects she seems to have been very much like Mohandas Gandhi who made his own trips of inspection into the Indian equivalent of the Virginia coal mines and the New York City tenements.

Franklin ran for the vice-presidency in 1920 and lost. The loss was expected; he was at that point positioning himself for later political

---

30 *Without Precedent,* 7

opportunities rather than trying seriously to become Vice-President. Eleanor in the meantime was increasingly unhappy with the idea of spending so much of her time in New York attending or giving an endless cycle of teas and luncheons and dinners. The terrible realities of war had made such a life impossible for her, and she instead began to improve herself in many practical ways. She organized a schedule of activities for herself: she decided to learn (finally) to cook, she attended business school, and she took courses in typing and shorthand. She also became involved in the League of Women Voters and met two life-long friends who were also to become her mentors, Elizabeth Reed and Esther Lape. Both women were political activists and veterans of the suffrage wars, and both added immensely to her political education.

In spite of her emerging activism, her political education was still insufficient. When Franklin came out publicly for women's suffrage she was shocked. She had always assumed that men were superior to women and knew more about politics than women. Further, she was still far from a confident, self-asserting woman who would be apparent in the 1930s. She admits that she had already "lost a good deal of my crusading spirit where the poor were concerned, because I had been told I had no right to go into the slums or into the hospitals, for fear of bringing diseases home to my children...."[31] In fact it was Sara Roosevelt, her mother-in-law, who cautioned her about disease from her charitable work. At that time Eleanor was increasingly busy with her social activism but still had not freed herself fully from the yoke of her mother-in-law's opinions and demands.

Eleanor soon added the Women's Trade Union League, the League of Women Voters and the Democratic State Committee (where she became finance chairman) to her activities. Franklin had been struck down by infantile paralysis in 1921 and Eleanor had became a very active campaigner for the Democratic party in New York even while he was struggling literally to get back on his feet. Her enormous energy and vitality and her ability to counsel others carried her successfully through her very busy schedule. It also allowed her some semblance of a family life and the opportunity to maintain a prodigious correspondence with her friends and admirers. In the midst of all this activity her outstanding

---

31 *The Autobiography of Eleanor Roosevelt*, 68

abilities as an advisor became increasingly recognized and admired. Great mentor that she was, it must be recognized that her abilities as an advocate of causes, the other side of the Idealist's competency repertoire, were also impressive.

As advocate she had become an increasingly important voice for women's issues. The most immediate arena for these was the place of women in New York's Democratic Party. The voice was no longer the timid parroting of men's perspectives, but a determined—but always gentle—assertion of women's rights. During the 1924 state Democratic convention she addressed a women's group:

> It is always disagreeable to take stands. It is always easier to compromise, always easier to let things go. To many women, and I am one of them, it is extraordinarily difficult to care about anything enough to cause disagreement or unpleasant feelings, but I have come to the conclusion that this must be done for a time until we can prove our strength and demand respect for our wishes.[32]

How remarkable it must have been to hear the quiet, high-pitched voice of Eleanor Roosevelt talking about "demanding" respect! How striking the transformation from the Victorian age leftover to this political and social activist. (FDR commented tongue-in-cheek about feminist political activity in general: "It's only the beginning. Once they mount the soapbox, mark my words, they never get off."[33])

It quickly became evident that Franklin, in spite of his handicap, was determined to re-enter the political arena. Despite Eleanor's own interests, and though she did not care for the burdens of being a politician's wife, she devoted great energy to his campaign when he ran for the governorship of New York. It was due partially to her very effective and vigorous support and her own considerable popularity that he was elected Governor in 1928. But Franklin's successes were only one part of her life now, not its center. Her activities were more and more shaped by her own idealistic credo that focused interests in the well-being of children, of the poor and of the economically and politically oppressed, and by her commitment to various political reforms, including legislation for equal pay for women, child labor amendments, and political support for other planks espoused by women reformers.

---

32 *Love, Eleanor: Eleanor Roosevelt and her Friends,* 87
33 *Love, Eleanor: Eleanor Roosevelt and her Friends,* 86

By 1930 the Great Depression was beginning to overshadow the lives of millions of people. For the next decade there would be ample opportunity for social causes, as the numbers of the poor, the unemployed, the dispossessed, and the hungry grew constantly and everywhere. The presidency of Herbert Hoover had attended the coming of the Depression and was crushed by it. When the jaunty and confident Franklin Roosevelt campaigned against Herbert Hoover in 1932 he easily defeated the dour Republican. Roosevelt's campaign song was "Happy Days are Here Again" and though the bouncy, cheerful little ditty was being sung years too soon, FDR had become President of the United States. That meant of course that the vital and compassionate and immensely popular Eleanor Roosevelt was First Lady of the land. Whatever the nations's circumstances, the presence of Franklin and Eleanor Roosevelt meant to many that there was again hope for something better.

The two Roosevelts provided a remarkable complementarity. Franklin was urbane, witty, a wheeler-dealer Artisan who maneuvered people with consummate skill. Eleanor was warm, gracious, open, often naive, a woman whose contacts with people were always open and intensely personal. Franklin attempted a wholesale scatter-gun assault on the Depression from his office in Washington. Eleanor often travelled out among the impoverished and debilitated, always responding personally to the individual human beings she encountered, always touching the hearts of those around her. Over the years Franklin introduced massive, energetic, though often hastily conceived and poorly implemented programs for the American populace. Over the years Eleanor performed thousands of small—and not so small—favors for the people she met in person, for those who wrote to her, for people she merely heard about. Franklin could use people and dispose of them when they were no longer useful; Eleanor loved many people and wanted desperately to keep contact with them. Always Franklin acted as the consummate politician, weighing and balancing economic need and political advantage. And always Eleanor acted with remarkable grace, deflecting attention from herself and finding ways to nurture and honor those whom she helped.

For example, a group of recently-settled refugees from Hitler's Europe wrote to her asking if she might speak to them. They had little

hope the busy First Lady would do so; theirs was not a large group nor
an influential one. They were therefore quite pleasantly surprised when
she agreed to appear. In her speech of welcome she displayed her
Idealist empathic understanding of their situation, saying:

> We Americans are well aware that this is not a one-sided relationship.
> We are offering you a home and a haven, to be sure. However, you, in
> the United States tradition of immigrants, are bringing us your skills,
> your talents and your cultures. We are grateful to you for broadening
> our scope and enriching our country which consists of newcomers just
> like you.[34]

Another example: one of her favorite charities for many years was
the Wiltwyck School for Boys in New York, whose purpose was to
reform delinquents from the city. Eleanor would on occasion have the
boys brought to her home at Hyde Park for a picnic where she would
personally barbecue and cook for them and read them stories. After one
such visit a boy was found to have stolen a silver dollar and was
required to send the dollar back to Mrs. Roosevelt with a note of
apology. She replied to the note immediately, saying that "she was so
glad to have it back for it belonged to one of her sons who had gotten it
from his father for a good report card."[35]

And another: a woman who had done volunteer work in Italy after
the Second World War found and adopted a young Italian orphan. But
when she tried to bring little Elena home to the United States she was
denied permission. The adoptive mother is said to have written
thousands of letters and to have made extraordinary efforts to get
permission to bring Elena to this country. Fortunately she met Eleanor
Roosevelt who was instantly interested in her story and promised to do
whatever she could. It took seven years, but a bill was finally taken
through the Senate which made Elena's immigration possible. When
Elena, now eleven years old, arrived her mother wrote to Eleanor to
thank her. Eleanor Roosevelt's gracious reply was "I am so glad that
your child finally has come home."[36] Always there was that grace and
warmth in her actions, the minimizing her own contribution, and the
unceasing and compassionate interest in others and their struggles.

It is fascinating to read Eleanor's descriptions of Franklin, most of
which are quite gracious. The Idealist cast of her portrayals is obvious

---

34 *A Woman of Quality*, 44
35 *A Woman of Quality*, 30
36 *A Woman of Quality*, 47

and often charming. Note for instance the following comment about Franklin's interest in politics: "...the science of government was interesting—and people, the ability to understand them, the play of his own personality on theirs, was a fascinating study to him."[37] Franklin, was in her view "particularly susceptible to people, took color from whomever he was with, giving to each one something different of himself. Because he disliked being disagreeable, he made an effort to give each person who came in contact with him the feeling that he understood what his particular interest was."[38] Her comment that Franklin was drawn to the "science" of government shows her Idealist's propensity for attributing desirable characteristics to others. Franklin, of course, was not in the least interested in the *science* of government. Eleanor herself set up the distinction when she commented on his love of the *game* of politics: the wheeling and dealing, the maneuvering, the seeking for advantage. She was quite accurate in noting that he disliked being disagreeable: almost always the price of being disagreeable is the surrender of advantage. Tactics, the pursuit of advantage in the moment, and not technology or personal warmth, were his abiding love. But rarely have the maneuvers of the "susceptible" Artisan been so graciously described.

It is characteristic of Eleanor that she would portray so warmly what some others disliked so fiercely. She was almost uniformly gentle in her few critical comments about others. Her assessment of Richard Nixon therefore stands out in an almost stark fashion to those who know her writing style and the importance she attached to personal convictions:

> I regard Mr. Nixon as a very able and dangerous opportunist, but since 1952 he has learned a great deal. He now knows the importance of gaining the confidence of people and he has worked hard at it and made progress. This still does not make me believe that he has any strong convictions.[39]

She was even more pointed in her comments about Herbert Hoover in 1928, though they were made during a political campaign. Her observations are such a wonderful example of an Idealist criticizing a Rational that they cannot go unremarked:

---

37 *The Autobiography of Eleanor Roosevelt*, 66
38 *The Autobiography of Eleanor Roosevelt*, 129
39 *The Autobiography of Eleanor Roosevelt*, 358

On things material and commercial he has conducted endless researches, he has prepared yards of charts and reduced statistics to the last decimal point but on the great fundamental human problems of life he shows no such interest, perhaps because they cannot be charted and reduced to figures. He has indeed the engineer's mind and problems which cannot be solved by algebra and mathematics do not attract him.[40]

With rare exceptions such as the above Eleanor Roosevelt's kindness always showed through, no matter what error or awkwardness she might bring with it. By the time her husband reached the presidency Eleanor was writing two different magazine columns (In *The Ladies' Home Companion* and *Woman's Home Journal*), she had at various times two radio shows, she made hundreds of speeches, gave hundreds of lectures and made countless personal appearances of all kinds. She made little money from her commercial work (the radio shows and columns and some lectures) and much of what she did make went to charities. Thus the claims some made that she was using her position as a powerful politician's wife to make money were erroneous. In fact she was, like most Idealists, never very good with money and rarely seemed to know in any practical terms how much she was receiving or how much she had.

In spite of her popularity it must be admitted that her writing, especially her early writing, was sometimes rather trivial and poorly thought out. Though she increasingly devoted her writing to serious matters some of her earlier writing consisted of anecdotes about a grandchild cutting her finger on a piece of paper, of Eleanor's growling like a lion to please another grandchild, and so forth. Her speaking voice was also unfortunate—squeaky, sometimes falsetto, clearly poorly trained. She had a laugh which would insert itself into her speech for no apparent reason and to the considerable annoyance of many listeners who were already struggling with her somewhat unpleasant voice. For a while she took speech lessons which helped in some degree, but her voice would never be pleasing to listen to. Nonetheless her awkwardness and errors were more than offset by what one speech teacher called "the warmth, sincerity, and earnestness prevalent in her voice."[41]

---

40 Speech given in 1928, quoted in *Anna Eleanor Roosevelt: The Evolution of a Reformer*, 175

41 *Anna Eleanor Roosevelt: The Evolution of a Reformer*, 235

When Eleanor cared deeply about people or causes she could be remarkably forbearing, almost blind to their defects. She could even be considered self-deceiving, for it was difficult for her to accept evidence that the beneficiary of her caring was unworthy of it. One of the most famous examples of this difficulty was her relationship with the American Youth Congress in the 1930s. The American Youth Congress was a communist-infiltrated and communist-dominated organization and the evidence for the communist takeover eventually became so obvious that there could no longer be any real question about the matter. But Eleanor, with her fondness for, (indeed idealization of) youth, had affiliated herself with the American Youth Congress emotionally and publicly, and staunchly refused to acknowledge that it had become a communist front organization. The recognition came only slowly and painfully and it was not until in 1940 that she quietly ended her association with it.

It was sad that her hopes for the future, so invested in youth and in her belief in the power of democratic discussion, had to be cut loose from the American Youth Congress, which promised so rich a collaboration of both. As is so often true of Idealists it was hard for her to turn her back on anyone about whom she cared—or to realize that she should consider doing so. She had in plenty the Idealist's lofty credulism and at times she could be quite naive and almost embarrassingly gullible.

All the same, she was an increasingly astute political force. She did learn from her mistakes as well as from her successes and of course she knew well how to work with people face to face. She also had a way of working with Franklin that deserves our admiration, for though she never really understood his Artisan character she did know how to influence his decisions. So effectively did she arrange for certain people involved in movements important to her to meet with the President that she was thought by some observers to be insensitively pushy. Apparently some even felt a bit sorry for the poor, dominated Franklin, which shows how poorly they understood this irrepressible Operator. One of her biographers commented, "No one who ever saw ER [Eleanor Roosevelt] sit down facing her husband and holding his eyes firmly [saying to him] 'Franklin, I think you should'...or 'Franklin surely you will not'...will ever forget the experience."[42] Through her own personal impact she became, in the words of an admiring columnist, a "Cabinet Minister without portfolio—the most influential woman of our times."[43]

---

42 Quoted in *Without Precedent*, 10-11
43 Quoted in *Without Precedent*, 11

She also developed and maintained both spiritual and practical leadership over a network of reform-oriented people, largely women. Over time she became a consistent and increasingly effective advocate of equal rights for women, children's welfare, civil rights, assistance to the poor, and a diversity of other humanitarian projects. Still, though the years in Washington were busy and rewarding ones for her the social advocate; Eleanor Roosevelt, the Idealist woman in search of her true self, found them much less satisfying:

> On the whole, I think I lived those years very impersonally. It was almost as though I had erected someone outside myself who was the President's wife. I was lost somewhere deep down inside myself. That is the way I felt and worked until I left the White House.[44]

Only an Idealist would be likely to write these words, and it is an Idealist who is most likely to feel anguish about being "lost somewhere deep down inside myself" like some Genie trapped inside a bottle. Perhaps it would have gone much better for her had her relationships with her children been easier and more rewarding. In spite of her graciousness with others she was uncomfortable and somewhat stiff in her relationships with her own children. She had great difficulty responding to them in a warm, close way and was almost incapable of being playful with them. Her own childhood experience was lacking in such warm and playful moments except for brief times with her father and the occasional, playful but less personal times with her uncle Ted. Nor did she seem able to enjoy her children's affection for her. Eleanor was uncertain about how to mother her children, and her oldest daughter Anna remembers that "...she did not know how to let her children love her."[45]

This was after all the Eleanor who had written that, for the eight years her mother lived, she felt a "curious barrier" that kept her distant from her mother and brothers. Her mother Anna, she recalled,

> would read to me and have me read to her, she would have me recite my poems, she would keep me after the boys had gone to bed, and still I can remember standing in the door, often with my fingers in my mouth, and I can see the look in her eyes and hear the tone of her voice as she said, "Come in, Granny." If a visitor was there she might turn

---

44 *The Autobiography of Eleanor Roosevelt*, 280
45 *Without Precedent*, 6-7

and say, "She is such a funny child, so old-fashioned that we always call her 'Granny.'" I wanted to sink through the floor in shame.[46]

Given her childhood background, there should be no surprise when one reads that "Looking back I see I was always afraid of something: of the dark, of displeasing people, of failure. Anything I accomplished had to be done across a barrier of fear."[47] Even so she doesn't seem to recall moments of being terrified by her father's reckless driving, being disappointed by his broken promises, or being left by him with the doorman at his club while he wandered off, forgetting to return for her (it is quite in character for Idealists to repress most unpleasant events and all traumas.) Perhaps it is understandable that she would have difficulty establishing warm and playful relationships, or that she would sometimes express her sadness that she could never learn to "let go."

Her comment about Allenwood has a Guardian resonance: "If I lived up to the rules and told the truth, there was nothing to fear." That was probably an accurate assessment of the situation, but the wording of the statement shows her effort to understand life in Guardian terms. Of course the effort was bound to fail; the Idealist perspective would inevitably discover itself. We can hear it already undermining her Guardian training in her description of her outlook at the age of twenty:

> I had painfully high ideals and a tremendous sense of duty entirely unrelieved by any sense of humor or any appreciation of the weaknesses of human nature. Things were either right or wrong to me, and I had had too little experience to know how fallible human judgments are.[48]

As for duty, her friend and biographer Joseph Lash writes, "A person's duty was goodness, Eleanor said repeatedly...."[49] The injunction is not merely to "be good," but to pursue "goodness" itself. And how is this goodness to be understood? Over and over again Eleanor relates it to the growth and expression of one's unique individuality. In *You Learn by Living* she attributes her own Idealist search for self to others. "There is a desperate need for identification and recognition as an individual all through life to people who, because of circumstances or some limitations in themselves, have not learned to

---

46 *The Autobiography of Eleanor Roosevelt*, 10
47 *The Autobiography of Eleanor Roosevelt*, 12
48 *The Autobiography of Eleanor Roosevelt*, 41
49 *Love, Eleanor: Eleanor Roosevelt and her Friends*, 212

feel they have developed as individuals or have been so accepted."[50] One observer notes that "on the issue of women's equality, as in so many other areas, ER most often affirmed the inalienable right of the human spirit to grow and seek fulfillment....Throughout, she demonstrated a capacity for change grounded in a compassion for those who were victims."[51]

Education, she seemed to feel, should direct itself to this self-realization. She believed she had had great good fortune "to be under a really great teacher [Mlle. Souvestre] for the years that I spent in Europe. It was not the actual subject which mattered, it was the inspiration of her personality and character, and the fact that she created in her pupils a curiosity and gave them the tools with which to satisfy it."[52] She commented once that "the basis of all real education is the contact of youth with a personality which will stimulate not only to work but to thought." After all, she continued, "no matter what young people study, the important thing is that the study should be vitalized for them by the personality of the teacher."[53] Finally, then, the importance of the individual came through; it was who you were that counted, not the rules and regulations you proclaimed. "The influence you exert is through your own life and what you've become yourself."[54]

The struggle between her Guardian upbringing and her Idealist temperament was resolved, more or less, by her use of words like "duty" to clothe Idealist perspectives. Thus the "duty" to "goodness" was a disguised version of the Idealist's pursuit of growth and self-expression. But the resolution was probably never a comfortable one. The apparent emotional barrier between her and her children, her difficulty with asking for—let alone insisting on—what she herself, Eleanor, wanted for herself, and her uncertainty about trusting her own sense of appropriateness in her personal life, all are evidences of the conflict. Again, she could only note her regret that she could never really let go, express herself freely, openly, spontaneously.

One can imagine how difficult it must have been for her in 1918 when Eleanor discovered that Franklin was having an affair with Lucy

---

50 Quoted in *A Woman of Quality*, 29

51 William H. Chafe, *Without Precedent*, 26

52 From a speech quoted in *Anna Eleanor Roosevelt: The Evolution of a Reformer*, 10

53 Quoted in *Anna Eleanor Roosevelt: The Evolution of a Reformer*, 21

54 Quoted in *Without Precedent*, 26

Mercer, Eleanor's own social secretary. Eleanor apparently ran across some correspondence between Franklin and Lucy while Franklin was ill. According to various reports Eleanor offered to divorce him, but he refused the offer. According to these accounts, his mother Sara was able to work out an agreement between Eleanor and Franklin, which held the marriage together, at least in name if not in spirit. But estrangement is the most powerful defense Idealists have against threats to their self esteem, and Eleanor's discovery of the affair estranged her from him permanently. Eleanor and Franklin thereafter lived, in their son James's words, in "an armed truce" and only "as business partners."[55]

The estrangement was not a matter of mere resentment or jealousy. Idealist wives of wayward Artisan husbands (unlike their Guardian counterparts) may forgive their spouse for breaking many rules, and even moral rules, but not for infidelity. With integrity as the basis of their self-esteem Idealists cannot ever mend the rift in relationship. Eleanor was sometimes described as insensitive with her husband, pushy about her projects and causes in spite of his physical illness. Those who saw her this way (though they were few) considered her to be cold and thoughtless. Perhaps they were recognizing the "armed truce" and were captivated sufficiently by FDR's charm that they thought the problem lay only with Eleanor.

For his part, Franklin had no way of understanding how his philandering could cause a permanent rift. A temporary one perhaps, but certainly not permanent. But then, no Artisan has ever understood or will ever understand what the Idealist calls the "deep and meaningful relationship." He might have heard the expression many times, but he would also have shrugged it off as one of those strange quirks that characterize "women." Artisans rarely if ever take themselves as objects of study, and Franklin was no more likely to have noted that his wife and he did not share a single trait of character than he was likely to be aware of his own traits.

In 1936 FDR was running for his second term as President. The estrangement was complete and Eleanor could confess to being "indifferent" about her husband's chances for re-election. "I realize more and more that FDR's a great man, and he is nice, but as a person,

---

55 *Without Precedent*, 191

I'm a stranger, and I don't want to be anything else!"[56] Even so the marriage was not totally devoid of contentment. Throughout the years Franklin and Eleanor maintained an effective partnership and usually remained allies even if they could not be true intimates. Franklin's political career and Eleanor's humanitarian work gave them many opportunities and good reasons to collaborate. However, though he seems from time to time to have made a gesture of reconciliation, she would have none of it. The permanence of the rift was as natural and complete for the Idealist as it was galling and puzzling for the Artisan.

What finally shows through in any study of Eleanor Roosevelt, what must always be kept in mind, is that one cannot understand her influence in terms of regional or temporal circumstances. It was not just that economic conditions, power bases, or social movements had arrived at some particularly promising stage of development. Rather, there was something about her presence which had its own special character, its own ability to move those around her to love, to loyalty, to action. Her genuine interest in others, her compassion, the degree to which she could be moved by the people she met was truly extraordinary.

Though most of those who knew her well seemed naturally to love and respect her, she was a woman with whom few people ever felt they were comrades, people who could be both her equal and her intimate. Her close friend Joseph Lash noted how difficult it was to simply include Eleanor as one of the gang, no matter how much she might ask to be seen that way:

> With Earl [Miller] and me she would ask for an old-fashioned, try puffing on a cigarette, do household chores, but there was always a slight distance that separated her from those who loved her.[57]

When we read the voluminous correspondence she carried on, with political and social activists, with strangers making requests of her, with her admirers or with her friends, she reminds us increasingly of Mahatma Gandhi. He too offered a love and friendship marked not by camaraderie and playfulness or by an egalitarian style, but by a loving compassion that seemed almost to reach out past individuality itself. It is as if she became her mission in life in the same way that Gandhi became

---

56 Quoted in *Without Precedent*, 21
57 *Love, Eleanor: Eleanor Roosevelt and her Friends*, 400

his. Each was almost an avatar of different aspects of the Idealist temperament: his, the aspect of vision; hers, that of compassion.

The Earl Miller mentioned in Lash's comment was a Player Artisan and a "man's man" who was a bodyguard for Franklin Roosevelt and who became a close confidante of Eleanor's. He was also something of an inspiration to her, someone who could cheer her up and challenge her to take a few minor, pleasant risks from time to time. There was some talk that they had a sexual relationship but that appears most unlikely. Miller has denied such a relationship vigorously and seems to have held her in a combination of respect, loyalty, and affection. Certainly she returned his affection and respect but the idea of a sexual liaison seems little short of absurd.

Still there is a thread here: Earl Miller, the Player and her beloved father Elliott Roosevelt the Player. Her husband Franklin was the third Artisan in her life, her uncle Theodore a less important fourth. The only other really important man was probably Louis Howe, who was likely a Rational. Howe was Franklin's most valued political advisor and eventually served Eleanor in a similar capacity until he died in 1936. Three out of four of the important men in her life were Artisans, two of these were Players. Even the Operator FDR she could see as a "gay cavalier," someone to whom she could, in their early years, sign a letter "Little Nell," her father's favorite term of endearment for her. Perhaps only such men could hope to animate the playfulness in this very serious-minded Idealist; perhaps even they eventually could not leap the gap from advisor or inspirer or cheerleader to intimate. Eleanor was perhaps finally lost within the partial self the public knew so well.

It is striking that someone who could become so beloved by so many seemed to have so little natural political sense. It was in this area that her Artisan husband, her suffragette woman friends, and the Rational "king-maker" Louis Howe were so important to her. With their help she developed a political sagacity which enhanced her Idealist qualities. It was important for her to have such people available. She was at her best calling attention to social abuses but weak in promulgating practical solutions. In fact her solutions were sometimes impractical and on occasion could even be absurd. The historically-minded might like to read up on the Arthurdale community for unemployed families she helped to establish at the depths of the Depression. It was not only unable to sustain itself, but it cost more to establish and maintain than did far more affluent communities in the same area. It was designed impractically, and expensively, and situated with inadequate regard to opportunities for employment for its occupants. Eleanor didn't have the knowledge of economics or law, history, philosophy, or public administration, business and financial institutions. Yet her Idealist recognition of the human side of events gave her an insight lacking the more academic or business-like. An admirer comments that with all her weaknesses Eleanor Roosevelt was "the personification of virtually unblemished kindness, generosity, and in the best sense of that over-used word—goodness."[58]

Franklin Roosevelt died April 12, 1945, a few months before the Second World War ended. Though Eleanor Roosevelt thereby lost her "political base," her work and her influence never diminished. After World War II Truman nominated her as one of the United States's delegates to the newly-organized United Nations. There she worked with a delegation attempting to construct a declaration of human rights that would embody standards that all of civilized humankind would accept as sacred and inalienable. Over the several years it took to accomplish the task, years requiring enormous patience, arduous work, and great tact and delicate diplomacy, she became extremely closely identified with the declaration and her personal presence and remarkable energy and commitment contributed greatly to the final success of the project.

The declaration of human rights was very important to her, but she was also strongly dedicated to the cause of world peace. She had many years earlier commented about leaving her children during wartime that:

> It was a sort of precursor of what it would be like if your children were killed. Life had to go on and you had to do what was required of you, but something inside of you quietly died.
>
> At the time of World War I, I felt keenly that I wanted to do everything possible to prevent future war, but I never felt it in the same way that I did during World War II. During this second war period I identified myself with all the other women who were going through the same slow death, and I kept praying that I might be able to prevent a repetition of the stupidity called war.[59]

---

58 James R. Kearney, *Without Precedent*, 64-65
59 *The Autobiography of Eleanor Roosevelt*, 251

World peace may be considered her final, overarching cause, though her face-to-face compassionate activity never diminished. Her commitment to peace did nothing to make her interested in appeasement, however, or to delude her that peace was merely a matter of holding pleasant wishes. Her experience in the United Nations and elsewhere after World War II convinced her that a peaceful world required that we match our own determination and strength against the violently aggressive behavior of the Soviet Union. Thus, even while many other liberals were pushing for accommodation, Eleanor Roosevelt supported President Harry Truman's consistently strong stands with respect to the Soviets. The political and social education of Eleanor Roosevelt had made more obvious her Idealist character; it had also made more obvious to her the value of careful and unceasing planning, hard work, and iron commitment.

Her resolve may have been strengthened by her view of what she saw in the Soviet Union: a kind of cradle-to-grave regimentation, a destruction of individuality which could only be horrifying to an Idealist. She saw a systematic, nation-wide program of "Pavlovian" conditioning which would produce—and in her view was producing—very docile, easily manageable citizens with no real individuality. Her horror was not just of the possibility of Communist world domination, but also of the loss of personhood the Soviet child-raising techniques suggested to her. Though one can question the power of Soviet "Pavlovian" conditioning, one must still be moved by the powerful images Eleanor Roosevelt's words evoke:

> ...by the time he is seven years old the child is completely regimented. The Soviet children have little or no desire for freedom. Their conditioning and training has been carefully thought out to prevent deviation of any kind, on any level, from birth to death.[60]

She saw the democratic nations as the polar opposite of this Orwellian nightmare, and perhaps as the only force which could withstand its grim voraciousness. She was quite explicit about this, and again her Idealist perspective shines through:

---

60 *The Autobiography of Eleanor Roosevelt*, 391-2

> To me, the democratic system represents man's best and brightest hope of self-fulfillment, of a life rich in promise and free from fear; the one hope, perhaps, for the compete development of the whole man.[61]

The Idealist Eleanor Roosevelt saw the struggle between democracy and communism as one in which both food and ideas, both the body and the mind, are the issue. Victory in one of these matters without victory in the other could never be sufficient to give rise to "the complete development of the whole man." She saw that one must provide not only economic aid to the world but also a vision of what it means to be a human being as well:

> Some leader must appear from the West who can put into words not the advantages of any form of economy, or any degree of production, but the inspiration of belief in the dignity of man and the value of the human individual. This is the basic difference; this is what we of the west must really fight for, and speak out about in ringing tones.[62]

The ringing tones in this statement are Eleanor Roosevelt's, the inspiring and compassionate Idealist, educated to the difficult world of politics. In spite of disappointment and horror she remained incapable of cynicism and held her understanding of politics within the framework of her Idealist temperament and character. It is understandable that President Harry Truman would call her "First Lady of the World" in recognition of her compassion, her energy, her resolution, and her beneficent influence in so many different areas in the world.

It was as if the worst of Franklin Roosevelt's cleverness, manipulativeness, and lust for the exercise of power were presented in a mirror, transformed into generosity, devotion to others' well-being, and constant concern for the disadvantaged. Eleanor the Idealist was the antithesis of her husband Franklin the Artisan in temperament and character. Franklin may have held the reigns of official power, but Eleanor was, by her very character, profoundly well suited to offer America and the world what one author called a "genuinely earnest sense of compassion for human suffering."[63]

---

61 *The Autobiography of Eleanor Roosevelt*, 401
62 *The Autobiography of Eleanor Roosevelt*, 434-35
63 James Kearney, *Anna Eleanor Roosevelt: The Evolution of a Reformer*, 276

Bibliography

Abramowitz, M 1970	*Eleanor Roosevelt and Federal Responsiveness to Youth, the Negro, and Others* (Dissertation, University of California, San Diego)
Beasley, M 1987	*Eleanor Roosevelt and the Media: A Public Quest for Self-Fulfillment*
Berger, J 1981	*A New Deal for the World: Eleanor Roosevelt and American Foreign Policy*
Black, R 1940	*Eleanor Roosevelt, a Biography*
Davidson, M 1969	*The Story of Eleanor Roosevelt*
Douglas, H 1963	*The Eleanor Roosevelt we Remember*
Fabor, D 1985	*Eleanor Roosevelt, First Lady of the World*
Flemian, J (ed)1987	*Eleanor Roosevelt: An American Journey*
Goodsell, J 1970	*Eleanor Roosevelt*
Graves, C 1966	*Eleanor Roosevelt, First Lady of the World*
Gurewitsch, A 1974	*Eleanor Roosevelt: Her Day, a Personal Album*
Hareven, T 1968	*Eleanor Roosevelt: An American Conscience*
Hickock, L 1980	*Eleanor Roosevelt, Reluctant First Lady*
Jacobs, W 1983	*Eleanor Roosevelt: A Life of Happiness and Tears*
Johnson, G 1962	*Eleanor Roosevelt*
Kearney, J 1968	*Anna Eleanor Roosevelt: The Evolution of a Reformer*
Lash, J 1964	*Eleanor Roosevelt: A Friend's Memoir*
Lash, J 1971	*Eleanor and Franklin*
Lash, J 1982	*Love, Eleanor: Eleanor Roosevelt and her Friends*
MacLeish, A 1965	*The Eleanor Roosevelt Story*
Roosevelt, E 1940	*Christmas: A Story by Eleanor Roosevelt*
Roosevelt, E 1961	*The Autobiography of Eleanor Roosevelt*
Roosevelt, E 1977	*Mother R: Eleanor Roosevelt's Untold Story*
Scharf, L 1987	*Eleanor Roosevelt: First Lady of American Liberalism*
Steinberg, A 1958	*Mrs. R, the Life of Eleanor Roosevelt*
Youngs, J 1985	*Eleanor Roosevelt: A Personal and Public Life*

Scharf, L 1987   *Eleanor Roosevelt: First Lady of American Liberalism*

Steinberg, A 1958   *Mrs. R, the Life of Eleanor Roosevelt*

Youngs, J 1985   *Eleanor Roosevelt: A Personal and Public Life*

Eleanor Roosevelt grew up in a staunchly conservative culture, one that by design suppressed a great deal of the individuality of its members, and especially its female members. Yet Eleanor Roosevelt's unique Idealist character was dramatically apparent in her words and in her deeds. Powerful as her influence was, there was another person whose life offers us an even more compelling example of the Idealist presence on the world stage. Mohandas Gandhi, the sainted Mahatma of India, also never held high elective office, never belonged to a strong party organization, never campaigned for office. Yet his work led directly to the independence of the Indian subcontinent from Great Britain, to the creation of the nation of Pakistan, and to social reforms that have strongly and permanently influenced Indian history and culture. Gandhi shows us with remarkable richness the political and social impact the Idealist can have, and because of this the life of the gentle Mahatma has a powerful claim to a place in this work.

Mohandas K. Gandhi

"To see god face to face"

Born October 2, 1869
Died January 30, 1948

I count the days with Gandhi the most fruitful of my life. No other experience was as inspiring and as meaningful and as lasting. No other so shook me out of the rut of banal existence and opened my ordinary mind and spirit, rooted in the materialist, capitalist West as they were, to some conception of the meaning of life on this perplexing earth.[64]

These are the words of William L. Shirer, a vastly experienced observer of the political world, an historian for over fifty years, and an author whose *The Rise and Fall of the Third Reich* won him the Pulitzer Prize. Who was this Gandhi, this man whose spiritual character so

---

[64] *Gandhi: A Memoir*, 250

profoundly and enduringly influenced the worldly William Shirer as well as millions of others?

But the question is not encompassing enough. Gandhi was not only a great spiritual leader; he was also a surpassingly successful social reformer and an extraordinary statesman. To understand Gandhi we must therefore ask not only about the spiritual character of his life, but also about his social and political behavior. This is the man, after all, who almost single-handedly freed India and its five hundred million people from their two and one-half century subjection to the British Empire. And this is the man who accomplished that remarkable feat without raising an army, without firing a gun, or taking a hostage, and without ever holding significant political office.

This is he about whom Albert Einstein said, "Generations to come will scarce believe that such a one as this ever in flesh and blood walked upon this earth."[65]

This is the Mentor Idealist, Mohandas Karamchand Gandhi.

Mohandas Gandhi was born October 2, 1869, in Porbandar, India, the youngest of four children. He believed he was blessed to have had the parents he did. His mother he characterized as possessing great saintliness and his father he saw as short-tempered, but a truthful, brave, generous, and absolutely incorruptible man. There was nothing else about which the young Mohandas felt he could boast. Though they were hard-working and reasonably comfortable by Indian standards, his family was not well-to-do. His family was widely respected in their community, though not of the highest caste. As a youngster Mohandas was at best an indifferent student, bright enough, but the victim of extreme and even painful shyness.

> I used to be very shy and avoided all company. My books and my lessons were my sole companions. To be at school at the stroke of the hour and to run back home as soon as the school closed, — that was my daily habit. I literally ran back, because I could not bear to talk to anybody.[66]

He was also tied to a standard of truthfulness that did little to help him socially. In his autobiography Gandhi commented that "I do not remember having ever told a lie, during this short period [from age six to twelve], either to my teachers or to my school-mates.[67]

---

65 Quoted in *Gandhi: A Pictorial Biography*, 175
66 *Gandhi, An Autobiography*, 6
67 *Gandhi: A Memoir*, 6

His characteristic shyness and truthfulness continued unabated into his teen years. In the India of Gandhi's youth, what we would call "high schools" were subject to visits from governmental monitors. Their task it was to examine the school's students to see if the proper standards of learning were being maintained. It was not an uncommon practice for teachers surreptitiously to "help" the students during such testing in order to make the school look better. During one such examination Gandhi was struggling with a word on a spelling test. Gandhi's teacher tried subtly to encourage him to copy the word from his neighbor. But Gandhi didn't get the message,

> for I had thought that the teacher was there to supervise us against copying. The result was that all the boys, except myself, were found to have spelt every word correctly. Only I had been stupid. The teacher tried later to bring this stupidity home to me, but without effect. I never could learn the art of "copying."[68]

This sort of "stupidity" would not ultimately be a problem for Gandhi the Idealist, however. Intellectual virtue was fine, of course, but it was a secondary virtue for him. Intellect had its utility but it was not what was finally central to his life, as Gandhi remembers:

> I had not any high regard for my ability. I used to be astonished whenever I won prizes and scholarships. But I very jealously guarded my character. The least little blemish drew tears from my eyes. When I merited, or seemed to the teacher to merit, a rebuke, it was unbearable for me. I remember having once received corporal punishment. I did not so much mind the punishment, as the fact that it was considered my desert.[69]

The young Idealist responded to the heart of the matter: it was his *self* that was at issue. Attributes such as intelligence or courage or cleverness might be comforting and useful but they were not the unique, pure self he was already devoted to realizing.

> What I want to achieve—what I have been striving and pining to achieve these thirty years,—is self-realization, to see god face to face, to attain Moksha.[70]

The word Moksha can be translated approximately—and incompletely, for it is rich with meaning—as salvation; freedom from

---

68 *Gandhi: A Memoir*, 6
69 *Gandhi, An Autobiography*, 15
70 *Gandhi, An Autobiography*, xii

the cycle of birth and death; freedom from the temporal and mortal world of illusion, of ordinary experience."

With characteristic passion Gandhi continues,

> I live and move and have my being in pursuit of this goal. All that I do by way of speaking and writing, and all my ventures in the political field, are directed to this same end.[71]

Consider his Truth that is behind the truth, his Reality more real than everyday reality, the Certainty he has beyond certainty. Notice too the fervor of his vision, his joy in its scope. Only an Idealist would write these lines:

> All that appears and happens about and around us is uncertain, transient. But there is a Supreme Being hidden therein as a Certainty, and one would be blessed if one could catch a glimpse of that Certainty and hitch one's waggon to it. The quest for that Truth is the summum bonum of life.[72]

Because he was a remarkable example of the Idealist temperament, the young Gandhi could hardly expect completely to avoid blemishes to his character. In later years he remembered with special distress a young friend (or so he seemed to Gandhi at the time) who was able to blandish him into sinful ways. His ostensible friend even tried to set Gandhi up with a prostitute. He failed in that venture but was successful in convincing the young Idealist to try including meat in his diet. Meat was forbidden to Gandhi but his young friend's clever arguments made it seem acceptable, at least for the moment. Gandhi was briefly persuaded to eat meat, but eventually came to detest his own behavior, and recovered from his errors more convinced than ever of the inviolate fitness of his beliefs.

There was one fall from grace which he committed without being talked into it and which he remembered ever after. It was an act of petty theft, the guilt for which assailed him so terribly that he finally wrote a letter of confession to his father. (He had to write; he could not bear to speak the words aloud.)

> He read it through, and pearl-drops trickled down his cheeks, wetting the paper. For a moment he closed his eyes in thought and then tore up the note....I also cried. I could see my father's agony. If I were a painter I could draw a picture of the whole scene today. It is still so vivid in my mind....Those pearl-drops of love cleansed my heart, and washed my

71 *Gandhi, An Autobiography*, xii
72 *Gandhi, An Autobiography*, 250-51

sin away. Only he who has experienced such love can know what it is.[73]

It is a moving testimony which speaks to the reader of Gandhi's remarkable way of giving meaning to events. His father's tears were for Gandhi the expression of terrible disappointment, but they also expressed a disappointment grounded in unending love and therefore in forgiveness. Those tears were Gandhi's penance, done for him by his loving father, and bear a striking similarity to the Christian rendering of Christ's sacrifice on the Cross. It was a heartbreaking and a beautiful experience for the young Gandhi.[74]

> One thing took deep root in me—the conviction that morality is the basis of things, and that truth is the substance of all morality. Truth became my sole objective. It began to grow in magnitude every day, and my definition of it also has been ever widening.

While these convictions were growing in him the young Mohandas was also growing into his place in his family and society. Gandhi was married at thirteen, to a girl he knew only vaguely, as was the custom of his social class. The marriage had been agreed upon by their families some time earlier, and he and his equally young bride, Kasturbai, were wed in a traditionally lengthy celebration.

Their marriage endured until Kasturbai's death some sixty years later, but it was marked by not a few powerful disagreements and, as his work carried him from place to place, numerous prolonged separations. Gandhi confesses that as a newly-married youngster he was very intent upon "playing the husband." He swaggered into the role with a prideful, possessive and jealous passion and a vehemently dictatorial style, not uncommon to husbands of his social class. He also admitted later to a relish for the sexual side of marriage which, he confessed sheepishly, he was able to surrender only after many years of prolonged struggle.

Idealist or not Gandhi had been raised in a traditional Hindu Indian culture. Husbands and wives in that tradition were not "equals" in the fashion which is often idealized in the West. It was only after some years that Gandhi learned to bring reasonable grace and compassion to his relationship with his wife. For her part Kasturbai was a strong woman who was quite capable of resisting her husband's more

---

73 *Gandhi, An Autobiography,* 27-28
74 *Gandhi, An Autobiography,* 27-28

unreasonable dictates. During the early years of marriage she often gave as good as she got in her struggle against his domination.

When Gandhi finished his schooling at eighteen, he was already five years a married man and a father as well. He needed to decide on a career, and his family and he agreed that he should study law. Law was a far less exalted goal than it might appear. Barristers were plentiful in India, their schooling was relatively brief and leisurely, and their training was far from arduous. But their status was greater than that of the common worker, and with enough perseverance a young man could make a decent living at the barrister's trade. So, in September of 1887, Gandhi sailed for England to be trained in law. He arrived wearing a new white flannel suit, convinced by his experience in the warm climes of India that all Englishmen wore white suits. He was mortified by the error but, still persuaded at his young age that the British Empire was enlightened and admirable, he bought new and stylish clothing, and continued for some time to attempt English ways.

While in London he studied law assiduously, but he also continued to pursue his deep interest in self-purification. As time passed he simplified his life more and more, restricted his budget ever more tightly, for he knew the cost of his education was a burden for his family, and immersed himself deeply in his experiments with dietary self-purification and health. Eventually he decided to live in one room in which he did his studying, sleeping, cooking and (usually) his eating.

Gandhi's interest in dietary matters proved to be intense and lifelong. He experimented continuously with diet and went to extreme lengths in his quest for the ideal dietary discipline. As the years passed he imposed more and more restrictions on himself. Fairly early in his "experiments" he attempted to live on a "pure fruit diet, and that too composed of the cheapest fruit possible. Our ambition was to live the life of the poorest people."[75] Raw nuts, dates, bananas, lemons and olive oil were the full substances of his diet—and of those who joined him in his "experiment," for even as a young man Gandhi had a way of attracting others to his side.

One finds no sanctimony in Gandhi's narrative about his life-long experiments with food. He focuses rather on the benefits to be reaped.

---

75 *Gandhi, An Autobiography,* 329

Even the everyday benefits are worthy of his mention: "The fruit diet turned out to be very convenient also. Cooking was practically done away with."[76] Nonetheless the Idealist understands that any worthy practice, including fasting, is a fundamentally spiritual exercise. Regardless of the physical benefits of any diet,

> it is certain that the mind is the principal thing. A mind consciously unclean cannot be cleansed by fasting. Modifications in diet have no effect on it. The concupiscence of the mind cannot be rooted out except by intense self-examination, surrender to God and, lastly, grace.[77]

The Idealist knows that acting because one "ought to," observing the forms but ignoring their significance, is worse than wasteful. "If physical fasting is not accompanied by mental fasting, it is bound to end in hypocrisy and disaster,"[78] he tells us. Life is a matter of personal meaning and personal purity, of the integration of the inner and outer, the private and public selves. But to pursue one's path, no matter how stringent, does not mean that one must suffer.

> Let not the reader think that this living made my life by any means a dreary affair. On the contrary the change harmonized my inward and outward life. It was also more in keeping with the means of my family. My life was certainly more truthful and my soul knew no bounds of joy.[79]

Diet and living style were finally not the issue, but rather spirituality, growth, oneness, the purity of the soul. These were not ways of sacrifice, but rather ways of growth.

In spite of the single-minded vigor of his search for spirituality and truth he was to the world around him still the same shy, tongue-tied Mohandas he had always been, and his shyness still posed problems for him. During his time in England the diet-absorbed Gandhi had joined a vegetarian society. There came an occasion when the expulsion of another member from the society was being considered. The grounds upon which expulsion was proposed were fundamentally irrelevant to the society's purpose and Gandhi, intensely absorbed in the issue, finally decided that he must speak out against the proposed expulsion. But the problem of his shyness remained.

---

76 *Gandhi, An Autobiography,* 329
77 *Gandhi, An Autobiography,* 329
78 *Gandhi, An Autobiography,* 332
79 *Gandhi, An Autobiography,* 55

I had not the courage to speak and I therefore decided to set down my thoughts in writing. I went to the meeting with the document in my pocket. So far as I recollect, I did not find myself equal even to reading it, and the President had it read by someone else.

This shyness I retained throughout my stay in England. Even when I paid a social call the presence of half a dozen or more people would strike me dumb.[80]

But Gandhi had an extraordinary ability to find a positive perspective about any event in his life, to find valuable meaning in what others might see as the most distressing happenings:

Experience has taught me that silence is part of the spiritual discipline of a votary of truth. Proneness to exaggerate, to suppress or modify the truth, wittingly or unwittingly, is a natural weakness of man, and silence is necessary in order to surmount it....My shyness has been in reality my shield and buckler. It has allowed me to grow. It has helped me in my discernment of truth.[81]

In 1891, after four years of study in England, Gandhi easily passed the bar examination and was formally admitted to the bar. The twenty-two year old Indian barrister immediately returned to India and took up the practice of law in Bombay. But his legal skills were not much better than his training, which had been, except for the intensive studies he undertook on his own initiative, desultory. Opportunities for making a living were meager. A new lawyer, he was advised, should expect to "vegetate" for three to seven years; only then could he expect to make a good living at the trade. His legal career was further impeded by his own impeccable and irrepressible honesty and his almost impossible shyness. After six months of struggle and in some despair he returned to Rajkot where his family had moved from Porbandar, and where he became little more than a clerk in his brother's employ.

At that time there were some 65,000 Indians in South Africa, some businessmen and many laborers, and inevitably there was legal work which needed doing. Through his family's connections with certain of these businessmen Gandhi was offered a year-long tenure in the Natal where his chief function would be to help with a troublesome legal dispute between two business in the Indian community. He gladly

---

80 *Gandhi, An Autobiography,* 60
81 *Gandhi, An Autobiography,* 62

accepted the offer and sailed for Durban in Natal, in white-dominated southern Africa.

Once there he became engaged not only in the legal work but also in the broader life of the Indian business community. And at last the paralyzingly shy young lawyer began to find his tongue.

> I had always heard the merchants say that truth was not possible in business. Business, they say, is a very practical affair, and truth is a matter of religion; and they argue that practical affairs are one thing, while religion is quite another. Pure truth, they hold, is out of the question in business, one can speak it only so far as is suitable. I strongly contested the position in my speech and awakened the merchants to a sense of their duty, which was two-fold. Their responsibility to be truthful was all the greater in a foreign land, because the conduct of a few Indians was the measure of that of the millions of their fellow-countrymen.[82]

It was by his own admission the first public speech of his life. The upshot of this speech, prompted by his passion for truth and his commitment to ethical behavior, was not only the revivification of truth and ethics, but the organization of an association of Indian businessmen which would provide political strength to its members. This was also most important, for there were several matters of some urgency to the Indian community (some as primitive but important as sanitation habits and facilities) about which they had not been able to take effective action.

Gandhi's passion for integrity was bolstered by his conviction that integrity was also a practical matter and that he could proffer arguments with which to demonstrate its practicality. His remarkable ability turned his Mentor's vision into a utilitarian world, to speak effectively of truth and of sanitation in the same sentence, was a hallmark of Gandhi's work all his life.

In all this, "Africa was the laboratory for India."[83] It was there that he began to develop the principles and methods that would find their fullest expression in India. Already his mix of the practical and the idealistic was evidencing itself, even in his handling of the legal dispute for which he had been brought to South Africa. It was a dispute between two Indian businessmen that was marked by its complex and

---

82 *Gandhi, An Autobiography,* 126
83 *Gandhi: A Pictorial Biography,* 33

inflammatory character. Still, after a great deal of work Gandhi was able—to the astonishment of the community—to persuade the antagonists to resolve the matter without going to court. His comment about the outcome is one not generally associated with lawyers:

> My joy was boundless. I had learnt the true practice of law. I had learnt to find out the better side of human nature and to enter men's hearts. I realized that the true function of a lawyer was to unite parties riven asunder....I lost nothing thereby [in future cases]—not even money, certainly not my soul.[84]

After all, he commented on another occasion, "My experience has shown me that we win justice quickest by rendering justice to the other party."[85] It is preferable to avoid contest and the possibility of causing hurt to another. Far better to reach always for understanding and compromise—without compromising truth or justice—and to rejoice when they can be achieved.

One suspects there may be very few Idealist lawyers for the same reason there are few Idealist politicians.

During his time in South Africa Mohandas Gandhi had seen the discrimination practiced by the white population against the "coloureds" (chiefly Blacks and Indians). In fact he had referenced it in his arguments with his fellow Indians about the importance of truth in business. But he became most personally involved with that appalling discrimination when he made a business trip from Natal to Pretoria, South Africa, in order to settle the legal matter just mentioned. He had of course always been seen by the whites as merely "coloured," and his profession made him nothing but another "coolie barrister." But he learned to set aside the matter of discrimination, at least insofar as it was practiced only against him. He seemed to be unconcerned with matters of status or position, and such idiocy left him largely unaffected.

So Gandhi arranged to travel to Pretoria on the matter of business. He bought a first-class ticket for the train from Durban, settled into his first-class accommodations, and prepared to enjoy the trip. But when the railway conductor discovered him he was quickly rousted out and told to take his place in third-class accommodations with the other coloureds. The coloureds always travelled by third-class, after all, and the Indian's presence in first-class was naturally an affront to the whites.

---

84 *Gandhi, An Autobiography*, 134
85 *Gandhi, An Autobiography*, 182

Gandhi refused to leave the first class seat for which he had paid, and was consequently and unceremoniously thrown off the train at the next stop. The stop was at the small town of Pieter Maritzburg, located high in the freezing South African hill country. Gandhi sat on the platform of the Maritzburg station, his luggage strewn about him, trembling in the bitter cold.

> I began to think of my duty. Should I fight for my rights or go back to India, or should I go on to Pretoria without minding the insults, and return to India after finishing the case? It would be cowardice to run back to India without fulfilling my obligation. The hardship to which I was subjected was superficial—only a symptom of the deep disease of colour prejudice. I should try, if possible, to root out the disease and suffer hardships in the process. Redress for wrongs I should seek only to the extent that would be necessary for the removal of the colour prejudice.
>
> So I decided to take the next available train to Pretoria.[86]

The remainder of his trip was no less eventful and no more pleasant. Near the end of the journey he transferred to a stage, the final means of transport to his destination. Here he was required to sit on top with the driver rather than inside with the whites. Even so one of the white passengers eventually demanded Gandhi surrender his seat so the passenger could smoke a cigar. Gandhi again refused to surrender his place and (as Gandhi put it) "had his ears boxed" by the angry white. Only the intervention of more compassionate whites prevented him from being again ejected from a public conveyance.

Gandhi had made his decision at Maritzburg: he would neither run away from nor submit to unjust law or custom. Nor, it is important to note, would he attempt to revenge himself upon their perpetrators. He would seek redress for wrongs "only to the extent that would be necessary for the removal of the colour prejudice" but never as a matter of personal satisfaction. With the actions now born of his emerging vision of social justice, Mohandas Gandhi, the painfully shy young "coolie barrister," began to foreshadow Mohandas Gandhi, the inspirational spiritual leader and immensely effective social and political reformer. The great Mahatma Gandhi had sat in embryonic form on the freezing railway platform in Maritzburg.[87]

---

86 *Gandhi, An Autobiography,* 112

87 The term "Mahatma," with which Gandhi was eventually universally honored, was applied to a person venerated for his great wisdom and saintliness. Shirer translates the word as "great soul."

As he continued his remarkably effective and inspiring organizational work his reputation grew. He became immensely popular among the Indians in South Africa, and his services were so much in demand that his one-year tenure as a legal trouble-shooter turned into a remarkable three-year social reform mission. In 1896, he returned briefly to India, but had hardly settled down before he was called back to Africa to help further with the reform work there. So famous—or notorious, depending upon one's viewpoint—had he become that his arrival in Africa was greeted with a near-riot in which he only narrowly escaped being beaten to death by an angry mob of whites.

It was absolutely typical of Gandhi that he refused to become angry or vindictive toward the whites who had threatened his life. When it was suggested that he take legal action against the members of the crowd, some of whom could be identified by witnesses to the event, he replied, "I do not want to bring anyone to book. I am sure that, when the truth becomes known, they will be sorry for their conduct."[88] Again, typical of him was his response to being assaulted outside the residence of South Africa's President Kruger. During his time in the capitol of South Africa Gandhi had frequent occasion to walk past Kruger's residence. There were always guards surrounding the place, and on one occasion a guard took it upon himself to walk over and shove the unsuspecting Gandhi into the gutter. A white acquaintance saw the incident and offered to serve as a witness in court so charges could be brought against the guard. Gandhi declined the opportunity to retaliate. "What does the poor man know? All coloured people are the same to him. He no doubt treats negroes just as he has treated me. I have made it a rule not to go to court in respect of any personal grievance. So I do not intend to proceed against him."[89]

There is no suggestion here that Gandhi was seeking to be a martyr. When he wrote later about the incident he said, "But I never again went through this street....Why should I unnecessarily court another kick? I therefore selected a different walk."[90] And in such matters he could certainly exercise the restraint demanded by common sense. But he

---

88 *Gandhi, An Autobiography,* 195
89 *Gandhi, An Autobiography,* 130
90 *Gandhi, An Autobiography,* 131

could never be cowed and he continued his work in South Africa regardless of the dangers involved. He did not return to India again until 1901.

Once back in India he undertook a lengthy railway tour of the country to familiarize himself more thoroughly with conditions in his own homeland. This time he chose to avoid the comforts of first-class travel. Instead he booked the third-class rail accommodations which were used only by the poorest Indians. These accommodations were terribly uncomfortable, characterized by jammed compartments, ill-repaired cars, and grossly inadequate sanitary facilities, as well as the physical dangers associated with crowded and abused travellers and invariably hostile treatment by railway officials. Though he knew largely what to expect Gandhi did nothing to make his lot more comfortable than that of other third-class passengers. He travelled, he watched, and he learned.

He was capable of great compassion and had a remarkable ability to move people, but Gandhi never saw himself simply or even chiefly as a social reformer, and certainly not as a political activist. He was still a seeker after self-realization, which was ultimately intertwined with the search for God. Gandhi tells his readers this quite explicitly when he writes of the active role he took in social and political reform.

> If I found myself entirely absorbed in the service of the community, the reason behind it was my desire for self-realization. I had made the religion of service my own, as I felt that god could be realized only through service.[91]

And again,

> The little fleeting glimpses, therefore, that I have been able to have of Truth can hardly convey an idea of the indescribable lustre of Truth, a million times more intense than that of the sun we daily see with our eyes....To see the universal and all-pervading Spirit of Truth face to face one must be able to love the meanest of creation as oneself. And a man who aspires after that cannot afford to keep out of any field of life. That is why my devotion to Truth has drawn me into the field of politics; and I can say without the slightest hesitation, and yet in all humility, that those who say that religion has nothing to do with politics do not know what religion means.[92]

---

91 *Gandhi, An Autobiography,* 158
92 *Gandhi, An Autobiography,* 504

As time passed he undertook many other first-hand inspections of the conditions under which most of his fellow Indians lived. He did so most typically by subjecting himself to the same conditions as those whose difficulties he was investigating. Soon he was accompanied by volunteer teachers whose job was to increase the common people's literacy and to help them acquire some basic skills in taking effective social action. Gandhi's volunteers also provided medical supplies, education about disease, and the connection between disease and poor sanitary conditions. (Sanitation had been a matter of concern to him since his earliest days in Africa.)

Gandhi's work, however, was not intended to be practical work laced with piety. In fact the converse was the case. On one occasion, for example, he was witness to the sullying of a sacred cleansing ceremony and became very angry. He decided to atone personally for the behavior of the transgressors. "He vowed never to eat more than five articles of food in any twenty-four hours—a vow he kept to the end of his life.[93]

In this we find more evidence of the Idealist emphasis on purity, of the soul or spirit or self, to be sure, even when demonstrated through the purification of the body. And it is a particularly Idealist trait to consider that one might purify the world by purifying one's self.

Along with such measures, however, Gandhi's actions began to take on an increasingly direct political cast. This was especially evident when he became involved with the Indian Congress. This was a British-sponsored committee whose chief function was to rubber-stamp British political and economic decisions. It was a noisy but ineffectual political body which, Gandhi once said, would meet three days every year and then go back to sleep. Somehow in the midst of all this activity Gandhi the barrister also managed to set up and maintain a reasonably successful law practice in Bombay. The practice itself came to focus more completely on rectifying the social injustices he observed. But it also prospered sufficiently that Gandhi became a modest financial success. Still, as time went on the barrister had little and less time for professional success; he was busy changing a world.

It was about 1915, on his return from one of his trips to South Africa, that he had begun teaching widely his strategy of non-violent

---

93 *Gandhi: A Pictorial Biography,* 54

non-cooperation, which he called "satyagraha." "Satyagraha" is a word coined by Gandhi, a combination of two other Indian words. Gandhi could find no single word which conveyed quite what he wanted it to. The meaning of "satyagraha" is very rich and to translate its nuances into English is an almost impossible task. In rough terms "satyagraha" means "passive resistance," but it is resistance as an enriched and ennobled act. *Not* to obey is taken to be quite different than simply to *dis*obey. To do what is right, what is ethically demanded of one may mean to ignore the laws of the land. But such an act, said Gandhi, is quite a different matter than to deliberately and wantonly disobey the law.

Satyagraha also calls upon one to act in such a way as to do no harm to others, to subject everyone to the force of truth and love. Therefore to ignore unjust laws does not mean to take upon one's self the right to do damage to others. Even those who attempt to uphold unjust laws should not be made victims of violence. One is reminded of the "flower children" of the sixties. A memorable photo comes to mind of some of these people, most of them still in their late teens and early twenties, attempting to disarm a line of national guardsmen by stuffing long-stemmed flowers into the barrels of the guardsmen's rifles. There are some parallels in that image with Gandhi's satyagraha, though perhaps the full power of the term cannot be understood unless one also remembers another photo, this one taken one tragic day at Kent State University.

It is tempting to translate the term as "civil disobedience," but the English term is far too weak. Gandhi meant to call attention to resistance as a highly disciplined, courageously ethical act of non-obedience, carried out in a non-violent manner. The principled, ethical quality of satyagraha may perhaps be understood with more immediacy if one notes Shirer's potent two-word translation of the term: "soul force."

This increasingly well-articulated strategy of non-cooperation with unfair and oppressive laws repeatedly called him to the attention of the authorities. As a result he was thrown into jail, time and again over the next two decades. William Shirer added up the figures and discovered that Mohandas Gandhi spent almost six and one half years in British and South African prisons and jails. Shirer's exact accounting of Gandhi's imprisonments: 2,089 days in India, 249 days in South Africa.[94] Nevertheless, Gandhi was in no manner precipitous or thoughtless about the employment of the satyagraha strategy. He warns us sternly about its use:

> Before one can be fit for the practice of civil disobedience one must have rendered willing and respectful obedience to the state laws. [Compliance out of fear of the consequences of disobedience is not] the willing and spontaneous obedience that is required of a Satyagrahi. A Satyagrahi obeys the laws of society intelligently and of his own free will, because he considers it to be his sacred duty to do so. It is only when a person has thus obeyed the laws of society scrupulously that he is in a position to judge as to which particular rules are good and just and which unjust and iniquitous. Only then does the right accrue to him of the civil disobedience of certain laws in well-defined circumstances.[95]

There could be no mean-spiritedness in such an approach. There could be only the pursuit of justice and the removal of the sources of injustice. These sources were not to be found in the nature of individual human beings; individuals, no matter how disturbing their conduct, were inherently deserving of our respect and our compassion. A man and his deed are two distinct things. Therefore whereas a good deed should call forth approbation and a wicked deed disapprobation, the doer of the deed, whether good or wicked, always deserves respect or pity.

> It is quite proper to resist and attack a system, but to resist and attack its author is tantamount to resisting and attacking oneself. For we are all tarred with the same brush, and are children of one and the same Creator, and as such the divine powers within us are infinite. To slight a single human being is to slight those divine powers, and thus to harm not only that being but with him the whole world.[96]

The British government in India did not look kindly upon Gandhi's efforts, no matter how high-principled his strategy, nor would he have wished it to do so. Thus in 1922 he was brought to trial for three newspaper articles he had written in which he "attempted to bring about disaffection for His Majesty's government." At his trial Gandhi simply pleaded guilty. Then he put the government—and the judge—in an awkward position when he said (and only part of his eloquent statement is offered here):

---

94 *Gandhi: A Memoir*, 221
95 *Gandhi, An Autobiography*, 470
96 *Gandhi, An Autobiography*, 276

I am here therefore to invite and submit to the highest penalty that can be inflicted upon me for what in law is a deliberate crime and what appears to me to be the highest duty of a citizen. The only course open to you, the judge, is either to resign your post and thus disassociate yourself from evil, if you feel that the law you are called upon to administer is an evil and that in reality I am innocent; or to inflict on me the severest penalty, if you believe that the system and the law you are assisting to administer are good for the people of this country, and that my activity is therefore injurious to the public weal.[97]

The judge, caught in the awkward position his defendant intended for him, sentenced Gandhi to two years for each of the three offences: a total of six years. The judge announced his sentence in a lengthy statement which clearly conveyed both an apology for the sentence and his considerable respect for the Mahatma. He was in effect trapped into admitting that he was upholding a law in which he could not fully believe.

Perhaps the most famous example of Gandhi's satyagraha campaign was the highly-publicized "Salt March" he made in the spring of 1930, an event ably portrayed in the film *Gandhi* just a few years ago. The British maintained the right in those days to be the sole makers, distributors, and sellers of salt throughout India. (Just to round out the picture, the British also reserved the right to collect tax on the sale of salt.) Any Indian who produced his own supply of salt was therefore a lawbreaker who could be punished with a fine, with jail, or with both. Gandhi felt that this law was a bald, blatant example of British political and economic oppression, that it was especially oppressive to India's poor, and that it was a law richly deserving of satyagraha.

Thus in March 1930 he made his famous and well-publicized 220-mile walk to the sea. As he and his few followers slowly paced off the distance others joined in the walk, which gradually became something of a procession. Some villagers along the hot and dusty way might sprinkle water on the roads in front of him to help keep down the dust; others would throw leaves and flower petals before him to ease his path. All along the way more people joined in the walk. There were several thousand people in the procession by the time the journey ended at the edge of the sea. Once there, and under the eager eyes of thousands, Mohandas Gandhi gathered up a small handful of salt from the water's edge.

---

97 *Gandhi: A Memoir*, 83

As he marched Gandhi had captured the attention of the entire Indian subcontinent. To do this he needed only to walk to the sea and take up a little salt. The act was done, the law had been set aside by this one aging man. Granted the walk was a long one; a short trip would have lacked sufficient drama. The handful of salt was, as things are measured, utterly trivial. The importance of the act was found not in its difficulty or scope but rather in what it symbolized. Much like the reform movement in India, the Salt March was a slow, inexorable progression during which Gandhi came to represent the best of India. His actions were the actions of India, his heart was the heart of India, his setting aside the law of the British was, therefore, India itself setting aside the British law. It was as if India itself reached out and quietly laid claim to its own.

Part of Mohandas Gandhi's brilliance was his remarkable attunement to those symbols which had the greatest impact on the people of India. It was this sensitivity to the nuances of symbol that enabled him so sublimely to combine symbol and his own person. The Salt March demonstrates beautifully his Idealist's gift for symbolic communication. The Idealist's universe, as William Blake put it, can be found in a grain of sand. Similarly, the spirit of India can be found in a single man's March, and India's freedom from subjugation could be found in a single man's gathering of salt from the sea.

It is not merely that the sign stands for the reality. Each participates in some profound way in the being of the other. Thus the symbolism used so routinely and sometimes so powerfully by the Idealist is not mere simile, no matter how artfully constructed it may be. On the contrary it is the simple expression of what is truth self-evident— at least to the Idealist.

Idealists, especially Mentors, often lead by example, and Gandhi's entire life was clearly devoted to this kind of leadership. Whether he demonstrated the discipline of proper diet, the importance of acceptance, or the duty of non-obedience, he demonstrated them, he lived them and modeled them. Gandhi had the Idealist's ability to unite people who might belong to very disparate, even dangerously polarized groups. This was an important ability, for India is composed of many disparate groups, including Moslems and Hindus who are capable of murderous savagery toward one another. He united these elements not through legislation or rhetoric, not by cajoling or cleverness, but by his own personal presence, his own personal example. The Salt March was a wonderful example of this leadership.

The Salt March inspired demonstrations and civil disobedience all over India. The British government had to take violent and massive measures to suppress these outbreaks and before long the jails in India were filled to overflowing with demonstrators. Clearly the British diplomatic intelligence was far less than Gandhi's, whom they once again jailed. He was not given a trial, in important part because the government did not want to give him the opportunity to deliver another speech. But jailing Gandhi this way only strengthened his position: he was a martyr in the eyes of the people of India who already loved him for his courage, his vision, his sacrifice, and for his love of them.[98]

Gandhi was by then worshipped by millions of Indians, especially the poor to whom he devoted so much of his time and energy. The Mahatma had become a man that the Boer government in South Africa and the British government in India had to deal with thoughtfully and gingerly. So well-loved and respected had he become that on several occasions he forced the British government to bow to his requests by the simple expedient of fasting publicly until it did so, and on several occasions he successfully employed the same approach with masses of angry and violent Indians as well. No one was quite safe from the Mahatma's loving insistence, and no one could doubt that he would die rather than break his fast before his conditions were met.

It was wise to recognize his absolute determination. He was merely a powerful fanatic to many observers, of course, but from the perspective of temperament theory one can gauge the almost perfect expression of Gandhi's Idealist style. Gandhi was seeking after true knowledge of God in all his activities, and for self-realization, and finally (if there is ever a finally for the Idealist) for Truth itself and release from the world of illusion. The quest was, at its root, not for three distinct outcomes, but for three aspects of the one. That quest he

---

[98] Technically, by the way, this high-handed British behavior was quite legal. There was a law which allowed the government to hold without cause anyone "at the pleasure of the government." This old law actually meant at the pleasure of the powerful merchants of the East India Company which was for many years the de facto ruler of India.

could not surrender any more than he could surrender his very identity, even if its fulfillment meant the loss of his physical life.

> For it is an unbroken torture to me that I am still so far from Him, Who as I fully know, governs every breath of my life, and Whose offspring I am. I know that it is the evil passions within that keep me so far from Him, and yet I cannot get away from them.[99]

He was already fify-six years old, and his passionate search was as intense as ever.

Winston Churchill, the brilliant and pugnacious Artisan Prime Minister of England, detested Gandhi. He hoped fervently that Gandhi would finally overdo things and starve himself to death, but he dared not let the Indian mahatma do so in a British jail. That would have led to horribly violent uprisings all over India and insurmountable political problems for Churchill. On one occasion, under the impression that Gandhi was dying, Churchill ordered that the Mahatma be released from prison where he had undertaken a three-week fast. Somewhat later the angry and impatient Churchill, still frustrated at his inability to eliminate this dreadful gadfly, sent an angry wire to his Indian Viceroy demanding to know why Gandhi wasn't dead yet!

Political activism had come slowly to Gandhi, but it was an inevitable consequence of his social activism. During his first two or three decades of life Gandhi had considered himself a good citizen of an essentially just and benevolent British Empire. The Empire had its flaws and made its errors, he thought, but these would be eliminated by its governing officials if only they were brought properly to official attention. But as he saw the pattern of British resistance to change, he realized that the Empire's intransigence was quite deliberate. Its discrimination against its "coloureds" would not succumb to enlightened administration, for there was no enlightened administration.

Characteristically, Gandhi's disillusionment did not lead him into despair but rather led him to a new vision, a new goal which would shape the course of much of the rest of his life: India must be freed entirely from British rule.

From that time forward Indian independence was in his mind no matter what social reforms he undertook, no matter what oppressive

---

99 *Gandhi, An Autobiography*, xv

laws he attempted to have repealed, no matter whether he was active in Africa or in India.

Gandhi worked intensively to bring about a peaceful Indian independence. In 1931 his efforts brought him to a political conference being held in London at which he hoped to generate significant movement toward independence. But he was not taken seriously and in spite of his arduous labor none of his hopes were realized. William Shirer was witness to the London conference and gives us a glimpse of Gandhi the Idealist there. He portrays Gandhi as a humorous, bubbling, man with a twinkle in his eye, an indefatigable and optimistic catalyst for action, and a saintly ascetic. Shirer's notes from the conference recorded that Gandhi appeared to be sleeping no more than four hours a night, and that

> ...he seemed fresh and relaxed, bubbling with confidence and often humor—how often those days, as I recall them and as my notes show, he broke into a peal of laughter.[100]

In the early part of the conference Gandhi maintained himself thus. But his failures there burdened him terribly. His 62nd birthday fell during the conference, and though it was cheerfully celebrated by his friends and admirers Gandhi seemed unusually discouraged. At one of the several birthday parties held in his honor he made a rather grim and disillusioned speech to his guests, something quite unusual for him. Then, according to Shirer,

> ...he hurried back to his East End settlement to attend a final birthday party, this one given him by the children of the dock workers who lived in the neighborhood. These were the sort of occasions he liked—among the poor. Once more, as he squatted with the children and talked and joked with them, he was his radiant, beaming self. I felt it was the happiest part of his anniversary day.[101]

Gandhi the Mentor could work, inspire, catalyze the ideas and actions of others. He could also lose his spirit, however temporarily, in the face of others' intractable meanness and cynical maneuvering. But the Idealist still had his special love for children and the poor. Such people were still the innocents of this world, they were still his occasion for hope, their appreciation could still transfuse his spirit with life.

---

100 *Gandhi, An Autobiography*, 131
101 *Gandhi, An Autobiography*, 193

Gandhi returned to India on December 28, 1931, convinced that only massive popular resistance to British rule would be effective. The route of traditional formal political action, meetings, conferences, and so forth, seemed bankrupt. But on January 4, 1932, before he could take extensive action, he was again arrested and jailed, again without trial. But it was too late; his disappointment was clear to the millions and his calls for action were irresistible. The British began to panic: within two months Lord Willingdon, the British Viceroy of India, had jailed 35,000 Indian leaders.

But Gandhi in jail was as potent as Gandhi at large. He had for some years been especially interested in improving the lot of India's "untouchables," the most disenfranchised and least regarded group of people in all India's caste-ridden population. In September of 1932 there was a measure before the authorities, and sponsored by the British, which would isolate these "untouchables" even further from their fellow Indians. On September 13 the Mahatma announced from his jail cell that he was undertaking a "fast unto death" until the measure was properly considered by the Indian authorities. The fast was frighteningly debilitating for him; it appears that he almost died in consequence of it. But it was a very effective move; the measure was dropped, and an outpouring of new acceptance of the "untouchables" swept through India.

But Gandhi had not done with using himself as a kind of spiritual hostage: as sometimes happened, he heard a voice, and the voice this time told him he must fast further. He was still in prison and the British government feared he would die there, so they simply released him. He continued his fast, was terribly weakened, but slowly recovered.

Such was the style of the Mahatma, Mohandas K. Gandhi, and the next fifteen years of his life continued in the same vein, though with more political work of a less dramatic character. For our purposes it is enough to know that he continued his trebly-determined life until it ended: his constant work toward social justice and economic improvement for the downtrodden of India; his unending struggle for India's national independence from Great Britain; and underlying and powering both, his lifelong pursuit of his own complete self-realization.

Perhaps Gandhi might have acknowledged that the first and the third of these goals were ultimately—and properly—out of reach. But the second: quite another matter! "Just remember this, my friend," he had said to Shirer at the London Conference. "Just remember what I've harped on so often, even though you don't believe me: I shall see India free! Before I die!"[102] And on August 15, 1947, when Mohandas Gandhi was seventy-seven, he saw his goal accomplished. Lord Lois Mountbatten stood before the news cameras of the world and in solemn ceremony officially announced the end of British rule in India.

Kasturbai, his life's companion, did not live to see the event. She had died more than two years earlier, in February of 1944. She might have lived longer, but for religious reasons, and because he thought it was already too late, Gandhi forbade the use of antibiotics. She died in his arms.

Though India's independence was the fruition of a lifetime's work, Gandhi was horrified by the events which quickly followed. The majority of Indians (about 80% of the population) were Hindus, while the remainder were mostly Moslems. Tensions were high between the two factions and it had already been established (to Gandhi's deep regret) that immediately upon independence India would be divided into a predominantly Moslem state, Pakistan, and the predominantly Hindu state of India. The bifurcation came about at the insistence of influential Moslems, for in spite of Gandhi's best efforts the suspicions and antagonisms between the Hindu and the Moslem populations were very deeply rooted. Gandhi could subvert mindless force and violence, even cause an empire to release its grip on another land. But he could not resolve the problems associated with the differing beliefs of the Hindus and Moslems. Ideas as potent as his now openly opposed Gandhi's own ideas. Idea defeated idea, ingrained religious belief broke inspired spiritual vision.

With the declaration of India's and Pakistan's statehood, twelve million Moslems began the journey from every part of India to the borders of their new country. For many of them it was a long, arduous and dangerous trek. For a half million of them, men, women, and children alike, it was a fatal one: they were slain by hostile Hindus before they could reach the safety of Pakistan. Meanwhile other Moslems vented their own generations of anger upon the Hindus, loosening a flood of murder, rape, torture and destruction as they made their way toward Pakistan. Gandhi was almost broken by these appalling events as well as by the collapse of his hopes for a unified India shared peacefully by Moslem and Hindu.

---

102 *Gandhi: A Memoir*, 66-67

As in a play whose climax has been reached, the end came quickly. On January 30, 1948, less than six weeks after India's independence, Mohandas K. Gandhi was walking toward the place of his evening prayers. As always he moved through a crowd of worshippers and of admirers and of the merely curious. An assassin (who was also a Hindu, fortunately; it is terrible to think what would have happened had he been a Moslem) found it easy to step up to the Mahatma, raise his pistol, and fire three bullets into Gandhi's chest. Gandhi cried out "Oh, God!" and fell to the ground, mortally wounded. He was dead in a matter of moments.

Mohandas K. Gandhi had lived, and now he died, seeking

the Absolute Truth, the Eternal Principle, that is God...I have not yet found Him, but I am seeking after Him. I am prepared to sacrifice the things dearest to me in pursuit of this quest. Even if the sacrifice demanded be my very life, I hope I may be prepared to give it.[103]

The day after he was slain an editorial appeared in the Indian newspaper *The Hindustan Standard*. Alone in the middle of an empty page it stood, its dark brevity heavy against the white page:

Gandhiji has been killed by his own people for whose redemption he lived. This second crucifixion in the history of the world has been enacted on a Friday— the same day Jesus was done to death one thousand nine hundred and fifteen years ago. Father, forgive us.

Bibliography

Andrews, C 1929	*Mahatma Gandhi's Ideas*
Bahattacharyya, S 1929	*Mahatma Gandhi, the Journalist*
Basham, A 1988	*The Father of the Nation: Life and Message of Mahatma Gandhi*
Bedekar, D 1975	*Towards Understanding Gandhi*
Bourke-White, M 1950	*Halfway to Freedom*
Bose, N 1974	*My Days With Gandhi*
Brown, J 1977	*Gandhi and Civil Disobedience*
Catlin, G 1950	*In the Path of Mahatma Gandhi*
Chatfield, C (ed) 1976	*The Americanization of the Mahatma*
Chaterjee, M 1983	*Gandhi's Religious Thoughts*
Das, A 1979	*Foundations of Gandhian Economics*

---

103 *Gandhi, An Autobiography*, xiii-xiv

Datta, D 1961	*The Philosophy of Mahatma Gandhi*
Dey, M 1948	*Portraits of Mahatma Gandhi*
Doke, J 1959	*Gandhi: An Indian Patriot in South Africa*
Edwards, M 1986	*The Myth of Mahatma: Gandhi, the British, and the Raj*
Erikson, E 1969	*Gandhi's Truth*
Fischer, L 1951	*The Life of Mahatma Gandhi*
Fischer, H 1983	*Mahatma Gandhi: Personality and Leader of his Time*
Ganguli, B 1973	*Gandhi's Social Philosophy*
Gandhi, M 1945	*An Autobiography*
Gupta, S 1968	*The Economic Philosophy of Mahatma Gandhi*
Houssain, S 1937	*Gandhi, the Saint as Statesman*
Iyer, R 1978	*The Moral and Political Thought of Mahatma Gandhi*
Jones, E 1948	*Mahatma Gandhi*
Keer, D 1973	*Mahatma Gandhi: Political Saint and Unarmed Prophet*
Koestler, A 1960	*The Lotus and the Robot*
Nanda, B 1958	*Mahatma Gandhi: a Biography*
Nanda, B 1985	*Gandhi and his Critics*
Nehru, J 1966	*Mahatma Gandhi*
Patel, M 1953	*The Educational Philosophy of Mahatma Gandhi*
Power, P 1961	*Gandhi on World Affairs*
Radhakrishnan, S (ed) 1939	*Mahatma Gandhi: Essays and Reflections*
Roland, R 1924	*Mahatma Gandhi: the Man who Became One with the Universal Being*
Sethi, J 1989	*Gandhian Critique of Western Peace Movements*
Sheean, V 1955	*Mahatma Gandhi, a Great Life in Brief*
Shirer, W 1979	*Gandhi: A Memoir*
Shuckla, C 1949	*Conversations of Gandhi*
Verma, S 1970	*Metaphysical Foundation of Mahatma Gandhi's Thought*
Walker, R 1943	*The Wisdom of Gandhi*

A Backward Glance

Eleanor Roosevelt and Mohandas Gandhi: neither Idealist was a President, nor a head of state anywhere. Both were still profoundly influential, by virtue of their benevolence, their empathic style, the strength of their personal vision. They remind us that *election* is only one form of *selection*; and, as history has demonstrated, not always the most important form.

Chapter Six

PATTERNS REVISITED

Back around the turn of the century three Americans, William James, John Dewey, and Charles Peirce, made up a distinctly American brand of philosophy, best known today as "pragmatism." They were less interested in traditional questions of truth than in "heuristics," the study of methods that *work*. The pragmatists postulated that as we grow up we acquire a repertoire of means, a sort of toolkit of useful things to do. Having acquired our tool kit, we look around for things that we can fix with it. They said that we do not first look for problems to tackle and then come up with solutions, but rather we have solutions and we look for problems we can use them on. In this sense, *temperament* determines which of the four toolkits we will pick up; *character* is the toolkit to which temperament has led us.

As Harry Stack Sullivan once said, "people are more simply human than anything else."[1] The Presidents, all of them, were and are simply human, just like the rest of us. Just as we all do, the Presidents of the United States continue after they become President to do what they were good at doing before they entered the presidency. They come to the office equipped with their repertoire of useful methods, and they are inclined to apply them to whatever problems those methods fit. And they tend not to notice the problems, of which there are always many, that they are not equipped to handle. As they must, whether Presidents or plumbers, people will always act in character.

Given that there are four temperaments, then it is possible that each of the four is better suited than the other three to deal with some particular kind of situation, that each character toolkit is best suited for a certain type of problem. When it is time for long-range planning, for a

---

1 See Sullivan's *Interpersonal Theory of Psychiatry*

sea change in the political architecture or course of a nation, we might expect that a Rational would make the most fitting candidate for office. When it is time for fast and vigorous action rather than reflection, when a political or military gunslinger is needed to respond quickly to immediately pressing challenges, then it would appear that an Artisan is the most suitable selection. When matters are moving in a productive direction and it is important to stabilize and regulate social interactions at home and abroad, it would seem to be time to elect a Guardian.

It might also be that an Idealist president would be most suitable when the relationships between people of different countries, especially face-to-face diplomatic relationships, are critical. For example, what might have happened to Wilson's Fourteen-Point plan had it been presented by a benevolent Idealist such as Eleanor Roosevelt or Mohandas Gandhi instead of the uncompromising Guardian Wilson? And what might have been possible if a talented Idealist had been able to talk with Northern and Southern hotheads in the middle 1800s? Perhaps a half million lives would have been saved.

Of course one assumption of the democratic process is that the electorate will usually choose the candidate best equipped to deal with current problems. Washington, for example, was a wonderful presidential choice for the earliest days of the nation, and Lincoln's presidency 72 years later was something of a gift from heaven for a nation doomed to civil war. Harry Truman was an unusually steadfast character, just the type to tackle Stalin's aggressive moves, and the brash John Kennedy may have been just the man to outwit the rash Nikita Khrushchev.

Perhaps the electorate recognizes in some way the differences in character, and responds, however instinctively, to these differences in its choice of presidents. Is this in fact what has happened? Has the electorate tended to choose Artisans when there was need for quick and decisive action, or Guardians during times when stability was most important, or Rationals when it seemed time to consider the direction the nation was moving?

As the discussion proceeds you may wish to use the following listing to help you recall the sequence of temperament and prior work experience of each President.

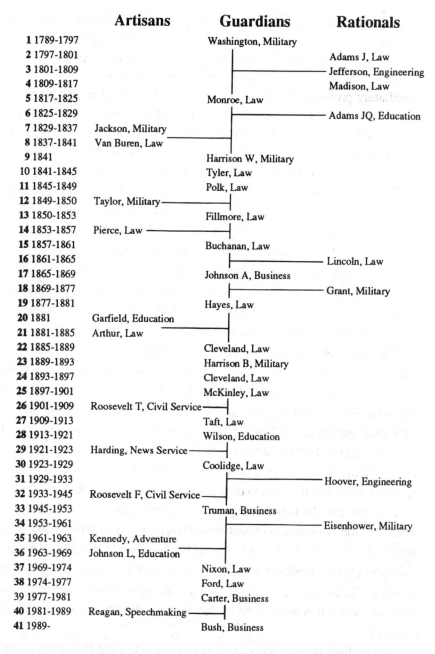

		Artisans	**Guardians**	**Rationals**
1	1789-1797		Washington, Military	
2	1797-1801			Adams J, Law
3	1801-1809			Jefferson, Engineering
4	1809-1817			Madison, Law
5	1817-1825		Monroe, Law	
6	1825-1829			Adams JQ, Education
7	1829-1837	Jackson, Military		
8	1837-1841	Van Buren, Law		
9	1841		Harrison W, Military	
10	1841-1845		Tyler, Law	
11	1845-1849		Polk, Law	
12	1849-1850	Taylor, Military		
13	1850-1853		Fillmore, Law	
14	1853-1857	Pierce, Law		
15	1857-1861		Buchanan, Law	
16	1861-1865			Lincoln, Law
17	1865-1869		Johnson A, Business	
18	1869-1877			Grant, Military
19	1877-1881		Hayes, Law	
20	1881	Garfield, Education		
21	1881-1885	Arthur, Law		
22	1885-1889		Cleveland, Law	
23	1889-1893		Harrison B, Military	
24	1893-1897		Cleveland, Law	
25	1897-1901		McKinley, Law	
26	1901-1909	Roosevelt T, Civil Service		
27	1909-1913		Taft, Law	
28	1913-1921		Wilson, Education	
29	1921-1923	Harding, News Service		
30	1923-1929		Coolidge, Law	
31	1929-1933			Hoover, Engineering
32	1933-1945	Roosevelt F, Civil Service		
33	1945-1953		Truman, Business	
34	1953-1961			Eisenhower, Military
35	1961-1963	Kennedy, Adventure		
36	1963-1969	Johnson L, Education		
37	1969-1974		Nixon, Law	
38	1974-1977		Ford, Law	
39	1977-1981		Carter, Business	
40	1981-1989	Reagan, Speechmaking		
41	1989-		Bush, Business	

As an additional refresher, here are the Presidents grouped in terms of operational and speech habits:

UTILITARIAN METHODS		SANCTIONED METHODS	
Directing	**Reporting**	**Directing**	**Reporting**
ARTISANS		**GUARDIANS**	
(CONCRETE SPEECH)			
Operators	**Players**	**Monitors**	**Conservators**
Jackson	Taylor*	*Washington*.	Fillmore
Van Buren	Pierce	*Monroe*	Buchanan
Roosevelt T	Garfield.	Harrison W	*McKinley*
Roosevelt F	Arthur	Tyler	Taft*
Kennedy	Harding	Polk	Ford
Johnson L	*Reagan*	Johnson A	Bush
		Hayes	
		Cleveland	
		Harrison B	
		Wilson	
		Coolidge	
		Truman	
		Carter	
		Nixon	

Directive	**Reporting**	**Directive**	**Reporting**
RATIONALS		**IDEALISTS**	
(ABSTRACT SPEECH)			
Organizers	**Engineers**	**Mentors**	**Advocates**
Adams J	*Jefferson**	(None)	(None)
Adams J Q	*Madison*		
Grant*	*Lincoln*		
Hoover*			
Eisenhower*			

The names in italics are of the Presidents who served more than four years in office.[2] Those with asterisks after them are the names of those men who are not considered professional politicians.

---

2 On the whole, the odds for re-election to the presidency are modest. Only eighteen men of the forty who have become President have served more than four years in that office. Only thirteen, Washington, Jefferson, Madison, Monroe, Jackson, Lincoln, Grant, Cleveland, Franklin Roosevelt, Wilson, Eisenhower, Nixon, and Reagan were elected to two or more terms of office. Teddy Roosevelt, Coolidge, Truman, and Lyndon Johnson were elected after they completed the terms of their deceased predecessors.

Of the forty men who have been American Presidents, twenty have been Guardians, twelve have been Artisans, and eight have been Rationals. Assuming that the Guardians comprise roughly 45% of the population, the Artisans, 40%, the Idealists 10% and the Rationals 5%, then it appears that the percentage of representatives of each temperament in the White House (with the exception of the Idealists) has been largely a matter of chance. Over the long run the voters don't seem to prefer one temperament over another.

That is, we are not surprised to find twenty Guardian Presidents. We might expect to find a few more Artisans, about sixteen, rather than twelve, but the discrepancy is not shocking; the proportion is about right. But we would anticipate only two Rationals, rather than the eight who were actually elected, and we would expect to find about four Idealists rather than none. We have some understanding of the absence of Idealists. Can we arrive at an explanation for the "extra" Rationals?

Four of the first six Presidents were Rationals, and two were Guardians. The remaining four Rationals are scattered among the thirty-four Presidents following Adams's time. Given their small numbers in the population, this is still more Rationals than we would expect. We might also wonder how it is that four Rationals assumed the presidency in those early years, and that Rationals were in office twenty-four of the first forty years of the American presidency.

If we remind ourselves of a few facts, the matter becomes reasonably straightforward. First, the men who became Presidents show the following clusters of pre-presidential experience:

Artisans	Rationals	Guardians
3 law	3 law	12 law
2 military	2 military	3 military
2 education	1 education	1 education
2 civil service	2 engineering	4 business
1 news service		
1 adventurer		
1 speechmaking		

Half of our forty Presidents came to the nation's highest office from a background in law. One of them, the Guardian William Howard Taft, went on to become Chief Justice of the United States Supreme Court after his term in the Oval Office. But law is a many-splendored thing;

like medicine and engineering, it has many branches and specialties. Law for Rationals is nothing like law for Guardians, since the two temperaments are diametrically opposite in most respects: the Guardians tend to be drawn to contractual law and the litigation of local disputes, while the Rationals are interested in national and international law more than in contractual, and in legislation than in litigation. The four Rationals schooled in law—Thomas Jefferson, James Madison, John Adams, Abraham Lincoln—focused almost exclusively on constitutional law.[3] Artisans have no special interest in contract or international law, but tend to prefer tort law, the excitement and the challenge of the courtroom duel.

The voters have also elected eight generals to the presidency. It was their success as military leaders, in fact, that helped make them attractive to the voters. These men came to office after commanding hundreds, thousands, and in the case of Grant and Eisenhower, hundreds of thousands of troops. In fact, the success of these two generals largely explains the statistically "extra" Rational Presidents: Grant and Eisenhower were highly visible and very successful generals, and therefore were almost automatically worthy presidential candidates. Without their successes, the number of Rational Presidents since the early days of the nation would be in keeping with their numbers in the population at large.

Since legal and military experience gave rise to twenty seven of our forty Presidents, we rightly ask whether such experience is the best preparation? How do education, civil service, and business, for instance, compare with legal and miliary backgrounds? This question is not easily answered because the competencies required for successful presidential opperations are so varied. Some presidential objectives require the tactical skills of the Artisan; others the strategic skills of the Rational, and yet others the logistical skills of the Guardian. How do the various experiential backgrounds develop these character-specific talents? The answer to the question is inordinately complex, so we can only touch upon it here.

First, in the case of Guardian Presidents, we might guess that legal, military, and business experience would be useful in sharpening the Guardian's inherent logistical skills, so that nineteen of the twenty Guardian Presidents may have profited from such experience. Laws of

---

3 Of course each of these men, by virtue of the times in which they lived, had special reason to be interested in constitutional law especially.

any kind are, after all, standards of conduct, just the sort of thing that interests Guardians. And the military, at least short of battle, practically runs on standard operating procedures. Likewise, the achievements of successful businessmen, like Carter and Bush, may well have been more by dint of standard logistical actions than tactical maneuvers or strategic plans. Which leaves the educator Wilson, who, among the twenty Guardians, was without legal, military, or business experience. But he was a college administrator, and that experience, if not his teaching, may have prepared him somewhat for the job that lay ahead.

As for the Rationals, three of them had legal training, which doubtless stood them in good stead, if only because of their great concern for constitutional and international law. Indeed, constitutional law was the major issue, especially for John Adams, James Madison, and Abe Lincoln. The one Rational educator, John Quincy Adams, was (like his father) an extremely learned scholar and professor of rhetoric and oratory. Even so, it is doubtful that his scholarship turned him into a competent president. His long years as minister to European nations must have helped greatly. Nevertheless, had he not been a brilliant scholar he might not have become the extremely effective minister whom George Washington valued so highly.

We find that the backgrounds of the Artisans are quite varied. There were three lawyers, two generals, two educators, two civil servants, one newsman, one adventurer, and one speechmaker. The three lawyers, Van Buren, Arthur, and Pierce were effective trial lawyers, in keeping with their Artisan tactical abilities. And it must be said that their attempts to advance their respective presidential agendas reflected some competency in legal maneuvering. Next, of the two Generals, Jackson and Taylor, only Jackson seemed to have profited from his experience as a tactical commander, and in the case of the two Artisan educators, their youthful excursion into education apparently had little effect on their acquisition of tactical skills. Garfield became a master speaker, and Lyndon Johnson a master legislative manipulator. But these developments clearly were not because of their brief tour of duty in education, a tour that was decidedly out of character for both Artisans. In contrast, the experience of the two Roosevelts in civil service was just the thing to prepare these wily Operator Artisans for their spectacular presidential tactics, just as Kennedy's youthful adventures prepared him for his brief but highly tactical performance in Washington. Then there was Reagan. Did his long experience as a speechmaker help him advance his political agenda? By making so many speeches in his folksy manner, he seems at least to have convinced a lot of people that his agenda was worthwhile. So speechmaking, at least in this case, may have been just as good preparation for the presidency as law, the military, education, or business.

Returning now to the question of the numbers or proportions of Artisans, Rationals, and Guardians in the presidency, we may wonder at the preponderance of Rationals among the early Presidents. The Guardian Washington's election for two terms of office (and for three, had he wished) was based on his peers' recognition of the specifically Guardian character of his virtues, which were exactly those needed at that time. The new nation desperately needed a stable and trusted man at the top, a solid, measured patriot like Washington, a man largely disinterested in tampering with ideological issues. This was a recognition held by the political power center of that time, that small group of people such as Thomas Jefferson, James Madison, Alexander Hamilton, and Benjamin Franklin, a group of men, mostly Rationals who had masterminded the revolution, adopted the Articles of Confederation, and designed the Constitution.

Since most of the nation's leaders were to be found among these men, and since they were mostly Rationals, Rationals tended to be elected President. As more non-Rationals gradually involved themselves in government, the proportion of non-Rationals who looked like potential candidates naturally increased. Thus the large proportion of early Rational Presidents has been followed by a relative absence of Rational Presidents since then, only Hoover and Eisenhower having been elected in the twentieth century.

Thus, after Washington's two terms of office, the next five presidential terms were held by Rationals: John Adams, Thomas Jefferson (twice), and James Madison (twice). The times were still unstable, the country's relationships with other nations troubled, a strategy for surviving in the community of nations was still being formed. Though a few tacticians might have been handy (as General Jackson was during the War of 1812), the issues were mainly strategic and Rationals were probably the best choice for the still young nation. Then came an eight-year time of relative peace and prosperity and, appropriately in terms of character, the election and re-election of James Monroe, the country's second Guardian President. The hold of the Rationals was broken.

So far we might claim that men of the most appropriate character were selected by some sort of recondite wisdom of the electorate. The nation's voters somehow knew that Rationals were needed, so they elected Rationals. But the truth seems to be more down-to-earth: the men elected to office during those first forty years were already recognized as heroes and patriots; their talents were well recognized, and they shared with each other access to the political power structure. Because of this the likelihood of their election by the people approached certainty, regardless of their character in relation to the needs of the times. They did not need to convince the electorate to win the presidency, as much as they needed to persuade one another.

Since Monroe's time the election of our Presidents has probably become more a matter of in-house politics and back-room wheeling and dealing than a demonstration of concern for the national welfare. Political coalitions arose to support certain political ideologies, but they quickly developed a primary interest in their own survival. The American political party apparatus emerged, helped along by Artisans like Van Buren (understudy of Aaron Burr and baron of Tammany Hall), and political parties became more and more influential—and more and more self-serving political machines. Eventually, it would now appear, candidates were selected for four primary reasons. First, because their politics were palatable to the party bosses; second, because they might be electable; thirdly, because they were manageable; and finally (in several cases), because their party owed them the favor. The appropriateness of their character to the needs of the nation seems to have been (and, some will claim, typically still is) quite far down the list of criteria for the selection of presidential candidates. Most important may be how well they will serve the political machine.

Further, for more than 150 years the candidates finally selected have had to belong to one of the two major parties. In the twentieth century, of course, this means either the Democratic or the Republican party. No third political party has had the strength to elect its candidate to the presidency. Even the enormously popular Teddy Roosevelt failed to regain the presidency when he abandoned the Republican Party in 1912. With very few exceptions, presidential candidates have had to be mainstream politicians relying heavily on their party's machinery to win elections. Even the occasional military hero, though he may have been as resoundingly popular as Andy Jackson in 1828, Ulysses Grant in 1868 and 1872, and Dwight Eisenhower in 1952 and 1956, required the support of party machinery. If we want to know what is most important in selecting presidential candidates, we must look at what the immediate concerns of party bosses are, not at national needs or a potential candidate's character.

What presidential candidates' managers have done with their candidates' character offers interesting, though perhaps unappealing, lessons in the workings of American politics. For example, the hell-raising and egalitarian Artisan Andy Jackson was a military hero who could be portrayed somewhat reasonably as "a man of the people." It was not out of line to pronounce the stolid, and utterly accountable George Washington "the father of his country." Ulysses Grant's strategic military genius was touted as the promise of brilliant political leadership. And the stubborn honesty of the Guardian Grover Cleveland was portrayed as outstanding probity.

These depictions were largely reasonable as well as politically useful. But in politics accuracy gives way rather quickly to expedience and, when expedient, to absurdity. For instance, the rather inept Guardian William Henry Harrison was presented as a latter-day Andy Jackson, a ridiculous comparison on the strength of their characters alone. The wolf-like Artisan Zachary Taylor was offered up as a military hero, which was true, and by some sort of alchemical connection, as a statesman, which was nonsense. And the fox-like cleverness of the Operator John Kennedy could also be confused with statesmanship, another failure to distinguish one sort of capability from another.

Finally, then, political expediency tends to distort—often quite deliberately—the character of political candidates. Perhaps the greatest connection we can discover between character and political behavior is to be found in the recognition that politicians play with character as cynically as they play with everything else associated with politics.

Presidential Character and the Character of the Times

The old argument over whether the individual shapes history or whether history shapes the individual is unlikely ever to be resolved in a manner satisfactory to everyone. All the same, it seems clear that the character of the President can have a powerful impact upon the course of events and the temper of the times. Once again, the steadfast and industrious Washington stands out as a man whose character provided virtues nearly perfect for safeguarding and stabilizing the fledgling nation. Lincoln's long range perspective, his Rational's strategic frame of reference, and his ability to stay aloof from the Civil War's whirlpool of hatred, not only shaped history during his life, but have been immensely important to the entire course of the nation's subsequent history.

The wolf-like Andy Jackson's zest for evening the score, his Artisan charisma and egalitarian view of government did much to make electioneering more populist—and fun-filled—than it had been before. But his high-handed promoter behavior also helped precipitate an economic crisis that made the tenure of his hand-picked successor, Martin Van Buren, most difficult. And Jackson's eight years in office, with the Red Fox of Kinderhook whispering in his ear, also solidly institutionalized the spoils system: government positions given to political supporters as a means of self-serving political patronage. Political patronage and its close relative, political corruption, have been problems in American politics to this day.

The eight Presidents from Jackson's time until the Civil War were either Artisans or Guardians, none of whom could find an adequate solution to the problem of slavery. Every one of these Presidents was trying either to maintain the status quo or to foist off on the country some temporary palliative. Perhaps no one could have made a difference, for the problem was horrendous, and Lincoln himself acknowledged during the Lincoln-Douglas debates that he didn't know what to do about it. If there had been an Eleanor Roosevelt or a Mohandas Gandhi available, a diplomatically astute Idealist who could have worked face-to-face with the major advocates of each side, then perhaps a peaceful solution could have been worked out and a half million lives could have been saved.

In later days Kennedy's Artisan disregard for Eisenhower's well-laid plans led to the Bay of Pigs fiasco, a debacle which has haunted the United States' Caribbean relationships ever since. But that same Artisan character also led to Kennedy's Operator-fashioned tactical victory in the Cuban missile crisis, with results whose importance transcend the merely military. The Artisan Lyndon Johnson's politics of personal power resulted in some unpalatable manipulations, but also led to a powerful civil rights program, something in which Johnson himself had a personal interest.

Arguably, then, the character of the Presidents has played a major role in shaping American history, and presidential character will doubtless continue to do so. How an informed electorate might take advantage of this idea, however, is difficult to imagine. No temperament guarantees success or failure, no character is free of flaw or of virtue.

Goodness and greatness, triviality and meanness, are not to be found in any particular temperament, but rather in how the individual unfolds that temperament.

As we said at the end of the last chapter, the Idealist's political vision exists largely as a personal expression, so Idealists who seek some special political goal are more likely to generate movements or organizations than to join them. This was the case with Eleanor Roosevelt, who initially fell back on the power she had through Franklin's position, and Gandhi, who labored for years to generate a movement. The success of these personally-inspired movements depends upon the strength and expression of the vision that inspires them. But it is unlikely that any vision will be powerful enough to offset the dominance of the political party system in the United States, so there is little likelihood that an Idealist will ever attain the presidency.

The conspicuous absence of Idealist Presidents underscores that people choose to become—or avoid becoming—involved in politics for reasons specific to their temperament. There do seem to be character-related motifs which determine the choice to enter or to avoid political life.

Guardians, for instance, are sensitive to their place in the social hierarchy. They work hard to get and keep their rightful place in their group, and the prestige and dignity which properly accompany that place. As in the case of James Polk, Grover Cleveland, Woodrow Wilson, and Richard Nixon, they sometimes look to politics as a way to do this, since they may find in politics a chance to be of service and to be recognized for it with enhanced prestige and higher status. People can also try for advancement by gradually earning recognition as good employees, or in politics, as good party men. People can even aspire to the CEO position: the top, the final recognition, the highest status possible with its attendant prestige—in American politics, the presidency itself. Given all this, we might expect the political life to capture the interest of many Guardians.

Artisans, in contrast, are more likely to be drawn to the excitement, the contest, the game. They will usually be the political wheeler-dealers, typified so well by Martin Van Buren and Lyndon Johnson. They are the supreme opportunists and they are attracted by the opportunities that political life offers. Politics, especially national politics, is the opportunity to score big, to have fun, to adventure, to enjoy. Best of all it is their chance to impress, to influence, to have impact.

Rationals usually find less personal satisfaction in political office. They are more likely to seek office in order to execute some strategy, whether political or economic. They may have some sort of vision or master plan for the well-being of the nation; or they may wish to bring reason and coherence to the office in place of what they see as the blunders or the lack of direction of the incumbents. Or they may aspire to the presidency as the final evidence of their own competence, their own capability, their own vision. Of course what is most likely is that, like John Adams, they will combine both personal aspiration with some broad strategy in national or international politics.

Presidential Character and the Laws of the Land

It is difficult for all of us, even specialists, to know about the thousands of laws our Legislators have adopted, let alone understand them. Yet every one of these thousands of laws is designed to keep us from doing certain things with others people or with our possessions, or to require of us that we do something. We are limited by law in what we can say, where we can go, how we can serve others, and how we can indulge, defend, and avenge ourselves. Even more, these thousands of laws limit us in what we can do with our money, securities, supplies, equipment, and buildings. In the United States legislators are charged with enacting these limitations on our options, while the judiciaries interpret them, and executives enforce them. The President, the nation's chief executive officer, has the job of enforcing the laws as they are created by legislators, and as they are interpreted by judiciaries.

Any President will enforce certain laws aggressively, others passively, and still others, only reluctantly. With few exceptions (such as the irascible John Adams), Rational Presidents displayed a reluctance to enforce laws constraining economic activity. The Sherman Anti-Trust Law, for instance, has not been favored by Rational Presidents, though most of those Presidents were militant about enforcing laws limiting the government's own enforcement actions. Artisan presidents, on the other hand, were more aggressive in enforcing laws limiting the options of corporate officers, and less so with laws limiting the options of individuals. Recall Andrew Jackson's assault on the United States Bank, for example, and his advocacy of individual rights, and the delight the "rugged individualist" Teddy Roosevelt took in assaulting the monopolies a half century later. Guardian presidents, in contrast to both Rationals and Artisans, sought less to limit corporate and government agents, and more to limit the moral latitude of individuals and groups.

If we consider that laws concern themselves with constraints on either social or economic actions, then we can place one's preferences about enacting and enforcing laws in a matrix. The matrix also demonstrates correlations between these preferences for social and economic limitations, and political party and presidential character.

More Social and More Economic Limitation	Less Social and More Economic Limitation
More Social and Less Economic Limitation	Less Social and Less Economic Limitation

Generally speaking, political parties in America and Europe have devised social and economic policy platforms that represented their stances with respect to various issues. These platforms inevitably favor certain kinds of laws and decry others. Political groups usually emerge from a broad consensus about specific issues, and only gradually become organized, distinguishable entities. Their names are usually meant to indicate something of their stand on issues, though they often end up representing quirks of their platforms or candidates, or are truncated mottoes. Thus they acquire names such as Christian Democrats, Communists, Constructionists, Democrats, Democratic Republicans, Fascists, Federalists, Libertarians, Progressives, Republicans, Populists, Socialists, Tories, Whigs, and so on. The names have changed and sometimes simply disappeared over time, so that John Adams was our first and last Federalist President, Thomas Jefferson our first Democratic Republican, Andrew Jackson our first Democrat, William Harrison our first Whig, and Lincoln our first Republican.

But the political party structure in the United States has become effectively stabilized, at least on the national level, as a two-party structure. Thus all Presidents since Lincoln have been either Republicans or Democrats, because these two parties have emerged as the only parties powerful enough to elect their candidate to the presidency.[4] (The old

---

4   The last time a third party (Republican Teddy Roosevelt's hastily constructed Progressive Party) managed to garner a significant number of votes, the result was to split the Republican vote between Teddy Roosevelt and the incumbent William Taft. Woodrow Wilson, the Democratic candidate, was elected partially as a result of the split.

Democratic Republican party of the founding fathers may be said to have re-emerged in the 1970s and 1980s, renamed the Libertarian Party, though on the ballot in most of the fifty states it so far manages only a few million votes each election year.) In spite of these changes and vagaries, however, we can map all political parties onto another matrix showing the kinds and degrees of limitations the parties advocated.[5]

Those parties that advocate decentralizing governmental power, which goes hand-in-hand with their advocacy of minimal limitation of both social and economic options, are located in the lower-right cell of the matrix. In contrast, those parties which champion greater limitation of social and economic privilege, and its almost inevitably attendant advocacy of centralization of power, are found in the upper left corner of the matrix. The other two political stances promote a mixed bag of legislative options and limitations. Conservatives (and others located at the lower left) advocate less economic limitation and more social limitation, while Liberals (and others at the upper right) favor more economic limits and fewer social limits.

| | | **Social Privilege** | |
		Central Control	Local Control
Economic Privilege	Central Control	Socialist Communist Fascist Collectivist Centralist	Liberal Democrat Social Democrat Labor Progressive
	Local Control	Conservative Republican Christian Democrat Whig Tory	Libertarian Democrat-Republican Anarchic Libertarian Individualist Decentralist

---

5 In his *The Lessons of History*, Will Durant tells us that freedom and equality are mutually exclusive: as one waxes the other wanes. Thus the greater the freedom to produce and exchange goods and services, the greater will become the disparity between the more productive and the less productive. According to Durant, the more productive, when left to their own devices, quickly outdistance the less productive in acquiring assets. Wherever laws have been adopted to reduce the disparity, there has followed a steady reduction in the quantity and the quality of production, and therefore of consumption. Equality was achieved, but it was equal impoverishment, the price payed by any nation that seeks to equalize consumption by limiting production. The Soviet Union and its Eastern European satellites stand as excellent and painful examples of this phenomenon.

In the heat of a political campaign, matters are never as straightforward as they are presented here. Further, though party platforms included planks that advocated various limitations, and insist on certain requirements, Presidents have often avoided committing themselves openly to such limits. On the social side, such as regulating medical, engineering, and law practice, or licensing the sale and use of chemicals and weapons, few Presidents have actually taken clear and consistent stands. This is true also of the economic side, where limitations on the freedom of private groups and individuals to dispose of their assets were usually imposed hesitatingly and enforced sporadically. Nevertheless few Presidents, if any, consistently held to the principle of least government, just as no President has advocated total government control of all economic actions in the private sector. (A case can be argued for extraordinary presidential domination of important elements of the private sector under emergency conditions. Lincoln's suspension of habeas corpus and Franklin Roosevelt's coercion of industry at the outbreak of war are examples of such deliberate domination. All the same, none of these Presidents *advocated* regular government control of the private sector, and especially the economic behavior of that sector.)

The Rational president is more likely than others to advocate maximum options for the private group or individual, both in matters of trade and in matters of social comportment. In the Rational view, government is best kept to a bare minimum. Its intent should be little more than to keep the peace within and between groups. Thus it is the Rational who is most likely to champion the position insisted on by the Rational Jefferson that the least government is the best government. Even so, when their pragmatic sense required them to do so, Rational presidents have opted for extensive, even if temporary, government intervention in the conduct of the nation's citizens. The most obvious case of the principled pragmatism of the Rational's dealings with the laws of the land is Lincoln's behavior at the outset of the Civil War. In order to save the country, he believed, he had to set aside important parts of the Constitution (suspending habeas corpus and by-passing the Legislature to manage federal funds, for instance). But this was a matter of temporary though overwhelming necessity, not advocacy.

The Guardian Presidents have been more vigorous in applying laws limiting social interaction than they were in applying laws limiting the disposal of possessions. (Nixon's wage and price controls and tax-credit revocations are unusual in this regard.) On the social side, George Bush's vigorous attempt to limit the production, sale, and use of narcotics is a typical example: here was moral turpitude that could be attacked (and *should* in his view be attacked) without significant criticism, even from those who thought that prohibiting narcotics increased demand for them, and who claimed that drug control efforts had generated a level of criminal activity which overshadowed the crime wave related to the illicit sales of alcohol in the 1930s. Neither Artisan nor Rational Presidents, on the other hand, have paid special attention to laws designed to keep people from overindulgence in anything. It is likely that they figured that people who did that sort of thing had to face the natural consequences of their actions, and that there was little need for government interference. But Guardians, including Guardian Presidents, are typically reluctant to allow nature to take its course in the case of licentious behavior.

As for the Artisans presidents, with their only fleeting interest in the principles of governance and their constantly shifting alliances, it is hard to predict and impossible to explain their applications of law. The ostensibly liberal John Kennedy, for instance, surprised his party by reducing instead of raising taxes, and gave private enterprise a tremendous capital boost by allowing investment credits on tax bills. And three of the more spectacular Operator Artisans, namely Jackson and the two Roosevelts, were quite unpredictable in almost everything they did in application of law. Most recently Ronald Reagan, the inimitable Player Artisan, spoke frequently and even eloquently of reducing the size and power of the Federal government. But, though he spoke out for reducing governmental borrowing, spending, and printing money, the government, including his own administration, continued to grow in size and power, continued to borrow enormous amounts of money, continued to print money and lend it to banks, and continued to spend all the money it could capture.

Character In Depressions And Wars

The United States has had at least four significant depressions and at least nine important wars. (The exact count depends on who is doing the counting; one person's severe depression may be another's mild recession, and one's war may be another's border incursion.) In each of these instances the President has behaved in character. In fact the character of the President has strongly influenced the course and conduct of the wars of the United States—and in certain cases, whether or not the war has occurred in the first place. This is probably not true of economic depressions, however. Chief executives still behave in character, but it seems that depressions will run their course largely unaffected by the actions of the nation's chief executive.

Artisan Character and the Politics of Depression

The Artisan Andrew Jackson saw the financial structure of the country in a rather provincial way. For him the financially powerful Eastern United States, especially in the form of the Bank of the United States, was not part of a complex, dynamic economic system. In his eyes it was a deadly, many-headed "Hydra," a monster cruelly victimizing Jackson's friends and neighbors, just as it had victimized him. So the outrageous and outraged wolf-like Operator attacked the Hydra, just as he always attacked his enemies. In spite of his political rhetoric, he was again a duelist seeking revenge; his world was the simple world of honor, challenge, retaliation, winning, and pride: in a word, a world of *contest.*

Jackson won, as he did in his duels, but the fight was very difficult and the cost to the nation very high: his actions helped to precipitate and probably to prolong a severe economic depression.

When in 1837 the shrewd Martin Van Buren, Jackson's anointed successor, entered office on Jackson's heels, the economy was beginning a downward spiral. Jackson had already taken action to head off the problem, but people took his moves as a signal that the government was going to restrict the availability of credit, and that the banks would start calling in their loans. When Van Buren, whom most considered merely Jackson's mouthpiece, assumed office, panic ensued. Banks and mercantile houses began to fail, there were riots over surging costs, banks suspended payments in hard currency, and it looked as if there would be a total economic collapse.

The Panic of 1837 was followed by a prolonged depression comparable to the Great Depression of the 1930s. Some thought that the revival of the national bank system (which Jackson had angrily destroyed) would help revive the economy, and Van Buren was pressured heavily to reinstate it. But the national bank had been

Jackson's pet peeve, and Van Buren wanted to keep the still-powerful Jackson's support. He also wanted to avoid a rupture with Thomas Jefferson, who was usually opposed to increases in governmental power, including governmental intrusion into economics or economic policy. So he refused to be stampeded by the pressures for reform, and so kept both political allies.

Van Buren was not callous about the welfare of the United States or of its citizens. He was an Operator Artisan, and he did not register the broad scope of a national depression in the same terms as a Rational would have, or with the same interest in conserving commercial and economic resources as a Guardian. For Van Buren, as for Jackson, the depression was at root a concretely local, tactical, political matter, a matter of alliances to be made, advantage to be gained, losses to be avoided or minimized.

By contrast we can consider another Artisan, the wily Franklin Roosevelt. He faced an agonizing economic depression when he came to office in 1933. But the political circumstances were different, and there was none of Van Buren's reluctance to act in Franklin Roosevelt's approach. Quite the contrary, Roosevelt had been mandated to act, for he had won the election by presenting himself as an inspiring and energetic activist, and by promising that he would act quickly and decisively. The people's mandate was *to act*; and to act *now*. And Roosevelt acted. He pulled out his executive shotgun and fired it at everything in sight.[6] He increased his political and administrative reach by greatly increasing the size of the executive branch. (When he died a dozen years later he left behind a large executive bureaucracy which has never shrunk.) And from the very beginning he vigorously pressed a willing Congress for vast bodies of legislation designed to finish off the depression.

Congress was always anxious to protect its power, and had resisted the threat of a powerful presidency for many years. But now it was overwhelmed by the immensely popular FDR, who arrogated to the presidency not only the right to pressure the Congress, but the right to act broadly without consulting the Congress at all. As one presidential scholar said of Roosevelt, "In the first Hundred Days he gave Congress a

---

6 During his first few months in office there were panic-induced runs on banks all over the country. In response to the panic Roosevelt made a radio address which showed him at his charismatic best. He was able in that talk to inspire confidence in the government's ability to handle the situation, and thereby to avert an even greater run on the banks. According to some that single address may have been the most important financial act of his career.

kind of leadership it had not known before and still does not care to have repeated."[7] Roosevelt may have had no comprehensive economic strategy, but his tactical virtuosity, his ability to make the most effective political moves, was remarkable.

There are a few who have argued that his uncoordinated actions may have impeded recovery. But the consensus is quite the opposite. Whether or not this is so, the fact remains that his actions, like those of Jackson and Van Buren, were in perfect keeping with his Operator character: politically and tactically astute, though not especially strong in rationale or in long-range vision.

Rational Character and the Long View of Depression

The Rational Ulysses Grant had been President for four years when the Panic of 1873 struck and a severe depression followed. The presidency, as Grant understood it, was not an activist or policy-making position. In Grant's terms, as in the terms of so many at that time, the Presidency was an *executive* position, charged only with the execution of the will of the Congress. He might abhor the depression; it was nevertheless none of his official business until Congress, through the enactment of legislation, told him differently. Thus the depression could follow its course, unimpeded by significant actions from the President. The wide-ranging vision of the Rational was on the more distant fields of foreign policy anyway, for it was in that area that Grant believed the most important questions of national survival would be found.

President Herbert Hoover, an Organizer similar to Grant, had been Secretary of Commerce during the tenures of Harding and Coolidge, which were in general times of prosperity. He was recognized as an active and brilliant organizer, and the optimism of the times served to enhance his reputation. So when the Great Depression of 1929 began, it looked as though Hoover would be just the man to tackle the problem. The nation's depression, after all, would merely require one more large-scale organizing effort of the sort at which Hoover was so expert.

But such was not to be the case. Hoover, like many Rationals, abhorred big government, which he strongly believed posed a greater

---

7 Clinton Rossiter, *The American Presidency*, 140. Quoted in *Congressional Quarterly's Guide to the Presidency*, 461.

threat than any temporary economic downturn could. He held the cure, big government, to be worse than the disease, depression. And though the "downturn" quickly showed itself to be quite serious, Hoover had a Jeffersonian faith in the ability of the people to take care of themselves. He therefore worked to generate community-level or local government level organizations which would address problems without the interference of big government. And since the Congress was in his view closer to the people than was the presidency, he also wanted the Congress to be an active agency for economic change. In this way the country could deal with its difficulties and avoid the danger of a presidency which would become inevitably more and more powerful as it dealt with the nation's economic problems. Given that his relationship with the Congress was not very good, and that he was not a professional politician to begin with, he had little influence on the Congress even when he did try to move it to action. Like Grant before him, he was deliberately an executive rather than a legislative President, and like Grant before him, he put himself in a position in which he could not be powerful.[8] (Hoover, after all, saw the presidency as "the inspiring symbol of all that is highest in America's purposes and ideals,"[9] and did not want it corrupted by excessive power.)

Though Hoover was frustrated by what he saw as the intransigence of Congress, he avoided attacking it openly. "I had felt deeply that no President should undermine the independence of the legislative and judicial branches by seeking to discredit them," he later wrote.

Hoover was an organization builder, not a politician. He could not act in the vigorous and bold tactical style of the Artisan politician, and the dangers his Rational's long-range outlook showed him would have prevented him from doing so even if he could. It is after all the architect of government who understands the importance of limiting the powers of government, and the lesson is not lost even when convenience would suggest gathering power in the hands of one individual or group. The Rational is not as politically astute as the Artisan, but instead weighs and

---

8 He did agree to a few moves that Congress made, including a protective tariff that in the long run only made matters worse. He also consented to establish the Reconstruction Finance Corporation, but this organization loaned money to railroads and banks, whose collapse threatened long term disaster. Though it was probably a good economic strategy, it was a political disaster, for it suggested that Hoover favored the rich and cared nothing for the poor.

9 *From George ... To George*, 6.

Guardian Character and the Morality of Depression

Shortly after President Grover Cleveland took office in March, 1893, a nationwide financial panic struck. It bankrupted major industries, closed banks, shut down businesses, and threw millions of people out of work. President Cleveland, a staunch and steadfast Guardian, believed that most of the difficulties facing the nation were the consequence of irresponsibility and chicanery. His Monitor Guardian's perspective focused on others' foolishness and wrongdoing, including especially the foolishness and wrongdoing of politicians. He was therefore proud of his record of vetoes, which was longer than any President's up to his time. He believed that the primary cause of the depression had to be some sort of reprehensible behavior, and he fastened on the Sherman Silver Purchase Act of 1890 as the culprit and sought its immediate repeal. He called a special session of Congress to consider the repeal, but beyond such "negative" measures he largely refused to take action to alleviate conditions. In a world such as Cleveland's, in which moral turpitude and wastefulness are the problem, what is needed is to undo wrongdoing (and if necessary, to punish it), rather than to produce something new. The solution to Cleveland's depression was the vigorous undoing of wrongs done.

Conditions always exist in the viewpoint of an observer, and observations will always be made in keeping with character. "Depression" will be for one kind of President, as it was for Van Buren and Roosevelt, a political threat, to be dealt with in political terms. It may call into question the balance of powers of the three branches of government, or raise the menace of a dictatorial presidency for Rationals such as Hoover. It may be the sad but inevitable consequence of wrongdoing to a Guardian like Cleveland. The *words* spoken may be the same; "depression" comes as easily to the lips of the Artisan as to those of the Guardian, for example. But the *significance* of the depression will be determined chiefly by one's character.

Action may *look* similar among people of different temperaments, by the way. Van Buren and Cleveland and Hoover, though of three different temperaments, took much the same action in the presence of a depression: they refused to act. Only Roosevelt took a vigorous role, and only because to do so was politically expedient (and, no doubt, great fun). But the ways in which these men came to their decisions were rooted in very different ways of making sense of the world, profoundly shaped by their temperaments.

Presidential Character in American Wars

The Constitution gave to the Congress alone the right to declare and to finance war, while the place of the presidency with respect to war was left rather ambiguous. The President was the designated commander-in-chief of the armed forced of the United States, but the options and the obligations that went with this role were not well specified. The lack of specificity has meant that the President's war powers were subject to considerable interpretation, and in these interpretations we again find interesting demonstrations of the impact of temperament on history. The United States has been involved in many conflicts, some quite small cross-border incursions, and several others, enormous conflagrations which spread around the entire globe. Exactly how many of these there have been depends on the observer, but the following seems a reasonably realistic listing.

Wars Presided Over by Artisan Presidents

1941 Franklin Roosevelt: World War II
1962 Lyndon Johnson: the Viet Nam War
1983 Ronald Reagan: the Grenadan Raid

Wars Presided Over by Guardian Presidents

1845 James Polk: the Mexican War
1898 William McKinley: the Spanish War
1917 Woodrow Wilson: World War I
1950 Harry Truman: the Korean War
1969 Richard Nixon: the Viet Nam War
1989 George Bush: the Panamanian Raid
1991 George Bush: the Iraquian War

Wars Presided Over by Rational Presidents

1803 Thomas Jefferson: the Barbary Coast War
1812 James Madison: the British War
1861 Abraham Lincoln: the Civil War

Artisans at War

War broke out in Europe in 1939, and had already been killing thousands in the Far East, where Japan sought to secure a permanent position on the mainland and to conquer China. Initially Franklin Roosevelt may have thought the United States could avoid involvement in these wars, but when Poland and France fell and England was left, isolated and hungry, to face a powerful and triumphant Germany (and a weak Italy), he apparently changed his mind and began to take action. But he had to be careful about how he moved. He was able, to begin with, to tamper with the United States' neutrality laws to favor the Allies at the expense of the Axis, and he arranged the Lend-Lease program which provided Great Britain with a fleet of fifty vitally important anti-submarine destroyers. He also ordered the United States Navy's destroyers to escort American ships to protect them from German submarines, and housed an important British intelligence effort on United States soil. The canny Roosevelt took all this action with *no* declaration of war against the Axis, *no* formal partnership in war with the Allies, and *no* decisive sanction from the Congress.

Then, on December 7, 1941, the Japanese attacked the American naval and military bases in the Hawaiian Islands and the Philippines, most notably the naval base at Pearl Harbor. Immediately after the attack, FDR asked Congress for a declaration of war against Japan. Then Hitler, a few days after Japan's attack, declared war against the United States, and Roosevelt's hands were freed completely: he could now openly bend all the resources of the nation to the defeat of the Axis powers, continuing the policy that he had been pursuing somewhat covertly for several years.

The Allies, bolstered by the enormous resources of the United States, of course won the war in Europe and the Far East. But world peace was more elusive than military victory. The French had colonized portions of southeast Asia before World War II, thus the region's older name, "French Indo-china." (Today, the same region is divided into Viet Nam, Cambodia, and Laos.) After World War II ended the French had their hands full trying to suppress the Communist-backed guerillas trying to gain control of the region. President Eisenhower did not want to see the French presence in southeast Asia diminished, but he knew there were limits the United States must observe in its efforts to assist them. To offer economic assistance might be helpful but to send combat soldiers, he believed, would be a tragic error.

But even with assistance the French could not maintain their hegemony, and Indo-China broke up in 1954. The government of the newly-formed South Viet Nam proved unequal to the task of suppressing Communist insurgency, and in 1961 the restless Artisan President John Kennedy, stirring with awareness of a challenge unanswered, ignored Eisenhower's earlier assessment. Kennedy gradually added military "advisors" to the United State's assistance to the South, advisors who were soon actively involved in combat. Eisenhower had sent about 800 men to Viet Nam during his administration; Kennedy increased the number to more than 16,000. When the Artisan Lyndon Johnson succeeded Kennedy in 1962, the South Viet Namese government still seemed destined to fall to the insurgents. President Johnson's choice was either to cut and run, or rise vigorously to the challenge.

The aggressive Operator of course took the second option. He tried to stave off the South Viet Namese defeat by sending in more United States ground troops, at first only a few more, and then larger and larger numbers of them. Along with them went air and naval forces and enormous financial resources. More than a half million Americans finally saw duty in Viet Nam. But the conflict dragged on, and though the South Vietnamese and the United States were not exactly losing, "not losing" could never be equated with winning. Faced with the quagmire of Viet Nam, with severe economic difficulties, with the fierce protests at home about the war, and with the disarray within his own political party, and unable to come up with any promising course of action, even the clever and competitive Lyndon Johnson had to admit defeat, and decided not to run for re-election. (He thereby abandoned the presidency and the war to the Guardian Richard Nixon, who subsequently met his own painful political defeat.)

Even with the strange redefinitions of the word "war" which the last forty years have wrought, Reagan's adventure in Grenada in October of 1983 cannot qualify as more than a raid. It has been characterized by some as another unjustified American intrusion into the territory south of the United States' borders, and by others as a daring and worthy action to prevent a communist takeover of a neighbor of the United States. Reagan the Player saw a public relations victory and a chance to eliminate a small enclave of communism, and perhaps a bit of face-saving for the tragedy in Lebanon a few years earlier. With no public discussion with the disorganized Congress, he took advantage of the opportunity, claiming that the United States was suppressing illegal communist rule and protecting young American citizens attending medical school in Grenada. The surprise was almost total: most Americans had never heard of Grenada or of the hospital there, let alone worried over the possibility that the place might be infested with communists. But it was a rather popular action, for most people apparently agreed that we saved Grenada from communism and restored our national dignity at the cost of very few casualties.

The three Artisan Presidents show the willingness of the Artisans—indeed, their appetite—to ignore the rules in favor of expedience, to maneuver extensively behind the scenes to promote their initiatives, and to rise to challenges with as much forcefulness as they can muster. If we observe them closely we see in their behavior, as we saw in Jack Kennedy's behavior during his Cuban embargo, the very personal, immediate, exciting quality of the Artisan's involvement in conflict.

This is a strikingly different quality than we will find in the behavior of the Guardian at war.

Guardians at War

By 1840 the United States had grown out of its defensive posture. It was no longer a new and fragile country trying to preserve itself, but a vigorous, sprawling entity of considerable power. There was spread widely across the land the notion of "manifest destiny," and in keeping with this notion the Monitor Guardian James Polk deliberately precipitated a war with Mexico. Polk had campaigned on a platform of fulfilling the nation's "manifest destiny," of admitting Texas to the Union and annexing as much territory as possible, ranging, if it could be done, all the way to the Pacific Ocean. The nation was destined, he proclaimed with the advocates of the expansionist doctrine, to extend itself all the way across the continent, "from sea to shining sea."

Polk was a strict Constitutionalist, and though he wanted to act, he didn't want to violate the letter of the Constitution. He asked for and got the nation's first *joint* congressional approval (both houses agreeing as one unified body) for a secret agreement with Texas, and though the joint approval was not an action sanctioned by the Constitution, neither was it forbidden. And, of great importance to the Guardian, it offered some legitimacy for Polk's highly controversial actions. Polk then provoked Mexico into attacking United States army units, and Polk could claim to Congress that Mexico was the aggressor. Congress promptly declared war, Mexico was badly defeated, and the United States added to its territory Texas, and what is now Arizona, California, Colorado, New Mexico, Nevada, Utah, and part of Wyoming.

The Guardian's acquisitiveness was irrepressible here, just as his patriotism was unquestioned and simple. Once his actions could be made legitimate, the rest followed almost predictably.

It was not until 1898 that the Congress declared war again. This time it was a Conservator Guardian who stepped before the Legislature to ask for a declaration of war. But it was not by choice; unlike James Polk, William McKinley was pressured into that action. Initially McKinley resisted the widespread call for war against Spain, but finally succumbed to political necessity. He was a career politician and a loyal member of his political party, which wanted the war, and he knew that to resist further would be both futile and politically suicidal.

Expansionism was rampant again, and Spain was guilty of ruthless suppression of the Cuban people. The Spanish proved willing to negotiate a peaceful withdrawal from Cuba rather than go to war with the United States, but the public's enthusiasm for war was at fever pitch, and when the *U. S. S. Maine* mysteriously blew up in Havana harbor, there was no longer room to talk about peace. With great sadness, for he had seen war and its horrors first hand, McKinley asked for the declaration of war. Congress declared war enthusiastically; the United States Navy and Army went into action against the Spanish; and the United States was everywhere triumphant. The war was gratifyingly short, casualties were few for the Americans, and victory included Spain's departure from Cuba and its surrender to the United States of most of its possessions in the Caribbean and the Far East. (McKinley, by the way, pressed Congress to include Hawaii in its flurry of annexations, and Congress responding happily, so that in 1898 the Hawaiian Islands became a territory of the United States. Other new possessions included Puerto Rico, Guam, and the Philippines, whose people McKinley felt it was his duty to civilize and Christianize.)

Only sixteen years later, in 1914, the First World War broke out in Europe. The Monitor Woodrow Wilson worked to keep the United States officially neutral until 1917, while he sought a diplomatic settlement for the dreadful war. But Germany's provocations against neutrals, and the United States' rather aggressive insistence on its right to trade with Germany's enemies, eventually led Congress to declare war.

Wilson was far from enthusiastic about the war; in fact he was disgusted with the war aims of both sides, which he saw as cynical and self-serving, and his Fourteen Point peace plan offered, by his lights, the only acceptable conditions for a just and lasting peace. With it the Monitor Guardian would show the Western world the path to peace. But Wilson did not sufficiently account for the war-weariness and vengeful feelings of the victors, nor for the cynicism of their diplomats. Wilson's was a world in which God's plans counted, and in which Woodrow Wilson could presume to speak for them. The United States helped win World War I for the Allies, but Wilson's exalted perspective of his place in world events cost him the Fourteen Points, his health, and perhaps even his life.

Less than a generation later the cost of Wilson's failure became clear: World War II erupted and more than fifty million people died. The war ended formally in 1945, but some have claimed that in fact it never ended at all; we just changed enemies. The United States' former ally, Stalin's Soviet Union, proved to be a more devious enemy than the Axis, and no less ambitious. Monitor President Truman was a feisty man; he knew right from wrong, and he wasn't about to let anyone weaken or destroy the democratic governments of the United States or of any of its allies. When on June 25, 1950, communist North Korea invaded South Korea, Truman immediately gave the go-ahead for United States forces in the area to assist the South Korean army to repel the invasion.

The United States was again at war, and some claimed, as some always do about any conflict, that the Korean matter was not worth a drop of American blood. But, Truman recognized, South Korea was a formal ally, the United States must stand by its friends, and South Korea's fall indirectly threatened Japan. Further, Truman believed, the attack was part of a new communist offensive that extended from Europe into Asia. If you don't stop your enemies when they first move on you, Truman might simply ask, then when *will* you stop them? On June 27,

1950, he went to the United Nations and soon the Security Council agreed to intervene in defense of South Korea with troops from many U.N. nations.

Instead of a war the conflict was officially termed a United Nations "police action." The Congress never *declared* war. In fact Truman moved so quickly that initially he failed to act in consultation with the Congress. The conflict ended in a military stalemate, but the consequences of Truman's intervention were not merely military. South Korea has remained a buffer between the communist and the capitalist countries in the Far East ever since. United States troops have been stationed there in a guardian capacity ever since, and South Korea, like Taiwan, Japan, Hong Kong, and Singapore, has become a prosperous participant in the West's capitalist economy.

When the Artisan Lyndon Johnson declined his chance at another term in office in 1968, he passed the job of commander-in-chief of the armed forces in Viet Nam to the Monitor Guardian Richard Nixon. Nixon claimed to have a secret plan for bringing about "peace with honor," a claim which helped him win the election. The plan amounted to one last crack at breaking the North's will with massive bombing, giving the South Vietnamese additional economic assistance, and pulling United States military forces out of the country. But even with the aid, South Viet Nam fell to the North quickly. The United States was, in many eyes, humiliated, but it was finally free of one of the worst wars in its history. The long view prevailed: the war could not be won, and Nixon made an attempt to find a face-saving way to abandon the hopeless conflict. All that could be done was to allow the persistently feeble and corrupt government of South Viet Nam to disappear into the trash bin of history.

Among the warlike actions of the Guardian Presidents there have been the very recent actions of President George Bush in Panama and in the Persian Gulf War. These actions will probably be seen ultimately as the result of Bush's moral convictions, which are quite strong, and his Guardian's concern for property and prosperity, which appears to be equally strong. Clearly Bush does not enjoy war; in both Panama and the Persian Gulf, and for better or worse, he has been eager to end the conflict as soon as he can, and, in the Gulf War, has even been criticized for quitting before delivering the knockout punch.

Unlike the Artisans, then, the Guardian Presidents have generally been reluctant to go to war and eager to end it. The single exception to this is James Polk, but even here, though Polk's patriotic acquisitiveness led him to instigate a war, it was clearly a war which promised to be an easy one. Polk's patriotic "manifest destiny," Wilson's moral and religious fervor, and Truman's and Bush's angry determination to preserve and protect what was right and good, prompted these Guardians into warlike postures, while sheer political weight pressed McKinley into a reluctant and half-hearted request for war. Further, the Guardian Presidents have shown no love for war or excitement about it once it was under way. It was for them a necessity, never an adventure.

Rationals at War

Early in his presidency the Guardian George Washington had declared American neutrality in a conflict between the French and the British. The Rational Thomas Jefferson was discontent with Washington's declaration: in fact he thought it was unconstitutional. If only Congress can declare war, Jefferson reasoned, then the President could not unilaterally forbid war. But this was exactly what Washington had done with his declaration of neutrality, and in this single stroke Washington had set the precedent that the President could make foreign policy, and would never again be seen as merely the executor of the congressional will.

Jefferson's concern was typical of the Rationals: though he might agree with Washington's opinion that the United States should avoid the conflict, his wide-ranging perspective concerned itself very directly with that more abstract matter, the nature of the relationship of the President, the Legislature, and the people. The Rationals must understand the immediate in terms of the remote, and the most fitting with regard to the one may be very troublesome with regard to the other.

As President, for example, Jefferson rather consistently consulted with the Congress before taking action. This helped to preserve the balance of powers the Constitution intended. But during his presidency he faced the problem of extensive and increasingly troublesome piracy against United States shipping. In 1801, American merchant ships in the Mediterranean were being attacked by pirates from Tripoli, Algeria, Morocco, and Tunisia. In effect most of the North African coast was at war with the United States. Jefferson recognized that the nation's maritime economy was at stake, and, of equal importance over the long run, the reputation of the country itself. The upstart United States could not afford to be seen as a weakling, unable to take care of itself in the community of nations. It was important to act, and Jefferson was not eager to confront a divided Congress which might debate matters endlessly. But there was that Constitutional matter of Congress's unique power to declare hostilities against foreign states, which Jefferson did not wish to ignore. Instead he dispatched a squadron of U. S. warships to the Mediterranean, giving its commander instructions to offer the rulers of the Barbary Coast states payment to stop their attacks. However, he quietly added to his instructions this codicil:

> If you find on your arrival in Gibraltar that all the Barbary Powers have declared war against the United States, you will then distribute your forces in such a manner, as your judgment shall direct, so as best to protect our commerce and chastise their insolence—by sinking, burning, or destroying their ships and vessels wherever you shall find them. [10]

Of course Jefferson's instructions described what was already the case, so the outcome was largely forgone. Jefferson was soon able to reported to Congress that the Navy had captured a pirate ship which had attacked an American merchant ship. But, he regretfully reported, the United States navy had let the pirate go free; Congress, after all, had not declared hostilities. Congress was impressed with the Navy's success and angered by the release of the pirates, and it quickly authorized naval war against the Barbary powers.

Though troubled by Washington's declaration of U.S. neutrality, which he saw as a usurpation of Congressional power, Jefferson could mastermind the technically unauthorized aggressive response to the Barbary Coast pirates. His concern over Washington's action was in keeping with his abstract, strategically-oriented world-view, while his own presidency required of him action for the short term, action which raised the problem of reconciling the immediate with the strategic. This is often the struggle of the Rational: to take effective concrete action without violating abstract principle. In the long run, the Rationals' principles are always pragmatic, and their pragmatism is always principled, so they can usually find a way to fit the two. In fact, to understand the Rationals requires understanding this complementary interaction of principle and practice. We can see this in Jefferson's actions: he needed to take action, but he did not want to diminish the

---

10 Quoted in Congressional Quarterly's Guide to the Presidency, 534.

powers or moral authority of the Legislature. His small deception allowed him to satisfy both requirements.

Less than a dozen years later another Rational President, James Madison, reluctantly came before Congress about the matter of war. At that time the British were still struggling with Napoleonic France, and the British navy was attempting to blockade the entire coastline of Europe, from the Baltic to the Mediterranean, and to defend British colonies and shipping in the Caribbean. Britain's ships and men were not sufficient to meet these arduous demands, and they had tried to make up the deficit by taking American ships and impressing American sailors into the British navy. Furthermore, there were rumors that Great Britain was supplying arms to hostile frontier Indians, who were reputed to be on a killing spree. War fever was running high in many parts of the United States, and the pressure on Madison to ask Congress to declare war was enormous.

Madison knew it would be unwise both militarily and economically to go to war, and he worked hard for a diplomatic resolution to British-American problems. But most of the country was eager for war, and it was a campaign year and he was running for re-election. His party continued to press him, and he eventually succumbed: he went before the Congress on June 1, 1812 with a list of grievances. Reporter Rational that he was, he did not quite ask Congress for a declaration of war, but instead presented the list and left it to Congress to decide what action to take.[11] If he could not stop them from their foolishness, at least he did not exhort them to pursue it.

His action was surely not the action of a powerful or clever tactician; there was no fox in him. Madison was a brilliant political philosopher and highly important to the framing of the Constitution. But this Rational was not (as most Rationals are not) a good politician. In agreeing to go before the Congress he abandoned his own stance and violated his own judgment. His natural concern with the long view gave way to the pressures of those more interested in the immediate; patient strategy was abandoned to angry tactics.

---

11 The Congress did have to give the matter some thought, for the war was not everywhere a popular cause. For instance, in the Northeast some were talking of seceding rather than going to war, and the governors of Massachusetts, Rhode Island, and Connecticut refused to authorize the use of their troops for war.

In 1861 the United States began the bloodiest war it has ever experienced: the Civil War. When the South seceded, newly-elected President Abraham Lincoln acted with admirable dispatch and effectiveness to arm the North. But he also trod heavily on the fabric of the Constitution in doing so: without the authorization of the Congress or the Supreme Court he issued calls for volunteers, suspended habeas corpus, and imposed martial law. Further, a joint session of Congress had been called to debate the problem of Southern secession, and Lincoln postponed the session for two and a half months so that he could act without organized political resistance. In this bold action on the one hand, and in his constant concern about the danger of presidential usurpation of power on the other, he reminds us of Thomas Jefferson. Like Jefferson handling the Barbary Coast situation, Lincoln acted high-handedly. But like Jefferson, Lincoln strongly advocated limiting presidential authority.

Lincoln wrote to a friend about his actions at the beginning of the war that "...I felt that measures otherwise unconstitutional might become lawful by becoming indispensable to the preservation of the nation. Right or wrong, I assumed this ground and now avow it."[12] He was principled, as was Jefferson, but like Jefferson, he was pragmatic as well, and we see again the Rational's complementary relationship of abstract principle and pragmatic action.

This is the same Lincoln, incidentally, who had a few years earlier absolutely rejected his law partner's assertion that the President should have the right to decide for himself when he must exercise extraordinary authority. It is questionable whether a Guardian who held Lincoln's view of presidential limitations could have acted as high-handedly as Lincoln later did. In fact the Guardian Presidents who preceded him were (with the singular exception of Polk) largely hamstrung by their conception of the presidency as an intentionally weak office. On the other hand one can well imagine that an Artisan who thought the presidency was meant to be a weak office could have set aside, perhaps permanently, the question of original intention in order to take expedient action. Recall, for example, President Zachary Taylor's angry promise to lead an army and to personally hang anyone who attempted to bring about secession.

---

12 Quoted in *Congressional Quarterly's Guide to the Presidency*, 536.

The Rationals, with their strategic view, did not always, or even often, take the popular view, which tends to the short term. But over the long term their decisions have usually been sound, even while the observer may question the apparently peculiar integration of principle and practice that marks their behavior.

More Simply Human

Lincoln's Gettysburg Address may be the most elegant speech ever made by an American President. In only a few words it reminds us of the vision of individual freedom to which so many of our nation's founders dedicated their lives, and it reminds us of the sometimes heartbreaking price of maintaining that vision. As we have seen, both our utilitarian and our sanctioning Presidents, each according to his character, his toolkit of solutions, has attacked the perennial problems of freedom in accord with his characteristic perspective. Most of our eight Rationals and twelve Artisans have struggled against government encroachment upon the individual's *freedom to act*, while most of our twenty Guardians have demonstrated the characteristically Guardian concern for the individual citizen's *freedom from want*. And being, as Harry Stack Sullivan said, more simply human than anything else, each has acted as his temperament dictated. Each has used his characteristic toolkit on the kind of problems he characteristically recognized, sometimes for better, sometimes for worse.

It has been said that the office of the presidency sometimes reaches out and changes the man who occupies it. We saw this in the case, for example, of "Chet" Arthur, the petty politician who came to office as a result of a murder, and who, in spite of his questionable background and cynical outlook, brought credit to himself as President. Any of us might hope to be so moved were we to find ourselves occupying the office; any of us might hope that we would prove equal to its terrible demands and its remarkable promises. But whether or not our future Presidents prove equal to those demands and promises, it is clear that presidential performance will always be in keeping with the character of the man or woman who holds the title, *President of the United States*.

Appendix A

A BRIEF TEST OF CHARACTER TRAITS

A questionnaire follows that will help you determine your own temperament. You will find instructions for scoring the questionnaire on the page following it. *First* complete the questionnaire, and *then* read the scoring instructions.

Pick the *one* word in each row that *best* fits you, and circle the letter in front of it. Please use a dictionary for unusual words and skip any items that do not apply to you.

I prefer to be:	E	seemly	Q	efficient	Y	pleasing	B	effective
I prefer feeling:	X	inspired	A	excited	D	concerned	P	calm
I take pride in being:	A	a winner	D	accountable	P	competent	X	authentic
I'd like being a:	E	magnate	Q	wizard	Y	sage	B	prodigal
I'd rather be:	P	pragmatic	X	ethical	A	practical	D	traditional
There's virtue in:	Z	goodwill	C	boldness	F	ownership	R	independence
I'm confident when:	C	dashing	F	included	R	self-willed	Z	in rapport
I most often look for:	X	my identity	A	adventures	D	security	P	proof
I'm proud of being:	Y	genuine	B	ahead	E	dependable	Q	capable
I'm best at:	C	expediting	F	monitoring	R	organizing	Z	mentoring
I often crave:	A	spontaneity	D	ceremony	P	achievement	X	love
I put my trust in:	D	authority	P	reason	X	intuition	A	luck
I am a good:	B	crafter	E	inspector	Y	counselor	Q	sequencer
I can be:	B	impetuous	E	dispirited	Q	preoccupied	Y	alienated
I'd rather be a:	P	genius	X	prophet	A	virtuoso	D	dignitary
I'm better at:	D	logistics	P	strategy	X	diplomacy	A	tactics
I count more on:	B	chance	E	certification	Q	logic	Y	instinct
I like being seen as:	R	progressive	Z	altruistic	C	urbane	F	forbearing
I'm better acting as:	Z	an envoy	C	a player	F	a broker	R	a planner
I tend to be rather:	X	credulous	A	optimistic	D	pessimistic	P	skeptical
I'm often:	A	cynical	D	fatalistic	P	solipsistic	X	mystical
I often speak in:	B	street talk	E	polite terms	Q	shop talk	Y	metaphors
I like myself more if:	D	prosperous	P	autonomous	X	benevolent	A	nervy
I often search for:	Q	evidence	Y	Self	B	risks	E	safety
I like being seen as:	R	generative	Z	unworldly	C	worldly	F	dedicated
I have more faith in:	Z	feelings	C	the breaks	F	licensure	R	grounds
I often yearn for:	R	attainment	Z	affection	C	whims	F	rites
I'm better at:	Q	devising	Y	championing	B	adapting	E	supplying
I often want more:	A	pleasures	D	services	P	problems	X	romance
I'm more capable in:	Z	personalizing	C	thematizing	F	standardizing	R	systemizing
My words are often:	D	conventional	P	technical	X	allegorical	A	lingo
Trouble is often:	Y	paradoxical	B	farcical	E	predestined	Q	meaningless
I tend to seek:	F	immunity	R	corroboration	Z	uniqueness	C	gambles
I'm rather often:	Q	a doubter	Y	a believer	B	buoyant	E	leery
I often speak:	Z	figuratively	C	in slang	F	establishment	R	in jargon
I'm self-confident if:	P	self-directed	X	empathic	A	impactful	D	belonging
I often feel:	Q	tranquil	Y	enthused	B	elated	E	serious
I have a hunger for:	Y	caring	B	impulses	E	rituals	Q	accomplishment
I often speak of:	P	entailment	X	cues	A	facets	D	amounts
Sometimes I get:	Z	estranged	C	reckless	F	downcast	R	distracted
I'm better at:	B	composing	E	insuring	Q	configuring	Y	conciliating
Bad times are often:	R	random	Z	inexplicable	C	a mockery	F	inevitable
Maybe I'll become:	C	top dog	F	an official	R	a mastermind	Z	a seer
My best ability is:	D	stabilizing	P	patterning	X	humanizing	A	fashioning
I'd be good as:	P	a marshaller	X	a teacher	A	an expediter	D	a supervisor
I can do well in:	X	advocating	A	improvising	D	providing	P	contriving
I'd like to be:	C	a virtuoso	F	a magistrate	R	a genius	Z	an oracle
I prefer to feel:	F	solemn	R	serene	Z	fervent	C	thrilled
There's virtue in:	B	daring	E	affluence	Q	independence	Y	kindliness
I emphasize:	C	description	F	evaluation	R	definition	Z	interpretation
I'm better at:	F	providing	R	inventing	Z	revealing	C	performing
I like being seen as:	Y	warm	B	sophisticated	E	staunch	Q	productive
I'm confident if I'm:	E	a member	Q	strong-willed	Y	sympathetic	B	impressive
I like myself if I'm:	R	skilled	Z	sincere	C	competitive	F	responsible
Under stress I can get:	D	depressed	P	preoccupied	X	confused	A	impulsive

Determine your score by adding together the number of A, B, and C responses, then the D, E, and F responses, then the P, Q, and R, and finally the X, Y, and Z responses.

The largest of these sums indicates which of the four temperaments you have identified yourself with.

A	+ B	+ C	=	The Artisan temperament.
D	+ E	+ F	=	The Guardian temperament.
P	+ Q	+ R	=	The Rational temperament.
X	+ Y	+ Z	=	The Idealist temperament.

Appendix B

THE CONTRIBUTIONS OF ISABEL MYERS

During the late 1940s and early 1950s Isabel Myers devised her *Myers-Briggs Type Indicator*, a self-report inventory which permits the classification of people into sixteen types. She developed the types from her explorations of the concepts Jung presented in his *Psychological Types*. The soundness of her work may be seen in the fact that her types easily sorted into the four categories described long ago by Hippocrates.

Myers defined four types of personality calling them "sensory perceiving" (SP), "sensory judging" (SJ), "intuitive thinking" (NT), and "intuitive feeling" (NF). These expressions are now commonly used by all sorts of people in all sorts of enterprise, including educational and governmental institutions, business and industry, churches, and the military.

What Myers called the SP has much in common with what Keirsey calls the Artisan. She regarded people of this type as adaptable, artistic, athletic, cool, easy going; acting with effortless economy, enjoying life, gifted with machines and tools, good natured, having no use for theories, knowing what's going on, looking for workable compromises, open minded and persuasive, seeing needs of the moment, realistic about immediate situations, sensitive to color, line, and texture, storing useful facts, tolerant, unprejudiced, and wanting first hand experiences.[1] Some of the SPs were said to be rather unfeeling and unsentimental, more "thinking" that is, and hence SPT.[2] These have much in common

---

1 Page A5 in *The Myers-Briggs Type Indicator*.
2 See pages 196-207 in *Please Understand Me* for portraits of the four "SP" types.

with Keirsey's Operator Artisan. The rest of the SPs were said to be more tender and sentimental, more "feeling," hence SP^f. These resemble Keirsey's reporting Artisan, the Player. Using the Myers terms the Operator Artisan Presidents, such as Jackson, Van Buren, and the Roosevelts would be called SP^{t}s, while the Player Artisan Presidents, such as Taylor, Garfield, and Reagan would be called SP^{f}s.

There are parallel overlaps of Myers's SJ type with Keirsey's Guardian. Myers saw the SJ as conservative, consistent, dependable, detailed, factual, hard working, non-impulsive, non-distractible, painstaking, patient, persevering, routinized, sensible, stable, thorough, good at maintenance, good at citing cases, and good at meeting the visible needs of others.[3] As in the case of the SP, Myers believed that some of the SJs were more unfeeling and unsentimental than the rest, or as she put it more "thinking" hence SJ^t. The others she thought of as more sentimental and "feeling" hence SJ^f.[4] The sentimental kind of SJ (the SJ^f) parallels Keirsey's reporting Guardian, the Conservator, while the unsentimental SJ (the SJ^t) parallels the directive Guardian, the Monitor. Thus the Monitor Guardians, such as Washington, Polk, Wilson, and Truman are in Myers's terminology the SJ^{t}s, and the Conservator Guardians, such as Mckinley, Ford, and Bush are SJ^{f}s.

Myers's NT type of personality parallels Keirsey's Rational personality. She regarded the NT as: abstract, analytic, complex, curious, efficient, exacting, impersonal, independent, ingenious, intellectual, inventive, logical, scientific, theoretical, research oriented, and systematic.[5] Myers had some the NTs more "judging" than the others, hence NT^j, and some more "perceptive" thus NT^p.[6] The NT^p corresponds to Keirsey's reporting Rational, the Engineer, while the NT^j corresponds in some degree with his directive Rational, the Organizer. In Myers's terminology the

---

3 Page A6 in *The Myers-Briggs Type Indicator*.
4 See pages 188-196 in *Please Understand Me* for portraits of the four "SJ" types.
5 Page 56 in *The Myers-Briggs Type Indicator*.
6 See pages 178-188 in *Please Understand Me* for portraits of the four "NT" types.

Organizer Presidents, such as the Adamses and Grant, are the NT^{J}s while the Engineer Presidents, Jefferson, Madison, and Lincoln, are the NT^{P}s.

Myers's NF type corresponds rather well with Keirsey's Idealist temperament. Myers saw herself as an NF and saw the type as: creative, enthusiastic, humane, imaginative, insightful, religious, subjective, and sympathetic, as well as capable of research, teaching, preaching, counseling, writing, psychology, psychiatry, and linguistics.[7] Some of the NFs were more "judging" than the others, thus NF^J, while the rest were more "perceptive" and therefore NF^P.[8] The NF^P parallels Keirsey's reporting Idealist, the Advocate, and the NF^J parallels the directing Idealist, the Mentor. Thus the Myers' NF^J is represented by the two Mentor Idealists presented in this book, Eleanor Roosevelt and Mohandas Gandhi.

Myers seemed more concerned with the talents and vocational contributions of the types than with other attributes. In her two books *The Myers-Briggs Type Indicator* and *Gifts Differing*, everybody has good intentions and is capable of doing good works, and are therefore more to be judged by their virtues than by their vices. Indeed, being a born Idealist herself, she was careful to avoid comment on anybody's shortcomings. Myers's very positive look at personality helps to account for how well her views have been received throughout America and in the last several years in many other countries as well.

It cannot be denied that there are some very difficult problems in correlating the *Myers-Briggs Type Indicator* with the *Brief Test of Character Traits*. The latter is based on the quadratic theory of behavior originated by Hippocrates in the sixth century BC and advanced by Adickes, Spränger, Kretschmer, and Fromm in the twentieth century. In contrast the Myers-Briggs test is based on a typology devised by Carl Jung in the early part of the twentieth century. Jung's theoretical base is causal-elemental while Keirsey's is field-systemic. This is an irreconcilable theoretical

---

7 Page 56 in *The Myers-Briggs Type Indicator*.
8 See pages 167-178 in *Please Understand Me* for portraits of the four "NF" types.

difference that makes any correlation between the Jungian-based tests and the Hippocratic-based tests all but impossible.

Keirsey's distinction between "utility" and "sanction" has no place in the Jungian ideology or in the Jungian tests, nor does his distinction between "directing" and "reporting."[9] The tentative suggestion made by some that "judgment" is in some degree the equivalent of "directing" is of little use. The Conservator Guardians, for instance, although they may be judgmental, are not at all directive in their interactions. And the Operator Artisans can be both judgmental and quite directive in their interactions. Thus the notion of "judgment" simply doesn't work very well in the Keirsey characterology. The same may be said for the distinction "thinking" versus "feeling," so prominent in the Jungian scheme: no place can be found in the quadratic theory, so the distinction is best left to the Jungians.

On the other hand Jung's distinction between "sensation" and "intuition" has been quite useful in Keirsey's characterology, albeit in the form of his distinction between "concrete" and "abstract." And as long as Jungian terms such as "sensation" and "intuition" are seen as metaphors, little harm is done to test construction. Unfortunately, they do tend to become reified, to the final confusion of everyone.

Incidently, Jung's distinction between "introversion" and "extraversion" does have a small place in the Keirsey system, but has to be replaced with two distinctions, namely "assertiveness" versus "attentiveness" and "gregariousness" versus "isolativeness." Assertive persons tend to blurt out their own message without invitation and not listen very long to another's message. In contrast attentive persons tend to listen patiently to what others have to say and to say little even when requested to speak. On the other hand gregarious persons, whether assertive or attentive, frequently seek the company of others, including strangers, while isolative persons frequently seek privacy and when in the company of strangers, friends, and neighbors do not

---

9 The *Myers-Briggs*, the *Grey-Wheelright*, the *Singer-Loomis*, the *Murphy -Mysgeier*, and others.

stay long. While these are interesting distinctions, we have not made much of them in this book since these characteristics are least noted by biographers, and since they are least essential to understanding issues of temperament and character.

Finally, it should be recognized that great credit is due Isabel Myers for breathing life into what seemed a dead issue. The works of Adickes, Spränger, Kretschmer, and Fromm lay unused and gathering dust on University library shelves until she aroused national interest in personality typology.

Appendix C

A BIBLIOGRAPHY OF SURVEYS AND COMPARISONS

Barber, J 1977	*The Presidential Character*
Barzman, S 1970	*The First Ladies*
Bassett, M 1969	*Profiles and Portraits of American Presidents and their Wives*
Bauer, K 1974	*The Mexican War, 1846-1848*
Boller, P J 1982	*Presidential Anecdotes*
Boller, P J 1984	*Presidential Campaigns*
Boller, P J 1988	*Presidential Wives*
Burne, A 1938	*Lee, Grant and Sherman: A Study of Leadership...1864-65 Campaign*
Caroli, B 1987	*The First Ladies*
Commager & Nevins 1986	*A Pocket History of the United States*
Cooke, D 1975	*Atlas of the Presidents*
Cunliffe, M 1987	*The Presidency*
Dickerson, N 1976	*Among Those Present*
Donovan, H 1987	*Roosevelt to Reagan*
Durant, J & A 1955	*Pictorial History of American Presidents*
Durant, W 1968	*The Lessons of History*
Garraty, J 1989	*1001 Things Everyone Should Know about American History*
Hershan, S 1970	*A Woman of Quality*
Hoff-Wilson, J (ed) 1984	*Without Precedent*
Hofstadter, R 1946	*The American Political Tradition*
McPherson, J 1988	*Battle Cry of Freedom: The Civil War Era*

Miller, D & J 1989 — *From George To George; 200 Years of Presidential Quotations*

Miller, M 1973 — *Plain Speaking*

Moses, J, Cross, W 1980 — *Presidential Courage*

Nelson, M (ed) 1989 — *Congressional Quarterly's Guide to the Presidency*

Neustadt, R 1980 — *Presidential Power*

Paletta, L & Worth, F 1988 — *World Almanac of Presidential Facts*

Pratt, J 1935 — *The Expansionists of 1898*

Rosenman, D & S 1976 — *Presidential Style*

Schram, M 1987 — *The Great American Video Game: Presidential Politics in the TV Age*

Shenkman, and Reiger — *One Night Stands with American History*

Thompson, C 1929 — *Presidents I Have Known*

Tugwell, R 1964 — *How They Became President*

Wecter, D 1941 — *The Hero in America*

Whitney, D 1990 — *The American Presidents*

BIBLIOGRAPHY OF WORKS CITED

1001 Things Everyone Should Know about American History, John A. Garraty, Doubleday, NY, 1989

Abraham Lincoln: The Prairie Years and the War Years, One-volume, Carl Sandburg, Harcourt, Brace, NY, 1954

Among Those Present, Nancy Dickerson, Valentine Books, NY, 1976

The American Political Tradition, Richard Hofstadter, NY, 1948

The American Presidents, David C. Whitney, Doubleday, Garden City, NY, 1978

The American Presidents: Biographies of the Chief Executives from Washington through Bush, David C. Whitney, 7th ed., Prentice Hall, NJ, 1990

Anna Eleanor Roosevelt: The Evolution of a Reformer, James R. Kearney, Houghton Mifflin, Boston, MA, 1968

Atlas of the Presidents, Donald E. Cooke, Hamond Inc., Maplewood, NJ, 1975

The Autobiography of Eleanor Roosevelt, Eleanor Roosevelt, Harper, NY, 1961

The Autobiography of Martin Van Buren, John C. Fitzpatrick, (ed), 1920

Battle Cry of Freedom: The Civil War Era, James M. McPherson, Ballantine Books, NY, 1988

The Collected Works of Abraham Lincoln, 9 vols. Roy C. Basler (ed), New Brunswick, NJ, 1952-55

Congressional Quarterly's Guide to the Presidency, Michael Nelson, (ed), Congressional Quarterly, Inc., ,1989

Dasher: the Roots and Rising of Jimmy Carter, James Wooten, Summit Books, NY, 1978

Diary and Letters of Rutherford B. Hayes, Charles Richard Williams, (ed), 5 vols., Columbus, OH, 1924

Dwight D. Eisenhower: Hero and Politician, Robert F. Burk, Twayne Publishers, Boston, MA, 1986

Early Reagan, Anne Edwards, William Morrow, NY, 1987

Eisenhower: Portrait of the Hero, Peter Lyon, Little, Brown, Boston, MA, 1974

Eleanor and Franklin, J. P. Lash, W.W. Norton, NY, 1971

The Eleanor Roosevelt Story, Archibald MacLeish, Houghton Mifflin, Boston, MA, 1965

Fall From Grace, Shelley Ross, Ballantine Books, NY, 1988

The FDR Memoirs, Bernard Asbell, Doubleday, Garden City, NY, 1973

The First Ladies, Betty Boyd Caroli, Oxford University Press, NY, 1987

The First Ladies, Sol Barzman, Cowles Book Co., NY,1970

A Ford, Not a Lincoln, Richard Reeves, Harcourt Brace Jovanovich, NY,1975

The Fox at Bay: Martin Van Buren and the Presidency, 1837-1841, James C. Curtis, University Press of Kentucky, Lexington, KY, 1970

Franklin D. Roosevelt's Own Story, D. Day, Little Brown, Boston, MA, 1951

From George ... To George: 200 Years of Presidential Quotations, Donald L. Miller and John Sargent (comps), Braddock Communications, 1989

Gandhi: A Memoir, William L. Shirer, Pocket Books, NY, 1979

Gandhi: A Pictorial Biography, Gerald Gold and Richard Attenborough, Newmarket Press, NY, 1983

Gandhi: An Autobiography: The Story of My Experiments with Truth, Mohandas K. Gandhi, 1927, 1929. One volume, Beacon Press, Boston, MA, 1957

George Bush: an Intimate Portrait, Fitzhugh Green, Hippocrene Books, NY, 1989

The Generals: Ulysses S. Grant and Robert E. Lee, Nancy Scott Anderson and Dwight Anderson, Knopf, NY, 1988

The Great American Video Game: Presidential Politics in the Television Age, Martin Schram, William Morrow, NY, 1987

Harry Truman and the Crisis Presidency, B. Cochran, Funk and Wagnalls, NY, 1973

Herbert Hoover, Eugene Lyons, Doubleday, Garden City, NY, 1948

Herbert Hoover: A Public Life, David Burner, Knopf, NY, 1978

The Hero in America, Dixon Wecter, Scribner's Sons, NY, 1941

The Higher Realism of Woodrow Wilson, Arthur Link, Vanderbilt University Press, Nashville, TN, 1971

Hold On Mr. President!, Sam Donaldson, Random House, NY, 1987

How They Became President, Rexford G. Tugwell, Simon and Schuster, NY,1964

I'll Never Lie to You: Jimmy Carter In His Own Words, Robert Turner, Ballantine Book, NY,1976

The Impeachment and Trial of Andrew Johnson, Michael Les Benedict, W.W. Norton, NY, 1973

In Lincoln's Footsteps: The Life of Andrew Johnson, Bill Severn, Ives Washburn, Inc., NY,1956

James Earl Carter: The Man and the Myth, Peter Meyer, Sheed, Andrews and McMeel, Kansas City, KS, 1978

Jerry Ford: Up Close, Bud Vestal, Coward, McCann and Geoghan, NY, 1974

Jimmy Carter: In search of the Great White House, Betty Glad, W.W. Norton, NY, 1980

Jimmy Carter: The Man and the Myth, Victor Lasky, Marek Publishers, NY, 1979

John Fitzgerald Kennedy, As We Remember Him, Goddard Lieberson, Atheneum, NY, 1965

John Kennedy: A Political Profile, James MacGregor Burns, Harcourt, Brace, NY, 1960

Kennedy, Theodore C. Sorensen, Harper and Row, NY, 1965

The Life of James Monroe, George Morgan, Boston, MA, 1921

Lincoln Talks: An Oral Biography, Emanuel Hertz, Bramhall House, NY, 1986

Looking Forward, George Bush (with Victor Gold), Doubleday, Garden City, NY, 1987

Love, Eleanor: Eleanor Roosevelt and her Friends, Joseph P. Lash, Doubleday, Garden City, NY, 1982

Lyndon, Richard Harwood and Haynes Johnson, Praeger, NY, 1973

A Man Called Intrepid: The Secret War, William Stevenson, Ballantine Books, NY, 1976

Martin Van Buren, Edwin P. Hoyt, Reilly and Lee, Chicago, IL, 1964

Meet Calvin Coolidge, Edward Connery Lathem, (ed), Stephen Greene Press, Brattleboro, VT, 1960

My Brother Lyndon, Sam Houston Johnson, Cowles Book Co., NY,1969

Nixon Agonistes, Garry Wills, Houghton Mifflin, Boston, MA, 1969.

One Night Stands with American History, Richard Shenkman and Kurt Reiger, William Morrow, NY, 1990

The Ordeal of Power: A Political Memoir of the Eisenhower Years, Emmet J. Hughes, Atheneum, NY, 1963

Past Forgetting: My Love Affair with Dwight D. Eisenhower, Kay Summersby Morgan, Simon and Schuster, NY, 1976

Pictorial History of American Presidents, John and Alice Durant, A. S. Barnes, Cranbury, NJ, 1955

Plain Speaking, M. Miller, G.P. Putnam's Sons, NY. 1973

A Pocket History of the United States, Allan Nevins and Henry Steele Commager, Pocket Books, Washington Square Press, NY, 1986

Presidential Power: The Politics of Leadership From FDR to Carter, Richard E. Neustadt, Wiley, NY, 1980

The Presidency, Marcus Cunliffe, Houghton Mifflin, Boston, MA, 1987

The Presidency of Martin Van Buren, Major L. Wilson, Regents Press of Kansas, Lawrence, KS, 1984

The Presidency of William McKinley, Lewis L. Gould, Regents Press of Kansas, Lawrence, KS, 1980

Presidential Anecdotes, Paul F. Boller, Jr., Penguin Books, NY, 1982

Presidential Campaigns, Paul F. Boller, Jr., Oxford University Press, NY, 1984

The Presidential Character, 2nd ed., J.D. Barber, NJ, Prentice-Hall, 1977

Presidential Courage, John B. Moses, M.D., and Wilbur Cross, W.W. Norton, NY, 1980

Presidential Style, D. Rosenman and S. Rosenman, Harper and Row, NY, 1976

Presidential Wives, Paul F. Boller, Jr., Oxford University Press, NY, 1988.

President James Buchanan: A Biography, Phillip Shriver Klein, Pennsylvania State University Press, University Park, PA,1962

Presidents I Have Known, Charles Willis Thompson, Indianapolis, IN, 1929

Profiles and Portraits of American Presidents and their Wives, Margret Bassett, Bond Wheelwright Co., Freeport, ME, 1969

The Pygmalion Project, Love and Coercion Among the Types, Vol. I: *The Artisan,* Stephen Montgomery, Prometheus Nemesis Book Co, 1989

Random House Dictionary of the English Language, 2d. ed., unabridged, Random House, NY, 1987

Reagan, Lou Cannon, G.P. Putnam's Sons, NY, 1982

Revolution: Reagan's Rise to Power, Martin Anderson, Harcourt, Brace, Jovanovich, San Diego, CA, 1988

Richard Nixon: The Shaping of his Character, Fawn M. Brodie, W.W. Norton, NY, 1981

Roosevelt to Reagan: A Reporter's Encounters with Nine Presidents, Hedley Donovan, Harper and Row, NY, 1987

Strategies of Psychotherapy, Jay Haley, Grune and Stratton, NY, 1963.

Thomas Jefferson: An Intimate History, Fawn M. Brodie, W.W. Norton, NY, 1974

Thomas Woodrow Wilson: 28th President of the United States: A Psychological Study, Sigmund Freud and William. C. Bullitt, Houghton Mifflin, Boston, MA, 1967

Ulysses S. Grant, Henry Thomas, Van Rees Press, NY, 1961

Websters New Collegiate Dictionary, G. and C. Merriam Co., Springfield, MA, 1980

William Howard Taft: In the Public Service, David H. Burton, Robert E. Krieger Publishing Co., Malibar, FL, 1986

Without Precedent: The Life and Career of Eleanor Roosevelt, Joan Hoff-Wilson and Marjorie Lightman (eds), Indiana University Press, Bloomington, IN, 1984

A Woman of Quality, Stella K. Hershan, Crown Publishers, NY, 1970

Woodrow Wilson: A Brief Biography, Arthur Link, Quadrangle Books, Chicago, IL, 1963

World Almanac of Presidential Facts, Lu Ann Paletta and Fred L. Worth, Ballantine Books, NY, 1988

Credits

PORTRAITS OF
TEMPERAMENT

Portraits
of
Temperament

DAVID
KEIRSEY

The Guardian
The Artisan

Keirsey • Bates

PLEASE UNDERSTAND M...

Portraits of Temperament is David Keirsey's most recent thinking on the ingrained attitudes and habitual actions of the four basic personality types, which he now renames the Artisans, Guardians, Rationals, and Idealists. Keirsey summarizes the four temperaments, showing how the behavior of each is either concrete or abstract, cooperative or pragmatic, directive or informative, and finally, assertive or responsive. The book includes two brief self-scoring personality tests to assist in observing the differences and similarities among us.

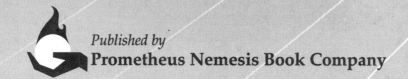

Published by
Prometheus Nemesis Book Company

LOVE, COERCION, AND THE ARTISAN

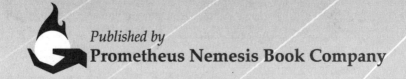

The Pygmalion Project: Volume I, The Artisan, by Dr. Stephen Montgomery (the editor of *Please Understand Me*) investigates the styles of love and coercion among the Keirseyan temperaments, taking famous characters from literature and film as provocative case studies. **Volume I, The Artisan** approaches the art of loving from the Artisans' point-of-view, by examining their playful and charming way in relationships with Guardian ("SJ"), Rational ("NT"), and Idealist ("NF") partners. Begin by completing Keirsey's new personality test, and then read about the Artisan mating game, how they delight and dismay their loved ones, as presented in the pages of D. H. Lawrence, Ernest Hemingway, F. Scott Fitzgerald, and eight other authors. More importantly learn more about Keirsey's concept of the Pygmalion Project—how we try to sculpt our loved ones into copies of ourselves, and how we are manipulated by them in return. If you've ever been in love with an Artisan (or ever been fooled by one), *The Pygmalion Project* will prove fascinating reading.

Published by
Prometheus Nemesis Book Company

THE GUARDIAN'S
PYGMALION PROJECT

The
Pygmalion
Project
Love and Coercion
Among the Types

VOLUME TWO

The Guardian

Stephen Montgomery

The Artisan

KEIRSEY

PORTRAITS OF TEMPERAMENT   Keirsey • Bates

PLEASE UNDERSTAND ME

T he second part of Dr. Stephen Montgomery's quartet on love and coercion among the types focuses on the Guardians' ("SJ") uniquely responsible style of caring for others. Montgomery (the editor of *Please Understand Me*) has selected characters from works of Jane Austen, Sinclair Lewis, Virginia Woolf, and half a dozen other authors, to bring to life the Guardian's parental way in love and marriage, and to illustrate their earnest style of interpersonal manipulation—what Keirsey calls the Pygmalion Project. The book examines the Guardians both as instigators and as victims of marital games with the Rationals ("NTs"), the Idealists ("NFs"), and particularly with the childlike Artisans ("SPs"). If you have a Guardian spouse (or even a Guardian parent), *The Pygmalion Project: Volume 2, The Guardian* will help you understand and appreciate them.

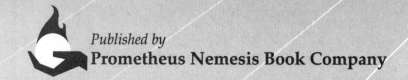

Published by
Prometheus Nemesis Book Company

PLEASE UNDERSTAND ME

CHARACTER & TEMPERAMENT TYPES

SEARCH FOR YOUR STYLE

Begin by completing the questionnaire on page five. Then read a picture of your way (p. 167–206). You may even enjoy talking with spouse and offspring and friend of your DIFFERENCES.

The authors are trainers of therapists and diagnosticians of dysfunctional behavior at California State University (Fullerton Campus). Impatient with the maturity theories of Freud, Maslow, Erickson, Sheehey, Levinson, and others, they insist that not everybody goes through the same phases of growth to maturity. "You may have an identity crisis or two, but I won't, haven't, and can't. And it's not because I'm fixated, arrested, or hung up at some immature stage, passage, or season of my life. I hear different drummers."

Professor Keirsey is a long time clinical psychologist of the gestalt-field-systems school. After 30 years of treating hundreds of teaching, parenting, marriage, and management problems, Dr. Keirsey now challenges the reader to "ABANDON THE PYGMALION PROJECT," that endless and fruitless attempt to change the Other into a carbon copy of Oneself. "It's OK," he says, "to marry your opposite and beget children who are far from being chips off the old block, but it is not OK to take marriage and parentage as license to SCULPT spouse and child using yourself as a pattern to copy. PUT DOWN YOUR CHISEL. LET BE. APPRECIATE."

DAVID KEIRSEY

MARILYN BATES

Keirsey adopted the theory of Psychological Types of Carl Jung and the pioneering (and best selling) method of measuring type of Isabel Myers in 1955 and ever since has adapted his clinical practice to the perspective of Jung-Myers typology. PLEASE UNDERSTAND ME provides a useful vocabulary and phraseology for applying the Jung-Myers concepts of type. The Myers-Briggs Type Indicator (Pub. by Consulting Psychologists Press, Palo Alto, Ca.) is distributed and researched by the Center for Applications of Psychological Type, Gainesville, Fla. 32604, P.O. 13807.

Stephen Montgomery, PhD, (Editor)
Prometheus Nemesis Books

DISTRIBUTED BY **PROMETHEUS NEMESIS BOOK COMPANY**
Post Office Box 2748, Del Mar, CA 92014   ISBN 0-9606954-0-0

ORDER FORM

| | Units | Total |

Please Understand Me Keirsey & Bates 208 pages—$11.95
National Best Seller. Over one million copies sold. A 25 year clinical study of differences in temperament in mating, parenting, teaching, and leading. Includes the *Keirsey Temperament Sorter.*
Versteh Mich Bitte Keirsey & Bates 276 pages—$11.95
German translation of *Please Understand Me.*
Por Favor Comprendeme Keirsey, Bates 238 pages—$11.95
Spanish translation of *Please Understand Me.*
Presidential Temperament Keirsey & Choiniere 610 pages—$15.95
Depicts temperament-determined lives of 40 U.S. presidents, from youth to old age. Authors found there were 20 Guardians [SJ], 12 Artisans [SP], 8 Rationals [NT], and *no* Idealists [NF]. Presents the lives of Eleanor Roosevelt and Mohandas Gandhi in lieu of the missing Idealist presidents. Includes *A Brief Test of Character Traits.*
Portraits of Temperament Keirsey 124 pages—$9.95
The four Hippocratean temperaments are named Artisan, Guardian, Rational, and Idealist, each with two variant patterns of behavior based on differing kinds of ability and interest.
The Pygmalion Project: 1 The Artisan Montgomery 180 pages—$ 9.95
Volume 1 looks at Artisan [SP] relationships with Guardian [SJ], Rational [NT], and Idealist [NF] types, using dialogue and scenes from novels, plays, and films, from D.H. Lawrence, Hemingway, Fitzgerald, & others.
The Pygmalion Project: 2 The Guardian Montgomery 258 pp—$9.95
Volume 2 looks at how Guardians [SJs] go about loving the other three temperaments as shown in dialogue and scenes from fiction and film, from Sinclair Lewis, Evelyn Waugh, Jane Austen, and others.
The Pygmalion Project 3 The Idealist Montgomery Printed Spring 1993
Volume 3 looks at love between the types from the Idealist [NF] point-of-view, with examples from E.M. Forster, Tolstoy, Dostoevsky, and others.
Abuse it—Lose-it Keirsey 20 pages—$2.00
Applications of the principle of logical consequences and the abuse it—lose it method for developing self-control in mischievous school boys who are all too often stigmatized as cases of "attention deficit disorder" and then drugged into obedience.
Drugged Obedience in the School Keirsey 8 pages—$ .25
A comparison between drugging mischievous school boys with cocaine-like narcotics, especially Ritalin, and the abuse-it-lose-it method of teaching self-control to school boys.
Temperament in Leading 48 pages—$ 3.00
Styles of management and teaching, from *Please Understand Me.*
The Sixteen Types 48 pages—$3.00
From *Please Understand Me* , featuring portraits of the 16 types.
The Keirsey Temperament Sorter $.25
A self-scoring test to identify 16 types, from *Please Understand Me.*
The Keirsey Temperament Sorter on Disc $7.00
Specify Macintosh (Hypercard) or IBM.
A Brief Test of Character Traits $.25
A self-scoring test to identify 4 types of temperament: Artisans, Rationals, Guardians, and Idealists, reprinted from *Presidential Temperament.*

Name	Shipping		Subtotal	
	Order Subtotal	USA	Abroad	
	$ 00.00 - $ 49.99 — $2.00	$ 3.50	7% Sales Tax (CA Only)	
Street or Box	50.00 - 99.99 — 3.50	6.00		
	100.00 - 149.99 — 4.50	9.00		
City State Zip	150.00 - 199.99 — 5.00	10.50	Shipping	
Mail order and check (U.S. Dollars only) to Prometheus Nemesis Books, Box 2748, Del Mar, CA 92014. CALL 619-632-1575; FAX 714-540-5288			Total Enclosed	